GEOFFREY DAWSON AND OUR TIMES

OTHER BOOKS BY THE SAME AUTHOR

UPHILL

STRUGGLE

I LOVED GERMANY

IMMORTAL YEARS

TRANSATLANTIC LONDON

Biography

FRANCIS YEATS-BROWN

1935

GEOFFREY DAWSON AND OUR TIMES

JOHN EVELYN WRENCH

With a Foreword by

THE RT. HON. THE EARL OF HALIFAX, K.G., O.M.

Speak of me as I am; nothing extenuate
Nor set down aught in malice.
(*Othello*, V, 2.)

With 20 *Illustrations*

LONDON
HUTCHINSON

Hutchinson & Co. (Publishers) Ltd.
178-202 *Great Portland Street, London, W.*1

London Melbourne Sydney Auckland
Bombay Johannesburg New York Toronto

First published 1955

Printed in Great Britain
by The Anchor Press, Ltd.,
Tiptree, Essex

TO

MY WIFE

Tibi quae, sive lucente benigno sole sive tempestate minante, cum tenerum tum seniorem, me, velut sidera nautas, direxisti.

CONTENTS

LIST OF ILLUSTRATIONS

FOREWORD

BY THE RT. HON. THE EARL OF HALIFAX, K.G., P.C., O.M.

FRIENDS of Geoffrey Dawson have long wished to see something written about him, and will be grateful to Sir Evelyn Wrench for enabling them to realize their desire.

The story of his life is allowed largely to tell itself from his own diaries and letters, so that the reader gets an impression personal and direct. And that is a true impression to give. For Geoffrey Dawson had a straightforward and unaffected approach to life, devoid of desire to create effects or score points, and retaining always a judgment of men and affairs that was balanced, well proportioned, and supported by principles so firmly grounded as to be instinctive. Keenly alive to the enjoyment of many different sides of human affairs, he was equally at home in *The Times* office, or at Oxford in Magdalen or All Souls, or on the Governing Body of Eton, or in Yorkshire on the slopes of his beloved Penyghent, and brought the same qualities of simplicity, poise and wisdom to whatever might be the task that each setting demanded.

I have always thought it a great tribute to him that he should have impressed, as he did, two men so different as Lord Milner and Lord Northcliffe, and that he did so surely says much for his gifts of head and heart. One consequence of these gifts was worth a great deal both to himself and to the public whom as editor of a great paper it was his task to serve, and this was the complete confidence that he won from those set in authority, in government or administration. Throughout his career this was one of the principal secrets of his work; nowhere to be shown of greater value than during some of the very difficult days of the 1914–1918 War. For it could and did mean much for the national advantage at that time to have someone in the unique position of Editor of *The Times*, ready to support any action that the situation plainly demanded; quick to discourage intrigue from whatever quarter; and trusted by many in the highest and most responsible posts who had little trust for one another.

Control of and responsibility for the production of a great paper can never, one might guess, be carefree. The opportunities of dropped bricks are too many; and wherever these are dropped, it must be the editor who *vis-à-vis* the public has to take the blame. Nor for a special reason can there have been any paper of which this was more true than *The Times* at critical periods throughout Dawson's editorship. Its position was constantly and widely misunderstood, so that in many quarters the paper and its editor were, as no doubt they still are, supposed to stand in some particular relation to the Government. Special weight was held to attach to opinions expressed in its leading articles, on the assumption that these carried some quality of government stamp, if not approbation.

Of this confusion of judgment Dawson often had to bear his full share, which certainly cannot have made it more easy at times of acute controversy to keep the waters of counsel clear. For the frequent consequence was to involve the editorship in a double criticism. Those who favoured Government policy were annoyed when *The Times* was not wholehearted in its support; while those who disliked Government policy tended, in spite of occasional criticism in the paper's columns, to regard *The Times* as a concealed ally of the Government, approving and abetting evil courses. Such misunderstanding, as might be anticipated, could be particularly embarrassing in the field of foreign affairs which throughout Dawson's time perpetually filled a large place in the sum of current events. The tormenting problems that arose as the immediate aftermath of the First World War soon merged into those that after uneasy years became in their turn the setting of the second. Often political and economic complexities ran together, demanding different, if not incompatible, solutions. And always on any international issue, the Foreign Secretary knew that, whatever might be the disclaimers, much foreign opinion would go on believing that the voice of *The Times* was the voice of the British Government.

Nor was it only on foreign soil that questions were continuously arising to test editors and statesmen. In the dark days of December 1936, when monarchy and people passed together through the tragic trial of the King's abdication, nowhere did the steady judgment of the nation find more true reflection, and more unswerving support, than in *The Times*. And through the preceding years between the wars, India; the conditions of Imperial trade; the industrial and agricultural needs and capacities of the United Kingdom; the rights and duties of organized labour in the world that many had hoped to make new; the economic crisis from which emerged the National Government of Mr. Ramsay MacDonald; these with much else occupied the stage and clamoured for the attention of all who might direct or influence policy.

In no case might the argument be one-sided; often it was made heated by its extension to the merits or demerits of particular personalities. A motley, uneven and exacting field; in which it was the inescapable duty of the Editor to sift chaff and grain, and to supply the readers of *The Times* with the material on which sound opinion could be reasonably based.

Readers of Sir Evelyn Wrench's study of Dawson's life will be able to form their own conclusions as to the methods by which the latter tried to discharge his task, and the remarkable degree of success which he in fact achieved. I do not doubt that those who knew Geoffrey Dawson best will gratefully acknowledge in what Sir Evelyn Wrench has written, a faithful picture of a friend, who gave much to friendship and drew much from it. They, no less than those who only knew him less intimately or not at all, may profit from the story of a life lived in single-minded devotion to duty, in loyalty to the standards by which his course was set, and free from any motives smaller than that of public service.

PREFACE

THIS book has been written because I thought that the story of Geoffrey Dawson should be told while some of his most intimate friends and colleagues were alive and it would still be possible to draw on their personal knowledge. I first met Geoffrey Robinson, as he then was, in June, 1908 (he was Editor of the *Johannesburg Star*), when he was paying the first of many visits to Sutton Place, near Guildford, then the home of Lord and Lady Northcliffe. It was at Sutton Place that Northcliffe finally decided to appoint Geoffrey Editor of *The Times* and I was staying there, as was Geoffrey, for the week-end of Saturday, September 21st to Monday, 23rd, 1912—the first day of his Editorship at Printing House Square.

There are many persons much better fitted to write Geoffrey's story than I am. My qualifications, such as they are, include a great admiration for him, both as a man and a journalist, and the fact that I was very close to Northcliffe during the immediate years after his acquisition of *The Times*. Apart from Lady Hudson (formerly Lady Northcliffe), there is probably no one left who saw more of both men in those years than I did.

Writing about Geoffrey's relations with Northcliffe has not been easy for me. I am still devoted to "the Chief's" memory. I can never forget his extraordinary kindnesses to me as a young man—I joined his staff at the age of twenty-one in 1904. As a gatherer of news, or as the possessor of an insight into the mind of the masses, I have never met his equal. He was a genius at getting the best out of young men.

As far as possible I have tried to let Geoffrey tell his story in his own words. From the outset I refer to him as "Geoffrey". It would have been confusing if the book had recorded the doings of "Robinson" up to 1917—the year in which he changed his name—and thereafter those of "Dawson"—at least so it seemed to me. Geoffrey, unlike some of his predecessors, had other interests apart from Printing House Square. No one can have been more devoted to Eton and Oxford than he was and the devotion was mutual. Few distinguished journalists, surely, had they allowed their names to go forward, could have become either President of Magdalen, Warden of All Souls, or

Provost of Eton. From the letters he received from those associated with Magdalen, All Souls and Eton it is evident that one of those great positions might have been his.

This book could not have been written without the help of Cecilia Dawson, who has placed all her husband's diaries, memoranda and letters at my disposal. The debt I owe her and her family is immense. To Lord Halifax, one of Geoffrey's closest friends, I am most grateful for writing the Foreword.

In accordance with the tradition and rule of *The Times* names of the writers of leading articles in the paper are omitted, except in the case of the Editor.

Marlow,
May, 1955.

E. W.

P.S.—A full list of acknowledgments to those who have helped me or given permission for the reproduction of letters, documents or extracts from their writings appears on pages 17–18.

ACKNOWLEDGMENTS

It would be difficult to thank adequately all those who have helped me in the task of writing this book. Many at Printing House Square have gone out of their way to provide information—among them I wish to mention the Chairman, Colonel the Hon. J. J. Astor, and Mr. John Walter; also Sir William Haley, the Editor, who was never too busy to see me and to advise, and who encouraged me when I was rather appalled by the magnitude of the task I had undertaken. I am especially indebted to two members of the Board, Lord Brand and Sir Campbell Stuart, for their assistance. My debt to the former is very great, for he also helped me with advice about Geoffrey's life in South Africa and in recording the work of the Kindergarten. Very many of the great "company" of *The Times* made possible my work by their sympathy and help. Mr. Dermot Morrah, on the staff of *The Times* and also the Editor of the *Round Table*, read my proofs and was a mine of information, and Mr. J. S. Maywood, the Librarian of *The Times*, provided me with information which I could not have obtained elsewhere. Among former members of the staff of *The Times*, I am very grateful to Mr. Wickham Steed, Editor from 1919–1922, and Mr. W. F. Casey, Editor from 1948–1952; above all, to Sir Bruce Richmond, the originator of the Literary Supplement and an assistant editor, who has read through my typescript and given invaluable advice; to Lord Altrincham, the late Mr. L. S. Amery, Sir Frank Brown, Captain A. L. Kennedy, Miss Mary Mills (Geoffrey's secretary during his first editorship), Mr. Alan Pitt Robbins, Mr. Charles Morgan, Mr. Bernard Darwin, Mr. John Stevenson in Canada and Sir Arthur Willert for letting me see his files relating to the period when he was *The Times* representative in Washington.

Among those, not connected with Printing House Square, who have helped me in various ways, are the following:

Professor W. G. S. Adams, former Warden of All Souls; R. A. Austen-Leigh; Sir W. L. Andrews of the *Yorkshire Post*; the Hon. Anthony Asquith; Lady Cynthia Asquith; the Argus South African Newspapers; Lord Baldwin; Lord Beaverbrook, for encouragement and advice; Lord Burnham; Miss E. Moberly Bell; Mr. G. W. Buckle; the Hon. Margaret Bigge; Mrs. Charles Brodribb; Sir Max Beerbohm;

the Archbishop of Canterbury; Richard Church; the late Sir Henry Craik; Lionel Curtis (intimate friend of Geoffrey since Kindergarten days); Henry Chisholm; Lady Curzon; Mrs. Neville Chamberlain; Lord Derby; Mr. Patrick Duncan; the Dean of Westminster; Mr. Peter Davies; Sir Anthony Eden; Lord Esher; Mr. Claude Elliott, Provost of Eton; the late Bishop Furse; Mr. Justice Feetham (member of the Kindergarten); Major Edward Ford; Lord Fisher of Kilverstone; Dr. Philip Gosse; Count Grandi; Mr. Rupert Hart-Davis; Mr. Richard Herpers, Secretary of Columbia University; Lord Hardinge of Penshurst; Mr. Geoffrey Harmsworth; Lady Hudson (formerly Lady Northcliffe); Mr. Maurice Headlam; Dr. Thomas Jones; Miss Isabel Loam, Senior Assistant, Public Library, Reading; Lord Long of Wraxhall; Lady Milner; Sir Dougal Malcolm (member of the Kindergarten), for his help throughout and for placing his papers at my disposal; the Rt. Hon. Malcolm MacDonald; Mr. Arthur Mann; Mr. Anthony Marlowe; Lady Milford; Sir Harold Nicolson; Countess Roberts; Lady Rumbold; Mr. J. C. Smuts; Lord Stanhope; Mr. Robert Sencourt; Mr. John Sparrow, Warden of All Souls; the Dowager Lady Tweedsmuir; Sir Godfrey Thomas; the Public Trustee (Northcliffe correspondence); Lord Wigram; Sir William Wiseman; Mr. G. M. Young.

Finally to my friends who have helped me with the proof reading, correcting, etc.: my colleague of forty years, Mr. Eric Chaplin, Managing Director of the *Spectator* for over twenty-five years; Mrs. M. J. Baylis, Editorial Secretary of the *Spectator*, for invaluable help in obtaining permission to reproduce letters and papers, and for sorting and typing documents; to Mr. Charles Davenport, Senior English Master at Sir William Borlase's School, Marlow, for help at every stage of the way; to Mrs. E. M. Smith and Mrs. J. Robinson for their help in the immense task of typing the manuscript.

E. W.

I

YOUTH AND YORKSHIRE

ON the 25th October, 1874, the feast of St. Crispin and the anniversary of the victory of Agincourt, Mary, the wife of George Robinson, gave birth at Dyneley House[1] in Newmarket Street, Skipton-in-Craven, in the West Riding of Yorkshire, to her first child, a son. The baby was christened George Geoffrey.

His father was generally spoken of as "Colonel" Robinson, or referred to in Skipton as "Black George", because of his black beard, and to distinguish him from another Colonel Robinson who lived in the neighbourhood. He was an ardent supporter of the Volunteer movement, and very active in public affairs. He was a devout churchman and a keen freemason. He was a governor of two schools in Skipton (the Grammar School and the Girls' Endowed School), and also of Giggleswick School. He had been educated at Preston Grammar School and at Giggleswick, of which Geoffrey later also became a governor. In 1851 Mr. Robinson entered the bank of Messrs. Alcock, Birbeck & Co., at Settle. In 1858 he became the Managing-Director of the Craven Bank at Skipton (subsequently the Bank of Liverpool and now Martins Bank);[2] he married in 1873 Mary Perfect of Langcliffe Hall, a mile from Settle. She was the third surviving daughter of William Mosley Perfect, banker of Pontefract and solicitor in Blackburn.

Geoffrey's pedigree has not been an easy one to disentangle, well-documented though it is. The Rev. Richard Dawson, of Halton Gill and rector of Bolton-by-Bowland, married Mary Long,[3] the daughter of the Rev. William Hutton of Maids Moreton in Buckinghamshire, in 1774. Their youngest child, Elizabeth Hutton (1780–1866),

[1] The house is now a private hotel.

[2] Geoffrey always took a great interest in the old family bank, and in addition to his regular banking account at Coutts's, kept a subsidiary account there.

[3] She had assumed the name of Long.

of Marshfield, Settle, Yorkshire, purchased Langcliffe Hall, and in 1860[1] she bequeathed her name and her property to her next of kin, William Mosley Perfect, Geoffrey's uncle, and his mother's brother. On coming into his inheritance in 1869 he assumed the name of Dawson. He died at sea, off Madeira, in April, 1900 (unmarried), and Margaret Jane Perfect, his eldest sister, then inherited Langcliffe Hall and changed her name from Perfect to Dawson. Her sister, Katherine Elizabeth (the "Kitty" of the letters), when her elder sister, Margaret, died in 1917, passed on the inheritance of the Dawson Trust to her nephew Geoffrey, and in 1917 he assumed the name of Dawson—he was forty-two at the time.

Geoffrey spent the first decade of his life at Dyneley House. With a growing family, his father, when he was able to afford the outlay, built, in 1884, a new home called "Overdale" on the road from Skipton to Bolton Abbey; it was named after the neighbouring moor. Here he brought up his family in the simplest possible way—he had a strict code of right and wrong and good sense of values. The nurse who brought up the whole family was a young Cumberland woman, the daughter of a farmer, called Margaret Nicholson. She ruled the nursery with loving care but also with uncompromising discipline. She remained a faithful friend of all the family at Langcliffe for sixty years. Geoffrey's love of walking, riding and exercise grew from the long walks of his boyhood and never changed. He liked shooting in the same way—for the day out in lovely country with good friends. Wherever he was on the "Twelfth", whether in South Africa or elsewhere, he always thought longingly of Penyghent and the surrounding moors.

With the exception of Geoffrey the children of George and Mary Robinson had more than their share of ill luck. Three of them died early. The only daughter, Mary Kathleen, to whom Geoffrey was deeply devoted, married Commander Valentine Phillimore, R.N., in 1908. There is this curious entry in his diary on June 16th, 1908: "K's Wedding Day—a most successful function, though the whole thing for some reason depressed me frightfully"—a curious instance of premonition, for within a year his sister was dead. His youngest surviving brother, Francis Bertram, died at the age of thirty while engaged as a civil engineer in the task of constructing a harbour in Brazil. Ralph, two years his junior, served in the Imperial Yeomanry in South Africa and with the Duke of Wellington's Regiment in the first

[1] Langcliffe Hall had belonged to Pudsey Dawson (1752–1816), who became Mayor of Liverpool. His son, also Pudsey Dawson (1778–1859), sold Langcliffe and it was purchased by Elizabeth Hutton, a member of another branch of the Dawson family, in 1860, and she bequeathed it to Geoffrey's uncle, William Mosley Perfect, as stated above.

World War in France. From infancy he was afflicted with a terrible stammer and never achieved the success for which his abilities seemed to fit him. He wrote a text-book on the new Lewis machine-gun used in the First World War, and a history of Coutts's Bank.[1]

The interplay of heredity and environment over a number of successive generations must have helped to implant in Geoffrey an unusually deep affection for his native countryside. An early Dawson ancestor was Christopher, born at Halton Gill in 1531, who also possessed property in Wensleydale and was buried in 1620 by his wish at Arncliffe "according to the use of my elders". Another Christopher, grandson of the first, bought the manorial rights of Halton Gill from the Earl of Cumberland in 1629, and built the old hall at Halton Gill in 1641, which still stands and is part of the Dawson estate. Josias Dawson, great-grandson of the first Christopher, married Mary, the only daughter of William Forster of Langcliffe Hall, and thus Langcliffe Hall came into the possession of the Dawsons. There is an interesting picture at Langcliffe of Major William Dawson (1676–1762), friend of Isaac Newton, who could understand Newton's *Principia Philosophiae*. Major Dawson had an arbour specially built in the garden at Langcliffe for his famous friend, and there Newton and he used to discuss philosophic and other matters, or there Newton would be left in solitary meditation.[2]

Halton Gill always had a special place in Geoffrey's affections. It is a little hamlet consisting of a group of grey farm-buildings at the top of Littondale, surrounded by rugged and russet fells and green pastures. It possesses a tiny church which shares the building with the local school. In it are twelve desks for the child population—and a wireless set. The original Dawson home is now occupied by a farmer and hams in bags are still suspended from the rafters. The weekly laundry hangs from lines from the beams for the final drying. In a world of change it is reassuring to find changeless Halton Gill. Small wonder that

[1] Ralph Mosley Robinson, educated at Charterhouse, a scholar at Worcester College, Oxford, died at Great Missenden, Buckinghamshire, on January 15th, 1936, at the age of fifty-nine. Geoffrey was staying at Langcliffe, when he received "the appalling news that Ralph had died an hour ago of a sudden heart attack".

Ralph Robinson had been a full-time member of the staff of the *Encyclopædia Britannica* (at 125 High Holborn) during the preparation of the Eleventh Edition under the editorship of Hugh Chisholm. Ralph visited Printing House Square occasionally and was much liked there. In 1929 his *The Penn Country and the Chilterns* appeared, and three years later *A History of the Ancient Parish of Giggleswick*. He was buried at Kettlewell, in Yorkshire, where he was patron of the living.

[2] Major Dawson is said to have planted there an apple tree to commemorate the story that Newton discovered the law of gravitation as a result of watching an apple fall while sitting in his own garden. Two trees said to have grown from cuttings from Major Dawson's tree survived to modern times. ("You Don't Know Your Yorkshire", Ben Rhydding in the *Yorkshire Evening News*, 27th August, 1948.)

Littondale and Geoffrey's moors in the heart of the Pennines meant so much to him.

Geoffrey's paternal grandfather, Dixon Robinson, born in 1795, lived at Clitheroe Castle, Lancashire, where he was Gentleman Steward to the Honor of Clitheroe.[1] Both of Geoffrey's parents were in fact born in Lancashire. The Robinsons and Perfects were closely connected with the soil and were wool-brokers, probably in the beginning through lending money to farmers before their season's wool-clip was ready, in the days when the only method of transporting wool in the dales was by pack-horse. From being wool-brokers his forebears came by easy stages to the counting-house.

It was through Geoffrey's paternal grandmother, Matilda Ingram, the wife of Dixon Robinson, that he inherited his academic leanings and the love of the Classics, though these particular ancestors were associated with Cambridge and not with his beloved Oxford. His Ingram grandmother died in 1886 when Geoffrey was in his twelfth year. Her father, Geoffrey's great-grandfather, was the Rev. Robert Acklom Ingram, born at Wormingford, Essex. He was Senior Wrangler in 1784 and fellow and tutor of Queens' College, Cambridge, and subsequently rector of Seagrave, Leicestershire. His father, Geoffrey's great-great-grandfather, born at Beverley, Yorks., was the Rev. Robert Ingram, Fellow of Corpus Christi College, Cambridge.

Langcliffe Hall is a mile from the little town of Settle, and actually gives on to the road, but on the other side the Dawson property stretches for miles over moor, fell, and dale to Halton Gill and beyond. Geoffrey's book-lined study opens out of the Hall at Langcliffe and is kept very much as it was in his day, with a large open hearth where through the long autumn, winter and spring a cheerful log-fire burns. It was there that, on rare occasions, he "scribbled" leading articles for *The Times* when he was in residence. A telephone was not installed in the house until after the death of his Aunt Kitty[2] in her eighty-ninth year. She regarded the telephone as the invention of the devil. Out of consideration for her Geoffrey refused to install one, and during her lifetime, whenever he had to speak to Printing House Square, he would walk willingly to Settle Post Office, over a mile away—a very great inconvenience to an Editor of *The Times*.[3]

[1] Clitheroe belonged for many years to the Buccleuch family and finally came into the possession of the second Lord Montagu of Beaulieu (he died in 1926), a pioneer motorist and subsequently a friend of Geoffrey's. Clitheroe Castle was purchased by the town as its war memorial in 1919 and the building in which Geoffrey's grandfather, Dixon Robinson, lived, when Steward to the Honor, survives.

[2] Katherine Elizabeth Perfect (1845–1934).

[3] Cf. p. 320, *infra*.

If Geoffrey was the lucky member of the family, it was due to his own powers of concentration that he won scholarships both at Eton and Magdalen. In this sense he was self-made, although admittedly fate put great opportunities in his way, of which he made the utmost use. In the closing years of the nineteenth century the family must have lived an almost Jane Austen kind of existence, and in the later stages of the Victorian era the various families with which he was connected passed quiet, uneventful and well-ordered lives: the Robinson family in Skipton, and fifteen miles away the aunts at Langcliffe, and, at Skipton Castle, their cousins, the Barretts. There was much coming and going between the various families for tea-parties, croquet, archery, or perhaps a large garden-party where the male guests were attired in "toppers and frockers", meeting in support of good causes and of course much church-going on Sundays.

II

AYSGARTH, ETON, AND ALL SOULS

HIS parents acted wisely when they decided to send Geoffrey (in 1883) to Aysgarth Preparatory School. His very successful career was in part due to the fact that he went to Aysgarth when the Rev. Clement Hales, a remarkable teacher and famous at that time throughout Yorkshire, was headmaster. Geoffrey had received an excellent early training both from his mother and from governesses at home; the headmaster recognized in him a clever and hard-working boy who had the makings of a scholar, and it was a proud moment for the school in 1887 when three Aysgarth boys won first, third and fourth scholarships at Eton, Geoffrey obtaining the third position in the Election. When he arrived at Eton as a Colleger he little thought how important a milestone in his career he was passing.

Geoffrey was not very good at games.[1] While he was a pretty good "field" player, being a fast runner, he did not shine at "the wall". He was, however, very keen on Field Sports, and used to listen eagerly to schoolfellows who were ready to talk about shooting and sport generally. "His eyes used to brighten (his very bright eyes were a distinguishing feature) when he talked grouse."[2]

Geoffrey was a pupil of the late Edward Impey (who actually survived him). Impey prophesied a successful career for him,[3] and

[1] His name does not appear in any of the athletic records, nor in the list of teams, e.g. the College Wall XI.

[2] Information supplied by a contemporary, who was in the College Election in 1887 and was also at Oxford with him. He also says Geoffrey soon became known to his tutor and friends as "Robin", because his friends thought that he looked like a robin; a more obvious reason is that it was an abbreviation of his surname.

[3] The list of Geoffrey's academic distinctions at Eton is considerable. In 1891 he won a Strafford Shakespeare medal; in 1892 he was bracketed 5th in the Select for the Newcastle Scholarship, and bracketed 3rd for the Latin Prose Prize; in 1893 he was top of the Select in the Newcastle Scholarship, i.e. 3rd among the competitors, and Wilder Divinity Prize (which is given on the Divinity papers in the examination); First Prize in the History Examination, Jelf Prize for original Latin Verse and Latin Essay Prize (all the above were School prizes). The *Eton*

Geoffrey was certainly lucky in having him as his mentor and friend. He could not have had a more helpful tutor, and Impey once said to an intimate that ever since Mrs. Robinson had brought Geoffrey to Eton a close and lasting friendship developed between them.

The following extracts are taken from Geoffrey's letters to his mother from Eton:

June 29, 1890.

My dear Mother,

. . . Now I must tell you about the Review last Monday. It was a long trudge up into the Park, a long way up a road parallel to the Long Walk, but we thought it was well worth it in the end. It was a big swell affair. When we arrived there was a long line drawn up. Four squadrons of "The Blues" (Horse Guards) with their mounted band, a lot of footguards and our Volunteers (Eton Volunteers), each with a band.

After a few minutes we saw a cavalcade coming across the Park—the Prince and Princess of Wales and the two young Princesses, the Duke of Clarence . . . the Duke of Cambridge, Lord Wolseley and a heap of others.

Just then the Queen was seen coming in the other direction with her bare-legged Scot and suite . . . then there was a royal salute with the Prince of Wales at the head of his regiment, and then the whole business had to be gone through again (I mean the reviewing). Then the whole lot marched past with the Prince at the head and then the Cavalry charged past. I never saw anything so wonderful, you could get no idea of a charge at the Military Tournament. You wonder that anything could possibly withstand them. Then they did pursuing practice at the canter—all their swords flashing regularly—up and down while they were more spread out, and covered a huge space.

July 12, 1891.

The review on Monday was glorious. The Emperor (the Kaiser) came with the Duke of Connaught and a staff, all riding beautiful horses into College Field. It is the only time I have seen the sacred grass trodden by a horse. One fellow, as you may have seen in the papers, put in a blank cartridge in the firing exercises, which somewhat amused the Emperor. He made a nice little broken English speech at the end.

In October, 1893, Geoffrey came from the foundation of Eton to that of Magdalen. The entries in his diary for 1894 are sketchy, but they serve to give an indication of his interests. He was evidently

College Chronicle in its first number of the Michaelmas Half 1893, in which there was a review of the Summer Half, remarks that the majority of the School prizes in the Summer Half were gained by Robinson, K. S. (Information kindly supplied by Mr. C. A. Elliott, the Provost of Eton.)

working hard, especially at the Classics. His holidays were spent in Yorkshire.

All through his life Geoffrey rejoiced in opportunities of going to Italy. A letter to his mother remains recording a visit with his Aunts:

Hotel d'Angleterre,
Rome,
March 29, 1896.

I have been roaming about the Capuchin establishment since lunch with Spencer-Smith. . . . We were to have gone to St. John Lateran at 5 to see the Chief Penitentiary, whatever he may be, received by other Penitentiaries, but decided that it wasn't *assez bon* in this rain and hail.

We had a tremendous day yesterday. Drove about 10 to the Vatican and spent the morning in the Sculptures—Belvedere, Apollo, Laocoon, Antinous, Caesars, and that lot, and after lunch Kitty took me for half an hour to the Capitoline Museum, to see the Dying Gladiator. They were awfully fine, but I don't really appreciate them as I should like to. I much prefer these old churches to anything else so far. We strolled through a ripper yesterday on our way back from the Capitol—Ara Coeli—with wonderful old pillars and mosaics—and a miraculous cure-working image, which a monk showed us for a consideration, and spat under the altar as he did it.

We saw two the day before, one where St. Peter is supposed to have been beheaded, and another, St. Onofrio, given up to Tasso.

We were to have spent this afternoon loafing round the Palace of the Caesars on the Palatine, that I might impart the wise words of Augustus Hare. He was awfully good and it was great luck my getting in for it. He is staying now at the Italie, where the Spencer-Smiths are, and is a very old friend of theirs.

The whole crowd of both our hotels turned out into the Colosseum last night about 9 to see it by moonlight, it was simply splendid, but we rather thirsted for the ghost of a lion or two, when an American (?) sat down and began to play the banjo. They write their names all over St. Peter's, the Leaning Tower of Pisa, the Arch of Titus, every bit of the Forum, and even on the *skulls* of the Capuchins. Would you believe it? The latter are not nearly so gruesome as you'd think, being far too small to be life-like. They must have fasted more in those days, I think.

It is very irritating getting no English newspapers, till you've ceased to care. I don't yet know what won the Grand National or the Boat Race, but I am wearing a chaste dark-blue buttonhole.

Geoffrey began his proper diary-keeping in 1897. From that year, till a week before his death, we have a complete record of his life.[1] They were "one day on a page" diaries. At the beginning he wrote in a large hand, and each page contained from forty to sixty words, but

[1] The only gap is for the two years 1919 and 1920. These diaries were lost.

later on he managed to write each day between 150 and 180 words on a page.

He was now twenty-two, but a study of his records does not reveal any marked views on the kind of career that he wished to take up. True, while still at Oxford, he went to discuss the possibilities of the Indian Civil Service with the authorities. He certainly was already much interested in Empire matters and listened to a debate at the Union on naval defence and attended a meeting of the Navy League. While in London he visited a friend at the Colonial Office and another at the Treasury—a year or so later when he passed his Civil Service examination, friends in both these departments helped him to leave the Post Office.

Geoffrey spent three periods of cramming at Wren's Collegiate Establishment of which Walter Wren was the Principal, at 7, Powis Square, Bayswater, the first period in July, 1897, of brief duration, the second in the autumn and a final and decisive period in the summer of 1898. For some unknown reason in the first spell, after a couple of days at Wren's, Geoffrey wrote "decided on going home and chucking it for this year if it wasn't to be the Indian Civil Service". What the definite reason responsible for this action was cannot be stated. The late Sir Henry Craik, who subsequently had a successful career in India, becoming Governor of the Punjab and Political Adviser to the Viceroy, and was at Wren's with Geoffrey, thought the decision was due to family reasons. Geoffrey's widow suggests that owing to his mother's delicate health (she died in 1903) he probably decided not to take a job which would mean permanent residence in the East.

Mr. Wren, crippled by paralysis, moved about the establishment in a wheeled-chair, and was a formidable figure; although he did not take any active part in the teaching at this period, he kept a strict eye on everything, carefully watching the progress of each candidate, and was a shrewd prophet as to the place each would probably take in the list.

Despite his previous resolution not to return to Wren's in 1897, Geoffrey was back there in October. He was now living in rooms at Marlborough Mansions, opposite Christ Church in Victoria Street, and thence he used to cycle each day to Wren's. In the evenings he visited both the Eton Mission at Hackney Wick and Oxford House at Bethnal Green, where he played games with the lads and, important from the standpoint of his future career, saw something of the squalor of the East End.

The early months of 1898 were spent by Geoffrey in Skipton reading seriously for his coming Civil Service examination; but he managed to get some hunting—and shooting. He attended steeplechases, point-to-points, and hunt-balls, and engaged in a few games of golf—"played shockingly" (he never was a keen golfer). On February 25th he became, like his father, a freemason, but did not, apparently, keep up his freemasonry for long.

While cramming for the Civil Service examination, at Wren's from April to August, 1898, Geoffrey kept a record of the number of hours spent daily in reading; the highest total was 10½ hours, the average entry was 7 or 8. He kept a careful list of all the papers in the Civil Service examination and made disparaging remarks for the most part on his efforts. After perusing his comments: Greek Language and Literature "fetid papers"; Mental Philosophy "rather bad"; English Literature "matter inferior"; Criticism and Creation "miserable effort"; Latin Translation and Latin Composition "two diabolical papers", the reader would never have expected that he would pass out tenth in a list of ninety-four successful candidates. On the final day of the examination, devoted to English Literature, he "finished 6 quills" and nearly six note-books.

On September 25 he returned to London and another important milestone in his life is passed:

> *Sept. 26.* London. A very busy day. Interviewed J.E.T. at the Colonial Office, then a medical, long but successful process, and got the last Home Civil Service vacancy namely at the G.P.O.

Refreshed by his visits to Yorkshire, he returned to Oxford and plunged into another examination which lasted three days, this time to compete for an All Souls Fellowship. The papers included "an English Essay, Latin, Greek, French, German and Italian translation, interspersed with a horrid *viva*"; an entire day and a half of history and a general paper.

On November 1st he moved to rooms at 13, Bruton Street, and went to report for duty at the General Post Office, where he was introduced to the various officials. He joined the Secretary's office as a 2nd class clerk, his commencing salary was £150 a year, and he worked in the Headquarters building at St. Martin's-le-Grand.

On his return to the G.P.O. from lunching with a friend in Cannon Street, Geoffrey found "a flood of telegrams" to say that he had been elected to All Souls. That afternoon (November 3rd, 1898) he wrote to his mother:

> Cocoa Tree Club,
> 64, St. James's Street, S.W.
>
> My dear Mother,
>
> Wires from Lang, Fletcher and Co., just arrived at G.P.O. to say that they have given me a Fellowship of All Souls and I must go

down there tonight. So I am off by the 4.45 but will come back by first train tomorrow to Bruton Street. Rather splendid isn't it? I feel supremely happy.

Ever your loving,
G. G. R.

The College of All Souls of the faithful departed of Oxford, commonly called All Souls College, was founded by King Henry VI (also the founder of Eton), by a patent of foundation bearing the date May 20, 1438 (fifty-four years before the discovery of America by Christopher Columbus). The co-founder was Henry Chichele, Archbishop of Canterbury, by whom the college was endowed and its statutes bear the date of April 20, 1443. "It was a Foundation designed in part for the offering of prayers for all the souls of the faithful departed, and especially for the souls of Henry V and of Thomas, Duke of Clarence, and other nobles and faithful subjects of the realm who had died in the French war."[1]

Throughout his diaries Geoffrey makes constant references to All Souls. He recognized to the full the debt that he and other Fellows owed to Sir William Anson, Warden when he was elected, whose death in 1914 he so deplored. To him that remarkable man was always "our beloved Warden", and when he died he regarded his loss as irreparable.[2] For thirty years Sir William had presided over All Souls with firmness and tact, and gave benign and shrewd guidance to the College. Two autobiographies by Geoffrey's contemporaries have recently appeared, and in both of them there are references to the happy and very special influence which All Souls exercised on their lives. The late Lord Simon and Mr. L. S. Amery were both elected in 1897, the year before Geoffrey's election. Many friendships between brilliant men were first made at the College. Here Geoffrey met Arthur Balfour, John Morley and many others. At All Souls, too, one of the most important events in Geoffrey's life took place, in October, 1922, when R. H. Brand,[3] on behalf of Major J. J. Astor, invited him to return to Printing House Square for a second term of office as Editor.

In 1932, Geoffrey's colleague and friend, Charles W. Brodribb, noticing what an extraordinary influence the Fellows of All Souls had had on current events, especially since about the 1860s, was

[1] *Vide* Statutes, made by All Souls College, Oxford, and approved by the University Commissioners in pursuance of the University of Oxford and Cambridge Act, 1923.

[2] He was succeeded by Dr. F. W. Pember, who remained Warden till 1932. No better choice could have been made. He only died on January 19th, 1954, in his ninety-second year.

[3] The "Bob" of the diaries. One of Geoffrey's most intimate friends, since South African days. Now Lord Brand.

moved to write, for his own amusement, a skit entitled "Government by Mallardry—A Study in Political Ornithology". (The Mallard is the ancient emblem of the College of All Souls, and figures in the ritual of the Fellows' meetings.)

After pointing out that illustrious "Mallards" abounded in all departments of State and every profession, and ranged over Europe, the Dominions, and America, Brodribb dubbed them, in his semi-serious concluding passage, "an unofficial club for running, or helping to run the destinies of the British Empire".

Brodribb had no connection with the College but recognized in its Fellows an aristocracy of talent which was not disbanded after three or four years of University life, but maintained its corporate spirit through perennial reunions.

What an exceptional advantage it was for a future editor of *The Times* to be admitted at the age of twenty-four to the lifelong membership of such a society!

It is small wonder that years later Geoffrey said that the two events in his early career which he looked back upon with the greatest pleasure were his election to All Souls in 1898, and his appointment as South African Correspondent of *The Times* in 1906.

III

THE COLONIAL OFFICE—1899–1901

GEOFFREY'S parents were very proud of their son's achievements in 1898 and came up to London for a few days, and he took his father round the Central Telegraph Office where he was then working. As the old year closed, however, a cloud appeared on the horizon. Geoffrey had slight trouble with his superiors at the G.P.O., who had heard that he was receiving communications from an Official at the Treasury. Apparently one of Geoffrey's friends in Whitehall advised him of a vacancy there and was pulling strings on his behalf. Certainly his heart was not in his work at the G.P.O.[1] and he consulted the Civil Service Commissioners, early in the new year, about the possibility of a transfer to a department which stirred his imagination—the Colonial Office—under Joseph Chamberlain, whose magnetic personality naturally attracted a young man with Imperial leanings.

By the 25th January the Colonial Office was formally demanding Geoffrey's services, and within three weeks he was able to write (Feb. 18, 1899) hopefully to Aunt Kitty:

> 13, Bruton Street, W.
>
> I am still hanging on in the Post Office where they don't want me, and go daily to jog the Civil Service Commissioners as the Colonial Office are very much overworked. They say they will be about two days longer, so I am going to take a day's leave and hunt with the Bicester on Monday.

On March 1st Geoffrey bade farewell to his friends at the G.P.O., and the following day began work at the Colonial Office, and spent most of the morning being taken round and introduced to everyone. He arrived there at the very moment when it was entering upon one of the most important phases in its history. The relations between the Transvaal Government and the United Kingdom, the Suzerain Power, were becoming strained. At last there seemed a chance of wiping out

[1] At the same time A. B. Walkley was on the staff of the G.P.O. before he became dramatic critic of *The Times*.

the stigma of Majuba and redressing the grievances of the Uitlanders. Six weeks after Geoffrey's arrival in Whitehall the Great Petition with 21,000 signatures arrived in the actual room where he was working at the Colonial Office. He was thinking of little else but South Africa. His reading included Kipling, James Bryce's *Impressions of South Africa*, Robert Baden-Powell's *Matabele Campaign* and much else. The South African Department was working overtime; one Saturday he put into code and cipher seven telegrams to the High Commissioner. Even Earl's Court staged a "Savage South African Show", where on hot summer evenings he and his friends water-chuted, switch-backed and "shot" white rabbits and macaws.

John Bull's patience had been tried to the uttermost. Not only *The Times* thundered but youthful Alfred Harmsworth[1]—then in his thirty-fourth year—proprietor of the *Evening News*, and, since 1896, of the rapidly growing *Daily Mail*, proclaimed with all his understanding of the mind of masses and with a mastery of the technique of influencing his vast public, that the time for deeds and not words had come. Finally, on 11th October, 1899, just over seven months since Geoffrey had joined the Colonial Office, Kruger's Ultimatum expired and war with the South African Republic had begun.

The early war news told of armoured trains destroyed, of heavy casualties at Glencoe, at Elandslaagte and elsewhere, of many Gordons and men of other regiments killed, of defeats and withdrawals. Not since the Crimea had the British people passed through such black weeks. Early in the new year came the news of a repulse by White's gallant men of an attack on Ladysmith. In late February at last, much good news from South Africa arrived—Cronje had surrendered and two days later (March 1st), the relief of Ladysmith by Dundonald with some of Buller's cavalry caused great jubilation, flags were hung out, bells rung and shouting mobs watched the illuminations. The tide had turned.

Some entries from Geoffrey's diary record these events:

March 8. . . . To the office via Buckingham Palace to see the Queen arrive on a two-day visit, great enthusiasm without, and Lords and Commons singing God Save the Queen within.

May 18. A skeleton drill at Somerset House . . . hear about 10 the first shouting for the Relief of Mafeking.

May 19. Rejoicings everywhere, cabs, houses, etc., a mass of flags. I was at the office till after lunch—then back to change . . . catch special for Battalion drill at Wimbledon. . . . To "The Rivals", at the Haymarket, excellently played . . . patriotic airs etc. Charlie (Phillimore) and I strolled round the illuminations.

[1] Subsequently Lord Northcliffe.

May 21. . . . office early and then about 1 p.m. opened with my own hand the official confirmation of the relief of Mafeking. Up with our new flag at once—the other offices following suit a little later.

June 5. 4th of June at Eton. I made off there at 1.7 p.m. . . . Official news of the occupation of Pretoria arriving as we drove through Pall Mall. . . .

In July, 1900, Geoffrey spent ten days under canvas at Minster Camp, near Sheerness, doing a course of musketry, with much drilling. By camp-fire one evening on "Spion Kop" there was a successful sing-song. In odd moments, curiously enough, Geoffrey did his first book reviews in camp. He had been asked by his friend, Richard Austen-Leigh, to review for the weekly, *Public Opinion,* then owned by Messrs. Spottiswoode, "a wildly sensational book called *Caged*". During the next two years he did several reviews for this weekly.

Early in the new year alarming news came from Osborne, and members of the Royal Family hurried down to the Isle of Wight. The Queen was obviously dying, and on January 20th, her grandson, the German Emperor, arrived. On January 22nd, 1901, the end came and with it the end of an epoch.

A world without Queen Victoria seemed impossible to imagine. Geoffrey's generation accepted her almost as a permanent feature of their lives. Their parents had been born in her lifetime, or indeed in many cases since she came to the throne. Her death made a tremendous impact on countless millions; especially in the British Empire which had reached new heights of development and achievement in her reign, and her subjects, wherever the Union Jack flew, suffered a sense of deep personal loss.

Geoffrey thus describes the days following her death:

Jan. 23 and 24. Two most depressing days at the office, blinds drawn all day—blackest of black-edged paper—Minute guns and bells tolling, and telegrams arriving galore from Colonial Mayors and Jewish communities. On Wednesday His Majesty arrived from Osborne and took the oath to the Lords of the Council as Edward VII. On Thursday at 9 he was proclaimed King at St. James's. . . . Houses of Parliament sat both days and took oaths of Allegiance—and the walls were covered with proclamations. So much work to do that I found I soon got hardened to expressing the views of *His* Majesty's Government.

Jan. 27. Oxford. Chapel 8.45, the new prayers sounding very strange. . . .

On May 24th, Geoffrey went to Waterloo to see Milner arrive from South Africa on leave. "Most of the Cabinet and the House of Commons there and crowds outside." Ten days later Sir M. F. Ommanney, Permanent Under-Secretary of State at the Colonial Office, told him he was to go temporarily as Assistant Private Secretary to Joseph Chamberlain, which stroke of good fortune Geoffrey records, somewhat inadequately, with these words, "which office I accepted with gratitude".

Milner's visit necessitated much extra work in the South African Department as there were many youthful place-hunters clamouring for interviews. These applicants had to be "combed" and lists prepared of suitable people already in the Civil Service. The life of a member of Chamberlain's staff was a thrilling one and one never knew who would be the next caller, come to pay his respects to the great man; it might be Sir George White, the defender of Ladysmith, or Lord Scarbrough with a scheme for the settlement of Imperial Yeomen in South Africa, or Geoffrey might be sent on some mission for his Chief, such as leaving his card on the United States Ambassador, when the news of the death of President McKinley was received.

But Geoffrey's days as a Civil Servant in London were numbered, as the following extracts from the diary show:

> *Sept. 24.* Found a telegram to Mr. Chamberlain from Lord Milner, asking him to let me go out as Private Secretary for a year at £1,000. Talked to Ommanney when he came up at 1, and found him on the whole inclined to recommend it.
>
> *Sept. 26.* Another influx of visitors to see the Chief. However he had time to approve my going out to South Africa and I wrote home and to the Warden of All Souls.
>
> *Oct. 22.* . . . I said good-bye to most people—and then after dressing and dining hastily at the re-opened Cocoa Tree to "Sherlock Holmes".

It is impossible to exaggerate the importance of the year 1901 for Geoffrey; in it he stepped out of the Home Civil Service and set out with enthusiasm to take up the task of serving as Assistant Private Secretary to Lord Milner, in South Africa.

None of Milner's young men had had a better preparatory training for his job than Geoffrey. He had spent over two years in the South African Department of the Colonial Office (excepting the four months when he acted as Assistant Private Secretary to Chamberlain, then immersed in South African problems). He had read much about South Africa and was fully posted, of course, with all the day-to-day cables, despatches and discussions both before and after the outbreak of war.

When the opportunity came of serving with Milner, it may truly be said that circumstances were urging him into a field of activity admirably suited to his tastes and talents.

IV

WITH MILNER IN SOUTH AFRICA—1901–1905

WHEN Joseph Chamberlain accepted the post of Secretary of State at the Colonial Office, in 1895, he showed clearly how important, in his view, were Empire problems. His action had stirred public opinion. Many factors were responsible for the growth of interest in Imperial developments and in the expansion of Her Majesty's Realms beyond the seas. For a time "Little Englanderism", as expounded by Goldwin Smith and others, was widely accepted—but a new era was soon to begin. There had been the humiliating defeat of British arms at Majuba, in 1881, and the sacrifice of General C. G. Gordon, through unpreparedness, at Khartoum in 1885. Gordon's death, however, had been avenged by Kitchener's victory at Omdurman, in 1898, and there was a growing interest in the affairs of "Greater Britain".

Towards the latter half of the Victorian era John Macdonald in Canada, Alfred Deakin in Australia, Richard Seddon in New Zealand, Cecil Rhodes in South Africa, and Cromer with his inspiring proconsulship in Egypt, had taught the British public to gaze on far horizons. Other factors in educating it were of course Charles Dilke's *Greater Britain* and John R. Seeley's *The Expansion of England*, while Rudyard Kipling reached an even larger public. The founding of the Royal Colonial Institute (in 1868), and of the Imperial Federation League (in 1884), which owed so much to the inspiration of George Parkin (born in Canada)—were symbolic of the increasing realization of the importance of the Empire. Finally the influence of the South African War itself, and the part the Colonies (not yet called Dominions) had played in sending contingents to fight alongside the troops from the Motherland, encouraged all who were working for Imperial unity. The "outer fringe" of the Empire was, in the national life, what the frontier, ever pushing westwards, was in the life of the United States. Imperialism was in the air, and even the Administration of the United

States, under President McKinley, had adopted an expansionist policy[1] which had resulted in the annexation of the Hawaiian Islands in 1898, and the acquisition of the Panama Canal under Theodore Roosevelt, a disciple of Mahan, and therefore a fervent apostle of expansionism.

When Geoffrey set out for South Africa he cannot have known Milner very well; he would only have seen him probably at a few official interviews at the Colonial Office. Milner had a genius for selecting the right type of young man, and he had obviously heard about Geoffrey's background and capabilities when he was at the Colonial Office in the summer of 1901. An exceptional relationship was to develop between the two. It has been compared almost to that of father and son; they seemed to understand each other by instinct. His new Chief shared many things in common with Geoffrey. They were both devoted to Oxford, where Milner had had a brilliant career, having won most of the great University prizes and having obtained a first class in Greats and been elected a Fellow of New College. In those days Geoffrey, of course, had no thought of adopting the profession of journalism as a career. His interest in the Press must, however, have been stimulated by the knowledge that at the age of twenty-seven his new Chief had worked for the *Pall Mall Gazette* under John Morley; and later had served under that great journalist, W. T. Stead.

Geoffrey, just twenty years Milner's junior, arrived in Cape Town a few days before his twenty-seventh birthday. It was four years since Milner had been appointed High Commissioner in South Africa by Chamberlain. From Milner's letters, in due course, we shall see some of the ideals which that great statesman steadfastly held before him. Few men had given more thought to the future of the British Empire, and above all to the relationship of the two sections of the white race in South Africa. Every act of Geoffrey's new Chief was influenced by the thought of the part that the British Empire might play in preserving peace and helping subject peoples to nationhood, and in spreading British ideals of justice and freedom throughout the world. Once peace was achieved in South Africa it was obviously our duty to strengthen those elements in South Africa which were prepared to throw in their lot with the British, and establish South Africa as a firm bastion of our World-State free from Downing Street interference.[2]

[1] Largely due to the teachings of Admiral A. T. Mahan who believed in the fundamental importance of the expansion of the two Anglo-Saxon World States in the best interests of civilization. His book, *The Influence of Sea Power upon History* (1890), had a lasting effect on British thinking.

[2] *Vide* "Lord Milner's High Commissionership", *The Times*, April 4, 1905. Lord Milner said: "South Africa can prosper under two, three or six governments, though the fewer the better, but not under two absolutely conflicting social and political systems, perfect equality for the Dutch and British in the British Colonies, side by side with permanent subjection of British to Dutch in one of the Republics."

When Sir Alfred Milner (he was created a peer by King Edward VII in 1901) arrived in South Africa in May, 1897, the Afrikander sentiment throughout Cape Colony mainly supported Kruger, whose goal plainly was a Dutch-controlled South Africa. Milner, ever slow to act until he had studied all aspects of the problem confronting him, patiently and unremittingly reviewed the entire field of British policy. He saw "everybody", was conciliatory and sought to learn, at first hand, every facet of opinion. Within twelve months his mind was made up. This was no hasty decision. There was no room in South Africa for divergent loyalties.

Milner proceeded to put his plan into operation. Briefly it was: (*a*) to obtain moral support in South Africa in an attempt to bring pressure to bear upon the Transvaal in the direction of Reform; (*b*) to convince the Conservative Government in the United Kingdom and British public opinion at home that his diagnosis was the correct one; (*c*) to enlist on his side the moderate element among the Dutch in the Cape Colony and the Orange Free State.[1]

In March, 1898, Milner delivered to a Dutch audience one of the most notable speeches in his career at Graaf-Reinet, in Cape Colony. He deplored the suspicious and unprogressive policy of the South African Republic, under President Kruger, which was the root of the trouble. He urged his hearers not to encourage the Transvaal Government by espousing its cause in every quarrel, but, as real friends of the South African Republic, to induce it "to assimilate its institutions and what was even more important, the temper and the spirit of its administration to those of the free communities of South Africa, such as were to be found in Cape Colony or the Orange Free State". The speech made a tremendous sensation. Milner's campaign was making progress. Towards the end of the war Milner returned to the task of shaping South Africa's destiny with Geoffrey as one of his assistants.

On his arrival, in November, 1901, Geoffrey wrote:

My dear Mother,

I have just sent you a telegram at vast expense announcing my safe arrival at my journey's end. It took place last night, but can only telegraph here between the hours of 3.00 and 4.00 p.m. when the Censor attends at the G.P.O. . . .

One afternoon at Cape Town I saw Rhodes's house and property and a

[1] *Vide* article entitled "Lord Milner's High Commissionership" in *The Times*, April 4, 1905. Also "Lord Milner and His Work", by Sir Percy Fitzpatrick, three articles published in the *Cape Times*, February 13th, 16th and 17th, 1925, and issued in pamphlet form.

cottage he has built on it for Kipling, all perfectly lovely and gardens and views which can't be beaten anywhere. . . . *In the train.* Practically all the first day's climbing through the Karroo, rocky brown hills with patchy heath growing on them, then in the north of the Colony you begin the smooth grassy veld more like the Berkshire Downs than anything else and that goes on right through the Orange River Colony up to here. . . . They (the troops) were sniping from the blockhouses as we went up, they seem to fire away at each other every night up there and no one seems any the worse, but it is rather thrilling lying in your carriage and listening to it in the dark.

Of course we never saw a Boer or a column all the time, no signs of war but the block-houses all the way up the line—two or three to the mile, sometimes more—ragged Tommies sitting outside them and marvellous contrivances of dummy khaki figures, dummy guns, and barbed wire fencing hung with sardine tins etc., to give them the alarm. Where the so-called road runs beside the line the veld is literally strewn with dead animals, but there are no burnt farm-houses or other horrors of war to be seen and the land looks thoroughly fat and prosperous especially the Orange River Colony. . . .

It was very odd after all the sea and train and hotel, waking up this morning in an ordinary English bedroom and having tea brought to your bedside by an ordinary white man—really the view from the window is vast (you can see the Forts at Pretoria) and it isn't very un-English except that there are no fences. There are plenty of trees out this way, and no houses beyond.

We each have our own room in the High Commissioner's Office and there seems to be a fair staff of clerks, typewriters, orderlies and messengers of various kinds. I gather that it (our abode) is a one-storeyed cottage with one big sitting-room, three bedrooms, bathroom, an attic and a bit of garden and a glorious view.

There are sentries and outposts everywhere, but no big bodies of troops, as all able-bodied inhabitants have had to join the Rand Rifles. You have to have a permit to ride, drive, bicycle, to go by train and to exist in the town at all.

Rand Club,
eadem. Johannesburg,
29th November, 1901.

The work I do here is of a very miscellaneous character. I'm turned on to writing memoranda and despatches on every conceivable subject—generally about five minutes' conversation which I have to remember as well as I can—and there are practically no works of reference here, or cupboards, or writing papers or anything else. I work at a trestle-table in an empty and fairly cool room which I have to myself and keep my papers in despatch boxes around me on the floor. My only continuous job is to act as medium between H.E. and the Johannesburg Municipality who are rather an ill-assorted and cantankerous crew. . . .

Lionel Curtis[1] states that he got Milner, who had decided to take the Municipality under his wing, to appoint Robin (i.e. Dawson) "who is a very able youth, as his secretary for Municipal Affairs", and that in consequence things went much more smoothly.

One of Geoffrey's first excursions on the veld is thus described:

> Wonderfontein. . . . Breakfast in the train then drove in cape carts to the springs with an escort of mounted infantry. . . . Glorious hot day, quite good weather for the Transvaal, with gorgeous snipe bog and rocky gorges beside it. Eagle's nest and many strange parti-coloured birds and a fine speckled snake in the water at the drift. After a sandwich lunch we explored the caves, one really fine one, running its head to Mafeking. Not unlike Clapham (near his Yorkshire home), with a river running far away inside, reminding one of "King Solomon's Mines". Exciting drive back over the veld with our faithful escort spread out in a fan round us.

In these early days Geoffrey saw much of Basil Blackwood and F. Perry, who came also from Oxford and the Colonial Office and who was also a Fellow of All Souls. He was Lord Milner's Imperial Secretary. He was described to the author by Geoffrey's old Tutor at Magdalen, Dr. C. C. T. Webb,[2] as "one of the ablest men he ever met". There are many references to Perry, with whom, at dinner on one of their first evenings, he had a "long philosophical discussion on what constitutes happiness".

In March came the news of the death of Cecil Rhodes, and "crowds of people came to call" on the High Commissioner, and he and his entire staff went to a packed church for the memorial service, when the sermon was preached by the Bishop of Zululand. During May there was great activity in connection with the negotiations for the ending of the war. Milner went to Pretoria and Geoffrey joined his Chief at the Agency there on May 26th, when he found "them all in the midst of telegrams. . . . Negotiations going slowly—rather better than they might have done". H.E. said "that of course the real fight was between him and Lord Kitchener—the Boers were simply supers looking on. . . ." Smuts and Hertzog were two of the delegates.

Two short entries in the diary record the end of the war:

1902.

May 31. H.E. went off about 7 to Pretoria . . . the Boer delegates came back likewise, and the TERMS OF SURRENDER were signed at midnight.

[1] Vide *With Milner in South Africa*, L. Curtis (Blackwell, 1951), p. 328.
Lionel Curtis, member of the Kindergarten, and called by his intimates, "the prophet"; there are constant references to him in Geoffrey's papers. On several occasions I have consulted him about Geoffrey's part in events.

[2] He died in 1954.

Sunday, June 1. FIRST DAY OF PEACE. I heard of it first on getting down to the office about 11.00. Darragh announced it from the pulpit.

In June, H.E. and Geoffrey dined with Kitchener and were present at the ceremony of the Inauguration of Civil Government at Pretoria, when there was reading of Letters Patent and the taking of oaths. In August, Geoffrey dined with Monypenny,[1] Amery and Herbert Baker.[2] In November, evidently the Colonial Office was trying to persuade Geoffrey to return to England, for he writes, "Fear my days in South Africa are numbered."

The year 1903 opened most tragically for Geoffrey. On January 2nd, bad news of his mother—"too feeble to write"—reached him and he cabled to find out how matters stood. Six weeks later there was another cable. Geoffrey was thoroughly alarmed and told his Chief, who was "most kind about it" and arranged for him to go home by the next mail. He wrote on February 17th, "Felt all night that it was too late and had a poorish time walking round and about the house." The next day the telegram arrived with the dreaded news that all was over. On the Saturday he went to church at 12 p.m.—the exact time of the funeral at Settle, where his mother was buried.

Fortunately for Geoffrey his work was interesting and there was plenty of it. Joseph Chamberlain had been at Johannesburg in January when he first became anxious about his mother's health, and there were many functions in connection with the visit. On March 17th the Customs Conference at Bloemfontein unanimously affirmed that there was a shortage of available South African labour, a step which ultimately led to the importation of Chinese labour, which was to play so important a part in British politics the following two or three years.

Geoffrey wrote to his father (April 5th, 1903):

> . . . Very little going on here except a bit of an outburst on the Asiatic question. . . . I think there's very little doubt now that it will come to Chinamen in time.
>
> It would release an immense quantity of niggers for agriculture etc., which they much prefer and I think it ought to be possible to keep the yellow men for unskilled labour pure and simple and to ship them home again when they have done it. It would certainly mean a great increase of skilled white labour in the mines because so many low-grade properties

[1] W. F. Monypenny, assistant to Buckle—whom the latter at one time hoped would succeed him as Editor of *The Times*—had served as correspondent in South Africa for the paper. Wrote first two volumes of life of Lord Beaconsfield.

[2] Subsequently Sir Herbert Baker. He was the architect of many of the best buildings in South Africa, including the Government Offices at Pretoria, and Groote Schuur (the home of Cecil Rhodes at Cape Town and now the residence of the Premier of the Union).

could be started, but you can't expect a labour agitator to look as far ahead as that, and he's nothing else to agitate about at present.

The tempo of Geoffrey's life at this period reveals itself in a further letter to Kitty (June 14th, 1903):

> I've had rather a satisfactory week consisting of a good deal of solid work and a good game of Polo on Saturday afternoon to wind it up. Feel rather as if I'd been through a mangle today and so I'm afraid do my ponies, but it is a grand game that can cram a whole week's exercise into 50 minutes. H.E. has spent nearly all day today working, bad for him. I dragged him out for an hour's walk after tea all along the ridge, such a glorious view and sunset. Church bells are very badly needed in this country to give a Sunday evening a proper peaceful finish. There is no town to be seen from our end of it but lots of little groups of farms scattered over the 40 odd miles between us and the mountains, and I think some of these millionaires must be induced to give a peal to knock out the noise of their beastly stamps (i.e. the machinery crushing the rock from which the gold was extracted). Perhaps it would offend the Dutch puritanism but they'd soon get used to it.

On August 12th Geoffrey sailed in the *Saxon* from Cape Town on his first leave since his appointment—but of course his mother's death must have weighed very heavily on him all that summer and especially at Skipton whither he went straight from the ship and was welcomed at midnight by his father and sister. In mid-September Geoffrey joined his family at Marienbad, the Bohemian spa; H.E. was also visiting Europe, and was at Carlsbad nearby. The day after his arrival, Milner came over to lunch and told Geoffrey, as had been correctly stated in the Press, that he had been offered the position of Secretary of State at the Colonial Office, in succession to Joseph Chamberlain. H.E., to Geoffrey's relief, had refused the offer, which in his view would have been fatal; this was no time to leave his key post in South Africa and to join Balfour's Unionist Administration, then in a somewhat parlous state.

On October 6th, Alfred Lyttelton accepted the Colonial Secretaryship, which Geoffrey held was as good an appointment as could have been made. Geoffrey spent most of his leave in Yorkshire and sailed with Milner from Southampton, aboard the *Dunottar Castle*, arriving at Cape Town on December 15th, "the ships all dressed in the bay, guard of honour and bands and drums". A week after Milner's return, the opening of the Chinese labour debate took place in the Legislative Council, and on the last day in 1903 Milner attended a meeting of the Executive Council to pass the Chinese Immigration Ordinance.

The policy of importing Chinese coolies to work in the mines on the Rand became a subject of acute controversy in Great Britain throughout 1904. Evidently, in South Africa, members of commercial and technical associations protested at the delay in obtaining assent to the Labour Ordinance, and Milner received deputations on the subject. Geoffrey received letters from home seeking enlightenment and he thus referred to the subject in letters (January 25th, March 20th and June 25th) to Langcliffe:

> As for your questions, I believe it is all right about the Chinamen coming, don't think there is any necessity to indulge in long negotiations with the Chinese Government, who have everything to gain by it, and as to their working underground I understand that the Northern Chinese is all right, but not the Southern who is a fat and timid creature.

> . . . It is impossible to say when we shall see our first Chinaman. Perhaps in a couple of months with luck and if nothing goes wrong in the meanwhile. He'll be a more popular man here than he ever was in his yellow Empire and probably will be received with brass bands, and a shouting crowd. They seem to be still talking an immense amount of rubbish about it in England. . . .

> . . . On Wednesday I went out in Lady Farrar's motor to see the first train load of Chinamen arrive on the Rand—very amusing after all the fuss we've had—to see a train steam slowly across the veld and disgorge 300 live pigtails. They seemed to be a docile and phlegmatic people, settled down at once, in the rooms in the compound, hung their straw hats on pegs, unpacked their wicker baskets, and they are now after two days, very zealous about their work. . . .

On August 30th the *Johannesburg Star* published a leading article by Geoffrey, written by him at the request of the Editor, on the departure of Sir Arthur Lawley on leave; of interest, as probably the first time he ever wrote a leader in that publication, of which he was to become editor the following year. Geoffrey was much amused by comments made to him by his friends who had no idea of the identity of the writer.

During the latter part of 1904, Geoffrey, who kept in close touch with his many friends in England, was convinced that the days of the Balfour Administration were numbered; how large a majority the Campbell-Bannerman Administration was to obtain in the "Chinese

Slavery" Election of January, 1906, even he could not have anticipated. The year ended with talks with the Boer leaders.

The first three months of 1905 were spent by Milner in clearing up after his eight years in South Africa. No small task, especially as events had not turned out as he had hoped. He would have preferred that the British Administration should have been fairly established before the inevitable introduction of responsible government. With the growing realization that a Liberal Government would be in power in Great Britain after the next election, events moved rapidly in South Africa. The beginning of February was taken up by an Inter-Colonial Railway Conference, when many of the leading statesmen, including Jameson and Smartt, participated in the discussions. Before embarking on the farewell functions, Lord Milner and Geoffrey went for a three-day trek to Potchefstroom, Venterskroon and Vereeniging. It was an intimate interlude in which they could discuss the future and survey H.E.'s work with its disappointments and successes. Geoffrey, the extrovert, kept a full account of these days. How one wishes that for once he had really let himself go in his diaries and told us what were his own feelings at this great turning-point in his life. Certainly he was, as always, responsive to the beauties of nature, as the following entries in the diary show. H.E. and he had ridden eighteen miles from Potchefstroom through "glorious green gorges" to Venterskroon, where they spent the night:

Feb. 14. . . . very jolly, 4 or 5 houses, good little hotel—we had a cottage next door. Heavy rain all afternoon but we gladly read and slept and walked after it had cleared in the evening, along the riverside. Quite a glorious sunset and a heavenly peaceful moonlit night. Bridge after an indifferent meal and a pyjama walk with H.E. before turning in.

Feb. 15. Venterskroon–Losberg. . . . Across the plain to the great hump of Losberg, visible all the way . . . a walk with H.E. to see the sun go down and the moon come up from the mountain top. A wonderful view all round and the colouring of sky and veld-fires and mountains never to be forgotten. Great talk at dinner on the nationalities and languages of Eastern Europe. Then bridge and bed.

During his month of leave-taking, Milner was delighted by the announcement that Selborne was to succeed him. A week later there was another pleasant surprise—a telegram from Dougal Malcolm, Geoffrey's intimate friend and a Fellow of All Souls, to say that he had been appointed Private Secretary to Selborne, an event which Geoffrey referred to in his diary as "a real good job". The following day, March 10th, was a very important milestone in Geoffrey's career, how important in its ultimate consequences he cannot, at the time, have had any conception. Probably on their trek, when they were having intimate talks, Lord Milner must surely have discussed the subject of the *Star*. Anyhow, on March 10th, Geoffrey lunched with Sam Evans and Lionel Phillips[1] "who definitely broached the *Star* project"; this remark surely shows that Geoffrey already knew what was in his Chief's mind.

Lord Milner was strongly in favour of the scheme as it would ensure that his policy would receive adequate attention in the columns of the *Star* after his departure, and the paper in Geoffrey's capable hands would form a rallying point for those who fervently desired to keep South Africa within the British Empire. Geoffrey was in due course appointed Editor by the Chairman of the Argus Printing and Publishing Company, at a salary of £2,000 per annum (and after a year, if both sides were satisfied, £2,500 per annum).

Lord Milner's final departure from Johannesburg is thus described: "About 5.00 p.m. we set off in two carriages for the station via the Wanderers which we reached in a terrific storm. Volunteers lining the streets—vast crowds—and a very impressive send-off from the station. At Pretoria an equally depressing downpour, quite spoiling the bands, guards, bonfires and guns."

At Delagoa Bay a large banquet was tendered to Milner by the Governor-General, and afterwards the Portuguese Authorities escorted him to the S.S. *Koerber*, "running a torchlight procession round us—and so good-bye". Geoffrey enjoyed the journey up to Nairobi in the cow-catcher with H.E., Sir Donald Stewart, the Commissioner of the East African Protectorate, and Monson, who had been with him at Aysgarth and Eton; especially as they "rolled into the plains to game country, a truly wonderful sight, everywhere herds of hartebeest, wildebeest, zebra, Grant's and Thompson's gazelles, ostriches, etc.".

Milner's term in South Africa may be said to have been divided into six periods: (*a*) the year of study and careful survey in which he sought to obtain an accurate conspectus of conditions; (*b*) the eighteen months after his Graaf-Reinet speech, during which period he feared war was inevitable owing to the refusal of Kruger and his followers to give way on the Franchise question; (*c*) the first months of war with a succession of disasters for British Arms, which showed that a new fighting

[1] Sir Lionel Phillips, identified with the Witwatersrand gold industry from early days. At one time he was President of the Chamber of Mines. He was one of the first Uitlanders condemned to death, after the Jameson Raid, by Judge Gregorowski, and subsequently released.

machine must be created if victory was to be achieved; (*d*) then a year of war after the tide began to turn with the capture of Cronje, the Relief, first of Ladysmith and then of Mafeking, and finally the entry of Roberts into Pretoria (in June, 1900); (*e*) the last year of war preparing for peace, during which he laid his plans for the post-war era; (*f*) finally the three years of rehabilitation and reconstruction, regarded by many as Milner's greatest achievement in South Africa.[1]

It will have been seen that Geoffrey joined Milner's staff seven months before the signing of peace and he was closely associated with his Chief in these vital years of reconstruction. He had immense admiration for Milner's complete absorption in the task of rehabilitation of the Transvaal, Orange River Colony and the areas in the neighbouring Colonies devastated by national war. He concentrated on the restoration of the gold-mining industry and on the introduction of scientific methods in farming. How successful these methods were may be realized from the statistics of the period. After the acute depression in the immediate post-war era, by the time Milner sailed from Delagoa Bay in April, 1905, the industrial well-being of the Transvaal was already well ahead of the pre-war days. The gold industry showed a better record in 1904 than it did in 1898. More new industries had been started in the last year of Milner's regime than in the preceding twenty years, and scientific methods of farming and improvement in stock had been introduced on a widespread scale. The antiquated and wasteful methods of the backveld Boer were already passing away.[2]

During a week of sightseeing in Cairo, Geoffrey spent a happy afternoon inspecting the Sphinx and exploring the Pyramids—he "climbed the big one, more for the good of the system than anything else—quite worth doing for the view of Cairo, and (at your feet) the dividing line of the desert and sown";[3] galloped across the desert to Moses's Spring; visited, on donkey-back, the bazaars of the perfume-vendors and of the goldsmiths and made the usual round of mosques and museums. He went to lunch "with the Lord[4] and his lady, just their two selves. He unusually agreeable, talking about the formation

[1] *Lord Milner and the Empire*, by Vladimir Halpérin. (Odhams, 1952.) *Vide* Part 2, p. 124.

The work of reconstruction after the Boer War; Monsieur Halpérin thinks that the importance of the effort made by the British during the period of reconstruction has not been realized and regards this work as providing one of the most illustrious pages in the history of British Imperialism.

[2] *National Review*, May, 1905, p. 461. An article by Geoffrey under the *nom de plume* of "Transvaaler" entitled "Political Parties in the Transvaal".

See also "Lord Milner's High Commissionership", *The Times*, April 4, 1905.

[3] The area of cultivation.

[4] Lord Cromer.

of his Civil Service by discriminating jobbery, the gradual decay of the French language in Egypt, South Africa, etc.".

He had several talks with H.E., of whom he finally took leave at the Khedival Club on April 29th, and a week later arrived in London and spent his first night on British soil "in my old rooms in 2, Ryder Street among my own furniture and pictures".

One of the first letters written by Milner to Geoffrey is that of the 27th May, 1905, from Cadenabbia, on Lake Como:

> . . . Many thanks for your letter, written just before leaving Egypt. I hope you know that, if you look back with pleasure upon your time with me, I do so just as much. Your work was absolutely first-rate, from start to finish, and I feel that, despite the difference of years, we have formed a companionable friendship, which I hope will always continue. . . .

V

EDITOR OF THE "JOHANNESBURG STAR"

GEOFFREY spent his well-deserved holiday in 1905 mostly in London and Yorkshire, with visits to Oxford, Eton and to the houses of a few friends. He spent as much time as he could spare with his father at Skipton, or with the aunts at Langcliffe. His main purpose, however, was to seize every opportunity of studying the details of newspaper production in the offices of the London dailies. He renewed contact with Fleet Street friends and visited them in their homes and offices. He especially concentrated on the immediate hours before a newspaper goes to press; there are many entries in his journal of long evenings spent at Printing House Square, or of talks with H. A. Gwynne at the *Standard*, or with Fabian Ware at the *Morning Post*. He lunched with Leo Maxse[1] in Montpelier Square, for whose *National Review* he had already written; he discussed foreign affairs with Valentine Chirol and W. F. Monypenny. When he returned to South Africa he had, therefore, a comprehensive view of the actual working conditions of most of the leading newspapers, and at the back of his mind were plans for improving the contents and layout of the *Star*.

In June, while staying with Humphry Ward (who wrote articles for *The Times* on art and literature), and his wife, Geoffrey found the Moberly Bells there. This was probably the first time he had met the the Manager of *The Times* away from the office. At the Colonial Office he had a talk with Alfred Lyttelton, Chamberlain's successor, and he attended a great Tariff Reform meeting at the Albert Hall, and listened to a stirring speech by his former chief. One of Geoffrey's last evenings in London was spent with Milner, no doubt discussing the problems which would face the new Editor of the *Johannesburg Star*, and from him he received a farewell blessing a few hours before catching the

[1] He was a close friend of Geoffrey's; when he came to live in London he often used to play lawn tennis with Maxse before beginning his day's work. In 1921 Lord Milner married Maxse's sister, Lady Edward Cecil.

boat train for Southampton, whence he sailed to South Africa in the *Kildonan Castle*.

On October 10th, 1905, Geoffrey arrived at Cape Town, on his third visit to South Africa and his first as Editor of one of the most important newspapers in the country. He was still in his thirtieth year when he set out for Johannesburg; he spent most of the two-day journey in reading the files of the *Star* in order to bring himself up to date with local current events. Within four months he had proved himself to be an able political journalist and controversialist and had been offered and had accepted the position of Johannesburg correspondent of the *Daily Telegraph*.

His first leading article in the *Star* was on the all important subject of "The Liberal Party and Chinese Labour". He explained to his readers the significance of the recent victory by a Liberal candidate in the Barkston Ash Division in the West Riding of Yorkshire, hitherto regarded as a safe Conservative seat.[1] Asquith had stigmatized "Chinese Labour" in the Transvaal as a most gigantic blunder, and young Mr. Churchill (the same age as Geoffrey) had stated that if the Liberals were returned to power the importation of Chinese coolies would cease and that they would all be returned to China within three years.

The following day he met for the first time at dinner young Edward Wood (with his parents, Lord and Lady Halifax), who later as Lord Irwin was to become one of his most intimate friends and for whom he had the utmost regard—a regard which never wavered.

Having gained a new friend he presently lost the society of an old one when Arthur Lawley and his family left the Transvaal. Lawley had been Lieutenant-Governor under Milner and represented to him a distinguished official with the same broad outlook on Imperial problems as his former chief.

In December the attention of the leaders of the mining industry was naturally centred on the utterances of the members of Henry Campbell-Bannerman's Administration and particularly on their policy of "arresting" Chinese labour. Geoffrey was genuinely alarmed at the consequences which might result from the repatriation of the Chinese coolies. He had, when with Milner, lived through the years of acute depression and had rejoiced when better times came as the result of the presence of 44,000 Chinese on the Rand.[2]

[1] The Conservatives regained the seat at the General Election a few weeks later.

[2] The following comparative figures were quoted by Geoffrey in a leading article on the subject of Chinese labour:

	1898	1905
Number of white men employed	10,701	16,593
,, ,, Natives ,,	82,105	90,998
,, ,, Chinese ,,	—	44,609

The following letters home describe events after his return to South Africa:

25th October, 1905.

My routine is to breakfast here, where I have a bedroom for the moment, get to the office before nine and lead a dog's life till 12.50 when my first edition appears. Then lunch at the Rand Club and see people, then back to the office. The second edition comes out at 2.50 and the third at 5.30, the latter much the best as a rule as containing all the cable news. The editorial staff is the same for all. The strain of things is over by lunch time, but there is always plenty to do—letters to answer, people to see, reporting to arrange and so on. It is rather an interesting job, but will certainly turn my hair grey in a month or two! . . .

Xmas Eve, 1905.

. . . People *are*, as a matter of fact, coming round fast to the idea of Responsible Government, and of course it is better than that the whole country should be ruined—but I am all for sticking to the constitution for as long as possible. . . .

31st December, 1905.

I'm glad you approve of the education policy of the *Star*. The thing is dormant now owing to the refusal of the Boers to come in—a great tactical error on their part, I think. This new Government at home seems about as bad as it can be. . . . We are not fussing yet about Chinese Labour, but the feeling is strong and difficult to restrain. What those idiots won't see is that to paralyse the mining industry is not to ruin the "Randlords" who could all retire rich men, whatever happened, but to ruin the white miners, professional men, traders etc. and generally to eliminate the British population of South Africa.

The new year opened auspiciously for the *Star*, and its sales had increased by over a thousand copies a day since his advent. In January he informed Lionel Phillips, a personal friend as well as a director of the *Star*, of the invitation to him to become the Johannesburg Correspondent of the *Daily Telegraph*; an offer which he gladly accepted because, at the back of his mind, he hoped that, one day, it might be a ladder back to journalism in London.

He wrote (February 25, 1906) to his father:

I've been pretty busy, have written a leading article every single day and sent, I think, three long cables in the course of a week (to the *Daily Telegraph*).

Lord Milner is to talk to the Lords tomorrow I see—how I wish I could hear him! In the long run I don't think there will be any effective interference with Chinese Labour, but if they give us a Boer majority for the sake of anti-Chinese verdict, heaven help us.

Geoffrey received this letter (2nd March, 1906) from Mr. L. S. Amery (in London)—which was to play so important a part in his career:

> . . . The *Star* has been quite excellent throughout this campaign and I shall be looking forward to your leaders as they come in during the next fortnight. I am afraid things here are in some ways very disheartening. The Government mean to do the right thing more or less, but they show absolutely no firmness towards the small and noisy section of "malignants" in the party who crack the whip almost daily whenever the Government does not please them. Asquith's speech some nights ago was simply made to pacify these people who were indignant with Winston Churchill.
>
> . . . Quite strictly *between ourselves* Moberly Bell has been thinking of transferring his nephew from Johannesburg to some other part of the world in connection with the mutation of our correspondents which is to take place in the course of the year. Would you, in that case, be able to act as *Times* correspondent? Monypenny used to do it, but I do not think he found the extra work impossible, besides I imagine that you could, without difficulty, devote part of whatever *The Times* gave you to extra assistance in the *Star* office. I shall be very glad if you would let me know what you think about this as soon as you can. . . .

After a few months at the *Star* Geoffrey began to feel quite at home in the maelstrom of South African politics. It was not as though he had to deal with a series of new problems, although before long the prospects of federation became within the range of practical politics. Events had moved quickly since the resignation of Balfour on 4th December, 1905, and the coming into office of the Liberals under Campbell-Bannerman on the following day; but the broad outlines of the cause he was championing were the same. The fundamental question was, of course, whether the British elements would unite in time in order to check the manœuvres of the Dutch party—*Het Volk*—an oligarchy, self-constituted and consisting of seven men, which ensured, at a critical juncture in the *post*-Milner period, that the ranks would be closed and the Afrikanders would rally round their leaders in their determination to obtain Responsible Government at the earliest possible moment. With the coming into power of the Liberal Party in Great Britain, their task became immeasurably easier, and all they had to do was to sit tight.

The vision of a strong British-controlled South Africa as a powerful unit in the Empire and a bastion of British Imperial power, might have been possible of realization if South Africa had not become a party issue at home; but in order to bring about such a state of affairs a steady influx of carefully selected British settlers throughout the country would have been essential; with time to strengthen the ranks of those relatively small sections of the Boer community, who would have been ready to work for a complete fusion of the two white races into a self-governing and united federation of the four separate colonies; and a consistent education policy, under British control, which aimed at capturing the mind of youth. But events did not shape themselves as Milner and his supporters hoped during the immediate post-war years. The chauvinistic Dutch *Predikant* and the backveld Boer were not ready to forgive and forget and to settle down in the best of all possible worlds.

In the early days of his editorship Geoffrey was in the forefront of the battle for the Milner ideal—and it was a very splendid ideal, i.e. that of an entirely self-governing unit, closely allied with its Sister-Nations across the seas, in a British World State working for world peace. But as events were to prove, both in South Africa and Canada centrifugal tendencies were too strong, and the influence of the French-controlled Government in Canada, and of the Dutch-controlled Government in South Africa played an important part in shaping the ultimate evolution of the British Commonwealth into a group of loosely knit and semi-independent states, only willing to come together in face of a great external danger such as that which confronted the Empire in 1914, and the Commonwealth in 1939.

In the early days Geoffrey and some of the leaders of the British element were inclined to class all the Dutch together as inevitably seeking to weaken the ties between South Africa and Great Britain. In 1906, in the midst of the bitter controversies over the constitution, the size of the electoral districts, the rights of voters, and "One Vote One Value",[1] the educational policy, the retrenchment in the Civil Service (which inevitably implied the gradual elimination of the British-born official in favour of the Afrikander), how could they have foreseen the enlightened leadership of Louis Botha and J. C. Smuts? These two great South Africans believed in the vision of a United Commonwealth in which their country could and would play a leading part.

Letter to Kitty (April 22, 1906):

> I am full of work—and things seem rather better on the whole. The Boers are giving themselves away more and more and our own people are getting under way and pulling better together. But it really is an *exasperating* place. What with this poisonous Government at home, the rotters out here—people who won't see or don't want to see, or can't be bothered—it is sometimes almost maddening. Besides it is a hard strain

[1] Equal legal rights implied that "every voter, be he rich or poor, Boer or Briton, farmer or miner" should have exactly the same share of Parliamentary representation—in other words that "One vote shall have one constant value".

to keep one's temper and not let private feelings make one unfair in the paper. I shall return to you quite soon I think—with white hair, no digestion, no temper and no illusions—and become something peaceful like a gardener or a sexton!

Empire Day (May 24) was celebrated by the holding of a banquet by former members of Milner's staff. More important still, it was the occasion of Geoffrey's lunching with Montagu Bell and his wife, "to talk with him about *The Times* work" in South Africa, a subject which had already been referred to by Mr. Amery.[1] Montagu Bell had represented *The Times* in South Africa for the previous five and a half years and was about to leave the country to become Editor of the *North China Daily News and Herald*, the leading British newspaper in the Far East.

Geoffrey wrote to Kitty (May 24, 1906):

The news of the day is that *The Times* have asked me to take over their South African work, which is a very great pleasure to me, so you must . . . take to the best newspaper in the world. . . . Nothing has really pleased me more for a long time (not since All Souls I think, which I shall always look upon as the greatest possible stroke of good fortune).

Evidently his resignation from the post of correspondent of the *Daily Telegraph* was speedily effected, for on May 31st he despatched his first cable to *The Times*.

Henceforth, in the columns of the *Star* Geoffrey took every opportunity of referring to the problem of federation, which would ultimately, in his view, be established in South Africa. He considered it was not altogether a disaster for South Africa that she would come late into the circle of the great Union of self-governing colonies, for it gave her a wonderful opportunity of profiting by the mistakes of her predecessors.

On June 17 he wrote to his father:

. . . Robert Brand, who is secretary to the Inter-Colonial Council and a member of my College of All Souls, is coming to bear me company next week. My nearest neighbour—a couple of hundred yards away—is Charlie Villiers who was at Eton with me and is also living an isolated life. . . . It is simply ripping being in the real country and I feel pounds better already. . . .

My only amusing day has been Tuesday when I motored to Vereeniging with Phillips and the Fitzpatricks to the Sammy Marks's, agriculture

[1] *Vide supra*, p. 50.

and tree planting, very interesting. We left at 7, breakfasted on the veld, spent the day farming and (thanks to two breakdowns) weren't home again until 9 at night, very good for the system. The system will want keeping up just now, for *The Times* job is going to be no sinecure. I had several letters from Amery this mail and they want a great deal more than the occasional telegrams I used to dispatch to the *Daily Telegraph*. However, with the aid of shorthand and typewriting which are indispensable in this modern world, I shall try to keep them posted up. I am training myself to dictate decent reading matter—rather difficult but an enormous saving of time and labour.

idem.

July 15, 1906.

I got back from my wanderings yesterday . . . it was a delightful trip in glorious country and very good for mind and body. From Pietersburg, which we reached on Monday morning, we moted (*sic*) away north-east to a place on the edge of the plateau where a cart and mules awaited us. Everyone said that it was the *Ultima Thule* of motorists.

. . . The natives who abound in those fat tropical valleys have of course never seen a motor before and ran shrieking down the road in front of us. When they found that it would overtake them however fast they ran, they hid behind bushes and prayed to the motor-devil to have mercy on them! It was an amazing experience. Tzaneen is now a Government experimental farm, a new enterprise which is likely to do well. But the great industry is tobacco and with Government capital there has lately been established a really up-to-date factory where the cigars, cigarettes, snuff etc., are turned out on the spot down to the boxes and tins. . . . Lionel Phillips . . . is really a delightful travelling companion, so clever and keen about everything and full of reminiscences of the days when he explored that country on foot.

It was in the beginning of September, 1906, that the members of the Kindergarten (i.e. those young men who had been on Lord Milner's personal or official staff from 1901 onwards) first approached Lord Selborne very privately with the proposal that they should prepare a memorandum on the whole question of the federation or union of the four independent colonies and how this great and difficult project could be brought about. In the evening of the same day (as his diary shows), Geoffrey and others of the Kindergarten dined with Lionel Curtis and sat up till all hours discussing the problem.

It is impossible to over-estimate the importance of the part played by the members of the Kindergarten, in paving the way for the closer union of South Africa after Milner had left. From the latter part of 1904 onwards Robert Brand, John Dove,[1] Philip Kerr,[1] and Richard Feetham[1]—with one or two others—set up a joint establishment in Johannesburg for themselves. Until the middle of 1906 they occupied rented quarters. At the end of 1905 Feetham acquired a plot of land on the outskirts of Parktown (a suburb) in what is now Valley Road, about three miles from the centre of the town—on which Moot House, designed by Herbert Baker, was built, and from June or July, 1906, that building became the abode of the fraternity, and a meeting place where they, and other members of the Kindergarten (including particularly Patrick Duncan,[2] Lionel Curtis and Lionel Hichens,[3] who were then working in Pretoria as Colonial Secretary of the Transvaal, Assistant Colonial Secretary and Colonial Treasurer), discussed problems of the day, more especially, of course, those connected with the "Closer Union" of the four Colonies. As the house was from the start intended to serve as the centre of such discussions, Feetham named it "Moot House".

It was at Pretoria that the very private meeting referred to already took place. Its object was to consider whether any steps could be taken to open the way to serious consideration of "Closer Union". It was decided at this meeting that it was desirable that some attempt should be made to prepare a survey of the existing situation in South Africa, which could be utilized in some way to enable the South African public to appreciate the gravity of the position which would have to be faced in regard to the mutual relations of the four South African Colonies, as soon as the Transvaal and the Orange River Colony passed out of the Crown Colony stage into the Responsible Government stage—a development which, as the result of the advent to power of the Campbell-Bannerman Government, was now to be expected in the very near future. This led to the production of a document which became known as the *Selborne Memorandum*. Those present at the meeting (excluding Selborne himself) became a committee for the preparation of the proposed survey—no doubt with the addition of one or two who happened to have been absentees.

[1] John Dove, destined to be Editor of the *Round Table* from 1920 till his death in 1934. This is the first reference to Philip Kerr, the future Lord Lothian, who was one of Geoffrey's closest friends till his untimely death in 1940, when Ambassador in Washington. Lothian was Editor of the *Round Table* from the date of its founding in 1910 to 1916. He was secretary of the Rhodes Trust from 1925–39. Richard Feetham, Deputy Town Clerk of Johannesburg in 1902. Had a distinguished legal career in South Africa—compare *infra* p. 73.

[2] Sir Patrick Duncan was Treasurer of the Transvaal in 1901. He remained in South Africa. Cf. *infra* p. 73.

[3] Lionel Hichens was a member of the Ministry of Finance in Cairo before becoming Colonial Treasurer of the Transvaal. He was Chairman of Cammell Laird & Co. from 1910. He was killed in an air-raid in London on October 14, 1940.

Lionel Curtis, who was at that time comparatively free from other duties, was, by common consent, appointed as draftsman, and immediately settled down to the task. At that time he became temporarily one of the inhabitants of Moot House and did most of his work there. Evening meetings were held from time to time at Moot House—at which those present would normally number perhaps eight or ten—for the purpose of discussing and criticizing Lionel Curtis's draft as portions of it became available, and he used to revise these in the light of the discussions.[1]

Mr. Lionel Curtis, who was one of the chief actors in these stirring events, writes:

April 10, 1953.

. . . When the Liberal Government announced that they would grant Responsible Government to the Transvaal and Free State as soon as voters' rolls could be made, I resigned my appointment as an official of the Transvaal Government and joined Selborne's staff. He sent me to visit the four South African Governments, and report on the situation. When I had done this I returned to the Moot House. . . . There we drafted a report to Selborne on the situation. We argued that the Liberal Government were right in conceding Responsible Government to the conquered governments as soon as possible, but added that, if nothing more than this were done, the ex-Republics[2] and the British self-governing Colonies would be at war again in a few years.[3] The only way these four self-governing territories could avoid another South African war was for the four governments to merge their sovereignties in one South African Union.

Our memorandum convinced Selborne who said that he would publish it. When he did so he said that it was drafted by his young men, but as he agreed with it he would initial it. It thus came to be known as "The Selborne Memorandum" but everyone saw from his general statement that he had not written it and that it was the work of his young men, one of whom was Geoffrey Dawson.

Before the Memorandum was published I went to stay with Jameson,

[1] The above information concerning the beginnings of the "Closer Union" movement is based on letters received from the Hon. Richard Feetham. Full details of the *Selborne Memorandum* can be found in Basil Williams's Edition of that document, published by the Oxford University Press in 1925.

[2] The ex-Republics, having no direct access to the sea, except through the Cape Colony or Natal or through the port of Delagoa Bay in Portuguese territory, were already coming into violent controversy with Cape Colony and Natal over Customs Duties and Railway Rates. Various Inter-Colonial Conferences had already been held in the attempt to find solutions. The Kindergarten were fully acquainted with these problems at first hand through those members who were conducting the Transvaal Government and through others who were concerned particularly with Railways.

[3] Other members of the Kindergarten did not share these alarmist views, and did not believe that there was an actual danger of war.

who was then as Prime Minister resident at Groote Schuur. I showed him the memorandum in print and asked him to write to the High Commissioner that the relations of the four self-governing Colonies had reached a deadlock, and ask him as High Commissioner to review the situation. The object of this was to give Selborne a reason for publishing his memorandum.

Meanwhile I had seen Francis Malan,[1] the leader of the Afrikander Bond, the left wing of Merriman's opposition, and a man of outstanding importance. He was Jameson's bitterest enemy who lost no chance of attacking him in the Assembly. I got to know him and went walks with him with Jameson's approval, because I found that he was at heart an enthusiast for South African Union. One day Malan and I were sitting on the seat where Rhodes used to look north and dream of uniting South Africa, when I took the proofs of the *Selborne Memorandum* out of my pocket, and gave them to Malan, asked him to read them and meet me in three days' time at the seat. I then told Jameson what I had done. "Quite right," was his cheerful reply.

I found Malan (three days later) sitting on the seat with the *Selborne Memorandum* in his hands. For five minutes he said nothing, so when I could bear it no longer I said, "Well?" "Publish it," said Malan in a low voice. I returned to Groote Schuur and told Jameson, who said, "Tell Malan that if I am still Prime Minister when we get a National Convention to draft a Constitution for the Union, I will ask him to come with me as my partner."

It must have been at this stage, and before the *Selborne Memorandum* was published, that Malan made his speech advocating Union, upon which "Robin" (Geoffrey) wrote his leader in the *Johannesburg Star*. Throughout November the *Star* continued to work for Federation, and leading articles appeared on November 3rd, 5th and 27th dealing with the problem which dovetailed into Geoffrey's own views concerning the unity of the Empire as a whole. Many of the extreme Nationalists in South Africa must have rubbed their eyes at this moment in South Africa's history, for the advocates of Union were to be found in both camps; small wonder that, later on, when the Union was formally inaugurated in 1910, there was a feeling of optimism about the future co-operation between the two white races in South Africa.

Geoffrey had now completed more than a year as Editor of the *Star* and he could look back with satisfaction on much of his work. During the year, quite apart from his activities outside the office and keeping contact with leading members of the community, especially those who were advocating closer relations with the Empire, he had

[1] Then Editor of *Ons Land*, the organ of the Bond, and not the ex-Prime Minister of the Union of South Africa.

himself written 209 leading articles, no mean achievement in the circumstances.

Geoffrey received this letter (11th January, 1907) from Lord Milner in London:

It is perfectly disgusting how I've treated you, but my correspondence is too much for me altogether. It has not decreased since I left South Africa in anything like proportion to the decrease in the assistance I formerly had in dealing with it. This is not a hint to you to come home, because you are infinitely better employed where you are, but merely to apologize. What I want you to realize are the following things:

(1) Although I seem to take no notice, I follow South African events closely; read my weekly *Stars* . . . and my letters from you, and others, and your telegrams in *The Times*, most religiously. If I make no comment on your proceedings, it is simply because I am almost invariably in complete agreement. Once only during the last few months have I been distressed, and indeed fearfully upset, by something done by our friends in the Transvaal. It was the action taken against Pim. Now I see from your last letter that you take exactly the same point of view as I do. It is merely one case in point; the understanding is practically complete, though the means of communication are so imperfect.

(2) I have kept comparatively quiet about South Africa though I am boiling inside, simply from policy. I never open my lips about it at all unless I am absolutely compelled. I have come to the conclusion that, having regard to the overwhelming, though fortunately decreasing, force of rotten Radical opinion, any little good I can do by calling the attention of our own feeble forces to South Africa is far more than outweighed by the impetus which my criticism gives to renewed vicious activity of the other side. A time will come, no doubt, for slaying the Philistines, but it is no use hitting them when you cannot slay them, or even hurt them seriously. . . .

Geoffrey wrote to Langcliffe (March 10th, 1907):

. . . We had a Kindergarten dinner to Patrick Duncan on Monday night after he had handed over his office to . . . Smuts. They jeered at "Lord Milner's Young Men" and Smuts turns out to be exactly Duncan's age! . . .

June 16, 1907.

Parliament resumed itself on Friday with prayers read in Dutch only by the Speaker (who speaks English as well as you or me). Botha then made a pleasant statement which you can read in the papers, and then the House adjourned to a garden party given by Mrs. Botha, where the Republican flag floated side by side with the Union Jack over the tea-tent, and the band did *not* play God Save the King when Lord Selborne arrived. We are getting on! . . .

June 30, 1907.

. . . I wish I knew (1) how to make speeches, (2) when the next General Election will be. Nothing would give me such complete satisfaction as to be able really effectively to show up the "triumph of Liberalism" in South Africa. People are flocking to Canada, Australia, anywhere. I have heard several of them say that the one place they will never live in again is England. Of course it is absurd to suppose that England is the same thing as a Radical Government, but they feel they've been sold by their Mother Country (some of them not for the first time!) and you can't get away from that feeling. . . .

Early in July the *Selborne Memorandum* (or Federal "Egg") was ready for publication, and Geoffrey despatched "a colossal telegram to *The Times* about it, as well as dealing with it at great length in the *Star*".

In August, 1907, Geoffrey was receiving disquieting news from his aunts about his father's health and was contemplating going home when a cable informed him that such a step would be useless as "a week would decide" one way or another. He therefore decided to carry out a long-arranged visit to Rhodesia. It was while at Salisbury that he received the news of the death of his father, and his diary of September 11th records that he "caught 9.30, a rotten train . . . the funeral was at 12.30, carriage happily to myself—read and thought—a gloomy day". It was curious how most of his early sorrows were associated with South Africa. It was there also that he heard both of his mother's and sister's deaths.

Geoffrey received the following important letter from his former Chief, explaining his outlook on the situation in South Africa:

47, Duke Street, S.W.
14th September, 1907.

My dear Robin,

I don't know that I can, in a letter of any reasonable length, answer the very fundamental question contained in your letter of Aug. 15.

You, no doubt, will answer it for yourself in time, and better than I can. But I am not sorry for the opportunity of putting my own ideas on the subject into order. In so doing I shall no doubt show you the train of thought which Lionel Phillips summed up in the rather misleading formula that "getting on with the Boers is our only course".

My view is that the policy, to which we devoted years of labour, and which was worth it (for it was a big policy which, if successful, would have made a material difference to the Empire and to the World) must be regarded as a thing of the past. I never had any doubt about it from the first moment that the election returns of January, 1906, began to come in, though the disaster has been more rapid and more complete than I imagined. Still, the elements of the case are very simple. To reap the fruits of the war, and make a *British* South Africa which would have been a source of strength to the Empire as a whole and a factor on the side of consolidation and not of disintegration, we required a consistent policy for at least 10 years. This was only possible if (1) the Unionists remained in office, *or* (2) South Africa ceased to be a burning question in British party politics, so that the Unionist policy might still be carried on, as it sometimes has been in other cases, even with a Liberal Government in office.

But the game was always a difficult and a hazardous one, the British position always a very weak one, as even among our own people there were not more than 1 in a 1,000 who understood it. When our feeble forces, opposed to the strong and united forces on the other side, were suddenly subjected to a deadly fire from behind, when the whole power and influence of the British Government were thrown into the scale against the solution of the South African question in a British sense, the thing became perfectly hopeless, and a total collapse of what you may call the Milner policy and fabric was inevitable. I always knew it, the moment I saw a Liberal Government with an immense majority, and the *South African piece still on the boards*. You, I think, also always knew it.

But while the great final, and hopeless, fight was on, we did not say so, even to one another. But now that it is over, we can afford to take stock of the situation frankly.

One thing which is quite evident is that the South African British are entirely relieved by what has happened from any obligations to the mother-country and can afford to think only of themselves. Indeed, even for the few of them who may remain at heart devoted to the Empire, the best course is not to think, for the present, about those wider issues, which South Africa can no longer—in our lifetime at any rate—influence for good, and which will be decided, wrongly in all probability, but still in any case decided without her. They should devote themselves wholly to the problem of making life in South Africa, regarded as more or less a foreign country, bearable for self-respecting British men and women, not disposed to part with their own national feelings and traditions. If they could only stick together, even a considerable minority of them, they would, I think, be in a first-class position to do this—to exercise a great influence upon the political and social development of the country—regarded as a foreign country—and at the same time to be materially very happy and comfortable. Look at the French in Canada! Are not they in a golden position, of which by a "loyal" but self-respecting policy they have made very good use.

The British party, if it continues to exist, would necessarily be an

Opposition party, until, that is, the Boer phalanx itself splits up, which the very completeness of its victory may cause it to do sooner than I once anticipated. But there is opposition and opposition. Opposition to the Boers because they are what they are, i.e. Boers and not British, is out of date. The fight is no longer for predominance. That is settled. The point is that, accepting Boer predominance, not as a desirable thing, but as a fact, a British party, as well conducted as was, on the whole, the Progressive Party this season, can do a lot, and an increasing lot, as the old issues recede, to influence any Transvaal or other South African Government on all these *material* questions, which after all form the usual staple of political controversy in young countries. Every government will want to be on some sort of decent terms with the representatives of the industrial community. . . . I am not arguing for a *submissive* attitude towards the Government, quite the reverse. You will get nothing that way and if the proprietors of the *Star* wanted to truckle, you would be quite right to chuck at once, as I know you would chuck. And, of course, seeing what a lot of our people are, there is an immense danger of this. But, if I am against a submissive attitude, I am also against beating the air, and flogging dead horses. . . .

No doubt you have one or two very bad years to live through, and perhaps the constitution of our people may be (too) feeble to stand them. But I am not without hope. Many of them did so well, despite the most appalling handicaps, during this very first session. And I have some confidence in the indomitable insubordinateness of the Johannesburger—in many respects it has been a great weakness to us, but it should at least prevent the policy of "taking it lying down" being carried to extreme lengths. And I think it should always make a plucky and critical stand up to the Government attitude, the *paying* attitude, pecuniarily as well as politically, for a Johannesburg paper. . . .

In the immediate weeks before sailing home on leave the entries in his diary are mainly concerned with the progress of the campaign for federation and record "great palavers" with the members of the Kindergarten about Lionel Curtis's new "egg" (the *Selborne Memorandum* and subsequent discussions), and finally in early May he records "Closer Union everywhere"—and on May 5th the passage by the Pretoria Conference of the famous Closer Union resolution.

On May 20th Geoffrey sailed for England. The vessel berthed at Southampton on June 6th, and the same evening he was dining with a small party at All Souls.

VI

MEETING WITH NORTHCLIFFE—1908

SUCH momentous events in Geoffrey's life resulted from his meeting with Northcliffe, in 1908, that it seems desirable to interrupt the sequence of this narrative and describe briefly the latter as he appeared to an intimate at the time. Geoffrey, as we have seen, was returning from two and a half years' strenuous work as Editor of the *Star*; within these thirty months he had undoubtedly made good and had fully justified Milner's confidence, when he recommended him as a young man who would make an efficient editor. It is a tribute to the confidence placed in Milner's judgment by the Board of Directors of the Argus Printing and Publishing Company—successful business-men in the world of Johannesburg finance and mining—that in March, 1905, they should have appointed to the editorship of their newspaper a young civil servant, who, although a very successful private secretary to the High Commissioner, had had no previous experience of journalism.

The gamble was fully justified, however, and Geoffrey took to the task of editing the *Star* as a duck to water; and not only won an exceptional place for himself in the life of Johannesburg but attracted outside attention to his work, and after acting as South African Correspondent to the *Daily Telegraph* for four months, transferred his allegiance to Printing House Square, an allegiance which was to last almost as long as life itself. Including his representation of *The Times* in South Africa he worked for the paper for thirty-two years.[1]

[1] If we include Thomas Barnes's years as theatrical critic and Parliamentary writer he too served *The Times* for thirty-two years; George Buckle joined the staff of *The Times* in 1880—he became Editor in 1884—he therefore also shared with Barnes and Geoffrey a term of thirty-two years. The only editors who exceeded their term of service of thirty-two years were John Thadeus Delane who, if we include his year of probation, served *The Times* for thirty-seven years, and W. F. Casey, who joined the staff in 1913 and only retired in 1952; he therefore served the paper for thirty-nine years. Thomas Chenery (1826–84), Buckle's predecessor as Editor, served *The Times* for thirty years; twenty-four as correspondent and six as Editor. Chenery was Editor from Jan. 1, 1878, until his death on Feb. 11, 1884, at the age of fifty-nine. Wickham Steed joined the staff in 1896 as correspondent; he therefore served the paper for twenty-six years.

On getting home in 1908 Geoffrey spent three nights with his aunts at Langcliffe—his first visit to Yorkshire since his father's death—but was back again in London by Thursday, June 11th, to dine with the Northcliffes at 22, St. James's Place, famous as the former home of the poet Rogers. Mr. Amery, with whom Northcliffe discussed his plans for *The Times*, had talked to him about his friend "Robin" (Geoffrey) of South African days. These circumstances give point to the diary entry of June 11th, 1908, ". . . Decided to move my things down to Amery's flat in the Temple—dined with the Northcliffes."

By the time Geoffrey had received the following letter (19th March, 1908) from Mr. Amery in South Africa, he must certainly have heard rumours of the sale of *The Times*:

> 2, Temple Gardens,
> London, E.C.
>
> . . . the great event of the past week as far as we are concerned has been the triumphant carrying through of Moberly Bell's scheme for *The Times*. I heard of it as soon as I came back, but it was still in a very uncertain stage then, and though Pearson was practically routed, other dangers still loomed in the foreground. The main point is that unlimited money has been found by people who are anxious to preserve the character of the paper and are quite content to leave its direction in the hands of the present staff, with the addition of Monypenny who has always been regarded as being on the staff though temporarily seconded to South Africa for the life of Dizzy, and is quite likely to become editor if anything happened to Buckle. They have not put me on that list, presumably because I have become too much of a politician. As a matter of fact, I shall be doing a good deal less on the paper in future, confining myself rather to special articles on the questions I am most interested in and not doing regular night-work. For the present, moreover, I have got somehow to polish off my sixth volume[1] and shall not even have time to write articles. . . .
>
> What are your plans about coming home this summer?
>
> Yours ever,
> L. S. A.[2]

Northcliffe regarded 1908—as well he might—as his *Times* year.[3] Geoffrey, who for nearly two years had acted as *The Times* correspondent in South Africa, must often have wondered what the future held in store for "The Thunderer". As early as January 5, 1908, the

[1] This refers to *The Times History of the South African War* in seven volumes.

[2] In a letter to me (12th July, 1952), Mr. Amery wrote: "What I saw of his (Geoffrey's) work on the *Johannesburg Star* when I was staying with him in 1907 made me urge him on Northcliffe when I was not willing to take *The Times* editorship myself."

[3] See Author's *Uphill*, p. 219.

following paragraph had appeared in the *Observer*—then owned by Northcliffe:

> It is understood that important negotiations are taking place which will place the direction of *The Times* newspaper in the hands of a very capable proprietor of several popular magazines and newspapers.[1]

Unknowingly at the time, I played a part in a mysterious exchange of telegrams and urgent messages which passed between George Sutton and Kennedy Jones in London, who were carrying on negotiations with Moberly Bell for the sale of *The Times* to Northcliffe—then referred to as "X", and Northcliffe's Austrian valet (on behalf of Northcliffe), Joseph Brunnbauer, staying with his employer at the Ritz Hotel, Paris. Northcliffe thought highly of Brunnbauer, who used to glide about the passages at Sutton Place, wearing fur-lined slippers, and occupied a privileged position in the establishment, for Northcliffe used him for many errands.

A very important telegram sent by Kennedy Jones (in the negotiations for the sale of *The Times*) on Wednesday, January 8, 1908, owing to very bad weather in the Channel, did not reach the Ritz Hotel until the morning of Thursday, January 9, 1908. The telephone between Paris and London was out of action, and just as I was having my breakfast (I had only arrived in Paris late the previous evening), I received a note from Northcliffe saying that he was sending me back to London with an important note for Sutton.

Details of Kennedy Jones's telegram to Brunnbauer will be found in *The History of "The Times"* (Vol. III, p. 536), and of the Chief's reply which necessitated my return to London and involved me in one of the stormiest crossings of the Channel I have ever made—I would, however, have been quite reconciled to the discomforts had I realized the importance of the memorandum I was carrying.

Geoffrey, who was never enamoured of the popular press, was evidently concerned by the rumours circulating about *The Times*, when he sailed for England in 1908; he must, however, have been somewhat reassured by Mr. Amery's letter. He must also have been very anxious to meet Northcliffe, the new power behind the scenes at Printing House Square; had Northcliffe not acquired *The Times* Geoffrey might never have succeeded Buckle.

Geoffrey's first meeting with Northcliffe went off happily—their mutual devotion to the Empire was a strong bond—and for the next five years their relationship was happy (the storm clouds began to gather early in 1913, as we shall see later), and Geoffrey recognized him

[1] See *The History of "The Times"*, Vol. III, p. 513.

as an unrivalled news-gatherer and organizer, and a man with great driving power. From the first Geoffrey formed a firm friendship with Lady Northcliffe.

Northcliffe—only nine years Geoffrey's senior—in 1908 was at the height of his power and still retained a youthful zest and charm which could be very stimulating. In those first happy months of contact and growing friendship, Northcliffe must have appeared to him, as he did to so many of his staff, the ideal chief to serve. He was always at his best with young men. His presence was very arresting. The steely blue eyes, which lit up his face when he smiled or was in bantering vein with his favourites; the clear-cut features, before he put on flesh and his neck and cheeks became somewhat massive; the Napoleonic lock of hair hanging over his broad and imposing forehead; his square-tipped fingers, and capable podgy hands which could play the piano so charmingly, and the small feet; his flattering and complete absorption in the problems of those with whom he talked, one of his most endearing traits. A man of magnetism, who, when the Jekyll was in control, could win real devotion from his employees and whose solicitude for their troubles and anxieties, and his extraordinary generosity and help in times of tribulation, forged real bonds of affection with them. Northcliffe often would wear a dark blue suit, a red silk tie with white spots, trousers not braced enough; a homburg hat somewhat pulled down over his eyes, and, as likely as not, he would be smoking a German cigar bought in Coventry Street for the price of fourpence!

He could, when really interested, be a most entertaining conversationalist, though he was at his best when talking *à deux* about some subject in which he was really engrossed. He would discuss with equal enjoyment the Empire, home politics, Napoleon, Pepys (his favourite bedside book at the time); America, a country with which he had very many links; the frailties of human nature and its unpredictability, and women.

It was above all the boyishness in Northcliffe in these years which was so attractive. He was to many of his young men like a carefree elder brother or light-hearted and stimulating young uncle. Never was he more alive nor more magnetic than in the first eighteen months of his ownership of *The Times*, which at first he proudly proclaimed was to him a hobby; what a palatial steam-yacht or racing-stable was to other rich men. He was like a happy boy who had longed for some object, a motor-cycle, a gun, a pony, or a motor-boat, to whom a fairy godfather had provided the object of his desires. Subconsciously Northcliffe certainly had long watched events at Printing House Square with deep interest. He had a great admiration for "The Thunderer" and he knew as much about its past history, probably, as any member of its staff. He had a high veneration for the qualities of independence of Thomas Barnes, whom he certainly regarded as the greatest Editor of *The Times* when he acquired control.[1] But he certainly thought that some of the methods adopted in recent years for improving its financial position lacked dignity. No one knew more about publishing encyclopædias and popular historical works and serial publications than Northcliffe, who had made vast sums of money out of them; but there was a proper setting for everything, and a properly controlled *Times* should not, in his view, have had to resort to "high-pressure transatlantic salesmanship"[2] to enable it to make ends meet. What *The Times* needed in 1908 was, in Northcliffe's view, greater dignity and above all expert guidance, which he was convinced he could supply.

Northcliffe, who used to refer to Carmelite House—the headquarters of the Associated Newspapers in 1908—as "the dog-fight", thought that a more serene atmosphere should pervade Printing House Square. In the early years after his acquisition of *The Times* he did not propose to assume direct editorial control and talked of establishing a board of trustees to control it and preserve its continuity for a few score years. When he wrote to Wickham Steed[3] in September, 1908: "I am not, nor never shall be, the 'Chief' of *The Times*; do not interfere in the conduct of the paper. . . . *The Times* is conducted entirely by Messrs. Walter, Buckle, Bell, Chirol and Monypenny who understand the task better than I ever could," he was no doubt perfectly sincere in what he said. Nevertheless in those first years of his control of *The Times* his fertile brain was constantly occupied with plans for its future. In April, 1908, within a month of his acquisition of control, he was talking about some of the changes he was going to make, and a particular conversation stands out in my memory. During a two-hours' walk near the Moorish ruins at Alcala, ten miles from Seville, he opened his heart and discussed his problems and the difficulty of finding his "generals" for various undertakings, among them *The Times*. (At that time he had not yet met Geoffrey, though he read his cables from South Africa with close attention.)

Geoffrey's second week-end (the first had been spent at All Souls) was spent with Milner at Sturry, his home in Kent. They were alone, and as it was nearly three years since their last meeting, there was very much to talk about. Geoffrey wrote: "I thought him very well and keen and cheerful except indeed about South Africa. As full as ever of work and enthusiasm about the Empire generally." In July he was

[1] During this period I was in intimate association with Northcliffe and travelled with him in France, Spain, Canada, Newfoundland and the United States, and had many talks with him about *The Times* and his plans.

[2] This refers to *The Times* Edition of the *Encyclopædia Britannica*.

[3] *The History of "The Times"*, Vol. III, p. 652.

again at Sturry when Mr. Amery was also there and the talk was chiefly about the Empire and "the possibilities of a real Imperial Parliament and Government and how to produce them". Geoffrey also visited Sturry in September to take farewell of Milner before he set out on his lecture tour in Canada. Geoffrey's third week-end was spent with the Northcliffes at Sutton Place, near Guildford, where the house-party included the Leo Maxses, Owen Seaman, Lady Dorothy Nevill, Sydney Holland and myself. On Sunday a large number of guests turned up for lunch including Monsieur Delcassé, the Garvins, Austen Chamberlains, Arthur Lees, Walter Harris (*The Times* Correspondent in Morocco) and others. Geoffrey went for a walk with Northcliffe, the first of very many during the next ten years.

This week-end at Sutton Place with the Northcliffes was the first of many visits up to the outbreak of the First World War. It was either after this or a subsequent week-end that Northcliffe, with one of his flashes of intuition, said to me (I was one of the party), "Evelyn, this afternoon you have seen me walking about with the future Editor of *The Times*."[1] Certainly Northcliffe was greatly impressed by Geoffrey's poise, good judgment and imperturbability at their early meetings, and he recognized him as a very reliable correspondent. Sooner or later despite his genuine conviction, as expressed to Wickham Steed, that he did not intend to interfere with the "old gang", he was already thinking about the future editorship. He wanted a younger man—to Northcliffe in 1908, then in his forty-third year, G. E. Buckle, at fifty-four, seemed elderly in aspect and elderly in outlook, and when he finally parted company with him in August, 1912, Buckle was only fifty-eight. Mr. Dermot Morrah, to whom Geoffrey was devoted, and who is still a distinguished member of *The Times* staff, related the following amusing story to me:

> I well remember the following remark of Buckle, made to me in 1932. "Geoffrey Dawson is fifty-eight today (October 25th) and has shown no sign of retirement; Barnes died at fifty-eight;[2] Delane went mad at fifty-eight; I resigned at fifty-eight, and no man can edit *The Times* after fifty-eight and live!"[3]

[1] It was not till July 27, 1912, that Northcliffe offered Geoffrey the Editorship. *Vide infra*, p. 82.

[2] As a matter of fact Barnes was only in his fifty-sixth year when he died.

[3] He might also have added that Chenery died at fifty-nine.

VII

THE UNION OF SOUTH AFRICA

THERE was still vital work for Geoffrey to do on the *Star* in connection with the "Closer Union" of the four Colonies. The members of the Kindergarten who remained in South Africa had not been idle during his absence, and undoubtedly the cause of Union was receiving much support; and it was felt that a unified South Africa might surely be kept within the Empire.

The following letter to Kitty from Muizenberg (24th November, 1908) gives a picture of events as Geoffrey found them in South Africa:

> All the world is at Cape Town, where the great Convention reassembled yesterday, and I had practically decided to spend a few days here and am more than glad that I did. In the course of a long day I have managed to see a good many of the people who are in it—a great palaver with Farrar, a few words with Smuts and Lord Selborne (who came on board early this morning) and a luncheon party with Patrick Duncan, Lionel Curtis, R. H. Brand and Philip Kerr—all that remains, in fact, of the Kindergarten. Now I have come down to spend the night with Herbert Baker, the architect of Groote Schuur and all good houses in South Africa, who is alone in his cottage on the beach at Muizenberg.
>
> Tomorrow I shall see Jameson, Fitzpatrick and the others, but I feel already that I have picked up most of their mysterious proceedings, and should be a much better journalist if people would tell me fewer secrets! . . .
>
> On the whole things seem to be going pretty well and much more rapidly than the outside world supposes. . . . I fancy that a constitution of some sort will be ready for public discussion pretty early in the year and may be in England for confirmation within twelve months from now. (This is strictly confidential.)

One of his first leaders on returning to Johannesburg was entitled "Brotherly Love", in which he dealt with the wonderful spirit of co-operation existing between the Dutch and British delegates, as shown for example in the "mixed" bathing on Muizenberg beach and the "laager of Transvaal delegates at Rondebosch, where General Botha and Sir Percy Fitzpatrick are said to preside over the common meals, the mutual admiration of Dr. Jameson and ex-President Steyn. The truth is that Cape Town is simply palpitating with brotherly love".

Geoffrey closed his working year with a leading article in the *Star* on December 31st entitled "The Year of Union", in which he recalled two important dates, May 5th, 1908, which stood out as the first landmark in the story—the day on which one of the recurrent interstate conferences adopted the principle of Closer Union; and October 12th, 1908—the day on which the Convention actually came into existence.

In March, 1909, there was a Conference of the Closer Union Societies, whose members were entertained by the Mayor of Johannesburg. After three days of discussion, the Conference passed a unanimous resolution in favour of union. On March 30, a special "Union" Session of Parliament was opened in the four Colonies.

Letter (March 7th, 1909) to Aunt Kitty:

> Such another busy week as you will doubtless gather from the constant odds and ends that I send to *The Times*. There has been a great gathering of Closer Union Societies—for which the Kindergarten is mainly responsible—and we have all had to play up to entertaining delegates and keeping their noses straight.

In May the Governors of the four Colonies met at Bloemfontein, and when the crucial issue of "equal rights" was reached, the Transvaal delegation, under the leadership of Botha, delivered an ultimatum and finally on May 7th equal rights was adopted. Four days later the Act was signed, and Geoffrey "scooped" the new draft for the *Star*. A week later he sailed for England in the *Walmer Castle*—"a tremendous boat-load of friends and acquaintances".

Geoffrey had run things fine, for the *Walmer Castle* only arrived at Southampton on June 5th, 1909, a dozen hours before the British Press gave its memorable inaugural banquet of the Imperial Press Conference at the White City. Those who were privileged to be present on that occasion will never forget the address of welcome given by Lord Rosebery, which Geoffrey refers to in his diary as "a wonderful speech" and was regarded by Northcliffe as the best speech he had ever heard. Rosebery gave a most moving picture of the old land which many of his hearers were visiting for the first time—the vision of a peaceful England with its picturesque old-world hamlets nestling round the village church. How little those present—excepting perhaps Northcliffe, who later in that very year in speeches and interviews in Canada and the United States dwelt on the inevitability of war with Germany—could have foreseen this peaceful island turned into an armed-camp in two World Wars within the ensuing thirty years.

On this visit to England Geoffrey crowded very much into seven weeks. Apart from the main functions connected with the Imperial Press Conference he managed to make many useful contacts. He breakfasted with Lloyd George; dined, together with some selected Empire press delegates, with H. A. Gwynne (Editor of the *Standard* and later of the *Morning Post*) to meet Lord Charles Beresford, Bonar Law, Leo Maxse and Milner; he saw Buckle several times and wrote a leader for him on South Africa, which was the first leader he ever wrote for *The Times*; he breakfasted with the "Doctor" (Jameson); attended a "*Kinderfest*" at Norfolk House, and on his last day in London he breakfasted with Smuts and Brand, and finally dined with most of the Kindergarten and Milner, F. S. Oliver and Jameson at "The Bachelors' "—"an extraordinarily good evening".

On 24th July, he sailed in the *Kenilworth Castle* and wrote the following letter to Kitty (July 27th, 1909):

> . . . Touching the prospect of work in England, of which you ask, the idea is to extend further the Imperial side of *The Times* which has been lately and gradually evolved out of the "Foreign Department". One man—Grigg—is at present in charge of the news from the Dominions, to which he makes periodical excursions with great difficulty of arrangement. It is suggested that I should be associated with him jointly and that we should take it in turn to work in the office and make trips to Canada, Australia or South Africa. It is the first thing I have struck which rather appeals to me and I think there is a reasonable chance of it coming off. However, it's hardly ripe yet, and I can't go away till things are settled in South Africa, or put the *Star* in the cart by leaving it without a decent successor. Don't mention this to anyone because it is still rather in the air and it would make it more difficult to achieve if it were more generally known. I have told Lionel Phillips of its possibility in strict confidence, so that preparations for filling my place, when the time comes, may be in train.

Geoffrey certainly was not an ambitious man. As late as the 25th July, 1910, in a letter to Mr. Amery, he thus describes his ambitions when he returned to England, after giving up the Editorship of the *Johannesburg Star*: "Remember that, one way or another, I propose to devote my life to our common cause—in journalism, politics, or any way that offers. 'Business' is out of the question as a *profession*. I can't do it and it bores me. As you know, I am more or less independent ultimately, and therefore don't worry about such things as pensions or provision for old age. The essential thing is hard and steady congenial work at once and at least £1,000 a year to add to the £300 or so which I derive from other sources now. This is a tall order, I know. . . . The *ideal* thing would be a £1,000 billet on *The Times*."

From the above it is clear that when he left South Africa a few months later he had no idea that he would be appointed Editor of *The Times* within two years, at a salary greatly in excess of the £1,000 mentioned above.

He was back in Johannesburg on Friday, August 13th, and probably as a result of his discussions in London he began ventilating the idea of Jameson as an Opposition leader. He expressed the view that "no true Coalition, meaning the equal co-operation of the two great South African parties in the same ministry, could have been effected without him".

On the 19th December, 1909, Geoffrey received a Christmas letter from Milner:

> . . . Blessings on you generally. The longer you can go on "keeping your end up", I know how precarious it is, the better for South Africa and the Empire. When you can no longer fight profitably in that quarter you will be an immense reinforcement to our side over here.
>
> Not that we are weak over here at the moment. We are putting up a devilish good fight. I don't for one instant expect to win. If we can substantially reduce the majority (i.e. of the Liberal Party)—I always said it would take two Parliaments to run it out—we shall have done very well. The combination against us is tremendous, but it lacks inner unity, which we are acquiring, and in time I believe the weight of argument will smash it up. Don't be disappointed if the first batch does not go too well. Once more heartiest good wishes and all affection.

While waiting for the arrival of Lord Selborne's successor, Lord Gladstone, Geoffrey and his friends picnicked on the top of Table Mountain. On May 17, Lord and Lady Gladstone arrived and were welcomed with due ceremony. The new Governor-General, as son of W. E. Gladstone, was assured of a warm welcome on the part of the Dutch in South Africa. Two days later Geoffrey met the Gladstones, and while at Groote Schuur he wandered about the lovely grounds, and, with Jameson, inspected the Rhodes Memorial and Swan's newly arrived "lions" (in stone).

The eve of Union Day (May 31st) was spent at the *Star* office in Johannesburg, and naturally entailed the sending of a long cable to

The Times and the writing of a leading article on this great moment in the history of South Africa in which Milner's Kindergarten, including Geoffrey, had played so important a part. A new chapter was opening. The miracle had happened. Less than eleven years since Kruger's Ultimatum, Boer and Briton were jointly rejoicing in the birth of a new South African Nation, based on equal rights for the two white races. There was also a suitable recognition of the spiritual side of the occasion and religious services were held throughout the land. Messages of congratulation from the sister nations in the Empire poured in. The British Lion had indeed lain down with the South African Springbok. The years of bitterness in the immediate post-war years were, it was hoped, a thing of the past. There would, please God, provided the extremists were kept in check, be no return to the post-war (aftermath of Boer War) era with its lingering hates and distrust of the other side. These and similar thoughts pervaded Geoffrey's writings. But during these final months in South Africa there were still problems that had to be carefully watched and reported. In a leading article of July 31, Geoffrey pointed out that the removal of British teachers, engineers, and policemen, was one of the Transvaal Government's most regrettable acts. Nothing had done more to convince the backveld that Englishmen and Dutchmen could live and work together than the efficient, sympathetic and unobtrusive work of the teachers, engineers and policemen of British blood, and now they were being sent home.

In August he was engaged in a long correspondence with *The Times*—no doubt about his work at Printing House Square after his farewell to South Africa at the end of 1910. The sands were running out. Geoffrey felt now that his job in South Africa was done. On the 20th September he sent a letter resigning the Editorship of the *Star* to the Chairman of the Board, and duly received an acknowledgment expressing the sincere regrets of the proprietors of the *Star* the following day.

On October 31st, he was in the City Hall of Cape Town where the Duke and Duchess of Connaught were being officially welcomed to South Africa. The next four weeks were spent on the Royal train. Geoffrey could not have devised a better method of gaining a final survey of Africa, south of the Zambesi, than as Correspondent of *The Times* during the tour—he little thought that he would never see South Africa again. There were bands and bunting everywhere, civic receptions, deputations of Boers and Basutos, inspections of police; tea on Kandahar Island, and a realistic hippo hunt on the Zambesi; native dances and general palavers. "Many little informal receptions at wayside stations. H.R.H. jumping out at all of them and shaking hands and talking with the first man who came handy." Then there was of course a visit to the tomb of Cecil John Rhodes in the Matopo Hills.

Geoffrey's last months must certainly have been strenuous, because, quite apart from the Royal Tour, he had his own farewells to think about. He had to hand over the Editorship of the *Star* and attend farewell parties and presentations. He took farewell of the readers of the *Star* on his own thirty-sixth birthday, writing his last leading article entitled "The Task Ahead". He touched on the possibilities before the young South African nation as a partner state within the Empire. "This is South Africa's opportunity to win her place among the nations—the chance of showing, once for all, that she has men with bigger ideas than the narrow racialism of the Beyers and the Bosmans. Is she going forward or going back?" That was his final message to his readers.

His last morning in Johannesburg included his farewell to Mr. C. Marx, Chairman of the Board of the *Star*, and a presentation from the Journalists' Association. At the railway-station he found everyone connected with the *Star* "forming a line far down the platform and making much noise as the train went out". On board the *Walmer Castle* were many more people to wish him God-speed—Patrick Duncan, Richard Feetham, Herbert Baker and countless others. The vessel remained for hours embarking Christmas mails, and as they left the harbour, Table Mountain and all the sea-front camps on Bay Coast "was looking too glorious in the setting sunlight". This was the final parting. How much Geoffrey had learnt about South Africa since that day nine years ago is thus described by Mr. Lionel Curtis: "We drove from the local station in Cape carts. Robinson (afterwards Geoffrey Dawson) of Magdalen, who had just come out from the Colonial Office, drove the mules in my cart standing up in front, shouting and belabouring like any coster, and tearing over quagmires and rocks."

While Geoffrey was exploring the south bank of the Zambesi at the Victoria Falls with the Duke of Connaught's party, an event was taking place in London which was to have a lasting influence on his career—the appearance of the first issue of the *Round Table*: "A quarterly review of the Politics of the British Empire", on the 15th November, 1910. The *Round Table* magazine issued naturally from the activities of the Kindergarten in South Africa. After the establishment of Responsible Government in the Transvaal and Orange Free State most of its members continued their work until the new Union Constitution was actually in force. Thereafter they found that their particular work in South Africa was done. Patrick Duncan,[1] who was,

[1] *Vide* footnote, p. 54 *supra*.

till Responsible Government came, Colonial Secretary of the Transvaal and Richard Feetham,[1] who had been Town Clerk of Johannesburg but had already joined the Transvaal Bar, both determined to stay on in South Africa. Duncan also began to practice law in the Transvaal but later went into politics as a supporter of Smuts, and ultimately became Governor-General of the Union, while Feetham became a judge of the Appeal Court of South Africa and Chancellor of the Witwatersrand University. Curtis and Kerr had already resigned their positions in the Government service to devote their whole energies to the attainment of Union and, when that was accomplished, they came home. Brand's work as Secretary of the Inter-Colonial Council and Railway Committee of the Central South African Railways, in which he had Philip Kerr as his assistant, and also as Secretary of the Transvaal Delegation at the Convention, ceased too with the Union, and after coming home with his Delegation for the presentation of the Constitution to the United Kingdom Parliament, he also remained at home, as did both Hichens[2] and Dove, the then Town Clerk of Johannesburg, who later edited the *Round Table* for some years.

Stimulated by what they had done and helped to get done in South Africa, this group of friends was fired by the belief that just as the South African Colonies had been united, so it should be possible to follow on with the Federation of the self-governing communities of the British Commonwealth. The writer indeed believes it to be true that the words British Commonwealth of Nations originated with them. Just as they had helped on the Union of South Africa through the medium of their magazine the *State*,[3] so now they thought that the best way of helping towards a still wider Commonwealth would be by founding a magazine in London devoted to that aim. The name, the *Round Table*, seemed to them best suited to symbolize all the self-governing nations of the British Commonwealth sitting round the same board. For this purpose it was determined to publish the *Round*

[1] *Vide* footnote[1], p. 54 *supra*.

[2] *Vide supra* footnote[3], p. 54.

[3] *The State* was a small monthly magazine, financed by some of the more well-to-do supporters of the Closer Union Movement and edited by Philip Kerr, afterwards Lord Lothian. It was intended to serve as the organ of the Closer Union Societies, and was frankly propagandist in the same cause. Its literary quality was high. Many of its articles, though all were anonymous, were written by other members of the Kindergarten as well as by the Editor; and its make-up was attractive. Its cover was adorned by a picture of G. P. Watts' statue of "Physical Energy"—the leading feature of the Rhodes Memorial in the mountain slope above Groote Schuur. It petered out after its object had been served by the achievement of the Union of South Africa; but it may be regarded as a precursor of the *Round Table* magazine.

Table magazine quarterly, and also to set on foot a series of Round Table Studies into the nature of Federation and the possibility of the federation of the Commonwealth. Philip Kerr became Editor of the *Round Table* magazine, and Curtis, who later became a Research Fellow of All Souls and Beit Professor of Colonial History, devoted himself to the Round Table Studies, which formed the genesis of his "Problem of the Commonwealth", "Commonwealth of Nations", "Civitas Dei", "Diarchy" and numerous other writings.

These two were therefore the publicists of the movement. The rest of the Kindergarten had to earn their living in various ways, but met frequently at monthly meetings to help to conduct the *Round Table* and also to keep abreast of what Curtis was thinking and writing about. Nevertheless they played an active and interested part with others who joined their group, for instance F. S. Oliver, who was an intimate friend and whose advice was of great value; Sir Edward Grigg (later Lord Altrincham), who was at one period Editor, and Sir Reginald Coupland, also Beit Professor of Colonial History, who too was at one time Editor. Geoffrey remained through the whole of his life a very active member of the Round Table group, attending its meetings whenever he could. The group gained a great deal from his knowledge and experience. Geoffrey himself was Editor after leaving *The Times* in 1919 and again acted as Editor on his final resignation from *The Times* (from 1942–44).

To the outside world it appeared that the members of the Round Table had identical views and that they subscribed to all the views expressed in the writing of their chief spokesman, Lionel Curtis, but this was not so. They all had a great admiration of Curtis and of his incomparable power of getting things done, whether as in the Union of South Africa, or in Reform in India, or in the Irish Settlement, in all of which he played an important part, but they did not subscribe to all his theories, whether of Imperial Federation or federation of the Commonwealth and European countries, or of the Anglo-Saxon countries with or without the European countries, or finally of world Federation. Philip Kerr probably went further than any of the others towards adopting these theories, though the experience he gained during his short Ambassadorship in the United States soon convinced him that any true federation with the United States was at present quite impracticable.

There were others, such as Lord Brand and Lord Altrincham, who thought any such objective as World Government at present not only quite impracticable but positively undesirable, since a World Government to be successful at all as a Government, must necessarily be a dictatorship. The majority, including these two, held the view that World Government, or even an Anglo-Saxon Federation were, in present circumstances, a Utopian dream and that, since even the most Anglo-Saxon of the Sister-States of the Commonwealth refused to contemplate any closer union than has been achieved at present, the practical objective to be aimed at must be, first, the maintenance and strengthening in every direction of the ties between members of the Commonwealth itself, and secondly, the search for the closest co-operation between all the free nations of the world.

In the first issue of the *Round Table* (published by the Arden Press at Letchworth), the purposes of the publication were thus stated: "To present a regular account of what is going on throughout the King's Dominions, written with first-hand knowledge and entirely free from the bias of local political issues, and to provide a means by which the common problems which confront the Empire as a whole can be discussed without bias." Each part of the Empire provided its own correspondents. In 1924 John Dove made some notes for a History of the Round Table, upon which the present account of the quarterly is based. Walter Hines Page, himself Editor for many years of *World's Work*, when United States Ambassador to the Court of St. James's, said, "The *Round Table* is, I suppose, the best review in the world." Some Continental publicists regarded its activities with bewilderment or suspicion. *Der Neue Merkur*, of Munich, regarded it as a mixture of Imperialism and Communism! On the other hand Monsieur Caillaux, at one time Prime Minister of France, held it to be a blend of Imperialism and reaction,[1] and spoke of evening gatherings, like the Round Table's, where people of great ability, for the most part old Oxford men and high officials, met and concocted vast schemes. The *Morning Post*, on April 10, 1923, stated, "It is run by a group of idealists who take a much greater part in the politics and policy of this country than is generally suspected." One reason for the mystery attending the purposes of the *Round Table* is no doubt the fact that its articles have always been anonymous, only the Board knowing the names of the writers.

Geoffrey's diaries often refer to meetings of the "moot" at Cliveden, overlooking one of the most lovely reaches of the Thames, the home of Lord and Lady Astor; and also at 4, St. James's Square, their London house; or perhaps the "mooters" would spend fruitful weekends at Hatfield with Lord and Lady Salisbury; or at Checkendon with Mr. and Mrs. F. S. Oliver amid the beechwoods of the Chilterns, and in later years at lovely Blickling, Lothian's home in Norfolk. Sometimes in London "moots" would be held at the home of Lionel Hichens, in Buckingham Palace Gardens, or in R. H. Brand's house in

[1] *Où Va La France? Où Va l'Europe?*—(*Edition de la Sirène*, Paris, 1922).

New Cavendish Street, once or twice in the Dawson home at 23, Sussex Place, or in the house of Dougal Malcolm.

Geoffrey's constant attendance at the "moots" was one of the main factors in enabling him, tied as he often was to his editorial chair in Printing House Square, to keep in touch with current events in both hemispheres.

It has sometimes been said that Geoffrey was not interested in European politics. It would be more correct to state that his first interest was the Commonwealth, and he was intensely alive to everything that affected it. The politics of Central and Eastern Europe, the nascent nationalism of the small States in the Danube Basin, and in South-east Europe, did not absorb him as they did, for instance, Wickham Steed, who probably knew more of the internal politics of the Austro-Hungarian Monarchy and its neighbours than any other living Englishman. But as soon as the interests of the Commonwealth were threatened, Geoffrey became absorbed in current, and possibly hitherto unfamiliar, problems, whether in Albania or Abyssinia, and no one had better sources of information when he needed them.

VIII

EDITOR OF "THE TIMES"

DURING his first months at Printing House Square, Geoffrey, for a short while at least, must have experienced the sensations of a new boy. True, he had been on the staff of *The Times* as correspondent in South Africa for nearly five years, and he was a close friend of Leo Amery, E. W. M. Grigg and other members of the staff. Rumours about his frequent meetings with Northcliffe[1] certainly circulated at Printing House Square, and he was already regarded by some as *papabile*, or in American jargon, as of "presidential timber". It was, however, a very different matter for a distant correspondent suddenly to find himself within the sacred precincts, and so accepted by the hierarchy. Geoffrey records in his diary that at the outset he sat at the feet of S. J. Pryor, a capable journalist whom Northcliffe employed to give expert advice on technical matters.

Geoffrey was attached to the Imperial and Foreign Department and acted rather informally as secretary or assistant to G. E. Buckle, the Editor; he worked for a while in Moberly Bell's room on the third floor. The two years, 1911 and 1912, may be said to be the two most important in Geoffrey's life, for they marked his "apprenticeship" on the staff of Printing House Square which led to his appointment as Editor in August, 1912.

Geoffrey had spent the Christmas (1910) holidays at Langcliffe with the Aunts, having gone there on the day of his arrival at Southampton, but he was back in London before the end of the year and stayed in lodgings in St. James's Place. He soon began picking up threads and dined with Brand in his flat, and on December 30th, after dinner at Brooks's, talked till midnight with Milner, who was anxious that Geoffrey should go to *The Times*, as a job which wanted doing and was not being done well and consistently (i.e. deal with Imperial matters at Printing House Square). Through his diaries it is possible to follow the steps which were ultimately to enthrone Geoffrey as *Jupiter Tonans*.

[1] Northcliffe had a high regard for Geoffrey. Behind his quiet manner he said he had one of the ablest brains in England.

Once again there were decisive talks with Northcliffe at Sutton Place, from January 5th to 9th, 1911. Northcliffe had evidently made up his mind that he wanted Geoffrey at Printing House Square. On the first day of the visit the two men were talking together most of the day. Northcliffe was at his best when discussing the past history of *The Times*, about which he knew much. He was entirely frank, talked of the great traditions of the Walter proprietorship, of his present difficulties, of the staff and of urgent problems. On Friday, Jan. 6th, Northcliffe definitely offered Geoffrey a position on the paper and pressed him to take it. Geoffrey's comment in his diary was: "Rather nervous about it but much too attractive to refuse." Ten days later he had a more formal meeting with the "Chief"[1] in his famous room, No. 1, in Carmelite House, in the presence of Moberly Bell and Reggie Nicholson, then Assistant-Manager, who succeeded the former on his death in April. Another week-end was spent at Sutton Place; this time the talks with Northcliffe were carried on in the presence of Nicholson, who now occupied a key position at Printing House Square. I was once again at Sutton Place and was vitally interested in observing the steps on the journey which were leading Geoffrey to Printing House Square. I had never forgotten the "Chief's" definite statement to me in 1908 that one day he would appoint Geoffrey to the editorship—I had only wondered why there had been so long a delay in putting this decision into operation. On February 13th Geoffrey had a further talk with Northcliffe at Carmelite House "covering very much the old ground—obviously very anxious to get things going better and becoming a little nervy about it. But he was as usual very pleasant to me. . . ." Geoffrey's first day at Printing House Square was Tuesday, February 14th, when he met the diurnal workers and attended the so-called Conference "when day meets night".

The following entries from the diary record the events of the next three days:

Feb. 15. Another day of rather tedious feet-sitting and finding my way about, everybody apparently working on his own without much direction and consequently a great deal of conversation and duplication. . . . Went to "Sumurun", the Arabian Nights Pantomime at the Coliseum.

Feb. 16. Another day in *The Times* office, still rather fogged and bemused

[1] By the year 1911 Northcliffe addressed Geoffrey as "My dear Robin" and up to 1918 Geoffrey always addressed Northcliffe, in his letters, as "My dear Chief"—as did most of those in key positions in the various concerns with which Northcliffe was connected. It was only when relations became strained early in 1919 that Geoffrey addressed him as "My dear Lord Northcliffe" and signed himself "Geoffrey Dawson".

with their extraordinarily messy arrangements for turning out that wonderful paper! . . .

Feb. 17. Further *Times* investigations, including a raid into the "Court and Social" department and an excellent luncheon in the office. . . .

During the first weeks at Printing House Square, Geoffrey tried to familiarize himself with all aspects of the editorial side; he was encouraged by Northcliffe to do so and he was very fortunate in having the help of Reggie Nicholson, a man of great tact and of real charm, who completely understood the difficulties of his position. Geoffrey went to the office at odd hours; on Sunday to talk with Lewis, the Sunday-duty man; another day, after dining with Capper, he remained at the office till 2 a.m., "when the first edition was printed and handed over to the sleepy newsmen, a very interesting but rather bewildering experience". Another evening he dined with Bruce Richmond[1] at his delightful house in Victoria Square. Then there were the frequent walks with Northcliffe on Hampstead Heath in early spring—so familiar to all his key men.

Seven weeks after Geoffrey's arrival at Printing House Square there occurred an event of major importance, the death of Charles Frederic Moberly Bell, the Manager, and one of the most loyal servants *The Times* ever had, whose death had undoubtedly been hastened by the strain of the previous years.

On his return from a visit to the Northcliffes in Paris, Geoffrey wrote to his Aunts (April 8th):

> I got back from Paris yesterday evening—only one day there and that the worst remembered by the oldest inhabitant—and the outward crossing was unspeakable. . . .
>
> I had to be back for various reasons and wanted too to go to poor old Bell's funeral. That tragedy must have happened very soon after I left the office on Wednesday and I didn't hear of it till I got to Paris. For him no doubt it was an ideal death—to drop down in harness without a moment's notice or pain—one of his inimitable letters half-written on his table—just at a time too when he must have begun to think of retiring, for I think he would have found retirement intolerable. But it has been a terrible grief and shock to everyone—and quite awful for his poor wife. She came to the funeral today and a very long business and a great company of people—and I have been walking about with Amery most of the afternoon since it was over.

In his diary the first reference to the difficulties of working with Northcliffe—and there were to be very many of such entries during the next eight years—was "a devil of a day with Northcliffe".

[1] Sir Bruce C. Richmond, Assistant Editor of *The Times*, originator of the Literary Supplement. Geoffrey was devoted to him.

After strenuous days at Printing House Square, Geoffrey frequently escaped to the country for week-ends; he stayed several times at Sutton Place, where he met many celebrities including old Lady Dorothy Nevill, full of reminiscences of the mid-Victorian era, the Max Aitkens, recently arrived from Canada,[1] and Sydney Holland (Lord Knutsford), who took him over the London Hospital. Geoffrey was always a welcome guest at Chequers, then the home of the Arthur Lees: as always he kept in close touch with Oxford and above all, with Langcliffe. He cordially shared Northcliffe's belief in long carefree holidays for hard-working journalists, and whenever the opportunity occurred he would betake himself to the fells of the West Riding, a practice he very sensibly continued throughout his working life.

In the summer of 1911, European problems were much to the fore. The German Emperor was indulging in sabre-rattling in West Africa, and in September the Office was "seething with excitement" over the outbreak of war between Italy and Turkey over Tripoli. Geoffrey took the occasion to have a long talk with General H. H. Wilson[2] about some of the war-clouds on the horizon and used to meet that eminent soldier from time to time. In the closing months of 1911 Geoffrey had a couple of meetings with Mr. Churchill, and discussed with that statesman his recent transfer to the Admiralty and subsequently the "clean sweep of the Sea Lords" which he was about to make.

Early in October, Geoffrey (who now occupied a small house at Number 2, Smith Square) decided to visit Ireland, as the Irish situation would, in view of the Liberal Government's pledges to introduce a Home Rule measure, soon occupy the centre of the stage. At Kilteragh he received instruction in the Irish situation from Sir Horace Plunkett and from J. E. Healy, Editor of the *Irish Times* and the Dublin correspondent of *The Times*—he could have had no better teachers. Much of the talk naturally centred round the attitude of Ulster and of Edward Carson. While those present were inclined to regard some of the speeches of the Ulster leaders as bluff intended to frighten the Liberal Government, there was agreement that they were taken very seriously by the grim Puritan rank and file in Northern Ireland, to whom they were addressed. Geoffrey, at first, must have been somewhat bewildered by the currents and cross-currents of Irish politics, unless his long experience in South Africa had prepared him for the depth of National feeling.

Within a year of joining the staff at Printing House Square Geoffrey was certainly associating with many men of importance, far beyond the scope of the "Imperial and Foreign" side of *The Times*. There were

[1] Probably his first meeting with Lord Beaverbrook.

[2] Who became C.I.G.S. during the latter part of the First World War.

Back row: Mrs. Nicholson (nurse) with Donald. She was for sixty years friend of the family and died at Langcliffe Hall in 1935; Mr. George Robinson, Kathleen.

Front row: Geoffrey, Mrs. Robinson, Ralph, Bertie

THE MILNER KINDERGARTEN, 1906

Standing (*from left to right*): The Hon. R. H. Brand (now Lord Brand), Sir Herbert Baker, R.A., and Mr. Lionel Hichens. *Middle row:* The Hon. Hugh Wyndham (now Lord Leconfield), Mr. Justice Feetham, Mr. Lionel Curtis, Sir Patrick Duncan, Mr. J. F. Perry and Sir Dougal Malcolm. *Front row:* Mr. John Dove, The Marquess of Lothian and Mr. Geoffrey Robinson (later changed his name to Dawson)

Photo by Sir Kendal Frank, 1902

Back row: Geoffrey Robinson (Private Secretary), Captain F. Henley (A.D.C.). *Front row:* Colonel Hon. William Lambton (later Maj.-Gen. Sir W. Lambton), Lord Milner, Colonel M. F. Rimington (later Maj.-Gen. Sir M. F. Rimington) many of his friends who must and did realize that some great change in his status was in the offing. I met him fairly frequently with the Northcliffes and he undoubtedly had made a great impression on the "Chief". On February 15th, 1912, Geoffrey had to deal with the "exciting news" that the Prince of Wales was to go to Magdalen; in March he was lunching with General H. H. Wilson, who told of incessant rumours "of a pounce by Germany in May"—an early reference to the likelihood of German aggression; and in the same month he saw *Milestones*, Arnold Bennett's play, "most attractive—the 3 ages of man, 1860, 1885, 1912—delightfully played".

It was in this period that Geoffrey was finding out for the first time that Northcliffe could, on occasions, be difficult. As early as the 11th January, 1912, there is an entry in the diary that "a very petulant telegram" had been received by Nicholson (the Manager) and Geoffrey's laconic comment was: "better ignored". On the 20th February there is this entry, "Another strenuous day of the usual kind—Northcliffe agitating about Repington and other troubles." By the end of March Geoffrey was evidently "stretching his wings", for in the absence of Capper and Freeman he took on their jobs. He evidently enjoyed the responsibility, for he wrote, "Good fun and an interesting paper." On this occasion (it was Sunday) there is a reference to the fact that before going to the office he had attended Evensong at St. Paul's—a practice which became part of his regular Sunday routine throughout the years. On June 2nd Geoffrey took charge of the Foreign page on a Sunday to release Edward Grigg, and later in the month he was "toiling at Printing House Square till the early hours of the morning in the absence of Capper[1] and Freeman[2]".

His friendship with the Waldorf Astors lasted from 1911, soon after his return from South Africa, till the end of his life. At Cliveden he took part in discussions on every conceivable subject and here the Round Table would assemble, sitting "obedient to Lionel Curtis in committees and summerhouses all morning". At Cliveden as early as 1912, Geoffrey was taking part in debates on a plan for India with ex-Governors and other experts. Certainly Cliveden provided Geoffrey, both before and after marriage, with a very stimulating background and a lovely setting for meeting old friends or making new ones. He met in these pleasant surroundings, or at number 4, St. James's Square (the London home of the Astors), people as varied in outlook as Bernard Shaw, "Jimmy" Thomas, Lloyd George, Will Crooks, Mrs. Wintringham and a host of others. Lady Astor was a genius at stirring the social melting-pot, and the last shreds of British reserve would

[1] John Brainerd Capper, Assistant Editor to both Buckle and Geoffrey.

[2] George Freeman, served as deputy to Geoffrey in 1918, and for some time under Steed. He was on staff when Geoffrey returned to P.H.S.

vanish—if indeed it had survived thus long—when the whole party was made to play musical chairs after dinner.

The following two extracts in the diary concerning meetings with Northcliffe—when the latter was finally making up his mind, if it was not already made up about Geoffrey's future—are of special interest as they were evidently leading to the momentous entry of July 28:

1912.

June 9. Sutton Place . . . a most interesting talk with Lord N. before dinner—full of ideas for *The Times*—most of them extraordinarily sound.

July 4. A long morning's talk with Lord N., his negotiations with John Walter, his future plans etc.: this in the streets, the Green Park, and finally in St. James's Place . . .

July 28. Sutton Place. Large party and a good deal of tennis . . . there was little time for serious talk as far as I was concerned, but it was clear that matters were settled so far as Printing House Square was concerned.

Throughout the days till August 8th, when his appointment as Editor of *The Times* became known, Geoffrey kept careful notes of his doings.

On July 29th he describes a difficult evening at Printing House Square: "Carried off Grigg to dinner and got hold of Capper afterwards, and finally of Buckle for a long and rather distressing talk in my room at the office. He was obviously sore about his own treatment, though entirely well-disposed to my succession."

On July 30th there was another agitating day in the office, full of "whisperings and rumours". He had talks with Bruce Richmond, Braham and Freeman—"about G.E.B.'s (Buckle's) going rather than my own accession which B.L.R. (Richmond) however assumed and supported". On July 31st he received a kind letter from Mrs. Buckle and dined with J. E. Mackenzie, correspondent at Berlin and always a strong supporter of Geoffrey's, whom he took to see Pavlova at the Palace and on to the Travellers' Club, where they found John Walter. On August 1st the Board received an admirable letter of resignation from Buckle; the task of providing an appropriate answer to it was entrusted to John Walter, Reggie Nicholson, F. W. Monypenny and Geoffrey. After the meeting he had a long talk with Monypenny, "who like everyone else was extraordinarily kind". Nothing stands out more during these days than the kindness shown to Geoffrey by the Buckles (with whom he dined on August 2nd), who did not allow their personal feelings to affect in the slightest degree the warmth of their welcome to him—generous treatment which he never forgot.

On August 9th a formal statement of the appointment was made. Geoffrey was literally "snowed under" with letters, telegrams and cables from South Africa and America.

The receipt of the following generous letter (14th August, 1912) from Buckle must have made Geoffrey very happy:

The Athenaeum, S.W.

My dear Robinson,

I do not think I have at all made clear to you how happy I hold myself in having you for a successor. If Monypenny were younger and stronger and had not got Dizzy (the biography of Beaconsfield) like a millstone round his neck, I should prefer him; and there was a time when my mind turned to Amery, but he has gone in another direction. . . .

Apart from your superior health and strength, you have an advantage over Monypenny in a much greater variety of interests. Politics absorb him to the exclusion of almost everything else. Those who know you or know of you are well disposed. To my personal friends among them I have warmly commended you; you will find a favourable reception from Balfour, Lansdowne, Bonar Law, Austen Chamberlain—and of course Curzon, Milner and Selborne, whom you know well—on the one side; and from Morley, Grey, Asquith and Haldane on the other. The Archbishop of Canterbury, whom I know well, will be very ready to help you. I have also bespoken the friendly interest of Stamfordham, the King's Private Secretary.

So you may start with great confidence, with the support of your colleagues and the benevolence of the world of politics. You will soon assimilate so much of domestic politics as is strange to you now; and you have a much wider range of intelligent interests than I have. To be followed by a man whom I like and respect so much, and an All Souls colleague, is indeed a real source of true satisfaction and pleasure to me.

You will be warmly welcomed by the staff, as indeed I expect you have already discovered. There will be no jealousy whatever, because there is no one who feels himself passed over or aggrieved; most of them had already anticipated your succession, though no doubt it has come sooner than any of us expected.

There is a similarly benevolent disposition to you outside. It is universally recognized that you are the right sort of man at the right sort of age. All the public comments that I have seen have been friendly. . . . I have no doubt you will gradually and insensibly get into the habit of regarding all public questions, not from your own personal point of view, but from an impersonal *Times* standpoint. "WHAT OUGHT *The Times*, with its history and traditions, to say about this?" has always been in my mind. So is the continuity preserved, which, in spite of old stories about Delane and his weathercock policy, is I think essential to the interests of *The Times* in the present day. . . .

There is no need to advise you to keep up our tradition of fairness in reporting speeches directed against the policy advocated by *The Times*, and in printing reasonable letters from all quarters. This is the ABC of *The Times* spirit, and must already be in your blood.

Try your best to keep *The Times* clear of special *Daily Mail* hobbies and policies. I fear you will not be able to do so wholly. I know you agree with me on the extreme importance of giving the lie to the taunt about a "twopenny halfpenny *Daily Mail*".

However, I must not run on and lecture you, but will remain,

Yours always,

G. E. Buckle.

Geoffrey received the following telegram from Lord Northcliffe: "August 9. Broadstairs. Am sorry to deluge you with this frightful cataract of publicity this morning dear Robin but it was necessary and will not happen again. Chief." He also received this letter (Aug. 8, 1912) from the "Chief" at Elmwood, St. Peter's, Kent:

My dear Robin,

Congratulations on your appointment. I hope and believe we shall work well together. I do not think that either of us are unreasonable people, and I know that we have many Imperial ideals in common.

I think that we ought to meet. I will be at my lady's cottage on Monday, the 19th, and shall be in London the following day. I am going abroad on the Wednesday for a very short holiday. I want to get back as soon as possible for *Times* matters, and expect to be home again about the date you mention in your letter. I want us all to make a tremendous struggle to maintain the price. . . .

From Lady Northcliffe:

My dear Robin,

You know how glad I am for you—(and indeed for all of us!)—that things are "as they are" at Printing House Square—and I need not tell you either that I shall watch it all with affectionate interest.

Molly.

Geoffrey's many friends vied with each other in sending cordial messages on his appointment as "Mr. *Tonans*". J. L. Garvin, Editor of the *Observer*, wrote that, "For two years I have said you would be, and ought to be Editor of *The Times*." John Buchan, no mean judge, said in a very cordial letter: "I congratulate *The Times* on getting the best Editor now in existence, and I congratulate you on having the most important journalistic post in the world. . . . I am delighted to think that your long and difficult years on the *Star* have borne this proper fruit." Milner wrote enthusiastically: "No need to tell you what I think. I have been praying hard for this consummation for months past, and while I realize all the difficulties of your position, I have the greatest confidence that you will make it a huge success. On the whole, I don't know that there is a finer chance in the whole sphere of public affairs."

IX

FIRST SIXTEEN MONTHS AS EDITOR OF "THE TIMES"

WHAT kind of a man was the new Editor of *The Times* and why was it that his countless friends—many of them cautious people, not prone to indulge in hyperbole—were so certain that he would make a success of his job? There was something fundamental in Geoffrey's character which inspired confidence. The men who had known him best believed in him most. Clement Hales at Aysgarth; Edward Impey at Eton; Herbert Warren at Magdalen; and William Anson at All Souls. Northcliffe once said to him, "Robin, I appointed you Editor of *The Times* because of your real Christian faith." It is certainly true that throughout his working life, Geoffrey's religion meant a great deal to him, though he did not talk easily about it.

From some of those who worked with him during his first term at Printing House Square (February, 1911–February, 1919) it has been possible to get a picture of his daily routine. For eighteen months he had filled a somewhat nebulous position, devoting himself chiefly to Empire matters and serving as assistant to Buckle. One of the first important jobs he undertook was the organization of the arrangements for the reporting of the Coronation of King George V. For the next fourteen months he worked in the editorial department until he succeeded Buckle. One of the first remarks Geoffrey made on entering the Editor's room in Printing House Square on Monday, 23rd September, 1912, to take up his post, was, "I must have space—more space." This remark applied to what he regarded as the inadequate writing-table, which filled him with dismay! Before long a table of immense dimensions was obtained, and there was a look of satisfaction on his face as he settled down at it. This desire for space and spaciousness ran right through his character; there was nothing narrow or mean or petty to be found in him. He imbibed something essential from the healing air and the environment of the dales without which he could never have become one of the great Editors of *The Times*—it gave him a sanity and imperturbability essential to his job.

During his first term as Editor the ordinary daily routine was somewhat as follows: soon after 10 a.m., personal letters were sent by hand to him at his house at 2, Smith Square; soon after 11 a.m., he would telephone to the office instructions about appointments, special messages for members of the day staff, or perhaps some changes in the distribution of the day's work. In those days it was the exception rather than the rule for him to come to the office before lunch. He usually came to the office about 3.30 to 4 p.m., when he would dictate letters or see members of the staff and would always attend the Editorial Conference about 5 p.m., instruct leader-writers, or, not infrequently, write a leader himself. If he was writing a leading article his secretary, in the outer room, would endeavour to keep him free from visitors. During his first term of Editorship, the following was his output of leading articles:

1912–13 . . .	10
1915 . . .	39
1916 . . .	78
1917 . . .	81
1918 . . .	74

The high-water mark of 81 in 1917 compares with his record output of 209 leaders in one year while Editor of the *Johannesburg Star*—though the leaders in the latter were much shorter than those in *The Times*. During his second period as Editor of *The Times* his most productive year was 1930 with 38 leaders.

Geoffrey usually left the office between 7 and 8 p.m., returning between 9.30 and 10 p.m., and remaining usually till the paper went to press. The lunch hour was usually kept for meeting some expert whom he wished to consult.

Throughout both his Editorships Geoffrey almost invariably—when he could find time to escape from Printing House Square—attended important debates in the House of Commons. He usually listened to them from the Press Gallery. The seat of the chief Parliamentary Reporter of *The Times* was immediately over the Speaker's chair and faced the seat in the Distinguished Strangers' Gallery, occupied by a member of the Royal Family. When Geoffrey arrived the Chief Reporter would give up his seat to the Editor, and listen to the debate from another part of the gallery. As a general rule, at the end of his visit, Geoffrey would slip down to the Inner Lobby to which he had the right of admission.

While Geoffrey was a Unionist and instinctively consorted with the most prominent members of the Party, he took special pains to make contacts with leading Liberals. Early in his Editorship, through Sir John Simon, also a Fellow of All Souls, he met Herbert Samuel, Runciman, Lord Lucas, Charles Trevelyan and Augustine Birrell. He already knew Morley and often corresponded with him. After two week-ends at Sutton Place, and one with the Arthur Lees at Chequers in glorious October weather with "bright sun and a nip of frost and mist in the Vale and flaming beeches on the hillside", Geoffrey, probably thinking that a Liberal environment would be a desirable change, went to stay with the Sydney Buxtons at Newtimber Place in Sussex, where he met Sir Edward Grey "shooting rabbits over beagles" and Lord Haldane "talking 'the deeper things of life'". He also saw Lord Chelmsford, Fellow of All Souls, from time to time. In November we find him dining with Lord Haldane, where he met the Asquiths, and relates that John Morley and the Prime Minister discussed "men great in literature who became great in affairs and held Dizzy, Thiers and Guizot unchallenged". Geoffrey made a point of dining in circles where he would meet the leaders of the world of politics and industry, and later on, particularly in his second Editorship, he made useful contacts with Labour leaders, especially with Ramsay MacDonald.

On Monday, September 23rd, 1912, his first day in the editorial chair at Printing House Square, Geoffrey began his diary with these words, "A definite plunge into responsibility for the paper—beginning at about 11.00 a.m., and getting to bed at 2.00 a.m." In the afternoon he fitted in a visit to Monypenny, who had just gone to a nursing home. On the second day Northcliffe was in the office. On the third he had a long talk with Valentine Chirol at Bruce Richmond's house and by the evening he was evidently becoming accustomed to his new position, for he wrote, "Quite a decent paper for once, and I began to feel a tighter grip on the job."

Very early in his Editorship Geoffrey had to adapt himself to the practice of withdrawing from the dinner-table punctually and unobtrusively to his friends. He had to be back at the office by about 9.30 to 10 p.m., if he were to do his final proof-reading and correcting. At public dinners only infrequently was he able to hear the words of the chief speaker.

In October Geoffrey had a long talk with Bonar Law, who was full of Edward Carson's sincerity and sense of responsibility. Like Carson, Law, as a last resort, was inclined to agree to the exclusion of Ulster from the operation of the Home Rule Bill. Another day Geoffrey had an interview with Lady Londonderry at Londonderry House about Ulster problems and we read of a discussion with Northcliffe "(in bed with worry and turning his face like Ahab to the wall) about the crucial problem of circulation and advertisements". In November Geoffrey lunched with Repington[1] when among the guests were Winston Churchill, Jack Seely and Lloyd George, "a table of obvious excitement to the lunchers at the Carlton. I had a great talk with L. G., who was evidently in a bellicose frame of mind and talked quite complacently about the rousing of the English national spirit for a war about the Balkans. He said he was in favour of national service—he was 'unorthodox' in that! Interesting, impulsive, human, rather tricky creature, I thought, very different from Winston". A few days later Geoffrey had, in the Buckle tradition, "a long and pleasant talk in the morning with Stamfordham at Buckingham Palace". They discussed the war and Parliament—the King's position with regard to Home Rule, and a dissolution, etc. Finally Stamfordham asked Geoffrey "What people thought of the King?"—a difficult conundrum! He parried it by saying that his only special knowledge was the great success of the Yorkshire tour. He said it would be repeated in Lancashire.

On December 16th, when speaking at Ashton-under-Lyne, Bonar Law "committed Food Taxes" to the responsibility of the Dominions, whereupon *The Times* pointed out that this would not do. This course did not make the paper popular in Food Tax circles. The Dominions, however, judging by the shower of cables received at Printing House Square, approved of the attitude of *The Times*. The diary entry for December 18, "I dined with the Northcliffes and told him what I intended to do," is of especial importance as it shows plainly that Geoffrey was completely in control of the situation and was in fact editing the paper according to his own views.

The first eight days of the year 1913 are of interest in the story of Geoffrey's career as Editor for, in this period, he made his first appearance as a writer of leading articles on problems connected with the internal politics of the United Kingdom. Hitherto his writings on the "Editorial Page" had been confined to South Africa or Imperial subjects. True, the issues of Preference and "Food Taxes" were also of deep concern to the Dominions, but in shaping the policy of *The Times* on this extremely important and controversial matter he was plunging right into the centre of the political arena. It is sometimes assumed that during his proprietorship of *The Times* it was Northcliffe, and Northcliffe alone, who shaped the paper's policy during the years 1912–19, but this is not the case.

Geoffrey learned from Arthur Steel-Maitland that Bonar Law had come into line with *The Times* policy. The policy of the paper was

[1] Lt-Col. Charles à Court, Military Correspondent of *The Times*.

based on two premises, admiration for Bonar Law's ability and courage and his desire to strengthen his leadership of the Unionist Party at this critical moment; and a recognition of the steady revolt in the ranks of the Party against the "Food Tax" element in Imperial Preference. *The Times* recalled that Bonar Law, after consultation with his colleagues, had in his Ashton-under-Lyne speech "announced on their behalf and his own that he could not say for certain whether or not duties upon foodstuffs would be imposed if, after the next election, his Party were returned to power". Geoffrey explained why *The Times* viewed this official pronouncement as mistaken. On every election platform the Unionist candidate would inevitably be confronted with the question—"If the Unionists win is there to be a tax on foodstuffs, or is there not?" He set out to influence opinion so that the Party would disavow "Food Taxes" for the present and advocate a system of Preference to be built up on a tariff "upon manufacturers and luxuries alone". By January 10th *The Times* was able to announce that the "Food Tax" question was settled.

Geoffrey's first essay at influencing home politics had therefore been successful without any assistance from Northcliffe. The happy outcome of the brief "campaign" gave him confidence in his own judgment and amply bore out Buckle's prophecy, "You will soon assimilate so much of domestic politics as is strange to you now."

In January Geoffrey spent a week-end at Tring with Lord Rothschild. He writes (Jan. 12, 1913) to Langcliffe:

Tring Park,
Tring.

. . . I find myself plunged in a large and distinguished party here. . . . It is not exactly a rest cure, but rather interesting and amusing but I've contrived to get a good deal of fresh air and exercise. The German Ambassador is full of gloom about the prospects of peace, which I think he honestly wants. I've had a good deal of talk with him and think he's thoroughly nervous and overworked already. A really delightful talk with Mr. Balfour last night, sitting next to him at dinner. He is absolutely satisfied with the way things have gone in the Unionist Party and quite certain that Bonar Law will be able to make a very clear and definite statement. I still feel that the danger is that he'll say something that can be explained in various ways. . . .

Such an odd ugly house this—full of monstrous furniture and hideous mid-Victorian ornaments, no doubt of priceless value—and among all the jumble the *most* glorious pictures you ever saw—the greatest of all the Gainsboroughs and some Sir Joshuas—perfectly lovely—and the portraits which Queen Elizabeth and Leicester had painted for one another. . . .

Geoffrey always enjoyed talks with Lord Roberts and there are many references to his campaign for National Service and preparedness with which he entirely sympathized. Military matters were certainly very much in his mind, stimulated in part by the one or two meals with Repington when he met many of the Service Chiefs and the French Military Attaché.

Geoffrey's political and literary contacts were made easier by his election to the Beefsteak Club in January, and to the Athenaeum in March, under rule 11. The month of February opened with a lunch with Mrs. Asquith—"the P.M. cruising with Winston off Scotland". It was not till his second Editorship that a real friendship developed between them.

A letter from Geoffrey to Langcliffe, written on March 8th, 1913, describes a dinner at Londonderry House:

> I am sure you are itching to know about my royal dinner party last night, so let me scribble before I go to bed. Imagine me in the first place arriving at Londonderry House in my best breeches and stockings, a gaping crowd outside and an array of powdered footmen about the steps. A few people already there that I knew, luckily—the German Ambassador (Prince Lichnowsky) and the Midletons and Lady Castlereagh and the others came thick and fast, and finally the King and Queen—shepherded, one in each direction by Lord and Lady Londonderry, round the circle into which we had formed ourselves and shaking hands with us all in turn. This was in Lord Londonderry's new room on the ground floor—just remodelled on the Castlereagh room in Dublin. And then to dinner at once—2 big round tables—the King with Lady Londonderry nearly opposite me at mine, which was something like this:

Lady Londonderry

Duke of Portland	H.M.
Lady Airlie	Princess Lichnowsky
Revelstoke	Duke of Devonshire
Lady Midleton	Lady Castlereagh
Ancaster	Ilchester
Acton	Lady Doreen Long
Leo Rothschild	Lord C. Hamilton

me.

> A very rich and sumptuous affair it was—glorious plate and glass and flowers and "soft music without", though of the food, alas, I can remember little except that it included salmon caught by our hostess, who only arrived from Ireland this morning.
>
> Personally, I had better company and was better amused than I expected. After dinner we all went up to the picture gallery at once and stood about and talked and smoked. The King, to my great trepidation,

sent for me at once and you may picture me carrying on a very conspicuous conversation with His Majesty in the middle of this throng—he mercifully doing most of the talking—about *The Times* and the changes in the Navy and the Midland Railway trouble and feeling on the Continent. It didn't amount to really very much, but gave me a very interesting insight into the Royal mind.

Then the Queen came up and I had a much more difficult 10 minutes with her; and then the King went off to play bridge and then the Queen sat down and we all thankfully did the same. He had said (very kindly) that he hoped I would go when I liked, as he knew I had to work, but it was rather a difficult thing to do—as a matter of fact I stayed to the end and had a very interesting hour or so talking books with Lord Rosebery. I had practically done with my leading articles in the afternoon and got to the office by midnight just in time to finish them off.

Certainly in the chronicle of the relations between Northcliffe and Geoffrey, the summer months showed but little diminution in the tension between them. With a sigh of relief on July 1st, Geoffrey enters the "Chief's" departure to Paris and a golf championship—"for he has been in an impossible state of nerves and contradictory suggestions". On July 11th "Northcliffe came back from Paris, apparently more peaceful, and I had a long talk with him". But a week later there is the entry, "N. appeared in the afternoon—rather ratty and dissatisfied"; and ten days later, "Left N. in his drawing-room in a hopeless state of confused objurgation of *The Times*," while on July 30th Geoffrey had a "worrying day in pursuit of N. who was upsetting everyone and invisible to me". This entry in the diary is of special interest as it records his first meeting with R. M. Barrington-Ward, who, in 1941, was to succeed him as Editor: "Aug. 5, 1913. A long day in the office—Grigg produced a young Barrington-Ward[1] (just through Greats) for my inspection at lunch, and I carried him off forthwith to write a (not bad) leader. . . ."

There were several meetings with Bonar Law. Geoffrey had a *tête-à-tête* lunch at Pembroke Lodge with that statesman, whom he found pleasant and communicative. A few weeks later there is another reference to Bonar Law ringing up and a lunch with him, when Geoffrey learned that Asquith had approached him and they both agreed that the proposals (concerning the Irish problem) must be carefully considered.

During the autumn the relations with Northcliffe were evidently none too easy, for Geoffrey, who did not indulge in self-pity, makes such references as these on different days: "N. on the telephone and

[1] The point in "a young Barrington-Ward" is no doubt that Geoffrey already knew B.-W.'s elder brother as a Fellow of All Souls.

general worry"; on November 21st, "office all morning. N. was there, with an exaggerated view of confusion in the office (largely caused by himself) and there was a great palaver with him, Reggie (Nicholson) and Chisholm".

After becoming Editor, one of the problems which was never for long out of his mind was Ireland, in view of the Home Rule Bill introduced by Asquith's Administration. In approaching the Irish problem Geoffrey naturally had the great advantage of having, in his years in South Africa, been in almost daily contact with a small nation passionately devoted to the doctrine of self-determination. Therefore at the back of his mind—and especially since the "closer union" talks during his Editorship of the *Star*—was some form of federal solution.

The Times stated clearly that Parliament would be no nearer to a solution so long as Ministers refused "to face the hard, unalterable fact of Ulster's organized opposition" to the Home Rule Bill, and proclaimed "As for Protestant Ulster, it is determined to resist it (the Home Rule Bill) to the death." By November 17th, Asquith, fully realizing the implications of the by-elections at Reading and Linlithgow in which there was a great access in the Unionist vote, was now ready to offer terms of settlement, and Bonar Law, representing the Opposition, was known to be ready to consider them. Throughout November and December Geoffrey was writing frequently on the Irish Crisis, and in a leading article headed "Mr. Asquith's Position" *The Times* recognized that the Prime Minister had spoken for the first time with genuine understanding of the cleavage between North and South.

X

THE ULSTER CRISIS IN 1914

DURING these years the Editor discussed every aspect of the Irish question with F. S. Oliver, a refreshing and unorthodox man of affairs who combined the direction of one of the most successful firms of drapers in London with the "hobby" of writing history. His life of Alexander Hamilton, the Federalist, won him fame as a historian, and, incidentally, a place in the inner circle of the Round Table group. Mr. Lionel Curtis, when discussing the work of the Kindergarten in its early days, said, "here we were trying to work out a new philosophy of the State and behold an unknown linen draper who had done it all for us".

Early in the Irish discussions, much as he deplored the fact (i.e. because it divided Ireland), Geoffrey realized that Ulster's claim for self-determination must be recognized if civil war was to be avoided. As early as the 17th October, 1913, he was writing to Lovat Fraser, whom he sent to Ireland on behalf of *The Times*: "What you say about the genuine dynamic force behind the Ulster campaign entirely confirms my view. . . . You say 'they mean to go as far as they are able'. I suspect that in point of fact a considerable proportion of them is quite prepared to be shot down rather than capitulate to superior force."

Of the position of Edward Carson he wrote: "Your notes on Carson's appearance are very interesting. I just missed him yesterday at Bonar Law's where I was lunching, but I heard the gist of his report. There is no doubt whatever that the responsibility of the whole business weighs upon him very heavily. Personally I think that he has played his cards exceedingly well." In a memorandum of a talk with Lord Morley, who spoke with a certain admiration for Carson, Geoffrey quotes the actual words of Parnell to the former: "I want all these Ulstermen in. Without them an Irish Parliament would be a trumpery, parochial affair. . . . His (Morley's) first and last words were that the Irish Question would only be settled by hard knocks. A rather depressing but friendly talk."[1] A day later Geoffrey was discussing Ulster with Lord Stamfordham, and in his notes of the conversation he observes that "H.M., like everyone else, was clearly attracted by the 'exclusion of Ulster' as the only remaining hope of peace".

Geoffrey had not been in Ireland since his visit to Horace Plunkett at Kilteragh in October, 1911. It was clearly essential that he should get an up-to-date picture of conditions there. He went to Dublin on January 6th, 1914; during the journey he re-read W. F. Monypenny's admirable little essay "The Two Irish Nations". Two days were spent in Belfast, where Geoffrey visited the shipyards of Workman and Clark, the York Street Flax Mill, and after dining with Craig, was taken by him to see some 200 men drilled by moonlight at Randalstown, twenty-five miles away.

Geoffrey never worked harder than in 1914. It was unfortunate for him that just at the moment when he was from time to time writing important leading articles himself on the Irish crisis, and was having innumerable interviews with leading statesmen, he should have been going through a period of intense strain in his relations with Northcliffe. When the time comes for a fair appraisal of his Editorship to be made, compared with that of his predecessors, this constant tension in which he had to work will have to be remembered. No previous editor had any comparable situation to face with, possibly, the exception of Buckle, during the last years of his editorship.[2]

After his return from Ireland there are frequent references to the Northcliffe situation. One day in January he records: "Fearful worry and chaos in the office. N. raging about and giving contradictory orders"; the next day "worried with all this lunatic raging and nagging"; on getting to the office he found that Northcliffe had goaded Braham into resigning. He had told him, among other pleasantries, that "he didn't like Jews in high places!" The third day running, Geoffrey recorded that he found N. holding an inquisition at Printing House Square "with Pryor at his side ticking off his personal dislikes". This ended in the dismissal of two members of the staff and "a general upheaval and disheartening of everyone". The following week a meeting of the Board was held when provision had to be made for the victims of the "recent cyclone". At this Board Meeting (Jan. 29th, 1914) Geoffrey spoke plainly on methods of retrenchment and the possibilities of real economy "as contrasted with dangerous pinpricks". That evening he wrote to Mr. John Walter on the subject: Geoffrey's

[1] On October 14th, 1913, after the Cabinet's first autumn meeting.
[2] Also under Northcliffe.

letter is printed in full in *The History of "The Times"*.[1] Its general purport was that many members of the staff were nervous and disheartened. The Editor's energies were being dissipated in attempts to avert resignations. If the Proprietors would frankly bring forward a plan for economy, and refrain from harassing individuals while it was being carried out, they would be able to cut costs and produce a better paper. As it was they were losing men of knowledge and judgment and concentrating on news gatherers. Both were equally necessary to the paper.

Meanwhile the problem of Ulster demanded attention and Geoffrey recorded a talk at Printing House Square on February 4th, 1914:

> The Archbishop of Canterbury came to see me . . . mainly to gather my views on the Irish Question which he suspected (I can't think why) of having undergone a change.
>
> I told him that I had never been in favour of the "exclusion of Ulster" and why, but that I thought it would avert civil war. I also tried to state the case for a General Election, which he thought was now barred by the Parliament Act, though it would have been possible a month ago.
>
> I agreed that the King was better employed in private pressure than in public action, from which he said that he had strongly dissuaded H.M. The most interesting part of the conversation, however, was what I gleaned from him. Asquith, it seemed (and as I had always stated), was prepared to go to great lengths in concession to Ulster. This would apparently be announced next week. The concession would take the form of virtual independence of Dublin—the right of veto on objectionable measures, I gathered, combined with a heavy bribe of additional Ulster members.
>
> The Archbishop also suggested that Asquith was prepared to exclude Ulster altogether for a limited number of years, and that Ulster (in his opinion rightly) would not have this. On the other hand, Asquith could not give exclusion with the option to come in later, which Ulster would no doubt accept. . . .

In February, 1914, Geoffrey spent two days with Northcliffe in Paris, when he evidently told Geoffrey, during a drive and walk in Fontainebleau Forest, of his plans for reducing the price of *The Times* to 1*d*. Evidently the talk did not clear up the difficult phase with Northcliffe, for on March 2nd he wrote: "worried all day. Garvin came and lunched—with the kindly intention of expounding N. and his own past worries with him. A very friendly and sympathetic talk".

The following days were full of references to discussions about Ulster and Asquith's Home Rule proposals. In the midst of them

[1] Vol. IV, Part I, pp. 142–44.

G. D. and Mrs. Dawson in the library—a painting by James Gunn

Penyghent in the West Riding

Langcliffe Hall, Settle, West Riding of Yorkshire, which Geoffrey inherited from his aunt in 1917, when he changed his name from Robinson to Dawson

Northcliffe, with his rare sense of timing, decided that the reduction in the price of *The Times* should take place on Monday, March 16th. The preliminary announcement of the reduction in price of "The Thunderer" caused a great sensation. On Sunday, March 15th, we learn from the diary that Geoffrey remained at Printing House Square till some thousands of the penny *Times* emerged. The machines ran through the night and stopped, according to his diary, at 281,000 odd about 11. a.m.

No sooner had the launching of *The Times* at a penny been accomplished with amazing success than the Government's intention of using the Army to coerce Ulster pitchforked Geoffrey into one of the greatest political crises of his life and one from which *The Times* emerged with great credit; for the Editor obtained one of the paper's greatest *coups*.

The acute "Army Crisis" lasted from Friday, 20th to Sunday, 22nd March, 1914. The first serious rumours that something was amiss reached Printing House Square about 11 p.m. on the Friday evening. Hitherto there had been reports of the movement of small bodies of troops and of naval activity but neither the Editor, the naval nor military correspondents could discover anything beyond "precautionary measures to protect arsenals and stores" (the official version of the War Office and Admiralty). Late on the Friday evening, however, excited messages came pouring in by telegram and telephone of the "wholesale resignations of officers at Dublin—the 5th Lancers, then the whole Cavalry Brigade and meetings of Ministers in London". Geoffrey, who had sent a member of the staff to interview Colonel J. E. B. Seely[1] (Secretary of State for War) and ask for the truth, "spent an agitated hour between my room and 'the stone', [2] fitting in such scraps of news as I could verify and altering the leader to suit". Eventually a statement was obtained from Colonel Seely to the effect that "appropriate action" would be taken.

Saturday 21st was a day of tremendous excitement and strain in London and Geoffrey had to abandon a week-end with Lord Roberts. His own house and Printing House Square becoming unbearable owing to continuous telephone calls, he escaped to the quiet of the Travellers' Club, and saw Lord Milner and General H. H. Wilson and others and heard details of the events in Dublin the previous day. General Paget[3] had met his brigadiers and colonels and had given them the option to undertake aggressive operations against Ulster or be

[1] Subsequently Lord Mottistone.

[2] A stone is a table on which a plate of iron (in early days a slab of stone) is mounted. It is here that type is assembled and made up into pages, and where final corrections can be made.

[3] Sir Arthur Paget, G.O.C. the troops in Ireland.

dismissed. Sir H. Gough had refused and had received unanimous support from the Cavalry Brigade. At 5 p.m. Geoffrey went to Buckingam Palace for a talk with Lord Stamfordham, who was deeply concerned and had never thought to live to see such a catastrophe. Violent letters and telegrams were pouring in at Buckingham Palace. The King had known nothing about the crisis till he read about it in *The Times* that morning. Geoffrey told Lord Stamfordham that in "his humble judgment there was no reason yet for drastic intervention by His Majesty". Finally Geoffrey dined *tête-à-tête* with Lady Londonderry.

On Sunday, March 22nd, in response to a message from the Archbishop he walked across to Lambeth in the morning. Dr. Davidson consulted him about the most useful course he (the Archbishop) might take; Geoffrey explained that at the moment he thought "the Army crisis was infinitely more serious than the Irish problem proper, that it was increasing every moment, and that something authoritative ought to be said to arrest it first thing in the morning, without waiting for the meeting of Parliament in the afternoon". The Archbishop undertook to go and see the Prime Minister and try to get something done. It was soon evident that he had been as good as his word, for while the Editor was presiding over the daily Conference at Printing House Square a message from the Prime Minister's secretary arrived asking Geoffrey to come to Downing Street to see Mr. Asquith.

Let Geoffrey tell the story in his own words:

A private and, it was hoped, unobserved entrance was arranged by the garden door and down I went. There, in the Cabinet room, I found the P.M.—obviously in a state of considerable agitation—pacing the room in a tight green smoking jacket, and puffing out his cheeks after his manner, while delivering himself of a statement designed, he said, to clear away current misconceptions. He told me that he proposed to see no other representative of the Press and that he would like *The Times* to correct the prevailing rumours about the action of the Government in moving troops, issuing warrants for the arrest of leaders, etc., etc., in the morning. I said that this could only be done on his (published) authority, and he assented, adding something to the effect that the King (from whom he had just come) saw no objection. I then offered to go away, reduce what he had told me to the form of a statement suitable for publication, and bring it back for his approval later in the evening. This he was inclined at first to think unnecessary, saying that he had complete confidence in my veracity and discretion, but I saw endless risks in any other course and in the end he agreed and we parted.

My office, when I got back to it, was full of excursions and alarms, to say nothing of people—Repington, Lovat, Amery and others clamouring to see me. However, I found time in the end to draft the requisite statement, and repaired once more under cover of darkness to the garden door of No. 10. By this time the P.M. was calmer and more expansive and dressed for dinner. I read over what I had written and he agreed with it practically without alteration—except for a passage attributing the Curragh business to an "honest misunderstanding", declaring that the Government had no intention of using troops against Ulster. This faithfully represented his earlier discourse to me; but he said that the matter was too delicate for formal statement; he had not heard Paget's side of the story; I might use it as an inference but not as a formal pronouncement. With that we parted again—he to dine with some colleagues at McKenna's house in my Square, I to ascertain from other sources what had really happened during the day and to compose a leader. The statement duly appeared in Monday's paper—to the unconcealed jealousy of the Liberal Press—and did something, I think, to calm things down. I attribute its origin largely to pressure from the King, reinforced by the Archbishop, and also to some extent to my talk with the latter in the morning. . . .

Geoffrey's diary emphasizes the great strain under which he was working during these dramatic days:

Mar. 24. Crisis raging. I worked literally all day. Wrote a leader and a half myself—heard, tracked down, and confirmed the story of Winston's naval coup (a squadron of battleships and a destroyer division to co-operate with Paget on land) and was generally distracted and driven to death. . . .

Mar. 25. Another full day in the Commons which produced *inter alia* a virtually complete admission by Winston of my "scoop" of this morning . . . another desperate night in the office.

Mar. 26. A game of tennis . . . in the morning; then home to think and work before getting down to the office for another desperate day there. x played up magnificently with *two* leaders—one a real classic. I had another "scoop" with the news of Haldane's intervention in the new (French's resignation) crisis.

The leading article—"The Plot that Failed" (March 25th)—made a survey of recent events. In the final paragraph *The Times* stated: "In the light of these latest revelations of what actually happened, it is frankly impossible to come to any other conclusion than that of a deliberate conspiracy to provoke or intimidate Ulster at a moment when the peace of the Province was neither broken nor threatened. Let us repeat that we acquit the Prime Minister, with his more responsible colleagues, of any effective share either in the conception or the mishandling of the plot. . . ." Three days later *The Times*, which had received letters stating that the King's name had been "used very freely in the catechism put to the officers in the Irish Command in the previous week", stated that certain Generals had "in all innocence" made this unwarrantable use of the King's name and concluded, "The simple truth is that in this, as in all other matters, the King has played a strictly constitutional part, and that in the fatuous and deplorable dealings of the Government with the Army he has played no part whatever."[1]

On the morrow of these exciting events Wickham Steed wrote to Arthur Willert, the paper's correspondent in Washington:

> *The Times* (Foreign Dept.),
> 29th March, 1914.
>
> . . . The drop in the price of the paper bids fair to be a huge success. We look like getting a regular circulation of more than 200,000. A fortnight ago Northcliffe's most sanguine estimate was 120,000. The rush has been frightful. We have to go to press at midnight, and messages that reach us after 10.45 p.m. stand little chance of getting into the paper, unless they are of vital importance. The Editor has been covering himself with glory since the Ulster crisis became acute. . . .[2]

Before the Easter holidays Geoffrey attended his first meeting of the Literary Fund Committee and then escaped to Yorkshire with R. H. Brand, showing him the sights of Craven. Easter Monday was spent at Portinscale where Geoffrey had an assignment with C. P. Scott, of the *Manchester Guardian*, and discussed Ulster with him for an hour or two, "finding a very narrow margin of difference in essentials" between their points of view.

Reading Geoffrey's journal at this period is a breathless undertaking and somewhat like looking through a quickly moving kaleidoscope. On April 30th he records that "Conciliation and federalism" are now rampant and that Lionel Curtis and Grigg are "very busy saving the State". In early May Northcliffe "returned from Le Touquet much displeased, of course, with the papers produced in his absence", and a few days later "two or three bad headlines in an otherwise blameless paper" caused a general atmosphere of gloom when Geoffrey lunched with him.

[1] The correctness of the statement is fully borne out by His Majesty's entry in his diary for March 21, as quoted by Sir Harold Nicolson in *King George V*, p. 238.

[2] Those who wish to study subsequent events in connection with the Ulster and Army Crises can do so in the columns of *The Times*. "The Plot and the Public" (April 20); "Admissions and Omissions" (April 23); "Ministers and the Crisis" (April 28); "Three Practical Problems" (May 4); "A Wasted Fortnight" (June 8).

The entry in Geoffrey's diary for June 28th is as follows:

> *June 28.* Sunday. Office and St. Paul's, in the morning. . . . When I came back I found the office convulsed with the news of the assassination of Franz Ferdinand and his wife in Bosnia. Steed was lost on the river till after 7 p.m., but I got Fraser, Flanagan[1] and others to work at once and we did it very well in the end.

[1] John Woulfe Flanagan had been writing leading articles for *The Times* since 1886 till he died on November 16, 1929. His earliest writing was mainly on Ireland, but as a result of his deep interest in, and considerable knowledge of, many European countries he gradually came to be regarded as principal leader-writer in this sphere.

XI

FIRST WORLD WAR 1914–1915

Cry "Havoc!" and let slip the dogs of war.
(*Julius Caesar*, Act III, 2.)

ON the morrow of the news from Serajevo Geoffrey played a "single" with young Barrington-Ward and then lunched with a group of South African friends, among them the Doctor[1]—"an amusing party". On June 30 he went to meet D. Keppel[2] "who was concerned about our treatment of the Court Circular!"—in many quarters the implications of the assassination of the Austrian Archduke were not realized. On July 2 Geoffrey's former chief, Joseph Chamberlain, died, and the following week-end, when staying with the Arthur Lees at Chequers, he noted "no-one thinking of anything else". On the 15th he paid his last respects to the memory of Chamberlain at the great service at St. Margaret's—"a wonderful gathering". That evening Geoffrey had to take the chair at the Magdalen dinner. He never enjoyed speech-making; but we find this entry in the diary which shows genuine surprise at the reception of his remarks: "My speech proved for some reason or other an astonishing success—at any rate I got letters about it for days afterwards. But it was a friendly and merry audience." In anticipation he had written to his Aunts, "Tonight I have the Magdalen dinner which turns out to be a tremendous affair—some two hundred—the Prince of Wales and a score of eminent persons besides—how I hate the prospect!" On July 9th, Geoffrey was picked up at the office by Lady Northcliffe and taken by her to the Salisburys' ball. In his diary a short newspaper cutting was attached to the day's entry:

THE PRINCE'S FIRST BALL

The ball Lady Salisbury gave at her town house in Arlington Street was, apart from two small dinner dances, the first dance the Prince of

[1] Sir L. S. Jameson.
[2] The Hon. Sir Derek Keppel.

Wales had been to in general society. It had all along been hoped that the Prince would be present, for he and Lord Cranborne, Lord Salisbury's eldest son, are close friends at Oxford. The Prince, however, is no dancer—he does not inherit the Queen's talent for waltzing. At Lady Salisbury's dance he did not waltz at all, but confined himself to one-steps, three of which he danced with Lady Mary Cecil, the daughter of the house. It was something of an ordeal for so young a boy and of so retiring a disposition as the Prince of Wales, for no one was allowed to dance until he began, and for a Prince who describes himself as a bad dancer this must have been a trial indeed. The Prince, however, is so natural and unaffected that he had the respectful sympathy of everyone. . . .

From July 17th to 24th the thoughts of the nation were primarily concentrated on Ireland. There were meetings of the Cabinet and much running to and fro. Geoffrey, accompanied by Brand, escaped for the week-end to Cliveden by the convenient midnight train. Just before leaving Printing House Square, F. E. Smith had been in to give him the latest facts. Despite the optimism in the lobbies, Bonar Law, on the telephone, "rather discounted it". On Sunday, July 19th, Geoffrey was back in Printing House Square early in the afternoon and spent "a rushing afternoon and evening in search of one of the greatest scoops of modern times"—the news that the King had convened a Conference of eight at Buckingham Palace.[1] "The *Daily Mail* had some of it, but no-one else." On Monday, July 20th, Geoffrey was in the House of Commons to hear Asquith, who was heckled about the premature news of the Conference appearing in *The Times*, announce its holding at Buckingham Palace. Geoffrey writes in the diary, "foreign situation very threatening—an additional reason for supporting King and Conference". On the first day of the Conference Geoffrey saw both Stamfordham and Bonar Law.

The following statement appears in *The History of "The Times"*: Dawson "was absent for the week-end of July 24–27, and on the 29th had been involved in a motor-car collision and had taken a day's rest to recover. Hence, at Northcliffe's wish, Steed was in charge of the paper from the morning of the 26th until the night of July 31st–

[1] The Conference assembled at Buckingham Palace on July 21st, when, after welcoming the members, the King withdrew. Those present were: (1) Representing the Government, H. H. Asquith (the Prime Minister) and Lloyd George (Chancellor of the Exchequer); (2) Representing the Opposition, Bonar Law and Lansdowne; (3) The Irish Nationalists, John Redmond and John Dillon; (4) Ulster, Edward Carson and James Craig. The chair was taken by the Speaker (James Lowther). After four meetings the Conference broke down on the delimitation of Ulster; and in essence on the question of the Counties of Fermanagh and Tyrone.

August 1st, during which period the crucial articles were required, and written on Steed's instruction by . . ."

Geoffrey's diary gives a different picture of the facts. On Friday, July 24th, he worked most of the morning, had a lunch-time meeting with Bonar Law and "a desperate afternoon" at the office. On Saturday he was at All Souls for the election of the new Warden, and on Sunday he returned to the office "just in time to get things straight". On Monday he had a talk with Northcliffe, an hour in the House of Commons, and worked until 2 a.m. On Tuesday the 28th he "concocted a peace-making leader on Ireland".

On the following day the war between Austria and Servia had begun. He was "at the office practically all day", and left by the 5.35 p.m. train for Lillingstone, Bucks, where he stayed the next day. On Friday, July 31st, he returned to "considerable excitement and confusion in the office. . . . Germany was well in it by this time. France threatened—British position quite undefined—a deep schism in the Cabinet. Grey struggling for peace. Winston making every disposition for war".

On August 1st Geoffrey wrote to his friend Maurice Headlam:[1]

> The Irish situation, and even the Dublin shooting, have been entirely eclipsed by this terrific situation in Europe. We have made as little as possible in *The Times* of a condition of affairs approaching to panic which prevailed in London yesterday. Small instances will bring it home to you when I tell you that the respectable Messrs. Coutts[2] refused to cash more than 10 per cent of our cheques on them, and that Fred Oliver, with whom I dined in the evening, was unable to change a "fiver" to pay for dinner at the Club. However, things are a little steadier in that respect this morning, though the situation abroad is steadily getting worse. . . .

> *Sunday, Aug. 2.* Office all day. The Cabinet was again sitting almost continuously. I saw McKenna before it met for the first time, Winston and Grey at 8 p.m. after its second meeting, when it had pulled itself together and Grey had given a written assurance of British support to Cambon.[3] He, with Tyrrell and F. E. Smith, were dining at Admiralty House. . . .
>
> *Monday, Aug. 3.* Bank Holiday!! a queer kind of holiday. I was at work all day and far into the night. London was crowded and busy, but not over-excited. . . . I went to the House of Commons afterwards to hear Grey—a very impressive and also very skilful speech, which completely united the House. It was a remarkable scene which I should be

[1] A contemporary of Geoffrey's in College, at Eton, and also at Oxford with him.

[2] In accordance with the agreement existing between bankers.

[3] The French Ambassador.

sorry to have missed. Later the Government, being by this time well in it, demanded Germany's intentions with regard to Belgian neutrality. Great demonstrations in front of Buckingham Palace in the evening.

To his Aunts Geoffrey wrote:

Printing House Square,
Monday, August 3rd, 1914.

My dears,

Many thanks. No, you can't help me in any way just now, I'm afraid, and the motor is more useful where it is. I am perfectly fit and well satisfied with Grey's speech of which I listened to every word this afternoon. Considering everything it was a great performance, and one which I hardly expected yesterday afternoon. Saturday was a black day for everyone who knew what was going on—more than half the Cabinet rotten and every prospect of a complete schism or a disastrous and dishonouring refusal to help France. The tide only turned yesterday afternoon, when Grey took the bull by the horns and committed us, and the evening Cabinet (fortified by the news from the Continent) brought over most of the wobblers. One or two will still go, I think, but all that will do no harm. Winston has really done more than anyone else to save the situation—I gather that he has done most of the fighting in the Cabinet, but apart from that he has been acting all the time ahead of the Cabinet and of Parliament.[1]

Friday was the critical night, when the Germans might, perhaps, have caught our second Battle-fleet on its way to join the first. We do not publish these things, but for your private satisfaction you may be glad to know that ships and men are complete in their places, and ready for anything—barring the Channel and stretching across the North Sea from Scotland to Scandinavia. The Army is mobilizing today and I don't think too much store need to be laid on the hesitation to promise an Expeditionary Force.

I am pretty well tied now—was at work all Saturday and Sunday (when we brought out a paper at 3 in the afternoon)—but I am only too thankful to have something useful to do when so many are clamouring to help. And I am necessarily on the move during the day—going to see Ministers and others so that it is not too sedentary a life. Obviously it is

[1] In retrospect in the letter to Leo Maxse, based on his contemporary records, Geoffrey made these further references to Churchill's part in the crisis: "He (Winston) regarded Grey as the strongest supporter among his colleagues, while Lloyd George, curiously enough, was leading the Peace Section of the Cabinet up to the last moment. Winston told me, I remember, that Arthur Balfour's attitude was 'splendid', and he was undoubtedly prepared to join A.J.B. in trying to form an alternative Government if things went wrong. However, the news that Luxembourg and Belgium were invaded settled matters very quickly. Lloyd George came round at once and so did most of the others."

no use talking about getting away in times like these. We must just see how things go.

Germany looks a *little* like wobbling tonight—probably the first shock of Grey's speech—but I don't count much on that. There can be no real doubt now that we're all in it up to the neck.

On Tuesday, August 4th, the day of the Declaration of War, he wrote from the Athenaeum:

idem.

I forgot to add last night—don't be alarmed about money and food. It only helps to create a rush and a panic such as there has undoubtedly been in London lately. The money stringency will be relieved directly by the issue of small notes and there need be no anxiety about food supplies. The sea routes are open to us while our fleets hold the North Sea and though we shall get nothing from Eastern Europe we have the rest of the World to feed us.

This is scribbled while waiting for a talk with poor old Morley. It is pathetic that he, the special friend of France, should be going out on this issue.[1]

Tuesday, *August 4*. A curt reply from Germany led to our Declaration of War as from 11 p.m. tonight—a difficult business to disentangle. Things moved so quick at the last and I was again in the office all day and all night. A meeting with Winston at 8.15 p.m. which led to my snatching a little dinner with him, his wife and mother and J. Churchill. Winston in very good form. A cheering crowd outside the Admiralty. X rising to the occasion with magnificent leaders.

Wednesday, *August 5*. FIRST DAY OF WAR.

(There is no other entry.)

On August 6th Geoffrey wrote from Printing House Square to Maurice Headlam:

My dear Maurice,

. . . I am more amazed and delighted every day with the way in which people have taken this crisis. So far as I can see there is absolute unanimity—for which I think a great deal of credit must be ascribed to Grey's personality—but there is very little of the Jingo business of music-halls and "mafficking" which discredited the South African War.

[1] In retrospect in the letter to Leo Maxse, already referred to, Geoffrey wrote thus of Lord Morley: "My second recollection is of meeting old Morley on the steps of the Athenaeum some few days after the war had begun, and of telling him, to his manifest surprise, that Beauchamp, Simon and Runciman had not resigned from the Government at the same time as himself. He had left the Cabinet under the full impression that they were all pledged to go together and had then repaired to his house at Wimbledon and heard no more till he happened to run into me!"

A vast crowd rolls round Buckingham Palace every evening and insists on the appearance of the King. The town is full of soldiers in Khaki, in which the whole Brigade of Guards is now clothed. So far as one can hear, the whole business of mobilization is going forward with the greatest smoothness and rapidity.

... The censorship is working rather crudely, and we are being asked to stop the most blameless messages; but that will right itself in time. These are strenuous days in a newspaper office, for the wildest rumours become current about midnight, and so one is at work almost all round the clock. Last night, for instance, it was reported on the authority of the police, the War Office, and the South-Western Railway that a railway bridge had been blown up by German spies at Guildford. With this combination of authorities, I was forced to believe there was something in it, and sent down two people at one o'clock in the morning to investigate. It turned out a complete mare's nest, and I am rather sorry for it. Nothing would have brought the war home so completely to people in the country districts.

In a memorandum Geoffrey recalled four strenuous Sundays in July and August which illustrate the rapidity with which crisis followed crisis. They were:

July 19th. The King, in the face of imminent civil war in Ireland, convened a meeting of party leaders at Buckingham Palace.

July 26th. War broke out between Austria and Servia: news of gun-running, rioting and shooting in Dublin.

August 2nd. The Cabinet, divided on the question of intervention in Europe, reached a decision after the invasion of Luxembourg.

A week afterwards—on Sunday, August 9—Geoffrey drove up to London from Cliveden in the motor which was to take a British General to embark for the Continent from Southampton.

Northcliffe always said the war would be a long one—of at least three years' duration. It is of interest to find how far out was Geoffrey in his calculations. His views were typical of the majority in those early months. In a letter to Arthur Willert, dated September 10, 1914, Geoffrey wrote:

I cannot tell you how long the war is going to last. When asked this question the other day I drew a bow at venture and said eighteen months. I was told by people who ought to be good judges that this was an excessive estimate. The real limit, I expect, will be found in the effect on Germany of a second winter. She is quite capable of weathering *one*. . . .

During August, 1914, Geoffrey spent two week-ends at Cliveden, where the Waldorf Astors made a room available for him and provided a horse to ride; there was also the likelihood of meeting some stranded American "refugees" (from the Continent) and thus keeping in touch with United States opinion; it was also a rallying-place for members of the Round Table; after a particularly heavy week he would very likely spend an idle Saturday morning on the river with Philip Kerr, reading *Henry V* or discussing Empire problems.

From very early in the war Geoffrey was much concerned by the bungles of the Press Bureau. Matters took a dramatic turn on August 30th; he had been staying at Hatfield with the Salisburys and returned to Printing House Square after a peaceful morning "to find a lurid Sunday Edition[1] with a gloomy despatch from Arthur Moore (one of its correspondents at the Front) and some *Daily Mail* additions inserted by Northcliffe. All had, however, been duly submitted to the Press Bureau and Freeman, in charge of the paper in the Editor's absence, had been requested to publish it." This was the dramatic despatch from France which told of the "Broken British regiments battling against great odds", and which, while proclaiming that the honour of our troops was untarnished, urged the desperate need of more men. The correspondent of *The Times* did not mince matters. He wrote:

> First let it be said that our honour is bright. Amongst all the straggling units that I have seen, flotsam and jetsam of the fiercest fight in history, I saw fear in no man's face. It was a retreating and a broken army, but it was not an army of hunted men.

When, on that Sunday afternoon, the average Londoner bought his issue of *The Times* he received one of the greatest shocks of the war. That evening Kitchener summoned Geoffrey for a talk in Carlton Gardens and discussed the damage done—"to which, however," wrote Geoffrey, 'the answer was complete", and then Kitchener discussed "rather heavily" the publication of casualty lists.

On Monday, August 31st, Geoffrey wrote:

> Violent attacks on *The Times* in all directions—a most distracted day. I went down to the House of Commons in the afternoon to see what could be done, and left Freeman to draw up a statement of facts, which we printed at night. Northcliffe raging about—himself the author of all that could fairly be charged against us.

> *Sept. 1.* More attacks and shoals of letters. (Kitchener went off to France, though this was the darkest secret.) I had another desperate day. . . . By circularizing our angry correspondents and keeping our end up

[1] In the early part of the war *The Times* printed a Sunday edition. On some occasions an edition at noon and two later editions were issued.

in paper, we fought the enemy as best we could and I think routed him. A very satisfactory talk with Brade[1] in the evening.

The History of "The Times", quite correctly, points out that Geoffrey himself "was not then a prolific writer; and made no personal contribution to the paper at all for the first six weeks of the war".[2] We are confronted, therefore, with this curious fact that Geoffrey, the very prolific writer in South Africa, during the first five months of the First World War wrote only five leading articles, one of which, "Antwerp and Public Criticism", was defending Mr. Churchill from what he considered the unfair attack of the *Morning Post*, which saddled him with the whole responsibility for the failure of the British Expedition thither; another was devoted to the defence of Prince Louis of Battenberg from unjust criticism; another was a tribute to the memory of Lord Roberts, a soldier for whom he had the deepest admiration and whose schemes he always sought to further. What was the cause of this disinclination to write on the mighty events which were shaking the very foundations of Europe? First of all there was the immense administrative work of transferring *The Times* from a peace to a war footing which left little time for literary composition (which Geoffrey always said was equivalent to severe physical labour). Secondly, Geoffrey was always diffident about asserting his own views until he was *certain of himself*. When he went to the *Johannesburg Star* in 1905 and plunged with confidence into leader-writing he was dealing with familiar problems. A World War, and especially one which had resulted largely from the permanent rivalry betweeen Slav and Teuton, was a very different matter. After becoming Editor of *The Times* he had moved cautiously and during the first months only wrote two leaders, both on Empire subjects.

Unlike Wickham Steed, Geoffrey had not lived most of his adult life in and around the foreign offices of Europe. Moreover world war was a new experience to his generation; not since the Seven Years' War and the Napoleonic era had the British Empire been involved across half the world. Geoffrey very wisely left the writing to the experts available. In *The History of "The Times"* there is this statement about his methods: "Dawson made a point of being accessible in the office from four to seven in the evening five days a week, as well as returning after dinner to go through the proofs of the leading articles of which he had laid down the substance in the afternoon. Indeed he laid down what he wanted said in leaders to such an extent as practically to dictate them; some time in 1915 this drew a long reasoned

[1] Sir Reginald Brade, Secretary of the War Office.
[2] Vol. IV, Part I, p. 239.

remonstrance from Lovat Fraser, who pointed out that such a degree of editorial dictation stifled the leader-writer's originality and initiative."[1]

Lovat Fraser very sensibly ventured to write frankly to Geoffrey in the following letter:

> I think that at present you are trying to do too much. The net result of the present method is that you are in effect providing all the leading ideas to which the paper gives publicity; and this at a time of unprecedented crisis and distraction, a time, too, when you are overwhelmed with *executive* responsibility.
>
> The method of G.E.B. (Buckle) was broader, and though he carried it much too far, especially towards the end, there were points about it worth considering. He always left his writers to work out their own articles and arguments, while invariably retaining *control* of *broad policy*. You will very often prescribe how a leader should begin, how it should end, and indicate the main arguments. I am sure you don't realize how often you do this, or how it paralyses the writer. He cannot then create anything. He echoes your ideas, very often quite imperfectly, but it is generally your leader, and not his. My own experience as an Editor is that you get better results if you simply satisfy yourself that your main policy is there all right, and never trouble about fine shades of meaning.
>
> You changed your method early in the Ulster business, and it has grown on you. It has gradually made you far less willing to look at ideas other than your own, and it has also prevented ideas from being offered to you. In my own case for very many months I have never made any *broad* suggestion. . . .
>
> I will try to be brief and practical. Without in the least lessening your own control, I think you should encourage, more than you do, the propounding of ideas. I don't mean little ideas, but the broader lines of policy. The decision and the ultimate responsibility must rest with you. When you have decided that you will adopt a suggestion, give the writer more freedom to work it out in his own way. This does not at all imply the adoption of Grigg's old idea of men other than the Editor having the *control* of policy, which I always saw to be quite impracticable. It only means that the paper will get a freer play of ideas. I expect you will think you have already done this, and I believe you really meant to, but in effect you haven't.
>
> . . . . .
>
> My points are really two: (1) more freedom to suggest with rather more certainty of having a ready hearing; (2) less definite prescription as to treatment, unless as sometimes happens, the writer presses for exact guidance. There are some occasions when it may be imperative for you

[1] *The History of "The Times"*, Vol. IV, Part I, p. 219.

to tell me exactly what you want said, perhaps because I don't know the subject.

The following is Geoffrey's characteristically genuine and modest reply (13th April, 1915):

My dear Fraser,

I am very much obliged to you for your notes. They seem to me perfectly sound and I entirely agree with them. My only difference with you is that I think the proportion of leaders in which you have been given an absolutely free hand is greater than you suggest. Still, no doubt, one is unconscious of the growth of habit and I am very glad indeed to have the reminder.

The real difference between me and Buckle, by no means to my advantage, is that I have written so many leaders myself that I begin to frame them instinctively in my mind.

However, the thing is very easily put right. I only beg of you never to hesitate to offer either ideas or criticism. You will never find them resented by,

Yours ever,
G. R. (Robinson).

Press and censorship problems continued to occupy Geoffrey's attention for many months. He was aware that on occasion the United States authorities could not understand Whitehall's attitude to American journalists and especially the activities of the censorship in handling the messages of newspaper reporters. Both Northcliffe and Geoffrey performed yeoman service in trying to make easy the path of the genuine American correspondent. Geoffrey was fully aware that care must be used and some quite innocent-looking message might be of use to the enemy; but he also knew, from personal experience, how much needless red tape had to be cut.

Several times after the beginning of the war Geoffrey regretted the extreme rustiness of his French and for a time, at least, tried to fit in an hour's French lesson a day. Relations with Northcliffe had their ups and downs. One morning in September he records "a walk with N. on Hampstead Heath. Territorials scouting behind every bush", and things seemed to be amicable for two or three weeks. On October 23rd he wrote: "A talk with Northcliffe, broaching the question of the Admiralty. I found him in the wildest state of mind denouncing Churchill, not as a bad First Lord, but as 'having spoken disrespectfully' of him, N.! and Prince Louis for being a German. . . . I tried to make an impression on him, but argument is of no use in his case. . . ."

There are several references to Lord Roberts, "full of strategy and longing to go to France—at 84!" As late as October 20, less than a month before his death, the gallant little soldier, if not wanted in France, was anxious to look after Home Defence. Geoffrey, at the Field Marshal's request, went down to Ascot to lunch with him and discussed "Home Defence, spies, etc."; the following day accordingly Geoffrey on his behalf went round to see Balfour, who was on a sub-Committee of the C.I.D.

The following three letters testify to Lord Roberts's amazing alertness:

28.10.14.

Dear Robinson,

Herewith Balfour's reply. Not very satisfactory. The fact is that the General Staff are overwhelmed with work and have no time to work out plans. I will call upon Balfour when he returns. Meanwhile it would help matters if some clever man in your office would prepare a memo. for me on the lines about which we were talking today.

Repington no doubt could help. I could then take it to Balfour as soon as he returns to London. It might be necessary to send it to him if he is likely to be long away.

Yours sincerely,
ROBERTS.

idem.

Ascot,
6.11.14.

Your leaders the last two days have delighted me. The country must be roused and the people must be taken into confidence—so long as preparations are made in secret—I mean such preparations as Germans assuredly know all about—I don't see how the nation could expect to respond.

idem.

Almond's Hotel,
Clifford Street,
Bond Street, W.
11.11.14.

I am going to France today to welcome the French troops and have a talk with French.[1] I shall probably return on Saturday and I should then much like to see you. There is one matter which requires to be settled without delay, not an easy one.

Three days after this last letter was written came the news of "Lord Bobs's sudden death in France and 'within the sound of the guns'".

[1] General Sir John French.

Then Geoffrey had "a sad and strenuous three hours, writing additions to his life, and a little leader and getting it into the paper".

Geoffrey received the following letter (January 20th, 1915) from the Field Marshal's daughter:

51, Upper Brook Street, W.

My dear Mr. Robinson,

I have never written to thank you for a dear letter you wrote me when my Father died—but I was very grateful for it. He was very happy those two days in France, and then he went without pain or the sorrow of parting, and with his great wish gratified, that he might die on service. And I too had one life-long wish gratified, that he should have no lingering illness, or know the sadness of failing powers, but it was hard to see him go and now the sadness comes back when I think what a joy it would have been to him to see his little grandson.

Thank you very very much once more, dear Mr. Robin.

Yours very sincerely,

AILEEN ROBERTS.

In October and November Geoffrey's records are somewhat scanty and the diary was only kept spasmodically, but we learn that Milner, who wanted to know how he fared on *The Times*, "hinted at two jobs—one in the City, one in the Civil Service". Geoffrey's comment was, "I told him I meant and ought to stick to the paper as long as possible".[1] On October 29th Geoffrey went to see the Prime Minister about the wisdom of holding up the news of the *Audacious*.[2] "He agreed with my doubts, said he'd shared them but had been converted by the arguments: (1) no lives lost; (2) express desire of Jellicoe; (3) Turkey more than ever on the wobble. This seemed reasonable, and he went on to discuss the war, the censorship, recruiting, etc."

On a visit in the autumn Geoffrey found Oxford "indeed 'translated', games going on, hardly any young man to play them, a hall porter in khaki, and a hospital in the Schools". In November he went with Lovat Fraser "to meet the Aga Khan and had a long talk afterwards with that entertaining deity", who was off to Egypt and India to try to counteract "German Mahometan intrigue". Also in November Geoffrey had his first meeting with Lord Fisher of Kilverstone, who "did all the talking and did it very well—an outline of his work and plans and a refutation of the rumours that the Admiralty was a one-man show, that he had quarrelled with Jellicoe, that the Fleet was now scattered, etc., etc. I thought he made a good case".

Fisher wrote this typical letter (25th November, 1914) to Geoffrey:

[1] Cf. *infra* p. 176.

[2] This super-Dreadnought struck a mine and within twelve hours foundered off Lough Swilly, Co. Donegal, on Oct. 27, 1914.

Dear Mr. Robinson,

I very seldom read anything but the enclosed caught my eye[1] and so excellent I send it hoping you and your friend Mr. Lovat Fraser may at least glance over it. I have not the faintest idea who wrote it (for all I know it may be one of you two!). Come some day, both of you and hear how the Dreadnought was discovered. So absolutely parallel to the discovery of the planet Neptune by Leverrier![2] Inexplicable perturbations of the heavenly bodies perturbed the astronomer, so also the "Dreadnought"! She wasn't born she was discovered—immortal! I had to hustle yesterday so could not do justice to the Biggest Thing in the world.

"The British Empire floats on the British
Navy and it floats on nothing else."

Yours truly,
FISHER.

idem.

The Admiralty,
Whitehall,
11.12.14.

Your kind letter greatly valued. Someday you'll love to hear the story! All the experts were d——d fools! *They nearly always are!!!* They can't ever believe that things done in a hurry are always done the best! Sturdee was there about 10 minutes before Von Spee—Nelson allowed 15 minutes!—so he said.

FISHER.

In November there was a "heated and exhausting wrangle in the evening with Northcliffe and Repington—N. wishing to publish the sinking of the *Audacious* and R. to make people's flesh creep about raids!" Geoffrey "had an article written, saying all I was prepared to say about either"—which shows that he could dig his toes in when the occasion demanded it.

Geoffrey made the following note on a talk with Bonar Law on December 29, 1914:

I suggested to him that the real weakness in the country just now was the failure of the Government to employ anyone but members of their own Party for really responsible work. No doubt Chamberlain, Walter Long, Selborne, himself and others had been invited at the beginning of the war to help on various Committees; but this was not really making full use of them. I called attention, for instance, to Selborne's recent

[1] An article on "The Triumph of the Big Gun" and also dealing with the "All-big Gun Ship."

[2] U. J. J. Leverrier (1811–77).

letter to *The Times*, urging that at least plans should be made for compulsory service if it were ever necessary, and wondered whether anyone was really entrusted with this business of looking ahead. Kitchener, of course, was entirely absorbed, and rightly absorbed, in the problems of raising men under the existing conditions and of prosecuting the war. . . . Ministers did not, in fact, accept responsibility for what they were doing, but perpetually made excuses and referred matters from one department to another. There was no co-ordination and no one was in supreme control.

He was inclined to agree with all this,[1] but I found him very much opposed at the present stage to anything like a Coalition Government. He said that he himself would feel very uncomfortable in it. He thought it would come in time—indeed the Liberals themselves must turn to it when they came to clearing up the mess at the end of the war. Meanwhile he defended his attitude of "No criticism" by pointing to the disaster which had befallen every political party in the past when it had opposed a popular war. This war was undeniably popular.

I agreed, but suggested that useful criticism could perfectly well be made without opposing the war, or, indeed, discrediting the Government.

1915

If the First World War could be divided into sections the year 1915 was certainly the period of national awakening; and in the task of mobilizing the nation no one played a more effective part, nor wrote to greater purpose, than Geoffrey. If he refrained from writing leaders during the first five months of the war it was typical of his dislike of embarking on a course of action without adequate preparation. By January, 1915, he was ready for his self-appointed task. He was clear about the course which the paper should follow. His name was but little known to the general public, although familiar in small and influential circles; he may well be regarded as one of the great anonymities of Fleet Street during the war years.

Let my position regarding the Northcliffe-Geoffrey relationship be quite clear. If, as the story unfolds itself, I seem to take Geoffrey's side, as I do, and frequently emphasize the impossible strain often placed on the Editor's shoulders by that man of moods, there is no intention of suggesting that close association with Northcliffe, however great an ordeal, was not also an unforgettable experience. Northcliffe has been described as the "greatest figure" that ever walked Fleet Street and there is much truth in that statement—if by "great" is meant

[1] Geoffrey's desire for a Coalition Government was realized in May, 1915. *Vide infra* p. 121.

the most efficient gatherer of news, with an uncanny instinct as to what would interest his public at any given moment. Undoubtedly at certain stages of the war he influenced the course of events. When Northcliffe became aware of the acute shortage of shells at the front or began to mistrust the ability of Kitchener adequately to fill the position of supreme Director of the National War Effort, he blurted out his convictions without counting the cost. He stunned his public. Indeed on the very day when the *Daily Mail* was burnt in the City of London and advertisers were cancelling their contracts by thousands, I recall walking with him through the peaceful passages and purlieus of the Temple. Never did Northcliffe appear to me of more heroic mould. Northcliffe knew his facts were right, he was intensely patriotic and nothing would deflect him from his purpose of telling the people the truth.

Geoffrey very soon discarded his early optimism about the duration of the war, and realized that the time for complacency had gone. There was an urgent need to arouse the nation to the great dangers which confronted it; to mobilize its strength and drastically to overhaul the methods then employed in the supreme direction of the war.

The first leading article in 1915, "The Compulsion Controversy" (Jan. 22), struck the note for the "motif" of the policy of *The Times* during the next two years, until Asquith had to make way for Lloyd George as war-time leader of the nation. In this leading article *The Times* welcomed Haldane's statement in the House of Lords that: "By the Common Law of this country it is the duty of every subject of the realm to assist the Sovereign in repelling the invasion of its shores and in defence of the realm. . . . Compulsory service is not foreign to the Constitution of the country, and in a great national emergency it might be necessary to resort to it." This was one of the principal themes which Geoffrey kept continuously before the readers of *The Times* till Conscription was adopted.

Another object for which Geoffrey consistently worked was the institution of a small War Cabinet, which would be in daily session, and on which the Navy and Army would be represented, which would thereby ensure the closest co-operation between the two Services, which hitherto had been lacking. He greatly disliked the cumbersome Cabinet of twenty-two or twenty-three members and became increasingly critical of Asquith's direction of the war effort. Thanks largely to the pressure of certain newspapers, especially of *The Times*, these reforms were finally adopted. The bungling which resulted in the withdrawal from the Dardanelles—a campaign finely conceived by Mr. Churchill—would not have occurred with closer co-operation between Navy and Army and the war might have been shortened by a year; and the general ill-success of British diplomacy in the Balkans, where Bulgaria joined the Central Powers and Greece refused to be drawn into the orbit of the Allies, gave force to the continued campaign for efficiency and a complete change in the personnel responsible for the direction of the war. By May, public opinion, as the result of events and of this enlightened campaign in the Press, brought about a Coalition Government, welcomed by *The Times* in a leader "The New Cabinet" (May 24).

His refreshing sense of humour stood Geoffrey in good stead, even when he was exasperated by some of the follies of the Press Bureau, and he must have enjoyed "scribbling" the leading article called "The Censor on Robert Browning" (Oct. 19, 1915). The previous day *The Times* had published a first-hand account of the fighting at Hulluch. In describing "the storm of bombs, shells, gases" which fell upon the enemy, the correspondent of *The Times* was rash enough to quote Browning:

> Twenty-nine distinct damnations,
> One sure if the other fails.

The message was duly submitted to the Censor, who passed it with the exception of Browning's quotation. Whatever the motive of the Censor may have been, the words "Twenty-nine distinct" were neatly rubbed out and the single word "different" inserted in their place. The Editor, with his tongue in his cheek, makes this admission, "We ourselves have been cautious of the Classics since the day when a quotation from Chatham was forbidden by the Censor, who seems to have confused the great War Minister with the naval base from which he took his title."

On January 18, Geoffrey had an entertaining lunch "with old Jacky Fisher". The following is the note he made of the talk:

Notes of a Luncheon with Lord Fisher. January 18, 1915.

On my way to luncheon I met Lord Morley in Bond Street, and walked with him as far as the Athenaeum. I thought him very old and feeble, and was rather glad to have the opportunity of piloting him across the streets. He spoke of Buckle's new volume of Dizzy,[1] which he had read and thought a good and interesting piece of work. . . . I talked to him afterwards about the war and the Government, and found him rather gloomy about both. He agreed with me that Asquith (who, he said, was no Pitt) would have been wise in his own interests to form a National or Coalition Government at the very outbreak of the war. This course, he told me, had actually been considered and discussed at the Cabinet meeting on Monday morning, August 3. On that occasion the

[1] The first two volumes were written by W. F. Monypenny, the last two by Buckle.

Prime Minister met his colleagues with the announcement that he had received the resignation of four of them—Lord Morley himself, John Burns, Beauchamp and Simon. He had thereupon pointed out to them that three courses were open to them. The first, which he would have adopted in normal circumstances, was to resign. But he did not feel that the other party possessed the men to carry on the war. The second course was to invite some of his opponents to join him. This he seems to have dismissed for the same reason, though, as Lord M. said, it was grotesque to suppose that the four vacant places could not have been better filled by men like Austen Chamberlain and Bonar Law. The third course was the one which he actually adopted, namely to fill the ultimate vacancies from members of his own party.

I had the best part of an hour with my host after luncheon, and found him obviously kicking against the conduct of the war by the "Board of Nine". Each of them, he said, had his own view of what should be done. They all delivered eloquent speeches—he recalled in particular one by Lloyd George, urging that the British Army should be sent to Montenegro. It was quite impossible to wage war under these conditions. The supreme control must be in the hands of a single man, and the best man in his opinion was Arthur Balfour. Balfour had come back to lunch with him the other day after one of these Board Meetings, and greatly impressed him by his clearness and courage. He had not known very much of him before.

He thought our land strategy so far had been a failure. There had been a great deal of talk of the failure of the Germans to reach Paris on the one side and Warsaw on the other. As a matter of fact what was wanted more than either was Antwerp—just as important today as in the time of Napoleon—and that they had got. The failure to save Antwerp had been a deplorable business. The essential principle in strategy was to go for the enemy's vitals, and in this case the decisive area of the war was in and around the North Sea. . . .

Incidentally he said that Grey had lost his nerve—would take no action for fear of offending neutrals—and that Asquith, with all his great ability, power of expression, etc., was not the man for the work, had no initiative, always voted with the majority in council, and cared most for keeping his party together.

Two characteristic letters from Fisher to Geoffrey are given here:

21.1.15.

I stumbled on the enclosed[1] half an hour before you came. I was the last midshipman to enter the Navy who was nominated by the last of Nelson's Captains at the request of Lord Nelson's own niece and I joined the *Victory*, Nelson's flagship, as my first ship and when I last had my flag flying at the main as a full Admiral it was on board the same

[1] Alas, there is no indication of its nature.

Victory, so you must not wonder I am saturated with Nelson and these bits I enclose I either wrote or gathered—a little garland of flowers—as a tribute and no doubt he knows!

Yours,
FISHER.

I have no other copy that I know of so kindly return.

idem.

5.3.15.

Enclosed[1] reaches me from the United States with great panegyrics of the astounding sagacity of the British Admiralty misleading the Germans! "*Toujours l'audace*"!

In haste,
FISHER.

The best thing you've done is leading article on "Indiscretion in high places"—it's damnable.

From time to time Geoffrey made a point of keeping in touch with Buckle with whom he discussed such matters as compulsory service and the need for a smaller cabinet.

In a letter (Jan. 20, 1915) to the Aunts he describes an early Zeppelin raid:

These are great nights. I have just come from watching a Zeppelin circling like a silver trout above this office, while the guns boomed all over London and the shrapnel made fireworks in the sky. At this moment a great fire is raging somewhere to the East of us and St. Paul's is a wonderful silhouette against the red glow. I had almost given up all hope of seeing a Zeppelin and am quite reconciled to being here and not at Langcliffe! It was a splendid spectacle. Surely some of our aeroplanes will catch her after so much worrying and in such a cloudless night.

Two days after acting as best man to Reggie Nicholson, who had succeeded Moberly Bell as Manager of *The Times*, Geoffrey spent ten days with the Army in Flanders. At Boulogne he saw his old friend Arthur Lawley, newly appointed Red Cross Commissioner, and with him at midnight he witnessed the arrival of a hospital train with many cases of frozen feet. At Bailleul he saw Sir John French and his friend General H. H. Wilson, to whom was due "most of our cohesion with the French". He visited the Whychaete-Messines ridge and Ypres, and

[1] The enclosure, from an American journal, described the alleged salvage of H.M.S. *Audacious* after she had been moved off Tory Island, Donegal. Actually, of course, the ship sank twelve hours after being struck, but her loss was not made public until the end of the war, and a dummy *Audacious* was constructed with the idea of misleading the enemy into the belief that she was still afloat.

came back cheered, like everyone else, by the spirit and infectious optimism of the Army.

By the month of March Geoffrey was getting his campaign for rousing the nation under way. He received the following letter (March 4th, 1915) from Sir Robert Baden-Powell:

Ewhurst Place,
Via Hawkhurst,
Kent.

Dear Robinson,

You may be surprised to hear from me, but I want to congratulate you on the line that you are now pursuing to wake up the average citizen to the fact that we are at war.

The worst danger to the country is the present apathy on the subject. In my small way I have been doing my best to bring it home through the medium of my small army of Scoutmasters throughout the Kingdom, and I am sending you a copy of our *Gazette* for this month which will show you what I have said to them on the subject, and which I hope you will find accords with your own ideas.

If we cannot get the Germans to make a raid on us the only other hope is, as you suggest, to send parties of working men over to France to see for themselves that war is going on, and to learn what war is like.

Geoffrey replied the following day:

My dear General,

I was delighted to get your letter and the copy of your *Gazette*. It was very satisfactory to hear that you agree about the importance of getting rid of the national apathy. I came back a week ago from a short visit to France very much impressed by what even the most friendly Frenchmen were saying on this subject. They are profoundly grateful for our assistance. But they say as a nation: "You have not yet gone to war at all. Don't you think it time you did so?"

Geoffrey certainly enlarged his circle in the war years, and probably as a result of reading E. T. Cook's biography of Delane, he was even more conscious of the importance of every kind of contact. At intervals he used to lunch and dine with Esher, who was extraordinarily well informed of events on both sides of the Channel. In April, Geoffrey listened to Curzon's account of his experiences in Flanders—"of which he talked like a schoolboy—the object of the war—Berlin or the Rhine?" He lunched "with old Cromer—very interesting on democracy, Dardanelles, the future of the Khalifate, etc.", met S. M. Booth, Lloyd George's "man of push and go", and had an "absorbing and rather reassuring talk about munitions".

The Bishop of Pretoria, who had just visited Flanders, returned to

London, seething with indignation about the failure of the nation to "get to war" and gave Geoffrey first-hand information about the shortage of high-explosive shells there. In May Geoffrey listened to a stirring sermon from Mike Furse in Upper Chapel at Eton and paid a visit to Slough for a long talk with Lovat Fraser about Northcliffe's attempts—"much resented by Fraser himself"—to instruct him behind Geoffrey's back during the political and munitions crises. Accordingly the following day, in order "to keep things on my own lines" (i.e. to prevent Northcliffe's interference), Geoffrey brought Fraser back to London with him "and wrote a leader myself *and* dictated a lot of stuff about the crisis—some 3 columns in all".

In June Geoffrey entered in his diary, "National Register for which *The Times* had worked, announced—*something* accomplished amid the prevailing gloom."

Apparently the Coalition, from which so much was hoped, was not working smoothly and there were rumours, in August, "of Cabinet ructions". Geoffrey therefore went to see Curzon, "who was said to be concerned, and found him scribbling in Carlton House Terrace in his shirt-sleeves, floor strewn with letters, as usual! He said no ructions so far; but he and others had felt it necessary to make a push to get big questions—e.g. National Service—faced. Prime Minister still strongly opposed to National Service, but Kitchener wobbling. If no action, then might be necessary to resign and agitate in the country". On August 16th Geoffrey discussed the Dardanelles with Balfour, "about which he was very anxious after the virtual failure of the new push last week, and Home politics. . . . He told me he had only twice left London since he took office—once to Windsor and once for a week-end with the P.M. *who had never mentioned the war*, though they were alone!" There was bad news from everywhere. A telegram from Robert Wilton, *The Times* Correspondent in Russia (18 August, 1915), referred to the presence of the Germans in Kovno and he also reported great pessimism in Petrograd and expressed fears about the alliance. Balfour told Geoffrey that the Foreign Office had received similar news. There was also general gloom caused by the heavy casualties during the abortive Gallipoli push.

Early in September *The Times* published a leader on the urgent need for reducing the size of the Cabinet. The following extracts are taken from "Notes of talks with Carson and Lloyd George, Sept. 15–16, 1915":

> A long talk yesterday morning with Carson and another with Lloyd George this afternoon. Carson is the only member of the Cabinet out of whom I get any real satisfaction in these days of drift, because he is the

only one who seems to see the situation clearly and as a whole, to be absolutely courageous and to care nothing for himself.

He was as depressed as usual about the conduct of the war—no plans or designs, a cumbersome Cabinet, watertight Committees, very much what I had written in a leader overnight. However, things were moving. He was drawing closer to Lloyd George, had had a long talk with him the day before, followed by a dinner and (apparently) an all-night sitting with Bonar Law and Austen Chamberlain. On the other hand he said his relations were worse with Kitchener, who resented inquiries, gave confused and contradictory answers, etc., etc.

I found him trying to sit down to a Memorandum on the whole question of Government machinery for circulation to the Cabinet, and begged him to go on with it and not make an unobtrusive exit to his cottage at Rye. There seemed less chance of this calamity than when I saw him a week ago. Evidently a strong nucleus was forming inside the Cabinet for more strenuous measures. Carson said he believed absolutely in L.G.'s disinterestedness and genuine zeal for the war. Some of his own people, e.g. Bonar Law and Austen Chamberlain, he said, felt as he did, but seemed to feel less keenly and to think it enough if they ran their various Departments efficiently. He thought things were really coming to a head, e.g. over National Service and the Dardanelles, and that it would be wise to go slow outside. . . .

I went to see L.G. rather vaguely, but found him very ready to talk in spite of a weary Trade Union meeting just finished. He gave me a most vivid summary of the war as he saw it—very much as stated in his famous "preface" published this week—Russia knocked out for the time being, Germans free to go to the Balkans? Italy? The West? He thought Balkans for choice, as I did. *No* plans made to meet these possible contingencies. Kitchener, he said, was now obsessed with the notion that the Germans had "shot their bolt" in Russia (see his yesterday's speech)—could neither get on or get out. L.G. very sceptical about this, but gave an inimitable account of Kitchener's indignation when challenged on any military opinion.

I asked him how he would put things right. He said: (1) "Conscription tomorrow"; (2) A conference of the real military heads of the Allies to take stock of the situation as a whole, instead of dealing, as at present, through second-rate "dug-out" emissaries. He thought Asquith would fight National Service to the last, and hinted (not obscurely) at the prospect that some half dozen of them would have to go to him and present an ultimatum of resignation. No doubt it would mean the breaking of that unity, which Asquith apparently counted above victory, but great wars had been won before in the face of opposition at home. . . .

I thought L.G. had aged since I saw him last some weeks ago but was full of fire and energy. He never gives me quite the same impression as e.g. Carson, of absolute disinterestedness, but I am sure that his first object is to win the war, and that for this he is prepared (as Asquith is never prepared) to throw over old traditions, ties and popularities. . . .

For a long time Geoffrey had been anxious that Milner and Lloyd George should meet, as he knew each of them would appreciate the other's desire that there should be a complete overhauling of the supreme direction of the war effort. The meeting took place on 30th September, 1915, and Geoffrey wrote this memorandum about it:

LUNCHEON—LORD MILNER AND LLOYD GEORGE

On Thursday, September 30, I effected a meeting between Lord Milner and Lloyd George. It had taken a little scheming, but each obviously wanted to get in touch with the other without doing it *coram populo*. My first suggestion—a luncheon at my house—was veto'd by Lloyd George on my warning him that McKenna lived opposite and might see his coming in and going out! Eventually we arranged to lunch with Lord Milner at 17, Great College Street, opposite to a blank wall. It was a very friendly and satisfactory affair—no checks or difficulties. We began on Egypt and its dangers, the Turks and Arabs, the Dardanelles (when both agreed that a most damnable situation was slightly eased by our naval attacks on the Turkish communications). Thence to the offensive in France, as to which Lloyd George was no more optimistic than Carson had been on the previous day. He agreed that in any event it made the need for men more urgent. Asquith and Kitchener were gambling on the result, and Kitchener no less than Asquith was to be reckoned as definitely hostile to conscription. Why? Lord Milner suggested (1) obstinacy and (2) fear of an immense and complicated task which he didn't understand. However that might be, said Lloyd George, there was nothing to be done till the battle was over. All the argument in the world wouldn't avail against the lulling effect of a victory. What constituted a victory? L.G. said K. definitely contemplated the "rolling up of the German Line"—not a mere advance of a few miles. Joffre had accepted this definition. The plan was his. The difficulty, of course, as we all agreed, was to get a clear admission of victory or defeat when the operations were necessarily hidden from the public and the truth would only leak out gradually. As for his own views, L.G. was emphatic that conscription was the only way. After thinking of nothing else for fourteen months he was satisfied that we couldn't win the war without it and should have our work cut out to win with it. He described the situation in golfing language as "Germans four up and five to play". Incidentally he paid a very high tribute to Curzon, Bonar Law, and Austen Chamberlain. The "Inner Cabinet" was inchoate and fluctuating in size. Four or five would be quite enough and they must have full responsibility.

To his Aunts Geoffrey wrote on Sunday, October 10, 1915:

. . . I have not been out of London at all, which is a mistake, and spent last night in writing an article instead by my own fireside. I want to

> make people see that they miss the target when they campaign against the Foreign Office or any other department in particular. It is the direction of the *whole* that is wrong. In fact it all comes back, as usual, to the fact that we have an Asquith instead of a Chatham waging war. It is a detestable job, this of mine, at such a time, and I feel that I am really paying the penalty for a misspent life. . . .

More and more Geoffrey was concentrating on the hopeless lack of co-ordination and direction in the Government and he had frequent meetings with Carson. On October 17, when staying at Walton, he walked over to see Lloyd George and had a general talk with him on the war situation. "C. P. Scott (of the *Manchester Guardian*) turned up while I was there . . . also Winston and F.E.—altogether a day of lobbying. I was back in the office by 3 p.m.—had a talk with Carson."

On October 18th there was considerable political excitement over Carson, who rang Geoffrey up at 11 p.m. to announce his resignation—"this apparently after formal application to Stamfordham, no answer being forthcoming from Asquith". The final breach had come over the question of the Government's military policy in the Balkans, but the fundamental reason, as the Editor well knew, was that Carson was "utterly sick of the failure of the Cabinet to frame and carry out a policy anywhere". At this period Geoffrey was in almost daily contact with him and was greatly impressed by him.

Geoffrey's relations with Northcliffe in 1915 had their ups and downs. On the whole they seemed to have culminated in a period of acute friction at the end of April, with spasmodic difficult phases in June and July and with a comparatively peaceful autumn. In view of subsequent events it is not without interest to recall that in August, 1915, Northcliffe said to me that "the then strongest men in the Cabinet were Lloyd George, Balfour and Carson". Certainly in October Northcliffe said he was seeing both Carson and Lloyd George frequently.[1]

On March 16th (1915), Geoffrey wrote: "To lunch with Austen Chamberlain who suggested to me afterwards that I should write the life of his father. He had asked Lord Milner, who was doubtful, and I was his second string. It had occurred to him that I might not find Printing House Square a bed of roses. I told him at once that I could not even consider it, was quite unequal to that kind of undertaking, and in any case intended to make as good a job as I could of *The Times*." In March and April there are frequent—at times almost daily—references to Northcliffe: "N. very active and rampageous on the telephone. I had to go and compose him as best I could. Find myself getting thoroughly

[1] *Vide* author's *Struggle*, pp. 143 and 145.

tired and nervy as the result of all this constant fuss. The labour of making bricks without straw is heavy enough in any case." The comments on the five successive days April 26th to 30th include: "came back to London at 1.00 and became involved in a typhoon with Northcliffe at Perth—raging about nothing at all and generally upsetting things and depressing me!!"; "the typhoon continued—violent telegrams about blameless leaders, etc., etc. I got into a hopeless state about ever doing anything with the paper"; "more telegrams from Perth, announcing N.'s early return—why?—and what is one to do against these brainstorms?" "N. arrived and I saw him in Fleetway House (Headquarters of the Amalgamated Press Ltd.), and succeeded in calming a not quite intelligible state of agitation"; "Another rather weary day and a further talk with N."

In May, 1915, within a few days of the Political and Shells crises, there are these comments:

May 17. N. at the office in rather truculent mood. However, his rages were soon swallowed up in a series of crises—munitions, Fisher's resignation (of which Lovat Fraser brought details), and on which we eventually wrote plainly.

May 21. Geoffrey saw Milner, Austen Chamberlain and Dudley Docker about munitions; Cromer about affairs at large; heard from Lansdowne that he would serve in the Coalition; "had a few words with Bonar Law on the telephone but the feature of the day was a general uprising against *The Daily Mail* for a disgraceful attack on Kitchener. It was burnt at the Stock Exchange, etc., etc. A peaceful and comforting dinner with Lord Milner".

In June there were running comments: "N. reduced to a state bordering on lunacy"; ". . . N. very much excited about the alleged 're-gunning' of the German Navy"; on June 26th from Cliveden ". . . drove myself over to spend the morning with N. who was as flourishing as the garden. Back for an afternoon of vigorous wood cutting"; on June 28th " . . . Hard at work in the office all afternoon—much interrupted from 6 to 7 by a desultory, lugubrious, and quite purposeless conversation between Northcliffe and Lovat Fraser who loafed into my room." On July 6th, Geoffrey writes: "Rather a worrying and agitated day. N. on the warpath about a long dispatch from Ian Hamilton (about the Dardanelles), though he had nothing in the end to suggest but what I had already told Fraser to write. However N. kept me on the go from early morning."

On July 15th Geoffrey was present at the luncheon given to Northcliffe to celebrate his fiftieth birthday at the Ritz, when Northcliffe proclaimed that he intended to continue his policy of criticizing the

Government till such a time as we applied ourselves as scientifically as Germany to carrying on the war. On July 16th Geoffrey wrote, "N. went off to Boulogne at dawn—a blessed riddance." In August Geoffrey wrote when Northcliffe was in Scotland, "Printing House Square had peace for fourteen days." On September 7th, "N. happily still away in Scotland and no troubles to speak of." On September 16th, Geoffrey spent "a weary afternoon listening to N.'s well-grounded complaint of a lack of 'features' in *The Times*. It is, of course, entirely a question of space and money! . . . Before that a long talk with Lloyd George".

The last entry in Geoffrey's diary for the year was:

> *Dec. 28.* Every sign of a new political crisis and a telegram from Freeman finally took me to London by the one train and straight to the office to deal with it. But it was virtually settled at today's Cabinet. Asquith off the fence at last on the side of compulsion.

XII

1916—TURNING POINT OF THE WAR

THIS year may be regarded as the turning point in the war from the standpoint of the United Kingdom and the Empire, in that the supreme direction of the war was drastically changed when Lloyd George succeeded Asquith as Prime Minister in December. John Bull, slow to wake up, is, according to popular belief, never at his best till his back is to the wall. By the end of the year a fundamental change in the national outlook had taken place, and no one had played a more decisive part in the metamorphosis than Geoffrey. His long and arduous training as a political leader-writer in South Africa was standing him in good stead. Throughout his career he never wrote more powerfully than in 1916; the great majority of the leaders in *The Times* were part of a carefully considered plan, firstly to awaken the country, and secondly to ensure that a nation in arms should have the most efficient leadership available.

Geoffrey's hand was much strengthened by the very important step taken by a small group of remarkable men. This entry in the diary may be said probably to be the most important in the year from the standpoint of his work:

> *Jan. 17.* The first of a series of private meetings—for the purpose of keeping in touch—between Lord Milner, Carson, Amery, Oliver, and myself. Meet at 7, talk for an hour, dine together afterwards if convenient. That's the plan. We met tonight at 17 Great College Street (Lord Milner's house) and had quite a useful hour.

This little group was in fact a kind of unofficial "Ginger Group", not however necessarily seeking office for themselves, but holding a watching brief for those who were determined that there must be a complete change in the methods of directing the British war effort. Right through the year they met on Mondays to discuss plans. Later on they called in other advisers, but in substance—apart from Mr. Amery's absence on active service—the group remained unchanged save for the addition of Waldorf Astor. This group was certainly unorthodox in its political beliefs and its one and only object was how best to devise the methods of achieving an early victory. It naturally owed much of its driving force to Lord Milner's unflinching purpose, to F. S. Oliver's genius and original outlook, and to Carson's dogged determination; but Amery's great knowledge of Empire problems, Waldorf Astor's wide experience and Geoffrey's extraordinary sanity and ability to put into words the aspirations of the group were also vital factors.

The main problems on which Geoffrey concentrated in *The Times* were really all part of the supreme one of securing a truly effective and efficient war Government. He advocated the need of overhauling the recruiting machinery, now that compulsory military service had been accepted by the whole body of ministers, and the abolition of such hardships as the calling up of the married men before the categories of single men had been "combed"; the urgent necessity of finding a war-time leader with driving force and vision, and with ability to inspire others; the creation of a supreme war cabinet of five or six men in place of the debating society of twenty-two to twenty-four departmental chiefs; the search for a successor to Kitchener, capable of filling this supremely important post under the conditions of world war in the new age of invention and scientific discovery; the reorganization of British air power, hitherto functioning as two separate sections, one under the Navy and the other under the Army, and their immediate fusion into a strong united body to have equal rank with the two Senior Services; and the creation of an efficient Ministry of Information, under an important member of the Government, with direct access to the Prime Minister. If Geoffrey was critical of Asquith, it was not from any personal animosity but solely because the former did not, in his view, possess the necessary qualities of a supreme war leader. He respected Asquith as a party leader or as a Parliamentarian but he was convinced that sooner or later, and the sooner the better, there must be a new leader.

From Geoffrey's diary we get a vivid picture of the year 1916, which opened with the news of the sinking of the *Persia* and the death of Lord Montagu of Beaulieu, whose obituary in *The Times*—"a handsome notice"—was provided by Northcliffe himself. Twenty-four hours later came the news that John Montagu "whom we memorialized so handsomely this morning" had turned up safe at Malta. A month later the following entry appeared in the diary:

Feb. 3. Lunch at 22, St. James's Place (The Northcliffes')—John Montagu there—still rather battered but very active. He gave an extraordinary account of his miraculous escape. They started thirty-three in a waterlogged bit of boat and were picked up eleven living. No food or drink for fifty hours—a ghastly picture of the dead, when thrown over, clinging like barnacles to the boat. Undoubtedly J.'s own seamanship saved him. He had to manœuvre the big ship alongside in the dark. He thinks he could just have lived till morning.

Geoffrey wrote one of his periodic surveys of the war to his special friends on January 9th, 1916, in which he referred to the evacuation of the Dardanelles:

. . . We have just had the news of the final evacuation of Gallipoli and of the loss of the *King Edward VII*. Ian Hamilton's long despatch was published on Friday after a good deal of chopping and changing up to the last moment. I hear that the Government did their best to make him take out his revelations of the deficiencies in his complement of troops. However, he stuck to his guns over this and on the whole, I suppose, produced a tolerably faithful and very picturesque account of that tragic business, though there is a good deal more to be said about his own general conduct of affairs.

During these anxious and momentous days Geoffrey never lost an opportunity of discussing any aspect of the war with the ablest and best-informed men in the country.

Jan. 25. A most interesting dinner with Lloyd George and Henry Wilson at Arthur Lee's—just we four. The talk was all of the chances of breaking through the Western front. H.W. said the odds weren't yet sufficiently in our favour, but could be made so by adding fifteen divisions to our 135 Allied divisions and diverting 20 German divisions to the Russian front. He was emphatic on "killing the Boche" and no "side-shows". The "Spring Offensive"—both from military and munitions point of view—is receding to August.

Among his varied meetings was a lunch to meet Raemaekers, the great Dutch cartoonist; and another with Harold Cox to talk economy; a lunch with officers in the R.F.C. (Royal Flying Corps) to get his views on the co-ordination of the two services under one Minister confirmed; several meetings took place *à deux* with A. J. Balfour to discuss the popular uneasiness about the Admiralty. On February 21st the Editor suggested that Jellicoe be brought back as First Sea Lord and Beatty be given command of the Fleet—changes which were made eight months later. In March he mentions another private talk with Balfour, who gave him an "amusing and I think accurate account of the activities of Winston and Fisher". The following day there is this entry:

Mar. 7. The day of Winston's disastrous coup[1] in the House of Commons. I heard A.J.B. and saw old Fisher, who was in the plot like a Chinese idol in the Gallery. The thing failed from the start but it was difficult to write about, because there is something in Winston's case.

In a letter to Mike Furse on March 3rd, Geoffrey wrote:

> ... "X" asks me in his present letter whether, amongst others, I do not think Chirol fitly rewarded by an honour for all his years of public service. This is delicate ground, and perhaps I had better refrain from saying what I really think, namely, that any working journalist who accepts an honour or reward from any Government is thereby depriving himself of half his independence and value.

There is no possibility of doubting that the sentence in the letter to the Bishop of Pretoria expresses Geoffrey's real views that for a working journalist to accept an honour was not in accordance with the traditions of Printing House Square. He entirely endorsed the reasons which prompted Buckle to refuse a baronetcy[2] and he admired the proud traditions of the Walter family likewise to refuse ennoblement. There are many references in his papers to his views on this, to him, important subject.

To his friends abroad Geoffrey wrote on March 22nd:

> ... All eyes here are still on Verdun, which has on the whole been a very satisfactory chapter. I am inclined to suspect that the fighting has

[1] This referred to the debate in the House on the Navy, when "Colonel" Churchill had come from the Front to take part in it, and had pleaded for more ships and had also suggested the recall of Lord Fisher. Sir Hedworth Meux had attacked the suggestion of bringing back Lord Fisher and concluded "we all wish him (Colonel Churchill) great success in France and hope he will stay there" (laughter).

[2] In December, 1919, Lord Lee of Fareham wrote to Geoffrey, on behalf of the P.M., Mr. Lloyd George, suggesting that he should accept an honour. Geoffrey replied:

9, Seymour Street.

My dear Arthur,

Don't think me ungrateful if I say I would rather be without any public "recognition" of such work as I may have done as Editor of *The Times*. My wife quite agrees, but we are nevertheless touched by your kindness in interesting yourself in it. Will you tell the Prime Minister?

Lord Lee wrote:

I am really disappointed—on public grounds—that you should not let your work be recognized but I quite understand and honour your motives for refusing. Some other way must be found of acknowledging the debt which we all owe to you for your courageous and extraordinary helpful direction of *The Times* throughout our greatest perils—and of emphasizing the misery that we all feel that you are no longer there.

been exaggerated on both sides, but there is no doubt whatever that the German losses have greatly outnumbered the French. The best estimate of the proportion is about four to one. This is a very different state of affairs from that which existed last Autumn, when the French suffered so terribly in Champagne; and the result on their *moral* has been very great indeed. . . .

All the news from Mesopotamia is bad. The last attempt to relieve Townshend was a complete failure, and bitter complaints are coming through about the inadequacy of medical stores and arrangements.

The main problems for us here are still the provision of men and munitions. . . .

Meanwhile Geoffrey continued his ceaseless contacts with men in power:

Apr. 14. Robertson (Sir William Robertson, Chief of the Imperial General Staff) came by himself to lunch with me and to have a long talk. . . . I had never bothered him before since the war, though I knew him in earlier days. He seemed to me very fit and very determined, not over worried but very conscious of the unequal task of arguing with politicians.

During Eastertide ominous events were taking place in Ireland. Sir Roger Casement was landed from a German submarine in County Kerry, where he was arrested. On April 24th (Easter Monday) the *Sinn Fein* Rebellion took place. The entry in Geoffrey's diary of April 24th shows that he had advocated (unfortunately without success) that special care should be taken in the United States in the presentation of news about the Irish Rebellion, which was becoming a serious affair.

The Irish Rebellion and the fall of Kut at last stirred the Asquith Government into action. On May 3rd Birrell, the Chief Secretary, resigned and the Prime Minister introduced his all-round Compulsion Bill. The following day there was a Ginger-Group lunch with Milner in the chair and Carson present.

On May 2nd Geoffrey wrote to his friends:

. . . Meanwhile everything was thrown into the shade for the time being by the outbreak in Dublin. It began at noon on Easter Monday—a very well chosen moment. Birrell I need hardly say was in England. The General Commanding was in England. Most of the officers had gone to the races. Wimborne was on the point of starting for Belfast, where Basil Blackwood was awaiting him. Consequently the rebels got a good start and nothing was seriously done to check them before about Wednesday. The first thought of the authorities was to close down on all news, so that it was Tuesday afternoon before anyone in England knew what was going on, and a good deal later before they realized how serious it was. . . . However, having once got to work, the military authorities seemed to have done extraordinarily well. The whole rising was smashed to smithereens within the week. . . . You will realize from the papers, when they reach you, what a ghastly business it has been. . . .

On the top of this week of horrors came the surrender of Kut, which at any other time would have excited an immense amount of feeling and indignation. As things were, the news was almost snowed under with other disasters, and no one paid very much attention to it. It seems incredible that any Government should survive three such simultaneous shocks. They had been responsible, directly or indirectly, for one of the greatest surrenders of British troops in history. They had allowed a revolution in Ireland to break out under their noses without the slightest attempt to check its perfectly obvious growth. Finally they had received a resounding slap in the face by being compelled to withdraw a Bill to which the whole Cabinet assented after the most tremendous fuss and crisis. Nothing seems to move them, or even seriously to shake them, though they have completely lost the confidence of the country. However, I am not without hope that the prompt retrenchment of Birrell may be the beginning of the end. Unquestionably all these failures spring from the same cause, quite apart from personal capacity—namely that the Cabinet is too large, too little united, and too much immersed in Departmental routine. What is needed, as I constantly point out, is a small strong Government of not more than half a dozen members, all of whom should be quite free from the ordinary cares of office. . . . Under present conditions there is no one to look ahead, make plans, and take precautions. Everyone I talk to seems to agree about this. The difficulty is to get a move on, and the real difficulty of getting a move on is that no one wants to return to a purely party Government, which we could get for the asking. Lord Milner and Carson could take quite enough Unionists into the Lobby at any time to make the position of Unionist Ministers untenable. . . .

During the year 1916, the relations of Geoffrey and Northcliffe seem to have been happier than they had been since the first months of his Editorship. Geoffrey was well established in his position, was playing an important part behind the scenes and many of the objectives for which he was working were coming within the range of realization. In March there were two appreciative references to Northcliffe's writings: "N. weighed in at night with an excellent message from Verdun which filled a good deal of the paper" and again: "lunched with returned Northcliffe . . . a most absorbing account of his experiences, which he was busily committing to paper".

On May 14 is an entry which does credit to both men. To Geoffrey for his temerity in speaking thus frankly; to Northcliffe, after the initial outburst, for realizing that Geoffrey was only concerned about the reputation of *The Times* and feared that Northcliffe's megalomaniacal tendencies were increasing.

May 14. . . . Found Northcliffe at the office and had a very plain talk with him about his unfair attacks on Curzon and his appalling bout of self-advertisement. He lost his temper at first, but otherwise took it well. I hope it may do good.

On May 25th Geoffrey was in the House of Commons to hear "Asquith's long-expected Irish statement—a rather comical outcome. He turned the whole business over to L.G. I had seen the latter for a moment in the morning and he told me that he had refused the Chief Secretaryship. Asquith obviously wants him out of the way". To his friends abroad Geoffrey sent one of his circular letters on May 30, from which the following extracts are taken:

For various reasons there is less controversy at home at this moment than for some time past. . . .

. . . Ireland has gone for the time being into a backwater owing to Asquith's ingenuous notion of turning the whole business over to Lloyd George. I am not sure, by the way, whether the notion was really quite so ingenuous as it appeared at first sight. It is not uncharitable, I think, to assume that the Government, while probably thinking Lloyd George the best man for the job, were not sorry to involve him in rather a risky adventure. Nearly everyone who has tackled the Irish question has burnt his fingers over it. On the other hand if Lloyd George by any chance were to make a success of it, some credit would accrue to the Government as a whole. . . .

It is difficult to see what Lloyd George will be able to achieve. Setting aside all the high falutin' nonsense that has been written about the dawn of a new era in Ireland, there seem to be two possible courses for any Government. One is to go straight ahead on the present lines, appoint a better Lord Lieutenant and Chief Secretary, maintain martial law as long as necessary, and do what has never been done in the last nine years, viz., govern the country as it was governed with general acceptance by recent Unionist administrations. The other course is to take the opportunity of making some progress on the lines which very nearly led to an agreement before the war—in other words, accept the Home Rule Bill as an accomplished fact on condition that special provision is made for Ulster. On the whole I am inclined to think that there are possibilities in this latter course. Ulster must be reckoned with sooner or later. Her work during the war, which has been unimpeachable, gives her stronger claims than ever to be left alone. . . .

On June 1st Geoffrey was dining with his friend Willie Bridgeman[1] who told him a rumour of a naval battle,[2] but all enquiries when he returned to the office failed to substantiate it. The entry in the diary for June 2nd is as follows:

> Office all day—growing rumour of naval battle. . . . At last, about 6.30 p.m. the Admiralty produced a dismal tale of British losses . . . at 1.30 a better communiqué came out and I sat down and rewrote a good deal of the leader for later editions. (Dined in an interval very heavy-hearted. . . .)

On June 5th Geoffrey dined with the "Ginger Group" and on returning to P. H. S. "invented a leader on a subject about which I felt profoundly, namely the bucking up of the nation by the hard fighting (whether victory or failure) we little knew what was happening to confirm this". The entry in the diary for the following day was:

> *June 6.* Wrote at home all morning—then, going to the club, heard of the tragedy of Kitchener, drowned last night in the *Hampshire*. I bolted straight to the office and was hard at work there all afternoon and night, revising and completing the memoir. . . . London was literally stunned by the news.

Geoffrey wrote a long memorandum, dated June 7–14, on the problem of the War Office after Kitchener's death; from it these excerpts are made:

> After announcing Lord Kitchener's death on Wednesday, June 7th, the *Morning Post* came out with a strong appeal that his successor at the War Office should be Lord Milner. I doubt whether it was a very wise line of approach, but it gave me the opportunity next day, Thursday, June 8th, of commenting in *The Times* on various names which had already been suggested, of showing that Lord Milner would probably make the best War Minister of all, but that it was difficult to imagine him in the present Cabinet without a very clear understanding about his position. In the next few days I had a good deal of evidence—some of it from very unlikely sources—of the popularity of the Milner suggestion

[1] William Clive Bridgeman (created Viscount in 1929) was a very old friend of Geoffrey. In 1916 he was Parliamentary Secretary to the Ministry of Labour, and subsequently held office as Home Secretary (1922–24) and First Lord of the Admiralty (1924–29). Every year he went to shoot at Langcliffe and the Dawsons were often guests of the Bridgemans at Leigh in Shropshire. Geoffrey and Bridgeman walked through the countryside they both loved. Geoffrey treasured Bridgeman's friendship and valued his sound judgment and delightful sense of humour.

[2] First mention of the Battle of Jutland.

with the general public. He himself told me that he quite agreed with what I had written in *The Times*, that he did not want office, and that he could not imagine it being offered to him. . . .

On Whit Monday, June 12th, I went to see Lloyd George at the Ministry of Munitions in the morning, and asked him how things stood. He began by saying that he did not want to go to the War Office—certainly not to a position so powerless as Kitchener's had lately become, and that his real desire was to get out of the Government altogether. He said that his work at the Ministry of Munitions had reached a definite stage at which it might well be handed over to someone else. The creative part was done. What was needed now was a good business head to keep things going. There were probably people who could do this better than he could himself. On the other hand the public needed to be kept in touch with the war. He thought he could do this from an independent position. Moreover he could supply what was wanted in the shape of organization outside, and that he would make a very useful combination with Carson. . . .

I could see that at that time Lloyd George was already flirting with the notion of an enlarged and glorified War Office, though he still had doubts whether the moment had not come for breaking with the Government altogether. He told me that he was just going to lunch with C. P. Scott, of the *Manchester Guardian*, and he would hear what he had to say about Liberal opinion in the provinces. . . .

That same night (Tuesday, 13th June) I had a telephone message from Arthur Lee implying that he was nervous about the prospect of Lloyd George leaving the Ministry of Munitions. He also said that he gathered from Lloyd George that I was in favour of his sticking to the Government and going to the War Office, and that Carson had independently given him the same advice. I told him there was evidently some misunderstanding; but the truth of course was that Lloyd George was becoming more and more enamoured of the idea of having the War Office. . . .

I went on to lunch with Arthur Lee (Wednesday, 14th June), who meanwhile had asked Lloyd George, but no one else. We talked of indifferent subjects during luncheon, e.g. the best biographies in the language, and L.G. said that the best biography he had ever read was of John Jones, the preacher, and was written in Welsh. When the room was cleared A.L. brought on the subject of the War Office by saying that he had read my note in *The Times* and saw some risk of disagreement between Lloyd George and me. Thereupon I held forth to the same effect as when I saw L.G. on Monday, and said that I saw great risk in his going to the War Office, that he would have much better scope for his powers if he went outside altogether, that his transfer would virtually perpetuate the present Cabinet, which in his own opinion could not win the war. A.L. chipped in from time to time on the importance of the Ministry of Munitions, that it offered more power than the War Office, and that it was easier to leave when the work was done.

But L.G., who had had a talk with Asquith the day before, was plainly dazzled by this time by the notion of a War Office with greatly extended powers. He said that these powers had only been curtailed because of Kitchener's peculiarities, and that he should see that they were restored. . . .

In order to clear his mind Geoffrey dictated the following memorandum on Wednesday, June 14, 1916. It will be seen that he did, in fact, foresee the kind of relationship which was to exist between Milner and Lloyd George in the last year of the war:

. . . Lloyd George has first refusal of the War Office. If he declines it, it will probably go to Bonar Law. . . .

If Lloyd George goes to the War Office, he is bound to make the position more important than his present place, in practice as well as in theory. He does not regard it as more important with its present limitations. Therefore, he will try, no doubt with Asquith's full approval, to get back some of the old powers of the Secretary of State. . . . I think he might easily come to grief at the War Office, and that this would be a serious matter for the country.

But the most serious consideration of all is that the transference of Lloyd George to the War Office would in practice mean the perpetuation of the present Government without much hope of improvement or change. . . .

I cannot help thinking that the best course of all—both for Lloyd George and the country—is that he should frankly come out of the Government altogether, and devote himself to the work which he can do better than anyone, and which he can only do in a position of independence. In conjunction with Carson he could not only do a great deal to keep the country in touch with the war, but he could get on with the vital practical matters of registration and organization. . . .

It seems to me essential to get Lloyd George bracketed with someone who thinks as he does about the war. He and Carson in conjunction would be immeasurably stronger than either of them single-handed. *The only alternative that I see is to get Lord Milner associated with Lloyd George inside the Government,*[1] by the appointment of the former either to the War Office or to the Ministry of Munitions. The two of them would either control affairs in the Cabinet, or would bring it down with a run if they were to resign together. But this seems rather a hopeless project and I think the former is better.

If ever there was a case of "intelligent anticipation" the last paragraph in the above document, written by Geoffrey to clear his mind, is one. Lloyd George was appointed to the War Office to succeed Kitchener and within six months Geoffrey's scheme for getting

[1] My italics. E.W.

Milner—the "someone who thinks as he does about the war"—within a small War Cabinet was realized.

Included in one of Geoffrey's memoranda to his friends, on August 3rd, was the following:

> . . . They (the Government) had another rebuff over the appointment of the two Committees to inquire into Mesopotamia and the Dardanelles. Asquith began by conceding the main point and was gradually driven from trench to trench until after about half an hour of it he had "walked" back nearly everything for which he had stipulated in his opening statement. I happened to be in the House and thought it the most complete surrender which I had ever seen on the part of an almost omnipotent Government. Quite apart from this minor question of the method of inquiry, the whole Mesopotamia business has greatly weakened their prestige. We have had an immense amount of information about it in this office, and I have really only used a fraction of it. The whole thing has been a most deplorable record of ineptitude and muddle, with a good deal of official callousness. I feel that our campaign on the subject has been of real service.

The entry for August 14th must be considered in association with that of May 14th, already quoted:[1]

> *Aug. 14.* . . . At Harrogate I got Saturday's and today's *Times* and nearly vomited over the sycophantic headlines imposed on two interesting telegrams from Northcliffe in Italy. I expressed myself freely to Freeman and Brumwell on my return and relations were a little strained.

On the following day there were further telegrams from N. and these, "presented with decency, had a great success". In September, after a visit to Langcliffe, Geoffrey dined with the Northcliffes, finding N. "in great form, tremendously impressed with Haig and with the efficiency of the Army". Early in the month Geoffrey had a long talk with L.G., the policy of the War Office then was "to try to get Bulgaria round (minus Ferdinand) to the Allied side. L.G. was interesting too on the question of 'no dealing with the Hohenzollerns' on which he thought it was worth while keeping an open mind". On September 3rd the "Great Zepp. *Strafe* had taken place in the early hours of the morning. Everyone went mad over it and the Enfield area was said to have been like 'a vast Derby Day'." Two days later Geoffrey wrote: ". . . in the office all afternoon—about my namesake (Robinson), the Zepp-strafer, now revealed and given the V.C., and about a ridiculous and petty agitation against the decent burial of his victims".

[1] *Vide supra*, p. 133.

VISIT TO THE FRONT

From October 5th to the 20th Geoffrey was once again on a visit to the B.E.F. He spent several days at G.H.Q. and an afternoon with Trenchard at the Headquarters of the R.F.C., with its great repairing sheds and special squadrons—"a wonderful organization and a wonderful set of men. I had several other talks with Trenchard, and it may be convenient to summarize the effect of them here. I came away with no doubt whatever that he himself was a really remarkable man. Everyone testified to the spirit which he had infused into the Flying Corps, and I was specially struck by the generous attitude towards people who must have been serious thorns in his side. . . . He is obviously nervous about the future. At the present moment our supremacy in the air is absolute. During the whole time I was in France I never saw an enemy machine. Our own 'sausages' sit in the air all day long just behind the fighting, and our aeroplanes are backward and forward over the German lines from dawn to dark. . . ."

"I had some talk with Sir Douglas (Haig) at dinner about the extent of his real information as to what was going on there (on the Eastern Front). He said he had none at all, and both the French and ourselves were hopelessly out of touch with Russia. The present channels of communication were unco-ordinated and in effect, there was great need for a thoroughly competent officer, with recognized authority, to tell us what Russia was doing. . . ."

"We reached Colincamps in the late afternoon, and there left the motor for a trudge towards the trenches. This was the best impression I had of the nightly movements of reliefs. Our path lay across a sort of rough moor-like track, filled with invisible guns which were firing incessantly. . . . Unfortunately our lateness made sightseeing a little difficult, but it was an interesting glimpse of life in the trenches and observation posts, at this point absolutely infested with rats, and the scene on the way back is not easy to forget. Silent companies of men—with their tin hats and full trench equipment—were filing in every direction across the moor, and the great shells screaming overhead, every flash by this time being plainly visible. . . ."

"During most of the time I was fortunate enough to see a good deal of Sir Douglas Haig. . . . I was with him at a time which must have been one of great anxiety—operations in progress every day, endless preparations for another advance, difficulties with the French, who were not up to time, and great doubts about the attitude of the people at home. In spite of all this he never showed the slightest trace of strain or discomposure, was never either elated or depressed, always seemed to have time for everything, and yet managed to put a great deal of steady work into an absolutely methodical day."

"He was in bed before 11 and told me he believed in plenty of sleep and always got it. He never smokes, drinks very little, is absolutely punctual, and seems to thrive on routine. The impression I carried away was that of a man in perfect health of mind and body, thoroughly realizing his task and trained for it just like a race-horse. There is no doubt whatever about the influence which his very steady character has had on all ranks of the Army."

After his visit to Flanders, Geoffrey was devoting much attention to the all important subject of Man-Power, which *The Times* kept constantly to the fore. With increased vigour, the Editor continued to press for the establishment of a proper Air Board.

One of the most important of Geoffrey's papers dealing with this period is the memorandum "The Political Upheaval of December, 1916", because it shows the exact moment when the members of the "Ginger Group" made up their minds that Lloyd George must withdraw from the "Government of Indecision":

> I date the actual beginning of the "crisis", so far as my own direct information goes, from Monday, November 27th, though, of course, it had been obviously blowing up for some time previously.
>
> On that night, Lord Milner, Carson, Oliver, Waldorf Astor, and I met for our usual Monday dinner at Oliver's house, and had with us also Henry Wilson, who had just returned from France. Carson was even more saturnine and serious than usual, and asked for our opinion on two points, viz.:
>
>> Should Lloyd George come out of the Government, which he was convinced was going the best way to lose the war?
>>
>> And was it, or was it not, desirable that Bonar Law should come with him?
>
> We were all absolutely unanimous that Lloyd George had very much better make a definite effort to set things right or to come out at once. We were also unanimous that Bonar Law should, if possible, be induced to support him—if for no other reason, because that would mean the bringing out of the old Unionist organization with its candidates and funds. The importance of this was obvious in the not impossible event of a General Election.
>
> Carson seemed to think us a little flippant and light-hearted about it; but we had all been so strongly of the same opinion for so long that it hardly seemed to need serious discussion. He was quite convinced himself and gave us to understand that he would at once urge Lloyd George to take action.

This I believe he did on the following morning, when I myself went and had a talk with Arthur Lee, who was very much in L.G.'s confidence. He was also quite definite that things had reached their limit. Incidentally he thought it a pity that L.G. and Northcliffe had not for some time been on speaking terms. I told him I thought there was not very much in this, and that so far as I knew Northcliffe, whom I had seen only a few times during the last weeks, was quite alive to L.G.'s great qualities and desire to win the war. In any case I said I was certain that a meeting between them could very easily be arranged, and on the following Thursday, when Northcliffe came up from the country for his weekly day in London, I suggested to him that he had better get rid of this impression of L.G.'s by going to see him. He was perfectly willing to do this, so I telephoned to Lee and they met on the following morning, just about the time when L.G. was finally submitting to the Prime Minister his plan for a stronger system of Government. After that they met frequently during the succeeding days, but nothing is more grotesque than to suggest, as various newspapers soon began to suggest, that L.G.'s revolt was the result of N.'s inspiration, or that the latter was in any sense the villain of the piece. It is true that the *Daily Mail* and the *Evening News* began a series of violent attacks on members of the present Government, and assumed a very intimate knowledge of L.G.'s intentions. But this had not in fact helped matters. If anything, it rather embarrassed L.G., as he himself told me afterwards, though it certainly gave some colour to the popular impression that the thing had been "engineered by the Northcliffe Press".

Before dealing with the remainder of his memorandum on the "Political Upheaval of December" we must, to preserve the proper sequence, refer to another memorandum Geoffrey wrote on "*The Times* leader of December 4th, 1916":

In his speech at the Reform Club Asquith made a great deal of the leading article in *The Times* of Monday, December 4th. It may be as well therefore to place on record the origin of this article and of the information contained in it, the accuracy of which is not in dispute.

Like the three or four preceding leaders it was written entirely by myself—half of it at Cliveden on Saturday night[1] and half in the office on Sunday afternoon and evening. It was absolutely "uninspired" (in the sense that no one suggested it to me) nor did it ever occur to me when writing it, that I was "giving away" information that was not known to a considerable inner circle. I had not seen, or held any communication with, Lloyd George himself for several weeks. Carson, on the other hand, I had seen constantly—I had a talk with him on the Sunday afternoon (December 10th) when I came back from Cliveden, and he of

[1] Geoffrey was at Cliveden both on Saturday, December 2nd, and Saturday, December 9th.

course was in close touch with L.G. But the question of the War Council or Cabinet—its size and composition—was one which we had discussed for months. Carson and I had always been keen about it and there was nothing new to us in L.G.'s demands.

G. R.

We now resume giving Geoffrey's remarks on the popular impression that L.G.'s revolt had been "engineered by the Northcliffe Press".

On Monday, December 11, N. rang me up from Sutton to ask if there was any news, and interrupted his question to say to a secretary (or telephone clerk), "Tell Mr. —— that I am very pleased with his article for the *Globe*."

Next day the *Globe* contained the following outrageous and (as N. knew) most dishonest puff. One would like to think that he had been consulted about some other article, but there was nothing else in which he could be supposed to take the slightest interest.

Copy of news cutting from the *Globe* of December 12, 1916:

THE GREATEST DICTATOR

Lord Northcliffe's Supreme Journalistic Feat

A journalistic correspondent writes:

I have read this morning that Lord Northcliffe has written an article on Mr. Lloyd George which will be read by eighty million people. The fact is mentioned only because it throws light on the power exercised by this single individual—a power which is in some ways greater to an inconceivable extent than any which any dictator in history has ever been able to wield.

This is frankly a journalistic diversion, and I make it with natural hesitation at a time when such gigantic world issues are at stake. But the simple truth is that Lord Northcliffe, by virtue of that power he exercises, is one of the chiefest figures in the great drama. There are those who contemptuously regard Lord Northcliffe as merely the personification of what one calls "the ha'penny press mind". Whether he is greater or littler than that it is anyhow an admission. He is at once democracy and also democracy's master; he is a million people's voices—but he is also the mouth which shapes what those voices utter.

And Lord Northcliffe has just brought down the Asquith Cabinet.

I know that the assertion will be jealously contested by those who would be his rivals; indeed, the statement is in some ways a generalization rather than a strict truth. The fact remains that it was after reading the now famous "leader" in Monday's *Times* that Mr. Asquith sent in his resignation. By that alone Lord Northcliffe (we speak now from the solely journalistic point of view) has achieved probably the greatest journalistic feat in history. He has out-lioned all the famous lions of *The Times* itself. There is no need to emphasize the magnitude of the deed. One only needs remark that Mr. Asquith's was the longest Administration of recent times, which is equivalent to saying that it must equally have been inherently the strongest. It collapsed in rather less than four days.

The facts are enough to support the contention I have put forward. Many may regard this man Lord Northcliffe as a Menace; they will fear the induction of a blood-lust. As to that one can only express the sincere opinion that hitherto Lord Northcliffe, in his own judgment, has done whatever he has done for the Empire's good. Whether his judgment was right or wrong, whether it will be right or wrong, is for History to show.

On December 4th—the day on which the famous leader appeared, the members of the "Ginger Group" dined together. The position was that Asquith was still negotiating and they directed their efforts "to keep L.G. firm"—a task entrusted to Carson. Geoffrey wrote a statement of the events which took place on December 5th:

. . . I went to the War Office where I had an appointment with Derby at 12.30. . . . I asked him to tell L.G., who had just come into the office, that I was there and should like to see him. Ten minutes later he brought back a message to say that L.G. would like to see me.

I found him "pale, but determined", very much in earnest, and quite clear about his own course. He told me that Asquith, who had agreed in principle to all his proposals on Sunday, had this morning gone back not merely on the details, but on the whole principle of the thing. That being so, he had no alternative but to back his opinion by resignation, and when I came in he was actually finishing a letter to this effect—a very good one, which he allowed me to read before sending it over to Downing Street by hand. In it he rehearsed his own plan for a small War Council. . . .

It was a good letter, stating the whole case without any sort of acrimony. L.G. told me that Asquith had practically come down to a mere reduction of the existing War Committee. . . . He (L.G.) was simply out to get an effective form of Government. He asked me if I saw Northcliffe to convey to him that it did not help him when the *Daily Mail* and *Evening News* assumed too intimate a knowledge of his actions and intentions. Also that too much vituperation of individuals was not so useful as insistence that the whole system of Government was unsound and could not win the war. . . .

By dinner-time we heard that Asquith himself had resigned, and later in the evening that the King had sent for Bonar Law. . . .

Geoffrey's account of the events of December 6th follows:

After lunch I ran into Carson, going away from the War Office, and went for a bit of a walk with him. He told me that Bonar Law had made no serious attempt to form a Government, beyond making a formal and apparently abortive inquiry of Asquith whether he was willing to serve. There had been a fresh attempt to re-open discussion of the Lloyd George scheme, but he, Carson, had insisted that this could no longer be re-opened. Asquith, Balfour, Lloyd George, and Bonar Law had now been summoned to Buckingham Palace together, Balfour getting out of bed for the purpose. Asquith had apparently been working very hard to obtain pledges from his Liberal colleagues that they would serve under no one but himself, and had even approached certain Unionists with the same object. . . . He (Carson) entirely agreed with what I had written overnight about returning to a small Cabinet, and said that this was also Lloyd George's idea. Once this was settled—and he was contemplating a Cabinet of four—his intention was to bring a great deal of new blood into the Government outside the Cabinet. No doubt there was a strong impression that the end of it would be the return of Asquith. The Athenaeum, into which I looked for a few minutes, was full of this foolish notion, and some of the evening papers were openly predicting it.

Just before dinner—after a visit to the War Office, and the Colonial Office, both of whose occupants were flown—I ran Carson to earth again in the Carlton Club, and drove back with him to Whitehall. By this time, he told me, things had straightened themselves out. Asquith and his friends had been asked whether they would take any part in the new Government and, after taking time for consideration, had definitely declined. Lloyd George, Bonar Law, and Carson had thereupon held a meeting and had agreed that Lloyd George should be put forward to the King as Prime Minister. Carson told me that he himself had been very strong on this point as being the only straightforward course and the one which the country expected. Lloyd George had now been entrusted with the task, and Carson was going back for a further talk with him.

He told me in confidence, as an instance of Lloyd George's impulsiveness, that the latter had at once said to him, "Of course you will be Chancellor." Carson had replied that nothing would induce him to be anything of the kind. He did not want to have any cares of any sort or kind outside the prosecution of the war, and, if he must take office at all, would take it without portfolio.

The record of the events on December 7th follows:

A long talk with Carson in his house at tea-time. He had lost all interest in the so-called "crisis" and was thinking entirely about the war. But I roused him sufficiently to discuss some of the appointments. His own great anxiety was to get Lord Milner in, and as far as possible to get away from the old business of party "claims." . . .

. . . He (Carson) agreed also with my suggestion that patriotic Labour should be as strongly represented as possible, and that the country would welcome an infusion of new blood from the ranks of the best "business men". He said that Lloyd George had already achieved the former, and was doing his best to achieve the latter by sounding people like Sir Albert Stanley and Mr. S. H. Lever.[1] Bonar Law was going to the Exchequer and they were trying to get Herbert Fisher for the Education Office. . . .

The adhesion of the Labour Party, which was announced during the afternoon, made Lloyd George's success certain. My enthusiasm was a little damped late at night by hearing that practically the whole "old gang" of the Unionist Party was returning to office intact, with Balfour at the Foreign Office.

The main posts in the new Government were filled on December 8th. Geoffrey thought one of the weak spots was A. J.B. at the Foreign Office. Geoffrey's account of his talk with Lloyd George follows:

I told him that I thought he was paying far too much attention to the importance of an immediate Parliamentary majority, and that the whole Balfour, Cecil, Chamberlain, Long, Curzon list was a most serious blot on his Government. He was inclined to agree, but said that he must make sure of his backing at first, and that Balfour in particular had been extraordinarily patriotic and useful to him. He could not undertake the F.O. himself, but Balfour was an easy man to work with and would allow him without friction to do a great deal, especially as regards America. . . . He was on the point of seeing Herbert Fisher, in order to ask him to be Minister of Education. I told him I thought this a most admirable selection and reminded him that the idea had long ago been put forward in *The Times*. He hoped to get Lord Milner as First Lord of the Admiralty, and Devonport as Food Controller—both great sources of strength.

Pointing to the placards about "A Bad Balfour Rumour", which the *Evening News* was already displaying in Whitehall, he said that Northcliffe really must give him a chance. He had great difficulties in forming a Government at all. Northcliffe had always purported to believe that he, L.G., was the man to run the war, and he must let him try to do it in his own way. It would be time to speak if the thing was a failure after six months.

I asked him whether it was true, as various newspapers were suggesting, that he had given up the idea of a small Cabinet, and was going back to the old plan of a large Cabinet and a small War Council. He said no—the Cabinet would be a small one, and was itself to be the War Council. He proposed to give his whole time to it, and to leave Bonar Law to run the House of Commons. The weak Ministerial appointments, which he

[1] Subsequently Sir Hardman Lever.

admitted, would not matter so much as I supposed, if the Cabinet was really as predominant as he intended it to be. . . .

There must have been quick work on this Friday night, for Lord Milner, whom I saw on the following morning, told me that his intimation that he was wanted in the Government was a summons to the Cabinet at 11. An hour after getting this he had been summoned by Lloyd George to the War Office, and offered the only place he really cared about having, viz. a non-departmental membership of the Cabinet. He told me that he had made up his mind against the offer of any Department. He thought it would be sheer waste of what he could do best if he were to spend three or four months, for instance, in learning the details of Admiralty work.

On the Sunday afternoon, when I came up from the country, I had a further talk with Carson, who told me that they had got through more work at the Cabinet on Saturday in seven hours than in all the times he had been a member of it before. The official list of the principal offices came out that night—nearly all the new appointments quite first-rate, especially that of Prothero to the Board of Agriculture. We had constantly put him forward in *The Times*, to which he was a regular and much appreciated contributor. His inclusion, and Lord Milner's and above all the creation of a real War Cabinet, relieved from departmental work, were a real triumph for the paper.

And, we may add, for Geoffrey; for most of the aims for which he had toiled unremittingly had been realized.[1]

[1] Northcliffe, according to *The History of "The Times"*, freely said that Milner owed his seat in the War Cabinet to the Editor of *The Times*. *See* Vol. IV, Part I, p. 308.

XIII

1917—ENTER AMERICA—EXIT RUSSIA

THE year began very sadly for Geoffrey. During the last days of December he had been anxious about his beloved Aunt "Mag"; when he was at Langcliffe for Christmas she was evidently failing. He was back in London on the 27th December, and was deeply concerned by the letters and telegrams about her condition; he decided therefore that he must return, and accordingly arrived back at Langcliffe on New Year's Day, 1917, to find his Aunt suffering from pneumonia. During a temporary improvement Geoffrey sat by her bedside, when she would talk a little, "nothing very definite but full of love and thoughtfulness, so anxious that I should get out for a walk, not worry about her or about my work, etc., etc. . . . Sometimes she lay looking at the hills and said, 'So lovely, so lovely'." The end came in five days. "She looked so peaceful and satisfied and beautiful, as though she knew now that her life had been well and truly spent in working for others." In writing of her death to Maurice Headlam several months later he said: "a great grief, as she had been a second mother to me for years, and a terrible tragedy for her poor remaining sister (Aunt Kitty), who is far less strong and indeed quite unable to deal with affairs. . . . My Aunt left no will. . . . Under the terms of the entail I shall have before long to change my name to that of Dawson. . . . I am puzzled to know how to convince the world that I shall not be a penny richer for the transaction but rather poorer".[1]

Throughout the year Geoffrey was a very regular attender at the Monday dinner of the "Ginger Group", two of whom had become

[1] As a matter of fact it was not till the beginning of August that Geoffrey changed his name from Robinson to Dawson. A member of the staff of *The Times* sent me an office quip, current at the time:

"'Tis strange that a deed-poll under the law
Can change a robin into a daw."

members of the Government.[1] Apart from the usual members, among those who attended were Philip Kerr (then the Prime Minister's Secretary), Lord Brabourne, Maurice Hankey, Roger Keyes and Admiral Sims of the U.S. Navy.

In January there were several references to Northcliffe, who had been absent for a month. Geoffrey was going through one of his worst depressions—"the reaction after Langcliffe"—due of course to the death of his favourite Aunt. On January 29th there is a brief reference to returning from a visit to Cliveden to find "the usual cyclone in the office—N. issuing insulting rescripts etc.".

American and Russian affairs were naturally much in Geoffrey's mind. Arthur Willert, in Washington, wrote to him constantly: as far as Russia was concerned the fact that Lord Milner left London on January 19th, 1917, as head of the Allied Mission and spent some weeks in Petrograd meant that he had absolutely up-to-date and reliable information about the alarming conditions in that country.

In reply to a letter from Willert, Geoffrey wrote on January 23rd, 1917:

> Just a line to acknowledge the arrival of your very interesting letter of December 31st. Of course it has largely been put out of date by the President's last effort which reached us yesterday evening from the American Embassy. We followed the old line of being courteous and restrained, but I fancy that "peace without victory" is destined to live as a phrase side by side with "too proud to fight". The broad difficulty about all this woolly idealism is that the American people show no symptom whatever of being prepared to suffer anything for their ideals. That is what makes it so intensely unpopular in England, where the whole population is after all beginning to realize what war means. Personally, I believe that nothing would be so popular here as a real anti-American outburst and the sacking, let us say, of poor old Page's house. Heaven knows he does not deserve it. In my judgment it is a real and very rare example of the restraining influence of the press. . . . I am really getting more than a little disheartened about the whole question of propaganda between these two great countries. I am sure that this new Government realizes the urgent need for reform. The trouble is that the old system, or want of system, is so deeply established and so many-headed that it is almost impossible to make a fresh start. I keep worrying at it. But the difficulty still is to get a single chief responsible for the whole business.

[1] See *The History of "The Times"*, Vol. IV, Part II, p. 1068. There is this reference to Lord Milner's important role in the War Cabinet, "Lord Milner had attained office, passing in a fashion unprecedented except by the younger Pitt straight to the second position under the Crown. . . ."

Early in February in Great Britain there was very naturally great excitement over America's probable attitude to the new German decree of "unlimited frightfulness". The following letter (Feb. 2nd, 1917) to Willert gives Geoffrey's views:

> . . . What is Germany after? I find it difficult to agree with those who think that she has committed her worst and final error of judgment. To my mind she is acting in a perfectly logical manner—always granted, of course, that she is not troubled by any sort of humanitarian scruples. She cannot possibly go on with the war for more than a few months longer. That, I think, is as nearly certain as anything can be. Our evidence shows that she is in a far worse internal condition than any of us think it wise to say in print. She may very well conclude, therefore, that her only course (failing peace on her own terms) is to throw the last ounce into the struggle and the last ounce, and a very formidable ounce, is represented by *U*-Boats. . . .
>
> There remains America. But for practical purposes America cannot bring her weight to bear for several months—perhaps not at all during the period for which Germany can continue the war. . . .
>
> At any rate that is how I read the situation from the German point of view. You know a great deal more than I do about the American point of view. . . . All I can say is that if Wilson manages to get out of the situation without fighting with any sort of credit left, he will deserve all the statues that were ever erected to ingenuity.

In the field of American-German relations events were moving rapidly and no statue would be erected to Woodrow Wilson for keeping his country out of the war! Good Friday, April 6th, will always remain one of the most important dates in the history of the English-speaking world, for on it the Congress of the United States approved of America's entry into the war with Germany by 373 votes to 50.

During a visit to Ireland, in April, 1917, Geoffrey, piloted as usual by Healy, talked with the Chief Secretary (Mr. Duke)[1] on current affairs and met many of his former friends. He conversed with "A.E."; J. H. Campbell, the Chief Justice; the Provost of Trinity "in his delightful house and saw his silver and pictures"; the Archbishop of Dublin (Church of Ireland); Lord Wimborne, the Lord-Lieutenant, and Captain R. J. H. Shaw, who later joined the staff of *The Times* and became the paper's chief adviser on Irish affairs. Although, admittedly, Geoffrey consorted chiefly with Southern Irish Unionists, through Horace Plunkett's affiliations, he by no means imbibed only their views. In March, before his visit, he studied F. S. Oliver's pamphlet "Ireland and the Imperial Conference"; after his return *The Times*

[1] Harry Edward Duke, subsequently Lord Merivale.

published leaders on "American Views on the Irish Problem", and "Ireland! The Danger of Delay" (May 8th), in which it assumed that a scheme for the settlement of the Irish problem would soon be forthcoming. *The Times* therefore advocated a fresh start, and appealed to Lloyd George, "who has just won new laurels for British statesmanship abroad", to address himself forthwith to "the most difficult, and the most unavoidable problem that faces British statesmanship at home".

No one realized more clearly than Geoffrey the importance of a liberal and sane settlement of Irish affairs as a main factor in improving British-American relations.

If there was much rejoicing about the entry of the United States into the war by those who realized what this meant in long-term results, simultaneously the news from Russia was becoming more alarming. Considering the importance of the Bolshevist Revolution in 1917, it is regrettable that there are so few entries about Russian affairs in Geoffrey's diary. But Russia is not a subject upon which the uninitiated can lightly embark—it requires a lifelong study. Of modern Russia, as it was on the eve of the collapse of Tsardom, Milner, who returned to London on March 3rd, had as reliable information as anyone and fully realized that nothing, short of a miracle, could save Russia from collapse. He undoubtedly passed on his pessimistic views to Geoffrey, but unfortunately there are no entries of any kind in the diaries from February 21st to March 18th—an almost unprecedented occurrence. A leading article in *The Times* (May 12th) was couched in optimistic terms. It stated, "Those who believe in the future of Russia as a free and efficient democracy will watch the vindication of the new regime with patient confidence and earnest sympathy." It is interesting to find at this period Milner was writing to Sir George Buchanan, the British Ambassador at Petrograd:

> . . . I am afraid there is nothing now to prevent Russia passing through the usual stages of the revolutionary fever, which may take some years, until a new form of authority—probably despotic, but the nature of which is quite unforeseeable—emerges from the chaos. This naturally knocks the bottom out of our plans. The work which our Mission tried to do at Petrograd, and which was of course based on the hypothesis that Russia would continue to be an effective member of the Alliance, is all as dead as Queen Anne. We must for the present continue to carry out our part of the bargain, but it cannot, I fear, be long before the futility of continuing to send arms and munitions to Russia—when we know they will not be used against the enemy—must lead to a breakdown of the whole thing.[1]

[1] *Milner Papers, Private Letters, 1914–18*, Vol. IV.

Ever since the summer of 1915 there had been pessimistic hints about the alliance with Russia from Robert Wilton, *The Times* correspondent. As he moved about London Geoffrey made stray references in his private papers to contacts with Russians, or with people who had recently been in Russia. In July there are references to "increasingly bad Russian news" and by September, Wilton arrived in London from Petrograd and Geoffrey introduced him to Carson and others. "He had really come over in the expectation of a successful Korniloff rising and was very interesting about Kerensky and life in the Winter Palace."

Geoffrey, who in the immediate post-war years in South Africa had inclined to be very critical of General Smuts, had now a growing admiration for that statesman and took opportunities of discussing Empire affairs with him. He writes to Mike Furse (April 23rd, 1917):

> Smuts is making a great impression. He stands head and shoulders above all the other Dominion representatives for ability and grasp of the war. Personally I hope he will not be in any great hurry to get back to South Africa. I think that in his heart he would like to stay here for a bit, and there is a good deal of feeling in favour of giving him the command of the Army in Palestine. From all accounts nothing could be more statesmanlike than his attitude to the big war questions in the Cabinet. . . .[1]

There are the usual number of references to Northcliffe while he was in England, but for five months that restless genius was doing a good job of work as Chairman of the British War Mission in the United States. On May 30th Northcliffe told Geoffrey of his appointment and he saw him several times before his departure. He also arranged for Northcliffe to have an hour's talk with "Bob Brand and Gordon of the Canadian Munitions Board, who put him wise on various essentials". No one was better equipped to carry out these arduous duties in America than Northcliffe, and Geoffrey did all he could to see that he received adequate backing from the War Cabinet. From the personal standpoint he must have rejoiced in the five-months' hiatus, in which Northcliffe was usefully employed on the other side of the Atlantic, and when he (Geoffrey) could conduct *The Times* on his own lines.

The following entry in Geoffrey's diary shows that Lloyd George was desirous of keeping in touch with the "Ginger Group":

> *June 4*. . . . An interesting dinner at F. S. Oliver's—all the usual party—Lord Milner, Carson, etc., plus the P.M., who was in great form after

[1] No doubt Geoffrey received his information from Milner. The former antagonists had each grown to respect the good qualities of the other.

four days at Walton. He swore that his new peers hadn't paid for it—Lord M. only hoped they had. Talk mainly on possible Food Controllers.

Geoffrey wrote the following letter (holograph) on June 20th, 1917, to Bishop Furse:

A.J.B. is back (from America) after a real success, looking younger than ever, broadened in mind and very pleased with himself. I had an hour with him this morning and a most interesting account of everyone from the President downwards. Wilson is evidently a bigger man than we thought. Like L.G., and unlike "Squiff", he went all out when once he had taken the plunge. There are passages in Charnwood's new life of Lincoln (not a bad book), which are uncannily like him, but I don't yet credit him with being a Lincoln.

Well, we must hope for the best, since it's clearly America's role to fill up the gap made by Russia. That much-vaunted Revolution has saved Turkey, bolstered the Germans in the west, and jeopardized our armies in Mesopotamia and Palestine. We must needs applaud it, but its immediate effects are simply damnable.

The net result is that after a brilliant beginning we must go slow this year and nerve ourselves for another winter. . . . I feel desperately stale and don't look forward to it. . . .

P.S. I have had to change my name to Dawson to comply with a will made ten years before I was born and must probably do it soon. My creditors will think I've come into a fortune—whereas in fact I shall be poorer than before for the possession of 3,000 odd acres of rough land and the necessity of keeping things going for my remaining Aunt under the burden of the death duties. . . .

Henceforth there was a stream of American visitors to Printing House Square, and on August 3rd, Geoffrey records a two-hour talk with Sir William Wiseman, who occupied an extraordinary position in the field of Anglo-American relations after America's entry into the war. He enjoyed the complete confidence of the President and Colonel E. M. House, and was used as a go-between by the two Governments. I saw much of Wiseman's work, and have always thought that his great services to the nation were never adequately recognized.

Most of Geoffrey's fresh contacts naturally were in connection with the rapidly expanding war effort, and with persons engaged in establishing new departments of State; especially the Air Ministry or Air Board, as it was originally called, and for the establishment of which he had so effectively worked. Among the politicians he met for the first time were John Hodge,[1] "a good strong sensible creature,

[1] He was first Minister of Labour (1916–17) and became Minister of Pensions (1917–19).

according to Willie Bridgeman, who took me to him"; Neville Chamberlain, with whom he was later to establish a real friendship; Edwin S. Montagu, then running the Reconstruction Committee, as deputy for Lloyd George, later to take such a prominent part in Indian constitutional advance; and he had his first sight of the famous William Temple, in St. James's, Piccadilly, "who discoursed on Melchizedek and the Maccabees". One of the few plays visited is thus referred to, "In the evening—a rare occasion—Molly N. (Northcliffe) took me to the first night of Barrie's *Dear Brutus*—a very Barrie-esque and charming little play which I really enjoyed."

In view of the alarming situation in Russia Geoffrey obviously gave more attention to labour problems at home and especially to the question of unrest in the factories engaged on war production. There are references to talks with Shadwell and of meetings with "earnest young workers", friends of Alfred Zimmern, at St. James's Square (the Waldorf Astors'). In July he lunched with W. Nicholson and Lionel Hichens to discuss Dudley Docker's Federation of British Industries and, as a counter-weight to the employers' point of view, a few days later dined "with the young labour experts in St. James's Square". In August there are references to labour unrest and in the autumn entries in the diary about talks with Jimmy Thomas (to whom Waldorf Astor had lent his boatman's cottage) about railway troubles.

On August 4th Geoffrey wrote to Aunt Kitty:

> My own plans are terribly uncertain. The trouble is that a very critical meeting of the Labour Party falls that very day (August 12th), and I don't like the thought of being off duty. It is a frightfully ticklish situation. We can't afford a quarrel with Labour, or any other internal feud at this moment, when we are practically fighting the Germans single-handed. France is tired, Italy querulous, Russia running away, America unprepared. On the other hand we can't afford to let the sound Labour majority be bamboozled by the pacifists. They may go to Stockholm with every patriotic intention, but experience shows how easily they are diddled. . . . Meanwhile I am rather busy putting through the change of name business. The notice will be gazetted, I think, next Wednesday and I have taken an extract from it to send to banks, lawyers, clubs, directories, foreign correspondents, etc., etc., etc. A specimen is enclosed. I am taking advantage of a wet Saturday in London to make lists and dictate circulars. . . .

Geoffrey wrote the following memorandum of a talk with Lloyd George on August 30th, 1917:

> An hour's talk with Lloyd George this afternoon. I had noted down various points for him, but he began at once with a general exposition of

his views on the war—not too cheerful. The Italians were doing well—perhaps very well, but in his opinion we were stuck in Flanders, while France was tired and Russia hopeless. He did not set up to be a professional strategist, but one could not be closely involved in war for three years without forming views, and his views were opposed to those of the military text-books. The plan of going for the enemy at his strongest point was all very well in a war of movement and of comparatively small armies; but this was virtually a siege, and in a siege one looked for the weakest spot. That spot was Austria or perhaps Turkey. The soldiers must judge of the details in that respect. He had always taken that view—at conferences in Rome, Paris, etc., but there was formidable opposition. We might once have done something in the Balkans. Now we should do better if we were effectively helping Italy with heavy guns and shells. He was going to have another talk with Henry Wilson, for whom he professed great admiration. So, incidentally, he did for Haig, commending especially his courage and optimism, but he complained that the war had produced no really great soldier.

So we came round to the future of parties. . . . I asked him what he foresaw in the immediate future. Was he getting together any organization for an electoral emergency? Did he anticipate a strong Opposition organization under Asquith? L.G. said that, so far as he himself was concerned, he didn't want either to relapse into the old Liberal Party (which would be very glad to get him) or to be left entirely with the old Unionists. He kept recurring to the fate of Chamberlain,[1] who (according to L.G.) had placed himself in a false position when he joined the Conservatives and abandoned his old noncomformist backing. . . . His own view was that the old Unionist and Liberal Parties both contained elements with which it was impossible to work for reconstruction—the extreme teetotallers on one side, the rigid landlords and churchmen on the other. What he hoped to do was to get together soon a private meeting of some half-dozen friends from each of the old parties—say, his own friends and Lord Milner's—see whether they could agree upon a basis of reconstruction policy and, if not, then agree to carry on for the period of the war and part afterwards. He repeated that he had found nothing in Lord Milner's views to which he would not himself subscribe. . . .

Speaking of "war aims" L.G. expressed doubts of the wisdom of Asquith's recent categorical questions—were the Germans prepared to evacuate Belgium? He said he had always avoided it in his own speeches, lest the Germans should answer in the affirmative and do nothing else. He thought it a dangerous question (and the event seemed to prove his wisdom, for a fortnight later the Germans began to fly a great Belgian peace kite).

Geoffrey was with the B.E.F. in Flanders from October 23rd to October 29th, and most appropriately spent his birthday (October

[1] Joseph Chamberlain.

25th) at Framecourt "on the very field of Agincourt" five hundred and two years after that battle. The following letter to Langcliffe gives a summary of the week:

> . . . It was a thoroughly successful and useful little visit—hard work, rather—long and cold motoring and much crowded talks—but all most interesting and everyone as kind as possible. I made no attempt to see sights, except for one little run to the Messines Ridge, but managed to find all the people I wanted—Sir D.H. (Douglas Haig) and his Chief of Staff, Director of Operations, Intelligence, etc., both the Army Commanders—Plumer and Hubert Gough—and their people—Trenchard of the Flying Corps, Grigg, Simon Lovat and his foresters, Nash who directs transportation, Sir A. Lawley and the great hospitals in Boulogne, and, of course, our correspondents. . . . And the interruptions continue even on this side of the Channel. Our mechanics are even now in the cellar and I am waiting for the first gun! (There was an air-raid warning on October 29th.). . . .

On November 7th, Geoffrey wrote to the Bishop of Pretoria:

> They (those whom he met in France) were all in fine spirits—perhaps a little more so than the regimental officers, though there's not the slightest despondency anywhere. But the latter are inclined to resent the over-optimism of G.H.Q. about failing German *morale*, etc., and there are doubts of the wisdom (at this stage and with these numbers) of set-piece battles as against the trench-raid business. All are curiously aloof from all other phases of the war and hardly count, for instance, on America, which is going to be a tremendous factor sooner or later.
>
> Just as I left came the Italian *débâcle*, which has necessarily altered things greatly and at present for the worse. No one was to blame for it but the Italian troops themselves. . .
>
> However help had to be bundled off as quickly as possible and it's impossible yet to foresee the end of it. Meanwhile the whole thing has brought to a head L.G.'s old desire for an Allied General Staff—unimpeachable in theory, a possible source of friction in practice, and there are the usual makings of a row between him and the soldiers with the "old Gang". . . . And into this cauldron we have Northcliffe returning in a few days—hardly a pacific influence and probably more useful in America, where he's done very well.[1]
>
> . . . Philip (Kerr) becomes more and more indispensable to L.G. . . . I see very few people these days except on business or by accident. It's a

[1] Northcliffe undoubtedly did a good job as regards public relations, Press, etc., from his New York headquarters. He left the British representatives of the various Departments in Washington alone; he wisely left them to carry on their work without interference.

strenuous life and becomes more difficult as people's nerves wear thinner! Every blessing on you.

In November, the politicians were "whetting their knives for a crisis", but Geoffrey commented approvingly on the Prime Minister's handling of the situation. He also heard from Milner of the various difficulties which Lloyd George had to face and how he proposed to deal with them. Geoffrey gave much time to Americans and United States problems. He lunched with the Governor of Rhode Island, and with the Curzons to meet Colonel and Mrs. House (he had already met the former before the war). He had a long talk with Colonel House "settling channels of communication, etc.". On November 20th Geoffrey recorded a visit to "the P.M., full of beans after his historic Anglo-American Conference in Downing Street, but as difficult as ever to pin down to anything in particular".

Just when there was much political activity, Northcliffe arrived in London on November 12th from his successful mission in America. Lady Northcliffe and Geoffrey met him at Euston. Shortly after his return Northcliffe composed "a somewhat incoherent manifesto to the Prime Minister", which Geoffrey bowdlerized and improved, and during the following week there were frequent references to N.'s activities at the Headquarters of the British Mission to U.S.A. in Abingdon Street and elsewhere. At a Journalists' Luncheon given to Northcliffe on his return, Geoffrey, who was present, noted that Northcliffe delivered a "really admirable private discourse on affairs in America".

No death in 1917, apart from that of Aunt "Mag", affected Geoffrey more deeply than that of Sir Leander Starr Jameson: the passing of the "Doctor" was the removal of a bit of his own life in South Africa and brought back memories of all the early conflicts with the Boer leaders, and the gradually improving relations and increasing confidence between the two white races in which the "Doctor" had played so notable a part. On November 20th, Geoffrey . . . deeply concerned by news of the "Doctor's" illness, went round to see him, when he found him "in the afternoon as plucky and characteristic as ever".

A few days later he recorded in his diary:

Nov. 26. Jameson died at 2.15 in the afternoon. I was rather hopeless after his doctor's last report and the faithful Higg's message this morning. . . . I added a short leader. . . .

Nov. 27. Busy off and on with arrangements for a memorial service to the Doctor, working with his brother and Dougie (Malcolm) and Carnegie of St. Margaret's, which they chose. . . . We printed a picture of the tomb in the Matopos, which was to be the Doctor's last resting place.

If the newspaper reports of the Italian collapse were depressing, heartening communiqués about Allenby's Palestine Campaign were soon to cheer the Allies. Geoffrey was at All Souls on November 18th and his diary has this entry, "Chapel 8.45—and read the first lesson—most appropriate to Allenby's proceedings in Palestine!"[1] And twenty-four days later there were the joyful tidings of his entry into Jerusalem.

One of the most important events in the year from the standpoint of the Editor was the receipt of the famous letter from Lord Lansdowne, and Geoffrey's refusal to publish it in *The Times*; he "used to say in after years that his difference of opinion with Northcliffe over this matter was the sharpest they ever had";[2] Geoffrey's refusal was due to his conviction that if the letter were published at the very moment when the Supreme War Council began its session, it would, inevitably, lead to "very public discussions that should be avoided". What was more, almost certainly further letters on the subject would reach *The Times*, and the Editor would have to refuse to publish them as it would be embarrassing to print pleas for peace, before the Allies were ready with their own terms.

Geoffrey's account of the episode tells how on November 27th Lord Lansdowne handed him a letter which he hoped *The Times* would publish, dealing with war aims and the possibilities of peace. Geoffrey promised to discuss it the following day. He found it "a thoroughly mischievous production. . . . The general effect was an appeal for peace-making by some abatement of our war aims (as being proved by this time impracticable) and there were moreover some highly questionable suggestions of negotiations, e.g. over the well-worn and dishonest German demand for 'the freedom of the Seas'."

Geoffrey's objections to the letter were that it was

(1) calculated to suggest to the Allies (just assembled for the Paris Conference) a weakening in the strongest partner;

(2) certain to be used by the Germans as a tribute to their new conquests in Italy and their negotiations with the Russian Bolsheviks;

(3) likely to discredit Lord Lansdowne himself, especially as he had just been put forward by Massingham in *The Nation* as an appropriate Prime Minister in place of Lloyd George.

[1] First lesson Amos I *inter alia*: "The Lord will roar from Zion, and utter his voice from Jerusalem. . . . But I will send a fire on the wall of Gaza which shall devour the palaces thereof . . ." (verses 2 and 7).

[2] See *The History of "The Times"*, Vol. IV, Part I, p. 337.

When Geoffrey expressed these views, Lord Lansdowne alleged that Balfour and Hardinge would approve of the letter, though it emerged that neither of them had seen it, and that he had been discouraged "(presumably by A.J.B.) from expressing similar views at this stage in the House of Lords". Lord Lansdowne agreed to sleep over Geoffrey's comments.

Two days later on his journey north to Langcliffe Geoffrey found that the *Daily Telegraph* had published the Lansdowne letter.

On December 12th *The Times* contained a leading article, "The Lansdowne Letter—A Last Word", in which the paper finally went over the ground and explained the reasons why the letter had been refused. The leader pointed out again that the letter was offered to *The Times* by Lord Lansdowne within a few hours of the departure of the Prime Minister and the Foreign Secretary for Paris to attend a great Allied Conference. The fact that it had been published on November 29th (in the *Daily Telegraph*) could "only have strengthened the impression in Paris that the British Government knew and approved of the publication of the letter at so critical a moment, and must have formed a very serious embarrassment to them. . . ." "Our own objection to the letter, as we may now perhaps be allowed to say, was based as much upon its untimeliness as upon the unrepresentative character of its general appeal."

In December Geoffrey plunged into Irish affairs. He spent an afternoon discussing recent events with Londonderry "in bed in Park Lane" and the following morning was occupied with a talk to Horace Plunkett and R. J. H. Shaw on the prospects of the Irish Convention "which had come up against it".

On December 10th came the joyful news of the fall of Jerusalem, but shortly before Christmas Sir Eric Geddes "announced the loss of another North Sea convoy" and another day "an air-raid came before 7.00 and lasted till after 10.00—meaning complete paralysis of the mechanical staff". On December 20th Geoffrey listened to the P.M.'s "wind-up speech all the afternoon, and had tea and a talk with him in the House of Commons afterwards".

On December 28th Geoffrey wrote to Arthur Willert:

> . . . I gather that the future of the British Mission is being settled today—I mean whether Reading is to go out again or not. If in the end he refuses, I gather that Northcliffe is prepared to return, but that he is increasingly reluctant to do so. I have really seen extraordinarily little of him myself.[1] He has paid one visit to this office in the last couple of months and is apparently absorbed for the most part in the work of the

[1] Proof that the Editor was, in 1917, largely left by Northcliffe to do his job in his own way.

British Mission at this end. Just at the moment he is showering bouquets upon *The Times* and its staff and we are well content to be left alone. My own impression is that, after two or three months in England, he will probably do more useful work on your side, but I think he has a genuine passion to be in the thick of things over here and he is the victim of all kinds of people who tell him that his presence is indispensable. It is quite clear that we shall be in a poor way unless America gets into the war both thoroughly and quickly. If anyone can assist that process, as I believe Northcliffe can, there is no more vital piece of work.

XIV

1918—THE YEAR OF VICTORY

ON New Year's Day, 1918, Geoffrey wrote thus to the Bishop of Pretoria:

. . . It is New Year's Day; I have worked all through Christmas (never again may I spend another Christmas Day in composing leading articles!); I am beginning to feel thoroughly jaded and irritable so I am off at dawn tomorrow morning for four or five days on my native hills. Otherwise, and in general, I am really wonderfully fit, and the paper has been running very smoothly and successfully in spite of its terrible depletion of staff. (We have sent over 500 men from this Office to the Colours by this time—that is—more than the total number employed at the beginning of the war); the Editorial Staff has contributed something like forty officers, and we have accumulated quite a nice sprinkling of "Mentions", etc., for real good work. Grigg and my former Secretary, Barrington-Ward, both appear in the new list of D.S.O.s tomorrow morning.

Northcliffe, as you know, came back from America in November and seems to have practically made up his mind that he will not go back again. *But I have seen next to nothing of him.*[1] He is still very largely absorbed in the work of the British Mission and means, I think, to go on running it from this end. Fortunately, he seems quite happy about the conduct of the paper, for which I am grateful.

You ask me about labour. It is a large question, and you should read in particular the reports in *The Times* of an important conference held last Friday and Saturday. You will find a good deal in the speeches to disturb you, but I am inclined on the whole, and in spite of everything, to believe that the labour situation is really more satisfactory than it has been for some time. I may be quite wrong, but this is my instinct. If I had to define it, I should say that, as the result of a good deal of blowing off of steam, labour was settling down to some fairly sound fundamental war aims mixed up with a good deal of rather washy idealism, and that

[1] My italics.—E. W.

they were on the whole in closer sympathy with the Government. Lloyd George had a very frank talk with them in private after the Conference, and they all seem to have parted the best of friends. I am pretty sure too, though they will not admit it, that the Russian Revolution has had a very steadying effect upon them. You talk of the possible need for "real radical changes". I wonder if you realize how radical are the changes effected already, and what a tremendous revolution is involved, for instance, in the new Franchise Bill, which passed the House of Commons almost by common consent.

. . . Undoubtedly the surprise attack after the great initial successes at Cambrai was a thoroughly "regrettable incident". London was ringing with it—not (as the Higher Command would have us believe) from mere revulsion of popular uninformed opinion, but from the unanimous verdict of officers of all ranks returning from the Front. Your highly-placed soldier with his well-disciplined forces around him is sometimes apt to forget that a real blunder cannot be concealed so long as men are allowed to come home on leave. . . .

By the way, both Lawley girls appear in the *Gazette* tonight with the Royal Red Cross, and richly they deserve it. They have been nursing in France with hardly a break from the beginning, doing almost inconceivable hours at a stretch and living in great discomfort. I only wish these great out-pourings of honours could be limited to people of that kind. . . .

Geoffrey wrote the following letter to his Aunt (February 14th):

. . . I'm getting terribly bewildered with all my correspondence and normal affairs owing to these damnable squabbles and intrigues in high places. Partly because the P.M. is really seedy, and partly because so many of his colleagues are jelly-fish, they are contriving to mishandle a very strong case. Poor Lord Milner is bearing the whole burden of it and it is taking years off both of our lives! Yesterday, for instance, everything[1] was apparently settled at four o'clock and I wrote an "able exposition" of it. By six the whole business was hung up again and I set to again, more dead than alive, to explain how it *ought* to be settled! About nine I took Lord Milner to dine at the Travellers' and we reflected on all the myths and humbugs and intrigues that are round about. We should have won the war some time ago if there were about half a dozen Lord Milners to form a Cabinet—however, I think things should really straighten themselves out today. . . .

During the early months of 1918, Milner and his group were giving much thought to the problems of the general direction of the

[1] On February 11th, an article by Repington appeared in the *Morning Post* attacking the Prime Minister and Sir Henry Wilson in connection with the Versailles decisions to ensure liaison between the Allies. A debate took place in the House of Commons and the Versailles organization was held up owing to these squabbles.

war effort. True, their battle for a small Cabinet had been won with the accession to power of Lloyd George a year before, or rather with the direction of the war being placed mainly in the hands of two men, who differed profoundly both outwardly and psychologically—the Prime Minister and Milner.

On one occasion Northcliffe compared Lloyd George to a "dishevelled conjurer", an apt and amusing description. But magician though he may have been, and certainly a major factor in organizing final victory, even the Prime Minister could not produce out of his hat the "rabbits" required by the Allies in the early months of the year. A small Cabinet—and the very effective L.G.-Milner combination, so suited to the circumstances, combining as it did the real patriotism, Celtic fire, flair and buoyancy of the Prime Minister, with his partner's steadiness, force of character, clear-sightedness, great powers of concentration and long experience of administration—could not bring about victory till there was real unity of direction of the Allied Forces in France. This was one of the subjects to which all concerned with winning the war were giving thought. Not only the War Cabinet but the "Ginger Group" knew that something drastic would have to be done to avoid the repetition of the events which had occurred after the initial successes at Cambrai.

Public opinion in England was gradually dividing itself between growing criticism of the military conduct of the war and growing distrust of the Government.

The new Session of Parliament opened on February 14th and by the 16th Robertson had resigned and Wilson had been appointed Chief of the General Staff. Geoffrey commented:

> The whole business strikes me as a sound and even inevitable policy. . . . Lloyd George seems to have arrived at it largely by instinct as he generally does. He would certainly have conceded some vital points in it, especially during his illness, if Lord Milner, who arrived at the same conclusions by reason, had not held up his hands. . . .

The diary of 1918 had opened with the following entry, which showed that Geoffrey and the "Ginger Group" were in close touch with the Prime Minister:

> *Jan. 1.* . . . And at night an interesting little dinner with the Prime Minister in Downing Street (in the little panelled room used by Mr. Gladstone). Only Lord Milner, Fred Oliver, and Philip Kerr—a gathering arranged for the purpose of pressing on L.G. the need for certain changes of personnel.

At this time Geoffrey certainly was very appreciative of the Prime Minister's drive and his general outlook on the war.

Quite apart from the all important question of the Allied High Command there were many other subjects to occupy Geoffrey's attention. There was, for example, the curious and worsening state of affairs in Russia, and, with his keen sense of humour—always alive—he records a visit "to my church in the Square, where the 'Gloomy Dean' preached appropriately enough on Russian pessimism". Geoffrey discussed the deadlock in the Engineering Trade Union with J. H. Thomas; rejoiced in the fall of Jericho; recorded "The final collapse of the Bolshevists—Germany still invading Russia amid their frantic squeals". In early March the "Ginger Group" met for dinner at Carson's; in addition to the usual members, there were present Amery (just back from Palestine), Philip Kerr, and Austen Chamberlain.

There are more references to Northcliffe in Geoffrey's papers in 1918 than in any previous year. 1917, with the pleasanter atmosphere, due mainly to Northcliffe's long absence in America and his absorption in the work of the War Mission, was the period of calm before the final storm; certainly neither of the two men, during the first part of the year, could have realized whither their constant differences in outlook were leading them. In January, Geoffrey lunched with the Northcliffes "as of old" and he visited N. "in his new official palace, Crewe House"—the headquarters of the Department of Propaganda in Enemy Countries. At the end of February Northcliffe "made a rare appearance" at Printing House Square. Earlier in the month Geoffrey wrote to Lord Knutsford (Sydney Holland, Chairman of the London Hospital), and friend of the Northcliffes:

> My dear Sydney,
>
> . . . But what amazed me most about this anti-Northcliffe campaign is the stupidity of all its authors in giving their *bête noire* so tremendous an advertisement. Poor dear St. Loe Strachey solemnly writes an article last week (in the *Spectator*) warning the country against "a Northcliffe ministry". This week he gravely publishes letters discussing the likelihood of such an event. If he had an ounce of common sense, he would realize that Northcliffe has neither the desire nor the power to form a ministry, but that this kind of pompous controversy gives him precisely the position which he enjoys and which Strachey detests.
>
> I think that some day I must write a book about the real Northcliffe and the Northcliffe myth. Not even the people who know him best (like Strachey, for instance, who has lived alongside him at Guildford for years) seem to realize that there was never a less far-sighted schemer than Northcliffe in the history of the world. His strongest characteristic,

and the secret of his success, is that he is so extraordinarily sensitive to the mood of the moment. No one was ever less like a Machiavelli. What he really is, is a master of publicity, and that enables him to associate himself, and to be associated by others, with political movements and events with which in nine cases out of ten he has hardly the remotest connection. If Lloyd George had been wise, he would have asked him to undertake the whole business of foreign propaganda for the nation, and disregarded the jealousy of every other newspaper in the country. He could have justified his choice up to the hilt in that connection. No one would have done it better. . . .

The following two paragraphs appeared in the *Daily News*, and Geoffrey's comments on them (February 25th) show how much he disliked the constant references to *The Times*, as if it were merely a more expensive *Daily Mail*; and it is also of great importance in showing what a small amount of time Northcliffe was devoting to the editorial side of *The Times*.

Lord Northcliffe on Jericho (*Daily News*, February 25, 1918):

What, I wonder, is the secret of the fascination Bartimaeus exerts on Lord Northcliffe? On Friday the news of the capture of Jericho came through. On Saturday the *Daily Mail* devoted its first leader to Jericho. The writer began at the Book of Joshua, worked through the campaigns of the Jews, and the incident of Rahab, touched on the fall of the walls of the city, and reached his climax at the point when, "centuries later, in the fullness of time, the blind Bartimaeus waited patiently at the gate the coming of One Who should deliver him".

Simultaneously *The Times* leader writer was at work on the same theme, evidently with a more efficient concordance at his elbow. He, too, began with Joshua (of whom he observed that he was the son of Nun), got in the Amorites and the Canaanites, settled Rahab's business, fetched Zedekiah and Nebuchadnezzar into the picture, and so, as Mr. Pepys would say, to Bartimaeus. The *Evening News* on Friday, strangely enough, gave Bartimaeus a complete go-by, though it offered us Hiel and Segub, and various other compensations. Is Lord Northcliffe taking holy orders?

Geoffrey's comments (February 25th, 1918) under the general heading, "Campaign Against *The Times*—1918":

This cutting from the *Daily News* of today is a typical example of the ceaseless campaign which is waged against *The Times*—the object being to suggest that it is a larger edition of the *Daily Mail* and a mere item in the detested "Northcliffe Press".

I suppose that ninety per cent (at least) of the newspapers of England devoted their leaders on Saturday to the Fall of Jericho and that fifty per cent (at least) quoted Joshua, Rahab, Bartimaeus, etc. Our own admirable article was written by X. after discussion with me and the study of a concordance. I doubt whether he knows Northcliffe by sight. Certainly Northcliffe (who was probably in the country) hadn't a notion of X.'s subject or of what he was saying about it. There was no real similarity whatever with the *Daily Mail*, which I have looked up, for the latter was mainly a tirade against "our unimaginative methods" of publicity—But the impression of intimate association is spread.

I have often thought lately what a much better case could be made for the common inspiration of *The Times* with newspapers where no connection is ever suspected, e.g. on some subjects the *Morning Post* and on others the *Manchester Guardian* and the *Daily Chronicle*—morning after morning I have found identical arguments and even identical phrases, as of course is inevitable when writers and editors with the same general point of view come to deal on the spur of the moment with the same subjects. No notice is taken of these coincidences. The truth is that in nine cases out of ten both the subjects chosen and the method of treatment in *The Times* and the *Daily Mail* are as opposite as the poles.

But the idea is fostered, not only by Northcliffe's enemies, but by Northcliffe himself with unremitting diligence. He has visited *The Times*, I think, exactly twice since last May—a matter of eight months. He has hardly criticized the conduct of the paper (one of his few criticisms, made on his return from Paris, was that I ought to have published Lord Lansdowne's letter—to which, as we were told by a shrieking chorus, "Northcliffe had refused publication"!). He has hardly ever made a suggestion, and most of his telephone messages have been to ask for news from somewhere in the depths of the country. But his correspondence is largely conducted on *The Times* notepaper and his conversation, especially to American visitors, is that of Editor, leader-writer and proprietor in one. I have no objection to this shadow so long as the substance is sound, and am grateful for his actual confidence and aloofness, but the prevalent impression is not good for *The Times*. Nor is it really good for his own reputation, in which the record of really astonishing achievements in earlier life is being forgotten in the later atmosphere of bluff. Too many people know, for instance, that the famous attack on Kitchener in the *Daily Mail* was delivered after K. was "down and out" and really succeeded only in rehabilitating him for another year. A growing number know that there is not a scrap of foundation for the popular belief in a Northcliffe-Lloyd George intrigue to dethrone Asquith, that N. and L.G. were not in fact on speaking terms for months before that crisis, and that the *Daily Mail* barrage against the "Old Gang" began *after*, not before, the actual offensive. The public is not too careful about dates, and a master of publicity, which Northcliffe certainly is, can always associate himself prominently with the *fait accompli*.

As for N.'s enemies, their hatred of him has become an obsession which entirely blinds them to the fact that in perpetually talking about him, they are giving him precisely the advertisement which is the breath of his nostrils. . . . The simple truth, of course, is that reputations are not ultimately made in this way. They depend on the judgment of those with whom you work, and N. has actually *lost* ground by emerging from anonymous mystery into this glare of publicity—in many ways—his own legitimate ways as a newspaper expert—he has done wonders for *The Times*, but I doubt whether his personal credit stands as high as when he first became associated with it.

The great German Push began on March 21st and during the next ten days the Allies went through one of the most anxious periods in the war. The Germans outnumbered them two to one, and advanced on the Somme at a terrific pace. On March 24th Lord Milner left for Versailles, and returned to London two days later, having made on his own initiative the momentous decision that General Foch should be entrusted with the Supreme Command of the Allied Forces on the Western Front.

Naturally the great changes in the supreme direction of the war did not show results immediately. There were still plenty of anxious days to live through. On April 11th there was the comment "the battle going none too well". On April 12th "the news was very black and a Zepp-raid reported (It went across to Lancashire). Haig issued rather an alarming Order of the Day".[1] In late March there had been a note that "there was trouble from N.'s spasms". At Printing House Square on April 18th Geoffrey wrote "rather a hectic day—N. ramping on the telephone from the sea, though I calmed him with some serious considerations about the office". Geoffrey must have been feeling the difficulties of his relations with Northcliffe acutely, because on April 19th he wrote, "Brumwell talked severely to me on the question of my remaining in P.H.S. at all costs". There certainly must have been fears at the office that the Editor might feel that he could not continue under the proprietorship of Northcliffe.

On April 20th Milner ceased to be a member of the War Cabinet because he was sworn in as Secretary of State for War[2] on that day and *The Times* expressed the hope that the change would not be dearly bought "at the price of his absence from the Central Council of Government", although from every other point of view the paper held it to be an admirable thing that Milner should go to the War Office.

[1] Every position must be held to the last man; there must be no retirement. With our backs to the wall, and believing in the justice of our cause, each one of us must fight *on* to the end.

[2] Lord Derby had been Secretary for War 1916–18.

On April 20th Geoffrey wrote: "Up early and down to Broadstairs by 9 train to see N. I hadn't seen him for ages and found him still bad with bronchitis but otherwise better. We walked and talked—there was a gleam of sun—off and on all day till 5 when I came back. . . . N. obviously up against L.G., who'd evidently been dodging him . . . as usual, very much in earnest about the war and full of ideas."

On April 22nd Geoffrey was host for the Monday dinner, this time at the Athenaeum—"a full gathering, to which the P.M. asked himself at the last moment. It was a little awkward, but he talked well and straight about Ireland. I arranged it thus, ten in all:

Waldorf Astor	
Lord Milner	Carson
Bob Brand	Philip Kerr
Amery	Fred Oliver
Henry Wilson	The P.M.
G.D."	

In referring to the occasion in a letter to Langcliffe he said, "it became rather a serious affair and I think did a certain amount of good in getting L.G. and Carson nearer together".

St. George's Day supplied news of the splendid raid on Zeebrugge, which "filled the paper" that night. Other events in April included the resignation from the position of Air Minister by Rothermere, who had become involved in a controversy with General Trenchard: and further discussions on the eternal Irish question. In May there are various references to meetings with the Prime Minister; on the 3rd there was a dinner at No. 10 Downing Street with Lloyd George, Milner, F. S. Oliver and Philip Kerr, when the conversation was about Ireland. The following day a vast "Moot" assembled at Cliveden for "a more or less formal discussion on Lionel's (Curtis's) work in India" (whence he had just returned), which subsequently resulted in the introduction of Diarchy.

From the continued strain of his work Geoffrey escaped to Oxford for a "17-mile trudge" with Bridgeman to Dorchester (Oxfordshire) and Didcot. Throughout most of his working life he never lost his zest for long tramps, and he took refuge in violent exercise when office worries were becoming too invading. Of a Saturday in June spent with Northcliffe he wrote: "Set off 9.50 for Oxford and Lechlade to visit N. in his fishing retreat—a glorious summer's day in which we loafed by the river and through wonderful Gloucestershire villages. N. still bad, I thought, with his throat, though he professed himself full of energy and interest." In July Geoffrey's references to Northcliffe on three consecutive days were: "N. came and took me for a walk in the Park—very amiable and mild"; "N. very troublesome"; "a visit to N. at Crewe House in the morning. I thought him rather unbalanced and anxious to assert himself". Northcliffe's megalomania was evidently increasing, for on August 5th Geoffrey wrote, ". . . N. had had a real 'beano' in the paper—a full page advertisement (thinly disguised as an appeal for War Bonds) and he and his brethren cropping up in every direction! . . ."

If Geoffrey was primarily interested in the Empire he nevertheless fully realized that as a result of the war the world was entering upon a new phase in international relations. On August 1st *The Times* published a leader with the heading "A Patriotic Programme", showing that Unionists "had no monopoly of resolution" and that the League of Nations did not exclude patriotism—a problem which, we may add, has been occupying the minds of many political thinkers ever since.

During the latter half of the year there are fewer references to meetings with Lloyd George than in the previous months. True, he had a talk with the Prime Minister in July about propaganda by aeroplane; in October he lunched intimately with him and Philip Kerr; in November, on one occasion he met the P.M. quite by accident in Downing Street, and on November 15th he took an American journalist to lunch with him (the P.M.) and Lord Reading. On 26th September the Editor sent L.G. a memorandum on the case for an early General Election:

> The case for an early General Election seems to me to be greatly strengthened by recent Labour troubles, which to an increasing extent are said to be due to sheer Bolshevism and not to any genuine industrial grievance. It may be said that this factor adds to the element of risk which is inseparable from any general election at such a time and under such incalculable conditions. The answer, I think, is that this risk will certainly increase the longer an appeal to the country is postponed. You cannot avert an election for ever. You cannot even be certain of averting it till after the war. I put first and foremost among the arguments for having it *soon* the necessity for re-establishing the authority of Parliament against attempts to "hold up" the country by unconstitutional methods. . . .
>
> I think that there is no doubt that at this moment the Government would obtain a very substantial majority, and that in that case it would be in a far stronger moral position than it is today. It ought, of course, to take advantage of this to strengthen its own *personnel*, for some of its Members are misfits and some of them are inevitably tired. It seems to me to be a moot point whether at this late stage the Government should be reconstituted before or after an appeal to the country. A month or two ago I should have had no doubt whatever about the wisdom of the

former course, but there are obvious electoral disadvantages in a process of *dégommage* on the very eve of an election. In any case I think that the Prime Minister should make up his own mind in advance as to the best War Government he can form, and make it perfectly clear to all his colleagues that he intends to claim a free hand to reconstruct. . . .

It was not till the end of September that the diary assumes a really optimistic tone when good news was arriving from all quarters. On September 23rd Geoffrey records, "A wonderful week of victories everywhere—Allenby's in Palestine daily growing, Serbs and Allies pressing on from Salonika, and towards the end another great Franco-Italian push west of Verdun". Early in October Geoffrey spent the week-end with Northcliffe at Elmwood, in Kent, where relations were quite amicable, and where Geoffrey, the non-golfer, quite enjoyed a game in which he and Northcliffe's golfing instructor, Sandy Thompson, defeated Northcliffe and Steed. This must have been one of the last friendly meetings with Northcliffe.

From Wednesday, October 16th, to Wednesday, October 23rd, Geoffrey was in Flanders with the B.E.F. visiting Advanced G.H.Q., Cambrai, with the Fourth Army, Bruges, Ypres, and finally Wimereux. In a letter of October 18th to George Freeman, who acted as his deputy at Printing House Square, Geoffrey writes:

. . . They have little doubt here that the *Boche* will sue for an armistice and swallow what they regard as terms of severity. Foch, Sir Douglas Haig and Clemenceau are said to be agreed about them and the Government at home are to consider them tomorrow. My impression is that the soldiers' terms are likely to be easier for the Germans than those of their Governments'. There is a very strong feeling here (which, as you know, I've always shared) against the "No peace with the Hohenzollerns" cry. The soldiers' view is that you must have *a Government and not a revolution*, on which to impose terms, while I feel strongly that Wilson's concentration on it is dangerous because the Germans might concede it in return for more practical advantages. Everyone is agreed that an armistice will be *final*. Whatever might be the case at home, the French could never be got going again. And, by the way, they all agree that Foch's greatest achievement is not so much his "unified strategy" as that *he got the French to fight again* after a very bad reaction.

The Americans are badly stuck owing to inexperience and disorganization, no control of traffic, congestion of supplies, food not getting up, cookers looted on the road, etc. The impression here is that, while the material is magnificent, and the achievement of divisions, e.g. two here with the British, very good indeed, it would take another eighteen months to make an *American Army*. They feel, as you know, that the recent work of the British Army is not sufficiently understood by the Press at home. . . . But there is no doubt at all that the present situation is mainly a *British* triumph. This Cambrai bulge, from which I am writing, is almost wholly British, and Plumer has been the backbone of the Belgian bulge in the North. . . .

On the day after his return from France, Geoffrey lunched alone with Henry Wilson "to discuss his terms of armistice". On October 28th the news of the night was of Austria's virtual surrender, and on October 31st official confirmation came of Turkey's surrender. The diary entries for these ten wonderful days follow:

Nov. 6. Big events moving fast. The Allied memorandum to Wilson came out in the morning, with his covering note to the Germans, followed by the news that a German delegation had started for Foch. . . .

Nov. 7. Day of suspense, German delegates finding some difficulty in getting through. A Reuter rumour that they had signed got all over London about 4 but was promptly withdrawn. Tiresome Northcliffe debate in the Commons.

Nov. 8. Foch met Germans 11 a.m. and gave them 72 hours. Meanwhile Americans take Sedan.

Nov. 9. . . . And a great banquet in the evening—a notable triumph for L.G.—who was able to announce that William had abdicated, though there was no news yet of armistice.

Nov. 11. I heard from my office soon after 10 that the Armistice was signed at 5 a.m.—to begin at 11. I went out, just as the guns began to proclaim it, and the crowds ran to Downing Street and especially to the Palace where there was an amazing scene. A wonderful day altogether, though it was dark and drizzly later which moderated the "maffick". Frank Cobb and Lord Milner lunched with me—a most satisfactory talk and I dined with Waldorf, Carson, Fred Oliver and Amery.

Nov. 12. N. back from Paris. He asked me to come for a walk and I strolled with him for half an hour, discoursing on indifferent topics. Then a talk with Townshend of Kut, who was wilder than ever, and (quite by accident) a meeting with the P.M. in Downing Street. . . . Among other things I wrote a little leader on the King's obvious and amazing popularity. Dinner with Lionel Phillips and others at the Ritz and a difficult struggle back to the office through the maffickers.

Nov. 13. . . . Crowd still merry-making by night with unabated enthusiasm.

Nov. 14. . . . on to a great Labour Demonstration at the Albert Hall—pretty harmless though it had a Bolshevist element. N. arrived—apparently much incensed by my very uninteresting leader—said he'd served notice on L.G. that he could no longer support him. How can *The Times* keep pace with these personal squabbles.

Apart from the heavy task of guiding *The Times* during these momentous weeks—writing frequent leaders himself—in November he wrote fourteen leading articles in seventeen days—relations with Northcliffe were becoming increasingly difficult as will be seen by the following extracts from the diary:

Nov. 15. More talk with N.—nothing to get hold of—but his attitude was partly explained by an incoherent letter from Rothermere which reached L.G. during lunch[1] and was passed across for me to see.

Nov. 17. Rather a harassed day—beginning with a message from Mr. Davy[2] at Broadstairs asking me to remember that *The Times* "was regarded as Lord N.'s personal voice in every quarter of the world", and ending in a successful refusal to have my leaders edited over the telephone. How can one work under these conditions?

Nov. 18. More or less peaceful day after the storm and an effusive bulletin from N. about my conduct of the paper! What a man!

Nov. 20. . . . a talk with N. about provision for the Peace Conference. He seemed very anxious to justify himself. . . .

Nov. 26. . . . On to P.H.S. where my days and nights are spent in ceaseless worry and vigilance. Dined with Smuts . . . an interesting talk.

Nov. 28. . . . Then to the office, where in the course of the afternoon I had a long and perfectly reasonable talk with N. on all kinds of subjects concerned with the future of the paper.

Nov. 29. . . . N. was as usual crabbing *The Times* and I had further trouble on the telephone on returning from a cheery dinner with Borden and some of his Canadians at Claridges.

Dec. 13. Rather a weary day. . . . N. was at the office in the afternoon and I had some disconnected talk with him. He was condemning the sudden turn-over of the Beaverbrook and Rothermere papers to L.G. and extolling the sobriety of the working man—with both of which sentiments I heartily agreed.

Dec. 18. Some rather querulous messages from N. in Paris. I devoted myself mainly to seeing that *The Times* gave a good welcome to Haig and his generals on their return tomorrow.

Dec. 27. . . . N. there (P.H.S.) in rather evil and petulant mood, which it is to be hoped was mollified later by his inclusion in a State Banquet to the President at Buckingham Palace.

The following letters were exchanged between Geoffrey and Dr. Furse.

From the Bishop:

[1] Geoffrey had been lunching with the Prime Minister and Lord Reading.
[2] Northcliffe's private secretary.

November 5th, 1918.

. . . I do hope you've got back your sleep. . . . I don't wonder it deserted you. My wonder all along is how you've managed to keep going all these four years past. To be Editor of *The Times* would be bad enough. To be so from 1914–1918 far worse.—To be so with N. as Chairman of Directors with the *Daily Mail* constantly getting you into the soup seems to me to be beyond human endurance. But I think you must have had some cause for thankfulness. When history is written *The Times* will come out of it all very finely. . . .

Geoffrey wrote from Langcliffe in reply:

December 23rd, 1918.

Your letter of November 5 turned up here yesterday and for once I have a chance to write to you in comparative peace. Heavens, what these last few weeks have been! Much the worst time I've ever known in spite of the glorious victory, and I've been very near the breaking-point once or twice—both physically and professionally!

If you hear, one of these fine days, that I've abandoned *The Times* you'll know that it's not the result of sudden pique but of a deliberate and growing sense that I can't carry it on under the present conditions as it ought to be carried on. I had a pretty stiff struggle during the election campaign, when N., who had set his heart on being "Peace Delegate" (why should he?), suddenly realized that L.G. wasn't taking any and began to try and torpedo him. We had some plain words on that subject and I bolted for a breath of air last week, while N. departed for Paris and began running Wilson against L.G. from there, crabbing all the British preparations and indulging in an orgy of self-advertisement. I never try to interfere with the paper when I'm away, but I foresee more rows when I get back, and I'm not sure that it isn't more honest to have no more association *at all* with a man whom at heart I regard as such a fraud!

However, it's no good anticipating troubles and I've had 2 years of comparative freedom, which have not been unimportant. I really shudder to think of the possible consequences of a megalomaniac, plus a personal quarrel with the Government, before the war was over! The Milner affair was part and parcel of the same story, but I needn't go into all that now.

My Christmas is rather a sombre affair—only an old Aunt living here now and she quite unable to get or keep any servants! My old nurse and her maid constitute the whole establishment at the moment! However, there's always a good deal to be done out of doors and we shall get the thing into orderly shape by degrees. I'm selling all the outlying land I can to try and pay Death Duties and have already turned a deficit into a balance, which is rather fun. I'm beginning to agree with George

Wyndham who held that public affairs were far less entertaining than local business and chiefly valuable as a training for it!

On December 28th[1] Geoffrey recorded the overwhelming victory at the Polls for Lloyd George. Every Liberal leader and every Pacifist Labourite was swept away. He saw the old year out at Printing House Square as usual "to the sound of a great clash of metal in the composing-room and the strains of revellers in St. Paul's Churchyard".

[1] The polling in the General Election took place on December 14th but the results were not declared until December 28th, as time had to be allowed for the collection of the ballot papers of the men on the Western Front who had voted by post.

XV

BREACH WITH NORTHCLIFFE

FEBRUARY 18th, 1919, may be regarded as the actual date of Geoffrey's resignation from the editorship of *The Times*; on that day he sent his formal letter of withdrawal to Mr. John Walter, the Chairman of the Board. From the end of January a study of the documents shows that nothing short of a miracle could have prevented the final rupture between Geoffrey and Northcliffe. It has been suggested in *The History of "The Times"*[1] that "it is curious that the Editor did not decide, after seeing Steed on the 19th (January), to go south to see Northcliffe. That he did not do so can only be because he felt unable to make up his mind what to say to him". This is no doubt true, but surely the fundamental fact, as we have seen from his letter to Bishop Furse of December 23rd and from his entries in the diary, is that he had completely lost confidence in Northcliffe, whom in the early years of their association he had regarded with affection, but now no longer trusted, and termed a "fraud"; he found Northcliffe's megalomania beyond endurance, knowing as he did the inside story of Lloyd George's access to supreme power. He was not prepared to serve as a cipher in a newspaper combine in which the voice of the proprietor alone counted. He was not craving for recognition of the part he had played in preserving the great traditions of the independence and the integrity of *The Times*. Much as he appreciated being Editor of the paper, there were lengths beyond which he would not go. During many of the most anxious moments of the war he had been Editor of *The Times* as completely as either Delane or Buckle. Any curtailment of liberty in future would therefore be intolerable. No one deplored his going more than Lady Northcliffe and she did her utmost to prevent Northcliffe from making the rupture final, but to no avail.

From the first Geoffrey had kept in mind Buckle's wise and friendly exhortation:

[1] Vol. IV, Part I, p. 463.

I have no doubt you will gradually and insensibly get into the habit of regarding all public questions, not from your own personal point of view, but from an impersonal *Times* standpoint. "What ought *The Times*, with its history and traditions, to say about this?" has always been in my mind. So is the continuity preserved, which, in spite of the old stories about Delane and his weathercock policy, is I think essential to the interests of *The Times* in the present day. . . .

Buckle,[1] very wisely, gave a specific warning; he foresaw the inevitability of the very situation, which did in fact arise: "Try your best to keep *The Times* clear of special *Daily Mail* hobbies and policies. I fear you will not be able to do so wholly, I know you will agree with me on the extreme importance of giving the lie to the taunt about a twopenny halfpenny *Daily Mail*." Geoffrey knew in his heart of hearts that he had consistently worked for that very object. Among the great quantity of letters he received when his retirement became known—and no editor can ever have received a more remarkable tribute to his work, both from the members of the staff of *The Times*, past and present, as well as from the public at large—none can have given him greater pleasure than this one from his predecessor, from 62, Oakley Street (February 24th, 1919):

Private

My dear Dawson,

I didn't say to you half of what was in my mind. I think that your Editorship of the paper throughout the Great War, with the permanent necessity of fighting on two fronts—for your country and for the dignity of the paper—has been a magnificent performance; and the manner in which throughout you have established a clear distinction between *The Times* and the other papers having the same chief Proprietor, has been beyond praise. Northcliffe has never realized the vital importance to *The Times* of its verdict being generally regarded as a corporate and not a personal pronouncement—not the opinion of an individual, even in Delane's greatest days, but of what Kinglake perhaps absurdly, but with an appreciation of underlying truth, called a company. You have, I feel sure, felt as I did, that in editing *The Times*, it was not so much important to emphasize what you as an individual thought but what ought to be the view of that great impersonal organ *The Times*. It will be your steady satisfaction, in after years, to remember that, in the most difficult circumstances, you held the banner of an independent corporate conscience aloft, and made all but the groundlings, who ignorantly or maliciously shriek "Northcliffe press", recognize it. So far as I can gather, the circumstances of your resignation are entirely in your favour and if

[1] Compare p. 83 *supra*.

he challenges . . . (?) you will emerge triumphantly. But, for the sake of the paper, I hope he will take it lying down. . . .

What I fear, in the interest of the paper, is that all the "old gang", your friends and mine, will follow you into retirement. Richmond, Flanagan, Shadwell, Freeman—will any of them remain? And, if they don't, will the tradition go on? . . .

Yours with full sympathy,

G. E. Buckle.

P.S. Please forgive bed-scrawl.[1]

A few days after the final resignation Geoffrey wrote a careful account of the events which led to it. The statement began with this general survey:

In February 1919 I resigned the Editorship of *The Times*, and, since it is not a position to be abandoned lightly or without many regrets, I am putting together at once some notes and correspondence of the previous three months in explanation of the change. It was due wholly to my growing conviction that it had become impossible to conduct *The Times* well—a sufficiently difficult business in itself—under the strain of incessant complaints from Lord Northcliffe, and that these complaints were inspired at bottom by personal vanity and the intention to use the paper for his own political aggrandisement.

To say that it was a "difference over policy"—the common ground of parting between Proprietors and Editors—would in this case be misleading. Certainly I should find it exceedingly difficult to define Lord Northcliffe's public policy during the last few months. Most of my efforts to discover it ended in complete agreement over the unimpeachable platitudes with which he always eluded any definite point. But I found myself more and more opposed to all his methods and to the private ambitions which seemed to lie behind them. Beyond telling me much earlier, on two different occasions, that he hoped to make such a position for himself as to be a British Plenipotentiary at the Peace Conference, he never confided any of his ambitions to me, and I paid no more attention to these remarks at the time than I did to many other of his very wild predictions about the war. It is clear enough now, however, that the idea was always in his mind, that it explains some incidents which are otherwise inexplicable, and that its final rejection by the Prime Minister was the origin of his attitude during the General Election and afterwards.

Our relations had sometimes been difficult before, and on one or two occasions nearer the beginning of the war I had seriously considered

[1] Buckle's letter was written in pencil from his bed. Permission to use this letter has been kindly given by his son, Mr. G. W. Buckle.

(but never hinted at) resignation.[1] What always stopped me in those days was the shaky position of *The Times* (due largely to its much exaggerated association with the *Daily Mail*) and the feeling that it was essential to make the best of it at such a crisis. After that the course became easier. There was no difference between us about any of the main features in the policy of *The Times*. Lord Northcliffe became, for instance, an enthusiastic supporter of the change of Government in December 1916, though he had little or nothing (contrary to the popular belief) to do with bringing it about and was not in fact on speaking terms with Mr. Lloyd George for several months before it occurred. In the summer of 1917 he went on a special mission to America, leaving no instructions whatever behind him so far as *The Times* was concerned. Nor did he once make any comment on its conduct while he was away. There was a brief explosion when he returned in the shape of an open letter to the Prime Minister; but I was not involved in it, and the following spring and summer brought another long period of relief while Lord Northcliffe was fishing in Gloucestershire and nominally superintending a Propaganda Department at Crewe House. The trouble began when these miscellaneous activities began to peter out, though they too were used to an increasing extent, as he afterwards wished to use *The Times*, for the purpose of establishing a political position for himself.

The following notes (as already indicated) were made in diary form at intervals between November and March and are transcribed exactly as they were written at the time. They date from a violent attack on Lord Milner in the *Daily Mail*, which first made me suspect a deliberate policy of overpowering the Prime Minister by discrediting his most disinterested colleagues.

It is eminently suitable that Geoffrey's story should have been begun on All Souls' Day, 1918, within a week of his return from the visit to France. While he was with the B.E.F. Northcliffe had "descended on P.H.S." and had insisted that his statement of peace terms—as a matter of fact written by Steed and "quite unimpeachable"—be published "with immense prominence and a commendatory leader". The same evening Philip Kerr visited Printing House Square and brought with him a statement from the Prime Minister, written specially for *The Times* and establishing the identity of Lloyd George's peace terms with those of Woodrow Wilson. In the end the Prime Minister's statement—to his subsequent great annoyance—was

[1] As early as October 21st, 1914, Geoffrey wrote in his diary: "He (Milner) was anxious to know how I fared on *The Times* and hinted at two jobs—one in the City, and one in the Civil Service as to which he had been asked to approach me. I told him I meant and ought to stick to the paper as long as possible." This entry is plainly relevant to Geoffrey's relations with Northcliffe, as referred to in the above statement of the events which led to his resignation. Geoffrey did not resign in October, 1914, because he felt *The Times* could not swop horses at such a moment. Cf. *supra*, p. 113.

Betsy, Belinda, Michael and Geoffrey

The . Times

No. 44263. London Wednesday May 5. 1926 Price 2d.

WEATHER FORECAST. Wind N.E.: fair to dull; risk of local rain.

THE GENERAL STRIKE.

A wide response was made yesterday throughout the country to the call of those Unions which had been ordered by the T.U.C. to bring out their members. Railway workers stopped generally, though at Hull railway clerks are reported to have resumed duty, confining themselves to their ordinary work, and protested against the strike. Commercial road transport was only partially suspended. In London the tramways and the L.G.O.C. services were stopped. The printing industry is practically at a standstill, but lithographers have not been withdrawn, and compositors in London have not received instructions to strike. Large numbers of building operatives, other than those working on housing, came out.

The situation in the engineering trades was confused: men in some districts stopped while in others they continued at work. There was no interference with new construction in the shipbuilding yards, but in one or two districts some of the men engaged on repair work joined in the strike with the dockers.

Food:-Supplies of milk and fish brought into Kings Cross, Euston and Paddington were successfully distributed from the Hyde Park Depot and stations. The Milk & Food Controller expects it will be possible to maintain a satisfactory supply of milk to hospitals, institutions, schools, hotels, restaurants and private consumers. Milk will be 8d. per gallon dearer wholesale and 2d. per quart retail today. Smithfield market has distributed 5,000 tons of meat since Monday.

Mails:- Efforts will be made to forward by means of road transport the mails already shown as due to be dispatched very shortly from London. The position is uncertain and the facilities may have to be limited to mails for America, India & Africa.

At Bow Street Mr. Saklatvala, M.P., who was required as a result of his Hyde Park speech on Saturday to give his sureties to abstain from making violent and inflammatory speeches, was remanded for two days on bail.

Full tram and (or) bus services were running yesterday at Bristol, Lincoln, Southampton, Aldershot, Bournemouth, Chelmsford and Isle-of-Wight, and partial services in Edinburgh, Glasgow, Liverpool, Leeds, Northampton, Cardiff, Portsmouth, Dover, N.Derbyshire and Monmouthshire.

Evening papers appeared at Bristol, Southampton, several Lancashire towns and Edinburgh, and typescript issues at Manchester, Birmingham and Aberdeen.

The Atlantic Fleet did not sail on its summer cruise at Portsmouth yesterday. The men went on shore duty.

Road & Rail Transport:- There was no railway passenger transport in London yesterday except a few suburban trains. Every available form of private transport was used. A few independent omnibuses were running, but by the evening the railway companies, except the District and Tubes, had an improvised service. Among the railway services to-day will be:- 9.30 a.m. Manchester to Marylebone 9.30 a.m. Marylebone to Manchester: 10.10 a.m Marylebone to Newcastle: 9 a.m Norwich to London: 9 a.m King's Cross to York: 5 p.m. King's Cross to Peterborough: 9 p.m. Peterborough to King's Cross. L.M.S. Electric trains between Watford and Euston and Broad Street will maintain a 40 minutes service. On all sections of the Metropolitan Railway except Moorgate to Finsbury Park, a good service will run to-day from 6.40 a.m. The Underground hope to work a six minute service on the Central London Line to-day from 8 a.m. to 8 p.m. between Wood Lane and Liverpool Street. The following stations only will be open:- Shepherds Bush, Lancaster Gate, Oxford Circus, Tottenham Court Road, Bank, Liverpool Street. A flat fare of 3d will be charged.

The Prime Minister had an audience of the King yesterday morning.

There was no indication last night of any attempt to resume negotiations between the Prime Minister and the T.U.C.

The Government is printing an official newspaper, "The British Gazette" which will appear to-day, price 1d. It will be distributed throughout the London Area.

Volunteers for the London Underground Railways and for L.O.G.C. omnibuses should communicate with the Commercial Manager's Dept. 55 Broadway, S.W.

The Prince of Wales returned to London from Biarritz last night travelling from Paris by air

The General Strike (1926) issue of *The Times*, known as "The little sister"

printed on a back page. On the day after his return from France Geoffrey lunched with the Prime Minister, who very naturally complained that "an inspired communication from the Prime Minister, which any other paper would have jumped at, was given less prominence than an occasional speech by Northcliffe" (the statement had been made by Northcliffe at a gathering at the American Officers' Club). Geoffrey replied that Northcliffe's speech had been presented to *The Times* as an important piece of official propaganda, revised and approved by the Foreign Office for the Director of Propaganda in Enemy Countries, and that it was for the Prime Minister himself to regularize the position if he disliked it.

Northcliffe had denounced Lloyd George for trying to "nobble" *The Times* in the Editor's absence and in particular denounced Philip Kerr as his instrument. Meanwhile Northcliffe had denounced Lord Milner for an untimely interview in the *Evening Standard* of which Geoffrey knew nothing but from quotations. He noted that the *Daily Mail* and *Evening News* were full of offensive references to Milner—apparently for saying that the German people were anti-militarist at heart.

On October 31st Geoffrey received from Mr. H. G. Price (Northcliffe's secretary) a three-column article on peace-terms, headed "From War to Peace by Lord Northcliffe": with an earnest request that it might have prominence on Sunday night. Geoffrey thus refers to the episode:

> . . . It turned out to be as unimpeachable as his speech, of which it was an expansion, but it was singularly unlike his style and was in fact the work of his Crewe House Committee.[1] The motive was no doubt to advertise himself as the real author of British peace terms, and he had taken immense pains to have it (the article) disseminated broadcast in America, etc. An amusing feature of the article was that it regarded a majority of the German people as being anti-militarist, the very view which he had been busily denouncing as "Lansdowneism" in Lord Milner.
>
> On returning to the office on Sunday, November 3rd, I found two more notes from Mr. Price—one recording some trivial correction in the article and one begging for a leader about it. This last request was a little difficult to gratify without any knowledge how far these peace terms committed the Government. However, they were announced as propaganda for Germany, so that (as the *Westminster* said next day) they were

[1] The article had, as a matter of fact, been compiled by various members of the Crewe House staff from Foreign Office documents. Geoffrey commented, "Its publication *urbi et orbi*, over his (Northcliffe's) name, seems to have been his supreme effort to appear before the universe as the sole author of British peace policy."

"pontifical" if not "official", and though there was nothing very new in them they were a useful summary. Chirol thought them good. . . .

On November 22 Northcliffe gave the first open sign of anxiety to figure personally and prominently in the Election campaign and expressed the wish that the Election news should be reported impartially and every reporter should be told to do so and that *every report attacking the Northcliffe Press should be given.*

By November 27 he had arrived at a satisfactory explanation of his obvious hostility to the Prime Minister (an explanation, it may be added, which did not tally at any point with the account afterwards volunteered to me by Lord Reading. Both the latter and Philip Kerr, who was in Paris at the time, gave me to understand that the "pursuing" was done by Lord N., for whom a luncheon interview was with difficulty extracted from the P.M. as he left for England. Reading said that it was a brief but most friendly luncheon party, with no controversial topics.) . . .

On Thursday, November 28, I had (for me) a long talk with Lord Northcliffe—all sorts of subjects, nothing very definite and no unfriendliness or apparent desire to interfere with the paper. Meanwhile the *Daily Mail* was vigorously running a number of Election "stunts"—"Hang the Kaiser", "Out with the Huns", "Germany must pay", etc., etc. . . .

On Sunday, December 1st, Northcliffe began the day with early telephoning, his usual practice when he had any special subject on his mind. Geoffrey told him frankly that he had no idea what his policy was and "where it differed from *The Times*" and suggested that Northcliffe should set it out in writing. A long letter arrived the same evening which Geoffrey admitted "did at least contain some sort of coherent ideas". They were briefly the very ideas which had formed the substance of the articles by Geoffrey in the summer, when he urged that the strongest possible Cabinet should be formed independently of party considerations. . . .

On December 2nd, Geoffrey "made a weary pilgrimage to see Northcliffe at Elmwood", near Broadstairs. Of this interview he wrote:

N. began with an outbreak about being determined to have his way, and if it came to parting, etc., etc., I told him it was no use talking like that, that, as he knew, I never had the faintest desire to stay with *The Times* if I was not wanted there, and that he need not consider me personally at all; then gradually got in all I wanted to say, viz. that he was not playing a straight game in his own papers by nominally supporting L.G., while doing everything to embarrass him and undermine him; that I could not run *The Times* as an appendage of the *Daily Mail*; that he was using great and difficult international questions as election cries, etc., etc.

He was extraordinarily elusive and difficult to keep to the point; tried at one point to suggest a compromise or bargain; told innumerable obvious lies (e.g. that he had only stood by L.G. because all the world was against him, etc.). I stuck to it that I wanted no concession, but only to know what he was aiming at, which of course he could not explain.

The following are some of the more important paragraphs in Geoffrey's memorandum:

When I went to Buckingham Street[1] (Dec. 3) I found that butter wouldn't melt in his mouth. I expounded my case for a strong Government (especially in view of the Peace Conference) which must in the circumstances be a *Coalition* Government; and could only be formed by *L.G.* He demurred at first, but eventually seemed to agree, broke out into a paean about L.G.'s energy and achievements and dashed off, primed by Steed, to see Masaryk. For a day or two his papers took on an entirely different tone.

This carried me to the end of the Election campaign on December 4. In the middle of the final week I wrote a long and balanced leader, saying precisely what I had already said to Lord Northcliffe. He was again at Broadstairs, and rang me up to say briefly that he profoundly disagreed with it. On the eve of the poll he arrived in Printing House Square, and said he would like to discuss the morrow's leader. I told him that I had already planned one on President Wilson's arrival!

. . . .

I escaped to Yorkshire for three or four days about Christmas, and my absence was the occasion for an appalling interview (appalling, at least, as presented in *The Times*) with President Wilson. . . . On the top of this, and of rather a blatant speech to his employees in Paris, N. returned to London well pleased with himself and issued on Christmas Eve a bulletin expressing his high satisfaction with *The Times*.

I want to take this opportunity of thanking every department of *The Times*—Editorial in all its branches, Managerial, Commercial, Advertising, Distributing, Reading, Type-setting, Stereotyping and Machining, for fine work during 1918, often under grave difficulties. I don't believe *The Times* was ever better produced, or was ever so high in public esteem.

January 6th, 1919. On Sunday afternoon, January 5th, 1919,[2] N. made what I hope was his final appearance in P.H.S. before going off to the South of France to recover his health and temper. I went over to see him, hearing he was about, and found him more incoherent than ever. He

[1] A war-time residence of the Northcliffes.
[2] This presumably was the last meeting between Geoffrey and Northcliffe.

began with the usual bluster—He wasn't going to go through the experience of the last month again—*The Times* had not spoken with his voice! He held me entirely responsible for L.G.'s great majority!!—and for the consequent trouble yesterday at Folkestone over demobilization!!! In future he was going to take a more direct hand in the conduct of the paper—would appoint a Managing Director of his own, whom he would train—was resigning his chairmanship of the *Daily Mail*—might even sell it—had had a huge offer, etc. I told him that I was under no illusion about the ownership of *The Times*. It wasn't my property and he could do as he liked. After this he became more reasonable, and produced some admirable sentiments about his feelings for the army and for the poor, his abhorrence of large fortunes, his zeal for research, his dislike of the narrow attitude. . . .

The position, therefore, at the time of Lord Northcliffe's final departure for France, was that after two very difficult months I still had some hope that a long rest would cure his disappointment, his want of balance, and his appalling megalomania. Certainly I was quite prepared to go on trying to make the best I could of *The Times*. It is, therefore, entirely untrue to suggest (as he afterwards did) that I took the opportunity of his absence to carry out a premeditated plan of resignation.

Lord Northcliffe was now abroad and cut off (according to prominently published notices) from all correspondence; but the announcement of the new Government on Saturday, January 11th, and the preliminary forecasts, produced a fresh convulsion. On the 10th came the following telegram:

> Private for Dawson from Northcliffe stop according to list published here this morning Cabinet even worse than I foretold you at Elmwood during election stop.

Two days later he telegraphed from Fontainebleau:

> When you were at Elmwood you said you could not understand what I was driving at when I urged stronger criticism stop you also said that I had in the past been sometimes right stop had you taken the line I wished this appalling result would not have been possible please take the trouble to read my daily articles through from the beginning and you will see that I foretold exactly what would happen Northcliffe.

Next came a letter (written, like much of his correspondence, on the notepaper of *The Times*):

> I am not given to saying, as most people do, "I told you so", but I saw the possibilities of the present deplorable Cabinet when I asked you to begin that campaign last summer.

I blame myself greatly for my lack of vigour in regard to *The Times* when I was ill at Elmwood in November and December. The sending of an emissary to me showed that George knew perfectly well that I was the only force that could stop his really timid nature, the timidity of which I know he is himself personally afraid. It is the timidity of the Gascons and of the Welsh which hides itself in brave words and gestures. Never again will I allow myself to be overruled in a matter like that. I am very willing to be led in matters that I do not understand, but I do understand character, else I should not have been able to erect so many different structures of different descriptions.

By the appointment of my brother[1] he has no doubt hopes of deflecting criticisms, by which I yet trust that I may be able to change the Government and avert a semi-revolution in England. The giving of office either to brothers or friends will not move me to the extent of a single colon or comma.

For the ungrateful and unjust treatment of your friend Astor, you have only yourself to blame; and I now earnestly commend to you a study of Welsh character and history. The Welsh are illusive, cunning and always ingrate. (12 January, 1919.)

This constant nagging bore no relation to anything published in *The Times*. I thought the Government in many respects a bad one and wrote exactly what I thought in a leader when the list was announced. . . . But the complete answer, of course, as I noted at the time, is that N. has utterly weakened his own position for criticizing the Government by crabbing it in advance after his quarrel with L.G. His *Daily Mail* articles, which he invites me to read, were devoted partly to the "Hang the Kaiser" cry, partly to sneers at the Tory Party, and finally to some pretty direct incitements of the troops to mutiny over "dilly-dally" demobilization. All of them were foolish. . . .

Then came the turning point. On the evening of January 29th I found at my house the following letter:

During my previous visit to Paris I saw that we were overstaffing our Government Departments. The matter had become common talk in French political circles. No less a newspaper than the *Journal des Débats* published a leading article about it.

I asked Steed to send a dispatch on the subject, which he did, and when I urged editorial comments you replied that you had received a letter from Lionel Curtis rebutting that dispatch.

In *The Times* of January 21st, which reached me yesterday, I find a laborious paragraph about the British Secretariat, dealing with that which I had anticipated weeks ago.

[1] Cecil Harmsworth, afterwards Lord Harmsworth, had been appointed by the Prime Minister Under-Secretary at the Foreign Office and Acting Minister of Blockade.

I have no intention of reverting to the unpleasantness of December last, but I assure you that I cannot acquiesce in any more of this kind of *non possumus*.

If you do not like my attitude, I beg you to do either one of two things—endeavour to see eye to eye with me, or relinquish your position.

The Times could have accelerated the Peace Conference had you followed up this dispatch by the editorial comments requested. Unless the Peace Conference be speeded, I can assure you from my knowledge of what is going on among our troops in France that we may have serious trouble.

My ownership and control of *The Times* are a great responsibility and as long as I have health I will act up to that responsibility to the full. In the last three months I have, against my will and owing largely to the inertia of ill-health, fallen far short of my conception of my duty. N.

I had said nothing to his previous complaints, but this letter seemed to require an answer. It was based on an almost wholly imaginary conversation. Some of the statements in it were simply untrue. I saw at once that he was working himself up into a state in which he would invent every sort of grievance against me, true or false, and that the only possible course was to send him a straight civil answer, placing the situation beyond any doubts. So, after sleeping over it, I replied by letter on the following day.

This passage, which you send me, is one that I wrote myself from Paris. I have never for a moment doubted your statement that many of our Departments there were over-staffed. It is quite true that I once read you a letter from Lionel Curtis justifying the size of *one* Department, viz. the Foreign Office, because I thought it would interest you as a point of view, but it is not true that you suggested any editorial comment on the subject or that I objected. The question was never even raised in the course of our conversation.

As for "not acquiescing in this kind of *non possumus*" I shall be only too willing, as you know, to give up the Editorship of *The Times* whenever the Proprietors desire it. If I had consulted my own wishes I should have done it before now, but I thought it would save trouble to remain here till you were well again and able to take a more active part in the conduct of the paper, as you told me that you intended to do.

G. D. 30 Jan.

I was quite aware that this would bring matters to a head and fully intended that they should be brought to a head.

Meanwhile my note of January 30 had reached Mentone, and on the morning of February 7 I received the following reply:

> Your letter received. I do not propose to terminate long pleasant relationship by acrimonious discussion as to what took place at an interview. You must allow me to say that it would have been fairer to the paper and to me to have told me of your wish to resign before I left England for a probable absence of three or four months.
>
> NORTHCLIFFE.

In other words—no comment on his old imaginary grievance, and a new complaint that I had not told him before he left England of a situation which had arisen out of his own messages from abroad!

I had no intention, however, of leaving him under any more imaginary grievances, so I sent him the following telegram at once:

To Viscount Northcliffe, Mentone. Feb. 7.

> Many thanks. You may be quite sure that I shall do my utmost for paper during your absence however long it may be necessary and shall neither tell staff my intention nor seek other work. But I thought it fairer in view of your letter to tell you that there should be no further occasion for complaint. I am truly worried on every personal ground that you should have found so many lately, DAWSON.

After this I heard nothing for three days, when a very formal confirmation of his message turned up by post (this was an exact copy of the message of February 7th):

> The control of *The Times* Company is in my hands by agreement, and I shall do my best in the matter of the selection of an Editor.
>
> I shall first offer the appointment to one or more members of the existing Staff and then, failing anyone's acceptance of the responsibility, seek outside help.
>
> NORTHCLIFFE.
>
> Geoffrey Dawson Esq. 6th February, 1919.

This was followed on February 13th by another telegram:

> Monday telegram received on getting your letter I replied to you and communicated with Steed whom I am meeting at Avignon on Thursday to discuss matters. NORTHCLIFFE.

While on the 17th I found yet another:

> Steed has accepted and will either write or see you speedily am sending you letter by John Walter. NORTHCLIFFE.

This finished the matter so far as I was concerned, and I was thoroughly relieved to have it finished so conclusively. What had happened was that Lord Northcliffe had risen with alacrity to the opening which I gave him on January 30th, thus leaving no room for doubt about his own desire for a break; had packed Campbell Stuart, his satellite, off to Paris, to offer the post to Steed; and had arranged to meet them both forthwith at Avignon. There was never any question, so far as I know, of Steed's readiness to accept the Editorship.

Next day (February 18) John Walter and Steed turned up in London. The former telephoned to me on his way from the station and I went round to lunch with him at the Travellers' Club. He told me of his sudden summons from Madrid to Mentone for purposes of consultation about the future of *The Times*, how he travelled in great discomfort for three days and nights, and arrived to find N.'s secretary drawn up to meet him—with the news that "his lordship had left by motor a few hours before"!

It was not, apparently, for another two days that they met, J.W. cooling his heels on the shore of the Mediterranean while N. was settling matters with Steed at Avignon. I gathered that in Walter's opinion he was thoroughly glad to be rid of me. Meanwhile, Walter, who had had no part in the decision, was sent home to carry it out. He brought me the following formal letters (composed after everything was arranged).

Mentone.

My dear Dawson,

. . . . . .

Against my doctor's orders, I travelled to Avignon on Wednesday and saw Steed on the following day. He is not anxious for the added responsibility but accepted it.

Walter is of the opinion that your kind and characteristic offer to carry on until my return should be accepted. But the date of that return is indefinite. I shall know better when my London specialist meets my doctor here at the end of the month.

My own view is that Freeman, if he wishes to serve under Steed, should be thrown upon his own resources as soon as you think fit. Walter, on the other hand, desires that you should give Freeman greater power, continuing to supervise his work till Steed returns to London.

I leave this matter to you and Walter to decide, knowing that you will both do your best for *The Times*.

I should have liked to have been in England to express more earnestly than I can do on paper my great regret that our association in journalism—to me a very happy one—should not have continued. I believe that I am credited with greater knowledge of the history of *The Times* than most of those who serve at Printing House Square, and, as I have said to Walter, it is my opinion that the paper has never stood in higher esteem both at home and abroad than under your leadership.

Yours very sincerely,
NORTHCLIFFE.

Geoffrey Dawson, Esq. 15th Feb., 1919.

Mentone.

My dear Dawson,

In my letter to you on the general subject of your resignation and the immediate conduct of *The Times*, I have not cared to mention pecuniary matters, which never have been discussed between us except when you have demurred at suggestions from me that you should receive a larger share.

The time has come, however, when money matters must be mentioned, and I have told John Walter that it is my desire that he should make any arrangement which is just both to yourself and to *The Times*.

Yours sincerely,
NORTHCLIFFE.

Geoffrey Dawson, Esq. 15th Feb., 1919.

To which next day I despatched an equally formal reply:

2, Smith Square,
Westminster, S.W.1.
February 19th, 1919.

My dear Lord Northcliffe,

John Walter gave me your two letters yesterday afternoon and I have since had a talk with him and with Steed. I agree with you entirely that it is far better, now that the latter is definitely appointed Editor, that I should hand over to him and Freeman as quickly as possible. Steed is also of the same opinion, and I propose, at his suggestion, to tell Freeman of the position this afternoon so that they may have a talk before Steed returns to Paris. It will be easier for him in some ways to take up the Editorship after a short interval, and I can gradually inform other members of the staff after he has left London. None of them is yet aware of the change, so far as I know; but it would obviously be impossible to keep it a secret for very long, and I felt last night that the arrival of Walter and Steed was already provoking curiosity in the office. I am sending Walter a formal letter of resignation of the Editorship and of my seat on the Board.

I am afraid you exaggerate altogether any services that I have been able to render to *The Times*; but I have done the best I could, and I am quite clear that any attempt to remain Editor in the circumstances would have been neither fair to the paper nor honest in me.

Yours very sincerely.

At the same time I also addressed to John Walter an official letter of resignation:

2, Smith Square,
Westminster, S.W.1.
February 18th, 1919.

My dear Walter,

I have been awaiting your arrival from Spain in order to tender to you, as Chairman of the Company, my formal resignation of the Editorship of *The Times*.

I need not trouble you with details of the correspondence leading finally to this decision. It is a step to which I had in any case been making up my mind for some weeks past—ever since it became clear that Lord Northcliffe was constantly dissatisfied with the policy of *The Times* on the ground that it differed fromh is own expression of opinion in other newspapers. Nothing is worse for a newspaper than any sort of internal friction, and therefore I wish to relinquish my position at the earliest date convenient to everyone concerned.

Will you allow me to thank you and your fellow Proprietors for the confidence, support, and unfailing personal kindness which I have enjoyed during the six and a half years of my Editorship?

My resignation includes, of course, that of my seat on the Board of *The Times* Publishing Company".

Yours very sincerely.

John Walter Esq.

In the afternoon of Feb. 18th Walter, Steed, and I met at the office. I told them that, while on February 7th I had offered to carry on the paper, there could be no question of that now that a successor was definitely appointed. They both agreed—as indeed did Northcliffe's letter of Feb. 15, brought to me (open) by J.W. I offered, at the same time, to save Steed any embarrassment by telling no one in the office till he had gone back to Paris, where he thought his presence more important than in editing *The Times*. This he then proposed to do on the following Friday morning. He kept putting it off, however—partly for the sake of reorganizing his Foreign Department, on which rather chaotic institution I'd lately had a report prepared—and it was not till Monday that he finally got away. Barring Freeman, therefore, whom I told at Steed's request, it was not till the latter left the office on Sunday evening that I was able to explain matters to some of the principal people in the office.

Meanwhile John Walter was obviously in difficulties about an announcement of the change and approached me once or twice on the subject. He suggested first having *no* announcement for a bit. I told him quite impossible. He then, after an interval, murmured something about the strain of the war and my feeling that I should seek some easier work! I replied that this was not true, and that, while he must do as he thought right so far as *The Times* was concerned, I reserved the full right to make my reason known. It was stated, I told him, in its simplest and least recriminatory form, in the letter which I'd written to him on the morning of his return. He said he agreed personally, but "thought Northcliffe wouldn't like it".

Accordingly on the Sunday, February 23rd, he produced a draft statement compiled by himself, Freeman and Steed (who had curiously added a phrase about his own close association with Northcliffe) and said they were all agreed that it wouldn't do to publish my letter in *The Times*. I said they must do as they pleased, but suggested as a journalistic point that it was unnecessary now to rehearse my early education and career since public interest in this respect was centred in my successor. These sentences were thereupon eliminated, and on Monday night the statement was duly printed in *The Times*, and sent to the Press Association without them, while I gave my own letter to the Press Association, together with separate copies for the *Morning Post*, *Daily Telegraph*, and *Yorkshire Post*, all of whom I asked to refrain from comment while just giving the facts. . . .

G.D.
March, 1919.

On February 25th, 1919, the following notice appeared in *The Times*:

Mr. Geoffrey Dawson has resigned the Editorship of *The Times*, and Mr. Henry Wickham Steed has been appointed to succeed him.

Mr. Dawson succeeded Mr. G. E. Buckle as Editor of *The Times* in August, 1912. His period of editorship was thus far shorter than that of Mr. Buckle (1884–1912), of Mr. Delane (1841–1877), or of Thomas Barnes (1817–1841); but it covered a chapter of English history more momentous than that recorded by any of his predecessors. This is not the place to assess the value of his work during the last seven years; but we may be allowed to observe that the position and influence of *The Times* today are due in no small measure to his energies, character and ability.

(Then followed two paragraphs about Mr. Steed and Mr. G. S. Freeman, the Deputy-Editor.)

Among Geoffrey's papers are several large envelopes containing letters from members of the staff of *The Times* on his retirement and from his large circle of friends and acquaintances and also from unknown admirers. It has been a privilege to read this collection of letters, and they bring home to the reader the tremendous shock caused by the notice of Geoffrey's retirement in *The Times*.

Hugh Chisholm, a former Editor of the *St. James's Gazette*, was offered the Editorship by Northcliffe in October, 1910, in the presence of Reggie Nicholson, then assistant Manager, but he had still five or six months' hard work in connection with bringing out the eleventh edition of the *Encyclopædia Britannica*. Chisholm made a very generous admission in a letter to Geoffrey on his retirement: "I can say to you now, more easily than before, that ever since I knew you, and increasingly as I have served under you, I have had no doubt that you were the right man for *The Times* and that I should not have been your equal in that respect."

The following are extracts from other letters:

From Mrs. Moberly Bell:

17, Carlyle Square,
Chelsea, S.W.

It is the worst piece of news that I have heard, and if V.C. (Valentine Chirol) had not broken it to me last night I really couldn't have stood this morning's announcement. I am quite sure you would not have given up, if things had not grown intolerable.

All through the war there has been such a feeling of confidence in *The Times*—and now with labour troubles I have always leant on *The Times*' opinions. All that has gone and we shall have no guide of any value. It is the worst day's work Lord N. ever did. When V.C. has gloomed about such a possibility I have always felt sure Lord N. could not be so foolish. I am dreadfully sorry.

From Sir Bruce L. Richmond:

3, Sumner Place,
S.W.7.

It seems a short time since I sent you a note that was to lie on your breakfast table on the first morning of your being Editor.

My regret in sending you this one today is tempered by the pleased vanity of the successful prophet when I remember the confidence I then expressed that the traditions of the paper were safe in your hands.

I do congratulate you most heartily on your six years' splendid work—regretfully I congratulate you also on your liberation from what must have been in many ways a beastly job.

But anyway you can look back on it with pride—and as one of your staff I hope you will also look back on some sides of it with pleasure.

I want to thank you for being so uniformly considerate to me and my corner of the paper. We are very grateful to you. Good luck to you in the fresh woods and pastures, wherever they may be.

Yours always,

B.L.R.

From Bernard Darwin:

Cambridge,

February 26.

Lying in bed yesterday with pseudo-influenza I opened *The Times* all unsuspecting to be suddenly stricken down with dismay.

From friends and acquaintances not members of the staff came the following:

From Sir Edmund Gosse:

17, Hanover Terrace,

Regent's Park, N.W.

Dear Dawson,

I have no right to intrude upon you, but I feel I must be allowed to say how much I have admired your conduct of *The Times* (when I have been able to detect your personal hand) through the war; and to thank you for your unfailing courtesy to myself. I am one of hundreds who will indignantly regret you.

From John Buchan:

76, Portland Place, W.1.

25th February, 1919.

My dear Geoffrey,

I was astounded at the news in *The Times* this morning. What has happened? I can well believe that you will be glad of a rest, but your resignation coming at this moment is a tremendous blow to me. . . .

You know what I think of your difficult work for the past four years. The country owes you a great debt of gratitude. Let us meet sometime soon, and tell me about things.

Yours ever.

From Lord Stamfordham:

February 24th, 1919.

My dear Dawson,

The King has heard with much regret of your retirement from the important position of Editor of *The Times*: though from what I told His Majesty he quite understands the reasons which have led to your decision. The King much appreciates your friendly and considerate assistance which could always be relied upon during the years that you have been at Printing House Square.

Yours very truly.

From Sir William Wiseman:

British Delegation, Paris,
Hotel Astoria,
March 5th, 1919.

My dear Dawson,

Since I saw the announcement of your resignation it has been on my mind to write you a line to tell you how sorry I was to hear of it, and at the same time to thank you for all the help you have given me the last two years.

I do not forget that it was due to your efforts that the Government was persuaded to send Lord Reading to America in the Autumn of 1917, when we had reached such a critical financial position with the U.S. Treasury. . . .

Some authorities detect the influence of Rothermere in his elder brother's decision to part with Geoffrey. It is said that one of those who moved in the same social circles as Geoffrey informed Rothermere that the former openly discussed his quarrels with Northcliffe and was very critical of the "Chief". This gossip was passed on to Northcliffe, for Rothermere was not a supporter of Geoffrey and, as *The History of "The Times"* states,[1] "he did not believe in the employment of strong editors". Northcliffe's mood in the latter part of 1918 probably caused him to pay more attention to Rothermere's words than he would have done in different circumstances. Others think that Geoffrey was not as discreet as he should have been in telephonic conversations at Printing House Square. This seems hardly likely to me. All who worked for many years for Northcliffe were fully aware of his system of "spies". Indeed when in a good mood, Northcliffe would often joke about them, and none of his intimates would ever have used the Carmelite House telephone exchange had he wished to discuss any matter not intended for the "Chief's" ears! The same must surely have applied to Printing House Square.

It is surely ridiculous to suggest that Geoffrey should not have discussed Northcliffe's opinions and policy with his intimates. Of course he did. Northcliffe's views were public property; he enjoyed the limelight in his latter years; "The Northcliffe Press" was constantly in the headlines and formed the subject of debates in Parliament and wherever persons interested in the progress of the war were gathered

[1] Vol. IV, Part I, p. 464.

together. It was hardly possible to discuss any important phase in political life or in current events without bringing in Northcliffe's name. How could it be otherwise? He did not spare his opponents and the Radical Press lost no opportunity of attacking him.

Without Geoffrey, or someone of his type, Northcliffe could not have carried on *The Times* in 1912. When he decided to part with Buckle he knew he would have to appoint a younger man with the same kind of academic background. When Geoffrey from the start made a success of his Editorship, Northcliffe was gratified; he took pride in the knowledge that he had picked the right man for the editorial chair. At some fairly early stage in their association Northcliffe may have wondered whether he had not perhaps appointed a man of too independent an outlook. Relations were none too happy in 1913. Geoffrey was fully prepared to shoulder all the editorial burdens at Printing House Square and the greater his responsibilities the more he throve. Several of the most successful causes sponsored by *The Times* under Geoffrey had nothing to do with Northcliffe, who for months on end was content to leave editorial matters to him. There came a moment, after his return from his successful mission to America in 1917, when he saw himself as occupying a key position in the supreme direction of national affairs and in the inevitable peace-making.

For some time he had been preparing to take a more active part in controlling the editorial policy of *The Times*. He certainly respected and had a genuine liking for Geoffrey, and if the latter had been prepared to become his mouthpiece and give up his own independence, there would probably have been no change of editorship,[1] but this was just what Geoffrey was not prepared to do.

There is surely little doubt that Northcliffe was perfectly genuine when he said to Steed that "Parting with dear Robin is a personal grief to me."[2] Later, when Northcliffe's mental illness developed after the return from the world tour in the summer of 1922, Steed was with him in Paris and fortunately kept a record of that extraordinary interview. Sometimes in the outpourings of one mentally deranged there is a modicum of truth. One of the observations Northcliffe made on that occasion was that in future he intended to be *Editor*[3] of *The Times* himself.

[1] *The History of "The Times"*, Vol. IV, Part I, p. 472, contains this passage: "but even now, i.e. on February 4, 1919, Dawson was sure that Walter would wish him to remain, and not sure that Northcliffe really wished him to resign. He was correct. What Northcliffe had counted upon was his being able to reduce the Editor to submission, to make him loyal to his own person and personal policy".

[2] Ibid, Vol. IV, Part I, p. 486.

[3] My italics.—E.W.

XVI

1919—MOROCCO AND MARRIAGE

THE immediate weeks after Geoffrey's retirement from *The Times* cannot have been easy. He had never worked harder than in the last weeks of the war and after the Armistice; then, above all, there had been the intolerable strain of the day to day situation with Northcliffe, followed by a spell of sleeplessness. I only saw Geoffrey two or three times in this period and I thought he looked abstracted. One occasion specially comes to mind. On November 7th, 1918, I had invited[1] Geoffrey to meet a small party of Editors of American religious papers at the "Cheshire Cheese" in Fleet Street. Among the British guests were Owen Seaman, of *Punch*; Leo Maxse, of the *National Review*; Lord Stanhope and Lionel Curtis. It was only a few days after the *Daily Mail's* violent attack on Milner, quite enough in itself to account for Geoffrey's mood. I did not, of course, know then that the much larger question of Geoffrey's whole future at Printing House Square was at stake. For the next four months Geoffrey was undergoing probably the severest strain he ever had to endure.

For three or four weeks after leaving Printing House Square he was busily engaged in clearing up his papers, bidding farewell to his friends on the staff and completing his records of the events which led to the final breach with Northcliffe.

A letter (January 27th, 1919) to Arthur Willert deals with some of the problems of peace-making in Paris where Geoffrey had been:

> I am sure that it is a good thing to keep on gingering up the Conference, but to us here the rate of progress does not seem by any means so slow as it does to you in Paris, nor do I feel that this criticism is really compatible with any strong claim for more representation of the smaller Powers. It seems to me that the real solution of this particular difficulty is to make a good job of the League of Nations, the charter and

[1] At that time, under Lord Beaverbrook, I was in charge of the British Empire and American Sections of the Ministry of Information.

Geoffrey with one of his Labradors

Geoffrey and Cecilia Dawson on Malham Tarn. The figure on the left is Michael Dawson

Geoffrey Dawson and Stanley Baldwin

safeguard of the smaller Powers. In other words, I feel that the fact that the League of Nations was taken first, and that it is apparently to be tackled in earnest, is far more important than the relative impotence of the smaller Powers in the preliminary Cabinet Meetings of the Conference.

Willert wrote to Geoffrey (May 10, 1919):

I write this on the eve of returning to the United States. . . .

I do not like the general outlook. It all seems to me still to resolve itself into the inability of those who run things to realize that politics and frontiers and *hoc genus omne* of problems really do not count until the world has food and work. Paris rather reminded me of a lot of old-fashioned butlers setting a picnic table on the slopes of a volcano in serene indifference both of dangers and of the fact that they had got no food for most of their patrons. You have been lucky to be out of it all. If it were not that the Germans are in a worse plight than us and seem no more able to adapt themselves to changed conditions it would be disheartening indeed.

You will hear a lot of talk about N.'s health when you get back. The fact is that his throat is by no means well and an operation is going to be needed. There seems to be no definite proof that there is anything radically wrong, but sinister possibilities cannot be overlooked. I spent some days with him in France. He was in better form than in the winter. . . . Do write to me and tell me of your plans and impressions of things. The latest rumour is that you are to be given a chance of filling the Ambassadorial gap in Washington. I wish it could happen. . . .

As already stated the years 1919–20 are the only ones for which we have no diaries and surprisingly few papers. Fortunately, as on other occasions, his letters to Langcliffe enable us to fill in some of the gaps. This one, written on January 18th, was from Paris:

. . . Paris is really indescribable—the Medes and Elamites and dwellers in Mesopotamia weren't in it! All the world is here and most of his wives and my head aches with the number of people I've seen in the 24 hours since I arrived. . . .

idem.

The Times,
22nd Jan.

I got back from Paris last night. . . .

The Hotel Majestic, where the British delegation lives, is really beyond all power of description. It's like a gigantic cinema show of eminent persons. Mr. Balfour strolling about with Evan Charteris and Ian Malcolm—Bikanir and Sinha with other Indian retinue. Smuts and Botha dining in one corner. Lord F. E. Smith flanked by a bottle of champagne in another. Labour members seeing life in Paris for the first time. Little Lawrence of the Hedjaz with his Arabs. Quite half the Foreign Office and a sprinkling of every other office, but this is only one of many similar invasions, from America, Italy, etc. . . .

Feb. 11, 1919.

. . . And now let me tell you betimes, and *for the moment in confidence*, that my days on *The Times* are drawing to a close. There is nothing to regret about it from my point of view—I was never more certain of being right, and I'm sure you'll agree when you hear the whole story. The gist of it is that Northcliffe has been quite intolerable during the last two or three months—continually nagging, wanting ridiculous policies, and generally making chaos. I won't do the thing unless I can do it well and I can't do it well under these conditions. The trouble came to a head over rather a trivial incident, but it was really inevitable sooner or later and I shall be relieved now to have it finally over. I don't want to sink into a journalistic hack, and there's lots of other work to do in the world. You'll find me, I hope, far less worried and better tempered in future than I've been lately and you'll also have more of my society, for I mean to take things easier this summer before getting into harness again. I've really rather worn myself out and must take a spell. . . .

Feb. 19, 1919.

. . . . Getting out of *The Times* is slow and rather nerve-racking work and the worst is still to come, viz: parting with the staff. However it's all going "according to plan" and I hope to be free within a week. After that I look forward to paying you a brief visit, but my vague idea is soon to go abroad into the sun. I'll do no more regular work till I've had a gigantic holiday, but I've a lot of paper to soil and a few records to write. . . .

idem.

Beefsteak Club,
Feb. 21st,
Friday night.

. . . It's a tiresome business this transition stage and I shall be profoundly thankful to have done with it. My successor was appointed with such promptitude that I have no longer the smallest doubt of the satisfaction which my opening gave. I still hope to come to you within a fortnight. After that, I think, Morocco.

Travellers' Club,
Tuesday, March 18.

I'll write again at greater length. This is just to say that I hope to sail for Gib.: from Tilbury on Thursday morning and that my first address should be:

Reina Cristina Hotel, ALGECIRAS, SPAIN.

R.M.S.P. *Arzila*,
March 26th.

. . . Lionel Curtis and I are all the better for our trip, already, and quite vague about plans. We shall probably go straight over to Algeciras, where the Lawleys and other friends are staying.

Algeciras,
Spain,
March 31st, 1919.

. . . The posts are appalling and the telegraphs worse. All Spain is more or less on strike. The whole staff of the place "went out" the day before we came and there was a question of rescuing some starving visitors and taking them across to Gib.: in the Governor's barge. However a few hours brought the strikers back—cheering and dancing jigs—and there has been no further *émeute* since L.C. and I arrived. It's a perfect place for a rest cure—a large low sunny hotel with glorious gardens, running down to a deep blue sea and the Rock facing it across the bay. And we lead a real lotus life—a long ride one day up and down rocky mountain paths and lunch high up in the cork-woods. Lady Lawley and the two girls and Lionel Curtis and I—and this morning I've been shopping with them by the aid of a *Spanish Phrase-book* in the very picturesque little town—oranges and cakes for a picnic tea. It's so like Italy you wouldn't know the difference—little whitewashed cobbled streets and courtyards and laden donkeys. Tomorrow we go fox-hunting.

Algeciras,
Spain,
April 8th.

. . . There are orange-trees abloom here, but it is the cork-woods in which we chiefly sit. You take a donkey or two to carry your lunch and coats and wander up stony tracks in rough mountain country (not unlike Scotland or the Lakes) with red-stemmed cork-trees everywhere. No roads at all and very little cultivation (unlike the Italian hillsides), but occasional strings of laden donkeys going up and down with jolly singing people. I had a great day's hunting on Friday with the Foxhounds—a 40-minutes' run on a little pulling Barb pony, as sure-footed as a cat with a most comical mixed field of sportsmen and sportswomen.

Tangier,
Morocco,
April 12, 1919.

. . . You can't imagine a more beautiful spot and the town itself is interesting beyond description with its little narrow streets and Moorish houses and motley crowds of Arabs, negroes and folk from the interior. I've been here a couple of days and hope to start within a week for Fez and Marrakesh, probably with Harris[1] himself and the Lawleys, travelling

[1] Walter Harris, *The Times* correspondent at Tangier.

by motor if the sun has dried the roads. That will mean about a fortnight's absence and I doubt whether there will be any chance of sending letters. . . .

Tangier,
Good Friday, 1919.

. . . Here I am again after another trip across the Straits and going on tomorrow to the French seat of Government at Rabat. I packed Lionel Curtis off home from Algeciras—most reluctant to go, as I was to part with him. However he would go, thought himself absolutely cured and wanted to get back to Paris. Now I'm off on tour with the Lawleys, but it's a complicated business. I've been vaccinated, photographed, identified in every possible way! Finally I had that rotten tooth pulled out this morning just before Church. It was bothering me again, so I strolled round after breakfast and found an American dentist (recommended to me by old Kaid Maclean, who used to command the Sultan's troops . . .). Quite a good little English Church here, did I tell you? We've been to it several times this week. I must tell Lord Ribblesdale how very well done I think his brother's tomb[1] just by the door. Since then Walter Harris has been in to make plans. . . .

How you'd enjoy this place with its motley crowds of Moors, and laden donkeys and camels sleeping under the Churchyard wall, and little narrow white streets and veiled women! I love it all. And by the same token I've never told you of my great day on Tuesday, visiting a wonderful cave in the mountains near Ronda with a French *abbé* and crawling about to see the drawings of deer, bison, and fishes done by primitive man at a date which is variously computed 50,000 to 100,000 years ago. They are fresh as when they were drawn: an amazing discovery which is the subject of several learned works but has been seen by very few eyes. I was lucky to get the chance, but it's no easy expedition and my *abbé* and I were out from 5 a.m. till nearly midnight and simply plastered with mud when we returned.

Casablanca,
Morocco,
26th April, 1919.

. . . We've been to Marrakesh, which is a joy reserved for very few, and what is more we've seen it under the best possible auspices, for my friend Harris was there and took us everywhere—to be received by the grand Bashaw, in his palace, to dine with some Moorish grandees, to see the ancient tombs of the Kings, and to wander about the most amazing streets and bazaars. It's a glorious city, built of rose-red brick, about the time of the Norman Conquest, in a great plain surrounded by hills—groves of palms and oranges in and about it, and the great range of the Atlas with snow-capped peaks lying 30 kilometres away.

Our Bashaw was a fine potentate, living in a house of marble and

[1] Hon. Sir Reginald Lister, H.B.M.'s Minister at Tangier, 1908–12.

mosaic, with rose-gardens in the courts. We were lucky to find him for he only returned a fortnight ago from a warlike expedition with 8,000 men across the very top of the Atlas, and discoursed to us with a gentle smile on the ethics of killing prisoners. He released one of them, by the way, in honour of our visit! I said to him (through an interpreter of course), as we came away, how beautiful I thought his house, and he replied in true Oriental style that it was *mine* and all that was in it! Our dinner party was great fun too, though I confess I think it a messy form of eating to sit on the floor and grab bits of stewed pigeon and chicken from a common dish. And the bazaars and lanes were an endless joy—utterly unspoilt—straight out of the pages of the *Arabian Nights*—donkeys and camels and endless chatter of grave Moors and blacker men from the South all in their long striped robes and yellow slippers—and baskets of oranges and pomegranates for eating and dyeing their leather. . . .

. . . . .

Within twenty-three days came the announcement of Geoffrey's engagement—hitherto he had been regarded by his friends as a "confirmed bachelor"—to Cecilia, the younger daughter of Sir Arthur and Lady Lawley. The announcement gave great pleasure to Geoffrey's friends for they realized that he could have married no one better able to share his interests in life or with whom he would have more tastes in common. His father-in-law was a Yorkshireman, coming from the East Riding (Escrick). His *fiancée* was, like Geoffrey, devoted to out-of-door life; she, as was natural in the case of a daughter of Lawley's, took a deep interest in South Africa and the Empire. Her father had been one of Rhodes' men in Rhodesia, having served as administrator of Matabeleland. After a year as Governor of West Australia, he had returned to South Africa, to serve under Milner, as Lieutenant-Governor of the Transvaal (1902–05). It was during this period that Geoffrey first met Cecilia Lawley. Throughout his diaries there are references to the family: in 1904 he goes "for a ride with the Lawley girls" and joins in charades at a friend's house; in May that year there is an appreciative reference to a speech made by Sir Arthur to some Boer delegates; in 1905 there are several references to further rides with the Lawleys; when Sir Arthur was appointed Governor of Madras, the event was referred to as a "horrid loss" and on December 4th, 1905, Geoffrey goes to bid them farewell at the station, and he writes "very sad at their going". Apparently for the next six years their paths did not cross, but on May 7th, 1912, Geoffrey dines with the Lawley family in London and writes "so nice to see them again". The following year, while staying at Lillingstone in Buckinghamshire, he "motors over to see Lady Lawley and Cecilia". On a visit to the B.E.F. in

France, in 1917, at the conclusion of his trip, while at Wimereux, he has "an early lunch with Sir Arthur and Cecilia, who'd been on night duty".

There was a strong streak of altruism in the Lawley family, and his *fiancée's* uncle, the fifth Lord Wenlock, had spent thirty years of his life in East End parishes, first in charge of the Eton Mission in Hackney whither Geoffrey frequently went during his term at the Colonial Office, and later both in Bethnal Green and Hackney Wick. This uncle was, like Geoffrey, an old Etonian, and officiated at their marriage service. The marriage took place—Geoffrey was in his forty-fifth year—at St. Margaret's, Westminster, on June 14th, 1919; appropriately enough the register was signed by Milner and Aunt Kitty among others. Lieutenant-Colonel Edward Grigg, formerly a colleague at Printing House Square, was the best man.

Lady Lawley wrote the following letter (June 15th, 1919) to Miss Perfect (Kitty) from 9, Seymour Street:

> The crowd was so great yesterday that I never had the chance of even saying a word to you and now hear that you have left London. I am so sorry for that, as my husband and I intended paying you a visit this afternoon—to talk the wedding over.
>
> I hope you were as happy about it yesterday as we were. Someone wrote that it was like betting on a certainty to wish them joy and though such things as "certainties" do not exist on this side of the grave, still I feel their future happiness is well assured—when two people are as much in love with each other as Cecilia and Geoffrey are, I think one need not fear for the future. He one in 10,000—and so is she!
>
> Please let me know if you are in London again.

The honeymoon was spent, first at Chequers, lent to Geoffrey and his bride by Lord and Lady Lee, and subsequently at Rest Harrow, Sandwich, lent to them by Lord and Lady Astor. The following letters to Aunt Kitty dealt with these happy weeks:

> Chequers,
> Princes Risborough,
> Bucks.,
> 16 June, 1919.
>
> I hope you weren't too much tired by Saturday—everyone seems to have thought it a nice cheerful wedding and I was really bewildered by the number of friends who turned up, without invitations or anything, on a fine afternoon. Chequers is simply perfect—too good to leave, but we go to Rest Harrow, Sandwich, Kent, tomorrow and no doubt it will be equally delightful. . . .

Rest Harrow,
Sandwich,
Kent.

. . . We don't want to leave here much before Thursday. I am cultivating golf, at which C. is an expert, and this afternoon we play a match for our only two bad wedding-presents. If *she* wins, I give her Mrs. Blank's shot pink flower vase. If I win (with a handicap) she gives me the Duchess of Blank's "ring-stand" which looks like a shelled tree-trunk in the Ypres salient.

We went to the evening service at Canterbury Cathedral yesterday taking tea with Lord Milner, at Sturry, on our way. He was rather depressed, poor man, by the prospect of another summons to Paris this morning and I think he was quite glad to see us.

Langcliffe Hall,
Settle,
Sunday.

. . . Returned (from the honeymoon) to a superb dinner. The "Band of Hope" which was celebrating Peace in the village came and serenaded us about 10.30, followed by most of the inhabitants! We greeted them on the doorstep and then retired to bed. This morning we went to Church at 8, but are shirking the morning service and writing letters. . . .

I foresee that you'll have to kick us out soon or we shall be too comfy to stir! . . .

The salver from the tenants is quite lovely, so are their candlesticks—an amusing product of Skipton! They'll have to be thanked individually and profusely. Indeed I'm overwhelmed with letters and business of all sorts and very glad of these quiet days to get it done.

Best love to you my dear and a thousand thanks for your hospitality.

XVII

INTERREGNUM—FEBRUARY, 1919, TO OCTOBER, 1922

GEOFFREY and Cecilia made 23, Sussex Place, looking on to Regent's Park, their London home and there he was busily engaged with his many interests, but as far as his career as a journalist was concerned, it was definitely a time of *reculer pour mieux sauter*. He did comparatively little writing during these forty-four months: an obituary notice in *The Times* about his neighbour in Yorkshire, Walter Morrison; an unsigned article entitled "Lord Milner goes" in the *Yorkshire Post*, dealing with the latter's retirement from the position of Colonial Secretary; an occasional article in the *Round Table*; he helped Owen Smith in connection with *The Guardian* and attended meetings at its office.

He had, however, many other interests. Above all he had a pleasant link with All Souls in his appointment as Estates Bursar on November 1st, 1919. He took his duties very seriously, and happy days were spent with his wife in the congenial task of visiting every one of the College's scattered farms in Romney Marsh. In that attractive corner of Kent he spent several days with some of the big sheep farmers discussing their flocks in which, as a Yorkshire landowner, he had a keen personal interest. On 22nd June, 1921, his appointment as Secretary of the Rhodes Trust was announced. A month earlier Milner had first proposed to him that he should fill the position recently vacated by Edward Grigg. He became a director of the Consolidated Gold Fields of South Africa and also joined the board of Trust Houses. On March 7th, 1921, he made his first appearance at a dinner of the Literary Society. As early as January 24th, 1921, there is this entry in the diary, "Presided over a large and long 1820 Settlers Committee."

The diary for 1921 opens with the following remark, "Diary resumed after a gap of two years—1919 (complete—with the Morocco tour and much else) and 1920 (just begun), having been stolen in a dispatch-box from 175 Piccadilly (then the office of the *Round Table*), with many other papers equally worthless to the thief."

It is a curious sensation to turn from the full entries of the Editor of *The Times* in the diary for the last weeks of 1918 to the stray jottings on a variety of subjects in the resumed diary of 1921. On February 24th he records a visit to Lord Milner, "who rather shyly imparted to me as a dead secret his arrangements for being married on Saturday". As a young man at Oxford Lord Milner had decided not to marry, so that he might devote himself entirely to the causes he had most at heart.[1]

Geoffrey received the following letter from Sir Edward Carson (27th May, 1921) on the latter's elevation to the House of Lords:

> Many thanks for your letter. You were quite right in being in doubt, as I am, whether I prefer congratulations or condolences but on the whole I think the time has come when it is necessary to have more rest.
>
> I can never forget what a valued friend you have always been since we met, and I hope I will now have more leisure to see you from time to time.
>
> We are, at present, very busy trying to get our new house in Kent into order, and my wife is moving in there today.
>
> I hope when she comes back we may arrange a little dinner and I am very anxious that I should see your and that you should see my "most attractive child".

In 1920, Geoffrey was sent by the Rhodes Trust to Malta to make the necessary arrangements for the granting of scholarships at Oxford to students in that island. His visit synchronized with the official announcement of the grant of the new constitution, in which he evinced the keenest interest. He spent a month in the island and wrote the following letter (April 22nd, 1920) to Mr. Amery:

> I spend an odd two minutes in reporting to you, *the Patron Saint of this Island*. My mission *in re* the Scholarship is duly accomplished and a good Committee of Selection in being. I am also steeped in Maltese politics and personalities. Moreover, I hope to start homeward, my ship to Syracuse being already two days late, and to be commencing with you in the course of a week or ten days. I'm very glad you sent me. It's an intensely interesting little place and you caught it just at the parting of the ways and in the hands of an admirable Governor.[2]

[1] Within sixteen days of his resignation from the Colonial Office Milner married the widow of Lord Edward Cecil and daughter of his old friend Admiral Maxse.

[2] Lord Plumer.

There are several similar episodes in the careers of Delane and Geoffrey; one of them is that each was offered an under-secretaryship by the Government of the day.[1] Delane was offered by Palmerston the post of Permanent Under-Secretary for War in 1862. On December 31st, 1920, Philip Kerr wrote to Mr. Lloyd George that he had seen Milner about the Colonial Office, the latter recommending Geoffrey as Permanent Under-Secretary for the Colonies, with Kerr supporting the proposal.[2] On January 19th, 1921, Geoffrey was recommended by Kerr to succeed him at the Prime Minister's Secretariat, though he doubted if Geoffrey could be paid enough money to enable him to accept the position. On the 4th February, 1921, Kerr wrote to Lloyd George on the Near Eastern question, and asked him to remember the suggestion that Geoffrey should be permanent head of the Mandates Section of the Colonial Office. On 14th February, 1922, Kerr informed the Prime Minister that he had had an informal talk with Geoffrey and that "he is not likely to take on the *Daily Chronicle*" (the suggestion was that Geoffrey should become political director).

The latter half of the year 1921 was not dominated, as far as Geoffrey's public career was concerned, by any one event. Punctiliously he attended his various board meetings and committees. He missed no function connected with the Rhodes Trust or the Rhodes Scholars; he kept in touch with Imperial events through the *Round Table* and was present at the periodical "moots". In the diary for October 26th, there is one of the rare references to Printing House Square, "lunch with Lowndes[3] at the Athenaeum and a gossip about *The Times*". While Geoffrey had no intention of ever returning to Printing House Square, he was naturally deeply interested in the welfare of the paper and of his former colleagues there.

The chief political events in the year 1922 were the termination of Lloyd George's premiership of nearly six years and his succession by Bonar Law on October 23rd, but in these events Geoffrey took no part. From his personal standpoint the two major events of the year were the death of Northcliffe in August and, as an indirect result, his own return to Printing House Square at the end of the year (though his Editorship is considered actually to have begun on January 1st, 1923).

Having placed "the two babies" with their grandparents, Geoffrey and Cecilia spent a happy month (April) abroad, mainly in Corsica. A

[1] Though, admittedly, in Geoffrey's case, the suggestion did not originate with the Prime Minister.

[2] This information kindly supplied by Lord Beaverbrook from the Lloyd George papers.

[3] Mr. F. S. A. Lowndes, husband of Mrs. Belloc Lowndes, who in his later days was in charge of the Obituary Department.

week was passed at Ajaccio, whence they made excursions through the lovely mountains, at the back of the town, going over "terrific roads, with amazing views, sometimes like Hex River or the Matopos".

Among typical entries in the diary are the following:

Apr. 14. . . . over another mountain range through a great forest of Corsican pines till we emerged above Spedale to a vast view over the southern tip of Corsica and the Straits and Sardinia . . . to Sartene, a small hill town where we found rooms in the Hotel de Provence and saw at night a wonderful Good Friday procession. Every window in the narrow street illuminated with lamps and candles—choir and priests bearing candles and chanting through the town—eight cowled men carrying a catafalque—and a red-cowled penitent with the Cross—finally a sermon in Italian to the whole populace in the market square.

Apr. 16. Ajaccio . . . down to the Grand Café after dinner and listened to an admirable violinist in a thick atmosphere of holiday-making and card-playing bandits.

Apr. 20. . . . we took our tea up the river and fished till dark, each getting one fair-sized trout. Came back to dine . . . and listen to an amazing concert by the inn-keeper and his whole family and the doctor lodger.

Two of Geoffrey's friends died in June, though in a very different manner. George Parkin of the Rhodes Scholarships died after "only three days' illness and no pain"; while on June 22nd "Desart met me and told me of the horrible news of Henry Wilson's murder,[1] half-an-hour before". For the next couple of days little else was talked about or thought of but of the murder. On June 28th he and his wife attended the funeral at St. Paul's—"a most wonderful and moving service".

Most of the months of August and September were passed at Langcliffe, though the Dawsons did spend a week with Archbishop Lang at Bellure in Argyll—the very best kind of preparation, had he realized it, before his return to *The Times* in December. There are several very appreciative entries in the diary—about the visit—of "swimming in a wonderful clear sea and tea afterwards on a heathery shore", and "C. and I had a long morning on the hill with Mrs. Macdonald, trying pointers and counting grouse".

A curious psychological problem is provided by the entries in Geoffrey's diaries for the period from August 13th (the eve of

[1] General Sir Henry Hughes Wilson, C.I.G.S. at the time of the Armistice (later Field Marshal). He incurred the hostility of *Sinn Fein* owing to his speeches on the Irish problem in Northern Ireland. He was assassinated by two *Sinn Feiners* on 22 June, 1922, on the doorstep of his London house, No 36, Eaton Place. He had been a friend of Geoffrey's for many years.

Northcliffe's death) to the end of the month. There is never a mention of his former Chief.[1] The period was spent at Langcliffe—whither the Dawsons had returned from Scotland on August 10th. The entries deal principally with the weather and the shooting; the guests at Langcliffe; how the sporting dogs behaved; the opening of a bazaar by Cecilia; the number of trout caught; the health of the children; the progress of the Vicar's fund for Church purposes; a visit to Lord Ribblesdale and other neighbours; estate matters and visits to Settle for daily errands and the Settle Livestock Show. Just the kind of entries which he would have made in a normal month of August. But, from his standpoint, the month was not normal. Since August 8th the well-informed knew that Northcliffe's end was near; on that day his friend Edward Grigg told Lloyd George that "Northcliffe might not last through the night." During the year, as we have seen, Geoffrey kept pretty closely in touch with friends who could tell him about conditions at Printing House Square, because he was deeply concerned about the rumours reaching him. Unfortunately there are no letters remaining from this vital period among Geoffrey's papers; even the invaluable Aunt Kitty, who kept every document about her dear Geoffrey, fails us, very naturally, for she was at Langcliffe. I have been unable to discover any references in the Dawson papers to Northcliffe's death—an event which took place at "Twelve minutes past ten" (from the bulletin signed by his two doctors) on the morning of Monday, August 14th, 1922, at No. 1, Carlton Gardens. At that hour Geoffrey was out shooting with his friend Willie Bridgeman. He must certainly have thought very much about Northcliffe's death and above all what the future had in store for *The Times* and all his friends at Printing House Square. Perhaps he made no reference to the event as he had been so completely disillusioned about the "Chief".[2] Things had turned out so differently from what he had hoped. There were no comments that he cared to make. The first entry in his diary with any bearing on Northcliffe's death is as follows:

> *Sept. 24.* Oxford. Church at 8 at St. Peter's in the East (congregation of 2 including me!). Then a morning in College with the Warden . . . to London at 1.00 . . . dined with Molly N. . . . staying behind for a talk with her (Molly N.) about his (Northcliffe's) wills and *The Times*.

[1] For another example illustrating how Geoffrey could be completely absorbed in his immediate surroundings *vide* p. 444.

[2] One of Geoffrey's intimates at Printing House Square writes, "It is my impression that this reticence about Northcliffe was no passing mood, but continued for the rest of Geoffrey's life."

XVIII

RETURN TO PRINTING HOUSE SQUARE—DECEMBER, 1922

THE story of how Geoffrey returned to Printing House Square, or rather, the events which were to lead to the purchase of *The Times* by Mr. John Walter, on behalf of himself and of a "secret backer"—who was in fact Major J. J. Astor, Chairman of *The Times* Publishing Company and Chief Proprietor from 1922—is most dramatic. It was a great day in the history of British journalism, when Mr. Walter and Major Astor acquired the paper and subsequently established a Committee of Trustees to safeguard the paper's future ownership.[1] It is usually only in the pages of fiction that a millionaire engaged in a big financial deal discusses his plans on the telephone, and that a member of the rival group, by a lucky chance, overhears a conversation which enables him to learn of his opponent's probable intentions. Yet such things do indeed happen in real life and, thanks to the alert and nimble brain of Sir Campbell Stuart, then Managing-Director of *The Times*, the way back to Printing House Square was made possible for Geoffrey.

Throughout the year 1922 there are occasional references to conditions at Printing House Square in his papers—but in those entrusted to me by his widow there is nothing to suggest that at any moment Geoffrey had the slightest idea of ever seeking to return to *The Times*. They are the kind of references one might expect to find in the records of one who had served the paper for over twelve years, or more than half of his working life. No one had entered more into the spirit of the Great "Company"—to use Kinglake's term—nor had better realized the importance to *The Times* of its verdict being generally regarded as a corporate and not a personal pronouncement. In no sense was Geoffrey trying to pull strings or to sponsor any group which might one day take over *The Times* if it ever should come on the

[1] Vide *The History of "The Times"*, Vol. IV, Part II, pp. 790–91.

market. Several of his friends and former colleagues were still on the staff, and when rumours about the conditions at Printing House Square and about Northcliffe's health began to circulate after his return from his world tour in the summer of 1922, he could not help hearing about them. I had severed my connection with Northcliffe about the same time as Geoffrey, after an association which began in 1904, and I remember very distinctly my bewilderment when I first heard of Northcliffe's alarming state of health in 1922. What would happen to *The Times* and the other vast enterprises of which he had been the chief proprietor?

After Northcliffe's death Geoffrey makes a few stray references to meetings with friends when obviously *The Times* and the future control of Northcliffe's holdings in it came up for discussion. On September 22nd he lunched with Freeman "at the Athenaeum where I saw also Buckle and B. L. Richmond and heard something of the chaos and intrigues besetting Printing House Square". On September 27th he lunched *tête-à-tête* with Kindersley, "very much concerned about *The Times*. Rothermere's purchase of the *Daily Mail*, etc., shares went through yesterday" (i.e. from Northcliffe estate). On September 28th Geoffrey wrote: "Rhodes Trust all morning looking in on John Walter and Lord Milner as I came down. Steed came to see me there." On October 12th, Geoffrey recorded that ". . . Steed also (was among the callers at the office of the Rhodes Trust)—with the latest news of *The Times* of which Rothermere was now in open pursuit", and on October 17th he lunched with Kindersley and Bob Brand.

October 23rd is important, for on that date Bonar Law succeeded Lloyd George as Prime Minister, as the result of a vote against Austen Chamberlain at the Carlton Club on the 19th; it was also of supreme importance to *The Times*, for on that day Mr. John Walter, acting on behalf of Major J. J. Astor—the "secret backer"—acquired the control of *The Times* thanks largely to Sir Campbell Stuart's handling of the affair.

For the full details of this momentous evening, which resulted in Campbell Stuart's getting to know the sum that Rothermere would be prepared to pay, the reader must be referred to the former's own story.[1] Here we can only record the mere facts. Stuart was dining with an influential friend, who, as a matter of fact, was a warm admirer of Geoffrey's and had greatly deplored Northcliffe's decision to part with him three years earlier, regarding his resignation as a "national disaster"; though he naturally had no idea in 1922 that there was any likelihood of Geoffrey's return to *The Times*. This friend, who had

[1] *Opportunity Knocks Once*, Chapter VIII, "*The Times*", pp. 91–162, Collins, 1952.

known Northcliffe well, was consulted by Rothermere as he, very naturally, wanted to find out what sum the group, with which John Walter and Campbell Stuart were in touch, would be prepared to pay. Hence the dinner *à deux* between Geoffrey's admirer and Stuart. After the dinner—which had been prolonged to well after midnight—the telephone bell rang in the adjoining room, and luckily for all who cared for the great traditions of Printing House Square, Stuart's host rushed in to answer the call, leaving the door open, and Stuart could not help hearing his remarks to the unknown listener at the other end of the line, "He started with £1,000,000 but is obviously prepared to bid £1,250,000." Campbell Stuart very wisely passed on the substance of the telephonic conversation to "Bobby" Grant, an American banker in London, who was advising Major Astor, and accordingly, when Rothermere's offer of £1,350,000 was made in Court, the representative of John Walter and of his "secret backer" made a similar offer and under the terms of Northcliffe's will *The Times* became their property. The future of "The Thunderer" was now assured.

Of all these exciting events during this dramatic week-end of hurried consultations between Grant and Astor and of the events in Court on October 23rd, Geoffrey must have been unaware. He and Cecilia were staying at Monk Hopton in Shropshire with Lord Wenlock,[1] one of Cecilia's favourite uncles.

There is nothing to show that Geoffrey knew anything about the details of the acquisition of *The Times* by John Walter with Astor's backing. The diary entries for October 25th and 26th follow:

> *Oct. 25.* Monk Hopton. My birthday—a glorious warm sunny one. We spent it most peacefully and happily—walking round farm buildings in the morning, blackberrying in the woods all afternoon—and reading in the evening.
>
> *Oct. 26.* Shot round Monk Hopton. An uncle and nephew arriving to make four. Some 12 pheasants and 3 rabbits rather a disappointing bag but we thoroughly enjoyed it. *Our last peaceful evening*[2] at Monk Hopton.

Geoffrey little knew how true the first four words of this last sentence were—though not in the sense he meant them. The events recorded in the diary during the following days are among the most momentous in his life, showing the steps by which he finally returned to the Editorial chair at Printing House Square:

[1] Lord Wenlock had not only married his niece and Geoffrey but was to christen their three children.

[2] My italics.—E. W.

Friday Oct. 27. Cecilia and I went out before breakfast with Sheba[1] in search of fallen pheasants—and flowers and packing filled the morning till we caught the midday train at Bridgnorth, I for Oxford and she for London. A large party in College, where I found a letter from Steed re *The Times* and after dinner sat till midnight with Bob Brand over the same topic. He was commissioned to ask me to return to it—a most depressing prospect which gave me a sleepless night.

During the next four days "Freeman revealed a horrid state of chaos in Printing House Square and seemed to have had hopes held out to him of succeeding Steed. . . ." Geoffrey also consulted Lord Milner, who emerged from "a long talk with Bobby Grant[2] with the conviction that on *terms* of security, freedom, etc., I ought to take the plunge".

Perhaps the greatest surprise I have experienced in my perusal of the diaries are the entries of October 27th when Brand, on behalf of the Proprietors, had invited Geoffrey to return to the Editorial Chair at Printing House Square: "a most depressing prospect which gave me a sleepless night" and that of October 28th, "a walk—still in the depths of gloom—with Bob and Dougie and Lang[3] on a gorgeous afternoon".

When Geoffrey was invited to come to Printing House Square for a second time, I had expected to find an expression of thankfulness or rejoicing, or an entry in the diary to the effect that the mills of God grind slowly. I have discussed these entries not only with Cecilia but with those colleagues, such as Brand and Dougal Malcolm, who knew Geoffrey best. There is no possible doubt these entries express his first reactions to the thought of returning to Printing House Square; had there only been the first entry, it might have been explained away as an impulsive first reaction after the peaceful, happy and carefree years since his marriage, of a shrinking from reassuming all the tremendous responsibilities of the greatest editorial position in the world. But twenty-four hours later there is still the even stronger entry "still in the depths of gloom".

Geoffrey's dislike of the thought of returning to Printing House Square was indeed genuine and due to several causes. Those final months with Northcliffe had been a gruelling experience. The strain of those war years with their responsibilities had been tremendous.

[1] References to Sheba in the diary are frequent. She was a black labrador and a great favourite. She was given to Cecilia as a puppy by General George Holdsworth, a very old friend of the family since Bulawayo days.

[2] Robert Grant, of the American Bankers, Messrs. Lee, Higginson & Co. Grant was a friend of Major Astor's and played a large part in the financial negotiations for the purchase of *The Times*.

[3] R. H. Brand, Dougal Malcolm and the Archbishop.

Since he had left Printing House Square he had married and now had the background of a happy home, surrounded with understanding sympathy and was the proud father of two children. One cannot understand Geoffrey unless one realizes what an enormous part his family played in his life after 1919. In addition, in the first twenty months, or so, after he had become the owner of Langcliffe (in 1917) he had not been carefree enough, owing to the war and his relations with Northcliffe (in 1918) to rejoice in all that the ownership of those beloved hills and dales meant to him. Why should he deliberately put his neck under the heavy yoke that editorship of *The Times* imposed? Why indeed? Is not that sufficient reason for the two entries in the diary?

Could conditions ever be evolved which would make Geoffrey, as Editor of *The Times*, the unquestioned master in fact of the editorial side? After three years of freedom and peace he would only go back to Printing House Square after definite and clear terms about the position of the Editor's powers and responsibilities had been agreed. It has sometimes been assumed that the memorandum containing his views on the matter was primarily the work of Lord Milner. During the days that followed, of course, Geoffrey discussed the offer of editorship with Milner, but also with F. S. Oliver, with his father-in-law, Sir Arthur Lawley; with Freeman, and also with friends such as Brand, Dougal Malcolm and others, but the memorandum of terms was the work of his own hand.

Geoffrey was determined not to consider returning to *The Times* unless the Editor was supreme on the editorial side, as was the Manager on the managerial side. In no circumstances would he return as long as there was a Managing-Director with powers such as those possessed by Sir Campbell Stuart during the last years of Northcliffe's life. In a memorandum to Major Astor, Geoffrey wrote:

> I gave a copy of the Memorandum[1] on the same afternoon to Sir Campbell Stuart, who now holds the office of Managing-Director, and learnt then for the first time how extensive his powers had recently been—especially over the Editorial side of the paper, which he estimated as occupying three-quarters of his time as against one-quarter devoted to the Management. My ideas, therefore, differed far more widely from his than I had ever imagined, and I should like to add my tribute to the readiness with which he has since agreed to waive them altogether and to resign the post of Managing-Director as from the end of the present year. I understand that his proposal is that he should then become an ordinary member of the Board of Directors, drawing the salary to which his contract entitles him till its expiry, but with no administrative duties and no greater powers than those of any other member of the Board.

[1] Memorandum to Major Astor and John Walter of 18th November, 1922.

It cannot have been easy for Sir Campbell Stuart to resign the position of practical dictatorship in which he had been placed by Northcliffe, but it speaks much for his good sense that he realized the implications of Geoffrey's view and voluntarily resigned his powers and thereby enabled him to return to Printing House Square on his own terms. It is not less than his due to admit that Sir Campbell Stuart's handling of the crisis in *The History of "The Times"*, caused by Northcliffe's death, must always be recalled with gratitude. Thanks to him, firstly the acquisition of the paper by Mr. John Walter, acting on his own behalf and on behalf of Major Astor, was made possible; secondly, as Geoffrey acknowledged in his memorandum, as quoted above, he realized that the only dignified action was "to waive them" (his extensive powers) and resign the office of Managing-Director.

Geoffrey's memorandum defining the editorship pointed out that the conduct of a newspaper has two objects: (1) To reflect and guide public opinion by producing a good newspaper. (2) To make money by producing a profitable newspaper. These were the spheres of Editor and Manager respectively, but they could not be kept entirely separate. The volume and character of advertisements, for instance, would concern both parties, and in a question such as "the amount of expenditure required to make the foreign correspondence worthy of a great newspaper, the Editor's and Manager's views should carry equal weight". Above all "every Editor worth his salt must have a free hand to conduct his side of the paper as he thinks best so long as he is in charge of it. The power of the Proprietors is exercised properly by the appointment and dismissal of the Editor, not by interfering with his work or doing it themselves".

No contract could be devised to guarantee smooth co-operation between Proprietor and Editor. This could only be founded on mutual confidence and constitutional procedure. The Editor was responsible for everything printed in the paper and must exercise a control commensurate with his responsibility.

In the midst of all these constitutions and talks Geoffrey and his wife escaped to Langcliffe for five days' electioneering prior to the General Election, which took place on November 15th, and resulted in a Conservative victory with Bonar Law as Prime Minister. The diary entry is: ". . . a glorious fine still sunny day for it (the Election). We spent the morning dispatching our pony cart to the hills, loading up (with voters) . . . and walking down to vote ourselves. More loading up after lunch and a final visit to the Committee Room . . . got in to London an hour late at 10.30 and at midnight we were watching the results shown at Selfridges".

On November 20th Geoffrey met Major Astor for the first time since *The Times* negotiations began. He thus refers to the talk: "He was very nice. . . . I gave him my note to study and offered, having done so, to see Campbell Stuart, who accordingly came to my office at 5. He of course realized that it upset the position of Managing-Director if my scheme was accepted. We argued, very friendly."

The entries in the diary for the next two days follow:

Nov. 22. Breakfast with Bob Brand and on to the city for a talk with him and Bobby Grant. By this time Campbell Stuart had abdicated, said he wouldn't be Managing-Director without full powers and wished to be an ordinary member of the Board. . . . Meanwhile a Rhodes Trust meeting all afternoon—all there except Kipling and clear that I ought to go (i.e. to *The Times*).

Nov. 23. Opening of Parliament by the King. We watched the procession from the Mall. . . . Then to see John Astor and tell him that it was only a question of setting down our agreement on paper—and a vain attempt to catch John Walter also.

After spending a pleasant week-end with the Beits at Tewin, Geoffrey returned to London late on Sunday evening, December 3rd, and then "went, like Nicodemus, by night to Printing House Square for a talk with Brumwell from 11.30 p.m. to 1.30 a.m."—Geoffrey's first appearance in the familiar surroundings since the terms of his Editorship had been settled. The next day he went for a talk, mainly about Reparations and the French visit, with Bonar Law, whom he found "very fit and cheerful".

On December 7th he was inundated with letters of congratulation on his return to Printing House Square—a paragraph in the *Daily Express* had announced his appointment as Editor by the new proprietors. During the next week he saw Bonar Law on four separate occasions; on one of them he "told me what had happened in his Prime Minister's Conference and did something to make it clear that British public opinion would not follow France into the Ruhr".

Some entries from the diary during the last days of a year so important in Geoffrey's life follow:

Dec. 22. Cecilia and I set off in the car soon after 10.30 . . . to Canterbury, where the Archbishop was clamouring to see me. . . . I got a walk with His Grace and a talk after tea-ing with the old Dean (Henry Wace, leader-writer since Delane's days).

Dec. 26. A delightful sunny Boxing Day for a change. Cecilia and I went with Ursula and her father for a tramp in Richmond Park—with Sheba, who found a cock pheasant! Lunching at Ham Gate in the car . . . and so to Printing House Square 4–7 and 9.30–12.

Dec. 27. An excellent game of tennis on rather a wet morning with Leo Maxse. . . . I sent Carnarvon a suggestion for taking over his Press work (in connection with the Tutankhamen discoveries—a great coup for *The Times*) . . . had a talk with the Prime Minister about the situation in Paris and Lausanne—both worse, and (in his opinion) connected, and got through some of the proofs of the *Review of the Year* in bed.

Dec. 31. . . . A cup of tea in the nursery—Belinda's first birthday and so to the office . . . and saw the New Year in (as so often before) in the Editor's chair. I put into the paper a short formal note of my return.

On this New Year's Eve, in the familiar surroundings, Geoffrey must almost have felt as if there had been no interregnum at *The Times*.

XIX

SECOND EDITORSHIP—FIRST YEAR

THE formal paragraph in *The Times* announcing Geoffrey's return appeared on New Year's Day, 1923, although he had, in fact, been working at Printing House Square since the beginning of December. The first entry in the diary for 1923 was:

Jan. 1. . . . On from the Rhodes Trust to Printing House Square after lunch. Sheba (the labrador) with me all day and took the Conference for the first time and generally played myself in as Editor. . . .

The following extract from a letter to Lord Long of Wraxall on January 5th, 1923, furnishes a good example of Geoffrey's perfectly genuine ability to regard himself objectively—a characteristic which remained with him all his life:

> There is a lot of leeway to be made up here, and I am not by any means clear that it is good for any paper to have an ex-Editor restored to it. Still, it ought to be less difficult for me than for someone who had never been here before, and in any case it was impossible to refuse.

Geoffrey must have been especially glad to receive the following letter (8th January, 1923) as representing a voice from the past and bringing back memories of his first weeks at Printing House Square:

> 17, Carlyle Square,
> Chelsea, S.W.
>
> Dear Mr. Dawson,
>
> You will have had hundreds of letters of congratulations to which please add mine—but the great congratulation in my mind is for my dear *Times*, that it has got you again and is in no danger of the degeneracy which threatened. It often made one unhappy to see the vulgarity creeping into it—for though it is clear from events that it was right in its opinion of Lloyd George it was losing its influence by the

way it expressed itself. It is splendid that those days are over and that my grey hairs may go down in peace to my grave.

I wish you a long and great success in the seat of the mighty.

Yours sincerely,

ETHEL MOBERLY BELL.

In a letter (February, 1923) from Rio Tinto, in Spain, in regretting his inability to do some reviewing for *The Times*, because he was involved in getting out "a little book of my own", Lord Milner wrote to Geoffrey:

> And many congratulations too on the already so noticeable improvement in *The Times*. I have heard this commented upon here by people knowing nothing at all of the inner history or of my personal interest in the matter.

The letters of congratulation on his return to *The Times*, and of congratulation to *The Times* on having him once again as Editor, came from far and wide, and within three or four months writers noticed, as Lord Milner had, a marked improvement in the paper. For instance, Lord Long wrote: "A few lines of warm congratulation upon the wonderful recovery *The Times* has made. It is a matter of ordinary conversation in places 'where men meet'. . . . I have been a reader of *The Times* now for forty years, and though I disagreed with the late Lord Northcliffe's methods and tactics, I never gave up the paper. . . . I really believe *The Times* has come back into its own and that before very long the position occupied by the newspaper and its Editor will be at least equal to that which marked the most powerful part of Delane's time and I suppose never was there a greater period in its history. . . ."

There were naturally many threads to pick up and many former friends to meet and problems to discuss. The diary entries are very much the same as they were during the first term at Printing House Square—the notes of an extraordinarily well-informed editor, who was interested in every aspect of life and had access to every section of the community. They convey a sense of continuity. Geoffrey had certainly lost none of his flair for "scoops" in the peaceful in-between years. One of the first things he concentrated on, as noted in his diary of December 27th, 1922, was an effort to persuade Lord Carnarvon to entrust *The Times* with the Press side—including, of course, the distribution of the photographic material—of his excavations near Luxor. By January 29th "the first big Luxor pictures" in connection with the amazing Tutankhamen discoveries, which thrilled the world, had arrived. On February 16th the Editor writes, "a great Tutankhamen message on which —— wrote and I contributed a short leader myself".

The diary shows that Geoffrey kept in fairly close contact with Bonar Law during the early part of the year. On January 6th and 9th he had long talks with the Prime Minister about the likelihood of a breakdown in the Conference in Paris; the growing tendency of Italy's representatives at international talks to become mere ciphers for Mussolini; the French advance into the Ruhr. Later in the month Geoffrey was summoned to "No. 10" on the 17th, 24th and 27th, as Bonar Law was anxious to explain the reasons which had prompted him to turn down the American proposals for funding the Debt, a matter which is dealt with in his memorandum of January 27th, which follows:

> The article in *The Times* of this morning, setting out as from "a Colonial" the case against settling the debt-funding negotiations on the American terms, was written by the Prime Minister.
>
> He showed it to me first on Wednesday 24th, saying that he had written it with the idea of anonymous publication, but had come to the conclusion that its origin would be traced. I asked him to let me show it to Mill, City Editor of *The Times*, and promised to restore it without saying anything to a soul about its authorship. Mill read it in my room at the office that night and at once suggested that it was the work of Beaverbrook!
>
> Bonar Law asked me whether after all I would publish his article—I said I would; I was all for letting the world know his arguments in a very difficult case, but would not myself undertake to support them. He seemed a little sad at this, but we parted friends and I carried out my undertaking.

In view of the great importance which Anglo-French and Anglo-German relations were to assume in the 'thirties it is of special interest to read Geoffrey's views in the Rowell Correspondence; the expression of the opinion of so eminent a Canadian lawyer as Rowell, who emphasized his countrymen's dislike of becoming involved in guarantees in Europe, was a lesson he never forgot. Newton W. Rowell wrote:

> January 30th, 1923.
>
> I have been following with the greatest interest *The Times* attitude on the present crisis, and wish to say how sane and sound it appears to one on this side of the Atlantic. It is difficult to realize that France would persist in the course she is taking, in the face of the attitude of other powers. . . .

Geoffrey replied to the above on February 13th, 1923:

What France wants most is security against future aggression. That being so, the only alternative to this attempt to dismember Germany seems to be some such pact as that which the Americans declined before. But one difficulty about this, quite apart from America, seems to be the attitude of the British Dominions, which would certainly have to consent. I imagine that that consent might be difficult to obtain at present, even though the Dominions would always in practice be involved in the case of such another unprovoked attack on France as Germany launched in 1914. I should much like to know what you have to say on this point. . . .

Mr. Rowell replied (March 14th, 1923) from Toronto as follows:

It may be as you say that the only alternative to the French attempt to dismember Germany is a Treaty of Guarantee such as you suggest, but I wonder if it is the only alternative. I am afraid the recent action of France has made such a treaty impossible; I should say it certainly has so far as Canada is concerned. I do not think that Canada would be prepared to join in such a treaty.

There is an influential party in France determined to bring about the dismemberment of Germany, on the plea of security to France against German aggression. They tried to secure this through the Peace Treaty but were only partially successful, thanks to the resolute stand of Wilson and, in a measure, of Lloyd George, but they have not ceased to work to this end. It seems to me it is a policy fatal to the future peace of Europe and is bound, in the end, to react more against France than any other country. It will not be possible to keep Germany down permanently, and if France now brings about her dismemberment she, in the end, will pay the penalty. One can only hope that a situation will arise which may make possible intervention, and that when that time comes the United States may be prepared to accept some measure of responsibility.

Cecilia, very sensibly, thought that change of scene was as good for Geoffrey—the Editor—as it had been for Geoffrey during the "interregnum"—so the twenty days from March 27th to April 15th were spent mainly at Rome.

They began their visit, on the afternoon of their arrival, by going straight to St. Peter's for the great *Tenebrae* service—the extinction of the candles, washing of the altar, the exposure of the relics, with beautiful Gregorian singing by two choirs. At St. John Lateran's they witnessed "a very inferior imitation of the Procession of the Cross", seen at Sartene, in Corsica, the previous year. An interesting afternoon was spent in "doing the Forum thoroughly" under the expert guidance of Dr. Ashby of the British School. Geoffrey had long talks with the British Ambassador; with Cardinal Merry del Val, "a courteous, fine-looking Cardinal, ready to discuss Russia, Fascism, the Ruhr and everything else". The Dawsons also dined one evening at the British Embassy to meet "the great Mussolini. . . . Difficult tri-lingual conversation but extraordinarily interesting".

Politically the year was important, for it witnessed among other things the retirement of Bonar Law, who, in April, had been ordered a cruise for his health. During his absence Lord Curzon had acted as Deputy Prime Minister. On the Prime Minister's return to London his physicians diagnosed cancer in the throat and Bonar Law resigned on May 20th. As will be seen from the following extracts from his diaries and documents, Geoffrey took a deep interest in the constitutional aspect of Baldwin's advent to power:

May 20. . . . Meanwhile Bonar, who returned yesterday suddenly and no better resigned by nightfall and I was on the telephone perpetually till midnight.

May 21. . . . A message from Stamfordham awaited me—I found him soon after four, trying to size up the situation for His Majesty and very distracted. He'd seen Willie (Bridgeman), Leo Amery, Salisbury, A.J.B. The problem was Curzon or Baldwin. By 7 when I saw him again, he told me the King (on telephone from Aldershot) had come down on the side of Baldwin. I wrote the first leader myself—with an interval for dining with Willie, who was also for Baldwin and the thing was practically settled by the end of the night.

May 22. . . . Meanwhile the King arrived and sent for Baldwin while the unfortunate Stamfordham took on Curzon! and soon after 4 Alec Hardinge rang me up to give me the official news.

The Times had published a leading article entitled "The King's Choice" (May 22nd), in which without infringement of the Royal Prerogative the paper clearly set forth the situation as it existed on Bonar Law's retirement. In sending for either Curzon or for Baldwin "the King would be acting strictly in accordance with constitutional precedents and with the facts of the situation". The article further pointed out that the days had gone by when the position of Prime Minister could be held to the public advantage by a member of the House of Lords. A further leading article appeared, "A Prime Minister in Being" (May 23rd), in which *The Times* dealt with the King's promptitude in offering and Baldwin's promptitude in "accepting" the position of Prime Minister. Geoffrey was therefore once again right in the heart of major political and constitutional events, studiously avoiding the limelight as was his custom. He, very sensibly, urged on the new Prime Minister the desirability of placing his Government on a broader and stronger basis than mere party considerations could suggest—he was probably thinking of Lloyd George's wisdom, during the war, in appointing such men as Milner and H. A. L. Fisher, who were not regarded as party men. Of Baldwin, whose promotion he regarded "as both astonishing and sound", he observed that he was a politician "singularly free from self-advertisement"—a quality which always made a great appeal to him. The diary entries for May 23rd and 28th follow:

> *May 23.* A message from Stamfordham and saw him about 12—much disturbed by Liberal suggestion that Baldwin had been forced on His Majesty by a "diehard" caucus. He described his very painful interview with Curzon yesterday. Then on to Downing Street to talk things over with Davidson[1] who showed me in to the Prime Minister himself—very composed, if rather subdued, and waiting for the Marquis's reply. He told me his plans for reunion.
>
> *May 28.* . . . A successful start to the Baldwin Government.

On June 17th Geoffrey had a couple of hours' talk with Baldwin and made a memorandum:

> Prime Minister at Chequers. Sunday June 17, 1923.
>
> An afternoon with the Prime Minister at Chequers, motoring over on my way from Oxford, where I'd seen him the night before and suggested a talk. No other man there—John Baird was out golfing—so I had him to myself 4–6, and sat and walked about the garden discussing all sorts of things and people. I set down some of them:
>
> The Ruhr: no news from France and no hurry for it. Baldwin was obviously not very hopeful and was thinking of the next stage in case of a breakdown. He was inclined for a public statement of British policy and a subsequent attempt to get other adherents to it. He was prepared to speak plainly to Poincaré, but saw no real settlement without France. Curzon was with him over this, but was difficult generally.

Then the conversations ranged over a number of subjects and show to what an extent the Prime Minister took Geoffrey into his confidence. They discussed squabbles in the Cabinet, and the relations between various politicians. It might come to a row between the Prime Minister and one of his colleagues. "What then? How would the public take that?" He, the Prime Minister, could probably get a peerage for Blank. He desired reconciliation with another leading member of the Party. Then there was the essential stupidity and narrowness of "X.". Who should be the next Viceroy? Who should have the post of Ambassador at Washington—where "it was exceedingly important to find a good man—and a good lady". Then there was "Y.", who was "a good

[1] Mr. J. C. C. Davidson (now Lord Davidson), who was Mr. Bonar Law's Parliamentary Private Secretary and later Chancellor of the Duchy of Lancaster.

platform man" according to Garvin but must be kept at a distance. In the discussions about finding a suitable Viceroy for India, Geoffrey suggested "Winston" because this great post required someone "with a spark of imagination"—a suggestion which, however, did not find favour. Then the conversation turned to the Dominions—a congenial topic—and to South African problems. He was entirely at home here and gave the Prime Minister an account of Smuts. Baldwin admitted his ignorance about the Empire and expressed a wish that the Imperial Conference could have been postponed. "What he'd heard of Bruce of Australia had impressed him (a man who'd rowed in the Cambridge boat!)".

Geoffrey's memorandum concluded with this paragraph:

> Of the younger men in Parliament he thought well of Billy Gore[1] and very highly of Edward Wood. Joynson-Hicks was doing well, but he hankered after Jack Hills. Of the Lloyd Georgians he was watching Hilton Young and Ned Grigg. Lloyd George himself he regarded as a real corrupter of public life and couldn't understand the spell. Like me he could no longer see him coming back quickly, as Bonar apparently predicted. . . . We discussed oratory and "first-class brains", for both of which he expressed great contempt. Altogether an interesting and extremely frank talk. I left him puddling off over the fields with Mrs. Baldwin to Ellesborough Church, as Cecilia and I did just four years ago.

In July Geoffrey received two letters from Mrs. Asquith whom he had known slightly during his first editorship; they were the forerunners of a very frank correspondence and show how strong her regard for him was. It was to him that she turned at the time of her greatest sorrow when her husband died. It is a tribute to their broad-minded outlook that both she and Lord Oxford had a real admiration for the man who probably had as much to do as anyone with the termination of the latter's premiership:

44, Bedford Square,
London, W.C.1.
July 15th, 1923.

Dear Mr. Dawson,

You will hardly remember me but I would very much like to see you before we all break up. Any morning between twelve and one, or if it suited you better I could see you after lunch at 3.30 or would you and your wife lunch one day? Could you lunch Thursday 19th at 1.30? Forgive my writing but I am impelled to do it because we *all* think you have done wonders with *The Times*, transforming it from the worst sort of wrong-headedness into the great paper it was.

[1] William Ormsby-Gore, subsequently fourth Lord Harlech.

I am so unhappy about the European situation that I implore you to use all your influence with the Prime Minister to act quickly and with great firmness over the deplorable French business. His statement was excellent; a cautious but solid step forward and I do hope he will not be afraid of his die-hards, whom he has got in the hollow of his hand. I admire and respect him and all wise opinion does the same, he has a *great* chance, and I do pray he takes it. France is not going to fight us and will feel moral isolation. The Ll.G-ites come to me and say "You prefer this 8th rate lot to us—join up and we'll sweep them out of office—the P.M.'s great pronouncement! what does it mean?—nothing." To which I answer "You aren't in a position to criticize anything. You asked for more money from Germany than France did, and but for your 1918 Elections or 'Make Germany pay the whole cost of the war', 'Hang the Kaiser', etc., France would not be in the Ruhr today. We are a small party but we delight in the P.M., and will back him to a man, he is the best find that this country has had for years." I only write this to show you *all* depends on the P.M.'s real courage. If I saw you I could tell you more. Europe is threatened with collapse and it is humiliating to be dragged at the heels of an ungrateful insolent French Government.

Forgive my bothering you and let me see you.

Yours in sincerity,
MARGOT ASQUITH.

21st July, 1923.

I can't tell you how relieved I was dear Mr. Dawson to get your charming letter—I was afraid you would think it cheek of me. If only Baldwin woos the votes of the Tory Industrials in the House of Commons and stands up against his die-hards, Derbys, Salisburys, etc., and is unwobbly he will remain in and do a lot of good, but if he is afraid of these latter or of France he is done and Ll.G. and Co. will intrigue and make it all very difficult for us.

From time to time Geoffrey exchanged further views with Newton W. Rowell of Toronto. In the following letter of July 20th, 1923, he deals with Baldwin and his predecessor in office and the condition of Europe:

. . . He has some of Bonar Law's qualities, but the public are inclined to think them more alike than they really are. Baldwin, in my opinion, is a much better judge of men . . . and he is very much more cheerful and robust. In domestic politics he has done exceedingly well since he took office, and I think he has done all that was possible in foreign affairs. It is a very considerable triumph to have got nearly the whole of Europe, always excepting France, round to the British view. The Italians are now definitely with us, and so at heart are the Belgians, if they were in a position to say so. . . .

Most aspects of the Indian problem were familiar to each member of the *Round Table* group, especially since Curtis's war-time sojourn in India. During his second term at Printing House Square, Indian political advance was constantly occupying Geoffrey's thoughts. He was destined to play a vital role in enlightening his countrymen, both during Lord Irwin's Vice-royalty, and in the 'thirties. Even in August, 1923, Lord Reading wrote to him from India, "I wish you could bring home the immense difficulties of keeping India within the Empire voluntarily and not by force".

The meeting of the Imperial Conference in London, was, as ever, a matter of deep interest to Geoffrey. Many references to it and to the individual Prime Ministers occur in the diary and correspondence. Of a visit to General Smuts he wrote to his friend, of South African days, Sir Drummond Chaplin:

> October 1st, 1923.
>
> . . . I had a long and interesting talk with Smuts on Thursday. As you may suppose, he is far more interested in the Ruhr and Corfu than in any of the domestic politics which he left behind him. His natural sympathies, of course, are strongly, and in the matter of the Ruhr, I think rightly, anti-French; and the result is to make him a tremendous British Jingo. He complains, for instance, that "we" are being dragged at the heel of the Latin races, that we are not speaking as the British Empire has spoken in the past, that we must assert ourselves and uphold the prestige of the Empire, for which we are trustees, etc., etc. . . .

After Baldwin had been five months in power in 1923, Geoffrey evidently, in view of the coming meeting of the National Unionist Conference at Plymouth, thought the occasion a good one for "gingering up" the Prime Minister. The major internal problem was unemployment, closely bound up with Foreign and Imperial relations. *The Times* referred to the fact that the cynics were talking already of a programme of faith and hope, while a brilliant cartoon of the week depicted the Prime Minister as "going nowhere in particular" but "just gliding about!" Geoffrey was determined, as far as lay in his power, to put an end to "the gliding about". After five months in office the Prime Minister could no longer face his party with "the beginner's plea for time". *The Times* demanded a clear definition of the Government's attitude towards "a condition of chaos in Europe", and expressed complete agreement with the views of those Dominion statesmen who admitted that the future of the Dominions was bound up in that of the United Kingdom, and that the ideal to work for was that of a Co-operative Commonwealth of Nations, each supplementing the others in every kind of international relationship. *The Times* expressed the view that whatever its shortcomings, the British Government was "the one stable factor in the European Kaleidoscope". Baldwin declared that his programme included the following proposed measures:

(1) Tax on manufactured goods with special regard to those imports that cause the greatest amount of employment among our people.
(2) Substantial preference to our Dominions.
(3) No tax on wheat or meat.
(4) Improve existing schemes of old age, ill health and unemployment insurance.
(5) Carefully investigate the best way to help agriculture and maintain the tillage of the nation.
(6) Develop our estates—our Empire.

Admirable aims from the standpoint of Printing House Square, and *The Times* therefore urged the Prime Minister to set up such machinery as would convince the country that they were not being invited to take a leap in the dark.

On November 5th the Editor was present in the Abbey for the funeral of Bonar Law, "a very beautiful service, Lang reading the lesson". On November 13th he and his wife went to the House of Commons to hear tributes to the ex-Premier.

Very soon after the death of Bonar Law the country became involved in an election, in which the Conservatives lost eighty-eight seats and were no longer in a majority, although with 258 seats they were still the strongest party. Labour had increased its representation in the House from 144 to 191; while the temporarily united Liberals numbered 158.

In retrospect, in the calm of his study at Langcliffe on December 20th, Geoffrey wrote a careful survey of the events which led up to the election and his part in them. He began: "Baldwin first broached his ideas to me on October 16. He put them rather vaguely, but very much as they afterwards took shape in his speeches—the hopeless problem of Europe, the difficulties for him personally of Bonar Law's pledge, his own belief in more general protection, the development of the Empire and its markets. A General Election would no doubt be necessary sooner or later."

Geoffrey thought Baldwin's policy and plans far too immature for immediate action, and that it was unwarrantable to risk upsetting the British Government, "the only fixed point in Europe". This view was strongly pressed in *The Times* on October 20th.

On November 5th Geoffrey produced "another warning leader"

which aroused criticism from many "enthusiasts", including Lord Milner, who thought it "completely off the rails".

Baldwin pursued his course, and made his dissolution speech on the 15th. "A characteristic utterance, not very impressive but transparently sincere."

"As to editorial policy," wrote Geoffrey, "I had no doubt that, once in the fight, which we had done our best to avert, there was nothing left but to back the Government all we could. They seemed certain to come back the strongest party and likely even to have a small majority. The alternatives were Labour, with their Capital Levy and other mischievous schemes, and the Liberals with no constructive policy at all. From every national point of view, and especially for reasons of foreign and Imperial policy, the best hope was that the Government should return as strong as possible. . . ."

The Election results swept away the Conservative majority, though they were still the largest party. Baldwin's first impulse was to resign and withdraw from the party leadership. Geoffrey promptly wrote a leading article affirming that it was still Baldwin's business to see that the King's Government was carried on:

> The next day was a Saturday (December 8). Baldwin went early to Chequers where Davidson (defeated most surprisingly at Hemel Hempstead), Neville Chamberlain, and others were going to see him. I myself went down in the afternoon to Buckingham Palace and had a long talk with Stamfordham, who was also revolving possible Prime Ministers in his mind (with an obvious preference for Coalition under an elder statesman such as Balfour, Asquith, Derby, Grey). I suggested, however (and he quite agreed), that all the arguments used against Curzon last Whitsuntide were incomparably stronger in the case of a Peer Prime Minister today. I also suggested (and he also agreed) that the King at all events should be very careful to give no ground for the impression that he was trying to avoid the necessity of asking Labour to form a Government. . . .
>
> After sleeping over it, . . . spent part of Sunday writing yet another leader urging the Government to "meet Parliament" as not merely the best tactics but the correct constitutional course. Lord Milner, with whom we dined, took exactly the opposite view. He thought that immediate resignation would stop intrigue, whereas I was becoming more and more convinced that the intrigue was started anyhow and would probably be successful if Baldwin were to disappear forthwith. In any case *The Times* came out strong in this sense on the Monday morning (December 10) and Stamfordham, to whom I had also written overnight to the same effect, rang me up early to say that H.M. was in agreement both with the letter and with the leader.
>
> So, I found, in the end was Baldwin himself when I saw him later in

the day. . . . I thought him far more settled, and on the whole happier, than on Friday. He had had a number of cheering letters and telegrams and felt that he had his Cabinet with him. They were to meet next day to settle their course of action, and he had no longer any doubt about its being the course already taken by *The Times*.

Next day (Tuesday, December 11) the Cabinet clinched the matter at once and unanimously.

In reply to a letter from Lord Robert Cecil[1] congratulating him on the leader in *The Times*, "Stalemate" (Dec. 8, 1923), Geoffrey replied:

It seems to me perfectly certain that we shall get back in the end, and should aim at getting back in the end, to the two-party system, which will presumably represent the division between constitutionalism and socialism. On the other hand, I see no good in attempting to produce that result this week. I doubt whether Asquith would drop Lloyd George, richly as the latter deserves it at his hands. I am quite certain that most Conservatives would refuse to serve in a Cabinet with Lloyd George. Above all, I think that any attempt at such an arrangement just now would open all the doors of intrigue, and that the safest, as well as the correct, constitutional course is for Baldwin to face Parliament and be beaten. The King would then presumably send for Ramsay MacDonald, who would be unable to govern without Liberal support and would therefore (if he undertook the task at all) gain some experience of administration with his wings clipped. I do not favour this plan with any notion of scoring off the Opposition, but simply because I feel it is the only way in which you will ultimately arrive at a strong reasonable constitutional party. . . .

Lord Robert replied (11th December, 1923) as follows from Paris:

Very many thanks for your letter of the 9th. I agree with you that MacDonald must be offered the Government, and personally I hope he will accept. Nothing is more dangerous than the existence of a large party in the State who have never had the responsibility of office and consequently do not know what can and cannot be done by the Government. My great anxiety is foreign affairs. MacDonald is too much under the influence of such men as Morel and may break the china. I have long felt that the only living Englishman who has the best chance of helping Europe through her prodigious difficulties is Grey, and though his blindness might prevent his being Foreign Secretary I do not see that it would be an obstacle to his Premiership, and really the European position appears to me to become more and more threatening.

[1] Now Viscount Cecil of Chelwood.

On December 9th, 1923, Geoffrey had written to Lord Stamfordham:

> Since our talk yesterday afternoon, I have been thinking over the situation and talking to various people about it. As is natural at this stage, they hold the most divergent views, but personally I have come to the very definite opinion that it is Baldwin's duty to King and Country, to say nothing of his own party, to carry on till he is defeated in the House of Commons. It seems to me that no precedent is of any value which is drawn from the early days when there was a strong Opposition emerging from a General Election with easy facilities for forming a new Government. Under those conditions it was right to let them get into the saddle as quickly as possible. But at this moment Baldwin still commands the strongest party, and it seems to me that the King has a right to press him to carry on. Moreover, this course puts an end at once to the vast amount of intrigue which is in progress; and when he is beaten, as he will and ought to be beaten, the choice of his successor becomes almost automatic.

The entry in the diary of December 13th follows:

Dec. 13. . . . went on to the Athenaeum to keep an assignation with the Archbishop of Canterbury, who had seen much of the Asquiths and something of Baldwin and Stamfordham. He seemed now to agree generally with what I had written in *The Times*, about which he was very complimentary.

After all these exciting events in the field of politics it must have been a welcome change for Geoffrey to spend a happy Christmas season with his family.

Dec. 24. Lunch—at the Athenaeum—Cecilia picked me up there to join the babies at a Christmas Tree . . . and the whole family dined with us before a most thrilling melodrama, "Good Luck", at Drury Lane with a real fire in a real prison, a real shipwreck and a real race with real horses for the Hunt Cup.

Dec. 25. Up at 7.0 and to Marylebone Church on a bitter cold frosty morning and back to find the babies absorbed in their stockings. . . . Later to see poor Lord Ribblesdale who was in bed and rather depressed and lonely but quite equal to an hour's talk about politics and Craven . . . we all dined—another family party—at Claridges.

Dec. 27. . . . Got in touch after some difficulty with Mann of the *Yorkshire Post* and gave him lunch at the "Travellers' ". His ideas on the political situation were much like mine. Then to a beautiful Carol Service at the Abbey.

XX

FIRST VISIT TO CANADA AND THE U.S.A. AND BALDWIN'S SECOND TERM

THE year 1924 was one of travel for Geoffrey and his wife. They spent three weeks in their beloved Italy, and in the autumn, two months in Canada and the United States. At home politics provided plenty of interest, for, in January, Ramsay MacDonald became Prime Minister—the first occasion on which a member of the Labour Party held that office—and in November, Baldwin, after his none too successful first brief term of office, became for the second time Premier; his administration was to last nearly five years.

The following letter to Drummond Chaplin gives Geoffrey's views on the political situation resulting from the fact that since the election in December, 1923, the Conservatives no longer had a majority over Labour and Liberal in the House of Commons:

January 4th, 1924.

> . . . All my efforts lately have been devoted to combating a very popular view that the Conservatives and Liberals should join hands forthwith in order at all hazards to keep Labour out of office. I really cannot imagine anything more immoral or utterly fatuous. It comes largely from the middle element in the City (where it is not shared, however, by Monty Norman, or any of the more intelligent people), from the unthinking, comfortable people up and down the country, who never bother to work or vote, and are now horrified by the prospect of Socialism. . . .
>
> Like everyone else, I think it more than likely that we shall ultimately develop a constitutional party ranged against Socialism, and for this reason I think it would be stupid to make enemies without cause in the Liberal ranks. But there is a world of difference between a combination of this kind in opposition to a palpable danger, and a purely artificial coalition based on nothing but funk. . . .

Geoffrey was evidently fully conscious that a new chapter in our Parliamentary history was beginning. He had a long talk at Number 10 with the Prime Minister, just back from Worcestershire; he found Baldwin's views unchanged, and determined not to make an approach to Asquith with a view to forming a Conservative-Liberal combination, as suggested by certain nervous people in the City. Through Gray,[1] a member of *The Times* Parliamentary staff, the Editor kept in close touch with Ramsay MacDonald and was thus able to give a fairly accurate forecast of the plans of the Labour Party.

On the day of the defeat of the Baldwin Government (January 21st, 1924) Geoffrey was watching the Parliamentary scene and listening to the Prime Minister's last speech while in office. The following day the first Labour Government was formed (it only survived till the beginning of November). *The Times*, in its news columns, dealt with its composition and emphasized the special position of Sidney Webb and Sir Sydney Olivier. It pointed out that the latter, like Sidney Webb, had been a Fabian even in his Colonial Office days, and, as a former Governor in the West Indies, had a wide experience and seemed, therefore, destined for the India Office. On the 24th in the leading article ("Men and Places"), in which the paper dealt with the new Prime Minister's appointments, it noted the arrival of the first woman on the Treasury Bench[2] and admitted that Ramsay MacDonald had "shown most successful cleverness in dovetailing its (the very miscellaneous character of his following) various elements into a composite whole".

Within twenty-two days of Ramsay MacDonald's appointment as Prime Minister, in a leading article—"Problems of Every Government" (February 13th, 1924)—*The Times* stated:

> The whole country shares his (the Prime Minister's) hope that a Labour Government, credited with unusual first-hand knowledge of the conditions and the requirements of the wage-earning class, may succeed, where others have failed, in contributing something substantial to the solution of such perennial difficulties as those of providing sufficient houses and sufficient employment to go round.

The paper dealt sympathetically with the Prime Minister's proposal to set up "a really authoritative committee" to consider the whole question of the National Debt, and of the effect of taxation on trade: it commended Ramsay MacDonald's attempt to make "a complete,

[1] J. A. Gray, formerly on the staff of the *Scotsman*. Subsequently connected with journalism in South Africa.

[2] Miss—later the Right Honourable—Margaret Bondfield, Parliamentary Secretary to the Ministry of Labour in 1924.

honest, able, scientific survey of our national finance" which obviously depends "wholly and solely upon the choice of men to conduct it".

During the weeks before the trip to Italy the diary records the usual round of varied contacts. As in the previous year there are many references to Tutankhamen, in connection with whose tomb there was trouble with the Egyptian Government at Luxor, where Howard Carter "finally lost his temper" with the authorities. On February 18th "more Luxor agitation" owing to the fact that *The Times* was the sole channel through which information and photographs were distributed, and Geoffrey inserted "a short note to dispel illusions about a 'Press Monopoly' "; and on February 22nd he had "rather a hectic interview with Lady Carnarvon about Luxor".

In March among the subjects occupying the Editor's attention was a slight racing accident to the Prince of Wales, on which topic he had exchanged letters with Stamfordham in the previous year; and Mr. Churchill's decision to stand for the Westminster constituency was the subject of two leading articles in *The Times*, "The Abbey Campaign" (March 6, 1924) and "The Abbey Result" (March 21st). In the former the paper explained that Mr. Churchill's "desire to return to the Conservative fold" had "not lately been concealed"; it recorded that Mr. Churchill, backed by the "Press Trust", was fighting the official Conservative candidate and thought that he would have been well advised to wait for a more suitable occasion; nevertheless *The Times* said, "The grave conflict with Socialism, which Mr. Churchill avows his intention of undertaking, is assuredly no chimerical or unnecessary crusade". Later, when Mr. Churchill failed by only forty-three votes to be elected, the paper stated, "No one, beyond a small embittered circle, desires to exclude his brilliance and his driving power from the House of Commons." Six weeks later (May 8) *The Times* was applauding Mr. Churchill's speech at Liverpool and expressing the hope that he would soon be back in the House of Commons.

Most of the month of April was spent by the Dawsons in Italy. During the last part of their visit they were joined by their intimate friends, Mr. and Mrs. William Clive Bridgeman. They visited Verona, Lake Garda, Padua, Ravenna and Venice. At Milan Geoffrey discussed "the tyranny of Fascism" with the correspondent of *The Times*; in some north Italian towns and tourist resorts he complains of "hotels full of Huns" or of attractive little places on Lake Garda "invaded by a pack of Huns" in motor-boats; at S. Vigilio he and his wife consorted with local Fascists; "just as we were thinking of bed about 10 came two serenaders with guitars to entice them (the girls) into the big room of a friend to which we all adjourned for a remarkable couple of hours. All the young men of the neighbourhood dropped in by degrees—

Alfredo the boatman, the local Fascist leaders, a Professor from Verona—and sang and danced, Cecilia with the star dancer from Brescia". At San Marino, "a most enchanting little mountain town with a view over the whole surrounding country as from an aeroplane", they saw everything including "the public offices and Duomo (where the two 'regents' are formally chosen)"; in Venice from a restaurant in the Piazza they "watched the lights of the gondolas like fireflies on the Grand Canal" and homeward bound had "a wonderful last gondola journey to the station before the steamers and the motor-boats were about".

There are several references to visits to Wembley Exhibition. On May 15th Geoffrey attended a large Government luncheon in connection with an Emigration Conference, where J. H. Thomas delivered a speech "full of robust Imperialism and misplaced aspirates". On May 28th he and John Astor went to *The Times* Pavilion to receive Their Majesties, and the King and Queen of Italy. King George said to Geoffrey that he was very glad to see him back at Printing House Square.

On June 26th the entry shows how useful his regular attendances at Round Table "moots" could be: "To a 'Moot' in Buckingham Palace Gardens (the residence of Lionel Hichens), a very full gathering with Lord Milner there[1] to talk Egypt and the Sudan—a very useful check on the leader, which 'X.' was writing meanwhile."

The following correspondence took place in June between Stamfordham and the Editor, who must have enjoyed justifying the use by *The Times* of a Johnsonian phrase:

Buckingham Palace,
21st June, 1924.

Dear Dawson,

Friday's report from the House of Commons describes how Lloyd George with a wave of the hand dismissed the interruptions caused in his speech and continued his review in "inspissated gloom". It is only in our very much up to date dictionaries that I was able to gather the true nature of Lloyd George's gloom! But are we to accept it as a recognized addition to the British Vocabulary? Possibly there is a special *Times* dictionary—if so perhaps you will send me a copy of it!

Geoffrey replied:

June 23rd, 1924.

"Inspissated gloom" is no new-comer to the English vocabulary. You may find the phrase, for instance, at least a century and a half ago in the

[1] It must have been one of the last gatherings of the Kindergarten attended by Milner.

works of Dr. Johnson, who complained of a scene in Macbeth that "the beetle and the bat distracted from the general idea of darkness—inspissated gloom".[1] My impression is that it is also used by Charles Lamb and other eminent English authors, but at any rate I am prepared to take my stand with Dr. Johnson.

Since the beginning of his first Editorship, Geoffrey had taken a special interest in Irish affairs. The fact that his fellow-member of the Kindergarten, Richard Feetham, had been appointed Chairman of the Irish Boundary Commission,[2] if anything heightened his interest in the problems with which that body would have to deal. When Mr. Justice Feetham was in London, he naturally saw him and heard at first hand of the difficulties which he was facing.

The Dawsons spent most of August at Langcliffe—and only had a few days in London at the end of the month before setting off for Canada and the United States on September 4th.

He wrote the following letter on the Irish Boundary question after his day spent with Lord Balfour on August 31st, 1924:

> I can throw rather more light on the Irish situation today than would have been possible if I had answered you yesterday, which I spent almost entirely in the company of Lord Balfour. . . .
>
> This is what he had to impart. By what is almost an accident he remembered and disinterred (with the aid of a more orderly secretary) the letter which F.E. (Lord Birkenhead) wrote to him when he returned from Washington in February, 1922, and found the Irish Treaty an accomplished fact. . . . It is the interpretation by a very eminent lawyer, who was at that time Lord Chancellor, of the actual words employed in the Treaty. I need not attempt to summarize the whole letter which I have seen. The broad effect of it is to show by precedents drawn from other Treaties that entirely different words must have been used if there had been any intention to leave the Commission free to take away large slices of Northern Ireland. "The Article," he says in one place, "contemplates the maintenance of Northern Ireland as an entity already existing —not as a new State to be brought into existence."
>
> Since discovering this letter A.J.B. has been in consultation with Winston and Carson. All of them agree that it is of the utmost importance and Carson apparently thinks that it may be sufficient to persuade Craig to appoint a member of the Commission after all. I must say I have my

[1] Geoffrey probably had in mind a familiar All Souls story of two Fellows who shared a taste for recondite language. W. P. Ker (Professor of Poetry), meeting F. Y. Edgeworth (Professor of Political Economy) at Oxford Station, on a day of heavy fog in London, said, "Well, did you find it caliginous?" "Yes," replied Edgeworth, "but not inspissated." This amusing anecdote was supplied by Mr. Dermot Morrah.

[2] June 5th, 1924.

doubts about this. I have often found Carson reasonable enough in private talk, but he is always apt to become extreme in public. However, he is certainly most anxious now that there should be nothing like a complete crisis and a general election over this business, which is indeed the last thing that can be of any real service to Ulster. Winston also seems to be working for peace, and Lloyd George (whom we encountered at Wembley yesterday afternoon) has apparently committed himself to supporting F.E.'s[1] interpretation of the Treaty in a public speech.

Whether the spell works or not, there is clearly nothing to be done but to make the most of it, so I devoted myself this morning to writing a leader[2] against the day of publication. When this will be I am not quite sure (I have written tonight to Winston, in whose hands the arrangements have been left). . . .

. . . . .

Few travellers can have walked down the gangway at the landing-stage of Quebec, dominated by the Heights of Abraham, better prepared for a tour of Canada than Geoffrey and his wife. Canadian problems had interested them, since South African days, in a special way, for both Canada and South Africa had two European Motherlands. In each case British settlement had only begun when European colonization had been established; in the case of Canada early in the seventeenth century; in the case of South Africa by the middle of that century.

The Dawsons arrived at Quebec on September 10th, and sailed from New York on October 25th in the *Olympic*, reaching Southampton on October 31st. At the outset of the tour they had their first contact with a North American business convention—an unforgettable experience for new arrivals from the Old World—when groups of insurance-travellers [*sic*], "morticians", "spectacle-makers" or "meat-packers", "dressmakers", or members of some other trade crowd the lobbies, vestibules and elevators of the hotels, with their women folk; and staid business men in silk knickerbockers, white stockings and parti-coloured boots and with paper caps and trumpets throng the corridors, each with his label. But fortunately the Dawsons, in company with Philip Kerr, escaped from the Conventionites and were able to feel the spell of old-world France in Quebec, and to visit the Heights of Abraham, where the fate of North America was decided.[3]

[1] Lord Birkenhead was still politically active and not, as the tone of the letter almost suggests, a distinguished figure of past history.

[2] The leading article, "New Light on the Irish Deadlock", appeared in *The Times* of September 8th, when he was off the "Banks" of Newfoundland in the *Carmania*.

[3] In the sense so often used by American historians, that the battle decided that French would not be the predominant civilization in North America.

At Montreal the visitors discussed world problems with Sir Edward Beatty, the President of the Canadian Pacific Railroad, and General Currie, President of McGill University. At Toronto much time was spent discussing Canadian and journalistic matters with sagacious Sir John Willison, the correspondent of *The Times*; at Niagara Falls they were lucky enough to visit the garden of a friend with "the most wonderful viewpoint in the world". At all the chief stopping-places telegrams from "the faithful Brumwell" greeted them with reports that all was well with the children.

Happy carefree days were spent in the Canadian Rockies, at Banff and Lake Louise. From the latter, where they were spending Michael's birthday, they "sent him his first cable and wished he might have so good a day as ours". In the Rockies they revelled in the clear atmosphere and the wonderful autumn colourings: they inspected the paddocks with Rocky Mountain sheep, goats and bison and explored mountain trails, taking their lunch with them "by the side of the path in company with a most engaging squirrel" (chipmunk); on another day they lunched "in company this time with three fascinating grey birds" (the Canadian jay). At Vancouver they witnessed the arrival of the Prince of Wales "amid scenes of great enthusiasm". At Cumberland on Vancouver Island, Geoffrey received cables at intervals which showed "that politics in England were irretrievably setting towards a crisis—just as we were at the remotest part of our journey". En route for home they left Canada by way of Moose Jaw.

On the first day in the United States Geoffrey wrote of North Dakota, "a much more cultivated country with groups of trees round every little homestead of small white houses and big red barn. . . . Wheat gradually giving way to Indian corn". At Chicago he met his former friend John W. Davis, now engaged on a strenuous Election Campaign, as Democratic Candidate for the Presidency. At Washington he was taken by Willmott Lewis, *The Times* correspondent, to see President Coolidge, "an unimpressive man" with whom he had a "rather dull conversation". He met many political leaders in the capital, among them Herbert C. Hoover (a future President) and Charles E. Hughes, Secretary of State. The visitors did the usual round of sightseeing in Washington and were taken out to charming Mount Vernon (the home of George Washington, on the Potomac) by Yoshida, the Japanese *chargé d'affaires*. At Washington Geoffrey was naturally much impressed by the Library of Congress with its spacious rooms and records and wonderful catalogue. In New York he was given "a tremendous luncheon at the *New York Times* office by Mr. Adolph S. Ochs and some forty of the staff—speeches! And an inspection of the whole vast and very wonderful office", later rejoining

Cecilia with whom he "went to the top of the Woolworth Building for an amazing view". And so after four very crowded days they went on board the *Olympic* shortly before midnight. The diary entry for October 25th begins, "First day at sea—begun in the small hours of the morning, as we moved down the river past the glittering sky-scrapers—a wonderful sight." Among the passengers was the Prince of Wales with whom the Dawsons dined—"quite a pleasant party; after which he took me to an uninhabited deck and talked America and English politics vehemently till midnight".

During the last three days of the voyage the thoughts of the travellers were concentrated on the General Election in Great Britain. On October 30th there were more wireless messages showing that the Election was "becoming a landslide and a Conservative majority overall of nearly 200!" On October 31st, the last day of the voyage, as the *Olympic* rounded the Isle of Wight, the *Repulse* dipped ensign and cheered.

Geoffrey must have regretted his absence from England during such an exciting election when Baldwin was given, after his disastrous experience a year earlier, what happens but rarely in life—a second chance. But exciting events were taking place and within seventy-two hours of his arrival in London the Labour Government had resigned. Entries in the diary during the first week after his return follow:

Nov. 4. Labour Government resigns . . . to Whitehall, where I had a talk with J. H. Thomas in his Colonial Office. He promised to make (and did make) a good speech at Sheffield tonight. . . . Ramsay MacDonald resigned at 5 and Baldwin accepted office. I had a long talk with him at 9 in Eaton Square and tried to give him some wise advice about his Government, which he took only in part!

Nov. 5. Coolidge had swept the States in yesterday's election. . . . I gave J. H. Thomas a pat on the back and pulled the legs of the place-hunters with Morgan's assistance under the title of "The Door-Step Club".

Nov. 6. . . . another talk with Baldwin and tea with him in Palace Chambers. He had practically finished his Cabinet—some daring rather good appointments, some duds, and some deplorable blots, as I told him. Thence to Printing House Square to write about it in such intervals as I could get from visitors and a Board and a great dinner given by Kindersley to Owen D. Young[1] (A.J.B. and all the ex-Chancellors—Neville and Austen Chamberlain, McKenna, Horne—and other eminent financiers).

[1] Chairman of the General Electric Company and a representative of the United States at the Reparations Conference in 1924.

During this week *The Times* published several leaders on the political situation, "Cabinet Making" (November 4th), "A Courageous Farewell" (November 6th), and finally "The New Cabinet" (November 7th). In the first of these leaders *The Times* dealt with the "amazing stroke of fortune" after the Conservative disaster of the previous year that this opportunity should have been presented to them by Ramsay MacDonald. The paper commented, "There is every reason, happily, to believe that Mr. Baldwin himself has no intention of initiating a period either of reaction or of mere tranquillity." The paper also urged the desirability of making use of Mr. Churchill's "wits, imagination, and driving power". In the short leader of November 6th, "A Courageous Farewell", *The Times* referred to the speech of J. H. Thomas at Sheffield as "a great ending to one of the few personal records in the late Administration which are not merely irreproachable but have a certain distinction". In the article on "The New Cabinet" the paper congratulated the Prime Minister on the daring appointment of Mr. Churchill as Chancellor of the Exchequer, and also welcomed the transference of Mr. Edward Wood (later Lord Halifax) to the Ministry of Agriculture.

Lord Esher[1] wrote (4th November, 1924) to Geoffrey from Scotland:

> I am sorry for poor old Baldwin, who had to adjust all these rival claims, and compose these evil passions! I only hope, for his sake, that he possesses the "let 'em go hang" pawkiness of old C.-B. Has he? There are two questions that he ought to put in the forefront of his programme. They admit of no delay; for big majorities have an unpleasant melting habit.
>
> (1) To establish the principle of consulting the Dominions on *every* important question of foreign policy, beginning with the attitude to be adopted towards Russia.
>
> (2) Amend the Parliament Act and reform the House of Lords.
>
> If he does not tackle these high matters, he will endanger the Empire, and pave the way for a bad Socialist reaction. However, no one knows all this better than you.

Geoffrey replied (5th November):

> I am even sorrier for Baldwin than you are for I have seen him at work. All the place-hunters are on his doorstep, while the country gents are shooting pheasants. He will not be able to think about policy till he gets all these people fixed.

On November 21st, Lord Esher wrote:

[1] The second Lord Esher.

East is East, and West is West, etc., etc. The "Liberal" elements in the Coalition never believed Kipling. They were furious when the King insisted on offering him an O.M.

Ramsay and his merry scoundrels took a much more practical view of India and Egypt. In old Kabul and Kandahar days, the Whigs always said, we must either *govern* or come away. No middle course is possible. It is disheartening to contrast Lyautey's government in Morocco, with our wishy-washy methods. However! What I really wanted to say was this.

There is an absolute necessity ahead for reconstituting the Committee of Imperial Defence on "Imperial" lines. It must be swept out and garnished afresh; and its principal members, after the Prime Minister, should be Dominion Representatives who should take precedence of Chiefs of the Staffs, etc., etc. This is the first step towards taking in the Dominions at the earliest possible stage of any discussion of matters that affect the whole Empire. Please think it out.

In the weeks after the Conservative triumph, Geoffrey was full of zest and discussed "opium" with Bishops Brent and Porter of the Protestant Episcopalian Church of America; encouraged me in my purchase of a controlling interest in the *Spectator*; gave invaluable help to the work of the Child Emigration Society; was present at the Founders' Feast at King's, Cambridge, and went with Walter Durnford "to a beautiful service in the candle-lit Chapel (almost nothing but Parry's long *magnificat*)". On December 16th he and his wife attended the Arthur Lees' Silver Wedding Feast, a great gathering, at which he "had Madame de Laszlo and Molly Northcliffe for neighbours and a very long talk with Austen Chamberlain afterwards". In December the Dawsons lunched with old Yarrow "on partridge cooked for 2*d.* by his latest (carbon) invention—and saw his traffic model and his motor periscope and discussed his latest hobby—the price of gold".

The following letter (December 29th, 1924) to a leader-writer is of interest because it gives Geoffrey's general outlook at the end of the year:

I gathered from our three-cornered telephone conversation the other day that you are prepared to write me a New Year's leader for publication on Wednesday night. . . .

I think that the keynote of your leader might be the immense importance of stability and continuity in the present condition of the world. It seems to me to be worth while sacrificing almost any single item of legislation or administration in order to achieve these objects. Baldwin has a heaven-sent second chance. The last thing we want, so far as this country is concerned, is any repetition of some risky experiment which would divide the Cabinet and throw the country once more into turmoil. I see no prospect of it myself, for I am sure that Baldwin has learned his lesson; but I think it is always worth while rubbing in the value, not as Bonar Law called it of tranquillity, but of stability and continuity.

. . . There is the real value of this year's Labour Government experiment in Foreign and Imperial Affairs, which I think will never again be discussed in the House of Commons with so little knowledge and sympathy as in the past. . . .

Clearly Geoffrey was pleased to see Baldwin back in power and he met him fairly regularly during the first full year of his second Premiership.

On occasions when there seemed to be too much complacency at "No. 10" the Editor of *The Times* was by no means loath to give a judicious prod to his friend, for whom he had a genuine liking, although aware of his failings.

Throughout his Editorship, in the tradition of Buckle, he kept in close touch with the King's Private Secretary, Lord Stamfordham. On New Year's Day, 1925, he received the following letter from Windsor Castle, which shows how the King's Private Secretary consulted him on such matters as the selection of suitable candidates for the "Order of Merit":

I must send a line of grateful appreciation of your leader in today's *Times* on "The Golden Bough". It is very helpful. You can imagine the difficulty experienced in selecting the *right* people for the O.M. For two years and more we have been endeavouring to get a consensus of opinion in Frazer's[1] favour—and, on the whole, succeeding in doing so. Some day I wish some unanimity could be arrived at as to "scholarship" and I shall look forward to a talk with you some day on the subject.

Geoffrey replied (January 4th, 1925):

I am glad you approve of the little article on "The Golden Bough". I confess frankly that I have never got through the whole of it myself; but I know enough about it to feel quite satisfied that the O.M. was worthily bestowed. As for pure scholarship, I doubt whether my own University can at present produce anything in that class, but I think you might do worse than make a few inquiries about A. E. Housman[2] at Cambridge and elsewhere. He was, by the way, an undergraduate at Oxford and is still an Honorary Fellow of an Oxford College, though he now holds a Chair of Latin at Cambridge. Incidentally he is one of our greatest poets. . . .

[1] Sir James George Frazer (1854–1941), scholar and anthropologist.
[2] A. E. Housman (1859–1936) was in fact offered the O.M. but refused.

The Times made its appeal on behalf of the "St. Paul's Restoration Fund" on January 7th—to which the public responded most generously. The fund made rapid headway—within a week donations amounted to £74,000—and by January 28th the sum of £200,000 was reached.

The diary records as usual a miscellany of events ranging from an international rugby match to an evening with Barrie, and a visit to Savoy Hill (the former quarters of the B.B.C.) where Geoffrey, "rather nervous without spectacles" contributed a sentence or two to the broadcast news.

Several Saturdays and Sundays were spent at All Souls with old friends, and on March 4th the Prince of Wales lunched at Printing House Square, and Lord Milner, just back from South Africa, was also present. It must have been his last visit to the office of *The Times*.

In a leading article (March 21st) *The Times* observed that Lord Curzon's death had removed "a great figure, rather than a great influence" for he was "a remote and magnificent personage", unaffected by popular approval, and the pomp and circumstance of his "official façade" was compared with the real man to be found by his friends behind the barrier of reserve—"perhaps the last of the great Viceroys of the old school".

In February and March the Editor was in touch with the Prime Minister. On one occasion they discussed at length "the Political Levy, housing and insurance". In a leading article, "Conservatives and Trade Unionism" (February 19th), *The Times* urged the Cabinet to consider very carefully their attitude to the Political Levy Bill, which was being promoted by a section of the Conservative Party. The paper dwelt on the fact that Conservative opinion as a whole was by no means sympathetic towards the Bill. It explained that in its simplest form, it sought "to transform the system under which trade unionists" might contract out of the political contribution levied by their unions into a system of "contracting in"; and in theory, it asserted, the change seemed eminently just and reasonable. *The Times* continued:

> For our part we hope sincerely that the Government will refuse to identify themselves with any such measure. The Conservative Party have infinitely more important work in hand than tinkering with Trade Union privileges.

In the article "We Stand for Peace" (March 7th), *The Times* dealt with the Prime Minister's great success in the House of Commons the day before—"a success of his own peculiar kind. But his success, which was very remarkable, was due at bottom to his own qualities, and in particular to that broad instinctive sanity—sometimes verging on sentiment, but never on pettiness—which always directs his outlook on national affairs."

The writer of the article went on to say that the Cabinet had, a week earlier—"very largely, it is said, because of the firm personal intervention of its leader"—decided that there should be no official support for Mr. Macquisten's Bill. The leader ended with the words, "It is a very long time since any speech in Parliament has made a more profound impression." Haldane referred to the speech as having "lifted public affairs to a higher level and recalled to me things that happened fifty years ago". At the conclusion of the speech Baldwin said, "Although I know that there are those who work for different ends from most of us in this House, yet there are many in all ranks and all parties who will re-echo my prayer, 'Give peace in our time, O Lord'."

The diary at this period shows how Geoffrey's attention was divided between political events and family affairs:

Mar. 3. A telephone message from Ronald Waterhouse on my return—I'd written to him yesterday to say I wanted to see the Prime Minister and went down and had half an hour with him at 1. Thence to the Travellers' to lunch with Steel-Maitland and talk about the Political Levy and the "Dole".

Mar. 5. . . . Our morning was quite overclouded by the loss in the Park of our very old friend "Squeaky" and we had another search and informed the police!

Mar. 6. Cecilia and I went down to the House again for the Political Levy Bill and a remarkable speech by Baldwin—very quiet, very impressive and extraordinarily effective. I wrote something about it at intervals at home and in the office during the afternoon.

The loss of Michael's "Squeaky", a little stuffed lion, was a matter of major concern to the parents. Most of one morning was spent by them, accompanied by the faithful Sheba, in searching for it in Hyde Park—but alas and alack without success. The following day a new toy was purchased, with some trepidation named "Squeaky the Second". On Saturday, two days after the "tragedy", a *dies non* usually as far as Printing House Square was concerned, Geoffrey was involved in office worries owing to depletion of the staff of the Foreign Department. The one bright spot in an otherwise tiresome day for the Editor of *The Times* is thus referred to in the diary, "On the other hand, 'Squeaky the Second', purchased for Michael with some doubt yesterday, is an immense success."

Geoffrey naturally felt very deeply the death of Lord Milner (13th May, 1925), the passing of the great public servant who had done his duty without personal ambition, whose one desire had been to serve his ideals; under whom he had worked from shortly after his twenty-seventh birthday for three and a half years, and whose memory always remained enshrined in his heart.

On March 20th he had dined alone with Lord Milner whom he found "rather aged, but very interesting about his South African visit". Ten days later he learned that Lord Milner was to be offered the Oxford Chancellorship. When he went to see his old Chief he found him "rather worried and disinclined". On May 12th there was a note in the diary recording the receipt of "a very depressing bulletin about Lord Milner". The following day came the news of his death and Geoffrey wrote in the diary, "I could do little but write a line to Lady Milner and revise the memoir and leader"—which he had written at Langcliffe when he first realized how serious was the nature of the illness. In the leading article he referred to the heavy toll the spring had taken of great public servants. He was thinking of Curzon among others; he wrote, "The death of Lord Milner, in retrospect, the greatest of them all."

He dealt with Lord Milner's genuine dislike of office and his innumerable interests—in business, in literature, in the guidance of such semi-public organizations as the Rhodes Trust, and above all in the furtherance of those great National and Imperial causes to which in one position or another he had devoted the whole of an extraordinarily consistent life. Of the South African period, about which he was so well qualified to speak, "that momentous proconsulship", he wrote, "and especially the rapid reconstruction which followed the long-drawn struggle . . . is a tale of patient investigation, definite decision, unswerving resolution, and singular efficiency". Finally he wrote of the character of his former chief and the part he played in the World War:

> How far-reaching that service became at the turning-point of the war, what a godsend that combination of cool judgment and knowledge with the Premier's flair and courage, how essential to victory the power of decision which at the blackest moment consolidated the direction of the Allied Armies . . .; but, when the story comes to be fully written, it may yet be found that nothing even in the South African chapter has left a more decisive mark on history than Lord Milner's work at Doullens and in Downing Street. . . .
>
> Even in the least creditable days of South African controversy Lord Milner's high purpose, his personal integrity, his complete indifference to his own fortunes had never been impugned. His bitterest critics—assailing his methods, his choice of assistants, his lack of sympathy with their own ideas—paid tribute to a rare association of first-rate brains and

unimpeachable character. That particular brand of qualities, which it is the fashion nowadays to regard as almost mutually exclusive in public men, does nevertheless come in the end to establish itself firmly in the mind of the British democracy. They never really knew Lord Milner; but they trusted him as few statesmen of our generation have been trusted, and they recognize his death as the falling of a pillar of the State.

On May 15th Geoffrey took Baldwin with him to All Souls where the Prime Minister meditated a speech on public service, in which he took Milner as a great example of devotion to the State, and on the 16th he and Cecilia attended the funeral at Canterbury Cathedral and afterwards at Salehurst; at the grave were gathered his old South African staff and a few others—"a beautiful peaceful spot at the edge of the cornfields". Two days later the Milner Memorial Service was held at Westminster Abbey.

On June 12th Geoffrey received a letter from Mr. Amery informing him that, if he was willing, the Rhodes Trust would like to appoint him as a Trustee. A few days later he replied:

My dear Leo,

You may take it that I am delighted to accept the kind invitation of the Rhodes Trustees that I should join their number. I am, in fact, both surprised and greatly honoured by the suggestion. My hesitation at first only came from the fear that I might not have time to do my share of the work; but I see no reason why this should not be managed and I am quite clear that I should like, above all, to be associated again with the Trust.

Geoffrey received the following letter from Lady Milner on October 19th:

My dear Mr. Dawson,

Among all Alfred's friends there was no one among the men younger than himself of whom he was so fond as you, or whose character and affection and ability he trusted more.

I have gone through all his few personal possessions. The few things he touched and handled and wore. I should like you to have something really personal.

He had three watches—you may remember—he wore them impartially and alternately, treating them with the greatest care and never altering the hands, so that often when he looked at them it was only his admirable arithmetical sense that enabled him to find out the time. I send you one, the one that was left him by his half brother, Charles

Cromie. He wore it constantly, it was one of his few family possessions. I should like you to have it in memory of him. . . .

Yours affectionately,
VIOLET MILNER.

Labour problems were much to the fore in the summer. The deadlock in the coal situation dragged on but, on July 31st, the Prime Minister announced in the House of Commons "the stoppage of the stoppage"—a temporary subsidy and a big enquiry. On 17th September Geoffrey had a talk with Baldwin just returned from Aix, "who wanted news which I couldn't give him". On September 23rd the diary contains the entry, "Another prod for our rather sleepy Government about the complacent spirit shown in their Party report and the simultaneous holidays of the whole Cabinet." The leading article in *The Times*, "Complacency" (September 24th), criticized the apparent complacency reflected in the recently published annual report of the National Union of Conservative Associations. It asserted that a complacent spirit might be adequate at Brighton, where the Union was shortly to meet, but not in other parts of the country, "but it will be surprising if echoes do not reach the Government of the real anxiety which exists among their supporters everywhere about the present industrial and political situation".

The paper then enquired what, in opposition to the incessant campaign of extremist propaganda, had the Government got to say on "the present position of the housing problem, a fertile source of popular unrest?" A statement towards the end of the article suggested that ". . . the real antidote to Communism was not repression, but a better alternative policy, and a wider popular knowledge that it is in fact being devised and diligently carried out. . . ." In the leader "Parliament Meets" (November 16th), after the three months' recess, *The Times* warmly endorsed the Prime Minister's attitude towards Labour, as exemplified in his "Peace in our time" speech in the House of Commons, on the Political Levy Bill. The paper regarded Baldwin's attitude, in spite of all that was said to the contrary, as "producing a atmosphere in which their (genuine grievances in the industrial world) redress would some day be discussed without passion. It is essential that he, and those who agree with him, should be thinking of the next constructive stage in the organization of peace at home".

Few events since he returned to Printing House Square gave Geoffrey greater pleasure than the appointment of his friend Edward Wood as Viceroy. In his mind he and Lord Milner had that quality in common which impelled them to hold office as a matter of duty without any thought of personal advancement. In the leading article, "The New Viceroy" (October 30th), *The Times* said, "Mr. Edward Wood is one of those rare characters in the public life of the country of whom all men speak so well that no great post falls vacant without the suggestion that he is admirably qualified to fill it." The Editor was convinced that the new Viceroy possessed just those qualities which would win him respect in India—a land where spiritual values count for much. "Mr. Wood's record," stated the leading article, "is precisely of that kind which should win him welcome from the outset from the people and the Services in India. He is known in this country as a man of the highest character, a popular administrator. . . . He has shown that he possesses both courage and sympathy. That he is also by heredity and habit a man of deep religious feelings is a quality which is no subject for public discussion, but is more directly relevant to administration in India than elsewhere. . . ."

With the appointment of his friend, whose outlook he shared on many problems, he naturally followed events in India during the new Viceroy's term of office with intensified interest. He and his wife spent three months on their Indian tour in the winter of 1928–29, and it is no exaggeration to say that the part Geoffrey played in furthering the Indian Settlement—not to be finally achieved till after his death—was one of his greatest contributions to the Commonwealth during his Editorship of *The Times*.

In the late autumn Geoffrey noted that the celebration of Armistice Day had been more serious than ever before, "a stiller silence, larger crowds, less junketing, more church services, ending in an admirable broadcast sermon by the Archbishop in Canterbury Cathedral". Geoffrey went to the House of Commons to hear the Locarno debate, "Austen Chamberlain very concise and good; MacDonald oratorical and petty; Lloyd George solicitous for the Dominions . . . only thirteen wild men voted eventually against approval of the Pact." At the end of the month he met Luke Thompson, M.P. for Sunderland, and discussed with him the serious state of the shipbuilding industry and the alarming increase in unemployment. When the change in the chief proprietorship of the *Spectator* took place, *The Times* printed a leading article (December 3rd), and rejoiced that it would involve no essential breach in a great tradition, and recalled the fact that in the hundred years since it was founded by Robert Stephen Rintoul, it had hitherto known but three proprietors.

On December 23rd Geoffrey received the following letter from Mr. John Walter:

> I want to take this opportunity of Christmas to thank you for the admirable judgment with which you have conducted the Paper during

the past year. Under your Editorship *The Times* has resumed its traditional function of leading and at the same time steadying public opinion. That dual task could never have been so difficult as now, but I am confident that there never was a time in the Paper's history when it was performed with greater efficiency and consistency, nor—may I add—when the tone of the Paper was higher or more pleasing to those of our readers by whose good opinion we chiefly set store. For all this I want to express my thanks to you. . . .

After three years of his second Editorship Geoffrey, during the Christmas holidays, wrote a "Retrospect" setting forth his views under "the new regime". After dealing with the very satisfactory state of the paper's finances and circulation, he dealt with the editorial side of Printing House Square. Some extracts from the memorandum follow:

EDITORIAL POLICY

This recovery has been assisted, of course, by greater stability on the Editorial side. I was quite clear when I came back that what *The Times* wanted first and foremost was a period of obvious steadiness, even stodginess, before it could become an active force again. No doubt it is of the essence of a successful independent newspaper that no one should be quite certain overnight what opinion it will express next morning. Nothing is duller than the conviction that it will support a party or an individual under all conditions. But the process of startling the public had been carried rather too far—or perhaps it would be more true to say that the very violence of *The Times* had become dull because it supported nothing that the Government might do and was out of touch with its own public through perpetual nagging.

In the last three years *The Times* has endeavoured to return to the tradition of fair play for the Government of the day without by any means following them at every point. It has had three successive Governments to deal with—Conservative under Bonar Law and Baldwin in 1923, Labour in 1924 and Conservative again in 1925. Its relations with each have always been friendly to the extent of having personal relations with ministers and the chance of setting out their intentions honestly. . . .

LEADER WRITING

For my own amusement, and because the occasion has often been important, I have kept a cutting-book of the leading articles that I write myself. There are not as many of them as I should like, for nothing is more satisfactory than the production of an effective leader. . . .

On October 22nd, 1923, there was an article of mine foreshadowing the Plymouth Speech which began the downfall of the Government and warning the Prime Minister against his plan of campaign. I wrote another warning article on November 5th, 1923, at the conclusion of this trilogy of speeches.[1] I dealt myself with the results of the disastrous General Election of December, 1923, and afterwards took the line very strongly that the Government should meet Parliament before resigning, as they eventually decided, after much hesitation, to do. . . .

In January, 1925, I wrote again on the perennial topic of "Consultation with the Dominions" and on Mr. Asquith's Earldom (January 26th). On February 10th came a difficult turning-point in the controversy over the proper use of our St. Paul's Restoration Fund—itself a most encouraging sign of the growing strength of the paper—and I took some trouble one evening at Langcliffe to set out the position of *The Times* and the limits of our responsibility. . . .

On October 30th I was suddenly confronted with Edward Wood's appointment as Viceroy and had to scribble something about him against time in the absence of anyone else who knew him. And the last two months of 1925 found me writing on such miscellaneous topics as the Guildhall Speeches, the meeting of Parliament, the disappearance of the *Corriere della Sera*, the Joynson-Hicks indiscretions, the Communist Trial, the change in the proprietorship of the *Spectator*, and the Native policy of the South African Government.

The last entry for the year recorded an afternoon and evening at Printing House Square, trying to get the paper away early with its annual review. "We succeeded so well that I was back in Regent's Park when the clocks struck midnight, walking Sheba the last few hundred yards home." (She had evidently been on one of her periodical visits to Printing House Square.)

[1] Mr. Baldwin's.

XXI

GENERAL STRIKE—POLITICAL AND PERSONAL MISCELLANY—1926–1927

TROUBLE had been brewing in the coal industry for some time. In the summer of 1925 the Cabinet offered owners and miners financial aid pending a Royal Commission. The miners were under the dynamic leadership of Mr. A. J. Cook, who had started life as a Baptist lay preacher, and described himself as "a humble follower of Lenin". The Royal Commission, under the chairmanship of Sir Herbert Samuel, presented a report on March 11th, 1926, in which it advocated an entire reorganization of the Coal Industry, the buying out of the royalty owners and the widespread introduction of technical improvements. The Commission also advocated a small reduction of wages, less drastic, however, than that recommended by the owners. The Government accepted the Report but the miners, under the leadership of A. J. Cook, refused to consider any reduction of wages, and by the end of April it was evident that the country was indeed face to face with a major disaster, in the form of a general strike.

Geoffrey wrote (February 10th, 1926) to Drummond Chaplin:

> . . . There is little news to tell you here. Herbert Samuel, who has been lunching with me, promised his Coal Report for the end of this month, so that it should be out about when this letter reaches you. Everything turns on that. It will be very exhaustive and (according to Samuel) very definite, providing not only for the whole future of the industry in years to come, but making concrete recommendations for that awkward period that begins in May. For the rest Baldwin and his Government are in a more than ever impregnable position for the moment. The Liberals are squabbling over the land. Labour is equally divided and its leaders are hopelessly ineffective. . . . And the Government is really solving its problems rather steadily. Housing goes on very well so far as England is concerned, and it is at last being tackled in Scotland seriously. Unemployment is rather better. The hubbub over education has subsided . . . on the whole the Cabinet is very popular and unprovocative. . . .

From the personal standpoint Geoffrey had several pleasant surprises and unsought honours. On February 10th, Sir George Murray wrote to inform him that he had been unanimously elected a member of the Grillions Club, an historic and select dining-club. Geoffrey received the following letter (February 19th, 1926) from the Archbishop of York:

> I am moved to send you a mere line to congratulate you on having been admitted to the elect people of Grillions—I think you will enjoy the Dinners. I always do. Sometimes as in February when you were elected there are really remarkable gatherings. On that occasion the Prime Minister, the ex-Prime Minister (Asquith), the Foreign Secretary, two ex-Lord Chancellors, two Archbishops, the Head of the Army, three Judges, and three of our most prominent men of letters—I like to think that I may sometimes have the chance of seeing you there on the too rare occasions on which I am able to be present. My love to Cecilia and my God-paternal benediction to the babe.

Grillions Club appears to have originated in 1812 with a few friends who were in residence at Christ Church, Oxford, during 1805–08 and who had assembled in London for annual dinners in the three following years. The first record of a meeting is on February 15th, 1813. The Club originally met at Grillion's Hotel in Albemarle Street (hence its name), and it stayed there till 1860. It changed its meeting place several times but in 1897 the dinners were transferred to the Hotel Cecil. It now has its dining-room and ante-room in Grosvenor House.

In February, Geoffrey was invited to join the Governing Body of Eton and remained a member till his death. Another pleasant surprise was the information from the President (Sir Herbert Warren) that he had been elected an Honorary Fellow of Magdalen, his old College, and while he was staying at Oxford a few days later the bells of the College were rung in his honour according to custom.

In March there is a reference to a meeting with Miss Shaw-Lefevre who gave him reminiscences of Delane. "She told me—oddly enough after my own effort (a leading article on 'A Tax on Betting') this morning—that Delane constantly wrote the Monday leader himself and talked it over with her at Ascot on the Sunday." On March 3rd the Duke of York (later King George VI), as head of the Industrial Welfare Association, made a well-planned tour of every department of Printing House Square. At the subsequent luncheon Geoffrey sat next to the Duke of York and found him "very pleasant and easy but nervy and fragile-looking".

From Geoffrey's mail-bag the following two letters are taken. The first (March 29th) was to Mr. John Walter:

> . . . Yes, I agree that Mussolini is most impressive and I am glad to know that he himself recognizes the general fairness of *The Times* in its dealings with Italy. No one can go there without being struck by what he has done. I myself travelled through the country from end to end just before the Fascist Revolution and was held up at every station by a strike. When I got to Rome everyone was on strike. In these days strikes are apparently unheard of. The trains run and the streets are swept. But the trouble about Mussolini is that he is reckoning entirely on his own personality, that he has no one to follow him, and that he is (I think quite unnecessarily) antagonizing the liberal-minded Italians by his dictatorship and especially by his dealings with the Press. It always seemed to me that it was not impossible for him at one time to put things on a basis which would last; and it is becoming more and more difficult, and meanwhile he looks like following the course of all dictators by going in for foreign adventure. If you did not see Borsa[1] on the way out, do try to have a talk with him as you return. He is always illuminating on this subject. . . .

In April the Dawsons spent a very congenial holiday in the Eastern Mediterranean. They visited Venice, the Dalmatian Coast, Corfu, Greece, Constantinople and Candia. On board the *Asia* on the second day of their Hellenic cruise he noted, "I passed three successive women reading Homer without a crib, which suggests the standard of the party!" A happy day was spent on the island of Corfu . . . "all as beautiful as it could be—perfect weather and amazing colours—oranges and lemons on the trees, a carpet of wild flowers, the sea wine-colour, and a range of snow mountains across it in Albania".

The entry in the diary for April 11th was:

> Dardanelles. A memorable day coasting round Suvla Bay, Anzac Cove, Brighton Beach, Lancashire Landing, Y and V Beaches and all the great scenes around Cape Helles. Brilliant weather, so that it was possible to see everything—the countless little orderly graveyards, the derelict rusty boats and barges on the shore, the dug-outs and trenches. Some of the Hellenists were more excited by an alleged view of the site of Troy! . . .

> At Sea April 16th.
>
> . . . We left Constantinople on Tuesday night after doing all that we could reasonably expect in the time—2 long visits to S. Sophia and to the wonderful old walls and gates of the city, several other mosques, a trip up the Bosphorus to the Black Sea; an ascent of the Galata Tower to see

[1] *The Times* correspondent in Milan.

the view. So much for sight-seeing. At intervals I had long talks with Lindsay, our Ambassador, and arranged a plan of campaign about our expelled correspondent (H. H. Macartney) which I hope he is launching by this time at Angora. . . . All Wednesday we were in the Aegean—Mitylene, Chios, Mudros, etc., and all yesterday ashore at Candia in Crete, whence we visited Sir Arthur Evans' exploration of the great Palace of Minos at Knossos. He himself was there to explain it and Cecilia and I and the Vice-Chancellor and some others lunched with him at the house which he built for himself hard by and means to hand over to the use of students from the British School at Athens. The scenery of Crete is magnificent. . . .

At the end of the tour Geoffrey succumbed to a severe attack of fever which necessitated an enforced stay of ten days at Fiesole, near Florence. On Wednesday, May 5th, when he was sitting in the Cloisters there reading *The Times* of Monday, May 3rd—the last issue of the paper to appear before the General Strike, although naturally he didn't realize that fact at the time—stirring events were taking place in Printing House Square—about which little was heard outside *The Times* office. On the afternoon of May 5th a deliberate attempt was made to set fire to the office when the machine-room was deserted except for a solitary attendant. A stream of petrol was poured into the building through the port. Lighted matches followed the petrol and a great blaze of flame roared up. Most fortunately the one man at work upon the machines—with great presence of mind—enabled the alarm to be given at once and five fire-engines speedily were on the spot and put out the flames.

The Dawsons returned straight from Florence to find the General Strike in full swing. Geoffrey regarded the manner in which *The Times* emerged from the ordeal as "one of the most singular and successful experiences of Printing House Square". The following extracts from the diary show the day-to-day events as they appeared to him at the time:

Friday, May 7. London once more. . . . I went down to Printing House Square, picketed and policed but full of good people carrying on with increasing success after a bad first night on Tuesday. I lunched at the House of Commons . . . and had a long talk there afterwards with the Prime Minister mainly on my own subject of publicity which in my view (and he agreed) was being mishandled by Winston (then Chancellor of the Exchequer) with his *British Gazette* run from the office of the *Morning Post*. He asked me to write him a letter for the Cabinet, and I left this in Downing Street at 8 on my way home to a hurried dinner. Office again till midnight.

Saturday, May 8. We sold 170,000 copies of our 4-page paper this morning

—nearly back to normal and a great achievement for our tiny band of pensioners and women. I went down to Printing House Square till we closed the office for 24 hours at noon, leaving of course a strong guard on duty . . . was involved in a correspondence with Winston, who sent a great reply to my letter to the Prime Minister. . . .

May 9. Strike . . . a walk with Cecilia before lunch round our barred and fortress-like Park to get passes for our household and the Gosses, whom we met. The Freemans came to lunch and drove me to Printing House Square afterwards for a hard afternoon of pushing and planning and talking and fighting for our paper and indeed for our existence against Winston's wild commandeering raids . . . went back till midnight to produce 250,000 copies.

May 10. Strike. Got Cecilia off at 8 for Crewe and Lancaster—sitting on her box in a crowded luggage van with a patriarch for driver and a young man from Balliol as guard. . . . More hostility from the *British Gazette* but growing support for us in the Cabinet. . . . All the Lords and Commons were packing for us at midnight . . . and even Clive Morrison-Bell, Winston's PPS!

May 11. Another peaceful and on the whole satisfactory day from the publicity point of view. From our own it was rather marred by the seizure (in the interests of Winston's *Gazette*) of about a quarter of our available paper stocks.[1] I duly recorded this in a dignified paragraph at night. . . . Otherwise I was in the office from noon till 1 a.m. when our titled packers and drivers were all at work again. . . . Much T.U.C. activity at midnight.

May 12. End of Strike. . . . An official announcement from Downing Street that the strike was abandoned; so we quickly put a new column of the news in this morning's paper. I brought the leader up to date in 10 minutes and by 3.30 we were selling the only evening paper in existence—some 80,000 of it in London—with bills everywhere. Then followed a strenuous afternoon. . . . I dashed down to Pall Mall for a talk with Herbert Samuel who had been getting on with the coal problem. In the intervals of all this I wrote another leader, while Campbell floated our plan for a National Police Fund. Got through just in time for a hurried dinner . . and was back in Printing House Square till 1 a.m. All our friends and undergraduates and schoolboys packing again.

May 13. A day of negotiations in every industry—except for the taxi drivers, who crept out of their holes with extraordinary promptitude,

[1] In its issue of May 15th, 1926, the *New Statesman* wrote: "It (the *British Gazette*) was supposed to be supporting the authority of Parliament, but it gave us nothing worth calling a report of the proceedings either of the House of Commons or of the House of Lords. For that we had to go to *The Times*. . . . It was scandalous that *The Times* should have been deprived of its paper supplies in order to enable Mr. Churchill to poison public opinion. We can only offer our gratitude and our congratulations to *The Times* for the struggle which it made in face of this robbery, and for the way in which it selected the comparatively small amount of news it was able to print, and maintained its best traditions of truthfulness and impartiality."

there was no settlement or resumption in any of them. Pybus was at it on our behalf with the NPA from morning till midnight, by which time the unions were ready to accept terms with the solitary exception of the packers, who had no sympathy from the others. . . .

May 14. Much better day than yesterday—settlements in all directions—led by the swallowing of some very stiff terms by the railway men—J. H. Thomas (who had called them out) being said to wish to "larn them a lesson" not to hustle their leaders. . . . Lady Violet Astor and Lady Maidstone joined our packers. Volunteers getting very tired and disappointed at the deadlock—as indeed were most of our strikers. . . .

We sold 400,000 this morning.

May 16. Printers' Strike ended. A morning of suspense (mostly spent in the office) waiting for the result of another meeting between NPA and unions. It ended in a settlement about 1—evening papers tomorrow, morning on Tuesday. One more night therefore of our wonderful volunteers. . . .

May 17. Back to normal. Men came in at 8, apparently tame, though there was an anxious moment in the evening when it came to taking plates cast by Casey[1] & Co. off the machines and packing papers for still unsettled wholesalers. However all went well in the end. . . .

In his account of the Strike, published at the end of 1926, "for private record", and referred to as "An episode in the history of *The Times*", Geoffrey, under the heading of "Exodus", begins in this manner:

"Of all the blunders committed (and since admitted) by the organizers of the General Strike of May, 1926, the attempt to suppress the newspapers was perhaps the most glaring. It was part of a deliberate policy long prearranged. In a scheme which had for its purpose the swift capitulation of the Government and the suppression of democracy, the forcible control of the normal channels of public opinion was indeed a very natural ingredient. But it failed, as the whole scheme failed, to take account of the risk of enlisting large bodies of strikers without a grievance. It underestimated the irritation likely to be felt by the general public at a plot to deprive them of any certain knowledge of what was happening. It broke down finally because some newspapers refused altogether to be suppressed. . . ." The Editor then goes on to explain that one of the decisions taken beforehand as an insurance to meet any eventuality was the installation at Printing House Square of six machines and mechanics capable of producing a "Multigraph" newspaper, which "saved *The Times* from any breach in a tradition of continuous publication which had lasted unbroken for more than a century. . . ."

[1] W. F. Casey, who succeeded Barrington-Ward as Editor in 1948.

The Times of Wednesday, May 5th, No. 44,263, shows what this famous issue and its successors looked like, and has become an object of value to collectors. It measured thirteen inches by eight. This "little Sister", as it was affectionately termed at Printing House Square, "stood for twenty-four hours between a long line of ancestors and the extinction of the race. She proved, in fact, to be the only regular London newspaper issued from its own office on the first morning of the General Strike". *The Times* Police Fund reached a total of over £230,000, subscribed by the readers of the paper as a tribute to the loyalty of the Police during the General Strike.

In its leading article on "The Nation's Victory" (May 13th), *The Times* dwelt on the implications of the end of the General Strike, described by Baldwin as a victory for the best part of the nation as a whole, and strongly supported the Prime Minister in his determination that there must be no talk of "smashing the unions" and "no malice or vindictiveness".

In the leading article "Changed Values" (May 21), on the adjournment of Parliament for its Whitsuntide recess, *The Times* stated: "After the experience of the last three weeks no one is likely to doubt that Parliament as such, and Mr. Baldwin's Government, both stand incomparably higher in the public mind today than at any time since the one was elected and the other formed. . . . There is equally no question that the general rise in values is led by the soaring reputation of the Prime Minister. . . . The plain Englishman whose modest claim to fair dealing was once derided by the intellectuals, who has promised nothing but an honest attempt to interpret what other Englishmen feel, is on a pedestal today such as few Prime Ministers ever scaled."

In the months following the General Strike a great variety of subjects are covered by the diary. In June Geoffrey dined at the Beefsteak "partly to see what that mixed company had to say about the Betting Tax, which was going through Committee"—a good instance of how, like Delane, he used the various social and political groups with which he associated to serve in the job of gauging public opinion.

In early November the Editor lunched with Arthur Balfour to meet Mr. Cosgrave, the Irish leader, and a Canadian and New Zealander, "a pleasant little party". Geoffrey was present at a protracted Mansion House lunch in honour of the Dominion Premiers, when "Lord Mayor Blades offered Hertzog Kruger's old waggon, which I saw just twenty-five years ago on Kitchener's departing train". In December, Geoffrey finished his little Strike Book.

. . . . .

In the year 1927 Geoffrey's correspondence with the outside world grew in unexpected directions and his mail-bag was enlivened by letters from Max Beerbohm, J. M. Barrie and Margot Oxford—who remained a frequent correspondent during the following decade. Henceforth his relations with the Asquith family remained very friendly and its members appreciated the generous leading article in *The Times*, "A Tribute to Lord Oxford" (July 30), when that veteran statesman was presented with a sum of money by his admirers, of whom Lord Reading had been the pioneer. *The Times* cordially endorsed this tribute to the former Prime Minister and regarded the presentation as a happy thought, including as it did colleagues and opponents alike. Friends of Lord Oxford conceived the idea—"based presumably on his retirement, his recent illness, and the fact that Prime Ministers are neither overpaid nor pensioned—of offering him an endowment for his declining years".

In the field of home politics Geoffrey certainly acted as a "Watch Dog" and on several occasions sought to keep Mr. Baldwin up to the mark. On February 17th he wrote "a talk with Baldwin . . . in his room at the House of Commons. He was as pleasant, irrelevant and unsatisfactory as ever. . . ." While on October 5th, the entry in the diary is as follows: "An hour with the Prime Minister in Downing Street. He was in excellent form, full of enthusiasm over his Canadian visit, and much more sure of himself. He outlined his speech for tomorrow and I made one or two suggestions. Then we fell to discussing the appointment of Bishops and Archbishops and of a new Regius Professor of Medicine at Oxford. . . ." Three specific occasions may be noted when the Editor felt it incumbent on him to be critical of the Government. The leading article in *The Times*, "Vacancy by Promotion" (January 15th, 1927), attracted considerable attention and was regarded by the *Manchester Guardian* (Jan. 18th) as being inspired by the Government and as "a sign that there is presently to be a reconstruction of the Government". The article certainly suggested that there ought to be a re-shuffling of offices. It ended with these words: "This New Year marks, humanly speaking, the central point of Mr. Baldwin's current term of office. It is an occasion when he might profitably survey the colleagues at his side, from the highest to the lowest, and consider whether none of them might be replaced with advantage—of his own initiative and not of theirs—from the extensive and singularly vigorous ranks behind him."

In March the Editor had to spend nearly a week in Paris dealing with the disorganization of the Paris office, caused in part by the resignation of Hubert Walter and the necessity of finding a suitable successor. Finally he decided to transfer H. G. Daniels from Berlin to the

French capital. During the two years 1926–27 Geoffrey had to give an exceptional amount of time to staff changes. He appointed Ebbutt[1] to succeed Daniels as Berlin correspondent. He was also concerned with appointments in Rome and the Balkans; in fact these changes almost "amounted to a general post in Europe", while on the death, in May, 1927, of Sir John Willison, the eminent correspondent of *The Times* in Canada, he appointed Mr. John A. Stevenson as his successor. The year was also remarkable for the fact that in the spring he had succeeded in persuading Robin Barrington-Ward to return to Printing House Square from the *Observer*, an event which took place in October. "A delicate business, conducted with great good will by Waldorf Astor on his part and with complete frankness on mine." I have mentioned the number of changes and additions which had to be made in these two years both at Printing House Square and in the representation of *The Times* abroad, to show that no Editor, even if he had been assisted by a specially appointed Foreign Editor, could have devoted more attention to the problems involved.

In the spring of 1927 the Dawsons spent three weeks in Provence and in exploring such attractive places as Carcassone, Avignon, Nîmes, Les Baux, Tarascon and Aigues Mortes. At Nîmes there is this entry in the diary:

> *May 1.* A very peaceful hot Sunday loafing in Nîmes—to a Calvinist service in the morning—a very eloquent old preacher in gown and bands. And after lunch we strolled across the street to the Arena, where a ridiculous game of bull-ragging was in progress before a vast crowd—a small, rather tame animal with padded horns and a small red cockade to be plucked from between the horns by a number of cautious young men, who displayed great agility in leaping the barrier. And so to sit over tea on a lovely evening in the garden by Diana's temple.

In June, Geoffrey and his wife watched the eclipse in company with J. M. Barrie, who was their guest at Langcliffe for the occasion. The following is the diary entry:

> *June 29.* (Eclipse–York.) A long and unforgettable day. We were up before 4 and off soon after the half hour—across the river to the hill above the Mains, and there, by amazing good fortune, had a perfect view of the eclipse with all the thrill of doubt till the end. . . . The flight of the curlews on the hill and the faint cheers from the school below are

[1] Norman Ebbutt served as *The Times* correspondent in Berlin until his expulsion in August, 1937.

> what I remember hearing at the critical moment . . . to York for the great St. Peter's Day service at noon: lunched with the Dean and Chapter. . . .

In July the Dawsons lunched with Lady Oxford, "who was very good on greyhound racing, which had thrilled her"; evidently fired by Lady Oxford's example, subsequently Geoffrey went with Lints Smith, Manager of *The Times*, to the Greyhound Races—"an astonishing spectacle. 80,000 people including many friends". In this period there is a reference to the Editor's search for young men for Printing House Square. He wrote, "I feel that the Kindergarten (of course nothing to do with the Milner Kindergarten) is beginning to function" and he referred to two important dispatches sent by young Barker from Vienna and by Riley[1] from Hankow.

Just when Baldwin was starting for Canada a leading article appeared in *The Times* with the object of persuading the Prime Minister to infuse fresh blood into the Cabinet—"Home Thoughts from the Sea" (July 20). In it the paper returned to the theme of the need for "an overhauling of the whole personnel of the Government; the withdrawal of Ministers who are either tired or misfits, or palpably out of tune with the times; the infusion of fresh blood into an organization which is ceasing to work as a team".

The following letter (July 21, 1927) was received by Geoffrey from Lord Esher, then in Scotland:

> That is a most remarkable article of yours in yesterday's *Times* (20th). The "Thunderer" of Delane's day—*redivivus*. The P.M. is a strange phenomenon. What is he? He cannot be the *fainéant* he seems. And yet? I very nearly added another effusion to my 6 letters to *The Times* of 1909–10, and then I thought "A quoi bon"? Does anybody mean business, or is the whole thing talk?
>
> Personally I think the Parliament Act (far from the intention of its framer) is a bulwark. Never again can an unscrupulous Minister force his way through safeguards. . . .

Geoffrey replied (July 22nd, 1927):

> I am glad that article interested you. It is only once in a blue moon that I can find time to write one myself, and this is a subject which I have very much at heart. I do not know what the Prime Minister is. His instincts seem to me to be nearly always right. Most of his public

[1] Frank Basil Riley, special correspondent in China, a Rhodes Scholar at New College. He disappeared from Chengchow on July 23rd, 1927, and it was assumed that he had been murdered.

speeches are excellent. Personally I have always found it quite impossible —much as I like him and well as I know him—to discuss anything serious with him in private. I am beginning to think that he is what the Americans call "a bad executive".

Also I have an impression, though I do not know quite enough about it, that the machine is all wrong. When . . . Marriott (Sir J. A. R. Marriott) wrote the letter which I printed this morning I could not help thinking how much better you would have done it. The Cabinet are overworked. . . . I entirely agree with you about the Parliament Act.

Probably the most important event of the year 1927 from Geoffrey's standpoint, although he may not have realized the fact, was the appointment of the Commission of Inquiry into the Indian Reforms, under the chairmanship of Sir John Simon. It meant, quite distinct from his growing interest in India during Lord Irwin's Viceroyalty, that there was an additional reason why he must give much thought to the work of the Commission and arrange for *The Times* to deal adequately with the tremendous issues involved. With the re-opening of Parliament, on November 8th, came the announcement of the Indian Commission in both Houses of Parliament and a leader on the subject appeared in *The Times* (November 9th), which congratulated the Government on the appointment of Sir John Simon, and thereby provided a complete answer to those who might scent a "Tory intrigue" in the premature dispatch of the Commission.

In the remaining weeks of the year there are frequent references to the Prayer Book Measure, which the Editor had supported from the outset and about which he had kept in close touch with the Archbishops. He was deeply concerned by the defeat of the measure in the House of Commons and did his best to comfort Dr. Davidson.

Geoffrey received several letters from Lady Oxford in 1927:

7th October.

Dearest Mr. Dawson,

I would so much like to see you and talk about lots of things. I go to Westgate, St. Mildred's Hotel, today till 11th and then here till 17th. We *can't* allow the old Foundling Hospital site and all the open spaces to be ruined by speculators. We have enough amateur speculators when we see Devonshire House, Grosvenor House etc. all disappearing. Lansdowne leaves a million, yet lets his house to Selfridge! Victor[1] owns all Eastbourne, yet sells Devonshire House. I wish I understood our upper classes. They do little to make one long for the House of Lords to have more power. Will Dorchester House be turned into a Girls' School?

[1] Duke of Devonshire.

It is all rather disgraceful I think. The filling-in stations which deform every village and all the lovely green places by their Aunt Sally faces. "Mobiloil! Shell! Pratt! Shell!" brick-red or gamboge yellow are heart-breaking and the bungalows creeping like microbes. I feel that England is commercializing itself in a horrible way, and it makes me sad. . . .

Yours in sincerity,
MARGOT OXFORD.

eadem.

6 a.m. 16th October, 1927.

. . . New friends are such a joy to me that you cannot imagine the pleasure I have had in getting to know you. Your paper did more to kill us during the war than ever Lloyd George did and yet it is the only paper.

You had nothing to do with all this,[1] but when I find you fair-minded and just over people and politics of course it is a joy to me. My *best* friends turned against us and said we were doing *nothing* in the war. If they had taken the trouble to come and see me at any time, 4½ a.m. or *any* hour they would have found me and my husband not having even taken our clothes off. . . .

Yours,
MARGOT.

23rd November, 1927.

I thank you. I can tell you exactly what the Liberal papers are at. They think Lloyd George will lead the Liberal Party and that if they can prove that Asquith and the whole of his family are rotten, full of spite, self-indulgence, and thwarted ambition they will prove to the world that their Hope and their Hero has been *maligned*. That he *was* the man that won the war, and that he is the *only* man who can save the country.

Lloyd George is a discredited man among people who are educated and know but except in the *Morning Post* he is boomed. Not by you but by Rothermere etc. The gaping public do not realize he is the biggest Bluff ever put across this country—(and a dangerous Bluff). The *Morning Post* attacks are coming out in a pamphlet I hear, and I only wish I was rich enough to distribute them. It makes my heart ache to think our papers are so vile as to abuse my Elizabeth and all of us, for the purpose of showing Lloyd George to be a victimized person.

Ever your grateful and affectionate,
MARGOT.

Geoffrey certainly enjoyed this correspondence with Max Beerbohm:

[1] This is not true. The Editor of *The Times*, as we have seen, played a great part in forcing Asquith to resign.

First unofficial Radio telephone message across the Atlantic. The conversation took place on January 7th, 1927, at 1.57 p.m. London time, and shows Geoffrey Dawson speaking to the late Mr. Adolph S. Ochs, publisher of the *New York Times*

Geoffrey Dawson is seated in the front row, second from the right

A letter not requiring an answer.

Villino Chiaro,
Rapallo,
October 2, 1927.

Cutting from *The Times* enclosed reading:

Thursday, September 29th.

SUCCESSORS OF THE VICTORIANS

Mr. Belloc on *British Literature*[1]

Dear Geoffrey Dawson,

British Literature!? Is this expression on the Style Sheet in Printing House Square? Are you so afraid of fussy Scotsmen? Or is it the Australians and Canadians who might bother you with protests? In any case, doesn't the expression chill you to the spine? I can't imagine it not having that effect on anybody accustomed, as you and I are, to the old, traditional, seemly and dear expression, English Literature.

It opens up awful vistas, too. Are we to have the British language, the King's British, the Merrie Empire—and so on?

All these questions are rhetorical. I repeat that this letter needs no answer.

Yours very sincerely,
MAX BEERBOHM.

P.S. I want to do a drawing of Lord Burnham seeing at the Guildhall "signs and portents which must encourage us as to the future of British letters and British art". And while I'm about it I must do another of him, seeing "no reason why we should not retain the pride of place which we certainly held in the last century and were fully capable of holding now. (Cheers".)

How (another rhetorical question) can clever and well-educated men sink to such imbecilities when they rise to their feet on festive occasions? The writer of a charming article on "After Dinner Speaking" in the aforesaid issue of *The Times* might say it's because "they see themselves in print". But surely if they did this they would acquit themselves better. I think the explanation is a simple one. They simply lose their heads.

M.B.

October 13th, 1927.

My dear Max Beerbohm,

It was delightful to see your handwriting even on the subject of "British Literature". I was absent, I hasten to say, or I hope I should have spotted it. For it isn't funk that does it, nor yet Imperial sentiment, but the solid phalanx of Scots sub-editors that dominates this and every other newspaper office. No other race can stand the strain and they must have their fling sometime.

[1] The two words "British Literature" are heavily underlined by Max Beerbohm.

As for Burnham, it isn't that he loses his head, for it wouldn't help him if he had it. No man who lunches and dines in public every day can avoid this sort of inanity. I seldom hear it myself, but foresee a whole evening of it on October 29th, when I am invited by the Lord Mayor to dine with him "in honour of Journalism".

Yours very sincerely,

G.D.

October 22, 1927.

My dear Geoffrey Dawson,

Not only for your delightful reply to my letter, but also now for that further specimen of Lord Burnham, very many thanks indeed.

What *will* he—what *won't* he—be saying at the Mansion House on the evening of the 29th? I envy you your presence there, and I do implore you to grant me a personal favour and have the vigorous Viscount reported verbatim for me in *The Times*! Thanking you in anticipation.

Yours very sincerely,

MAX BEERBOHM.

P.T.O.

Vague prevision of the end of the full report of Lord Burnham's speech:

I do not think it is too much to say, my Lord Mayor—and many of us will think that I do not go far enough in saying (Cheers)—that if Shakespeare himself were alive and living today among us he would pour out for us his wit and wisdom, his genius and his geniality, not in the form of dramas and—er—plays, or of sonnets and—er—poems, but rather in the form of signed and unsigned articles for the daily and—er—weekly press (Loud Cheers). I will go further (Cries of No!) I will go so far as (Prolonged interruptions among which, having spoken for 35 minutes, his Lordship, with a smiling face but a broken heart, resumed his seat, which collapsed under his weight).

At the close of the proceedings, before the singing of the National Anthem by the Corporation Choir, the Lord Mayor rose and announced that the fragments of Lord Burnham's chair would be sold by auction for the benefit of the Gog and Magog Orphanage Fund.

Lord Burnham, rising from among the fragments to return thanks, was again howled down; and the Editor of *The Times*, with flashing eyes, cried "Let's burn down the Mansion House, lads, and put an end for ever to all this foolery!"

At the time of going to press, the flames had not yet been extinguished, nor had any attempt been made to save Lord Burnham (of whom an obituary notice will be found on page 15) from the wreckage.

October 25th, 1927.

My dear Geoffrey Dawson,

I am again indebted to you. In a communication sent to you yesterday, I made mention of Lord Burnham's physical (as apart from his moral and mental) weight. But, not having seen him for years, I didn't know the extent to which this weight had increased. I gather from the photograph that he now equals the bulk of the first Viscount, whom he so amazingly resembles.

Anyway it is a joy to have this picture of him beaming and bulging among the Archimandrites—playing them all off the stage—bursting with the happiness that comes only to very able and successful men who have never been troubled with a thought. It does one's heart good to see such unadulterated, such uncontrollable happiness. And more than ever do I envy you your hearing his voluptuous voice at the imminent banquet.

Yours very sincerely,
MAX BEERBOHM.

A sudden doubt arises in me: Will he, after all, not be on the toast-list? Down, loathsome doubt!

XXII

DEATH OF LORD OXFORD—INDIAN VISIT AND AFTER

THE year 1928 opened for Geoffrey with the receipt of the following letters from Lady Oxford, watching over the sick-bed of her husband:

1928,
The Wharf,
Sutton Courtenay,
Berks.
(The first day of a year that can't be happy for me.)

Dearest Geoffrey,

You saw Elizabeth and you said little of what I told you. She is both very old, and very young for her age, and has no idea really of the situation here—though she is infinitely tender and understanding. Nor do I want her to, as I feel it may last several weeks as Henry was made by God to have lived 100 years. He has nothing that has in any way deteriorated, nor had any kind of stroke, but the blood vessels are all worn and slack and feeding the arteries and brain unevenly and perversely. Sometimes quite brilliant on his old colleagues, and full of intellectual scorn for Lloyd George & Co. Sometimes quoting Bacon on Judges, or Pope or Marvell; often laughing at life's little vanities, the cowardice of the Liberals, and confusedness and *lethargy* of the Tories etc. And at other times far away from me and very very unhappy.

Tuesday 3rd. I did not finish this as I'm so seedy myself that I hardly know why I write to you—only you are the first person I told (and I believe it will be a much longer thing than I thought) and you are so affectionate and understanding. Let Elizabeth tell you anything she likes, but don't you tell her anything I ever say or write to you (I have not one friend who can hold his or her tongue in the real sense of the word). Anyone can keep a secret but few recognize one and I would feel it an insult if you were to warn me. I'm not at all a snob, but if Henry dies I would like Lloyd George and Co. to realize what pigmies they are in comparison to him.

Once the House of Commons chucked us, and we went to the House of Lords, I realized Henry could never score off his Judas friends with any hope of having our scattered and camouflaged Party behind him, but I never thought it would have been like this. Elizabeth thinks if Henry dies he will be buried in Westminster Abbey and now that Bonar had this honour, it is not quite what it was. If Lloyd George were dead I would not care one way or the other, but now he is alive I would like this for Henry. This wish is not inspired by anything fine in me; it is purely the idea of impressing our enemies and may be impossible for all I know. I shall not warn you to say nothing even to Elizabeth, but when she spoke of it to me I felt a dim hope that it would enhance Henry's reputation and perhaps silence the malignant lies spoken and written about him.

Perhaps you'll be shocked at this, but I don't somehow think you will. No one outside a very small circle knows he is seriously ill, and I open letters every day asking him to speak and lecture in the Summer or Autumn etc. If you put Private and seal your letters to me no one opens them. The nights when I was sitting in his room in the dark and hoping he was asleep, he suddenly said "You know quite well I'm not dying—I'm dead." Another time: "I must give Baldwin a word of advice. He is letting his great opportunities slip through his fingers and is assisted in the folly by 8th rate men—I don't know who advises him."

Yours as you know,

M.O.

10th January, 1928.

I am not surprised that people love you (perhaps hardly a compliment!) for your heart and understanding are rare, and to me very healing —I don't think the end will come soon but I would like you to talk to Baldwin who really loves me and Henry. He withdrew the Tory in one tragic Paisley election to help us, but the Tories did not vote and their hatred of us made some of the Tory females vote Labour which they regretted. It is nice of you to say the Liberal Press which I loathe won't cavil over Westminster Abbey.

On January 11th, 1928, Thomas Hardy died, and in the evening Barrie visited Printing House Square, "anxious to move for his burial in the Abbey". Geoffrey went to the Prime Minister the next day to get his views about Hardy's funeral, and with Barrie visited the Dean of Westminster and obtained his ready consent to the Abbey funeral. Within a few days Geoffrey received these two letters (January 20th and 31st, 1928) from Barrie:

Just a line to thank you for all you did personally and in *The Times* for Hardy. One doesn't forget such things. It makes me more glad than ever to know that we are friends.

idem.

. . . Those two articles on Hardy's prose and verse in the Literary Supplement were probably the best things of the kind that ever appeared in a newspaper.

On February 3rd, the day of Haig's funeral at the Abbey, Geoffrey wrote in the diary: seats "exactly opposite the Unknown Warrior's grave. A beautiful simple service, but why wasn't the King there?[1] No one raised it in public, but we felt it acutely. . . ." Lord Wigram wrote to Geoffrey on 4th February, 1928, from Buckingham Palace:

There was one touching little incident in connection with the Funeral yesterday, which I think you may like to know.

Lord Haig's charger, which he rode in France and in the Victory March in 1919, was taken over by the King in 1920 and named "Haig". This horse followed the coffin and behaved splendidly until just at the moment when the coffin was being taken off the gun carriage to be placed in the railway van. He suddenly got restless and the three men with him had to hold tight on to his bridle, and as the coffin was being lifted he gave a loud neigh.

I knew the horse well and have ridden him in many parades and occasions since 1920, and I have never known him neigh like that before, or become restless. . . .

The day after Lord Oxford's death Geoffrey received the following letter from his widow:

The Wharf,
Sutton Courtenay,
Feb. 16th, 1928—5 a.m.

Dearest Geoffrey,

The anguish is over for me; and so is the joy. He became unconscious Sunday morning at 7 o'clock and died at 7 yesterday.

After what I had asked you it was a disappointment to find a little written statement with his will.

"I shall probably be buried at Wanborough, but wherever it is I desire the utmost simplicity. I do not want anything in the nature of a public funeral."

"Wanboro'" is a little Church Yard near Godalming where my two little babies—who only lived a few days—are buried.

As lately as September last year (1927) after spending an afternoon with Rosebery motoring back to North Berwick, I said to Henry:

[1] The Sovereign does not, of course, personally attend funerals or memorial services of his subjects, though he is often represented, and was in this instance by the Prince of Wales.

"When you are buried in Westminster Abbey you won't have a statue will you?"

H.—"God forbid! no statue there or I hope anywhere. There are far too many statues."

M.—"Could my name be on your plaque in the Abbey?"

H.—"No, darling—but you wouldn't mind that, would you?"

Of course I told him I was only laughing and we joked a little about it. He and I often spoke of it, never once did he say he objected to a public funeral. I was very ill in the spring of 1914 and I think he must have thought I was going to die. I wasn't in bed with any regular illness, but I had colitis of a very trying kind and prayed to die so as not to hamper him in Downing Street. He had obviously completely forgotten this; but his trustees asked me if they could possibly disregard this expressed wish and though I felt no one need know, and longed for the honour to be paid him (and the sort of triumph for the countless poor, loyal, loving Liberals who loathe Lloyd George and feel wounded and bitter over the way in which the Chief they adore has been treated by him) I felt it would not be quite straight of me to ask them to let him be buried in Westminster Abbey.

This letter is only to thank you for your great understanding and tell you that Henry had a real admiration for your work on *The Times* and said only a few weeks ago that he was glad Elizabeth and I had got to know and love you. (We suffered a great deal over *The Times* in Northcliffe's day but both he and I have—probably foolishly—always treated the Press with contempt and more than that.)

Ever yours affectionately,

MARGOT ASQUITH.

On May 19th, Geoffrey received the following letter from Cyril Robert Carter, Estates Bursar of Magdalen College:

I am writing to you on my own behalf to ask whether you would allow me to put forward your name for the post of President. Of course I do not know what the ultimate decision will be but personally I can think of no one whom I should like to see here in preference to yourself. I need not tell you what the position is. . . . Will you think it over?

Geoffrey wrote a short memorandum on the suggestion and the following day, when in Oxford, placed before Carter what he regarded as three unsurmountable objections:

(1) That he was not sufficiently eminent in the academic world.

(2) That, in his view, it was hard on those who had borne the burden and heat in the academic world that the plums should go to people outside.

(3) That he did not feel justified in leaving *The Times* at all events till he had collected "more young men to carry it on".

On July 12th, 1928, C. R. Carter returned to the subject:

Please excuse my bothering you. Craig tells me that he has seen you. I wish you would seriously reconsider the question of coming here. You are, to my mind, the one man for the job.

The Head of this College is no longer a figure-head only, but is a real force not only in the College but in the University and at large. We have the highest name in the University, far above that of any other College, and we should like to see it maintained.

Geoffrey concluded his statement:

Craig came to say that in spite of my talks with Carter (of which he knew) the Fellows had met and that there was a preponderating weight of opinion for me. Would I think it over again? I repeated the old arguments and undertook to write him—as I subsequently did. . . .

So I suppose it was definitely within my reach and I confess that in other circumstances I should have enjoyed it—far more than, e.g. All Souls, for the whole interest to me would have been in the undergraduates and not in the College and University business.

I mentioned the episode to John Astor and Bob Brand so as to assure myself that they wouldn't welcome the easy chance of getting someone younger for *The Times*, but they both assured me that this was not so.

G.D.

During the spring and summer the diary covers many subjects. In May, while at All Souls, he met Sir John Simon for the first time since his return from India; at a lunch at Printing House Square Geoffrey had as neighbour Conan Doyle, "who has lost all interest in crime as compared with mediums and is now getting in touch with the unfortunate Hinchliffe, who was lost with Miss Elsie Mackay in the Atlantic"; on July 10th the Editor saw "the Prime Minister in his room in the House of Commons (he wanted to talk about the vacant History Chair at Oxford and also about Bishops and Archbishops)"; later in the month he lunched with Stamfordham and discussed with him a project, near to his heart, about the possibility of making Dr. Davidson, on his retirement after serving twenty-five years as the ninety-sixth Archbishop of Canterbury, a lay peer. In a leading article, "The Primate and the Peerage" (July 23rd, 1928), *The Times* suggested that Dr. Davidson's services should, if possible, be retained in the House of Lords, which would be "manifestly stronger for his presence, owing to his wide experience, wisdom and moderating influence". Geoffrey always welcomed opportunities of discussing the reform of the House of Lords and he was, therefore, on familiar ground when he advocated that life peerages should be awarded to men of proved statesmanship, such as ex-Primates, ex-Viceroys, ex-Speakers, ex-Cabinet Ministers or ex-leaders of the great Trade Unions.

On July 26th *The Times* published the leading article "The Archbishop Retires", and two days later, in the article "Primate of All England", it welcomed the Editor's old friend, Cosmo Lang, as Dr. Davidson's successor, about whom there had never been any doubt, because of his natural gifts, quick intelligence, broad and tolerant understanding, "immense experience and a deep interest in public affairs" which "would have made him an outstanding figure in any society". On August 2nd *The Times* noted the general approval of Dr. Temple's nomination to the Province of York "except in the most rigid Conservative circles", where his "leanings to the Labour Party are viewed with suspicion."

In August, Geoffrey made this reference to the man who was ultimately to succeed him, "Barrington-Ward has been a tower of strength, a good administrator . . . and finding time to help me with two or three excellent and important leaders."

The Times suffered heavy losses in the editorial department—past and present—in the three years 1928–30, among them the death of Harold Williams (November, 1928), Valentine Chirol (October, 1929) and J. W. Flanagan (November, 1929). Certainly Geoffrey felt the loss of Harold Williams very deeply. There are a number of references to his illness and death in the diary. Quite apart from the deep personal sorrow, Geoffrey regarded Williams as being irreplaceable from the standpoint of *The Times*.

Of a talk with Baldwin on September 24th, 1928, Geoffrey wrote:

> I had a talk in Downing Street with the Prime Minister, who had just returned from Aix and Paris, and was looking extraordinarily well. I had various definite questions to put to him, and he answered them with rather unusual adhesion to the point.
>
> We discussed the members of his Cabinet and their state of health. I told him that he was going to the country with a set of crocks and had better take the initiative by announcing this fact and saying that his colleagues had worn themselves out in the public service. But I thought it probably too late now to introduce new blood to any great extent. His experiments might prove failures at the eleventh hour and some of the people who were left out might be disgruntled. Having let things slide so long I thought that he had better content himself with saying

clearly that if and when he was returned to power there would be very large changes in his team. . . .

We touched on House of Lords Reform—the Archbishop having told me the previous evening that Midleton and others were preparing an ultimatum against the Prime Minister's return. Baldwin himself had heard nothing of this and did not think much more of it than I did. I asked him whether he had ever seriously considered the plan which I had several times put forward in *The Times*—namely a gradual reform based on fresh power to nominate life peers. I had always thought it the right line of approach, and the one which was most likely to commend itself to the Labour Party. . . .

This entry (October 30th, 1928) in the diary refers to the centenary dinner to celebrate the founding of the *Spectator* by Stephen Rintoul in 1828:

A great dinner in the evening given by John Astor to celebrate the centenary of the *Spectator*. The Prime Minister was there and Hogg and Hewart and Barrie (next to whom I sat) and about 90 altogether—a very good party which I left reluctantly before it was over.

Ever since Lord Irwin's appointment as Viceroy Geoffrey's thoughts had been specially concentrated on India. Indeed, as a close student of Imperial relations and as a member of the Round Table, he could not but be interested in what was probably the biggest question which has confronted the Empire in the twentieth century. Was the Commonwealth great enough, as a permanent world state, to include within its orbit the ancient civilizations of Asia, alien in outlook in many ways and with an entirely different racial background, and yet—if its component parts could be kept together—capable of exerting a profound influence upon the future of the world? Whatever the final answer to that question, which, God willing, shall be answered in the affirmative, *The Times*, under Geoffrey, played no small part in the decade 1927–36 in making possible the settlement with India and Pakistan in 1947, by continuously seeking to keep before the British nation enlightened views. When he and Cecilia set out for India on 13th December, 1928, "very depressed at leaving the children", their visit was indeed *felix opportunitatas*. Geoffrey had long had such a trip in mind, while his wife, for her part, looked eagerly forward to returning to Madras and South India where she had spent happy years when her father was a very popular Governor. How opportune was the visit can be realized when we consider that subsequently India largely dominated the political horizon for the years up to 1935.

In the autumn of 1928, Geoffrey had

A long talk with Simon in the Law Courts, where he was clearing up before leaving for India: we discussed the programme of his tour and the probable time-table thereafter. The Commission would leave India in April. After that there would be the hubbub of the General Election. They would do very well if they got out their Report by the end of the year. Then, in 1930, there would be the Parliamentary Committee of both Houses and the promised delegations from India. He agreed with me that the issue of the Report, rather than the period of investigation, would be the time to have Graves in India. His impression was that Parliament, and indeed all England, would be more occupied with India very soon than it had been for many years past. We discussed the broad lines on which his mind was moving, and it was interesting to see the effect of contact with India on so conventional a Liberal. He was tremendously impressed with the size of the country and of its different Provinces, on which he had just expatiated in a speech at the Aldwych Club. It was futile to think of merely transplanting British parliamentary institutions. The probable policy must be to give the Provinces more power and to make them smaller, though he did not think that his Commission could go into the detailed question of their appropriate size.

The question of the Central Government was very difficult. He thought there must be a central Legislature of some sort, but did not think that it should be composed by direct election. He was considering various forms of indirect election. No doubt it was possible to run India from a single centre under a benevolent autocracy, but quite impossible to govern so large a country from one point through a representative Parliament. As he had said in his speech, Simon seemed very well satisfied with the growing response to his appeal for co-operation. Even as regards the convinced non-co-operators he thought there were some very good things in the Nehru Report, of which he had sent for copies. . . .

During the month of November the Dawsons were busy making preparations for their Indian visit, while Geoffrey was, naturally, much concerned about the King's health and kept in almost daily touch with Lord Dawson thereon. In a letter to Kitty dated 10th December he writes: "I am very anxious about the King, and altogether in a state of twitter as to whether I ought to leave the paper at this moment. Still, everyone seems to think it best to carry out the plan."

One of the last things Geoffrey and Cecilia did before leaving for India was to be present at the enthronement at Canterbury of Dr. Lang as Archbishop, "a most beautiful service". Afterwards they made a pilgrimage to the tomb of Chichele, the founder of All Souls, and saw the Milner Chapel.

On December 12th he wrote to Kitty, "The news of the King is certainly better these last two days and we hope to start 'according to plan' tomorrow." Geoffrey and Cecilia sailed in the *Orsova*, of the Orient Line, to Colombo. As the vessel passed Cape Guardafui he must nave thought of the journey with Milner in 1905—the last occasion on which he had passed through the Red Sea. How much had happened in those twenty-three years! They arrived at Colombo on December 29th—at a luncheon-party given in their honour Geoffrey plunged into Cingalese politics; their first evening ashore was spent at a wonderful entertainment given by the Police, "songs, plays, nigger minstrels, North American Indians dancing to the strains of the Eton Boating Song! . . . H.E. (Sir Herbert Stanley)[1] gave away cups at the end . . . and we sang 'Auld Lang Syne' amid scenes of great enthusiasm". At Kandy they visited the famous Temple of the Tooth, under the auspices of the Chief Priest, and spent the last day of the old year among the Buddhist antiquities at Dambulla and Anuradhapura:

> The former a series of sacred caves in the base of a rounded black rock—preserved everywhere—scenes in the life of the Buddha, as a baby, a young man, in contemplation under his Bo-tree, tempted of the Devil etc. and the horrid fate of those who offend against his code—lesser devils tormenting the sinners (very much as in the Campo Santa at Pisa and elsewhere). There were statues of the Buddha everywhere—one gigantic and almost filling the first cave temple, reposing on his side, and in the other caves whole rows of Buddhas in meditation. Votive offerings and modern gewgaws mixed up with ancient remains (as in the Temple of the Tooth, where the priest showed me a monstrous sham pineapple with exactly the same pride as he took in his sacred books of wonderful manuscript and great antiquity—some of them about 1,000 years old).

There are constant references in the diaries and records to wild life. The Dawsons saw rubber plantations and paddy fields—"very little other animal life (apart from oxen (Asiatic buffalo) wallowing in the pools) visible, though we heard a jungle cock . . . and there were white paddy birds in the swamps". On New Year's Day they motored through the jungle—"a fine jackal was sunning himself in the road and a gorgeous jungle-cock ran into the bush . . . lagoon by the sea, coconut palms everywhere, and a couple of mongooses".

In view of recent political developments in the Rhodesias and northwards it is of interest to find Geoffrey discussing with the Governor of Ceylon, as long ago as 1929, the double federation of Kenya, Tanganyika and Uganda, Southern Rhodesia with Northern Rhodesia and Nyasaland—perhaps ultimately combined with a capital on the Tanganyika plateau.

Geoffrey soon fell under the spell of India. He could not have

[1] An old friend of Geoffrey's since Eton days.

begun a pilgrimage through Southern India at a better place than Madura (where they arrived on January 3rd, 1929) under the guidance of their host, Robert Foulkes—the fifth generation of his family settled in the country, a rare type of unofficial public man, the elected chairman of the District Board, corresponding to the chairman of a County Council in England. "More talk with our host all day long—at breakfast under a tree in the garden with his monkeys and Malabar squirrel and deer all round us." At Trichinopoly the visitors were "greeted everywhere with garlands, salaaming elephants, and a native band. . . ." Of Madura he writes:

> . . . the great temple (an amazing place to which he took us last night at dark, when the lamps were lit and the whole vast place was thronged with worshippers in every court and corridor and tank) and two minor temples at some little distance from the town, both of great interest and beauty. Madura is a large, purely native town, given over for the most part to weaving a peculiar red cloth worn by all the women, streets lined with native bazaars and hovels, some modern factories (often owned by natives), no European shops or houses, dusty thoroughfares full of people, children, cows, donkeys, chickens, grain spread in the streets, temples everywhere, the towers of the big temple dominating the town, and little rest-houses for the passage of the gods from one to another at the festivals.

On methods of Government as discussed with his host he writes:

> So far as the districts are concerned he thinks the French system of individual Prefects with considerable powers has much to commend it. The people understand individual autocracy and a hierarchy of officials and councils multiplies corruption. Talking of the comparatively modern growth of anti-British oratory (rather than feeling) in India Foulkes attributed some of it to the disappearance of the last generation of Indians who knew by hearsay from old men of the chaos and unhappiness of conditions before the British came. In more recent times he thought Morley's *Recollections* had done infinite harm in disparaging the office of Viceroy and incidentally of other Governors. Till then the relations of Viceroy and Secretary of State had been a mystery.

The departure from Madura is thus described, "a crowd awaited us, and the sacred elephants trumpeted, and a native band brayed, and garlands of limes were tendered everywhere". Near Madras Geoffrey was introduced "to the entire hierarchy of tax-gathering etc., and witnessed harvesting and threshing with bullocks". At Ooty, a perfect morning, with brilliant sunshine, was spent "as we rose above the clouds, blue hills with red foliage, monkeys chattering at us and amazing views of the plains". Geoffrey the sportsman writes:

Shooting in Mysore and Madras.[1] Now comes an unexpected interlude of four days January 16–19 in the Mysore jungle, where we were lodged in a comfortable bungalow belonging to the Mysore Ironworks at Bhadrawati. . . . On the 16th we had a "chance" drive, which in its last few minutes produced a panther slinking noiselessly through some very thick bush in front of the tree where Cecilia and I were perched. I missed him but he went on into the open and F. Manners got him, so all was well and we returned in triumph. We had a wonderful visitation of jungle birds during that afternoon wait—some hornbills who frequented our tree and an enormous blinking owl, who sat on our very branch, and scores of others of every size and brilliant hue.

Jan. 19, 1929.—In the Mysore jungle . . . motored some 25 miles then trekked in a little bullock-cart and lunched and waited and finally had another thrilling wait in a tree top. We had two sights of tiger—one far away, out of shot, stalking majestically down the side of the jungle, the other suddenly appearing on the edge of my side of the ride in front of us, giving one roar at Cecilia (I could only see the top of her head) and then crossing the ride at a bound lower down, when I fired and missed her. She was not far away and presently another roar made me think she must be hit after all: but she cantered away behind, where F. Manners had a couple of shots and thought he too had missed till she was seen lying dead by a scout in a tree.

Calcutta—Jan. 26.—The Simon Commission. We arrived in Calcutta yesterday and were plunged at once into the orbit of the Simon Commission—a garden party given in their honour by a number of public bodies in the afternoon, dinner at Government House, at which most of them were present in the evening; two separate talks with Burnham and Simon this morning. I do not feel very happy about it.

During a ten days' stay at Delhi, as the Viceroy's guests, the Dawsons were able to study most facets of Indian opinion. They did the round of sights in Old and New Delhi, were present in "the Great Mosque" at the hour of weekly prayers. Geoffrey talked reform with Lord Irwin and with many of the leading men. While in Delhi they met again some of those they had already talked with on the journey in the South and Maharajahs, statesmen, civil servants, soldiers and business men from every part of the country. He described some of the problems confronting the Viceroy in the following summary:

. . . In January (when we were in Lucknow) Edward had opened the Assembly with a speech which created a favourable impression everywhere so far as one could tell. The snarling papers picked holes in it: but the *moderate* non-co-operators, who were said to be getting nervous

[1] At Madras the Dawsons stayed with Lord and Lady Goschen. They were invited to visit Mysore by the Maharajah (an old friend of the Lawleys), who arranged the shoot for Lord and Lady Manners and themselves.

about the extremists, seem to have seen a way out in the Viceroy's picture of his double duties to represent the King and to speak for the peoples of India. At any rate they seem to have approached him indirectly and in detail with an apparent anxiety to make a move. In any case Edward was determined to go on and began discussing with me at once the best approach to H.M.G. and their probable reception of his ideas. At this stage he evolved the further notion of trying to get all parties in England to combine before the General Election in statement of future *procedure* not *policy*—he had a phrase in his first draft about Dominion Status but this we removed.

I was no use to him of course about the situation in India, though it was soon clear that his sincerity and sympathy had given him a remarkable personal hold on all sorts and conditions of people. Everyone we met—politicians, Princes, Civil Servants—spoke of him with the greatest respect and affection. The one thing lacking, according to some, was that he should also be *feared*, and he himself quite agreed that his position would be stronger if he could find some good opportunity soon of showing himself resolute and tenacious. . .

While I was in Delhi the memorandum was revised in the light of recent events, and I contributed a draft of the sort of answer that the Prime Minister might make in the House of Commons before the dissolution—saying, if possible, that he had the concurrence of the Opposition leaders as well of his own colleagues—also of Simon. I attached great importance to this—indeed I thought it the first step to be taken.

. . . .

On the voyage home Geoffrey wrote a memorandum on India dated 25th March, 1929, from which the following extracts are taken:

It seems to me that a clear distinction should be drawn between (1) the problem of the forthcoming constitutional reforms in India and (2) *the method of approaching that problem*. The former is for the moment in the hands of the Simon Commission and any general discussion is to be deprecated until their Report appears. The latter, for various reasons, is becoming a matter of some urgency, and it is with this stage alone that the present Memorandum is concerned.

The position when I left India (March 16) is one of comparative political calm on the surface, but of expectancy beneath. The best opinion there is that a good many of the ablest non-co-operators are looking for a way out of a movement which has done them no good and has largely been a failure. They are a little frightened of their "Independence" wing and more than a little frightened of the rapid growth of Communism. They have compromised for the moment on the Gandhi demand for "Dominion Status by the end of the year"; but

Motilal[1] himself admitted to me that the demand was not seriously meant, and that what was really needed was an assurance that Dominion Status was on the way—or words to that effect.

The Viceroy's speech in opening the Assembly (January) had been very well received except by the professional naggers, and even they criticized rather because it had become a daily habit than because they had anything in particular to say against it. I happened, for example, to meet Chintamani (leader of the Opposition in the United Provinces and Editor of the bitterly hostile *Leader*) on the morrow of the speech, and it is typical of this attitude that he pronounced it "an excellent speech—far better than I dared to hope", in spite of having just published an article about it full of suspicious detraction. The Civil Servants and Europeans all liked it. Altogether it had a sedative effect, but the concluding passage about a Viceroy's double duty (to represent the King and also to represent the people of India) left behind it a general impression that something more was coming. . . .

. . . There has been an extensive arrest of Communist agitators (March 20) of which the bare news reached me in the Red Sea, though I had heard in confidence that it was in preparation.

The broad effect of all this, I hope, has been to suggest that the present Government of India is (1) sympathetic to Indian aspirations, (2) conscious of the problems of India as a whole, and not merely of the most vocal politicians in British India, and (3) determined to fulfil its first function of maintaining law and order. The Viceroy by common consent has succeeded in establishing a great personal reputation for sympathy and sincerity; but there has always been a doubt in India whether he is also a man of action and determination, as I think in fact he is. Certainly some sign of firmness was beginning to be needed, as he fully realized himself, and I feel that his anti-Communist "drive" has now placed him in a stronger position to do, without being regarded as "sloppy", what anyone wants if it can be managed—namely, to get the more reasonable non-co-operators back into the discussion of the next stage of the Reforms, or at all events to make it difficult for them to refuse.

There is a good deal of justification for making the effort. The British Government are greatly to blame for the manner in which the Simon Commission was launched. Everyone had been allowed to anticipate a "mixed" Commission. I feel sure that the "Parliamentary" inquiry, which was eventually adopted, was the only logical and practicable course, but no attempt was made either in England or in India to prepare the public for it. If the case had been clearly stated from the outset—the need of accurate information felt by a remote and ignorant Parliament; the absence, on the other hand, of any need for the participation in such an inquiry by Indians, living on the spot and familiar with own conditions; the rigid limitation of the function of the Commission to that of *rapporteurs* (as we called them in *The Times* at the outset)—if all this had

[1] Motilal Nehru, father of Jawaharlal.

SCARBROUGH

Geoffrey Dawson, Lt.-Colonel R. Lane-Fox, M.P. (later Lord Bingley), Neville Chamberlain, Lord Halifax and Sir Roger Lumley (later Earl of Scarbrough, K.G.)

Geoffrey bids farewell to Neville Chamberlain at Heston Aerodrome, on the occasion of his visit to Hitler

been emphasized from the beginning, then there would have been no substance in the cry of an "insult to India", which is now universal. . . .

And here it may be interposed that the uncertainty which exists at the moment as to the composition of H.M.G. a year hence suggests it would be of immense advantage if before the General Election an agreed plan of procedure in the matter of India could be formulated by *the heads of all three parties in England*. The Indian Opposition, it need hardly be said, is in active communication with our Labour Party, but Ramsay MacDonald is said to be discouraging extreme demands and the attitude of the extreme Indian Press towards him is very much that of the Soviet Press. . . .

There should, of course, be no question of turning the discussion into a "binding" or "decisive" Conference, though every effort would no doubt be made to represent it as such. The utmost that should be said—and I think that this should be plainly said beforehand—is that the outcome of such a discussion must necessarily carry great weight with H.M.G. but that the final responsibility rests with the British Government and Parliament (as indeed almost every Indian politician admits). The discussion, in short, would have for its purpose a final attempt to get at Indian opinion, and to convince Indian opinion of the sincerity and real difficulties of British opinion, made at an informal meeting on terms of perfect freedom and equality.

On 29th March, Geoffrey and Cecilia crossed the Channel and were met by their three most welcoming children and their grandparents. A further tremendous welcome with flags and streamers, prepared by the children, awaited them at Sussex Place.

A few days after his return Geoffrey was lucky enough to catch Sir Malcolm Hailey, just off to India, and had an "extraordinarily interesting talk" with him which confirmed most of his fleeting impressions. The first leader on India published in the paper, after his return, was "The Viceroy Takes Action" (April 13). It referred to Mr. Patel's legalized obstruction from the Chair and the firm action taken by Lord Irwin; it ended up with this tribute to the Viceroy, "the genuine sympathy with national aspirations, a natural gentleness and dignity of manner, unmistakeable sincerity . . . qualities" which in the three years since he left England had "made themselves felt, as every visitor reports, throughout the length and breadth of India". But the paper pointed out that onlookers "made a profound mistake who interpreted as lack of strength the innate kindliness of a great gentleman".

The first important statesman Geoffrey met after his return was Baldwin, with whom he discussed the state of politics and the Press, the Trade Delegation to Russia and other subjects. Two days later he spent a Saturday afternoon at Chequers, alone with Baldwin, who was succeeded as Prime Minister by Ramsay MacDonald in June; the entry in the diary for April 6th is: "I found him (Baldwin) very receptive and anxious about India and was duly indiscreet about Edward's (Lord Irwin's) ideas which appealed to him. We discussed Cabinet reconstruction, the Governor for India and every sort of topic." A few days later a leader appeared in *The Times* entitled "Reconstruction" (April 13th), which commented on the Prime Minister's (Baldwin's) mistakes and missed opportunities and explained why a reconstruction of the Conservative Government would not then be desirable. "There are many occasions, notably when the Prime Minister went to Canada the year before last, which gave him the chance of reviewing the condition of his team from a distance and of reforming it on his return. These chances were missed, and the consequences of this failure are not yet expended." True words, as was to be proved by the Election two months later, when Ramsay MacDonald became Premier for a second time; but on that occasion as head of the strongest party. *The Times*, however, insisted in this article that all that was decent or possible then was that Baldwin "should make it absolutely clear to the country that, if and when he returned to power, he does mean to reshape his Government drastically for another spell of work".

As part of the task of picking up threads, Geoffrey had a long talk with Stamfordham shortly after his return, and on June 18th a leader on the latter's eightieth birthday appeared in *The Times*, in which a tribute was paid to a career spent largely in service of the Crown. Lord Stamfordham was much touched, as will be seen by the following letter:

Windsor Castle,
Waterloo Day,
1929.

My dear Geoffrey,
If I may so call you!

You have done me a very great honour—the words of your leader in today's *Times* touch me greatly: but you put me into a higher class than I deserve! And then my warmest thanks to you and Cecilia for your very kind greetings. The feeling that one has such good friends prevents anyone from growing old even at 80.

It is rather a drawback not being in London in these days, but I must be there for two days next week and will try to see you.

The King is much better again and I wish the Thanksgiving Service could be next month.

Yours ever,
STAMFORDHAM.

On May 28th there is an entry about "listening to Ramsay MacDonald on the radio before returning to work"—this is one of the first references to a political broadcast at Election time; and two days later the following reference to the Election appears, "Then a long, hectic and rather gloomy evening—great Socialist majorities everywhere in the Boroughs till I finally returned home between 3 and 4 a.m. to find Cecilia with the wireless still recording results." The fact that Geoffrey had anticipated that Baldwin's missed opportunities would have dire consequences evidently caused him no satisfaction.

The diary during the first days in June is full of references to the Labour victory. In the leading article, "The Next Step" (June 3), *The Times* pointed out that there would be no combination of Conservatives and Liberals, such as Ramsay MacDonald had presumably feared the previous week, when he had protested against Labour "being put into the position of being the largest of three parties not having a majority". The previous day Geoffrey admitted that "like most other people I was torn with doubts whether Stanley Baldwin should meet Parliament or resign at once and kept on re-writing my leader" (in the diary for June 1st he understood that "the Prime Minister was undecided and Mrs. Baldwin urging him to go!"). The actual entries were as follows:

> *June 3*. . . . There was a Cabinet at 5 and it became known that Stanley Baldwin meant to go at once. . . .
>
> *June 4*. . . . Baldwin had gone down to Windsor to resign this morning. . . .
>
> *June 5*. Derby Day. . . . An easy journey and an excellent lunch after which we walked down to the Paddock, and saw most of the Derby horses and many more friends, and I saw the race quite admirably from Nancy's box. But it rained all day and Trigo won, and what with this and the advent of a Labour Government (as a porter remarked at the station) it was one of the worst Derbys of modern times.

On the morning of Derby Day a most excellent leading article appeared in *The Times* on "Responsibilities Overseas", in which the paper rightly dealt with the supreme importance of the qualifications of the next Secretary of State for India (who, as announced two days later, was W. Wedgwood Benn); it also urged the appointment of a separate Minister to be in charge of the Dominions Office and of the Colonial Office.

Ever since the death of Harold Williams there are many references in Geoffrey's papers to the gap in the Printing House Square Foreign Department which had never been filled. Certainly it was not from lack of trying to find a successor. In March, and in response to an enquiry from Geoffrey while in India, G. M. Brumwell, the acting Editor, wrote: "There is no sign of a Williams in the office or out of it, and that is a terrible source of weakness for it lays on the occupants of the Editorial chair a burden of unfair weight. . . . It has been rather a lonely time without your company and the impact of your mind. What really causes me more sleepless nights than the future of the Foreign Department is, who is to take charge here when you and I have gone. At present, I confess, I don't see the man. But I expect this problem occupies your thoughts too in the midnight hours." On June 30th there is this reference to Printing House Square in the diary, "Rather depressed by the state of the Foreign Department and the finding of a successor to Harold Williams." On July 22nd he wrote, "Barrington-Ward has done well in my absence though he realized the standing difficulties of late leaders and a weak Foreign Department." On December 4th Geoffrey wrote: " . . . I spent a long afternoon completing my notes on the Foreign Department. . . . I got Brumwell and Barrington-Ward in general agreement over the loosening of the foreign hierarchy."[1]

Two years after the death of Harold Williams, Geoffrey wrote:

> Above all, so is Harold Williams (i.e. irreplaceable), who had an astounding knowledge of foreign affairs, and an instinct for what he didn't know, with a special and most valuable capacity for dealing with the Dominions (he was a New Zealander by birth) and with the United States. His death is by far the most serious loss which the paper has sustained since I came back into it. It occurred just as I was preparing to start for a visit to India. There was no one in the office obviously fitted to fill the place. I therefore made at once a temporary division of his work and after much discussion and research decided to go on with it when I returned. . .

In July, 1929, Geoffrey wrote a memorandum to Lints Smith, the Manager, in which he gave his ideas on the future organization of the Foreign Department. He proposed the stabilizing of the then existing "working arrangement" and the abandonment "of the idea and title of a 'Director of the Foreign Department', which has become an anachronism, and dividing the various functions rather more precisely between the half-dozen members of the staff who nowadays carry on what used to be one man's task when the title was originally invented for Sir Donald Mackenzie Wallace". He outlined the position as it then was and explained that the foreign leaders would be written by a panel of experts on Eastern affairs, the League of Nations and Europe (Leo Kennedy), Anglo-American relations, Africa and Colonial problems. Geoffrey also referred to what he considered the most important addition to the staff during 1929, in the return to *The Times*

[1] *The History of "The Times"*, Vol. IV, Part II, p. 816, takes a different view.

of D. D. Braham, after sixteen years spent in Australia and a visit to the United States. He was a very definite asset to the forces at Printing House Square, as he at once fell into the position of leader-writer on a number of important Imperial and foreign subjects—the Naval Conference, the Imperial Conference, Russia (an old interest of his) and, of course, Australia.

In the memorandum Geoffrey thus set forth his views:

> The old theory of a "foreign leader-writer"—someone who was prepared to write on any subject or briefed by someone else—seems to me to be as obsolete as that of a "Foreign Editor". As a matter of fact most of the really effective foreign leaders even in the old days were written not by so-called "leader-writers" but by successive "Directors of the Foreign Department", e.g. Chirol and Williams. I am quite convinced that the only chance of keeping up the standard is that everyone should write as far as can be arranged on the subjects which he knows best and on which he has himself kept up close personal contact with the people concerned.

The memorandum ended with these two paragraphs:

> The suggestion has been made, and I think that there is a great deal to be said for it—it has in fact been put into practical operation lately—that correspondents visiting London with a number of miscellaneous points to discuss should always have a meeting at which these points could be raised and settled simultaneously by all those chiefly concerned with them in the office. It is said that in the past there has been a tendency for visiting correspondents to go from room to room in search of the most agreeable advice and instructions; and, though these additional private talks are obviously desirable, and any serious divergence of instructions has in fact been prevented by the concentration of formal communication in the hands of the Manager, I agree entirely with the view that correspondents should have a regular opportunity of meeting the office as a corporate body.
>
> It accords exactly with the underlying idea of these notes, namely, that the editorial staff of a newspaper cannot be organized in a rigid hierarchy like a bank or a Government Department, that the positions and duties in it must be far more elastic and must depend on individual interests and capacities, and that the fewer permanent titles there are about it the better. So far as the foreign side is concerned it seems to me that everyone should be prepared to write on his own subjects—which after all is the first and most important business of journalism—and that everyone should have in addition his allotted share of routine duties, which should in no case be so heavy as it has sometimes been in the past.

The month of July began with an hour's talk with Wedgwood Benn at the India Office; indeed Geoffrey seems to have kept in fairly close touch with the Secretary of State for India during the period before the meeting of the Round Table delegates in London. In a leader entitled "Rumours about India" (October 14th), *The Times* asserted there was no ground for the rumour that Wedgwood Benn proposed to visit India and thereby make the mistake of appearing "to anticipate the Simon Commission by a personal tour". We also find that in the Parliamentary correspondence (Oct. 31st), the paper writes sympathetically about Wedgwood Benn's activities and said that "unlike many of his colleagues, he had no hampering past so far as India was concerned". Geoffrey, of course, kept in close touch with the Viceroy who had returned to England for a while for consultations with the new Government.

In an important leading article, "The Ultimate Goal" (Nov. 1st), the paper dealt with the importance of the Viceroy's restatement (Lord Irwin at Delhi) of the ultimate purpose of British policy in India: "I am authorized on behalf of His Majesty's Government to state clearly that in their judgment it is implicit in the declaration of 1917 that the natural issue of India's constitutional progress, as there contemplated, is the attainment of Dominion status." The Parliamentary Correspondent (Nov. 4th) compared the Viceroy's statement, the object of the attack by those opposed to Lord Irwin's policy, with words used by Lord Birkenhead, when Secretary of State for India in 1927; and asked, "Is there any real difference, they (members) are asking, between 'the attainment of Dominion status as the natural issue of India's constitutional progress' (Lord Irwin at Delhi, 1929) and the 'precious promise of a Constitution which might bring India on equal terms as an honoured partner into the free community of British Dominions'?" (Lord Birkenhead in London, 1927).

Geoffrey must be allowed to tell the story of the "Indian Crisis" in his own words:

Nov. 2. I gave up Oxford early . . . my first miss of an All Souls Day when in England. . . . I amused myself by writing at intervals—largely to clear my own mind—a survey of the Indian crisis. The afternoon was entirely devoted to talking about it, for Baldwin (Leader of the Opposition) came to see me about three and stayed till 5.30.—rather worried about it all and by the intrigue behind it. He and Cecilia and I had tea together over the library fire.

Nov. 3. . . . Brumwell came to lunch, and carried off my "Bill" page (The Indian Crisis—Steadier Views) "lead" on India which came back for revision in proof about dinner time—It was clearly worth doing, for the Sunday papers were all wrong—(e.g. Garvin in a page of hysteria never once mentioned the Conference). As I wrote to Edward it was *Tempora contra mundum*.

Nov. 5. . . . got to the House of Lords for an hour of the Indian debate (Parmoor dreadfully prolix and F.E. simply deplorable). My contribution tonight (The Goal in India—Use of the word Dominion) to the "crisis" was to edit the sketch in that sense.

Nov. 6.—Office for an hour before lunch after putting down a few reflections on the Lords debate. We lunched with Nancy (Walter Elliot, Margesson, O'Connor, etc.,—all against Edward and *The Times*). Then Baldwin caught me for a few words at the Travellers' and I responded to an S.O.S. from Simon after inspecting the new Milner Relief in Westminster Abbey. The crisis was evidently fizzling and I wrote some political notes to this effect and some attempt at an analysis of the reactions in India.

Nov. 7. . . . Got to the House of Commons for the Indian debate 3.45 and sat through Baldwin, Benn and L.G. Then back to the office about 6 to furbish up a leader ("The Indian Reaction") . . . and to finish the Indian "Crisis".

Lady Oxford wrote the following letter (December 22nd) to Geoffrey:

I had 1000 more things I wanted to discuss with you, as I see you so seldom, and you are so busy in your own work and your own circle of friends (not alas mine, or we should meet oftener). You are one of the rare persons to whom one can say *anything*. Because you are a fine judge of character, which means a little *more* than people think. It means:

1. Preferences, but no exclusions.
2. It means imaginative insight into the *hearts* of men.
3. It means loyalty to what is good in *yourself* and in others.

There is an old Scotch saying, "There is now't so queer as Folk," and however much you may know of History, Languages, Art, and Government, this remains true. Human nature remains the most perplexing and the most *important* of studies.

When I die (and alas! I'm not young) you will have to write my obituary notice for your *Times*—and put in as few of other people's private letters as possible. I would like you to tell the truth (as nothing buries people more completely than false praise).

I would like you to say: "Lady Oxford, better known as Mrs. Asquith, was a woman of single mind; whose loyalty and devotion to her friends you could rely upon. She had a high standard of truth—never very popular—and could not only *keep* a secret, but could *recognize* one. There was no friend that she would not have defended in any company; and she had the rare virtue of gratitude to those who had befriended her.

She once told me that fortune tellers had often said stupid things about her, that she was fond of travel—which she never enjoyed—that she was a good linguist, which she was not etc! but they had *all* said—from the gypsy on the Derby Heath to the adventuress at a table—that she did not care for money, and that she had compassion for the foibles and failures of human nature. She had a lot of loose love to give. . . .

You have a heart as well as brains, and I never forget that by a strange accident you were the first person I told that Henry was dying. Nor do I forget your wonderful sympathy. I can't hear his name mentioned without emotion, and yet I long to hear it mentioned.

Forgive this egotistical letter.

XXIII

INDIAN ROUND TABLE—1930–1931

INDIA dominated the political horizon during most of 1930 and up to the time of the world slump in the autumn of 1931, when Great Britain went off gold. During this period *The Times* published a very remarkable series of leading articles on India.

Geoffrey received the following letter (written on January 7th at Astley Hall, Stourport) from Baldwin:

My dear Dawson,

I am sending up my Glasgow Rectorial. I have still to write an ending for it, but I read a leader of yours a few days ago on character, and oddly enough I had chosen that for my theme when I started the Address at Aix last August. I have to deliver it on Monday week, the 20th.

My staff in London feed me with the lucubrations of the Press Barons, Rothermere adopting my policy of '23 is comical. I have a pretty row to hoe among them all.

I should enjoy a talk with you when I get back which won't be till the 21st.

I sometimes wonder whether I am mad, or whether everybody else is!

Yours ever,
STANLEY BALDWIN.

A few days later Baldwin sent his completed Rectorial to Geoffrey whose comment was, "I feel that a dissertation on character is perhaps the best contribution that can be made to confused politics at the present moment."

On January 2nd, 1930, *The Times* published a leading article, "Lahore and After", and warned its readers not to underestimate the influence of the Congress Party, presided over by the "Young Harrovian", and suggested that there was still a chance of rallying reasonable opinion in consultation in the next stage of advance towards the ideal of an India, united and self-governing, within the Empire. It went on to say—with foresight in view of the events which took place in 1947—that the programme of Mr. Nehru could result in nothing but a series of revolutions and civil wars or else in an India permanently divided. In the early months of the year there are many references in the diary to the coming publication of the Simon Commission's Report and of occasional talks which Geoffrey had with Wedgwood Benn, then Secretary of State, about Indian problems. In the previous autumn Benn wrote to the Editor of *The Times* telling him how "deeply grateful" he was for his help.

On February 4th, after a talk with Sir John Simon, Geoffrey noted that he "seemed to be going towards sound conclusions". On February 17th there is a reference to the production of an India number of *The Times*—"the work of nearly a year". Geoffrey also noted that Beaverbrook *cum* Rothermere were "launching a new party"—" 'The Beavers', or 'United Empire Party' "; and by March 5th there is the entry "The United Empire Party had simply disappeared", and two days later he noted that "a definite Beaverbrook-Rothermere split was announced in the course of the evening". During the brief existence of the new party Geoffrey amused himself, in the issue of *The Times* of February 20th, by what is referred to in his diary as "My collocation of paragraphs in the Summary last night—the 2 noblemen with their new party and the 2 monkeys at large in London—had had an immense success and I received letters about it all day!" The comment of the *Manchester Guardian* was, "This, on the top of the crossword puzzles in Latin, ought to satisfy everybody that there is sparkle as well as thunder in the Thames-side air." Fleet Street was watching the columns of "The Thunderer" with delight. Both the *Star* and the *Daily News* made the most of these signs of humour in Printing House Square. Under the heading "Still at Large" the *Star* printed the following paragraphs:

> Was it only due to the long arm of coincidence that the two paragraphs reproduced below followed one another in this morning's *Times*?
>
> Lord Beaverbrook and Lord Rothermere have issued a series of statements about the formation of their new party and announce their intention to put a number of candidates in the field at future elections (Page 14).
>
> The two monkeys which escaped in London a few days ago are still at large (Page 11).

Punch, on February 26th, joined in the fray, and reprinted the famous two paragraphs with the following comment:

The general idea seems to be that this was a case of undesigned humour on the part of *The Times*. We ourselves shrink from endorsing the view lest we should be doing a grave injustice to our honoured contemporary.

On March 5, in "TODAY'S NEWS", *The Times* printed the following paragraph:

> One of the two monkeys which has lately been at large in London was recaptured last night by its owner, who had made skilful use of a trap baited with apples and bananas. The recapture of the second monkey is thought likely to be easier now that it is alone (Page 13).

The final episode in the story was the appearance in the columns of *The Times* of a report of some remarks of Lord Beaverbrook's on Empire Free Trade, which showed that his Lordship was certainly possessed of a refreshing sense of humour. At the end of his speech he said: "You know I have been a rebel. You know the monkey is in the cage." (Laughter.) In the diary of March 4th there is this entry, "Returned to Printing House Square to find that the monkey had been caught and so wound up the 'Monkey Saga'."

Despite these refreshing interludes of sparkle there were plenty of other matters, as usual, to occupy the attention of the Editor.

The second week in June was a period of intense activity owing to the forthcoming appearance of the Simon Report. For a couple of days Geoffrey had secluded himself from most visitors and on the three days—June 10th–12th—he produced four leading articles on this all-important subject: "The Importance of Unanimity", "Three Main Impressions", "All India" and finally "The Army in India". *The Times* laid special emphasis on the fact that the Simon Report would be found to be "without dissenting minute" which implied, therefore, that there would be no divergence in Great Britain about the essential features of the problem to be solved. From Mr. Sastri (the Indian leader) he received a depressing account of the Youth Movement and the growth of Communism in India, but noted that he was "cheerfully ready for immediate Dominion Status", and emphasized "the influence of Gandhi's selflessness and sees something of the same qualities in the young Nehru".

In "All India" *The Times* dealt with the inclusion of the Indian States in a common federal union with the provinces of British India; and finally in "The Army in India" the paper dealt with the part the army—a force of 60,000 British troops and of 150,000 Indian troops, led mainly by British officers—had played in providing for the security of the sub-continent. It then referred to the chequered course of the

"Indianization" of the Indian Army, and to the fact that the first grant of King's Commissions to Indian officers only dated from the year 1918.

Within less than a fortnight in a leader, "The New Way in India" (June 24), the paper dealt with the second part of the Report and therefore the termination of work of the Indian Statutory Commission, and stated categorically that there would never again be a "Simon Commission"; it then summed up the achievement of the Commission as setting "a new course towards the goal by translating mere ideas into a definite scheme of federal union" and referred to the method of federalism and the useful experience gained from a study of the subject as applied both in the United States of America and in the British Dominions. In July, and during the first days of August, *The Times* was again producing numerous leading articles interpreting the tremendous issues involved by the Report and preparing its public for the actual summoning of the Round Table Conference itself in the autumn. In the leading article "The Viceroy's Address" (July 10), *The Times* asserted that the Report did "in fact point the way—perhaps the only possible way—to the evolution of a Dominion by the same process which has already been proved in the case of Canada, Australia and South Africa". In the article "Choosing a Team" (August 5), the paper urged the importance of the personnel of the British delegation, representing the three parties, which would have to interpret "the broad outlines of what may be called a British policy for the present Indian situation".

In the leader "Britain at the Round Table", the fact is recorded that among the dozen British delegates would be the Prime Minister (Ramsay MacDonald), Lord Reading, Lord Zetland, Mr. Oliver Stanley and Lord Lothian. On November 6th, in "The Urgent Problem of India", *The Times* pleaded for an immediate meeting of the twelve British delegates before the Conference assembled. It also stated that the early arrival of the Indian delegates had enabled them by personal contact to realize that British opinion was "far more receptive and sympathetic" than they had sometimes been led to suppose.

The Times, which had been slightly critical of Lord Irwin in connection with the Government of India's Report, paid this tribute to the Viceroy in the leading article, "The Grand Parade" (November 22nd), "There has been no more remarkable feature of the Conference, as every member bears witness, than the spontaneous and prolonged applause which has greeted every mention of the Viceroy." It also referred to Lord Reading's allusion to "the dazzling swiftness" with which the East was changing and wrote appreciatively of the Prime

Minister as making a good chairman. The leading article, "The Conference Goes On" (December 13th), ended with a reference to the spirit of increasing good will which animated the whole Round Table, to the profound and sympathetic interest with which its fortunes were being followed by the British public.

There are of course many references to the Imperial Conference, which began on October 1st, but for once it took second place in the Editor's attention owing to the extreme urgency of the Indian "Round Table". On October 2nd he attended the unveiling of the bust of Northcliffe in Fleet Street, in the presence of a large company of journalists; on October 9th this entry occurs, "visit Stanley Baldwin, who'd written last night falling in with my suggestion of a *letter* (rather than a speech) 'restating policy' and was now contemplating an immediate interim statement welcoming the Dominion proposals". The following letters had been exchanged the previous day:

Private

Travellers' Club,
Pall Mall,
S.W.1.

My dear Dawson,

Were you joking when you said you had in mind the sort of letter I could write? I thought over what you said: there is much in favour of a letter as against a speech. If you were serious, do send me a draft of the sort of thing you had in your mind.

Yours ever,
S.B.

8th October, 1930.

My dear Baldwin,

No, I was not joking at all. In present circumstances I think a letter (as short as it can be made) to the Chairman of the Party by far the best method of conveying certain simple truths. Every newspaper is bound to give it prominence and it should of course be published textually by the B.B.C. Furthermore a letter enables the statement to be precise and beyond misinterpretation, while it avoids all the difficulties about audience etc. which are inherent in a public speech.

Geoffrey then explained that he had to go to Yorkshire but would, if Baldwin decided on adopting the plan, try and think out something in the train. On October 15th he had another talk with Baldwin, who was about to issue a further "statement of policy". On October 17th he published an article on "Mr. Baldwin as Leader". *The Times* observed that Baldwin had "cultivated the character of an amateur in politics to a point which is maddening to ardent politicians"; while his closest admirers "complain that they find it difficult to pin him to a serious discussion or to extract a definite statement of his views"; it then stated that Baldwin had carried loyalty to his former colleagues too far, and it was generally believed that the defeat of the Conservatives in the last election was due to the conviction that a victory for Baldwin would have entailed the reinstatement of the "same old gang".

The Times added that the prospects of the Conservative Party would be improved beyond all knowledge by the belief that "Mr. Baldwin was prepared to take office hereafter with a team that would be predominantly new and young". In the concluding part of the article it stated that Baldwin owed his position "to certain qualities of his own which do mark him out from his colleagues and to which history will attach no small importance in retrospect. None of the others has shown his power on occasion of rising to heights that are something more than oratorical". After referring to Baldwin's great wisdom in handling the period before and after the General Strike of 1926, it continued, "He has probably done more than any other Englishman to convince the labour movement that sincerity, good will and a genuine desire to improve the condition of the people may be found outside its own self-righteous ranks."

Towards the end of October Geoffrey found "politics getting very absorbing". On October 28th his diary recorded "an anti-Baldwin resolution passed by 44 members of the House of Commons", and on the following day he referred to "great political excitement over the anti-Baldwin intrigue". On October 30th he wrote, "a vast Conservative meeting was discussing Baldwin's leadership. He got away with it after a 'secret ballot' which was followed by a unanimous vote".

On November 12th the great Indian Conference was opened by the King and various of its members lunched at Printing House Square.

The year 1931 witnessed the final success of what we may term the Irwin-Baldwin-MacDonald-*Times* Indian Policy. Symbolic of the amount of thought Geoffrey was to devote to the Round Table Conference was the fact that the leading article in *The Times*, "Getting to Grips" (Jan. 3), in which the paper expressed surprise at the headway already made, stated, even if there were failure, "it is fair to doubt already whether the failure would be complete even if the Round Table were to break up in disorder tomorrow". Early in the year, however, *The Times* realized more than ever how intractable was the problem of the schism between Hindu and Muslim. At the same time it noted how definite was the advance made since the publication of the Simon Report, in the acceptance of the conception of responsible

Government by Indians at the centre, no less than in the Provinces. The paper also noted the welcome acceptance of a Federation of all India forthwith—"nothing more than a hopeful ideal till the Round Table was assembled in London"—and now recognized as a new factor of incalculable significance.

There are constant references in Geoffrey's diary, letters and memoranda to most facets of the Indian question. His admiration of the Viceroy's qualities never wavered and he knew, from what he had himself seen on his Indian tour, that Lord Irwin had indeed "stood between India and chaos" and that, thanks largely to him, "a greater storm", in the words of the Maharajah of Burdwan, had been surmounted than India had "seen since the Mutiny". When the Round Table was first suggested, *The Times* had supported the Viceroy and the Labour Government, then in power. Bitter were the feelings aroused, and at various stages of the controversy over India it looked as though the forces opposed to a fair settlement might triumph. Certainly if there had been any weakening on the part of *The Times*, Mr. Baldwin could not have rallied to his support the great majority of the party.

In one of the most important leaders on India published by *The Times*, "The Front Restored" (March 13th), it tried to analyse the circumstances "in which a Conservative Committee's resolution, almost universally regarded next morning as a complete reversal of policy, came to be suddenly thrown on the world last Monday (March 9th) night". The "front" had to be restored and this was done in the debate on the previous day, in which Mr. Baldwin rose to the occasion. *The Times* made this comment: "It is one of Mr. Baldwin's most unfailing characteristics that he never rises to the heights of which he is capable till the causes for which he stands seem almost desperate. His spiritual home is always the last ditch." In March the Rothermere Press became particularly active in its anti-Round Table campaign and a large meeting was held in the Royal Albert Hall, under the chairmanship of the Duke of Marlborough, while Mr. Churchill spoke with the deep conviction that he then felt in opposition to the Government's policy. When the Delhi truce was achieved as a result of the Irwin-Gandhi discussions the leader, "India and Party Politics" (March 5), appeared in *The Times*. In it the paper said that there were no doubts about the complete sincerity with which Mr. Churchill set out to marshal British opinion in support of a policy of repression. "It is certain that if India is to be saved to the Empire—as it would infallibly be lost if the Churchill school of thinkers were ever to have control—it can only be by the way that Mr. Baldwin broadly hinted in that very speech in the House of Commons for which he has been most abused." Excitement had reached fever heat by March 19th when the polling took place in the St. George's by-election and Mr. Duff Cooper was returned with a majority of 5710.[1]

Geoffrey received the following note (20th March, 1931) from Baldwin:

> At the end of this hectic eight days I want to thank you most warmly for the consistent support you have given me through a very difficult time.
>
> St. George's will do a lot of good.

A leader on "Lord Irwin's Return" appeared in *The Times* on 2nd May. The paper referred to the demonstrations of devotion displayed when Lord Irwin sailed from Bombay, "such as have seldom been accorded to any Viceroy": the paper also dealt with the fact that it was Lord Irwin "who gave the final freedom which has enabled India to frame a tariff better suited to herself than Lancashire". With foresight the paper also referred to "the great wave of Asiatic nationalism" which rolled up "with fresh volume for every attempt to ignore it".

On July 15th among the guests at the office lunch at Printing House Square were Lord Beaverbrook, Pat McCormick, Stafford Cripps, the new Solicitor-General. . . . Geoffrey wrote, "I liked Cripps and had some interesting talk with Beaverbrook about the future of newspapers, the Hitler movement, of which he didn't think much, etc., etc.".

On July 1st the Lord Chancellor (Lord Sankey) wrote to Geoffrey saying he would like to come round to see him for a talk about India. Two days later the Editor went round to his house in Dean's Yard so that they would be uninterrupted. Sankey was hard at work on the preparations for the Federal Structure Committee, which hoped to be able to make its report to a full meeting of the Round Table Conference assembling at the beginning of November. They discussed most aspects of the Round Table Conference. Geoffrey learnt that Gandhi quite definitely meant to come to London. The following brief extracts cover some of the matters discussed:

> The Lord Chancellor told me that his ambition was to prepare beforehand a constitutional scheme which would be agreed between all the British delegates, but to let it emerge so far as possible from the discussions of the Conference. I said that I agreed entirely with this plan. I thought it absolutely essential that there should be a complete preliminary agreement between parties on certain definite limits beyond

[1] The candidates were Mr. Duff Cooper, backed by the Conservative Party organization, and Mr. Ernest W. Petter, Independent Conservative, backed by Lord Rothermere.

which this country could not go. He produced a rough draft of the kind of document on which he was working—a constitutional scheme drawn in the form of a Parliamentary Bill with notes and comments and alternatives interleaved. . . .

He asked me what I should advise in the not improbable event of the Conference breaking down altogether. I said I should unhesitatingly go ahead with the establishment of provincial autonomy, about which everyone was agreed, and trust that matters might be improved by experience of it in practical operation.

XXIV

"THE TIMES" AND THE NATIONAL GOVERNMENT

THE *Times* under Geoffrey played a very important part in making possible the formation of the National Government in 1931 (a result of the world economic crisis which finally forced Great Britain to discard the Gold Standard).

During June and July there were signs of very serious financial troubles ahead. First came the welcome news of President Hoover's postponement of the war debt payments for a year, then ominous reports about a big bank in Berlin being forced to close its doors were circulated; in mid-July Philip Snowden, Chancellor of the Exchequer in the Labour Government, discussed with the Editor the French project of a loan to Germany, hedged round, however, with political conditions. Geoffrey must have left for Langcliffe on August 7th in a disturbed state of mind, for he had just had "an earnest conversation with Bob (Brand) on the critical financial state of the nation". On August 12th, after a "perfect day's shooting", this entry appears in the diary: ". . . The only thing to detract from complete holiday was a certain anxiety about affairs in London, where however everyone was at last realizing how serious the financial position had become. Ramsay MacDonald was returning from Lossiemouth and Baldwin from his journey to Aix. . . ." On the following day "more interesting and anxious letters" arrived from London. On August 17th these words appear in the diary, "My letters in the evening decided me to go to London tomorrow."

Among Geoffrey's papers is a memorandum about the "Financial Crisis" of Saturday, August 22nd and Sunday, August 23rd. In it he refers to a long talk with Reading whom he had not seen since the Crisis began. He found him showing considerable sympathy for the Prime Minister, who had to handle a following which had been taught that all the excitement about economy was merely "big business" and the bankers trying to make larger profits. Reading entirely agreed with the Editor's views, already expressed in *The Times*, about the extreme urgency of producing a scheme which would show foreign countries, and particularly the United States, that the Government was determined to put its financial house in order. The two men reviewed the figures which had so far been discussed. Originally the Cabinet had hoped to save about seventy-five million pounds, almost half of which was to come from cuts in the dole. But in order to propitiate the T.U.C. this amount had been whittled down to about sixty millions. The figure suggested by the City to impress the world was one hundred millions. Lord Reading, in reply to Geoffrey's question, thought a sum between eighty-two and eighty-five millions would just suffice.

His next talk on the Saturday afternoon was with Neville Chamberlain, from whom he sought to find out "what precisely the Government understood by the agreement for support of the Opposition" (the Conservatives). Chamberlain told him that Ramsay MacDonald suggested if he could get the Cabinet up to a figure which they thought tolerable would the Opposition undertake not to turn out the Government by combining with the Labour malcontents as soon as Parliament met. Chamberlain had told the Prime Minister that he should require time to consider this: but he told Geoffrey privately that he personally would be for agreeing to it if such a point were ever reached. Chamberlain was convinced that the Prime Minister realized to the full the extreme seriousness of the position and was prepared to go further than his colleagues, while Snowden (Chancellor of the Exchequer) had been more emphatic still and "had been very scornful of certain minor suggestions of economy from the Departments. . . ."

Of the momentous events of Sunday, August 23rd, and his part in them, Geoffrey writes:

> Clive Wigram rang me up soon after his arrival from Balmoral with the King and we had some preliminary conversation on the telephone. His Majesty was going to see the Prime Minister directly and was considering what line to take with him. He proposed to see Baldwin and Samuel later in the day, so as to have the views of all parties at first hand. I suggested respectfully that His Majesty should impress upon Ramsay that it was his business to get the country out of the mess and to dwell, with any flattery that he liked, upon the opportunity and the responsibility. The example of Scullin, who had become almost a popular hero by facing his problem in Australia, was one that might profitably be pointed out to him. I repeated the arguments that we had been using in *The Times* and said that I thought it was everything to get a plan of national economy put out in public by a Labour Government, since it was the only course that would have a permanent effect in reversing a policy of extravagance.

Clive Wigram said he quite agreed and would talk to the King on these lines at once.

Baldwin rang me up soon afterwards, came round to my house in the middle of the morning,[1] and stayed there talking till lunch time, when we drove down together to the Travellers'. He also agreed entirely with the views expressed above and was in hopes that the crisis would be temporarily settled on these lines by tomorrow. . . .

He then fell to discussing what should be the *personnel* of a new Government if by any misfortune he was to be called upon to form one at once, saying that it was easier for him to talk these matters over with me than with any of his political colleagues.

For several days after the decision to form a National Government was made Geoffrey remained in London. By the evening of Tuesday, August 25th, Ramsay MacDonald had seen the King and the principal list of appointments was out. Geoffrey bemoaned the fate which kept him in London and not "on the sleets" where the long-arranged field trials were taking place. He returned to Langcliffe on the 26th and the diary for the next ten days is devoted to the shoots on Penyghent and elsewhere, and to "a great trek"—a riding tour with Geoffrey, Cecilia and Michael "on our ponies, Edward (Halifax) and the Titchfields on their large hunters". After "a very breezy and wholesome week of riding and shooting" Geoffrey returned to London on September 7th.

The diary entries for these vital days follow:

Monday, Sept. 7. . . . I had an assignation in Leeds with Mann (of the *Yorkshire Post*), who entirely agreed with me about the undesirability of an early General Election, and I was in time to say this in *The Times*, to which I devoted a long evening on arrival. The news of the night was the lead given by His Majesty and the Prince of Wales in gifts to the Treasury. (The King decided that during the crisis the Civil List should be reduced by £50,000 and the Prince of Wales contributed a like sum.)

Thursday, Sept. 10. Emergency Budget Day. I began it with a long talk with Stanley Baldwin on the importance of going to the country as a National Government and not in three parties. He was very receptive, said it carried his own ideas much further and warmly approved my putting it to the Prime Minister . . . to hear Snowden's draconian Budget, applauded only from the Government benches and derided by a nasty-looking Opposition. . . .

Sept. 13. . . . to lunch with the Prime Minister at Chequers . . . and I had a couple of hours' heart to heart with Ramsay, who gave me his

[1] Sir Harold Nicolson (*King George V*, p. 461) states that Mr. Baldwin "had strayed off into the streets and could not be located: it was thus by one of the chances of history that Sir Herbert Samuel was the first to furnish His Majesty with advice". Mr. Baldwin finally saw the King at 3 p.m.

> whole story of the crisis and was very candid and receptive. He is quite prepared for a National Government appeal and to serve under Baldwin subsequently or alternatively to go round the Dominions. Personally he thinks a tariff essential and has set up a Committee to go into it. . . .

Geoffrey mentions in the diary that after lunching with *The Times* Correspondent in Madrid at the Travellers' Club, he "tried" his "General Election views" on five friends whom he found there—a method he often employed when engaged on preparing an important leader advocating a new approach to some political problem.

On September 15th he revised his General Election leader which urged an appeal to the country by the National Government as such, and not by a Party. The evening papers echoed this view, and many Conservative M.P.s declared their support of it.

Few leaders in *The Times* can ever have had more immediate results. In it the paper expressed the view that "even a premature appeal to the country would hardly be more mischievous than protracted uncertainty", and asked, "Is there any real reason why the appeal to the country, whenever it may come, should not be made—on a broad programme of reconstruction which will include a tariff—by the National Government as such?" On the 21st September, spent on his beloved Penyghent (near Langcliffe), the diary states, "*The Times* arriving just as I left the house recorded the final crisis and the abandonment of the Gold Standard"; later (September 26th), in the notes of the Parliamentary Correspondent, *The Times* returned to the topic of a National Government which was continually occupying Geoffrey's thoughts. The paper stated, "A great impetus was given yesterday to the growing conviction that the best hope of steady reconstruction at home, and of restoration of confidence in it abroad, lies in the prompt appeal by the National Government for popular backing."

On September 28th in the columns of the Parliamentary Correspondent the following statement appeared, "Not only this country but the whole world will be safer when once a National Government is established in Great Britain with a proper mandate for a five years' programme of reconstruction." On September 30th, again the paper said that recent events had "brought the prospect of a General Election definitely nearer on the only basis on which a General Election is tolerable—that is an appeal by Mr. MacDonald, as head of a National Government, for a popular mandate to go ahead with the work of reconstruction, and to use any and every means, including a tariff, which may be found to be necessary".

There were very crowded days after the Editor's return from

Yorkshire. In the closing days of September and the first week of October Ramsay MacDonald vacillated between throwing in his hand and carrying out the suggested Election programme, and Lloyd George seemed to be hostile to a renewal of the National Government.

Meanwhile letters such as the following must have cheered Geoffrey:

Osborne Cottage,
Cowes,
25th August, 1931.

Bravo, *The Times*! As a former member of the decaying profession of journalism, I offer my respectful admiration of your conduct during the past month. I doubt if there is a better or more important chapter in all your history.

Yours truly,
THOMAS MARLOWE.[1]

From John Buchan:

Elsfield Manor,
Oxford,
30th September, 1931.

Personal
My dear Geoffrey,

I have not always seen eye to eye with you in policy questions in the past year. But I want to say that I think your recent leaders on the situation have been the very best things done in British journalism for many a day. You have performed a great public service and if things go right it will be largely owing to you.

Yours ever,
J. BUCHAN.

From Lady Oxford:

Nov. 21. I must tell you that at lunch here yesterday—Buckmaster, Vivian Phillipps, Crinks Johnstone (an excellent fellow and one of our Whips) and Sir Hamilton Grant, were all loud in your praises. This gave me much pleasure. *The Times* has come out of all this confusion magnificently. I told them this National Government was *your* idea and one that I deplored as an Election cry but I had been *quite wrong*.

On October 8th Geoffrey found Baldwin finishing a good manifesto; the following day the Editor was again closeted with Clive

[1] Editor of the *Daily Mail* for over twenty-five years and highly respected by those privileged to work under him. One of the tragedies of Fleet Street is that he did not keep a diary and left no records of his remarkable career behind him.

Wigram at Buckingham Palace; on the 16th he referred to Snowden's short and devastating letter to the handful of faithful Labour candidates; on October 23rd persistent rumours reached Printing House Square of an eleventh-hour "bombshell" from Labour on the lines of the "Banker's Ramp".

On October 26th Baldwin rang up and suggested lunch at the Travellers', "where I found him rather overwrought after a great tour in the North, but very receptive and reasonable". The diary contained these entries during the next few days:

Oct. 27. GENERAL ELECTION. . . . I returned to the office from 9 to 3 a.m. and sat revising the paper from hour to hour, news, headlines and leaders as the news kept accumulating of an amazing rally to the Government—gigantic majorities everywhere and hardly an ex-Minister left in Parliament.

Oct. 28. . . . the election returns. These grew more and more wonderful as the day went on, the counties out-topping the boroughs with majorities rising in some cases to 50 and 60 thousand. Lansbury alone remained to lead the Opposition. . . . I had an interesting meeting with the P.M., who had flown from Seaham.

Nov. 1. . . . I had a useful talk with the Prime Minister on his return from Chequers and found he was really making a Government of his own and not a mosaic, but couldn't hope to finish it tomorrow. . . .

Nov. 4. Some writing at home (interrupted by a conversation, full of strange oaths, on the telephone with Jim Thomas), and a good talk later at the Privy Council office with Stanley Baldwin, who said he'd had the most unpleasant week of his life. Cabinet-making was still going on by communication with Lossiemouth. . . .

Nov. 5. . . . to lunch with Nancy and a typically mixed party—the Bernard Shaws, Mrs. Naidu, Ronnie Tree, Lady Margaret Home and Tom Jones. Some talk with Mrs. Naidu on India afterwards, and so to the office, where I eventually got a forecast of the new Cabinet (followed at 7 by the official list), and set Coote to write about it. A dash home in the midst of this, to find Cecilia arrived, to lay plans for the recovery of Nigger (the poodle) who'd run away yesterday afternoon, and to let off fireworks with the little girls, an immense success. Rather an arduous evening, what with Nigger (about whom wrote, telephoned and advertised!) and what with the new National Cabinet.

Nov. 6. The new Cabinet had an amazingly good Press, thanks largely to a common desire to make the best of it in the world. Now that it was out I set off with a more carefree mind to a General Purposes Committee at Eton (hearing just before my departure of Nigger's arrival at the Battersea Home). . . .

On November 19th Geoffrey had an interesting talk with the Prime Minister on India and the Statute of Westminster. Now that the

National Government was firmly established he was able to plunge once again into the affairs of the Round Table Conference, "getting pretty rocky". When the House of Commons passed the Statute of Westminster by 350 to 50, Geoffrey's comment was "thanks to an admirable speech by Baldwin".

The Editor had found time to write a leader on Gandhi—"A Delegate Among Delegates" (September 12)—in which he commented that it was not altogether unfortunate that the resumption of the Indian Round Table Conference should coincide with an acute political crisis in the country as the change of Government had enhanced rather than diminished the weight of the British delegation. In the leader "The Goal and the Pace" (November 28th), *The Times* stated that in its judgment Lord Irwin was right "when he dissociates himself with the view that the ideal of Indian hopes is to be a new and inferior grade of constitutional status". In December Indian matters were again much to the fore, and Baldwin asked Geoffrey to see him at the House of Commons to discuss the speech he was to make on India. On December 3rd the Editor listened to "an elaborate and mischievous speech by Winston and a reply by Simon in the India debate". On December 18th Geoffrey had a talk with Baldwin whom he found "tired but pleased with the way things were going and thought the National Government was really beginning to function".

XXV

1932—IMPERIAL ECONOMIC CONFERENCE AT OTTAWA, AND 1933: "A SEA OF TROUBLES"

AS far as the Editor of *The Times* was concerned the year 1932 was dominated by the preparations for and consultations about the Imperial Economic Conference to be held at Ottawa during the summer. The opportunity of talks between the Empire's leaders about economic co-operation seemed to him to afford a good occasion for strengthening the bonds between the Mother-country and the Dominions, now, under the Statute of Westminster, virtually independent states but bound together by a common allegiance to the Crown.

There are constant references in 1932 to the Indian situation in Geoffrey's papers, and in January the diary records that Gandhi was once more in gaol. Ireland was also a cause of concern because having achieved Dominion status, the Irish Free State, under de Valera's leadership, refused to settle down as a contented partner within the Commonwealth, sought to abolish the oath of allegiance to the King, and withheld land annuities due to Great Britain under the Treaty.

Apart from his daily work as Editor there were two literary tasks which claimed Geoffrey's attention in the early months of the year, both of them connected with Printing House Square. The first of them was the proposed *History of "The Times"*. This project was to be undertaken by Buckle, with the help of Dermot Morrah.

The other task which Geoffrey himself undertook was that of providing the memoir on Northcliffe for the *Dictionary of National Biography*. There are various references in the diary to mornings spent in trying to compress the great amount of material available. One of the last entries about the article occurred on May 9th, "I spent the whole morning in my pyjamas over the Northcliffe memoir . . . and broke the back of the difficult part about '*The Times* and the First World War'."

Those who sought to guide the Nation, both in its relations with other parts of the Commonwealth—such as India and Southern Ireland—and with Europe and Asia certainly had their hands full in 1932, the year in which Hitler rose to power, Japan embarked on an undeclared war upon China, and over-ran Manchuria with her forces, setting up a puppet Government there; and there were troubles in Austria and Spain. There was also the prospect of Great Britain being obliged to default on her debt payments to the United States.

In these days when Downing Street might be the centre of interest one moment and Tokyo the next, it was inevitable that the new methods of transmitting news would be more and more widely used. On February 1st the Editor was up at dawn and at the office by ten o'clock for a talk with Green (G. A. L. Green, Editor of the Cape *Argus*) at Cape Town by wireless telephone, which was inaugurated that day. On February 2nd Parliament reassembled and the opening of the Disarmament Conference in Geneva (while war raged in Shanghai) took place.

There were several talks with Sir John Simon, then Secretary of State for Foreign Affairs, about Geneva and the Far East, and from him the Editor learned of the dispatch of the Twelve Power Appeal to Japan. The international situation had gravely deteriorated in the years since 1919. After the first World War, problems of co-operation with the peace-loving nations seemed much simpler: statesmen were less confident of themselves in the 'thirties, owing to the disillusioning decade after Versailles. It is not easy to get a clear-cut impression of the principles which guided the foreign policy of either Great Britain or the other democratic powers.

Geoffrey at any rate did receive one partial and temporary clarification of some of Britain's aims. After a talk with Simon at the Foreign Office on March 14th, he wrote a memorandum in which he recorded that the Foreign Secretary had expressed his gratitude to *The Times* for its continuing support, and had then set forth the main lines of the Government policy: (1) to avoid at all hazards an open breach with Japan, (2) to convince the United States that Britain was doing the right thing, (3) to maintain as far as possible the prestige of the League of Nations and (4) to do this without letting the small Nations feel that the work was being taken over entirely by the Great Powers.

It is pleasant to record a purely social occasion in this year of bewildering cross-currents. On May 4th, 1932, Geoffrey was one of the guests invited by Barrie to his Adelphi flat. It was a men's dinner of thirty with speeches by Barrie himself, the Prime Minister, Stanley Baldwin, the Archbishop of Canterbury, Lord Grey and Winston Churchill. This was how the host described his party:

LORD GREY'S BIRTHDAY PARTY AND HIS CANDLES

My dear Lord Grey—our dear Lord Grey—I once thought of writing at the foot of the invitations to this birthday party the words "no candles". My canary said, "If you do that you will spoil the whole thing." And yet I think the candles are here: this company, Lord Grey, are your birthday candles.

The canary did not think that would do either. I ought to explain that my canary, like myself, is an Angus bird; indeed we both wish this party could have been held up there in our native Kirriemuir. In London after nightfall he and I are alone in this eyrie, and I sometimes have a sudden craving for food. I cook it myself, and if it smells of bacon, he wakes up, thinking morning has arrived, and comes out of his cage and we have our meal together, and naturally we fall into talk. The last time this happened he said to me, "Who is this Grey that is having a birthday?" and I said, "The famous statesman, you know," and he said indignantly, "No, I don't know." Presently he cried out, "You don't mean *our* Grey?" "Who is your Grey?" I asked. "The birds' Grey," he said, "the man the grey squirrels are called after." He burst into song. "Give him a Birthday Party by all means," he said, "but mind this, we are all in it, all the birds as well as you."

Here is a true story. One day in Downing Street during the war some other Ministers asked Lord Grey what he would do if the Germans won and said to him, "Unless you salute our flag you shall die." But Mr. Lloyd George, who was one of the company, and who I am very sorry has an engagement that prevents his being with us today, said, "The Germans would put a stiffer one to him than that; they would say, 'Unless you salute our flag we shall shoot your squirrel.' "

My canary—I can't get away from that confounded bird, so I shall sit down and leave what I was going to say to better hands. May Lord Grey continue to help humanity, which I take to be the statesman's special and glorious and terribly anxious province. May he long, on holiday, rod in hand, frequent the pleasant waters of a northern land. May his birds continue to gather round him—but he shan't have my canary.

J. M. Barrie.

On May 4th *The Times* published a very appreciative article about the Prime Minister. *Inter alia* it said, "Mr. MacDonald has so steadily gained in strength and public estimation since he took his great decision to face the country with a National Government that, if any man could ever be called indispensable to the State, he has won the title today." The Editor's diary contained an ominous entry in May when a correspondent came in to see him about "the Jews in Germany"; how ominous even he could not have realized at the time.

At the end of May and early in June there are constant references in Geoffrey's papers to the "most confused situation developing everywhere" or "Everything very confused and active in Europe and America—Hindenburg's absurd new Chancellor in Germany, no Government in France, Congress flouting Hoover".

Lord Wenlock, Geoffrey's father-in-law, died on June 14th, and Geoffrey and his wife were able to set out on their Canadian trip ten days later.

So much has happened in the world since the summer of 1932 that we are apt to forget the importance which our statesmen attached to the Economic Conference at Ottawa. From the very start Geoffrey had taken the Conference under his wing and was convinced that the British Delegation must be impressive. He attached the greatest importance to the presence of Baldwin as leader of the Delegation, and to work in the closest of co-operation with Neville Chamberlain, J. H. Thomas and the other delegates. Geoffrey and his wife went to Canada before the official delegation, partly for a change of scene, but also in order to get in touch with the Premier, R. B. Bennett (later Lord Bennett), with a view to paving the way. *The Times* was represented at the Conference by Dawson, by Mr. John A. Stevenson, resident Correspondent in Canada, and Mr. Alan Pitt Robbins, then the Parliamentary Correspondent of *The Times*.

Mr. Alan Pitt Robbins suggests that Geoffrey was probably never happier during his Editorship than in Canada and states that he was a constant inspiration to those who worked with him. He was delighted on reaching Ottawa to find that the circulation department of *The Times* had arranged for the paper to be sold in the streets by a youth in the familiar *Times* uniform. He was a very bright boy who incidentally managed to obtain the autographs of practically every delegate to the Conference, and before he left for England Geoffrey told the boy that if ever he came to London he would try to find him employment in Printing House Square, a promise which he duly fulfilled a year or two later.

The following extracts are taken from the report of the Conference written at sea by the Editor on the homeward voyage:

> . . . I felt that it was a good thing from time to time to get away from England and to look at the paper from a distance. . . . I spent about a week at Ottawa for a start and saw a good deal of the Prime Minister, who is for all practical purposes the Government of Canada. He asked me to lunch with him a day or two after I arrived, and said he'd "bring his Cabinet along". . . . he has enormous driving-power himself, and I formed the impression that he would get things done somehow in the end. He took me for a long *tête-à-tête* drive after the luncheon-party (with the members of the Cabinet), talking all the time, and giving a

most hopeful account of his views on all the points about which some doubt had been felt in England—that he had no notion of an exclusive Empire trade policy; that "Canada First" was a temporary (he thought at the time a necessary) slogan; that he was going to have no truck with selfish local interests; that he was determined to make the Conference a success; that it should be brief and businesslike. . . .

The Editor thus summed up the problems for the members of the British Delegation:

> So far as Great Britain is concerned the problem for Ministers will be to determine how far they can go (1) in maintaining the free entry for Dominion produce, which is to be terminated at present on November 15th, (2) in increasing in certain cases the preferences already given, (3) in extending the area of preference by levying duties on imports which are at present on the free list. The answers to all three must depend, of course, on the advantages secured in return for these concessions. . . .

He continued:

> . . . personally I should predict as successful an outcome as could ever have been expected—nothing spectacular, but a series of useful arrangements, ...
>
> . . . the solidarity of the British team soon became one of the outstanding features of the Conference. They all talked about it—not at all as people who wanted to put up a façade in front of internal squabbles, but with genuine enthusiasm, and a little surprise. . . . Stanley Baldwin was playing his usual role of the tactful skipper, keeping his hands pretty free from detail. . . . Jim Thomas was an immense success . . . his impromptu speech at the Government banquet—pulling the legs of the Irishmen and saying all the things about the British Empire and the British Constitution that only the " 'umble engine-cleaner" would have the hardihood to say—roused real enthusiasm from one side of Canada to the other. . . .
>
> . . . One broad effect of the experience at Ottawa should be to make the old free trade-protection controversy more unreal than ever as a dividing-line of parties.[1]

After returning to London Geoffrey wrote to J. W. Dafoe, the Editor of the *Winnipeg Free Press*. He said, *inter alia*: ". . . No one can regard it (the outcome of the Conference) as altogether satisfactory; but I am quite impenitent in my belief that it was well worth while—if only for its influence as a process of education.

[1] The National Government had abandoned Free Trade and imposed a General Tariff, which came into effect on March 1st, 1932.

"At all events I find it difficult to understand why our Liberal Free Traders need make it a breaking-point with the National Government. Ottawa was all up their street, so to speak, so far as the British delegates were concerned. Ministers who have been talking all sorts of loose Imperialism for years came back from Canada with a little first-hand knowledge and experience. I am bound to say that I think great credit is due to Baldwin and Chamberlain and the other delegates with a protectionist label for taking the stand that they did. I could see nothing to distinguish them in the end from Runciman and Thomas and the other traditional Free Traders."

The following extract is taken from the diary for September 23rd: ". . . I had about an hour with the Prime Minister in Downing Street at noon, and thought him in good form (I hadn't seen him since June). He regarded the secession of the Samuelites[1] as settled, didn't regret Herbert Samuel as an administrator and was thinking entirely about filling the vacant places and doing a bit of re-shuffling. We went through the names with general agreement."

In a letter to Geoffrey, the Prime Minister wrote, *inter alia* (22nd November, 1932):

> I will give you another point to think about which is causing me some trouble. The national propaganda is to all intents and purposes exclusively Conservative. When I was away in the summer I made it my business to see leading men from various parts of the country and also to look at newspapers published in Scotland. That made me understand what some of my most level-headed supporters had been complaining about that we were losing hundreds of political friends because the Government was nothing but a Tory one. Now if we are to keep a National sentiment in the country we must show to National Labour that they have not been absorbed in Toryism or that they have not been led up into a *cul-de-sac*, and this can be done only by platform propaganda. Therefore I must go on to the platform. That is why I went to Portsmouth on Saturday. It was one of the most profitable things that has been done for the Government since the election. For the same reason I am going to make a political speech in my son's constituency on Friday. With kindest regards,

Geoffrey's papers for the last three months of the year cover a very wide range of subjects. On October 4th there appeared a leading article in *The Times* entitled "Exit Mr. McNeil" (the Governor-General of Ireland). That morning, Sir Clive Wigram "rang me up at dawn to say that His Majesty gave me full marks for my leader which was to

[1] The Liberals, including Lothian, who resigned from the National Government.

be preserved in the archives as a statement of sound constitutional doctrine". Early in October the Lytton Report on Manchuria appeared and had to be dealt with adequately. On October 5th he noted that John Astor "looked in in the afternoon with possible ideas of a dinner to celebrate the new type"; thus referred to in the diary, "and so to the office for the exciting night of our change of type . . . tons and tons of metal replaced, and also to celebrate the Chairman's ten years' association with *The Times*". With the issue of October 3, 1932, *The Times* appeared in an entirely new type face, specified, originated and designed exclusively in Printing House Square and entitled "The Times Roman". At the same time the ornamental Gothic lettering of *The Times*, which had been in use at the head of the paper for 140 years, was suppressed in favour of plain roman capitals. Mr. Stanley Morison, the well-known typographer, was responsible for the introduction of these changes.

In October an important "moot" was held at Lord Lothian's place, Blickling in Norfolk, where most of the members of the Round Table were present. The "moot" was chiefly devoted to Manchukuo, the future of the British Empire and Curtis's forthcoming Conference in Toronto. On the third day Europe was discussed, as well it might be, for relations between France and Germany were becoming very critical.

During the next five months, national and international problems continued to worsen until, on March 1st, 1933, Geoffrey wrote:

> Dined with the Round Table. . . . Otherwise a sea of troubles—Germany still chaotic, the American banks getting deeper and deeper into the mire, Japan and China fighting merrily, the House of Commons sparring over Economy and Taxation, and everyone rather on edge.

When he quoted Shakespeare's words "a sea of troubles", Geoffrey probably recalled the next line in *Hamlet*—"and by opposing end them?" Certainly the vast majority of the inhabitants of the free states in the British Commonwealth, and in the United States, had no inclination to take up arms in a world of troubles in 1933 "and by opposing end them". It is easy enough to look back to the chaos in the 'thirties and blame the chief actors on the world stage in that decade for lack of foresight. Perhaps one can admit that the freedom-loving peoples were to blame for lack of intelligent anticipation of coming events; it is unreasonable, however, to suggest that the average citizen in the vast spaces of North America, Australia and South Africa, so remote from Central Europe, should have been ready in the mid-'thirties to go to war to stop an aggressor—or should have foreseen the rise of Nazi Germany to supreme power.

I have found no period in Geoffrey's long career as a journalist more difficult to write about. Europe and the world were assuredly passing through a "sea of troubles". There was much indecision in high quarters. When we look back upon the period immediately after the world slump we can appreciate the circumstances which brought National Government into being—the desperate economic plight of the United Kingdom. We can gladly admit that in dealing with the difficult problem of the Indian Round Table it performed services which we recall with gratitude. But this same National Government was not necessarily the ideal body for dealing with the incredible and unending difficulties of Central Europe. Even after the resignation of the free-trade Ministers it retained a "strong coalition flavour"—essential in providing a united national approach to the question of Indian self-government—but which made for indecisions and hesitations when dealing with the dictators, with the policy of Sanctions against Italy at the time of her invasion of Abyssinia and above all with Nazi Germany.

The problem of our relations with the United States and the solution of the War Debt problem received much attention in *The Times*. In a leading article entitled "Personal Contact" (February 14th), *The Times* referred to the visit to London of Sir Ronald Lindsay, British Ambassador at Washington, who had been in almost daily contact with members of the Cabinet and the War Debt Committee. The paper pointed out that "what America passionately desires, in short, is what we all desire. It is to be shown some means of escape from the stranglehold of the world depression". It continued: "The Prime Minister has long since been indicated by public opinion on both sides of the Atlantic as the principal British delegate to proceed, sooner or later, to Washington. . . . Mr. MacDonald is not only head of the British Government but the Chairman-designate of the World Economic Conference." The leader continued, "Is there any reason why he should not at once pay a short visit to President Roosevelt—not in any sense to negotiate a definite settlement, or even to make a beginning of it, but simply to try to arrive at some mutual understanding in the true relation of the Debt to the whole great problem of world depression which confronts both peoples alike?"

The entry in the diary for February 13th is as follows: "I sat down to a leader on War Debts, as the result of Saturday's talk (a Round Table dinner at 4, St. James's Square with the Waldorf Astors), and a week-end of reflection, suggesting that Ramsay should go across at the beginning, not at the end, his long suit being atmosphere rather than finance . . .; went down to the Travellers', where I found Ronald Lindsay (H.B.M.'s Ambassador in Washington), propounded my idea, which was new to him but not unacceptable: and thence to the office, where I was kept busy till after 6, when I went down and saw the Prime Minister at the House of Commons to make sure that he wouldn't kick.[1] I found him stretched on his sofa, a wearier Titan than ever, and Jim Thomas sitting beside him, with a whisky and soda in each hand! . . . There had been an answer on War Debts in the House and Hoover had made an immense speech so I was re-writing my informal leader till the paper went to press and wished I'd never begun it." The following day there is this entry in the diary: "My War Debts plan was going well. I wrote nearly a column of political notes explaining it afresh and had a capital telegram from Willmott Lewis (*The Times* Correspondent in Washington) giving the American reaction."

Two diary entries follow:

Feb. 28. . . . There had been a National (Conservative) Union and a heated debate on India, in which Winston's attack was narrowly repelled . . . spent a good deal of time over Germany, . . . and was visited on Philip's (Lothian's) introduction, by one Harrington Brown who had come straight from Berlin with tales of impending massacres.

Mar. 5. . . . A desperate afternoon and evening in the office—Roosevelt's (very stirring) Inaugural coincided with the climax of the banking crisis in America. The conjunction seemed to justify a second experiment with the double headline. Election Day in Germany (mercifully peaceful so far and decisive).

Hardly a day passed without reference to the European cauldron, and the diary twice records talks with me about the All Peoples' Association which was then making an attempt—it survived for seven years—to bring about a better understanding between the peoples of Europe, a project to which Geoffrey gave consistent support in *The Times*.

Shortly after the return of the Dawsons from a holiday in Spain and Morocco—the first since their honeymoon—the following entry appears in the diary:

May 7. Hever. A talk with John (Astor) after breakfast about his idea of the future of the paper (this rather brought to a head by letter from All Souls asking me to contemplate the Wardenship on the sudden death of Lord Chelmsford). He was obviously unwilling that I should go, even if I were willing myself; and suggested another 5 years

[1] Ramsay MacDonald did in fact visit President Roosevelt in April.

anyhow—so I wrote to Adams in the afternoon rejecting his flattering suggestion.

Geoffrey's letter referred to the future of *The Times*, and included the following passage: "It is quite clear that I cannot leave it at the present moment. I am under no illusion at all about the capacity of other people to make a better job of it; but there are all sorts of complications and problems to be settled and places to be filled before I could willingly hand it over, and I am satisfied that my resignation just now would be regretted by those with whom I work and to whom I owe so much."

Indian problems were very much to the fore in May and June. In the leading article, "The Conservative Choice" (June 8th), reference was made to the report of *The Times* Bombay Correspondent "that deep interest has been aroused in India by the prospect of an open struggle within the Conservative Party in this country for the direction of its Indian policy". This referred to the forthcoming meeting of the Central Council of the Conservatives on June 28th, when the decision would be taken "whether to follow Mr. Stanley Baldwin and the other Conservative leaders in the National Government, or to throw them over in favour of Mr. Churchill's leadership in Indian affairs". The article ended: "But to the broad question before the country—whether to go forward with determination and courage or to refuse altogether to face the difficulties of a stupendous Imperial problem—to this in the end there can be one answer only. No one is better able to give it than Mr. Baldwin, who perhaps is something more than a Party leader but who has an unerring instinct for the true tradition of Conservatism." The meeting was held at the Friends' House in Euston Road and in the end Lord Lloyd's resolution was taken to a ballot and defeated "by a comfortable margin of considerably more than two to one"—a great triumph for the policy of the paper. *The Times* in its comments (June 29th) said:

> Most significant of all, the whole available body of leaders of the great British Chambers of Commerce in India—the very people for whom Mr. Churchill and his friends profess their deepest concern—are telling us plainly that their Chambers of Commerce, whose interests are vitally concerned in the future of the country, "have after deliberate consideration decided to give support (subject to the amendments which they will put forward in evidence before the Joint Select Committee) to the proposals of His Majesty's Government, which in their opinion are those best calculated to achieve the common purpose of all shades of opinion in this country—namely, that India should remain a contented partner in the British Commonwealth of Nations".

Entries in the diary during the month of June deal with such varied topics as the lunch given by *The Times* to the Mount Everest flyers on the 8th June; and the ceremonial opening of the World Economic Conference by the King in the Geological Museum at South Kensington on the 12th June, followed by the Government banquet at Grosvenor House. Alas, within three weeks the Conference, which had aroused high hopes at the outset, was *in extremis*. Among the entries in the diary are the following:

June 13. . . . A desperate afternoon. I heard in the middle of it that the War Debt instalment due on Thursday had been settled by consent.

June 14. Debt agreement at last. . . . I had a talk to Dr. Dollfuss, the "Pocket Chancellor" of Austria, at his Legation and subsequently to Ambassador Bingham (U.S.A.), in his sick bed at Princes Gate. Dollfuss is very impressive—a determined little man with flashing eyes and a sense of humour; Bingham, a typical well-do-do American, almost lyrical about his President and Cordell Hull.

During June the following correspondence took place between Geoffrey and Lord Derby:

Coworth Park,
Sunningdale,
Berks,
4th June, 1933.

My dear Dawson,

I was writing—indeed had written—a letter to the Editor of *The Times* thanking him for the very interesting and instructive article about the Titan, when I was told it was you yourself who had written it. I write—as is much more pleasant—to an old friend instead of to an impersonal editor, to thank the writer. It really was charming. . . .

He is a great little horse—only 15–1 and speaking for him, I thank you for what you said—but even more do I thank you for the more than kind personal reference you made to me.

Ever yours sincerely,
DERBY.

Geoffrey replied, June 6th, 1933:

I am so very glad that you liked the leader about the little Titan. Nothing ever pleased me so much as this year's Derby—your winning it, Hyperion's height, and all the rest of it.[1] I only wish I had been there to see.

[1] Lord Derby won the classic race easily with his fifteen-hands Hyperion amid scenes of great enthusiasm.

And Hyperion interests me for another reason, which may be new to you. When I was first elected to All Souls many years ago, there was an old Fellow there, John Doyle by name, of a type which is not likely to be seen again. He was a bachelor, with a profound and miscellaneous knowledge of sport, and a learned but somewhat dull historian. He had a house in Wales, where he hunted a pack of harriers on foot. He bred fox-terriers. He also bred about one thoroughbred foal per annum and sold it at Doncaster, where he always took a lodging for the week. I was once there with him, and very interesting it was. Otherwise he used All Souls as his headquarters for racing during the summer, emerging from the Lodge in his old top hat to Epsom, Ascot, Newmarket and Goodwood. He never recognized the modern suburban course as being worth his attention.

It was the dream of his life to breed the winner of a classic race; but he never succeeded in doing this during his lifetime. When he died, however, (during the years when I was in South Africa) he had bred Rosedrop, who subsequently won the Oaks; and Rosedrop, as you know, was the dam of Gainsborough and therefore Hyperion's grandmama.

I will try to get you a copy of a little volume (long since out of print) and John Doyle's *Essays on Various Subjects*, which were published after his death. They deal among other things with the breeding of racehorses. I cannot help hoping that he saw the four flashing white feet from his grandstand in the Elysian Fields.

In October there are several references to talks with Baldwin on the tense situation in Europe. Indeed hardly a day passes without some reference to Nazi Germany which in the middle of the month announced her intention of leaving the League of Nations. Geoffrey was at Cliveden on October 14th "where we plunged into a gigantic party and the news that Hitler had suddenly run out of the Conference and the League. No one talked of anything else and the wireless was invoked to hear Hitler himself at 6.00". At Cliveden the following day the Prime Minister was brought over for "a somewhat woolly talk" with his hosts and a small party, including Geoffrey, about the German situation. On October 16th the "Crisis" monopolized attention in the world. On October 17th, Simon returned from Geneva and broadcast "not too convincingly"; a week later one of the most significant by-elections ever held in London took place in East Fulham where a "Conservative candidate converted a majority of 14,000 into a minority of nearly 5,000". When so strong a Tory stronghold could be lost in "a wild flood of pacifism", no Conservative seat seemed safe. During these anxious days the Editor had talks with Mr. Eden, the Prime Minister and others about the ever-changing European situation and a scare about German propaganda in France.

A leading article appeared in *The Times*, "What Is the British

Policy?" (November 17th), which complained that the British proposals on disarmament had never been presented to the world: "the world knows even less of what in the British view would represent a fair and reasonable offer to Germany today. . . . Whether Germany is soaring on a wave of moral regeneration, or sinking (as others allege) into a trough of barbarism; whether Herr Hitler means peace, as his speeches reiterate with apparent sincerity, or whether they are merely the cloak behind which his people are cultivating the will to future war—on any of these theories the case for plain dealing with Germany remains exactly the same."

The entry for November 27th was: "An afternoon in the office ending in a long talk with the Prime Minister in the House of Commons. He was worried about the position of his National Government and spoke more freely and definitely than usual. Baldwin made an admirable speech later in the evening." Geoffrey was evidently amused when he wrote on November 29th: "Dined at Grillion's. . . . Clive Wigram reported a glorious story reaching him from several quarters and said to emanate from George Lloyd that *I* was advising H.M. on foreign affairs and India!"

XXVI

1934—YEAR OF ASSASSINATIONS AND MANY AFFLICTIONS

Le despotisme tempéré par l'assassinat, c'est notre Magna Charta—(Words of a Russian noble to Count Münster on the assassination of Paul I, Emperor of Russia—1800)—could apply to Europe in 1934.

MR. STEPHEN GRAHAM has called 1934 "The Year of Assassinations", which it certainly was, but it was something more; it was a year of many afflictions in Europe and the greatest of these, had we but realized the fact at the time, resulted from the death of President von Hindenburg, at the age of eighty-six. Within an hour of his passing, Adolf Hitler was decreed supreme ruler of Germany, with the titles of Führer and Chancellor.

The most significant entry of the year in Geoffrey's diary occurred on June 1st, but he was naturally quite unaware of the importance of the prophecy made to him by Lord Trenchard, Marshal of the Royal Air Force, "who was very interesting and voluble about the Police, his new college (opened yesterday), his idea of retirement, his anxiety for the new section houses: and then Imperial Defence, co-ordination, Chiefs of Staff, etc.: (He believes now for the first time in a war within five years and ascribes it to the new spirit in Germany) and so to the office and got as much as possible done before the arrival of Roosevelt's Debt Message. . . ." Had Geoffrey been endowed with the rare gift of second sight and realized what an amazing prophecy he had just listened to and promptly acted upon it, British preparedness for the Second World War in 1939 would have undoubtedly been more advanced than it was five years later. But he was not a superman and possessed no such powers and therefore he no doubt listened with respect to the views of Lord Trenchard and returned to his editorial chair to deal with the immediate problems of the day.

The year witnessed many political assassinations, most of them in Germany. On June 30th Hitler got wind of a conspiracy and while the Storm Troopers were immobilized (on holiday), he decided to liquidate his former associate Ernst Röhm and others, whom he no longer trusted. A large number of prominent men were murdered (the official figure was given as seventy-seven). Hitler himself, escorted by Goebbels, had driven through the night to Röhm's villa in Bavaria, where its owner was shot at sunrise. Twenty-five days later Dr. Dollfuss, the "Pocket Chancellor" of Austria, with whom Geoffrey had talked at the Austrian Legation in London the previous year, was murdered (three months after he had assumed dictatorial powers). His assassins were captured and executed and died proclaiming "Heil Hitler!" On October 9th King Alexander of Jugoslavia, on a visit to France, was assassinated in company with Monsieur Louis Barthou (Foreign Minister) in Marseilles. On December 1st Kirof was assassinated in Leningrad and the Russian Terror took an anti-Semitic turn.

In the United Kingdom millions thanked their stars that the English Channel divided them from Continental Europe. As *The Times*, in its annual "Review of the Year", said, "It was a year of many discomforts and afflictions; but as they surveyed the plight of others the inhabitants of Great Britain might congratulate themselves that for all its faults theirs was still the best country to live in."

In Geoffrey's life it was a year in which more than ever he realized the supreme importance of the mission of the Commonwealth, in which citizens of every race, class, colour or creed could live in security under the *Pax Britannica*. He rejoiced during the late autumn, when he and all those who had been working for the revision of the Indian Constitution witnessed success crown their efforts with the passing, by the House of Commons, of the motion which held that the Report (India White Paper) provided the basis for the proposed Bill. There is no doubt that without the whole-hearted backing of *The Times* the White Paper would never have been accepted by the majority of the Conservative Party.

When reading contemporary documents for the year 1934, it is impossible not to contrast the difference in atmosphere between the decade preceding the First World War and the years preceding the Second World War. As we read through the records of the between-the-war years, however, there is a general *malaise*; most people were deeply concerned by the trends in Central Europe, as well they might be; but they seemed powerless to arrest them and indulged in wishful thinking about "collective security" and the possibility of preserving peace by the signing of treaties such as the Kellogg Pact. After the delirium of Armistice Day (11th November, 1918) and the ending of the war came the period of great disillusionment in the 'twenties. Where were the fruits of victory which politicians had promised, the homes for heroes, "making Germany pay" and President Wilson's idealism? The first real blow came when America turned her back on Europe.

How, after the great victory, had it happened that the United Kingdom, whose sacrifices for the common cause had only been exceeded by France among the Allies, emerged from the struggle much poorer; the vast loans she had made to her associates unpaid, and she herself heavily in debt to the United States and no longer in the proud position she had occupied as the leading world power in the reign of Victoria? The American people, after their "crusade" across the ocean, were more than ever isolationist in sentiment, and washed their hands of the affairs of Europe. The old world must look after itself. The refusal of the two English-speaking Commonwealths to guarantee France from aggression was one of the main factors responsible for the worsening conditions in Europe in the 'twenties and leading up to German rearmament and the rise of Hitler. The fervent hopes of the British electorate during the 'thirties were therefore inspired by the determination that "never again" should Europe be permitted to become involved in world war on the scale of the 1914–18 struggle. International co-operation; above all the attempt to bring France and Germany together; a just settlement—which in the eyes of the majority Versailles was not—that would seek to reconcile the "have-nots", was the dream that was kept constantly before the British people by statesmen and students of international affairs on the platform, in the Press and "on the air".

In the early months of the year, up to the death of Aunt Kitty on May 2nd, Geoffrey and his wife escaped to Langcliffe whenever possible to be near her. On January 15th, Geoffrey had to return to London, leaving Cecilia to look after Aunt Kitty for a further week. There were several other visits to Langcliffe, and by mid-March his Aunt was definitely feebler and he had to take over the task of writing letters and cheques for her. The diary of April 1st at Langcliffe is as follows, "Cecilia and I went to church at 8—a congregation of sixty (which, compared with the complaints in some old family diaries I have been arranging, doesn't bear out the popular belief in the recent decline in church-going)." During the days of waiting there were walks on the hillside near Langcliffe "melodious with grouse and golden plover, curlews and sandpipers—very lovely". His Aunt died on May 2nd and the entry in the diary on May 6th is as follows: "Up rather late after a sleepless night. We all went to the village church in the morning—matins followed by communion—the Vicar making reference in his sermon to Aunt K.'s life in the village—her sixty-four years of teaching in the Sunday School and her visits to those in sickness and trouble."

In January the diary records that the draft of *The History of "The*

Times" kept Geoffrey busy. In April he was discussing with Barrington-Ward office problems, among them the "History"—"now envisaged as a trilogy—Barnes, Delane, Parnell, etc.". Early in October, on a visit to All Souls, there is the following entry, "buried myself in Dougie's little sitting-room with the *History of 'The Times'*. I got through most of Morison's notes, made a list of points in the introduction (mostly wished on to me by others) and accomplished a good deal before dinner in Hall." The following day, "Then a long day with *The Times History* . . . for which by this time I had begun to sketch out an introduction." And on October 8th, "However the back of the accursed introduction was broken and I got the bulk of it typewritten before the night was out".

A leader in *The Times*, entitled "Half-way House" (March 7), surveyed the work of the National Government and explained how it had accomplished its first great task—that of recovery and "the business, that is, of extricating the nation from the appalling chaos with which it was threatened by a combination of world-wide depression and incompetent handling". The paper continued: "The second task is reconstruction—in other words, the business of ordering our social and economic life, our Imperial and international relations, to meet vastly different conditions which the post-war years have imposed . . . The record of the National Government in this sphere has been beyond all criticism. It has almost been too successful, for it has tended to obliterate the continued existence of a real emergency. Mr. MacDonald's courage in his original decision, the loyal self-sacrifice of Mr. Baldwin and his colleagues, the determination of all of them to sink old differences and work together for their country—these qualities have been justified over and over again."

In a leading article on Empire Day entitled "Youth and Empire", a sentence from Lord Milner's writings long ago was given and is of interest as showing the Editor's views on the Empire: "The British Empire, keeping the peace within its own borders, bound in its own interest, by the very nature of its constitution, to 'seek peace and ensue it' everywhere, is the most powerful bulwark in the world today against the spread of international discord. The maintenance of the strength, the preservation of a unity of the Empire is not the only contribution, but is by far the greatest and most practical contribution, which British statesmanship can make to the welfare of mankind." Then the writer pointed out how the Imperialism of both Lord Milner and Lord Meath was closely bound up with social reform. "The heart of the Empire must be sound if the Empire was to influence the world." The article continued: "In the world as it is today—to a greater extent even than in the days when Lord Meath and Lord Milner surveyed it—there are overwhelming difficulties in achieving anything like universal peace and freedom. For the moment an era of suspicious nationalism seems to make the ideal more remote than ever. But unquestionably the way to attain it lies through the gradual grouping of such nations as are prepared to work and trade together and to live at peace for all time with one another; and the one group ready formed for this great purpose—bound by all the ties of history, tradition, and complementary requirements—is the existing group of British Nations and Dependencies." The article finally dealt with the wide range of work ahead which included maintaining the link with the sister nations of the Dominions: in solving the native problem of Africa; "most of all perhaps in guiding and helping India through a colossal experiment in self-government".

During the year the Editor constantly saw the Prime Minister and Mr. Baldwin, his right-hand man.

If Geoffrey tried to concentrate on Indian problems during the year, there was hardly a day without disturbing news from Europe. A typical entry in the diary is that of January 27th: ". . . visiting the Foreign Office for a talk with Simon and Anthony Eden—I got out of it a copy of their statement of policy on Disarmament and some useful hints about the snags which they foresaw. Hitler was to celebrate his anniversary on Saturday: Mussolini was bursting with a statement of his own: the French Government was tottering (over Stavisky) and actually fell in the afternoon". Three days later Hitler delivered a portentous anniversary oration. February brought news "of a riot and bloodshed in Paris". On February 9th Doumergue formed his Government in Paris, including six former Prime Ministers, but there was more rioting later. On February 12th a day's General Strike took place in Paris, but this news "was quite outshadowed by civil strife in Austria, where the Government sat heavily on the Socialists". On February 20th Dr. von Müller of the *Neue Freie Presse* just back from Vienna, "and terribly concerned with events there", came in for a talk with the Editor.

In April Geoffrey went to the House of Commons to hear Neville Chamberlain "expound, without any frills or pleasantries, a most satisfactory Budget to an absolutely packed House—unemployment benefit to be restored in full; salary cuts to be restored by half; 6*d.* off Income Tax, 5*s.* off the £1 h.p. (motor licence)".

Two intimate friends connected with the *Round Table* quarterly died in the summer—John Dove, its Editor, and a friend of South African days, and F. S. Oliver, Geoffrey's constant associate in the campaign in the First World War to make more efficient the supreme direction of the British effort.

A very happy occasion was the conferring on Geoffrey by Oxford University the honorary degree of D.C.L. At the *Encaenia* (20th June) he and Cecilia met many old friends and the sun shone.

In introducing Geoffrey the Orator asked:

Quis est nostrum quin, quotiens "aurora novo conspersit lumine terras", Tempora instantia exspectet? By reading *The Times quid bono civi sentiendum sit ab ipso Jovis Tonantis ore ediscimus. Sed post siparium sedet vir hic egregius, qui omnia dirigit, qui res gestas aequo judicio examinat, qui populum ad meliora latens ipse hortatur.* As Demy of Magdalen, Fellow of All Souls and Rhodes Trustee Mr. Dawson is well known in Oxford. The Orator presented him as *virum ἀνωνύμῳ quadam auctoritate potentissimum, eximia sollertia et integritate diu spectatum.*

The Chancellor saluted Geoffrey with the words: *Vir literatissime cujus sub dicione Tempora non mutantur sed qualia ab incepto processerunt sibi constant.*

Who of us, when "dawn sprinkles the lands with new light", does not await the current issue of *The Times*? By reading the *Times* we learn from the very mouth of Jupiter the Thunderer what the views of a good citizen ought to be. But behind the curtain sits this outstanding man who controls everything, who weighs achievements with impartial judgment, and who, himself remaining hidden from view, encourages the people to better things.

The Orator presented him as a man most powerful by an anonymous authority (influence), long renowned for his excellent shrewdness (intelligence) and uprightness (integrity).

The Chancellor saluted Geoffrey with the words: O man of great learning, under whose sway *The Times* do(es) not change but remain(s) like itself as it has continued from the beginning.

Geoffrey received a kind letter of congratulation from John Walter (June 29th), and the following which must have been one of the last letters (May 25th) he ever received from Buckle, who died the following year:

I am delighted to see you are to have an honorary degree at the *Encaenia*. No one has a better right to this distinction, and it must be specially gratifying to you to receive it while still Editor. Your work at Printing House Square has been magnificent; first in keeping the old high traditions alive amid the difficulties of Northcliffe's generation; now for a dozen years in effecting the complete rehabilitation, so that the primacy of the paper is universally admitted and its financial position assured—a result due mainly to two men, the Editor and Chief Proprietor. . . . Let me repeat my warm congratulations. I expect you feel, as I did, that an honorary degree from his own University, especially when it is such a renowned and glorious University as Oxford, is about the highest and most satisfactory recognition of his work to which an editor of *The Times* can aspire.

Yours in sincere affection and admiration,

GEORGE E. BUCKLE.

The diary of July 1st records the receipt of the news of Hitler's new coup when Röhm and others were assassinated, and many arrests were made. On returning to London the Editor entrusted to —— the task of writing a leading article on the barbarous doings in Germany entitled "Medieval Methods". Reference was made to the fact that President Hindenburg had thanked the Chancellor. The writer of the article went on to say, "For this country at all events there is a very plain lesson—to remain faithful to our old method of Government by persuasion, to shun all short-cuts and violent remedies, and to recognize the dangers inherent in all quasi-military organizations for the pursuit of political ends." The article had begun by referring to the official announcement from Berlin proclaiming that "law and order prevail throughout the Reich. The whole nation stands in unprecedented enthusiasm behind the leader". Then it referred to the ruling triumvirate—Hitler, Goering and Goebbels. "What motives," the paper wondered, "prompted them to make their sudden onslaught upon their former associates", and it referred to the act as similar to that carried out by the O.G.P.U. police and observed that one dictatorship resembled another. *The Times* boldly stated, "Germany has ceased for the time being to be a modern European country." The following is the diary extract for July 4th: ". . . Berlin rather upset by my leader of yesterday, on which I had a perfect spate of congratulatory letters, and Ebbutt had plainly been 'told off' by the Hitlerites".

The diary of July 19th refers to Baldwin's statement of the Government's Air policy which was dealt with in the leading article "Air Defence" (July 20th), and referred to the increase of the R.A.F. by forty-one new squadrons during the following five years (by 1939). Thirty-three squadrons were to be allotted to Home Defence, bringing the total of squadrons used for this purpose to seventy-five. Geoffrey was evidently keeping in close touch with Baldwin, for he discussed defence problems with the latter the day before he made his air statement in the House of Commons which shows that he was fully alive to the extreme importance of speeding the air programme. As *The Times* explained, the reason for this step was that negotiations for international disarmament during eight and a half years had produced no results. In the article the hope was expressed that there would be improvement in the machinery of co-operation, not only between all arms of the British Services, but also between the British and Dominion

Air Forces. The diary for July 25th dealt with the worsening situation in Austria: "All communications closed about 6 p.m. and we lived on the wireless. It became clear in the end that a Nazi rising had been scotched, but that little Dollfuss had been killed. No time for more than a paragraph leader but we got in most of the news with the aid of the *Neue Freie Presse.*" A final entry for the month of July was, "The House of Commons was holding its last sitting and the murderers of Dollfuss were condemned and executed."

In the late afternoon of October 9th came the news of the shooting of King Alexander of Jugoslavia at Marseilles and of his death and that of the French Foreign Secretary Monsieur Barthou. The diary for the following day says, "Everything overshadowed by the Marseilles murders . . . passed the Ritz just as Queen Marie was emerging with the little King (Peter of Jugoslavia) *en route* for Paris."

Geoffrey's papers show how much his mind was dominated by the Indian problem during the last months of 1934. Earlier in the year the Joint Select Committee, under the Chairmanship of Lord Linlithgow, prepared its Report, which was supported by twenty-two of the thirty-one members. It recommended that there was to be no departure from three broad principles of the Government plan, provincial autonomy, all-India federation, and responsibility with safeguards. As late as October 4th, when the Conservative and Unionist Associations met at Bristol, as many as forty-nine per cent of the delegates voting were hostile or doubtful regarding the White Paper scheme, but with the issue of the Report on November 22nd this situation was changed and ten days later, at the Queen's Hall, Baldwin undertook to confer with the Conservative Party and the Central Council approved the general proposals of the Report by a seventy-four per cent majority. After a three-days' debate in the House of Commons, finally on December 12th, by 410 votes to 127, the House held that the Report provided a basis for revision of the Indian Constitution and authorized the Government to frame a Bill accordingly. Geoffrey was very keen that the Report should have the widest possible circulation and advocated that it should be issued at the price of one shilling. *The Times* eulogized it in a leading article.

Finally in the leading article, "Their Lordships Concur" (December 19, 1934), the paper concluded with these words: "But the outstanding feature of the divisions in both Houses is that 239 Peers and 410 Members of the House of Commons (exactly two-thirds of its whole strength) voted affirmatively and without reservation for the Government's policy. Two exhaustive debates, following seven years of hard investigation, having invested it at least with an unimpeachable mandate from the Imperial Parliament." Certainly no one during those seven years had worked harder than Geoffrey.

XXVII

1935—SILVER JUBILEE REJOICING —GERMANY REARMS—ITALY INVADES ABYSSINIA

MOST of us are escapists in ordinary life. Certainly during the latter part of the reign of Queen Victoria the British people dwelt on the pleasant things around them. Within the last fourteen years of the Queen's life her peoples, around the world, threw themselves with enthusiasm into the festivities and rejoicings of the Jubilee in 1887, and the Diamond Jubilee ten years later.

Her reign had witnessed unparalleled prosperity and development in the British Empire. The greatest Empire in the world relied on the unchallenged might of the British Navy for its defence. Why should not the Queen's realms continue to expand and prosper? In the latter part of her rule, however, there were clouds on the horizon. The expansion of Imperial Russia in Central Asia had gradually approached unpleasantly close to the frontier of Afghanistan (then regarded as a British "Sphere" of interest) and Kashmir. In South Africa there was the conflict between Boer and Briton. There was a remarkable increase in German prosperity and power in the three decades after the Franco-Prussian War. Fortunately Queen Victoria's grandson was on the throne of the Hohenzollerns and presumably she understood how to keep him in his place. Nevertheless, at the time of the Jameson Raid there were unpleasant indications that the young Emperor might prove difficult. In the year 1900, the last full year of the Queen's life, I was living in Germany and often had an unpleasant realization that the Germans were working harder than the people at home. Also that they were responding with enthusiasm to the extremely efficient propaganda of the German Navy League—which had a membership of over a million. In letters to my parents I tried to explain the reason why the Germans felt that their future lay on the water—but the activities of the *Flotten Verein* left uncomfortable feelings in my mind. When travelling in Russia, Austria and Germany in the years 1898–1900 I thanked God for the British Navy, and rejoiced in the happy conviction that Britain would never again be drawn into a struggle in Continental Europe, where the German army seemed supreme! Of course the British way of life was quite safe—this I took for granted. But I did sometimes wonder why all these great European nations were armed to the teeth, and what would happen if a clash came.

Four decades later when the peoples of the British Empire and Commonwealth threw themselves with enthusiasm into the celebrations of the Silver Jubilee they had good cause to rejoice. Their devotion to the King and Queen had grown with the passing of the years. In 1928 during the anxious months of the illness of King George V they realized how deep was their affection for the Monarch and his Queen. The King's annual broadcasts had further endeared him to the masses. When the British people eagerly took part in the celebrations of the Silver Jubilee, they could not help comparing their free institutions and privileges with the lot of the enslaved masses in Europe. Since King George came to the throne the Empire had withstood grave trials and dangers and seemed to be emerging successfully into better times. When Baldwin, on becoming Prime Minister for the third time, declared that our foreign policy was based upon our membership of the League, the overwhelming majority of the nation endorsed his view. What was more natural in this year of national rejoicing than that John Bull, like the Pharisee, should rejoice in the thought that he was not as other men? To be an escapist in 1935 was perfectly natural. The things that were happening in Europe and Ethiopia were bewildering. Let the British people concentrate on bringing back prosperity to their own country; develop the Empire to the utmost and help forward all who were seeking to promote understanding between the peoples of Europe. These were no ignoble aims and were enthusiastically endorsed by millions of British voters. They did, however, ignore one important fact: how was an inadequately armed British Empire and Commonwealth to refuse to be drawn into another world war if Continental nations resorted to aggression? When Mussolini decided to seize Abyssinia, and Hitler prepared to annex Austria and Czechoslovakia, despite solemn undertakings, what could the peace-loving Democracy of the United Kingdom, without adequate armaments, do to stop aggression? To that question we now know there was no solution, short of war; but in the 'thirties most of us felt there must be some peaceful way out.

In the immediate five or six years before the Second World War there is no doubt whatever that the policy of seeking to bring about conciliation in Europe, and better relations between France and

Germany, as advocated by *The Times* under Geoffrey, was in fact approved by the great majority of the British people.

At home, the year 1935 is remembered as the year of the Silver Jubilee which culminated in the great service in St. Paul's on May 6th; of the final passing of the India Act—the product of more than seven years of intensive enquiry and discussion—which received the royal assent on August 2nd; of the retirement of Ramsay MacDonald from the premiership in June, and the succession of Stanley Baldwin, who entered upon his third term as Prime Minister and decided in October to seek a fresh mandate for his policy of vigorous support of the League of Nations. The "Collective Security Election" in November resulted in an astounding victory for Baldwin.

Abroad, the year is chiefly remembered by Hitler's reviving Conscription in March, which resulted in the League Council condemning German rearmament; the increasing wave of anti-Semitism throughout the *Reich*; by the announcement that the German Air Force was equal to the R.A.F. in numbers; and by the aggression of Italy in Abyssinia, which began in January with the decision of the Fascist Grand Council to take military measures and culminated in the actual invasion of Ethiopia on October 3rd.

Geoffrey's diary for the year 1935 opens as follows:

> *Jan. 1.* The 150th birthday of *The Times*—The Anniversary Number and the publication of Volume I of *The History* brought a flood of telegrams, letters and (literally) bouquets all day. I was at the office coping with them morning, afternoon and night. . . .
>
> *Jan. 2.* . . . The telephone (56 Settle!) was installed at Langcliffe yesterday.[1]

Geoffrey had wanted to re-visit South Africa in the autumn of 1934, and had hoped to attend the meeting of the Empire Press Union in Cape Town in February, 1935, but owing to the very disturbed conditions in Europe he abandoned the idea. His visit, therefore, to Waterloo Station on January 18th to see off the "press gang" (i.e. the delegation going to the Empire Press Union meeting) must have filled him with envy. Probably there was no one present at the Radio-Telephone lunch who took a deeper interest in the proceedings: "Feb. 7th. . . . I to a Radio-Telephonic lunch organized by Evelyn Wrench of the Overseas League at which he and Kingsley Wood and Jim Thomas addressed us from our end and Hertzog, John Astor and Patrick Duncan from the Cape—a wonderful show."

[1] It seems incredible that the Editor of *The Times*, for all his first Editorship and the first twelve years of his second Editorship, should have been without a telephone in his country house. Cf. p. 22, *supra*.

Early in the year Geoffrey saw the Prime Minister and learned from him that he would soon have to give up the Premiership for health reasons. MacDonald preferred to carry on till after the Silver Jubilee when he would make way for Baldwin. On March 6th Geoffrey had a talk with the Prime Minister, at his invitation, whom he found "prostrate on his sofa at No. 10—a red dressing-gown and a khaki rug—lunch on a tray—general dejection—heavy cold on the chest".

The entry in the diary for March 12th is:

> ... Poor old Buckle was clearly dying and I spent some time revising his memoir. He died in fact just after I had left the office at about 12.30. A talk with Stanley Baldwin ... he thought the Prime Minister would last on over the Jubilee, and that he might then have to take over—very reluctantly. We discussed various possible Cabinet changes.

Throughout 1935 there are naturally constant references to Nazi Germany. On March 1st the *Reich* took over the Saar, in accordance with the result of the Plebiscite held there in January, which reached an overwhelming majority of votes for the return of the Territory to Germany. The diary for March 17th is headed "Conscription in Germany" and is as follows: "Cecilia and the little girls went off for the day with George Holdsworth among the lambs at Glynde and I remained to toil at the German 'bombshell' recorded last night—Hitler's decision to introduce conscription for an army of 36 Divisions. ... Went down after lunch for a talk with S.B. and the P.M. ... I urged them to go on with the Berlin Mission and if possible to strengthen it; but they saw great difficulties in this suggestion. Soon after 5 I had a long talk to Berlin over the telephone and found Ebbutt extremely calm. ... I went back to draft headlines ('gravity but not panic') and to revise the leaders." On March 19th Geoffrey wrote:

> I plunged into a difficult day at the office, protracted till long after midnight by conflicting news from the Continent. French and Italians both feverishly anxious to get us into an anti-German Conference, and the latest telegrams suggested that Simon had agreed. If so he had taken quite a different view yesterday.

Geoffrey, in the midst of the Silver Jubilee distractions, managed to write a memorandum on his talk with "Baldwin on Reconstruction" (of the Cabinet). It was dated May 6, 1935, and included the following paragraphs:

> I found S.B. alone in Downing Street on the pre-Jubilee Saturday afternoon and quite glad to unburden himself about his troubles. ... He

opened up at once on the subject of 4 problems in connection with the impending and long-expected reconstruction of the Government.

1. SHOULD WINSTON BE INCLUDED?

To this, contrary to some statements that had been made, he felt no personal objection, but Winston would be a disruptive force especially since foreign relations and defence would be uppermost. Moreover there was great feeling in the party about some of his recent activities against the Government's Indian policy. I suggested that the continuance of the Indian problem, even when the Bill was through, was sufficient argument for keeping him out for the present.
(On June 17, 1923, in a two-hour talk with Baldwin, at Chequers, Geoffrey had suggested the appointment of Mr. Churchill as Viceroy, *vide supra*, p. 219).

2. SHOULD L.G. BE INCLUDED?

On this problem also S.B. has a perfectly open mind. He doubts L.G.'s effective support though he admits his nuisance value in opposition. He thinks that L.G. and Winston *together* would be impossible.

3. Dealt with the problem whether an effort should be made to attract the Samuelite Liberals. Geoffrey suggested the value of using such men as Foot. Baldwin was "less convinced about Philip (Lothian), whom he likes but whose judgment he distrusts".

4. IS THERE ANYTHING TO BE DONE WITH REASONABLE LABOUR?

I thought it hopeless; but S.B. said (and I agreed) that some Labour leaders were no longer anxious to win the next election and that in these circumstances might conceivably be ready to come across.

He thought that under our democratic conditions the next administration must be prepared to spend money, though not to the extent that L.G. wanted. Monty Norman had been over to see him at Trent and was prepared to look into the prospects of a big loan, which, said S.B., should cover not only roads, settlement, etc., but defence, particularly aircraft, destroyers, and small cruisers, if no limitation in this direction proved possible and other nations went on building. He thought that such expenditure would be highly popular, that it would provide a great deal of employment next winter, and that it would serve the essential purpose of keeping our skilled artificers in being.

Incidentally he told me that Ramsay would like to stay on, though not as P.M. and that he was determined to fight Seaham again, a very courageous ambition. In this connexion we discussed some of the misfits in the present Government.

There were few journalists with whom Geoffrey would sooner discuss world affairs than Mr. Arthur Mann, the distinguished Editor of the *Yorkshire Post*. Frequently on the journey from Hellifield (the station where the fast trains stopped, near Langcliffe) Geoffrey and Mr. Mann exchanged views at Leeds—sometimes the conversations were heated because their views differed on the best way to deal with Germany. In the diary of April 10th there is this entry: "To Leeds, where Arthur Mann met me and took me to his office for a half-hour talk about European affairs. I don't think I shook his violent anti-Germanism much. . . ."

The following letter from Lord Snowden (May 1st, 1935) was received by Geoffrey:

> I feel that I must write to tell you what pleasure and satisfaction your recent leaders on the international situation have given to me. They have been magnificent in courage, impartiality, broad-mindedness and leadership. It is a great thing that one journal of outstanding international importance and influence should at a time like this speak the plain truth to our statesmen, and remind them of the mistakes of the past, and of the urgent need for a changed attitude of mind for a less provocative habit of speech and writing.
>
> I do share so strongly the view you put forward in your leader in today's issue that there is now a great opportunity for Britain to play a decisive part in a policy of detachment and independence. . . . Your recent articles are, I am sure, having a profound influence on important opinion in this country, though they are probably not making you more popular in official quarters.
>
> I should feel proud that the greatest English journal should show such conspicuous independence, and should be giving the country a lead towards a policy which alone can save Europe from the disaster which will certainly come upon her if the present policy is pursued.

On May 21st, Hitler made a long-heralded speech in which he declared that Germany would not come back to the League of Nations till the Covenant had been separated from the Treaty of Versailles. He further said that he was willing to join an "Air Locarno" and to outlaw the bombing of open towns. He would, he said, co-operate for world peace, but only if Germany had equality of rights.

Soon after the Jubilee the change of Government took place, as will be seen from the following extracts from the diary:

> *June 3*. A very political day. . . . I had a long talk with the Prime Minister who was clearing up—slightly sniffy about the Tory machine, but looking forward to serving under Stanley Baldwin (with special responsibility perhaps for the committee of Imperial Defence, etc.). I went on to see Stanley Baldwin himself who was worried but said he saw daylight and would finish the whole business on Friday (7th June).

June 7. Change of Government. A very smooth and swift affair, carried out with every detail of kissing hands, a Cabinet meeting, a Privy Council, etc.: between the rising of the House at 4 and the departure of Ramsay MacDonald for Lossiemouth and Stanley Baldwin for Himley soon after 7. What a contrast with the unhappy French, who did however form a Laval Government soon after midnight (the 3rd within a week!).

The leading article in *The Times,* "Change-Over Day" (June 7th), deals with the end of Ramsay MacDonald's Premiership and the appointment of Mr. Baldwin to his third term of office. The article concludes: "How much of the cohesion of the National Government has been due to Mr. Baldwin's temperament and character is a matter which history will assess and which perhaps only Mr. MacDonald can yet appreciate fully. . . . The situation, it may be said, was admirably suited to both of them, for Mr. Baldwin is entirely devoid of self-seeking and loyal service comes as second nature to him. That is one of the secrets of his strength in the country. But the different qualities, complementary with his own, of Mr. MacDonald will rightly stand beside him when history comes to take stock of this curiously successful duumvirate. . . . It needed courage of a high order to take the step which Mr. MacDonald took in 1931. . . ."

Mr. Baldwin's Government found plenty of problems confronting it, among them Mussolini's Abyssinian adventure: from several well-informed quarters the Editor received alarming accounts of the state of the Duce's mind. At the house of Captain A. L. Kennedy, Geoffrey met Hitler's Ambassador-at-large, von Ribbentrop, with whom he had a candid talk about the Anglo-German Naval Agreement, which was signed on June 18th. Under its terms Germany was to build her fleet up to thirty-five per cent of the naval forces of the British Empire, and it acknowledged her right to equal British submarine armament. (Later in the year it was stated that Germany already had twenty-one submarines.)

In the latter half of the year the long-expected Italian invasion of Ethiopia took place. Small wonder that the Editor noted, after a talk at the House of Commons, that Baldwin was "worried about Abyssinia and foreign affairs generally. He raised the question of the date of the General Election, and I said the sooner it was over the better".

The Times contained leading articles on the Italian problem on August 30th and September 2nd. In the former, "Italian Plans and British Opinion", the paper stated that Mussolini's remarks had clarified the situation which would confront the League Council the following week. "Signor Mussolini is out for blood. He means to have a war. It would hardly be unfair to say that he would be disappointed now if he were to achieve his designs on Abyssinia without a war." The article continued: "It is significant that in all this correspondence there is no division of opinion about the reckless immorality of the Italian preparations for war, undertaken and carried through without the slightest serious attempt at a peaceful settlement. . . . There are signs everywhere of a new appreciation of the inequalities left by the Treaty of Versailles in the distribution of mandates for colonial territories." After dealing with the expansion of a growing people (the Italian) and their claim for a share in the raw materials of Africa, the article (September 23) continued: "That claim—the inequality between the 'Haves' and 'Have nots' which affects other countries besides Italy—was never regarded with anything but sympathy here. . . . The fantastic notion of a European war, as an alternative preferable to an Abyssinian war, has never for a moment entered the head of any sober Englishman."

Other events in the autumn were the resignation of Mr. Lansbury, the Leader of the Opposition, who opposed the application of force to Italy, whereupon Major Attlee became the Leader of the Opposition. On September 11th at Geneva, Sir Samuel Hoare made his famous speech championing the rights of small nations. It was in this speech that he used the phrase "Collective resistance to all acts of unprovoked aggression", which became reduced and popularized in the words "Collective Security", a basis for the forthcoming election.

The "Collective Security Election" duly took place on November 14th and resulted in a majority for Baldwin of 247, although Labour gained 96 more seats than it held at the dissolution. On November 24th the Editor visited the Prime Minister in his new rooms at No. 10 and found him "quite prepared to talk seriously about his Cabinet changes and the organization of Defence—on which I had some ideas". Abyssinia continued to be the Government's main preoccupation in December. Early in the month Mussolini banned all British newspapers except the *Daily Mail*, *Observer* and one or two others.

The Hoare-Laval proposed compromise on Abyssinia, which resulted from the Foreign Secretary's meeting with Laval, the French Foreign Minister, in Paris on December 8th, caused a great outburst of public indignation. No one better voiced the nation's anger than the Editor of *The Times*, as can be seen from the diary:

Dec. 9. . . . A nasty international situation arising out of Sam Hoare's agreement with Laval and the calculated leakages in the French Press.

Dec. 10. . . . spent the afternoon probing the Hoare-Laval Peace Crisis, on which there had been two Cabinets. Edward (Halifax), whom I saw at

3, was worried like all his colleagues. Anthony Eden, whom I found later in the House of Commons, was putting the best face on it in a sudden debate . . . altogether a very difficult night. . . .

Dec. 11. Public indignation growing over Paris Peace Plan. A bad Press for the Government (I had extracts from it put together) and a volume of letters . . . lunch with Jim Stanhope, now in charge of the Foreign Office, at the Travellers' and a talk about the situation which was worse than I supposed.

Dec. 12. I sketched out a leader trying to show the Government the strength of public feeling and the only way to meet it. . . . Clive Wigram came to see me, sent by His Majesty who was also not unnaturally concerned and was anxious about the future of his Government. I walked with him (Wigram) across to Downing Street: looked in at the House of Commons, which was in a ferment . . .

Dec. 14. A quiet day at home spent mainly in a weary effort to write something useful about the deplorable plight of the Government. . . .

Dec. 15. . . . A morning at home wrestling with the Abyssinian problem. . . .

The Times on Monday, December 16th, contained one of the most famous leading articles written by Geoffrey entitled "A Corridor for Camels". It began: "The Paris dispatches add a curious postscript this morning to the White Paper which records Sir Samuel Hoare's telegrams to the belligerents. The suggested basis of negotiation, as everyone appreciated at once, did at least contemplate one highly important advantage to the invaded country. It provided, in the words of the telegram, that 'Ethiopia should receive, in full sovereignty, an outlet to the sea, with a strip of territory giving access thereto . . .' whether at Assab in Eritrea or at Zeila in British Somaliland, the port, with its indispensable corridor, was regarded as the one serious makeweight in a singularly ill-balanced project. But the latest news from Paris makes it clear that there was an intention, however far it may have gone, to deprive even this concession of most of its value. The Emperor, we are told, was to be informed 'at a convenient moment' (presumably when he had recovered from the first shock of dismemberment) that he was forbidden to build a railway along his corridor. It was apparently to remain no more than a strip of scrub, restricted to the sort of traffic which has entered Ethiopia from the days of King Solomon, a corridor for camels. . . ."

"The suggestion seems so incredible, so completely at variance even with the most cynical interpretations of a 'civilizing mission', that its origins should be investigated before there is any fresh attempt at peace terms." *The Times* evidently spoke for the nation on this occasion, when it expressed great concern over the Hoare-Laval 'peace proposals' in Paris. The paper emphasized the fact that any settlement based on the partition of Ethiopia would inevitably be rejected by the Empire and would fail to be endorsed by the League of Nations. The article brought forth letters of approval from a number of eminent men.

The Archbishop of Canterbury wrote:

Lambeth Palace,
December 13th.

My dear Geoffrey,

I have just read the article in *The Times* of this morning on "The Way Out". I can't resist the impulse to sit down at once and thank you for it. It expresses finely and calmly all that I feel—and strongly: I hope it will have its influence on the Government. I really cannot imagine—apart from suspicions as to France which I do not want to entertain—how they have changed their prestige and leadership for this humilitating position.

Yours in anxiety and gratitude,
COSMO CANTUAR.

Sir Horace Rumbold wrote:

December 13.

I expect you will receive a great many letters appreciative of your first leading article in today's issue of *The Times* headed "The Way Out". You have so exactly expressed what I and, I am convinced, very many of us feel about this latest phase of the Abyssinian business that we can only thank you and hope that the article will sink in.

I do not remember ever before feeling so disturbed and even humiliated as I have felt these last few days, and when these so-called peace proposals come to be illustrated in map form they will certainly arouse increased criticism and hostility.

Entries in the diary during the rest of December include the following:

Dec. 18. . . . The crisis was now at boiling point and after an hour at the children's play (in which Belinda and Betsy did "Red Riding Hood"—Betsy a perfect wolf—first in French and then in German) I went to see Sam Hoare at his house in Cadogan Gardens. He had made up his mind to resign and I urged him strongly to do it. Stanley Baldwin was coming round at 6 (probably more culpable than Sam). I went back to write about it . . . the news came out officially about 9.30.

XXVIII

1936—THREE KINGS

DURING the year 1936 the country had three Kings—to find a parallel one must go back to the year 1483, which witnessed the death of Edward IV, the deposition of Edward V in the Tower of London, and the accession of Richard III.

Abroad, the clouds on the international horizon gathered even more quickly. In 1936 Hitler re-occupied the Rhineland in March—an event which caused growing concern; the conquest of Abyssinia was completed and King Victor Emmanuel of Italy was proclaimed Emperor in place of Haile Selassie, the ruler of Ethiopia. Civil War broke out in Spain; British defence was speeded up, and the last weeks of the year witnessed the Abdication of King Edward VIII.[1]

On January 17th alarming news was received about the state of health of King George V. Ever since His Majesty first broadcast from Sandringham on Christmas Day, 1932, there was a link with his subjects, such as none of his predecessors had possessed. Some extracts from the diary describe these sad days:

Jan. 19. . . . The King was said to be much the same. . . . I talked with Lord Dawson and Clive Wigram at Sandringham and did not get much comfort from them. The Archbishop had gone there to stay.

Jan. 20. Death of King George. A long and difficult day. . . . There was no longer any doubt, even in the public bulletins, that the King was sinking fast. It was only a question of time—a terribly difficult question for *The Times* and we had to be prepared by 11 at latest for either event. He died at 11.55, when we had already printed some 30,000 copies: but Russell and his men worked magnificently and the change was quickly and smoothly made. Had written the leader—in 1928!—and it had been continually revised. A long memoir and four pages of pictures were already cast. We got them into more than 300,000 copies.

[1] Treated separately in Chapter XXIX.

Jan. 21. . . . Events moved rapidly in London. A Council for the new King's Declaration at 4—a meeting of both Houses of Parliament to take the oath at 6.

Jan. 22. . . . there was news of Accession ceremonies all over the Empire and wonderful tributes from foreign countries.

Jan. 23. From Sandringham to Westminster Hall . . . in the House of Commons by 2—a crowded, solemn and unanimous gathering—to hear Stanley Baldwin, Attlee and Archie Sinclair move the resolutions . . . Then I walked into Whitehall, and was near the War Office when the small but most impressive procession passed from King's Cross to Westminster Hall—just the R.H.A. gun carriage, Imperial Crown on the coffin, and the King and his brothers and King George's staff walking behind. . . .

Jan. 26. . . . to the Lying-in-State in Westminster Hall . . . the vast multitude of pilgrims on the Embankment and far over Vauxhall Bridge . . . a deeply moving spectacle.

Jan. 29. The circulation of the paper was round about 450,000 and St. John Hornby (one of the directors of Messrs. W. H. Smith), whom I met in the afternoon at a Treasurer's audit of the Royal Literary Fund, said that Smith's output that morning was the biggest on record . . . Late at night Queen Mary issued a moving message to the nation.

Geoffrey received the following letter from Lord Wigram, the late King's Private Secretary:

Personal

Buckingham Palace,
31st January, 1936.

My dear Dawson,

You wrote me a charming letter, which I did indeed appreciate. Thank you so much. I just feel numbed and lonely. I have lost not only a beloved master but a real true friend.

The late King was always such good company. His outbursts were violent at times but always generous. H.M. loved his *Times* and I don't think he felt happy at the end of the day if he had not studied his paper. More than once he said to me when I went to see him in the evening: "Now hurry up with your work. I have been busy all day and have not yet had time to read my *Times*."

The last time I talked to the King on the morning of his death, Monday 20th, he had *The Times* on his table in front of him opened at the "Imperial and Foreign" page and I think his remark to me, "How's the Empire?" was prompted by some para. he had read on this page. H.M. was not unconscious—he had perfectly lucid moments. His circulation just failed for a time when he faded away, but when the blood was circulating again he was quite normal, and knew what he was saying.

The Queen has been quite marvellous and I take my hat off to Her Majesty as one of the most courageous and plucky women I know. The strain has been awful but she has kept herself from breaking down by sheer will power. She has been too sweet to me and is always holding my hand and asking me "Are you all right?" At the end of the service at St. George's I was standing at the foot of the coffin which had been lowered into the vault. Before going out the Queen came up to me, just patted my arm and squeezed my hand—I very nearly broke down.

You always had the King's confidence though H.M. sometimes did not agree with your policy. When times were difficult H.M. knew that *The Times* would support him and took it for granted that I had seen Dawson about the particular question.

You may be sure that I shall always be grateful for all your help to H.M. and to myself.

Yours ever,
WIGRAM.

Early in the New Year Geoffrey went to the Foreign Office for talks with Mr. Eden (who had assumed his high office on January 2nd). There were very worrying and depressing months to be lived through after Italy's conquest of Abyssinia, when the League of Nations and all who had taken part in the imposition of "Sanctions" had to eat humble pie and recognize as a *fait accompli* the conquest of Abyssinia by Italy. Events in Germany continued to be ominous and *The Times* naturally, both in its Parliamentary notes and editorially, dealt with the problem of defence and the need for better co-ordination between the three services. In the diary the following entries occur:

Feb. 10. Lunch with Brumwell at the Athenaeum, where I found the Chief of the Imperial General Staff, somewhat ruffled by our campaign for the co-ordination of defence and Thursfield (the Naval Correspondent of *The Times*) reported that the Admiralty was still more disturbed. So we are getting on!

Feb. 11. . . . I had the best part of an hour with Stanley Baldwin in his room at the House of Commons . . . We discussed Defence (in very general terms) and the young King and his dangers, etc., etc.

On February 28th Geoffrey and his wife lunched with friends when Marshal of the Air Force Lord Trenchard, Admiral Strutt and others were present:

We had a good talk about "the co-ordination of defence" and the man to do it (still unchosen). . . . I left the office to go down to the Foreign Office for a talk with Anthony Eden, just off to Geneva to settle about an Oil Embargo and discussed that and Defence and the Franco-Soviet Pact with him.

The Dawsons were down at Cliveden on March 1st, when Samuel Hoare was among the guests and where there was talk about national security. *The Times* was devoting much space to the problem of re-organization of defence and the paper claimed that the whole-time devotion to this task of one particular Cabinet Minister had never seemed to be sufficient in itself. The leading article in *The Times*, "Mr. Baldwin's Choice" (March 14th), deals with the appointment of Sir Thomas Inskip, the Attorney-General, as Minister for Defence. In retrospect we can see that it would have been much wiser to appoint Mr. Churchill, but the leading article of *The Times* gives the paper's views at the time. "It is not difficult to follow the process of thought which had led the Prime Minister through many changes and perplexities, to the promotion of Sir Thomas Inskip to the Cabinet for the special work of the Defence Programme. He has considered others, of course, as many of us have done: but for various reasons—that they were Peers or otherwise without a seat in the House of Commons, that they were ill-adapted to team work or (what was equally important) to work with their particular team. (Obviously the paper must have had Mr. Churchill in mind.) . . . Above all that their appointment at this particular moment in the world's affairs might be misunderstood and misrepresented—for one or other of these reasons he dismissed them all in turn. He had every right to do so. The choice, as he told the House of Commons last week, is his 'sole responsibility'."

On the afternoon of Friday, March 6th, the Editor went down to the Foreign Office for a talk with Mr. Anthony Eden. . . . "Anthony Eden had had the German Ambassador in with warning of an important Message tomorrow and was staying handy during the week-end. We arranged to meet again on Sunday." Geoffrey was staying at Eton for the week-end, when the evening papers on the Saturday afternoon recorded Hitler's speech at noon and gave the news of the re-occupation of the Demilitarized Zone of the Rhineland. "We listened later to the wireless on these grave events." The entry in the diary for March 8th is: ". . . I took train for London directly after lunch and plunged into a desperate day's work. There was great hubbub in Europe and the French were growing more and more excited. Masses of news from everywhere. . . . Our correspondents both in Paris and (oddly enough) in Berlin were inclined to be a bit wild. I went down to the Foreign Office at 6 for a talk with Anthony Eden and found him in very good form, as he reported Stanley Baldwin also, and determined to bring good out of evil."

In the meantime Nazi Germany was not letting the grass grow under its feet. Goebbels was carrying on urgent propaganda among the German people advocating "Guns before Butter". In his speech

Hitler had denounced the Locarno Pact and the task of re-fortifying the Rhineland was begun immediately. Small wonder that the diary of March 15th reports "All Europe rather on edge and no one but Nancy (Lady Astor) would have selected this moment for a dinner party which Cecilia and I attended—sitting herself between the Belgian and German Ambassadors and having also van Zeeland (the Belgian Prime Minister who was my neighbour), Titulescu, Avenol, Maisky . . . Rosenberg[1]—some forty in all." On March 17th the crisis had moved forward to the extent of the sending of a German delegation and the following day Ribbentrop had arrived by air. Meetings of the League Council and the Locarno Powers took place. On March 19th, Ribbentrop put the German case to the Council which proceeded "rightly and in due form to condemn the coup".

The diary for March 20th contains the following entry: ". . . I saw him (Eden) at 7, feeling that he'd brought the French a long way, dined at the Beefsteak, and spent an hour at midnight with Ribbentrop at the Carlton. He was a good deal upset and made a strong case for Hitler's general attitude. I begged him to take his time and to keep negotiations alive."

> *Mar. 22*. . . . I went down to the Foreign Office at 6 for a talk with Anthony Eden who was grateful for our help and not without hope of keeping negotiations going. The telegrams from Berlin were not hopeless either. Leo Kennedy had apparently been flying with Hitler to Breslau.
>
> *Mar. 29*. . . . It was the day of Hitler's great "Election" in Germany, everyone driven to the polls and no alternative to vote for so that a 99 per cent "majority" was not surprising. . . .

By the end of April, and in early May, Italy's aggression in Abyssinia was again in the headlines and the Italians were getting close to Addis Ababa. On Saturday, May 2nd, during a week-end at Cliveden, there is this entry: "In these peaceful surroundings we heard at night of the sudden flight of the Emperor of Abyssinia to Jibuti and spent the rest of it (the evening) wrangling about British policy and Sanctions and the future of the League." Geoffrey was back in London on the Sunday morning and to be on the safe side wrote the greater part of a leader at his house by three o'clock, lunching off a tray. "I wanted to make the best I could of British policy, which could

[1] (1) Nicolas Titulescu, Rumania's most able statesman in the field of foreign affairs. (2) Joseph Louis A. Avenol, Secretary-General of the League of Nations, 1933–40. (3) Ivan Mikhailovich Maisky, Ambassador of U.S.S.R. in Great Britain, 1933–43. (4) Alfred Rosenberg, German writer, who was put in charge of all political and intellectual education in the Nazi Party. His main book was *The Myth of the Twentieth Century*, the chief exposition of National Socialist doctrines.

hardly have helped itself, but was clearly shaken. Barrington-Ward arrived from Oxford however: and Casey, Coote and Braham were all there: and we put together our sad tale of the Abyssinian collapse." Geoffrey certainly did not enjoy his part in preparing the leading article, "The Emperor Withdraws" (May 4), and admits that he was "Rather weary all day after yesterday's effort and depressed by the general state of the world." The article stated: "The critics would be on stronger ground if they were to argue that there was once a period, long before the Geneva speech so signally confirmed our policy, when Great Britain should have revised her commitments in the prospect of some such event as has since occurred; that in the light of these commitments she should have looked sooner to her own military strength; and above all that she should have made more certain betimes that her neighbours shared her own conviction of the sanctity of pledges . . . In the most conspicuous case of aggression which it is possible to imagine, she has tried out the whole present capacity of the League for effective common action. She has found it wanting and the case for its reconstruction, which has become more and more imminent, will hardly be disputed now. . . ."

In a leading article, "Mr. Baldwin's Role" (May 25th), Geoffrey referred to the general belief that the Prime Minister regarded himself as entrusted with two main tasks to be fulfilled before he could conscientiously lay down his office. The first was to stand at the side of the Sovereign (Edward VIII) during the early months of the new reign . . . and the second was "to make some definite contribution to the appeasement of Europe, which means first and foremost, so far as this country is concerned, the promotion of a better understanding with and between France and Germany."

On June 4th the paper recorded that Mr. Eden's discreet utterance on June 2nd "did contain four totally definite indications of the direction in which his mind was moving; (1) he refuses to despair of the League of Nations; (2) the manifest failure of the League . . . must be admitted and remedied 'in a spirit of candid realism'; (3) the limitations of effective British action must be clearly defined and (4) he supported the case for the prompt restoration of the national defences, which indeed is unanswerable from any point of view, and put in a special plea for strengthening the Territorial Army".

In a spirit of realism Geoffrey composed the leading article "The League and Germany" (July 6th), in which he dealt with the year's melancholy record. The Editor wrote: "Mr. Baldwin's constantly repeated phrase about 'bringing together France and Germany' represents the national instinct, as his phrases often do. It is also (as his phrases often are) so general and so unimpeachable that it requires definition and amplification. British opinion, then, accepts as an axiom the existing friendship with France. . . . It is prepared to go very far in guaranteeing the integrity of French territory. To put the obligation on no higher ground, the safety of Northern France and of Belgium, and for that matter of the Netherlands, is a recognized British interest, as it has been through the centuries. What British opinion is not prepared to accept is the leadership of France over the whole field of foreign politics, or to admit responsibility for all the liabilities which she has been accumulating since the war in the shape of alliances with the further side of Germany. And as for Germany, British opinion is determined, in spite of many set-backs, to come to grips with Herr Hitler's peace offer as representing the best immediate hope of the stabilization of Western Europe. . . ."

"Nothing has done so much to frustrate an Anglo-German *rapprochement* as the religious persecutions, the violent anti-Semitism, the general suppression of liberty, which have marked the opening stages of the Nazi regime. . . . There is no sympathy whatever with the forcible re-occupation of the Rhineland, in the face of pledges freely given, when it might have been accomplished beyond all question by negotiation and general good-will."

"In the quest for this co-operation there is no need to profess either trust or distrust at Germany's sincerity—and least of all to abate for a moment the resolute restoration of British armaments to an effective level. Everyone is agreed in these days that British foreign policy must have the backing of far greater strength to enforce it."

In June Geoffrey received the following interesting letter from Sir Horace Rumbold, a former British Ambassador in Berlin:

Personal

4, Grosvenor Crescent, S.W.,
June 13, 1936.

Dear Dawson,

. . . I have rather come to the conclusion that the average Englishman—whilst full of common-sense as regards internal affairs—is often muddleheaded, sloppy and gullible when he considers foreign affairs. One often hears such phrases as "the Germans are so like us". Nothing is more untrue. I could quote many points of difference. For one thing Germans have a streak of brutality which is quite absent in the ordinary Englishman. And Germans like or put up with things that are repugnant to the average man of this country. My point is, therefore, that we should know the people with whom we propose to deal.

Now Hitler has quite consistently applied the principles of *Mein Kampf* in Germany herself. He has now got to apply them in his foreign policy and that's where the trouble is coming. The value to us of an understanding with Germany is not only that it may bring peace and stability in Western Europe but that it may act as a drag on Hitler's adventures in Central and Eastern Europe. Once he embarks on any adventures in those regions war is, to my mind, a dead certainty. The ordinary Englishman does not realize that the German is an inexorable Oliver Twist. Give him something and it is a jumping-off ground for asking for something else.

I thought that after Hitler had reoccupied the Rhineland he had admitted that Germany had achieved *Gleichberechtigung*. But now I read that she still has not got it. Perhaps she will admit that she has it if and when Hitler's dream comes true and Europe is inhabited by a block of 250 million Teutons.

Forgive me for pontificating but I do feel that the public need enlightenment about Germany and Hitler, and the enclosed pamphlet gives them that enlightenment straight from the horse's mouth.

Yours ever,

HORACE RUMBOLD.

Germany and Italy by no means monopolized Geoffrey's diary and correspondence. He continued his search for suitable candidates for employment on *The Times* and in February he wrote "the young men are coming on". There are many references to the outbreak of the Spanish Civil War and the participation of Italian and German forces, when the British Government adhered to the policy of non-intervention. Among Geoffrey's papers during the months of June and July, 1936, are several letters concerning the possibility of his name being put forward as Provost of Eton. Geoffrey at once wrote to say that he was not in the running for the position. One of those who had broached the proposal replied: "On the other matter—I am sorry. Either at All Souls or at Eton I can see you presiding superbly; but plainly you are a heretic about all that." There the matter rested as far as Geoffrey was concerned.

In October Geoffrey was present at a small party at All Souls where two of those present were "all for supplying arms to the Reds in Spain!" There are also references to clashes between Sir Oswald Mosley's followers and the Communists and the Public Order Act which was passed prohibiting the wearing of political uniforms banning black, brown or red shirts. On November 2nd the Rome–Berlin Axis was announced and a couple of days later there was the welcome news that Franklin Roosevelt had been elected for a second term. In the autumn Japan signed an anti-Comintern Pact with Germany.

XXIX

THE ABDICATION OF KING EDWARD VIII

If in any cataclysm the Crown vanished, the Empire would vanish with it. It is a link which once broken can never be repaired, and so long as the tradition to which we have been accustomed, the tradition which guides those who sit on our august throne, so long as that tradition lasts, it will be blest to our country and no power on earth can break it. (Stanley Baldwin, May 3rd, 1935.)

King Edward VIII brings to the altar of public service a personality richly endowed with the fruits of travel and universal good will. He has the secret of youth in the prime of age. He has a wider and more intimate knowledge of all classes of his subjects, not only at home but also throughout the Dominions and India, than any of his predecessors.

We all look forward with confidence and assurance to the new reign. Under God's providence, Edward VIII will establish the throne more firmly than ever on its surest and only foundations—the hearts of his people. (Stanley Baldwin early in 1936.)

Very much has been written about the Abdication and much remains still to be written as the records of the chief actors in the drama come to light. Presumably we shall not know all the facts till some far distant date when the Crown Archives and the Cabinet papers are available. There are references to the Abdication in most of the contemporary biographies. This record is merely an attempt to tell Geoffrey's part, perhaps only second in importance to that of Baldwin, in the Abdication story.

Later Geoffrey wrote a private diary covering the period September to December, 1936, which he hoped would serve incidentally to answer certain statements which were current in various quarters afterwards —as for instance:

(1) that the long silence of the newspapers was due to some censorship or muzzling from outside.

(2) that it was due to collusion—an arrangement between themselves for common action.

(3) that this arrangement was shared by the Government, who used the Press for their own purposes.

(4) that it included the heads of the Church, who deliberately selected the Bishop of Bradford to break the silence.

(5) that *The Times*, and subsequently the Archbishop, were guilty of "hitting a man when he was down".

In Geoffrey's letters and papers from 1912 onwards there is nothing to show that he had anything but friendly feelings towards the heir to the throne, though in 1924 there are records of talks concerning certain episodes referred to by the American Press and its lack of reticence in the case of a public character who had probably received more adulation than any Prince in history, and had been referred to as "the most universally popular personality in the world". The Editor's first and only meeting with Mrs. Simpson was on April 24th, 1936, at a luncheon party given by Lady Oxford; he commented, "she seemed, pleasant, quiet and sensible".

One of the most important letters ever to arrive at Printing House Square must surely be the nine-page typewritten epistle, written on October 15th, 1936, and apparently read by Geoffrey on October 26th, for there is this entry in the diary: "After a spate of correspondence and cuttings from America which had been growing ever since my return (September 24th) went to Buckingham Palace at 11.00 for a talk with Alec Hardinge[1] and left with him a copy of the best letter I'd had about opinion and comment in U.S.A. on H.M. and Mrs. S. He undertook to put it forward and we had a long and rather depressing talk about it."

In the private diary referred to above Geoffrey wrote:

> When I came back from holiday in mid-September I found a stream of letters and newspaper cuttings from America trickling into the office about His Majesty's relations with Mrs. Simpson. They were based on certain items of published news—a dinner party at St. James's Palace (of which S.B. told me at the time that "while he and Mrs. B. were agreeably placed, it seemed odd to find Lady Cunard at one end of the table and Mr. Simpson at the other"): the King's trip to the Adriatic with the subsequent visit to Balmoral, in both of which Mrs. S. took part without "Ernest". Some of them were malicious, some exaggerated gossip, some pure invention. The stream of cuttings gradually swelled to a flood, and the letters began to include a number which were abusive and

[1] Major the Hon. Alexander Hardinge, the King's Private Secretary, now Lord Hardinge of Penshurst.

contemptuous of the British Press for its silence and others which were frankly distressed. These last came mainly from English men and women living in the States and across the border in Canada, where the papers were just as reticent as our own in spite of the full impact of American scandal. One effect of all this was a certain amount of pressure in England itself, where many people were receiving a similar mail, for some comment in *The Times* that would put an end to the mischief or bring it to a head. There was an obvious risk of some unfortunate explosion elsewhere, and I remember Barrie, who was my neighbour at a Literary Society dinner on October 5, telling me of his fear even at that stage that one of his own compatriots might think it is his duty to become another John Knox and denounce the sins of the Court from the pulpit.

For the moment at all events it seemed to me better to go on taking the risk, though it soon became impossible to think of anything else. To a few unknown, but obviously sincere and troubled, correspondents I sent a line of reassurance. Some of them, for example, enclosed a flat-footed newspaper statement that "Edward will wed Wally" and asked why the public at home were not as much disturbed by the news as they themselves. In a few cases like this I came to reply, in a more or less stereotyped form of words, that the British public would indeed be just as much disturbed if they had any reason to believe that the news was true. Hence, I assume, a long and wholly imaginary interview with me which a chain of American newspapers "carried" soon afterwards—to the effect that I (G.D.) had denied that Edward would wed Wally and had stated definitely that he would on the contrary marry a "hand-picked Balkan princess". Nothing of the kind, of course, had ever passed my lips or crossed my mind, but it was probably an expansion and perversion of one of my soothing circulars. The bulk of the letters called for and received no reply.

FIRST CONTACT WITH THE PALACE

Oct. 25. Towards the end of October, however, I received a long communication which seemed to me to sum up opinion in America so well that it ought to be seen by others. So on the morning of Monday, October 26, I took a copy of it to Buckingham Palace and begged Alec Hardinge to put it before the King. This he undertook to do, though I suppose that similar letters must have been reaching the Palace already. It was the first time that I had seen him for months and he told me something of his own anxieties and difficulties. I found him terribly distressed about the whole business. He said he had thought it best hitherto to say nothing to the King on his own account, but to maintain relations with him as his Private Secretary and thus be able to facilitate the access of Ministers and other more weighty advisers. I entirely agreed with this view, for it would be disastrous if there were no such channel of communication left: and went on later in the day to see the Prime Minister. To him I also gave a copy of the American letter, which he said would be very useful to him and might strengthen his hand in dealing with the King.

This is the letter referred to above, a copy of which Geoffrey handed to Major Hardinge and Mr. Baldwin[1] on October 25th, 1936:

October 15, 1936.

To the Editor of *The Times*.

Sir,

The present letter, touching as it does on what is in England a forbidden theme, is one that in the nature of things I cannot expect to see published in *The Times*, and it may therefore be a rather futile gesture to write it; and yet it involves issues of such great moment that I cannot help unburdening myself by bringing certain facts, for whatever the effort may be worth, to the attention of the organ that is traditionally regarded as the chief moulder of British public opinion—if indeed other correspondents have not already anticipated me in this.

I might begin by saying that I am a Briton who has been resident in the United States for several years. I have had a deep and continuous interest in everything bearing upon Anglo-American relations, and I have always sought, by depicting British public life in its most favourable aspects, to contribute in my small way to the furtherance of friendly sentiments between the two countries based on mutual respect. It has therefore been with great regret, and even with dismay, that I have watched in the course of the last few months the development of a situation that gravely lowers British prestige in American eyes. I refer to the poisonous publicity attending the King's friendship with Mrs. Simpson.

I am one of those who had a deep admiration for the present monarch when he was Prince of Wales: and looked forward to the day when he would bring a new vision and a new inspiration to the task of kingship. In common, I fear, with a great many others, I have been bitterly disappointed. The doings of the King, as reported in the American press, have in the course of a few months transformed Great Britain, as envisaged by the average American, from a sober and dignified realm into a dizzy Balkan musical comedy attuned to the rhythm of Jazz. It must be remembered that the American man in the street sees other countries through the medium of some outstanding personality who is "played up" by the press. To him Italy is Mussolini, Germany is Hitler, Russia is

[1] In a letter to me Mr. G. M. Young, Baldwin's biographer, writes (March 11th, 1954): "The workings of Baldwin's mind, as I have tried to bring out, were infinitely subtle, and I have often thought that what keyed him up in the Abdication crisis was his romantic attachment to Canada. If Canada goes—Canada, the eldest child of the Commonwealth—then everything goes. And he knew from his study of the Canadian press that Canada was alarmed and angry over the figure which the Crown was cutting in American eyes."

Stalin; for many years Great Britain was George V. I believe that when the throne is filled by a King like his late Majesty, a democratic monarchy has many advantages over a democratic republic. It serves as a convenient device for providing the nation with a colourful figurehead, escaping on the one hand the disadvantages of a personal dictatorship and on the other the drabness of a republic. There is no doubt that France, for instance, has failed to make much impression on American public opinion through her lack of an outstanding personality that would fascinate the American imagination. The average American cannot name the French President or Prime Minister, or for that matter, probably not even the British Prime Minister; but every American knows the name of the King of Great Britain. A monarchy, therefore, when presided over by a highly respected individual, can be of incalculable behoof in creating the intangible elements that make for international good feeling: this was pre-eminently the case during the reign of George V, who was admired by many and respected by all Americans, even by those who were aggressively republican in their political outlook. But, by the same token, a monarchy filled by an individual who has made himself the subject of cheap and sensational gossip can be of incalculable harm by adding to the difficulties of international understanding. On the morrow of George V's death, the Prime Minister delivered a moving address in which he said of the late sovereign: "He earned the loyalty and respect of all parties in the State, new and old. He hands down in turn to his son the throne he himself received from his father, and he hands it down with its foundations strengthened, its moral authority, its honour, and its dignity enhanced. It is an incomparable and awe-inspiring inheritance." I am not in a position to know whether British opinion at home considers that King Edward VIII is satisfactorily carrying on his father's tradition. But the prevailing American opinion is that the foundations of the British throne are undermined, its moral authority, its honour, and its dignity cast into the dustbin. To put the matter bluntly, George V was an invaluable asset to British prestige abroad; Edward VIII has proved himself an incalculable liability.

For several months now the American public has been intermittently titillated with unsavoury gobbets of news about the King and Mrs. Simpson; but in the course of the last three or four weeks there has come a perfect avalanche of muck and slime. The American public are notorious for the manner in which they can be suddenly swept by a "craze" on this or that subject. The prevailing "craze" today is the King and Mrs. Simpson: the popularity of the theme is no doubt in large measure attributable to the fact the lady is an American. First we had the news dispatches, suitably and abundantly illustrated by photographs; Mrs. Simpson accompanies the King on a yachting cruise, Mrs. Simpson accompanies the King when he goes to consult a Vienna ear specialist, Mrs. Simpson accompanies the King to Balmoral, Mrs. Simpson accompanies the King on the train back to London, the ubiquitous Mrs. Simpson is in the King's company on every conceivable occasion. If the

American "news-hawk" happens to be slightly malicious he will point a contrast between the King and Mrs. Simpson "merrymaking" at Balmoral while the "grief-stricken" Queen Mary prepares to leave Buckingham Palace. Then comes the juicier pieces of outright scandal. One journal facetiously suggests that Mrs. Simpson's aid be enlisted in the collection of the British War Debt to the United States. Another gives the alleged details of a conversation in which the Prime Minister reproves the King for his carryings on, and the latter curtly tells him to mind his own business. Another asserts that Queen Mary is being ousted from Buckingham Palace in order to clear the way for Mrs. Simpson's installation as the King's official hostess.

Another popular weekly magazine with a circulation of over two million publishes a sensational article about "the most envied woman in the British Empire". A chain of newspapers with a huge circulation is now publishing in daily instalments a popular "biography" of "the most talked of woman in the world". Advertisements in railway trains and other places scream out exhortations to buy this or that publication to get the inside story about the King and Mrs. Simpson. Distinguished Britons landing on American shores are beset by pressmen who ask them what the British people think about it all; and the next day appear accounts describing with malicious glee how the distinguished Britons struggled amid confusion and embarrassment to evade the question.

Nor can one simply ascribe this campaign of defamation, which is gathering volume like a careering snowball, to the sensational proclivities of the American press; for George V was never in my experience the subject of such publicity. As a matter of fact a sober newspaper like the *New York Times*, which has consistently sought to promote good relations with Britain, until quite recently eschewed Mrs. Simpson's name from its columns as rigorously as the British press; but it has now given up this voluntary censorship as useless and prints copious news about Mrs. Simpson on its front page, although in less febrile accents than the sensational press.

I have hitherto always sought to defend British institutions in general, and the British crown in particular, against the criticism of American acquaintances; but under the impact of the recent avalanche I have given up Edward VIII as a hopeless case, and bite my tongue into discreet silence when I hear the King of Great Britain made sport of by American jokesters. After all, before one can expect to persuade others to respect the British Crown, one must at least expect the example of respect for the Crown to be set by its chief custodian.

Of course, the really serious, even tragic aspect of the affair is not so much what is said of the King as an individual, but what repercussions these stories have upon the international scene. This may be difficult to measure, inasmuch as it does not impinge upon diplomacy in its formal aspect; but the murky quality of the atmosphere that has been generated is unmistakable. As I have already intimated, the average American sees in the sovereign a mirror and exemplar of British political and social life. His impressions of Britain are not founded on the activities of Mr. Baldwin or Mr. Chamberlain, about whom he knows little, but on the stories he reads about the King and Mrs. Simpson. In a few brief months Britain has (in his eyes) usurped the pre-eminent place in the realm of sordid intrigue formerly tenanted by some such Balkan State as Rumania.

In an epoch in which Britain's prestige has suffered severe reverses, especially through the setbacks endured by her diplomacy in the Italo-Abyssinian conflict, it can ill afford to sustain additional shocks that are all the more intolerable in that they are so gratuitous, so unnecessary, and could easily have been avoided by a little more self-discipline on the part of one individual.

I have spoken so far from the standpoint of Anglo-American relations, but there are also the Imperial and home viewpoints to be considered. I cannot discuss these with authority, but it would seem supererogatory to say that what has transpired can scarcely strengthen the ties of Imperial sentiment. Nor do I pretend to know much about the situation as it is viewed at home; I understand that little or nothing has as yet been published on the matter in the British press. I cannot escape the feeling, however, that if Edward VIII continues as he has begun, the British Court will eventually be once more enwrapped in the unsavoury atmosphere that surrounded it in the days of George IV—with the inevitable concomitant of widespread republican sentiment.

It may be presumptuous, and even impertinent, for a person far removed from the centre of events to suggest a remedy; but I cannot refrain from saying that nothing would please me more than to hear that Edward VIII had abdicated his rights in favour of the Heir Presumptive, who I am confident would be prepared to carry on in the sterling tradition established by his father. In my view it would be well to have such a change take place while it is still a matter of individuals, and before the disquiet has progressed to the point of calling in question the institution of monarchy itself.

Yours faithfully,

BRITANNICUS IN PARTIBUS INFIDELIUM.

The British Public for the most part up to December 2nd was unaware of what was going on in the Monarch's immediate circle, as no word about the subject had appeared in the British Press. Rumours were flying around in the clubs and there had been gossip in Fleet Street, and of course those with contacts in the United States, and to a lesser degree with Canada, heard enough to make them gravely disturbed. It is however true to say that the vast majority of newspaper readers in the United Kingdom knew nothing of what was happening. Hence the incredible state of bewilderment which followed the flood of publicity which broke in London on December 3rd. We must however retrace our steps to October 26th, the day on which

Geoffrey had been at the Palace and talked with Major Hardinge and the Prime Minister.

In his answer to the various statements about the "Baldwin Press" and about *The Times* in particular, the Editor wrote in retrospect:

> There was in fact neither censorship nor collusion from first to last. The nearest approach to interference from high quarters was probably the customary request from Buckingham Palace (as old as Queen Victoria) that the Sovereign's privacy should be respected by the Press during his annual holiday abroad. It was not of course observed universally, though the *Referee* was the only serious offender in England. As for the Government, the Prime Minister probably saw a great deal more of me at this time than he did of any other journalist; but that was due rather to an old friendship and habit of discussion than to the slightest desire to influence me. He never in fact told me any secrets, nor did I ask for them.
>
> The only collusion with other papers, so far as *The Times* was concerned, consisted of three or four conversations, of a purely personal character, with journalist friends; and it is safe to say that no one foresaw the Bishop's (Dr. A. W. F. Blunt's, Bishop of Bradford) address, which had consequences expected least of all by himself.
>
> Finally the one and only article in *The Times* which was in any sense critical was the final leader written on the night of the abdication. That was bound to attempt some estimate of the defects of character which had led to the crisis; but it gave full weight also to King Edward's good qualities, and it was the last word written on the subject.
>
> He (Mr. Baldwin) then told me, more fully than he ever spoke of later events, about his first private conversation at Fort Belvedere on the previous Tuesday, October 20, after one or two unsuccessful attempts to catch H.M. during the week-end. The latter had gone off (via Ipswich) to entertain a shooting party, which included Sam Hoare, at Sandringham, but returned specially for this interview, which seems to have been difficult but quite friendly. Its general lines were eventually disclosed in the House of Commons.

Oct. 27. I lunched with Neville Chamberlain, saw S.B. again for a few minutes, and went to a party at the Vincent Masseys'[1] for the express purpose of having a word with Mackenzie King, who had had an audience of H.M. in the morning. It had been hoped, as I knew, that the P.M. of Canada might have said something on this occasion about the growing anxiety in his own country. He was in a strong position to give such a warning; but it was quite clear from his conversation with me that he had done nothing of the kind—had indeed, if anything, made matters rather worse by discoursing on the King's popularity in the Dominions. This impression of personal popularity was in fact becoming a very dangerous factor in the situation, and

[1] Canadian High Commissioner and Mrs. Massey.

S.B. told me later that the only rift in his friendly conversation with the King was on some occasion when he warned him that it was not strong enough to stand the strain of his intended marriage.

It was on this day that the Simpson divorce went through at the Ipswich Assizes. They had rung me up from the office one night when I was about to ask how this now imminent event was to be chronicled in *The Times*, and I pointed to a perfect model—a paragraph with one headline—in the recent divorce of Mrs. "X". This was all in fact that the English law permitted, and so we acted when the time came.

Oct. 31. Then came a hurried week-end visit to Langcliffe for the consecration of our Churchyard extension by the Bishop of Bradford,[1] who was eventually to play so conspicuous, if unintentional, a part in precipitating the crisis on to the public stage.

Nov. 2. On the Monday I lunched alone with Lord Dawson, who was interesting on the subject of His Majesty's obsession. The Literary Society, with whom I dined that evening, was also absorbed in the same subject (to the complete exclusion of literature). "A" and "B", who were my neighbours, speculated on the possibility of some representation to the King by senior officers of the Brigade of Guards, who were, "B" said, the only people for whose opinion he had any respect.

Nov. 11. I had a talk with John Astor about this possibility of having to take rapid action, and got him to read what I had written so far. A talk also with the Archbishop at Lambeth, where he was sitting quite remote from the principal actors in the crisis, having made up his mind (wisely, as I thought) that any intervention on his part would do more harm than good. Apart from his ecclesiastical position his friendship with the late King had put him out of court. King George V, he said, had had many distressing talks with him about his successor's infatuation, which he thought had definitely shortened his life. He had not met King Edward since some general talk about the Coronation Service in July, but had seen Queen Mary once or twice. . . .

Nov. 12. This, and another visit (to the Prime Minister) on the following evening, were devoted largely to discussing the possible value of publicity. There were likely to be further popular demonstrations during the impending visit to South Wales and to the Fleet. If newspaper criticism were to begin before these engagements it might be taken as an attempt to undermine H.M.'s popularity in advance; if immediately after them, as an attempt to minimize his influence. It was a very difficult problem, on which S.B. professed himself quite unable to give advice. The press is an unknown world to him, and

[1] The Bishop of Bradford informed me (3rd March, 1954) that neither on October 31st, the day on which he consecrated the churchyard extension at Langcliffe, nor any other date, did he exchange a word with Geoffrey about the problem which ended in the Abdication, or about anything relating to it.

he wondered vaguely, supposing that it should ever become necessary for him to explain the position to the newspapers as a whole, what machinery was available for his use. As things turned out, the necessity never arose, and S.B. was able to keep his confidence for the House of Commons.

Nov. 13. Next day I paid another visit to Alec Hardinge at Buckingham Palace, and he showed me, since I happened to be there, the draft of a letter to his Royal master which he had felt impelled to write after a sleepless night. It was his first and only intervention—an admirable letter, respectful, courageous, and definite—a warning that the Press could not long be kept silent and that Ministers were about to take counsel together, a plain statement of the constitutional position, and an appeal to the King to get Mrs. Simpson out of the country quickly. He sent it off to Fort Belvedere that same Friday afternoon—and never had the slightest response or reference to it either in writing or by word of mouth.

Nov. 16. H. A. Gwynne, Editor of the *Morning Post*, asked for a talk at the Bath Club on the Monday morning, but had nothing particular to say. He himself was in favour of simultaneous common action by the newspapers when the time came and of direction by the Government. I pointed out the objections to this sort of official Press phalanx, but the main point of interest to me was the certainty that the *Morning Post* was going to do nothing without a lead.

I looked in later on Alec Hardinge, who had had no word whatever from Fort Belvedere, and felt that there was nothing more that he could do. Instructions however came later for a summons of the Prime Minister to the Palace at 6.30, and this turned out, as all the world knew later, to be the crucial interview at which the King declared his "readiness to go". S.B. told me of the summons as I passed him in the Lobby in the early afternoon, and telephoned late in the evening to ask me to come and see him again. It was a difficult moment—10.30—in the production of the paper: but of course I went down at once to the House of Commons and found him unusually depressed and worried. He told me nothing definite of his talk with the King, but broke out impatiently once or twice about his "obsession". He was to see H.M. again within a week and had left him something to think about. Meanwhile he made it clear for the first time that any Press comment at this moment might weaken his influence such as it was.

Nov. 17–19. He (Baldwin) left next day to make a speech in Scotland and the King left for his tour of South Wales. Barrington-Ward had a talk with his friend Walter Monckton, who gave him the same impression that I had received from S.B.—that everything was now tending towards abdication. H.M. had dined with Queen Mary last night after seeing the P.M., and was seeing the Duke and Duchess of York today.

Nov. 19. By Friday S.B. was back in London and I had another long talk with him that afternoon before he went down to ruminate at Chequers. He wanted to clear his mind on a number of cardinal points—to what proposal, and at what stage, the Cabinet (if it became a Cabinet question) could properly make formal objection; what would be the reaction to such a course in the country, etc., etc.

Nov. 23. The following week brought the crisis to a head behind the scenes and brought also some premonitory signs of knowledge in the Press. *The Daily Mail*, which had been running a weekly parade of the King's activities, opened it on the Monday morning with a monstrous attempt to contrast His Majesty's solicitude for the unemployed in South Wales with the indifference of his Ministers; and in the evening I got —— to put together a short leader, which I almost dictated and largely rewrote, on the impropriety and danger of this attitude.

It was a crowded day, which included another long talk with S.B. . . . He was clearly getting more and more worried, though he told me very little and confined himself, as on Friday, to discussing various possibilities and the popular reaction to them. He was quite clear however that I ought to give up a visit to Yorkshire planned for the week-end. . . . He was still against any publicity for the moment—at any rate pending his next talk with the King, which was fixed for Wednesday. Vincent Massey, though his own views were sound enough, was obviously divided in mind about the proper course for Canada, in this no doubt reflecting his Prime Minister.

Nov. 24. On Tuesday, realizing that there would be general silence at least for another day on the main crisis, I finished a leader of my own on Patrick Duncan's appointment as Governor-General,[1] but took the occasion to introduce one or two passages on the importance of keeping the Crown and its representatives remote from "glaring public scandal" and above "public reproach or ridicule". The significance of this and yesterday's leaders was not lost on the American Press or indeed on many people in England.

Nov. 25. Next day, Wednesday, the King definitely broached the project of a "morganatic" marriage to the Prime Minister and asked him to refer it to the Cabinet and the Dominions. I gathered this in a talk with S.B. on the following day. . . . Alec Hardinge, whom I had seen again earlier, confirmed this information. My only other talk on the Wednesday was with Margot (Lady Oxford), who was full of Mrs. S.'s good sense and good influence on H.M. and seemed to think even now that their relations need never provoke public comment.

Nov. 27. On Friday morning the Cabinet met specially to discuss the situation in pursuance of the King's request to the Prime Minister, two members being recalled from Provincial engagements. They let it be thought in the Lobby that this hurried summons was due to some new turn of events in Spain, and several papers innocently swallowed the dope and made a good deal of it.

Nov. 29. The week-end passed without further incident. The ball had

[1] Of the Union of South Africa.

been passed to the Dominions and they were busily returning it. I had a note on the Saturday from Alec Hardinge urging silence on his own advice and Walter Monckton's. On the Sunday afternoon I looked in on the Archbishop as I walked to the office and found him very anxious, as he was bound to be, but still taking no hand in public affairs. Arthur Mann of the *Yorkshire Post* came in to the office about 7 and appeared to be perfectly clear and sound. Meanwhile I got ——, who was surveying the Parliamentary week, to prepare the House of Commons, in a final sentence, for "proving itself a Council of State, which is able to demonstrate its solid strength in any crisis that may arise, whether foreign or domestic". This sentence also attracted a good deal of attention. On the Monday morning, November 30, St. Andrew's Day, we went down to Eton and I was not in London again till 4.

This, though none of us knew it, was the eve of the breaking of the storm. . . . The Dominion replies were coming in, and were all confirming S.B.'s view that "morganatic" legislation was impossible anywhere in the Empire. . . . When I returned to the office[1] after dinner I found on my table the report of an address delivered during the day by the Bishop of Bradford (Dr. A. W. F. Blunt) to his Diocesan Conference, in which he expressed his hope that the King was aware of his need for God's grace at his Coronation and his wish that "he gave more positive signs of his awareness". With this report was a long quotation from the leading article to appear in tomorrow's *Yorkshire Post*,[2] which went much farther than the Bishop and indeed revealed the whole course of the scandal in the American Press. It was reinforced, as the night went on, by similar quotations from other Northern papers.

This presented me with a difficult dilemma. *The Times* had kept silence now for something like three months in the face of a great deal of pressure and ridicule from both sides of the Atlantic. I had always felt very strongly that we must be the first to speak. The rest of the Press had quite openly been looking to us for a lead. And now the floodgates had unquestionably been opened, almost by accident, and there could be no further postponement of universal public comment. The problem, so far as *The Times* was concerned, was whether to begin it tonight or to leave it till tomorrow.

[1] Mr. Morrah recalls that the Editor remarked that he'd never known such a famine of news and he didn't know how to fill the paper. That night the Crystal Palace went up in flames, and the next day the Bishop of Bradford delivered his historic allocution.

[2] It is probable that had not the Editor of the *Yorkshire Post*, Mr. Arthur Mann heard of the Bishop's talk to his Diocesan Conference and devoted a leading article to it, the Bishop's remarks might have passed unobserved by the Metropolitan Press. Mr. Mann also circulated the leading article through the Press Association and sent a copy to the London morning newspapers. The curious thing about this episode is that when he made his speech, the Bishop had never heard Mrs. Simpson's name.

There was no one else in the office who knew anything of the situation from inside, and the first point to be ascertained was the probable action of other London newspapers. So I took the (to me unprecedented) course of ringing up Camrose of the *Telegraph* and Gwynne of the *Morning Post* and asking them plainly what they meant to do about it. My talk with Gwynne on November 16 had given me an excuse so far as he was concerned; but he had left the office before dinner, giving instructions that nothing was to be said. I had also met Camrose lately dining with Abe Bailey, so that it was quite easy to have a word with him. He was reluctant, he said, even to report the Bishop's address, which indeed, as I told him, I myself had not yet read fully; but he begged me to do so at once and to let him know my decision. After thinking things over therefore, and concluding that it was not a bad thing that the break had come in the Provinces, I told him (1) that it was quite impossible in my opinion to withhold publication of a pronouncement which would certainly become historic, and (2) that I had made up my mind to refrain from comment until the following day. He said he would take the same course; and, since it was certain that the Rothermere and Beaverbrook organs would not explode, I felt pretty confident now that the whole London Press was safe. All that *The Times* published therefore on the Wednesday morning was the Bishop's address in full, with the important passage extracted for the Bill page, and a prophetic leading article on the wonderful reception of the Duke and Duchess of York in Edinburgh.[1]

Dec. 2. Next day the flood of publicity broke in London. I put together a leader on "King and Monarchy" from fragments already written, trying to remember all through that, however familiar to me, the whole story would come as a shock to many readers of *The Times*. It was the first time that Mrs. Simpson had been mentioned except as a guest on two occasions in the Court Circular. The idea that the King might marry her must now be broached, but only as unthinkable. I had already cleared my mind by writing a paragraph to explain why, as King, he could *not* marry her, but this I deliberately kept till the following day. The article in general contained an account of the campaign in the American Press, an admission that it had a solid basis of fact, and a conviction that the institution was greater than the man.

. . . He (Baldwin) was going to see the King at 6, and had nothing much to tell me yet beyond reporting a solid front in the Dominions

[1] A member of the editorial staff of *The Times* recalls, as an instance of Geoffrey's foresight about the Abdication crisis, that a day or two before its outbreak, the Editor sent for him and said something as follows: "The Duke and Duchess of York are coming back from Scotland tomorrow. Will you write a little piece congratulating them on the success of their visit and welcoming them home? I think this is the opportunity you've been waiting for to try and spread the loyalty of our readers a little more widely over the Royal Family." After the Abdication some review remarked on it as a remarkable coincidence. It was scarcely that.

and the House of Commons. He seemed indeed to be nearly at the end of his tether and sat with his head in his hands on the table, probably just glad to have someone with him till the time that his interview came.[1]

In the late evening, as I was struggling with the paper, he rang me up twice himself—the only time, I think, that I ever heard his own voice on the telephone—to say that His Majesty was worrying him to find out, and if necessary stop, what was going to appear in *The Times*. He understood that there was to be an attack on Mrs. Simpson and "instructed" the Prime Minister to forbid it. In vain S.B. had explained that the Press in England was free, and that he had no control over *The Times* or over any other newspaper. When he spoke to me, full of apologies, the second time, it was to say that the King would now be satisfied, and leave the Prime Minister alone, if the latter would read the leading article for him. Could I possibly let him see it for the sake of peace? By this time, as I told him, the paper was just going to press; but towards midnight I sent a proof of the leader by messenger to Downing Street and heard no more about it.[2] S.B.—with Tommy Dugdale and all the other faithful staff who were supporting him—was able at last to go to bed.

Dec. 3. Next day, Thursday, the whole London morning Press was ablaze, the more serious papers taking the same sort of line as *The Times*, Rothermere and Beaverbrook hesitating, the *News Chronicle*, which boxed the whole compass during the week, supporting a morganatic marriage. I looked over the paragraphs which I had already written to explain the case against a marriage under whatever guise, and X kindly finished it off in the course of rather a hectic afternoon, while I devoted myself at intervals to setting out the facts of the situation in a series of notes for the Bill page.

At a lunch in the office I sat between Auckland Geddes, who was shocked by the whole business, and a Canadian, who reported a strong anti-King reaction among his own countrymen. Thence to the House of Commons, where the P.M. had a wonderful reception, but in answer to a question said that he had nothing yet to tell. The evening papers were all given up to stories and pictures of Mrs. Simpson. There was constant news till midnight of comings and

[1] In the diary the same scene is described in the following words: "I was brought back to the House of Commons for a half-hour's talk with the Prime Minister before he left for his difficult talk at the Palace. He was getting worn out and sat with his head on his hand, propped up by the table, but was quite clear about his course and reported a solid front in the House of Commons and in the Dominions. I went back to put together my leader, about which S.B. later reported H.M. to be very jumpy. He (S.B.) rang me up himself twice before midnight."

[2] Mr. G. M. Young in *Stanley Baldwin*, p. 239 (Rupert Hart-Davis), 1952, says: "At midnight a proof was sent to Downing Street. Baldwin had gone to bed, as he had on the night of the General Strike." In reply to my query about the matter Mr. Young wrote (March 11, 1954), "Yes—he was in bed when Dawson's article arrived and Barrington-Ward agreed with me that he never read it."

goings between the Palace, the Fort, Marlborough House, and Downing Street. All the Royal Family cancelled engagements.

Dec. 4. Friday was another trying day. The "Simpson Press" (as the *National Review* described them afterwards) had got going by this time, and there was a regular barrage of pleas for delay, for reference to the people, for anything that would keep a popular Sovereign (and, it was not obscurely hinted, get rid of a bad Prime Minister). The latter did a good deal to stem this rot by a plain statement made to a crowded House of Commons, pointing out that under our law the King's wife was Queen, and that neither H.M.'s Ministers nor the Dominions were prepared to introduce legislation to alter that position. The House, as I surveyed it, seemed to be quite solid behind him. His reception indeed was a most remarkable demonstration, and Winston, who made various attempts to intervene, was looking extremely glum.

Dec. 6. I spent the night with the Elliotts[1] and came up to London after service in Chapel and a visit to Clive Wigram, who had been trying to hearten the Duke and Duchess of York for their approaching doom. . . . The mischief-makers had by this time been reinforced by Tom Mosley's Fascists, who were organizing demonstrations in the streets. I drove round the town—Buckingham Palace and Whitehall—in the evening, and saw a number of small processions of young men with banners and a large crowd of bewildered people standing about on the pavements.

Dec. 7. The "Simpson Press" was hard at work all day and Bernard Shaw brought it the offering of an abominable skit of a conversation between His Majesty, Stanley Baldwin and the Archbishop, printed first by Beaverbrook in the *Evening Standard* and taken over bodily by the Rothermere papers next morning. The latter peer[2] was indeed so excited that he addressed two distinct and contradictory letters to himself in successive issues of the *Evening News*.

But the House of Commons, thanks largely to week-end visits paid by members to their constituencies, was far less disposed than ever to be affected by this sort of thing. I went on to the Gallery after my talk with Edward Halifax and witnessed S.B.'s reception, which was even more whole-hearted than that of Friday. He made a second statement, heard with general murmurs of approval and sympathy, though there was nothing very new in it. . . .

That night —— wrote an admirable first leader, rehearsing once more the case against a morganatic marriage. . . . Towards midnight came a statement from Mrs. Simpson, who by this time had arrived in Cannes, protesting her "unchanged attitude" of readiness to "withdraw from a situation which has been rendered both unhappy and untenable".

[1] Mr. C. A. Elliott, the Headmaster, now the Provost of Eton.
[2] The first Lord Rothermere, died in 1940.

Dec. 8. For some extraordinary reason this statement, which every newspaper printed as a matter of news, was hailed next morning by the *Daily Express*, and placarded all over London, as the "End of the Crisis". It meant, of course, exactly nothing, and was no doubt dictated from London by King Edward's constant solicitude for Mrs. S. I wrote the beginning of a leader pointing out that the situation was quite unchanged, and left others to finish it in the course of another crowded day. But there was little kick left in the opposition by this time, and we were all simply waiting for the crisis to end at Fort Belvedere and not at Cannes.

Meanwhile the harassed Prime Minister had made another journey to Fort Belvedere, where he stayed to dine with H.M., the Duke of York, and Walter Monckton, who had been staying there since Mrs. S.'s departure. He told me afterwards that the only cheerful member of the party was the King himself.

Dec. 9. Wednesday was a day of "Lull", as *The Times* leader in the morning described it. The lull indeed extended even to the more excitable newspapers, which had now come down, one and all, on the side of the Government. I went to the House of Commons again, but there was no definite statement yet, though the P.M. virtually promised it for tomorrow. So I devoted myself to sketching out a final leader against the news of the now inevitable Abdication, and meanwhile set Morrah to work on a survey of the vast mail, showing the successive waves of public opinion, which had poured into the office since the crisis began. It was quite impossible to acknowledge all these letters individually but it seemed desirable to set their various tendencies on record before making an end of the whole business.

(Geoffrey's ordinary diary (Dec. 10) began with these words: "Climax of the Crisis—King Edward signed his Abdication in the morning and his message was read in both Houses in the afternoon. . . . S.B. spoke for nearly an hour . . . very effective it was and the whole House extraordinarily good.")

The final act of Abdication came next day, being Thursday, I spent the morning over as much of the leader as could be written in advance and in getting things going in the Office so as to be free to finish it later. The scene in the House—the Prime Minister's entry with the Royal Message and his subsequent speech—has been described so often that it need not figure in this narrative. I only record my personal impression of S.B.'s almost conversational manner, of the characteristic untidiness of his scraps of notes, of the skill with which he told the whole story without a word that could give offence,[1] and of the simple sincerity of

[1] Mr. Young in his biography of Baldwin (Rupert Hart-Davis), p. 241, says: "'Whoever writes about the Abdication,' Baldwin said to me, 'must give the King his due. He could not have behaved better than he did.'"

certain memorable phrases. The whole performance reminded me strongly of Edward Grey's speech at the outbreak of the War.

He spoke for the best part of an hour, and I came back to the office as soon as the House adjourned for an interval of reflection. It was one of those rare occasions (the death of King George had been another) when it was clear that the public would read and think of one subject only next day. I therefore devoted myself first to arranging that all the subsidiary leaders should deal with some different aspect of the Abdication—getting Morrah to pen a paragraph of sympathy with Queen Mary, Radcliffe to point out the relief to work and industry in getting rid of uncertainty, Child to show that light followed darkness. It was also one of those occasions when the circulation of *The Times* was certain to be far larger than usual, as it always is at times of national crisis, so that we must reckon on going to Press not later than 11. I settled down in the end to the completion of my own contribution on "King Edward's Choice". . . .

The following is the final leading article written by the Editor on the Abdication Crisis:

KING EDWARD'S CHOICE (Dec. 11, 1936)

The momentous message which the Prime Minister conveyed to the House of Commons yesterday will bring a shock of distress to every household in the British Empire. It is not too much to say that far even beyond the Empire the whole world has been awaiting the news of the King's decision, for the most part with anxious good will and everywhere with a sense of the tremendous issues involved. Yet there must be many who have come to feel during the last few days, as the issues grew clearer and the first controversies died down, that there could be but one end to their vigil. Rumours of a different course, diligently spread and all too eagerly believed, were soon seen for what they were worth; and in the end the conflict in King Edward's heart—for there was no other—has led him to the choice which he himself has clearly concluded to be the better for the Monarchy and the Empire. None of us may constitute himself judge of the incalculable human emotions which have gone so far to jeopardize the very fabric of these great historic institutions. But at least we are all entitled to the conviction, which His Majesty certainly shares, that the institutions are incomparably more important than the happiness of any single individual, however closely he may have become identified with them and however strong his hold on the popular affections. Both Monarchy and Empire have been sadly shaken, but they can and will be restored. And they will be restored all the more rapidly because there is no longer the slightest doubt about the duty laid upon a stunned and sorrowing people. The King has made his own deliberate choice, and has pronounced it "final and irrevocable".

Printing House after bombing

Colonel the Hon. J. J. Astor, Chairman of *The Times*, and Geoffrey in their war-time quarters in Printing House Square

The Editorial Conference at Printing House Square

Geoffrey Dawson with Barrington Ward, who succeeded him as Editor of *The Times* on October 1st, 1941

The account which Mr. Baldwin gave of the events leading up to it was characteristic both of himself and of the King. He may have his defects as a party leader or as an administrator; but in handling a great national problem, in which the life and standards of millions of his fellow-countrymen are concerned, he has no comparable rival either among his own colleagues or in any other walk of public life. Every one of us may well be grateful that he remained in office with sufficient vigour to withstand the terrific strain of the last two months, and to have emerged without dividing the nation, which for a day or two was ripe for schism, or forfeiting the respect and affection of the King, with whom he was dealing for the most part single-handed, or conceding a jot of his own principles, which he knew at heart to be those of the people behind him. His narrative yesterday had none of the ornament of oratory. He explained that he had had no time for studied eloquence, and that is easily understood. Perhaps it was all the more effective for an almost conversational style.

At any rate, stage by stage, date by date, from odds and ends of notes, he unfolded in detail the story of his talks with his Sovereign, initiated (as he rightly conceived to be his duty) by himself, but by himself as an old and experienced friend and not as chief Minister of the Crown. From the first difficult approach in mid-October he carried it down to the time when a hopeless suggestion of compromise brought the Cabinet, and all the Cabinets of the Empire, into formal consultation at the King's own request. Lastly he told of his efforts during these last few days, when the King's dilemma had been laid bare in all its inevitable nakedness, "to help him" (as he said simply) to make the choice which he has not "made". Mr. Baldwin failed in his purpose; but he was absolutely justified in claiming yesterday that, where he failed, no other man could have succeeded. There was no real hope in the final appeal with which the whole Cabinet responded to the note of decision from Fort Belvedere. But the very fact that it came from Fort Belvedere is no less creditable to the King, who has scrupulously refrained from any public appearance which might encourage demonstrations. Clearly the last thing that he desires is to place any handicap on his successor. He pencilled a note only yesterday morning to commend the Duke of York to the support of the whole Empire. The very notion of a "King's Party", said Mr. Baldwin, is abhorrent to him—a warning which may be laid to heart by those, if there are any left, who need it.

It is well to remember these things, for they complete the picture of dignity with which the King, no less than Parliament and people, has comported himself throughout this sorry business. But let them be remembered in their true perspective against a background which can be nothing but dark. Above all let us have no talk of "romance" about what is indeed a drama, but a drama of the deepest tragedy. King Edward had most of the qualities that would have made a great constitutional Monarch. He had shown himself brave, completely free from pompousness, chivalrous where his affections were engaged, conscientious in his everyday public duties, attractive to a crowd, genuinely interested in the condition of the poor as he went about among them. He was unfortunate, no doubt, in some of his intimates; but he also had advisers who served him with courage and prudence, and it would have been well if he could have brought himself to prefer them to the others. Clarendon wrote of a popular favourite more than three hundred years ago that

> His single misfortune was (which indeede was productive of many greater) that he never made a noble and a worthy friendshipp with a man so neere his aequall, that he would frankely advize him, for his honour and true interest, against the current, or rather the torrent, of his impetuous passyons:

That is apt to be true of every man who holds a great position, and it is peculiarly true of King Edward. They profoundly misunderstood the earlier signs of division in this country who represented it as an issue between "the people's King" and a hide-bound set of aristocrats and ecclesiastics. It would be far more accurate to say that His Majesty's circle was too largely composed of men and women, some of them of high birth and all of them remote from "the people", who cared far less for his welfare than for their own amusement. The real clash was between the thoughtlessness of an exotic society and the hard core of a British tradition of conduct which is common to all classes in this country; but it must also be said in fairness that none of us can realize how hard is the path of a King in choosing good friends.

That, amid all his great qualities, there was also something lacking in himself is sufficiently shown by the unprecedented decision recorded this morning; for it is proof of obstinacy rather than of strength that it must have been reached in the face of a very human reluctance to abandon a position which afforded him so many proofs of success. For those of us who are more humbly and happily placed there is assuredly nothing but relief in being able to avoid the burdens of a Crown. What seems almost incredible is that any man who was born and trained to such high responsibilities, who had clearly the capacity to undertake them, and who had in fact begun to exercise them, with the complete good will of the nation, should sacrifice it all to a personal preference for another way of life. *Omnium consensu capax imperii nisi imperasset*—the well-worn quotation from Tacitus is irresistible. It can hardly have been a better verdict upon the Emperor Galba than it is upon King Edward that all men would have judged him worthy of the Throne if he had never ascended it.

Mr. Baldwin's last words were an appeal to the nation to rally round the new King; and beyond all question the uppermost feeling of the nation, after the first shock of distress at King Edward's decision, will be one of overwhelming sympathy with his brother. No doubt the Duke of York, who stood next to the Throne already, must have been conscious all along that some incalculable stroke of fate might at any time make him its occupant. That will not mitigate the reluctance with which he must always have regarded such a prospect, and which can only be magnified tenfold by the circumstances which have brought it to reality. To succeed a brother greatly beloved by the people, who is still living and whose withdrawal is regarded as a national calamity, without the smallest ambition for so stupendous a task, must seem the most cruel exchange for the relatively peaceful domestic existence—by no means free from devoted public service, but with none of the responsibilities of Kingship—which the Duke has enjoyed in the past. Being what he is, he will not shrink from a task which he will perform supremely well. Nor will his future subjects, being what they are, be backward in their support and understanding. The prayers and thanksgiving of the whole Empire went up last night for him and for his Duchess and their children.

. . . . .

The Abdication diary ends with the following paragraph:

And there the crisis was brought to an end as far as *The Times* was concerned. The Abdication Bill went through all its stages on the Friday morning (December 11) so rapidly that when I looked in at the House of Commons after lunch there was no one left in Westminster and the Duke of York was already King George VI. I spent the whole day in the office and listened there to the final broadcast from Windsor of "His Royal Highness Prince Edward" (as Reith announced him) before he sailed from Portsmouth at midnight in the *Fury*. On the Saturday morning came the Accession Council, and in the afternoon we heard the Heralds proclaiming the new reign at St. James's Palace. By Monday we were all back to normal. There were naturally comments in *The Times* on these events and on the smoothness and rapidity with which they had passed, but no further reference was ever made to the cause which had provoked them.

A flood of letters reached Geoffrey at the conclusion of the crisis congratulating *The Times* and its Editor on the lead they had given the nation during these anxious days. One of them came from the former Bishop of Bangor, Dr. Watkin Herbert Williams, then in his 92nd year, who in fact died eight years later in his 100th year:

60, Carlisle Mansions, S.W.1.

Sir,

I have been an admiring reader of *The Times* for 80 years. In my opinion your handling of this calamity, which has filled our hearts with sorrow, has surpassed anything achieved under the inspiration of any of your illustrious Predecessors.

Yours,

WATKIN H. WILLIAMS.

The Editor received two letters from Dr. Nicholas Murray Butler, President of Columbia University,[1] written on December 3rd and 22nd, 1936, from which the following extracts are taken:

I must give myself the satisfaction of congratulating you most warmly upon the remarkable editorial in this morning's *Times* ("King and Monarchy"), which is reproduced in full by *The New York Times* of today. I read it with a distinct thrill for it represents the old Thunderer at its best. What wonderful things the English character and the English tradition are when they really set in motion to reveal themselves for some high end!

It is too bad that this unhappy situation should have arisen at a moment when the world needs the entire strength and full prestige of England for reasoned and courageous resistance to the powers of reaction and despotism which are making so great an impression upon different peoples and upon some element of almost every people. . . .

In the whole history of the American people no public event, whether domestic or foreign, and whether concerned with war or peace, has ever so seized upon the interest and imagination of the people or has occupied so large a portion of the daily press as the recent happenings in England. Former Governor Alfred E. Smith of New York was speaking of all this the other day and said that while he himself had never been out of the United States, he had followed all these happenings with keen attention and had read every printed word that he could find concerning them.

. . . Our sober reflection here is that now that the excitement is over and the matter so superbly handled by Mr. Baldwin and his Government, as well as by English public opinion, it will all soon pass into history and no damage will have been done to British institutions. . . .

Surely the English character and English public opinion have never revealed themselves in stronger or better light.

. . . .

On January 4th, 1937, Geoffrey wrote to John Martin,[2] in Johannesburg:

[1] Permission to use these letters was kindly granted by Mr. Richard Herpers, Literary Executor of the late Nicholas Murray Butler.

[2] He was a director of the Bank of England from 1936–46. He was Chairman of the Argus South African Newspapers, proprietors of the *Johannesburg Star* (but long after Geoffrey was Editor).

. . . Of course there were also difficult moments in the week when the public crisis lasted—notably during the week-end when all the forces of evil were bent on getting together in a "King's Party". But Providence undoubtedly watches over this country—most notably in the present case by deciding that Lloyd George should have sailed for the West Indies and (with a certain touch of humour) by appointing a guileless provincial Bishop to open the floodgates without a notion of what he was doing.

XXX

1937—CORONATION OF GEORGE VI—NEVILLE CHAMBERLAIN SUCCEEDS BALDWIN

IN the diary for January, 1937, there are several references to the new Sovereigns. A visitor to Sandringham had informed Geoffrey how impressed he had been by the strength and confidence which King George VI had developed; a few days later the Editor had a talk with Baldwin, who also had just returned from Sandringham, and gave a very good report of Their New Majesties. On January 30th there is a note of talk with Clive Wigram about the dangers of over-working the new King. On May 14th there is a reference to a talk with the Prime Minister (Mr. Baldwin) "who was perplexed about the title of H.R.H. for Mrs. Simpson, which it seems is hers unless a special order is passed". On May 28th there is this entry, "Finally Letters Patent defining his title 'H.R.H.' and eliminating Mrs. Simpson." The marriage of the Duke and Duchess of Windsor took place in a French *château* in June.

There is a certain similarity between the internal and external events during 1937 and those of 1935. Two years earlier the British people had turned from the ominous happenings in Europe and Africa—the rearmament of Germany and Italian aggression in Ethiopia—to their very natural rejoicings connected with the Silver Jubilee. They were fully entitled to congratulate themselves on their lot compared with that of their neighbours—so long as they realized how perilous was the condition of a great nation without adequate defences. Once again rejoicing at home, however, tended to obscure ugly events in Europe and Asia.

At both ends of the continent of Asia the signs were ominous. Bloodshed and violence were occurring between Arab and Jew in Palestine, the mandated country for which Great Britain was responsible; while in the Far East Japan had embarked on a war against China. I happened to be in an ocean liner moored off Woosung, in the Yangtse River, in August 1937, whence my wife and I watched the Japanese aircraft bombing Shanghai during the early days of this undeclared war. There were no adequate forces to withstand Japanese aggression and a mortal blow had been given to the whole system of mutual aid, as represented by the League of Nations. In Asia, as well as in Europe and Africa, henceforth the law of the jungle would prevail.

The solemnization of the Coronation ceremony in Westminster Abbey on May 12th stirred the hearts of citizens in the Commonwealth in a very special manner. This was no mere pageantry, however splendid and impressive; the ordinary folk could and did rejoice in a great "Imperial and dynastic success", which served as a tonic and inspiration to countless millions. There was deep-seated rejoicing because of the conviction that King George VI and his Queen would provide the Commonwealth with all the benefits that had been associated with the reign of King George V and Queen Mary. As *The Times* well said, the Coronation ceremony marked decisively "the dedication once more of the Sovereign and the whole Royal Family to the Nation's well-being".

There were several references to meetings with the Prime Minister during the weeks before the Coronation, including a long talk about "his own retirement (should he go to the Lords?—I said emphatically yes); the '*Complete Peerage*' ". A few weeks later the Editor had another talk with Baldwin in the House of Commons. "He was like a schoolboy counting the days to his release and in very good form." Baldwin resigned on May 28th, when Neville Chamberlain succeeded him. The leading article, "Mr. Baldwin Withdraws" (May 28th), written by Geoffrey, gives an admirable picture of his friend, the ex-Premier. The article began: "Mr. Baldwin's plans for his resignation have been laid and known for so long that they can come into effect this morning with the least possible disturbance of our politics. . . . He was rightly anxious—more rightly than he knew—to see the Monarchy firmly established in a new reign. He also believed that he could do something personally to contribute to the appeasement of Europe. . . ."

"Parliament in fact is by far the best vantage-ground for a retrospect of Mr. Baldwin's leadership. Throughout all his years as Prime Minister the House of Commons has been his spiritual home. More than any of his predecessors to whom the title has been applied he has been a 'House of Commons man' . . . He has lived in it, dined in it, watched it, kept his hand upon it. . . . He believed profoundly in the democratic system, and the House of Commons was its mainspring and focus. His politics were those of the average moderate-minded Englishman . . . He made his periodical orations to great audiences up and down the country; but it was for the House of Commons—sometimes, as it seemed, on the spur of the moment, and nearly always at the last stage of some impending crisis—that he reserved the political utterances for which he will be remembered longest. . . ."

". . . Three conspicuous examples of his instinctive power of intervention in debate, each of them deeply characteristic of the motive behind it, must recur at once to everyone who remembers his handling of the General Strike in 1926, of the most critical moment in the India Bill of 1934, and of the Royal Abdication last year. . . . The crowds who gave him so signal a reception as he passed in the Coronation pageant knew nothing of his love of the classics or of his power of commemorating friends. They cheered him just because they had come to look upon him as the embodiment of their own best instincts, which were uppermost that day."

"His defects as Prime Minister are obvious enough. He was too typical an Englishman, perhaps, to take a sustained and detailed interest in foreign affairs. He made no obvious contribution to the cause of European settlement which was one of the main objectives of his last term of office. . . . There may well be tighter and tidier methods under a new regime. But no improvement in the efficiency of Government will quite compensate for the loss of those other qualities which have enabled Mr. Baldwin, on occasions, to rise to heights of national leadership attained by none of his colleagues and by very few of his predecessors. He has contrived to combine the guise of an almost rustic simplicity with rare political acumen, and apparent indifference to criticism with an uncanny power of routing his enemies in his own good time, a conversational style in expression with the genius of a bard for moving his audience."

Geoffrey had frequent meetings with Mr. Eden at the Foreign Office. There were many complex problems to discuss; the constantly changing situation in Germany, the Civil War in Spain and how to make non-intervention more effective; Franco-Italian relations; the gentleman's agreement between the United Kingdom and Italy under the terms of which the two Powers agreed to respect one another's rights in the Mediterranean.

One of the Editor's sources of information concerning Germany was Lothian,[1] who was strongly in favour of a policy of appeasement and of trying to arrange a satisfactory relationship with the *Reich*.

Geoffrey's views on the importance of reaching an understanding with Germany are given in a letter dated May 11, 1937, to H. G. Daniels, correspondent of *The Times* at Geneva. The Editor wrote:

[1] As far as I recollect from talks with Lothian, he did not pretend to be an expert on German affairs, apart from his talks with Hitler.

Personally I am, and always have been, most anxious that we should "explore every avenue" in the search for a reasonable understanding with Germany. So you will have my blessing in anything you can do to further this end. By all means go from Geneva to get a statement from the Chancellor if you think that it will be of any service. The more personal contact there is between the two nations the better. But let me add that in my opinion the worst possible way to an understanding is to clamour for the retrocession out of hand of all the former German colonies. I do not believe that this is what Germany really needs most, and in any case I should regard it as no more than an item for reasonable discussion as part of a comprehensive settlement.

In a further letter to Daniels written on May 23rd, Geoffrey writes:

. . . But it really would interest me to know precisely what it is in *The Times* that has produced this new antagonism in Germany. I do my utmost, night after night, to keep out of the paper anything that might hurt their susceptibilities. I can really think of nothing that has been printed now for many months past to which they could possibly take exception as unfair comment. . . . I shall be more grateful than I can say for any explanation and guidance, for I have always been convinced that the peace of the world depends more than anything else upon our getting into reasonable relations with Germany.

The Times contained a leading article, "Germany and the Press" (August 17th), which referred to the visit of the German *Chargé d'Affaires* in London to the Foreign Office to announce that his Government proposed to expel Mr. Ebbutt, the principal correspondent of *The Times* in Berlin. The case against Mr. Ebbutt "was frankly based on dissatisfaction with his published record of affairs in Germany". The leader then described how the Government-inspired Press campaign increased as the days passed: "It was conducted with a volume of abuse which can hardly be realized in more stable communities; and it was only when offensive epithets began to run short that it gave place to anonymous personal messages by letter and telephone—surely a singular pastime for a self-respecting people . . . it is permissible, perhaps, to remind these well-drilled German newspapers that *The Times* has stood rather conspicuously for an attitude towards their country which is by no means universal in England . . . The distinction which it has always drawn is between the internal affairs of Germany (which are her own concern) and those national activities—due to some extent, no doubt, to the character of her rulers —which may threaten the peace and security of other countries, or strike at the world-wide freedom of religious belief. There is too much reason to believe that Mr. Ebbutt's main offence has been his repeated exposure of these persecutions of religion which are the worst feature of the Nazi regime and which are bound to be a perpetual stumbling-block in the path of international friendship. . . ."

Geoffrey was naturally deeply interested when on November 2nd he heard that Lord Halifax was to visit Berlin on behalf of His Majesty's Government for a meeting with Hitler. The impending visit was announced in the House of Commons on November 12th, "and had a great welcome both in the country and (more surprisingly) in Germany". Lord Halifax was the emissary of Neville Chamberlain, acting on behalf of His Majesty's Government, and his mission was obviously of great importance. Its real purpose was to ascertain whether Hitler could be persuaded to pledge himself "not to attempt forceful solutions, in order to obtain his objectives", which might lead to war. For some time Ribbentrop had been busy in London seeking to create a friendly atmosphere towards the *Reich*. His propaganda had been carefully thought out. Nazi Germany undoubtedly stood as a wedge between Russian communism and the West, and this was a fact of which Geoffrey was fully cognizant. Even those who detested Hitler's methods had to admit that he had given back to the German people their self-respect. The majority of the British nation in 1937 was quite ready to endorse the argument that at Versailles Germany had been forced to sign a harsh peace, which in the view of the vanquished did not bear any true relation to President Wilson's Fourteen Points. There were, however, many who feared that at some future date the German people would seek to redress their grievances by force.

In the leading article "The Claim to Colonies" (October 28), the paper clarified its views. There was no support, it claimed, "in this country for the view that the peace of the world would be assured by a mere reversal of the colonial settlement of Versailles. . . . The truth is that British public opinion is probably far ahead of the Government in its conviction that a clear understanding with Germany would have consequences more profound and more conducive to a stable peace than any other single object of our foreign policy. There is little sympathy here with the view, which has sometimes seemed to prevail on the Continent, that the proper way to treat Germany is to ring her about with vigilant allied States, sometimes masquerading as the League of Nations, like trained elephants round a tiger in the jungle, to prevent her expansion in any direction beyond the limits imposed twenty years ago. She has broken these limits here and there already—broken them by methods which are creditable neither to herself nor to the rest of the world—and every article of statesmanship suggests that a halt should be called to a process which must otherwise lead inevitably to war and to the downfall of civilization in the West. Let us at least be clear at what point a stand should be made, and let us make a supreme effort, so far as Great Britain is concerned, to do what is possible for appeasement before that point is reached." It is proposed here to note that the word "appeasement" is used in the primary sense, of "bringing about a peaceful settlement". Bitter critics of this country's foreign policy on the eve of the second World War have since made it a mere term of abuse, signifying "the propitiation (at all costs) of him who is angry". It is a healthy corrective to refer to this sober statement of an unchallengeable aim by *The Times* in 1937.

There seems to be little doubt that if Lord Halifax, in November, 1937, could have promised Hitler that His Majesty's Government would not in any way interfere with whatever he might choose to do in the East, agreement could have been reached. But that was probably exactly what, for many different reasons, both practical and moral, it was impossible for Lord Halifax to say; although Neville Chamberlain was always ready to try to meet Hitler on the subject of trade. Certainly Hitler was constantly demanding more *Lebensraum* for Germany and Ribbentrop was frequently talking about "the encirclement of the *Reich*" and of the economic plight into which the Powers of Western Europe had forced her. Lord Halifax recalls that the British Government had many ideas about trying to help Germany in the economic field "but these of course came to nothing because it was not really in that sort of thing that Hitler was interested".

Students of *Mein Kampf* realized that among Hitler's main objects was a German hegemony of Europe and an eventual reckoning with France. The absorption of Czechoslovakia or its disintegration was an essential preliminary for the oil of Rumania and the granaries of Eastern Europe which were among Hitler's main objectives. Hitler certainly in the years before Munich desired the friendship of Great Britain and Italy. The Rome-Berlin Axis desired a strong Fascist Spain as this provided a constant threat to France on her Southern border—a grave strategic disadvantage. Realists, however, were convinced of Hitler's ruthless character and were convinced that he would hesitate at nothing in order to attain his objectives, and they recalled the fact that he gained power by deceit (at the time of the *Reichstag* fire) and strengthened his position in 1934 by the assassination of Röhm and others. Hitler, as a powerful dictator, held a trump card; he knew that he could do things which no democratic Government, responsible to the electorate, could do. He once said to Dr. Schuschnigg at Berchtesgaden, "I shall always get my way because I am ready to run the risk of war, and my opponents are not."

Perhaps we have wandered too far from our main theme but

hardly a day passed without some reference to Anglo-German relations and Geoffrey had many talks with the Prime Minister, Mr. Eden and Lord Halifax. On November 23rd, after the return of Lord Halifax, we read in the diary, "A talk in the House of Lords with Edward, who is, on the whole, well satisfied with his visit"; the following day the entry was brief, "Then a dart to the House to hear the Prime Minister say his piece about Edward's visit."

Shortly after a visit to Southern Germany with his family after Easter Geoffrey went to the House of Commons to hear Neville Chamberlain's last Budget speech in a crowded house—"threepence on the Income Tax and a new E.P.D." In the diary of April 21st we read:

> . . . To the Carlton Annexe to lunch with Anthony Eden and discuss the state of Europe. It is notably calmer for (a) British rearmament and (b) the Italian scuttle in Spain. He himself was in very good form and thoroughly sensible, . . . there was a good deal of agitation in the City and the House of Commons over Neville's new E.P.D. . . .

One of the problems to which the Government had naturally to devote itself early in the year was that of defence and to Neville Chamberlain, as Chancellor of the Exchequer, the task fell of making the necessary financial arrangements to provide for a loan to cover the cost of rearmament, not to exceed £400,000,000.[1] When the Chancellor of the Exchequer presented his Budget estimates he informed the House that £80,000,000 of the expenditure would be met out of this loan. He also devised a National Defence Contribution whereby industry was asked to make a special payment to the increased cost—a proposal which aroused criticism in the City.

In August Geoffrey visited the camp at Southwold whither he had been bidden to His Majesty's Camp for Boys—"H.M. was late—but in time to make a little speech to the boys before lunch after which we were all put up in turn to make speeches—a horrible ordeal!" During his holiday at Langcliffe Geoffrey had a daily telephone talk with Casey, at Printing House Square, after dinner owing to the disturbed conditions on the Continent. On returning to London on September 3rd he notes in the diary, "Had a talk on the telephone with Byas, '*The Times* correspondent' in Tokyo! We do this now every morning and save money on it, besides getting our news uninterrupted." In September the Hitler-Mussolini meeting took place in Munich when the Rome-Berlin Axis was celebrated. During the year the cause of international co-operation received a death blow when Italy left the League.

[1] Defence expenditure rose steadily from 1932 (when it was only £102,000,000) onwards. In 1936 it amounted to £188,000,000; in 1937, £280,000,000; and by 1939 it was £700,000,000.

XXXI

1938—THE YEAR OF MUNICH—ON THE BRINK OF WAR

DURING the year one international crisis succeeded another. Europe seemed constantly on the brink of war and yet somehow or other—many would say as the result of the democratic nations giving way to the dictators—a precarious peace was preserved. Undoubtedly the year was one of constant foreboding. The readers of *The Times* who had enthusiastically acclaimed the leading article "A Corridor for Camels", in December, 1935, witnessed the British Government eat humble pie and finally recognize the Italian Empire in Abyssinia in 1938. Once more Nazi Germany pursued its triumphant progress and by the end of the year was the dominant Power in Europe. In February Hitler became Commander-in-Chief of the German Forces. In March he achieved the *Anschluss* with Austria, which was merged in the Greater *Reich*. In May he visited Mussolini in Rome. In Spain, General Franco greatly improved the position of the Nationalists. The prestige of the League of Nations became grievously impaired.

On February 20th Mr. Eden resigned his position at the Foreign Office, to be succeeded by Lord Halifax. The Prime Minister continuously sought to get into direct negotiation with Hitler and Mussolini. In the Empire the opening of the great Naval Base at Singapore seemed to ensure that the Royal Navy would have an impregnable fortress in South-East Asia. In Europe in September, the United Kingdom and France acknowledged the right of the *Sudeten* Germans to self-determination and thereby made inevitable the dismemberment of the Czechoslovakian Republic, as created by Thomas Masaryk with so much enthusiasm after the first World War.

In September, Neville Chamberlain flew to Germany on three separate occasions, for talks with Hitler at Berchtesgaden, Godesburg and Munich, which resulted in an Anglo-German agreement being signed which, at the time, it was hoped, would ensure a peaceful solution of the points at issue between the two countries. Above all, the British Government, under Neville Chamberlain, in its attempt to prevent the outbreak of a second World War, adopted, like its predecessor under Baldwin, a policy of appeasement. The enthusiasm for the Munich Agreement was short-lived, for Germany, in November, embarked upon a widespread pogrom of German Jews professedly as a reprisal for the murder of a German diplomat in Paris by a Jew; the British public sorrowfully realized, despite his promises of a "Christmas of Peace", that Hitler, the destroyer, remained unchanged.

In many circles the power wielded by the occupant of the editorial chair at Printing House Square was realized in a new way. American journalists and commentators in the popular Press at home wrote about the great journalist hitherto regarded as "a man of mystery", who was now emerging from his anonymity, though through no desire of his own. The Abdication crisis had, of course, received enormous publicity in the American Press and American writers had placed Geoffrey in the small group of men who were supposed to control the British World. Some regarded him "as one of the dozen most influential men" in the land; others now considered the Archbishop of Canterbury, the Prime Minister, the Governor of the Bank of England and Geoffrey as the four most powerful men in the land. One popular journal claimed that he wielded "an influence fully equal to the Archbishop of Canterbury or any member of the Government".[1] Another writer, however, regretfully admitted that the Editor of *The Times* was still "surrounded by a heavy curtain of personal secrecy".

There was, however, another reason for the interest of the popular Press in Geoffrey—he and his wife were fairly frequent visitors to Cliveden and attended gatherings at the London home of the Waldorf Astors in St. James's Square. Geoffrey found this unsought publicity trying. In his diary for March 8th he wrote, "to lunch with Nancy and Waldorf—the P.M. and Mrs. Chamberlain, Tom Inskip, Edward Halifax, Philip (Lothian), Bob (Brand) and Tom Jones—the 'Cliveden front' in fact". On April 1st Geoffrey wrote: "lunching at St. James's Square: only Edward Halifax and Tom Jones there, but a group of photographers in the Square, with grotesque reactions in the *Evening Standard* and (tomorrow) in the *Daily Express*. This 'Cliveden Gang' business is becoming tiresome." It certainly was, but how to persuade the vast reading public that there was no such person as "the member of a Cliveden Set" was not easy. It was inevitable that the parties given by the Astors should come in for publicity because political leaders

[1] This recalls the view of Lord Lyndhurst, who had regarded Thomas Barnes in his last years as "the most powerful man in the country". *Vide* Greville's Diary. In *The History of "The Times"*, Vol. I, opposite p. 338, there is a reproduction of the page in which this entry occurs.

and prominent individuals in the worlds of literature and affairs, both in the Commonwealth and in the United States, sooner or later found their way thither.

The first major item of political interest in this eventful year was Mr. Eden's resignation from the Foreign Office in February.

> *Jan. 25.* . . . went for a pre-arranged talk with the P.M. in Downing Street. He was in excellent form and stood pat on appeasement with Germany—not, he said, getting much constructive help from the F.O.

In the news columns of *The Times* (February 21) there was a reference to the origin of the rift between the Prime Minister and Mr. Eden. The paper dealt with the divergence of views between them "extending over a matter of months", concerning the method of effecting a better relationship between the British democratic Government in the United Kingdom and the dictatorships established in Germany and Italy. The actual cause of the Cabinet meeting on February 19th was a visit paid by Count Grandi on the previous day to Downing Street, when he had talks with Chamberlain and Mr. Eden. They concerned, among other things, the situation in Spain where Italy had not, at the time, come into line with the other Powers in the matter of withdrawing what were known as her volunteers. "There have been other obstacles, such as the recrudescence from time to time of anti-British propaganda in Egypt and the Near East from Italian broadcasting stations and the concentration of Italian troops in Libya. . . . It is understood that the Prime Minister took the view that there was no essential reason why Count Grandi's visit should not be followed up at once; that anything which could be interpreted as a rebuff from the British Government would postpone the prospect of a general settlement in Europe; and that, in short, it would be one more case of an opportunity missed. Mr. Eden on the other hand, is said to have attached great importance to a preliminary agreement over intervention in Spain—at least to the extent of the adhesion of Italy to the system of timing the withdrawal accepted by the other Powers. Apart from this he felt, as his letter of resignation shows, that he and the Prime Minister were no longer working in harmony together; . . ." The entry in the diary for February 21st is:

> *Feb. 21.* . . . we (Geoffrey and his wife) went down together to a tense and crowded House of Commons where I stayed to hear Anthony Eden and Bobbetty (Lord Cranborne) make their resignation speeches and the P.M. follow on a motion for the adjournment. Truth to tell I didn't think any of them very good and felt that I could have made a better case for Anthony. . . . It seemed an unnecessary quarrel.

Early in February Geoffrey had an interesting talk with Sir Nevile Henderson[1] on the progress of Anglo-German "feelers" and "the idea of getting Goering over for the Grand National"; in this month there is reference in the diary to Leo Kennedy's return to *The Times* for a definite period to write on European problems, on which Geoffrey's comment was, "he will be invaluable this summer". On February 10th "the evening was thick with rumours of unrest in Germany". Two days later Hitler sprang another surprise by having a talk with Schuschnigg, and the following week there is the ominous entry "Austria worried". Geoffrey wrote:

> *Feb. 25.* . . . Cecilia and I lunched at 46, Bryanston Square to meet the (Ex) King and Queen of Spain. . . . The King a most intelligent and amusing little man, who gave us a priceless account of a visit to Rome when he and Dollfuss tried to keep up with Mussolini's goose-step. Thence I went to see Franckenstein[2] about his Chancellor's rather daring speech of yesterday: and thence to the office, where I found a formal announcement of Edward's appointment to the F.O. and fell to writing a leader about it myself.

By midnight on March 11th, Hitler had in effect completed a bloodless annexation of Austria, and by March 13th, "Mussolini had come to heel and Hitler was in Linz *en route* to Vienna".

In the leader, "A March and the Moral" (March 14th), *The Times* stated: "Herr Hitler has enjoyed two days of triumphal progress from the Austrian frontier. Our Correspondent leaves no room for doubt about the public jubilation with which he and his army were greeted everywhere—if any Austrian were against him on Friday (March 11th), they either hid their faces or were completely converted on Saturday and Sunday. . . . But the higher the value that is placed on their demonstrations, the more extraordinary it must seem that it was thought necessary to surround so spontaneous a welcome with all the paraphernalia of tanks and bombers and marching infantry. There must be many thousands of thoughtful Germans who are reflecting even now that these are the methods that brought them to grief in the past, and wondering whether they are really worth the accumulation of so much distrust and ill-will. . . ."

Geoffrey continued: "In any case a preliminary order to the Austrian Nazis to refrain from voting was followed on Friday by one ultimatum after another . . . and finally, though all these humiliating demands had been conceded, by the invasion of German troops and the arrival of Herr Hitler's deputy in Vienna. . . . There can be no

[1] H.B.M.'s Ambassador in Berlin.
[2] Baron Franckenstein, Austrian Minister in London.

dissent in any quarter from the British Government's view of the 'disturbing effects' which it must produce on Anglo-German relations and on public confidence throughout Europe. . . . But there is at least a moral to be derived from the very simplicity of the story, since it admits no other version. No country, least of all our own, can afford to be lulled into false security while these methods prevail on the neighbouring continent. It is not untimely that they should have been revealed in so blatant a fashion just when the British Parliament is engrossed in unprecedented estimates for the Defence Services. If there were ever any doubts about the colossal and most deplorable size of these estimates, *there will assuredly be no reluctance to pass them after last week's events.*[1] There will also be fresh support for the movement for a more rapid, effective, and even compulsory organization of the people of these islands for civilian service of the type demanded by modern dangers, particularly that of a panic caused by sudden air-raids. No precaution can be deemed irrelevant in the face of last week's warning, and the more complete the precautions the smaller the chance of war."

The diary entry for the day on which the above leading article appeared is as follows:

Mar. 14. Another arduous day—getting rid of my letters in the morning and lunching *tête-à-tête* with Sam Hoare (who was broadcasting an appeal for a million volunteers for A.R.P.) before going with him to hear the P.M. in the House of Commons. Incidentally I paid a call on poor Franckenstein, sitting like the last Roman Senator amid the ruins of his Legation.[2] The P.M. gave an impressive narrative of events in Austria, but wisely did not commit the country to anything but greater efforts.

Further entries from the diary for this disturbed month follow:

Mar. 21. . . . A *tête-à-tête* with Vincent Massey talking over the European situation and Canadian opinion, which he thought would support the Prime Minister's attitude of restraint . . . took a walk to the Tate Gallery before an assignation with the Prime Minister himself at 4. He said he had come clean round from Winston's idea of a Grand Alliance to a policy of diplomatic action and no fresh commitments.

[1] My italics.—E.W.

[2] A short leading article, "Baron Franckenstein" (March 15th), appeared in *The Times* in which the paper referred to the personal tragedy of the Austrian débâcle in the loss to diplomacy of one who had represented his country at the Court of St. James since the war. It stated: "The Austrian Legation has ceased to exist. For a brief period the swastika flew side by side with the national flag in Belgrave Square."

Mar. 23. . . . I went to the Travellers' where I found . . . Maurice Ingram among others—the latter very interesting on his talks in Rome. He was there when the blow fell on Austria and said the Italians were staggered and many of them indignant . . . the Prime Minister had a meeting with the T.U.C. with the object of speeding up rearmament.

. . . . .

The entire Dawson family spent most of April in Portugal. At Guimaraes they had a picnic lunch on a mountain—"great round Matopo-like granite boulders all round us and amazing views over the country in every direction". On Maundy Thursday they visited the Cathedral of Oporto where "A service was in progress, with many lighted candles and a Goya-like crowd of worshippers". Near Urguerica Geoffrey was again reminded of South Africa. He wrote, "The whole place—cottages dotted round a (radium) mine, and surrounded by scrub and trees with blue mountains in the distance, is curiously like some parts of South Africa."

After their return conditions in Europe seemed, on the surface, to be slightly easier, but all through the spring and summer months there are constant references in the diary to the motif of Czechoslovakia, and while the cauldron in Prague did not reach boiling point till September, it was certainly simmering for a long time and there were constant comments in *The Times* on the *Sudeten* problem (the right of the minority of three million Germans in Czechoslovakia to demand self-determination).

The Times wrote *inter alia*:

> The Governments which refuse even to entertain proposals of peaceful change must take their full share of responsibility if some such change is shown to be desired by a majority of the population. The object of national and international endeavour should be to try by all means possible to ascertain without pressure from any side, the true feelings of the population in the non-Slav regions of the Republic of Czechoslovakia.

On June 3rd *The Times* commented on the views of the Dean of St. Paul's, who had written a letter in support of a plebiscite for the *Sudeten* Germans—as a matter of justice and British tradition:

> A letter which was published from the Dean of St. Paul's yesterday was typical of many, and an effective expression of the view that the Germans of Czechoslovakia ought to be allowed to decide their own future even if it should mean their secession from Czechoslovakia to the *Reich*. With this view, the majority of Englishmen probably agree. The difficulties of holding a plebiscite were then set out.

On June 14th *The Times* stated: "The only question that really matters is: Do they (the *Sudeten*) really wish to remain where they are? Or have they the wish to be anywhere else? It is one of the mistakes of the Peace Treaties that though the principle of self-determination was much in evidence in Paris, the wishes of the Germans in Bohemia, as of their fellows in Austria, were never consulted: or, in so far as by their self-organized efforts those wishes found some expression, they were harshly brushed aside. What remains to be done is to rectify the errors of 1919, and to allow the *Sudeten* Germans peacefully to express their own views as to their future.

And on July 13th appeared the comment:

> The wishes of the Nationalities themselves ought to be the determining factor, and no solution should be considered too drastic which is desired by an overwhelming majority. But Herr Henlein himself has always maintained that he only demands full rights for his fellow nationals within the framework of the Czechoslovak Republic.

Geoffrey was on holiday mostly at Langcliffe from August 8th to September 6th.

Meanwhile the question of the *Sudeten* Germans was being officially examined, and by the end of August the editorial columns of *The Times* were making an effort to clarify some principles of policy concerning it:

> A permanent settlement, with all that it necessarily entails in the way of revision and change, is the aim of his (Lord Runciman's) mediation. The conception of strategic security must be illusory if it is itself undermined by disaffection from national groups.

. . . . .

After his month's holiday Geoffrey left Langcliffe on Tuesday, September 6th, and was at Printing House Square by 3 p.m. He spent much time revising the famous leading article which appeared in *The Times* the following day, in which the paper ventilated the idea, which had been revived on several occasions, of a secession of the *Sudeten* fringe to Germany thereby making Czechoslovakia a more homogeneous state. The article was perfectly consistent with the policy of *The Times*, but came in for much criticism.

We must now return to the diary:

Sept. 7. (Wednesday.) There was a hubbub, as I fully expected, over the morning's leader—reactions in Prague and Berlin, and the Foreign

Office went up through the roof—Not so, however, the Foreign Secretary, who came and lunched with me at the Travellers', and had a long talk. He is as much in the dark as everyone else, as to what is likely to happen next and discussed the question of his going to Geneva on Friday which I told him I thought would be a great mistake. . . .

There certainly "was a hubbub" after the publication of the leading article in *The Times* on September 7th. The lines chiefly responsible for the furore were the following:

. . . it might be worth while for the Czechoslovak Government to consider whether they should exclude altogether the project, which has found favour in some quarters, of making Czechoslovakia a more homogeneous State by the secession of that fringe of alien populations who are contiguous to the nation with which they are united by race. In any case the wishes of the population concerned would seem to be a decisively important element in any solution that can hope to be regarded as permanent, and the advantages to Czechoslovakia of becoming a homogeneous State might conceivably outweigh the obvious disadvantages of losing the *Sudeten* German districts of the borderland.

On September 7th an official statement was issued in London that the suggestion "in no way represents the views of His Majesty's Government". Among Geoffrey's papers are cuttings from several of the contemporaries of *The Times*. They are mostly written in somewhat similar terms to the effect that the article was one of the most damaging indiscretions in British journalism and that there could not have been a more deplorable misrepresentation of the British point of view. And yet the very suggestions which caused such a howl in the Press on September 7th were practically the terms as suggested by Lord Runciman, who, in due course, reported that the claim for self-determination of the *Sudeten* was substantially justified.

Geoffrey's diary for the day after the publication of the leading article of September 7th follows:

Sept. 8. Office morning, afternoon and night. Practically all our contemporaries had broken out in a volley of abuse of *The Times* for its suggestion that a revision of frontiers in Czechoslovakia should not be ruled out of discussion—a mild suggestion, often made before. This impelled me to write a par. as I read them, and to add another in the Rhodes Trust Office after a talk with Millar, and so to build up a scrappy 1st leader which at any rate relieved some of my weary colleagues. . . .

On September 13th the diary records that "negotiations in Prague were replaced by *Sudeten* rioting in various places and things began to look pretty black by midnight. I dined at the Beefsteak, where there was a very large company and returned to find a *Sudeten* ultimatum to the Czech Government about "special measures". Ministers were sitting late in Downing Street.

Geoffrey remained in close contact with Neville Chamberlain during the latter's premiership, lasting three years, and was in entire agreement with the policy of appeasement, and despite the stupendous difficulties he too was steadfastly seeking a way of escape from the catastrophe of another world war. A study of the records available certainly gives the impression that Chamberlain valued the Editor's opinion and was strengthened in his own views by the knowledge that Geoffrey agreed with his policy and would support it in *The Times*. That policy in so far as it consisted of "appeasement" was not new and was not—as is frequently suggested—Chamberlain's invention. Mr. Eden, at the time of the occupation of the Rhineland, told the House of Commons that "appeasement" was the policy of His Majesty's Government. In that respect Chamberlain was following the traditional practice of continuity in foreign policy. The difference that Chamberlain made (and in this he was wholeheartedly supported by Geoffrey), was that, instead of merely continuing to adopt a policy of drift, he was determined to act and in particular fully to probe the practicability of reaching a settlement with Germany.

There is no doubt that both Geoffrey and the Prime Minister felt that almost any sacrifice should be made to prevent Armageddon. They knew full well that the first World War had not, in fact, been the "war to end war", and they also were agreed that if a second World War were to begin it was impossible to foresee when or where it would end. They both were realists and were fully informed about the situation in 1938, and knew:

(1) The United Kingdom's armament weakness and general unpreparedness for air attacks.

(2) The strength of Germany especially in the air.[1]

(3) The alarming military, economic and political weakness of France,[2] who would certainly be unable to come to the aid of Czechoslovakia.

[1] On several occasions the late Lord Londonderry, Secretary of State for Air from 1931–35, deplored to me our appalling deficiencies in the air. He had always advocated that Great Britain should build a plane for every plane the Nazis constructed.

[2] Which facts were ignored by certain admirers of France in Great Britain who continued to believe in her up to her final collapse in 1940.

(4) The "no involvement" policy of the U.S.A.

(5) The Sister Nations in the British Commonwealth were not prepared to fight, to preserve Czechoslovakia, with its minority group of three million *Sudeten* Germans, who claimed the right of self-determination.

As I point out on several occasions, the really vital factor in Geoffrey's mind, which for diplomatic reasons could not be argued at the time, was his deep misgiving lest the United Kingdom Government should be led into war in circumstances in which the Empire might not support us. Mr. Dermot Morrah, who was in continuous touch with the Editor during the 1930's, thinks that after the *Anschluss* Geoffrey had no doubt that we should have to fight Hitler sooner or later. The Editor was very sensitive, and rightly so, to the views of eminent men from the Dominions who fostered this misgiving. If South Africa had remained neutral in a war fought for Czechoslovakia—and it was a very near thing even in 1939—and the United Kingdom had been denied the use of Table Bay, as well as Suez, the main strategic line of communication of the Empire would have been irretrievably lost.

If the entire nation was united behind Chamberlain in September, 1939, when war came, it was in no small measure due to the fact that every voter realized that no one had worked more consistently for peace than the Prime Minister.

In the light of after-events there have been many critics of the policy of appeasement, some of whom were silent prior to 1940. Some post-war commentators have criticized Chamberlain and Geoffrey for sins of omission which led up to the Munich Conference: but few of the critics have said what was the practicable alternative at that time and in those circumstances. This is not to say that more ought not to have been done to produce different circumstances, e.g. the more rapid conversion of national feeling from "peace" to "war"; and it is arguable that Geoffrey ought to have replaced the clock by a battle-axe. But when? Up to 1934, to most people it would have seemed outrageous. 1935? 1936, perhaps? But by then the Government had for three years been quietly modifying the "peace" policy (a modification doubted by some and opposed by others) and both Chamberlain and Geoffrey had accepted the view that, despite any reasonable settlement that could be proposed, the Hitler Germany might go too far. Hence the Defence White Papers—beginning in 1934 the policy that nowadays is called negotiating through strength, on which Geoffrey, in *The Times*, made the appropriate supporting comments.

Many critics of the Baldwin-Chamberlain policy say that His

Majesty's Government should have taken a stand against aggression. It is instructive therefore to recall that the White Paper in 1936 brought home to the nation the urgent need of a complete reorganization of our defences: it set forth what the Government considered essential. Two capital ships to be laid down in 1937; the number of cruisers to be increased to 70; an increase in naval personnel by 6,000; in the army four new battalions to be formed; improved equipment to be provided for the territorials; the modernization of coast defences and of defended ports abroad; the first line strength of the R.A.F. to be brought up to 1,750 aircraft (i.e. 250 more than the previous programme) exclusive of the Fleet Air Arm. Baldwin, in his speech on March 9th, 1936, after the reoccupation of the Rhineland by Hitler, in opening the two-day debate in the House of Commons—to which Geoffrey listened—was loudly cheered and said *inter alia*: "We shall, of course, continue to use our position, our prestige, and our influence to aid in the appeasement of international unrest . . . but no Government can overlook the possible danger of conflict somewhere in the world . . . if the countries of Europe desire to stop an aggressor, whoever he may be, by making that aggressor realize that his action will bring all the other members of the League upon him at once, the countries of Europe—and, as I say, it is a horrible thing to have to say—will have to be much more ready for war than they are today. In other words, to secure peace, and in the name of peace, you have to have increased armaments at hand and ready." The Government carried the motion by a majority of 218.

When the moderate proposal of rearmament was made by the Chamberlain Government, the leader of the Opposition on that occasion submitted the following amendment: "That as the safety of this country and the peace of the world cannot be secured by reliance on armaments but only by the resolute pursuit of a policy of international understanding, adherence to the Covenant of the League of Nations, general disarmament, the progressive improvement of international labour standards, the economic co-operation so as to remove the causes of war, this House cannot agree to a policy which in fact seeks security in national armaments alone and intensifies the ruinous arms race between the nations, inevitably leading to war; views with alarm proposals for the reorganization of industry on a war basis which will enormously extend the vested interests in arms manufacture and create a serious menace to organized labour and to trades unions' standards: and has no confidence in His Majesty's Ministers whose unworthy and ambiguous foreign policy has largely contributed to the present state of world unrest." (Mr. Attlee's amendment was supported by 155 votes to the 378 against it.)

Some critics say that we should have gone to war[1] when Hitler re-entered the Rhineland in 1936—when he was not ready. Perhaps a stronger policy then might have brought results: but this assumption is very doubtful. Hitler was fully aware of British unpreparedness and of the peace-loving qualities of the British voter. Anyhow, even if the British Government of the day had been prepared to challenge Hitler in 1936, there is no reason to suppose that the Dominions would have been any more ready to embark on a world war then than they were in 1938, and this argument was paramount in Geoffrey's case. Geoffrey was certainly influenced too by the thought that Nazi Germany served as a barrier to the spread of Communism in the West.

As for Chamberlain's decision, in the summer of 1938, to offer to see Hitler, it seems even more (notwithstanding the criticism of those who—ignoring the facts and circumstances of the time—say we should have "stood up to Hitler") to have been entirely in the common-sense English tradition, and as such, it naturally appealed to Geoffrey. To Chamberlain, with his matter of fact outlook, it was a logical and proper next step, even if a final one, to go to the utmost limits in pursuance of his determination fully to probe the practicability of reaching an understanding with Germany. Chamberlain knew, as Geoffrey undoubtedly knew, that in 1938 we were not in a position to say "No" to Germany: they both knew, however, that we should be able to say "No" in a year's time—and we did. The twelve months' interval obtained by the appeasement policy enabled the United Kingdom to build up the front line strength of our "Hurricanes" and "Spitfires" and naval escort vessels. If it had not been for this year in which to press forward with rearmament the victory of the "Battle of Britain" would not have been possible.

We now return to the diary:

Sept. 14. Prime Minister decides to visit Hitler. Edward imparted this momentous news to me at the Foreign Office in the afternoon under seal of secrecy till released but it enabled me to prepare for it, writing headlines and diplomatic notes and getting a leader started. It was a very great relief in every country in the world. . . .

Sept. 15. The Prime Minister went off at 8.30 a.m. for Munich and Berchtesgaden. It occurred to me that I might as well go home (to Langcliffe) tonight as tomorrow and laid plans to this end—visiting B-W. . . . The immense preparation at Berchtesgaden looked more and more like a 3 or 4 days stay: so I took, fairly contented, the 5 train to Hellifield, a tedious but sleepy journey, and it was not till I

[1] The possibility of the United Kingdom going to war without the Empire's support is also referred to on p. 374.

arrived at Langcliffe that Cecilia told me of a telephone call from B-W. to say that the Prime Minister was returning tomorrow.

Geoffrey had spent the morning on Dale Head, where he had a couple of drives, before bidding farewell to the shooters and catching the train to London:

Sept. 19. . . . I dined with B-W. on arrival and went on with him to the office to cope with the still critical situation. The Franco-British Plan —a slice of Sudetenland to Germany with a guarantee for the rest— was being considered all day in Prague after meetings of the 2 Cabinets in Paris and London. . . . A good deal of Left Wing (and other) opposition to the Plan was being aroused in England.

Sept. 20. . . . The Czechs were still considering the Plan, had practically accepted it last night, and were now said to be making reservations under Left Wing pressure. Their reply was received in London late, but not divulged and at about 11—just in time to get it into all editions—came the news that the Prime Minister was going to meet Hitler again (on the Rhine this time) on Thursday. Meanwhile the other Minorities (in Czechoslovakia) were pegging out claims.

Sept. 22. The Prime Minister's 2nd meeting with Hitler. . . . drove down to Heston to see Neville Chamberlain off to Germany. There was no great crowd there—his own staff (Horace Wilson, Strang, Malkin), the German Embassy, Corbin—but I think he was glad to see me and was very appreciative of the support of *The Times*. After that it was a day of waiting and suspense and a good deal of difficulty in constructing a paper. . . .

Sept. 23. Looked in on Joe Kennedy, U.S. Ambassador, on my way to the office and found him very vocal and excited and full of strange oaths. He had had Lindbergh with him, didn't see how we could go to war effectively, but supported all that "the old man" was doing. Later I lunched alone with another Ambassador, the Jap, Yoshida, just returning to Tokyo and very anxious to restore Anglo-Jap friendship. I told him plainly what stood in the way. For the rest a long, anxious waiting day in P.H.S. No further conversations at Godesberg but an exchange of letters (on the point of maintaining peace and order if conversations were to go on) and a final interview late—10.30—which turned out eventually to have lasted for 3 hours and admitted another ray of hope. . . .

Sept. 24. A morning spent largely on the telephone. Dorothy Halifax rang me up twice for "news!"—Edward having left the house at 9 and not been heard of since. He was meeting the Prime Minister at Heston. . . .

Sept. 26. This was a day of great and rapid events and immense activity everywhere. In the morning Roosevelt addressed an appeal for peace to Hitler and Benes and the Cabinet met and had further talks with the French. At midday Horace Wilson flew to Berlin with a personal letter from the Prime Minister. At 8 came Hitler's much-heralded speech—a truculent affair with a violent attack on Benes, but with some loopholes. At all events Joe Kennedy, who rang me up, thought so and Winston was reported to have described the speech as a climb down. I went and had a talk with Stanley Baldwin in the morning and received a visit from the 1st Secretary of German Embassy . . . at 1 a.m. our indefatigable Prime Minister issued an admirable statement from Downing Street involving the reconstruction of the whole paper.

Sept. 27. . . . Bruce came to see me (very worried about the risk of war and what Parliament might do). . . . I returned to the office to receive Freddy Maurice, who'd flown to Berlin with an offer of the help of the British Legion in supervising transfer. . . . The Prime Minister gave a rather depressing broadcast at 8.

Sept. 28 . . . was in the House of Commons by 2.30 for the Prime Minister's speech. It was a most dramatic occasion—the House and galleries absolutely packed—a long narrative from Neville, culminating in an account of his "last last effort" for peace in another message to Hitler and one to Mussolini (Roosevelt had also sent another excellent appeal). The answers came as he was speaking—pressure from Musso and an invitation from Hitler to Munich tomorrow. There was a wonderful demonstration at this, but the House was unmistakably with him all through. . . . Rather a happier evening and a very good paper.

Sept. 29. The Prime Minister went off to Munich at dawn, seen off by all his Cabinet: was in conference with Hitler, Musso, and Daladier by noon, and so continued throughout the afternoon and evening till agreement, which was now inevitable, was reached soon after midnight. . . .

Sept. 30. A bit of a walk with Cecilia across Hyde Park, where tremendous A.R.P. works were in progress,[1] on my way to the office to dictate letters and set out the lines of tonight's leader. . . . I was in the office again all afternoon and evening save for a brief excursion at 6 to see the Prime Minister's triumphant return from Heston to Buckingham Palace, where there were tumultuous scenes. He brought with him not only the Czech Agreement, but a declaration signed by himself and Hitler pledging the future of Anglo-German relations—a great achievement whatever the sceptics might say and did begin to say in their evening speeches. . . . The news coming in from all over the world was a stream of wild congratulations and 50 letters to *The Times* clamoured for a National Fund in Neville's honour.

. . . . .

On few occasions in peace-time can the inhabitants of the British Commonwealth and Empire have been so united in applauding the

[1] Ten months later when I was in Warsaw I saw no trenches.

actions of a statesman as they were when Neville Chamberlain returned to London with Hitler's agreement. President Roosevelt sent one of the shortest messages of congratulation to Mr. Chamberlain on September 28—"Good Man" signed Roosevelt. The Press in Great Britain and in the Commonwealth paid generous tributes to his achievement in reaching agreement. In the first flush of enthusiasm and after a tremendous ovation in an impromptu speech, "Chamberlain did make a *faux pas*".[1] The phrase "Peace in Our Time", which has so often been used against him, did express what millions hoped would be the outcome of the Munich settlement—anyhow in the immediate first hours after the Prime Minister's dramatic flight back from his final visit to Hitler. If Chamberlain used those words after the intense strain of those fifteen days of negotiations, he certainly, in his calmer moments, was not hoodwinked by Hitler. He pushed forward with the rearmament of the Royal Air Force and the two other Services and with organization of civilian defence. Few Prime Ministers of the United Kingdom can have ever received more cordial messages from the Dominions, and not even Mr. Chamberlain can have rejoiced over their arrival more than Geoffrey, who all through his Editorships was so sensitive to Britain's need for carrying public opinion overseas with us.

On the morrow of Chamberlain's return to London, the Dawsons escorted Lady Halifax down to Eton where they found some of the boys "who'd had a grand time, sandbagging, digging, going to cinemas, meeting the Prime Minister at Heston yesterday, etc.!" On getting back to London the Dawsons saw "Duff Cooper's resignation" on the evening paper bills. This event drew in its wake a resignation at Printing House Square: that of Anthony Winn, Parliamentary Correspondent of *The Times*. Winn and Duff Cooper were in fact personal friends, and the latter referred in his autobiography to the incident as follows:

> He is working on *The Times*. He told us that *The Times* are starting tomorrow morning a correspondence on the desirability of the Czechs handing over the whole of the Sudeten territories to Germany. . . . Oliver (Stanley) and I took so serious a view of it that we rang up Downing Street, where we heard the Big Four were in conclave and we told the Private Secretary what we had heard. He rang me back about twenty minutes later and told me that Edward Halifax had taken the same view of it as we had, that he had immediately got on to Geoffrey Dawson and spoken to him very strongly. It was too late to stop the edition, but Dawson had promised to do his best to "bottle up" the

[1] *See* "The Foreign Policy of Neville Chamberlain", *The Quarterly Review*, No. 600, April, 1954, p. 150, Robert Sencourt.

correspondence, whatever that may mean. I suppose only not to continue it.[1]

In referring to his own speech in the House of Commons on Monday, October 3rd, Duff Cooper wrote: [2]

> One further consequence of that speech should be recorded. I had, during the crisis, seen a lot of Anthony Winn, a hard-working journalist, many years younger than myself, who, having served his apprenticeship in the Provinces, had recently acquired the post, an enviable one for a man of his age, of lobby correspondent to *The Times*. He duly reported the speech, and what had been thought of it. I never saw what he wrote, but it did not accord with the policy of the paper. Not only did the editor suppress it but he inserted a concoction of his own in which the speech was described as "a damp squib" and headed it "from our lobby correspondent". Anthony Winn resigned his position. . .

Let us turn to Geoffrey's diary:

> *Oct. 3.* Parliament resumed after the crisis. . . . I went to the House of Commons to hear Duff Cooper (who spoke fluently for 40 minutes without a note but was not very impressive) and the Prime Minister. House much less emotional than last week, but very full . . . On the whole the debates in both Houses seemed to justify our heading "An Impregnable Case."
>
> *Oct. 4.* . . . I had a bad time with tendentious Political Notes and Sketch and at midnight received a long and pompous letter of resignation from Anthony Winn.
>
> *Oct. 5.* A morning visit to the office, where I dispatched a far too kind reply to young Winn accepting his resignation, which was really a great relief. . . .

In his letter of resignation Winn had asserted his fundamental disagreement with the paper's view of the *Sudeten* question. Unable to rejoice in "this peace" he found himself bound to resign from the staff of a paper "which was the first responsible advocate of secession and still has hopes of a genuine friendship with the Nazi regime".

He also accused the Editor of inserting into his account of Duff Cooper's resignation "two thinly-veiled sneers at a man who was abandoning his career for his principles".

In his reply Geoffrey pointed out that *The Times* had certainly not been the first advocate of the secession of the *Sudeten* Germans, and far from envisaging genuine friendship with the Nazi regime, it aimed

[1] *Old Men Forget*, p. 227. Entry of September 12th. Published by Hart-Davis.
[2] Ibid., p. 249.

at genuine friendship with the German people. As for the article on Duff Cooper, Geoffrey's comment that he (Duff Cooper) would now have more time to devote himself to literature was the only one which might conceivably be interpreted as a sneer and was certainly not meant to be one.

In the penultimate paragraph of his letter, Geoffrey observed that the relations of the Parliamentary Correspondent and Printing House Square might be difficult and delicate "but they have been maintained with mutual goodwill for a long period of years by those of us who realize that a newspaper staff must work as a team if it is to be effective" —and he certainly meant what he said. He never forgot Kinglake's reference to the "Company" of *The Times*. Geoffrey constantly added a few lines or sentences to emphasize some special point. His colleagues accepted these corrections readily as they recognized how to the point they usually were. This common practice at Printing House Square was, apparently, resented by Winn.

If there were some critics of the European policy of *The Times*, which there undoubtedly were, the great majority of the readers endorsed the paper's attitude. Geoffrey received very large numbers of letters congratulating the paper on its leadership in the autumn of 1938. Many writers considered the plight of Europe was in part due to the terms of the Versailles Treaty of 1919. Many correspondents rejoiced that the paper refused to stir up hatred and suspicion between the European Powers. Nevertheless days of reaction soon followed the wild enthusiasm aroused immediately after Neville Chamberlain's return. There was a very genuine regret for the decision which reduced the Czechoslovak Republic—which had seemed to have so bright a future ahead of it under Thomas Masaryk—to impotence. No sooner was the Anglo-German Agreement concluded at Munich than Prague had to concede the claims of the Polish Minority and a month later the Hungarian Minority asserted its right to self-determination and also in November a pact between Poland and the Soviet was re-established.

The country was still behind the Munich policy in the autumn as the by-elections showed. The fresh outbreak of anti-Semitism in Nazi Germany in November caused much concern in Great Britain and spread a sense of foreboding. There was apparently little likelihood of Hitler ever becoming a good European, and every speech he made only added to the indignation felt by the British public and made the nation gladly accept a great acceleration in defensive measures and acquiesce readily in an income-tax increased to an unprecedented level in peace-time.

Geoffrey spent a happy birthday (his sixty-fourth) with his family, "the faithful Nigger" (the poodle) bringing a silk handkerchief in his mouth to his bedside betimes. The evening was spent at Magdalen "to commemorate the 250th anniversary of the Restoration of the Fellows. A pleasant evening". The following day after "a more than usually feverish time" at Printing House Square there is this revealing entry: "The accumulation of work in the office and the repeated visits to Oxford, are becoming rather a strain"—one of the first occasions that Geoffrey admits to feeling the strain of his work. I cannot help wishing that he had realized how great was the cumulative strain of his twenty-two years of editorship which included the very difficult years with Northcliffe; the long and exacting campaign on behalf of Indian reform; the establishment of the National Government and the Abdication crisis. Various attempts had been made to get him to consider the possibility of letting his name go forward for influential posts at Oxford or Eton. Had he done so after the Abdication crisis, in my view years might have been added to his life.

The diary for the post-Munich months suggests no definite moment when the conviction became general that Hitler would disregard any pledges to achieve his aims. Certainly by early in 1939 many people realized that once again the free world would have to face a more dangerous Germany than even that of Kaiser Wilhelm and his Prussian war lords.

XXXII

1939—EVE OF SECOND WORLD WAR

THE fact that Geoffrey occupied the editorial chair at Printing House Square during the years before two world wars lends a particular interest to his Editorship and entitles it to be classed in a different category from those of his predecessors with the exception of Thomas Barnes, who, with the backing of John Walter II, made *The Times* into "The Thunderer".

The decade before the coming of the second World War had been one of progressive disillusionment with the exception of two interludes of national rejoicing at home during the Silver Jubilee festivities in 1935, and the Coronation in 1937, after the dark days of the Abdication Crisis. There was none of the enthusiasm in the first days of September, 1939, that there had been in 1914. The 'thirties had opened with the world slump which had shaken the financial foundations of the entire English-speaking world. "Human atomic bombs" in the persons of the dictators in Berlin, Moscow and Rome were at large and no one could foresee where the next explosion would take place. Down the ages mankind had been exhorted to be big enough to face its destiny, but the text-books contained no advice on how to deal with a Hitler, a Stalin or a Mussolini. If most nations refused to face facts in the years from 1930 onwards it was understandable—many of the ideals the previous generation had believed in seemed to be in jeopardy. It is all very well to say that when the dictators embarked on some fresh coup we should have stood firm. The fundamental mistake of the immediate era after the first World War, was that the idealism of Woodrow Wilson and all the champions of "collective security" ignored the vital fact that the moral standpoint was not enough if it were not backed by force.

What was the use of a Peace Ballot in the United Kingdom? The British Nation was a satiated power, a "have" nation—where peace propaganda was needed was in Nazi Germany, in Soviet Russia and in Fascist Italy. If only the dictators would leave the progressive nations alone! That was the futile hope. At few moments in history did the United Kingdom stand in a worse position for crying halt to aggression. Many behind the scenes knew that there was something rotten in the state of France—she had never recovered from her terrible losses in the first World War. The great American electorate was determined to keep out of European and Asiatic entanglements. My wife and I travelled widely in North America in 1937–38–40 and 41. The public sentiment seemed to become ever more strongly isolationist. As late as in April, 1941, when the proud city of Washington was looking at its best and tens of thousands of "war workers" (American workers engaged in producing war material for Britain) were crowding the streets to view the cherry blossom on the Potomac —the trees had been presented to President Taft by the Emperor of Japan—large processions of motor coaches full of American mothers were driving slowly through the main thoroughfares, with banners flying which proclaimed that they would not let their boys fight!

From Geoffrey's personal standpoint it was evident that by the year 1939 he was beginning to feel the terrific strain of editing *The Times* for over twenty-two years—how great that strain had been even he, probably, had not previously realized; but there are signs in the diaries after the Abdication that his body did begin to show signs of fatigue. In June he talks about his "intermittent sciatica", and later in the year he mentions that, after shooting, he "suffered at intervals from spasms in the leg and all the time from lack of practice and exercise". He had evidently made up his mind that he would be unable to occupy the editorial chair much longer.

There is the following reference in the diary to his position as Editor:

> *March 27*. . . . I looked in on Vi (Lady Violet Astor) on my way home to dinner—to impart to her my increasing years and my view that this must be the last of them in Printing House Square.

In a memorandum on "Second Retirement from *The Times*", 1938–41 (dated September 23rd, 1941), he wrote:

> Towards the end of 1938, when I was just 64, I came to the conclusion that it was time to think of making promotion for younger men and that 65 was approximately the proper age for retirement. I told the chairman

this, giving him in effect a year in which to find a successor—a choice about which we were not likely to differ. In the following April I wrote him (Colonel Astor) the following letter:

23, Sussex Place,
Regent's Park, N.W.1,
April 4, 1939.

My dear John,

I thought it was right to tell you before Christmas that I was within a year of the time which I had always regarded as the proper limit (if I should last so long!) of my Editorship of *The Times*. I gave the same intimation also to John Walter, who shares with you the duty of appointing my successor. Though I do not suppose that it will be a difficult matter, it seemed desirable that you should have ample notice of my intentions, and my object in writing to you now is only to put them on record beyond any possibility of misunderstanding.

I do not want to pretend that I have worn myself out in the service of *The Times* or that I am incapable of further exertion. In many respects I feel as young as ever, and I know how sorely I shall miss the work and interest and companionship of Printing House Square. Still less (need I add?) is there any question of disagreement or difficulty within the office. The confidence and generosity with which I have been treated by the Chief Proprietors and the Board have only been equalled by the wonderful co-operation of the whole staff. There is no rift, I hope and believe, between any of us.

But I have always had a horror of the sort of situation which I have seen in some other offices and businesses, where a man grows older and slower without realizing it himself, and his friends are too kind to point it out to him. It seems incredible to me, but it is a sobering fact, that it is thirty-three years since I began to contribute to *The Times* as its South African Correspondent and twenty-seven since I was first appointed its Editor. Moreover I am convinced that, in a large organization like that of *The Times*, there should be a steady flow of promotion if the staff is to remain contented and up to the highest standard of efficiency. It will always be difficult for Editors to suggest to their colleagues that the time for retirement comes to all of us unless they are themselves prepared to practise what they preach.

In saying this I must not be taken as subscribing to the dangerous heresy that everyone should retire at a certain age or after a certain period of service. There are obvious differences in this matter between the various professions, between this and that branch of the same profession, and between one individual and another. But the responsibility for editing *The Times* is so exacting, so continuous, and so delightful that the temptation to cling to it too long is peculiarly insidious. Nothing would distress me more than to feel that by yielding to it I was becoming a drag on the great institution with which I have been proud to be associated for so long.

I am clear therefore that you should regard this as the last year of my Editorship and should settle the precise date for my retirement as suits the paper best. I have said nothing of my intention to any member of the staff, for the reason that I am anxious to do what I can to make the change as smooth and inconspicuous as possible.

Yours ever,
GEOFFREY DAWSON.

Colonel Astor replied:

18, Carlton House Terrace, S.W.1,
April 5th, '39.

My dear Geoffrey,

Very many thanks for your letter which sets out the reasons for the decision you had previously spoken to me about.

I will tell the other Directors of it at an early date—and can imagine the dismay with which they will receive it. Their regret will certainly not be more personal or more genuine than mine.

If you had based your arguments on old age or its effects or shortcomings, I would have said that you obviously would have no case for many years. But when you talk of age, and its general applications, it is not so easy to argue.

There are many things I would like to say—and I hope to convey my sentiments some time!—but I think you know them, and thank Heavens the time has not come yet.

This is only to say that your letter fills me with intense regret and sadness. And I hate it.

Yours ever,
JOHN.

In his memorandum (of September 23rd, 1941) Geoffrey continues:

I kept Barrington-Ward informed of all that was going on and had no hesitation in commending him as my successor. He had been the obvious deputy man ever since 1927, when I brought him back to *The Times* from the *Observer* with this change in view. The whole office knew it and had latterly (since Brumwell's departure) been accustomed to his being in charge whenever I was away. He was duly selected and so informed.

Then, in September of the same year, came the war, with all the dislocation caused in the office at once by the departure of younger men for the armed forces and of various experts borrowed by Government Departments. There was general agreement that this was not the moment for a change in the editorship and that I should carry on for the time being. It must have been soon after the outbreak that I wrote the Chairman a letter of which the following is an extract:

> In this connexion you know my own position, though the office in general does not. It has of course been radically changed by the outbreak of war. I think you agree that I should not give up my work

here in present circumstances, and I should certainly be most reluctant to do so.[1] But, however that may be, you must regard as cancelled what you were kind enough to say about a pension when the time *does* come; and in the meantime I am entirely in your hands in the matter of salary.

I know that Kent has written to you to offer a large percentage reduction in his own case. Mine should naturally be larger. I have not considered it myself, and am *more* than ready to accept whatever you and the Board think reasonable.

In Geoffrey's book of cuttings is a short leading article taken from the *Evening Standard* of the 24th May, 1939, headed "Propagandist" and it shows how high was Lord Beaverbrook's opinion of Geoffrey as a propagandist.

The *Daily Telegraph* wants a Ministry of Propaganda to be set up in peace-time. It conceives such a department as a valuable addition to Britain's defensive structure. This newspaper, on the other hand, is opposed to a Ministry of Propaganda until war breaks out, for the oft-stated reason: "Thrice is he armed that hath his quarrel just." But if there is to be a Propaganda Minister, the greatest propagandist in the town is Mr. Geoffrey Dawson, Editor of *The Times*.

It is no slur on Mr. Dawson to say that. On the contrary, it is a declaration of positive and definite admiration. And never has Mr. Dawson's skill as a propagandist been shown to better advantage than during the past twelve months. You may disapprove of his views, although they are generally based upon common sense, but you must acknowledge the adroitness with which they are urged on the public. And, usually, Mr. Dawson wins through. His attitude prevails. Certainly, the popular Press is as nothing, in the way of propaganda, when compared with the unpopular newspapers. Put together the four popular papers, the *Daily Express*, the *Daily Mail*, the *News Chronicle* and the *Daily Herald*, do not carry nearly as much propaganda as the other two.

Geoffrey kept a very full diary for the year 1939 and it covers an immense number of subjects, though the items are of a more general nature perhaps than in 1914. On January 9th, after his conference at *The Times* office, he took tea with Edward (Lord Halifax) at the Foreign Office, "off on his visit to Rome tomorrow".

Towards the end of January the Editor spent an hour with Weizman (first President of the Jewish State)—"very impressive—as usual". There are references to several talks with R. H. Brand who, on January 21st, "carried me off for an hour's talk or more—very con-

[1] As a matter of fact Geoffrey continued to occupy the editorial chair till September 30th, 1941.

vinced about the German peril". The entry of January 23rd is as follows: "Rather a depressing day—by reason of rumours from the Continent and a bout of the 'jitters' in England. Edward with whom I lunched at Brooks's, was rather under the shadow of the Foreign Office; and indeed there was plenty of cause for anxiety. McDonald,[1] visiting the Foreign Office, brought back some rather over-categorical forecasts of German intentions. I kept them to myself, but they were distracting and people began to ring me up again to ask whether it was safe to go abroad. The Prime Minister broadcast an appeal for National Service for Civilian Defence . . . long prearranged to precede the issue of the National Service guide tomorrow." The diary for January 25th ends with the words "A more and more threatening situation in Europe". On January 26th the Editor commended Sir Samuel Hoare who "was delivering a good speech about the 'jitter bugs' and the strength of the Empire, and we gave this a good deal of prominence and comment". Later that same evening, Geoffrey had a talk with the Prime Minister "whom I found quite unrattled and not at all disposed to anticipate Hitler with a dramatic speech tomorrow night". Geoffrey was giving much attention to the problem of the settlement of Jewish refugees from the dictator countries, especially from Nazi Germany, a subject which he discussed with me on several occasions. He was interested in the possibility of a large tract of territory in Northern Rhodesia being definitely reserved for them. On another occasion he met friends to talk about the Syrians and the settlement of refugees in British Guiana.

The final entry in the diary for the month notes "a more cheerful atmosphere" in the City. The optimism, however, was of short duration for this entry occurs, "Not so reassuring was Bob. . . . It was a repetition of the case for a Continental army which he had poured out to me at Eydon,[2] and on many other occasions." I have read the interesting correspondence which passed between Geoffrey and Brand during the immediate years before the outbreak of the second World War. Through his banking connections and his visits to Paris, Berlin and Washington, Brand had special opportunities of correctly summing up the possibilities of the danger of a second World War. Certainly his warnings were fully borne out by events.

Defence problems were much to the fore early in February. Two articles on the subject by Liddell Hart appeared in *The Times*, and on the 7th the Editor had a talk with Inskip (Minister of Defence). At a Board luncheon at *The Times* office on February 9th Geoffrey sat next

[1] Mr. Iverach McDonald, then Diplomatic Correspondent of *The Times*; since 1952 Foreign Editor.

[2] Lord Brand's house in the country.

to General Ismay, Secretary of the Committee of Imperial Defence. On February 13th Sir John Anderson produced a limited scheme of camps for evacuation. On the last Sunday in February Geoffrey and his wife "paid a pilgrimage to Delane's tomb in Easthampstead churchyard, which needs restoration".

Early in March a major crisis in Central Europe drew the attention of all the world once more to Czechoslovakia. On March 10th the Premier of Slovakia, one of the minorities, had been dismissed by the President of the Republic, Hacha, the successor of Benes and a politician lacking firmness. He was summoned to Berlin by Hitler and by March 13th German troops had crossed the Czech frontier. By March 15th Hitler was in Prague and Czechoslovakia was "liquidated".

Geoffrey's day-to-day comments in the diary were as follows:

March 12. . . . Czechs and Slovaks were scrapping in Bratislava.

March 13. . . . Hitler was absolutely taking charge of the Czechoslovak trouble in his usual bullying way.

March 14. . . . news of the Czech crisis grew till midnight and after.

March 15. . . . I went down afterwards to the House of Commons and was lucky enough to get Cecilia into the Gallery too. Neville Chamberlain making a restrained but well-received statement on the invasion of Czechoslovakia (which Edward was doing in the Lords). . . . Hitler was by this time in the Castle of King Wenceslas.

March 17. . . . The Prime Minister was speaking in Birmingham, the eve of his seventieth birthday, and we listened to the broadcast,[1] which was world-wide, during dinner at Sarsden (near Oxford). He said all the right things about Hitler's broken pledges—rather as if speaking to a brief, as indeed he was. No doubt it put him right after his restraint in the House of Commons.

March 19. . . . The crisis was in full blast—Ministers and diplomats all working overtime: but there was no positive news. . . .

March 20. . . . At 5 I went down to the House of Lords to hear Edward, very good, though there was little positive to say—a tremendous audience of peers and prelates and a queue waiting at every door. The situation was definitely less tense.

March 21. . . . Meanwhile the French President and Madame Lebrun were arriving in sunshine and an enormous crowd was pouring back from the Mall . . . a party of French journalists supped in the office.

March 22. . . . I walked back along the Embankment and met the French procession, returning from Guildhall, in sunshine and splendour.

The month of March ended with a flamboyant speech delivered by Mussolini at a Fascist celebration in Rome, a talk with Sam Hoare

[1] There was hardly anything he would not sacrifice for peace, "but there is one thing that I must except, and that is the liberty that we have enjoyed for hundreds of years, and which we could never surrender".

concerned with his duties of supervision of Information—"if the worst should happen". A lunch with the Rothschilds in New Court, and on Tuesday, 28th March, an entry: "Some thirty M.P.s headed by Winston and Anthony, tabled a rather woolly resolution on the subject" (Defence and preparedness). "Meanwhile Madrid had finally fallen." On Wednesday 29th, Geoffrey writes: "The Winston-Eden motion was countered by an amendment with getting on for 200 signatures expressing confidence in the Prime Minister. The main news was Daladier's broadcast reply to Mussolini—conciliatory but quite firm." March 30th was "an anxious unsatisfactory sort of day. The Cabinet had an unexpected meeting in the morning and its Foreign Affairs Committee in the afternoon. The problem was the fear of a Nazi attack on Poland, about which the lobby was much excited." The entry for March 31st follows: ". . . Ned Grigg and I dashed off early to hear the Prime Minister's expected statement on Poland,[1] a very careful document, read to a crowded and very welcoming House. I looked in on the buzzing lobby before going back to Printing House Square to deal with it. . . ."

While April may not have been quite as stormy a month as March, it was not without its sensations. On the occasion of a visit to London of Colonel Beck, the Polish Foreign Minister, there were scenes of great activity in diplomatic circles and the implications of the British guarantee of support to Poland should its independence be menaced, were fully discussed. On April 1st *The Times* published a leader on Poland which caused some critical Foreign Office and left wing comment. The leader was thus referred to in the diary of April 3rd: "A good deal of to-do about Saturday's leader which was suspected (quite wrongly) of watering down the British declaration . . . it also ran the gauntlet in the House of Commons where there was a big debate in the afternoon and an admirable speech from the Prime Minister. . . ."

For several days there were "wild scares and rumours". Geoffrey, however, escaped to Langcliffe for a week at Easter and noted that the wireless at 9 p.m. on April 6th, recorded the last afternoon in Parliament—"the Polish Treaty made reciprocal." The entry for Good Friday (April 7th) was as follows: "Cecilia had heard on the telephone . . . that the Italians had suddenly invaded Albania, and the B.B.C. issued a series of bulletins. I got the facts, so far as they were known, from Barrington-Ward later in the evening and had a long talk about the

[1] In the House of Commons Neville Chamberlain said: "In the event of any action which clearly threatened Polish independence, and which the Polish Government accordingly considered it vital to resist with their national forces, His Majesty's Government would feel themselves bound at once to lend the Polish Government all support in their power."

paper and plans. There seemed to be no excuse whatever for this Good Friday outrage—at any rate none had been put forward."

In the diary on April 12th Geoffrey wrote: ". . . I lunched at the Travellers' where old Goodenough introduced me to two interesting sailors—Godfrey (Naval Intelligence at the Admiralty) and Troubridge, son of the Admiral (Naval Attaché in Berlin, where he reported the people passionately anti-war and with no stomach for a fight). . . . Edward has taken the measure of the Soviet, who are not out to help."

On April 13th the Prime Minister's statement proclaimed that Great Britain was also giving a guarantee to Rumania and Greece. There were great crowds in Whitehall and Geoffrey went to the House of Commons to hear the Prime Minister make "a good restrained narrative and declaration".

> *April 14.* A good reception for the British declaration, except, of course, from the Dictator Press.
>
> *April 15.* . . . dined at the Travellers' where the tape was gradually unfolding Roosevelt's personal message to the two Dictators.

In the leading article "The President's Message" (April 17th), the paper referred to the President's obvious great desire to help in averting "the disaster that impends" . . . The delivery of the speech was followed at once by the despatch of two personal messages to the leaders of the German and Italian peoples, copies of them being furnished simultaneously to the other European Governments. . . . "They contain a definite request which invites a definite answer . . . It is a palpable fact, and one which recent events make it impossible to ignore, that it is only from Germany and Italy that Europe has reason in these days to fear a flagrant act of aggression."

Few people can have been more pleased than Geoffrey when the official announcement of Lothian's appointment as British Ambassador to the United States was made. From the first Geoffrey had recommended Lothian as the most suitable candidate. In the leading article "The Washington Embassy" (April 25th) the Editor wrote: "Washington is one of the few capitals—perhaps the only capital left—to which the appointment of a British Ambassador from outside the regular Diplomatic Service will hardly be criticized even by those who belong to it . . . Washington is different . . . some of the greatest Ambassadors to Washington—James Bryce is the conspicuous example—have not been professionals. . . . Certainly it would be difficult to find a candidate more obviously fitted by temperament and training for this particular post than Lord Lothian must seem to those who know him best."

At the end of April Geoffrey writes that there was "intense activity and an obvious tending towards some form of compulsory training and service". On the 26th April the entry refers to "the Prime Minister's important announcement in the House of Commons . . . compulsory national training for all between 20 and 21 with other measures of 'preparedness'".

April 27. . . . A very satisfactory debate on Compulsion in the House of Commons with good speeches by Neville Chamberlain, Winston and Hore-Belisha.

April 28. Hitler's *Reichstag* speech in answer to President Roosevelt—much advertised, well circulated, conveniently in our hands by the early afternoon . . . to the office to read the speech carefully. . . . I decided to give the whole text and sub-edited it myself. It regarded the Naval Treaty (Anglo-German Naval Treaty of 1935) at an end—also the pact with Poland—but the rest was an elaborate vindication of German post-war policy, rather cleverly done.

April 30. . . . Edward came alone to lunch with us and we had a good talk about Poland, Ireland, Hitler's speech, and Maisky's return from Russia &c. . . . A tiresome (though relatively minor) worry was a message from Lumby (*The Times* Correspondent) to say that his presence in Rome was considered inadvisable by Mussolini for some trumpery reason. What fools they are!

May 2. . . . I called on Grandi (the Italian Ambassador) to talk about our own extruded Lumby. He was extremely friendly and obviously intended to be helpful. . . .

May 3. . . . The Prime Minister gave the usual answer on "encirclement", Poland, and the U.S.S.R. . . . At midnight came the news of Litvinoff's resignation (or extrusion) but the cause was still obscure. More silly reprisals on journalists and others between London and Berlin.

May 7. . . . I dined with Edward and Dorothy (Halifax) before going to the office to deal with the newly concluded Military Pact between the Axis Powers. It didn't alter the situation much, as Edward agreed, and the principal preoccupation was Russia.

May 10. . . . The Prime Minister made a statement on the negotiations with the Soviet. . . .

There are several references to the negotiations being conducted with Russia and on May 24th the Prime Minister "made a reassuring statement on the still continuing negotiations with Russia,[1] though

[1] When in Berlin early in July I was warned by a well-informed German friend (an anti-Nazi) to keep my eyes on Moscow. This friend implied that the Nazi Government was trying to cut the ground from under the feet of the British Delegation at the Kremlin. But the thought that the Nazis were seriously flirting with the U.S.S.R. seemed too proposterous for credence. Nevertheless when I was told by British friends in Moscow late in July, that there was a fifty-fifty chance of a treaty with the Soviet, I recalled my German friend's warning.

two weeks later there are entries "Russian talks still dragging on" and on June 20th, "a little talk with Edward (Halifax) who had little to report either of Tientsin or of Moscow, but confessed that he was batting on a sticky wicket". The diary for June 13th refers to the world situation thus: ". . . The news—Germany, Japan, Spain—was none of it very satisfactory." On the 21st Geoffrey attended the *Encænia* at Oxford where his sense of humour was aroused as he was seated between two Ambassadors—"Alba and Mr. (status) Quo.[1] What a world!" On the 22nd he was present at Waterloo in a private stand when Their Majesties the King and Queen were welcomed home from their very successful visit to Canada and the United States: "The scenes outside were tumultuous and lasted well into the night. We went to press early with the picture supplement of the amazing tour. It dominated the news not otherwise too good."

Geoffrey received the following letter (June 28, 1939) from Brand:

> One hears in various quarters that now that the Government have to face the consequences of their Polish guarantee, they may be hesitating. Heaven knows none of us want a war. But, if we have another Munich, then no one in the world will follow us, and Europe, East and Central, must all line up with Germany. The Peace Front disappears with appeasement. I heard the P.M. a very short time ago sing a Paean of Praise in honour of Munich as a great success, so he may want another. The Government must have willed the means with the end. Surely the only thing they *can* do is to stand up to their guarantee boldly. Perhaps that and its effect on Mussolini is the last chance of preserving peace: certainly it is the last chance of peace with honour. I do hope *The Times* will take this line. . . .
>
> I believe the moment is to the last extent critical and that we ought to form some form of National Government. If that is impossible owing to the P.M. then the Government should be strengthened by bringing in people like Winston, who will make a firm stand and will be known throughout the world to be ready for a firm stand. As at present constituted the Cabinet seem either "career" men or hopeless mugwumps.[2] . . .

Some extracts from the diary follow:

July 3. . . . The *Daily Telegraph* joined in the hue and cry for the inclusion of Winston in the Cabinet in order to impress the Germans. We continued the more effective process of calling attention to the growing strength of the British Army. . . .

[1] The Chinese Ambassador's real name was Quo Tai-chi.

[2] Mr. Dermot Morrah suggests that Brand was thinking of Geoffrey's favourite definition of a mugwump, "a politician who sits on the fence, with his mug on one side and his wump on the other".

July 6. . . . I went down to the House of Commons for a brief talk with the Prime Minister who was full of vigour, had no intention of being bounced into taking back Winston, didn't hope much of Russia but thought we should get agreement.[1]

July 13. . . . The Government announced Reserve Fleet Exercises in August–September.

July 21. . . . to see Philip (Lothian) who was much impressed by the imminence of the crisis, . . . a long talk with Professor Nock, whom I had met long ago in Rome, just back now from Germany. His main impression was of a people terrified at the thought of war—quite unlike 1914, he thought, but not likely to move against it. . . .

July 31. . . . I went to the office in the afternoon. A wind-up debate on Foreign Affairs was raging in the Commons. . . . In an interval I went down to hear the latter part of the Prime Minister's reply to Sinclair and Dalton, who had been casting every sort of aspersion on their country (and incidentally on me and "Scrutator"!).

August 3. . . . A foreign affairs debate was raging in the Lords and produced an admirable speech from Edward (by way of contrast with a rash prediction of Tom Inskip's, who was simultaneously proclaiming that "there would be no war").

August 10. (*The Times*) Film and Black-Out. Russell spent the morning being filmed solo and the whole conference assembled for this purpose at 3.15—an extraordinary performance— . . . "continuity girl" taking notes, brilliant lamps and cameras everywhere, Paul Rotha directing. This lasted an hour and was followed by 2 short scenes in my room (leaders with Barrington-Ward and letters with Gavin Brown). At every interval we prepared once more for the Black-Out and very early printing . . . at 11.20. p.m. with 1st Edition complete, and went with Cecilia to Primrose Hill, to see the lights going out in London and the flashing search-light beams. A very muddy walk back.

August 11. . . . Lunch at the Garrick with Vincent Massey, who had a project of buying American battleships (I suggested swapping them for a lease of naval bases).

August 21. Langcliffe . . . the news from my office after dinner decided me to go to London tomorrow.

August 22. . . . No doubt I was right to come at once and Brodribb was visibly relieved. Our late edition this morning (not available in Leeds) had carried the somewhat startling news of an impending Nazi-Soviet Pact and of Ribbentrop going to Moscow to sign it. This justified the suspicion of Russian good faith which some of us had long held and explained all their dilatory negotiations.

August 23. A great deal of telephoning and note-making at home before visiting the Prime Minister in Downing Street at 11.45. . . . N.C. seemed well and friendly—rather angry with all foreigners—Hitler and the Bolshies for their duplicity, the French for giving confidential

[1] *Vide* footnote *supra*, p. 392.

information away. He told me of his letter to Hitler being delivered by Henderson today. . . . "X" wrote on the Nazi-Soviet Pact. . . .

August 24. . . . Went on to the House of Commons to hear the Prime Minister and Greenwood—a one-day session, absolutely packed, to pass the Emergency Bill through all its stages in both Houses, which it did, by about 10 p.m. The situation was looking pretty black. Ribbentrop returning from Moscow, Hitler going to Berlin to meet him, anti-Polish campaign intensified in German Press. My own staff was becoming stronger. . . . Pronouncements by Roosevelt and the Pope. . . .

August 25. . . . The crisis grew and changed from hour to hour. A summons by Hitler to Nevile Henderson, who is flying to London tomorrow. Military demonstrations in Berlin. Anti-Pole, Anti-British Press campaign. More appeals from Roosevelt. At midnight the cancellation of Sunday's Tannenberg Celebrations.

Saturday, August 26. No visit to the office where there was a "victim" who read me the news at intervals. . . . Nevile Henderson arrived with Hitler's note at 12, was closeted with Edward and the Prime Minister and attended a Cabinet at 6.30. to discuss the reply. I dined with Edward and Dorothy (who cooked the meal to which I contributed some Woodside figs[1]). He went back to the Foreign Office to continue drafting at 10 and I walked most of the way home slowly and put some ideas for a leader on paper before going to bed.

Sunday, August 27. . . . I went round for an hour's talk with the returned Barrington-Ward very brown and fit. . . . The Cabinet met again over draft reply to Hitler and decided to meet finally tomorrow and then send Nevile Henderson back. He had had a shorter and not too satisfactory interview with the French Ambassador. . . . The Russian-German Pact with the Nazis was bringing us friends.

The Editor thus dealt with the political situation in a leading article "Sir Nevile Henderson's Visit" (August 28th):

Public attention must needs be concentrated, at this eleventh hour of the gathering storm, on the communications with the German Government which have been in progress during the last two days. . . . In the meantime, however, the mere news of the Ambassador's mission provides a basis for examining the British attitude towards negotiation.

It could hardly be better stated, or more concisely, than in the latest message to the German people which was issued at the week-end by the British National Council of Labour. "There need be no war," the message ran, "if the threat of force is renounced. But if Poland is attacked, Germany will be at war not with Poland only but, from the first day, with Great Britain and France, who both stand firmly by their pledges. We have no wish to destroy the German people."

[1] Lady Wenlock was living at Woodside, near Hatfield.

The article continued:

There is nothing in fact that might not be settled by the civilized method of negotiation if only there were confidence that negotiation would not be paralysed by threats of violence and that any resulting settlement would be honoured. It was not "Munich" that destroyed confidence in German good faith but the fact that the Munich Settlement was followed five months later by the brutal invasion of the very peoples which it was designed to preserve.

Monday, August 28. . . . The Cabinet met again to pass the draft to Germany and decided to have a sitting of Parliament tomorrow . . . to see Sam Hoare, who had issued a spate of regulations under the Emergency Act. . . . It was very sultry and there was a depressing prevalence of war preparations, crowds and hammering everywhere. . . .

Tuesday, August 29. Lunching at the Travellers'. . . . I found various Ministers, Jim Stanhope, Euan Wallace, etc., and Vincent Massey. . . . I also met Edward alone in St. James's Park afterwards and walked with him at his suggestion to the Foreign Office. The sitting of Parliament was very short, not informative, but quite unanimous. The German reply did *not* come in the mystery aeroplane, as the evening papers alleged, but was telegraphed much later and kept Edward and the Prime Minister in conference long after midnight. There were curious alternating waves of optimism and pessimism, but I did not feel that the outlook was very good.

Wednesday, August 30. . . . Lunched with Waldorf (Astor) at the Ritz to meet Congressman Hamilton Fish and his wife. . . . Both Fish (fresh from Berlin) and David (Astor) with his young German contacts were convinced that there would be no war. But McDonald brought rather gloomy reports in the afternoon from the French and the Poles.

Thursday, August 31. . . . A little before 10 p.m., the leaders being completed, the Germans broadcast their 16 points of a settlement with the Poles. They looked at first sight as at least a possible basis for negotiation. Then came the news that neither the British Government nor (till an hour ago) the Polish Government had had them and everything, so far as the paper went, was in the melting pot again. We got out a First Edition somehow, packed McDonald off to the Foreign Office for a midnight conference, and re-cast the paper once more. I got to bed about 2 pretty hopeless.

Friday, Sept. 1. . . . We had a meeting in John's (Astor's) room at 3.30 p.m. to discuss the stand-by Kettering arrangements,[1] about which

[1] *The Times* at that time had made complete arrangements, if Printing House Square was badly bombed, to transport itself to a newspaper office at Kettering. Happily, although Printing House Square was badly bombed, *The Times* was able to remain in London.

there had been some confusion of thought. I laid out the leaders as well as I could . . . correspondence with Germany which was issued as a White Paper when the House met at 6 p.m. I went down to this, heard Neville and Greenwood, and returned with further ideas for leaders. There was the first of the regular "Black-Outs" and I had some difficulty in getting back to Printing House Square from the Travellers' where I had been giving Bob (Brand) dinner. German troops had invaded Poland early in the morning, but it was difficult to get accurate news of the advance. Difficult also to declare war without the French, who were awaiting their Chamber tomorrow.

Saturday, Sept. 2. . . . had a talk with the Prime Minister in Downing Street, which was a hive of activity. . . . The Prime Minister himself wanted to unfold his plans for a War Cabinet, Labour on the whole preferring to stand out, Winston and Hankey to come in, a body of 6 with the Prime Minister, Edward (Halifax), Simon, and Chatfield. I fell to writing on all this when I returned to London and had had the latest news from the office. Parliament had been sitting and there had been some feeling in the House of Commons over delay. Edward was swept off to the Prime Minister just as he was coming out to dinner, and Dorothy and I dined at the Savoy Grill, where we encountered various Ministers preparing to meet again. . . .

Sunday, Sept. 3. WAR.

XXXIII

SECOND WORLD WAR—FIRST MONTHS

In the first months of the second World War the fog of war was "foggier than ever", to use Geoffrey's words. Certainly compared with the first weeks of the first World War the struggle of 1939 was indeed a strange one. The chief difference, from the writer's standpoint, is that one of the main sources of information in the years 1914–18 was the admirable periodic survey which Geoffrey wrote throughout the war, to a small group of friends abroad, explaining what was happening behind the scenes. In the second World War there are no such valuable papers.

Nothing seemed to go according to anticipation. Later on the first few months came to be regarded as the "phoney" war. Vast sums had been spent in equipping the population with gas masks, but there was no gas attack. Devastating raids on England had been expected on the outbreak of war, and balloon barrages above our big cities floated in the skies ready for attack, which did not take place. The long-prepared evacuation of children from the large towns was promptly and efficiently carried out, but as the days passed and no air-raids took place the return of the refugees soon presented a difficult problem.

Compared with the 1914 war the nation's "home front" was infinitely better prepared because, after Hitler's annexation of Czechoslovakia in March, in spite of his solemn pledges, the threat of a second World War became much more imminent. On the outbreak of war a civil defence army of two and a half millions of A.R.P. (Air Raid Precautions) workers was in existence; steel shelters to protect six and a half millions had been distributed; in addition, a very large number of Government departments and big firms moved to pre-arranged quarters throughout the country. By the third day in the war 200,000 beds were ready for civilian casualties in the event of air-raids. As the months passed and the *Luftwaffe* did not put in an appearance on a large scale, there was a steady return to normal in London and the big industrial cities.

The world had one of the greatest surprises on record when on August 21st, 1939, the Nazis, who had proclaimed that their mission was "to defend European civilization from Bolshevism", announced that they were about to sign a non-aggression pact with Soviet Russia. I was in Sweden when this amazing *volte-face* was announced and Swedish friends, who had heard the news on the wireless, came and congratulated my wife and me "on this act of treachery by Stalin (who had been negotiating the pact at the very moment when the Soviet had been discussing with Great Britain and France the signing of a treaty of neutrality) for there would now be no necessity for the Western allies to come to the rescue of Poland, in accordance with their former pledges". It was with difficulty that we explained that Britain and France would all the more feel that they must stand by their solemn engagement to Poland, now threatened on two sides.

The signing of the neutrality pact between Hitler and Stalin in Moscow on August 23rd meant that the threat of war, which had been growing for many months, had finally matured—but actually twelve extraordinary days passed before Neville Chamberlain, the man of peace, who had worked to prevent a struggle, as have few national leaders in history, declared on Sunday, September 3rd, that Great Britain was at war with Germany.

The second World War began more dramatically than the first owing to wireless when the nation shared the supreme moment and when Neville Chamberlain—"admirable in language and voice"—made his broadcast on Sunday, September 3rd, 1939, which Geoffrey heard in Printing House Square.[1] Never has there been a more dramatic meeting of the two Houses of Parliament than on that Sunday, at noon, when the Commons and the Lords heard respectively from the Prime Minister and Lord Halifax that the ultimatum to Berlin had remained unanswered and that Britain and Germany were at war.

On September 3rd, Chamberlain formed a War Cabinet of nine members, one of whom was Mr. Churchill, First Lord of the Admiralty —a post which he had held twenty-five years earlier on the outbreak of the first World War—and the following day the King broadcast a message to the nation in which he used the words "Stand calm, firm and united".

[1] I heard that the nation was at war at St. Paul's Church, Brighton, when the preacher was in the midst of his sermon. Suddenly the congregation heard the sirens and the atmosphere became electric. The priest asked the congregation to remain seated; he said that he did not think the sirens signified that there was an air-raid, but that they were intended to inform the public that we were at war with Germany, the Government's time limit having expired.

Apart from German activity at sea around Great Britain and Northern Ireland—Southern Ireland remained neutral—nothing dramatic occurred on the "home front", in marked contrast to what was taking place on the continent of Europe. September opened with the bombing of Warsaw by the Nazi Air Force on the pretext that the Poles had rejected the Führer's terms of peace, which they had, in fact, not even seen. On September 4th—the day after the R.A.F. raid on Wilhelmshaven—the first R.A.F. leaflet raid on Germany took place. On September 11th, the British Expeditionary Force, under Lord Gort, and under the supreme command of General Gamelin, crossed the Channel. On September 12th the Anglo-French Supreme War Council was formed. On the 17th Soviet troops invaded Poland and the following day Russian and German troops met at Brest-Litovsk. By October 1st the German troops had entered Warsaw and four days later Hitler arrived there. Poland was partitioned by the two "gangsters".

Some extracts from Geoffrey's diary during the first months of the second World War follow:

> *Sunday, September 3rd, 1939.*—WAR—I was in Printing House Square before 11.00 at which hour the notice to Hitler expired and heard the P.M.'s broadcast . . . 15 minutes later. . . . Thence Coote and I were going to the House, which was to meet at 12, when the sirens went for a very prompt air raid warning and the streets were cleared and London went to ground. However, we got there in time to hear the Prime Minister and Greenwood, Winston and McGowan. . . . The whole reconstructed Cabinet was announced in the course of the afternoon 9 (not 6 as the Prime Minister anticipated) in the "Inner Circle". . . . London more blacked out than ever.

The first leading article written by Geoffrey during the second World War, "The War Cabinet" (Monday, September 4th, 1939), began thus:

> . . . The most important step which awaited the final outbreak of war, the coping-stone of organization for an emergency, was the construction of an Inner or War Cabinet to take the main decisions and direct the national policy. . . . Mr. Churchill comes in now, as a matter of course, because he is a man of dynamic energy, most fertile imagination, and warlike temperament. These are qualities essential to a War Cabinet. They also provide sufficient reason why Mr. Churchill was not invited to join in the Government during the period of negotiation. He himself bore witness yesterday that nothing has contributed so much to the strength of the British cause in this grave crisis as the conviction, shared with our people by the whole world, that war has been forced upon

a Government completely unanimous and untiring in the pursuit of peace. . . .

Tuesday, September 5th. . . . Information and Censorship were committing incredible follies and a budget of letters testified to the ineptitude of the non-stop BBC bulletins. However Macmillan had this morning been appointed Minister of Information. . . . Smuts had defeated Hertzog[1] in the S. African Cabinet split and was becoming P.M.

Friday, 8th September. Office morning, afternoon and night—more struggles with the censorship, which develops new follies daily.

Sunday, 17th September. . . . When I got to London I heard that the Red Army had gone into Poland.[2] No one was clear exactly what this meant—a partnership of gangsters, or a warning to Germany.

Tuesday, 19th September. . . . I had a long talk later in the morning with Ned Grigg, who had been pressed by the P.M. to become Parliamentary Secretary to the Ministry of Information, a sticky job but one which I think he'd do well if he'd devote himself to a ruthless purge and reduce an enormous staff of highly paid essay-writing young men and women to a tenth of its size. Lunch later with Edward. . . . Edward not at all disturbed by the Russian move. We discussed the appropriate reply to a "peace" offer from these combined bandits.

Saturday, 23rd September. An invitation late last night to a night in the country took me down to Hever in time for lunch with John (Astor). . . . A little woodcutting afterwards with J. and then a long walk by myself, mostly on footpaths guided by a map, to the lovely little village of Chiddingstone and through some familiar coverts. After this I slept like a log in a chair before dinner, and had the luxury, rare in these days, of a hot bath and a change. The staff, except for one admirable footman, had disappeared, and a pack of evacuee children in the background was heard but not seen.

Wednesday, 27th September. . . . to the House of Commons. Another spate of questions about the Ministry of Information and then a singularly repressive and unimaginative Budget from Simon. Income Tax up 7/6, more surtax and death duties, and a few additions to tobacco, drink and sugar.

Thursday, 28th September. . . . A was writing on the surrender of Warsaw.

Friday, 29th September. . . . I went to lunch with Bob to consult him about *The Times* and my future thereon, and then to see Camrose and

[1] Hertzog had attempted to keep South Africa out of the war. Smuts had defeated him in a critical division in the Union Parliament, when a majority of 80 to 67 voted for S. Africa coming into line with the other Nations of the Commonwealth.

[2] The following day the Soviet forces occupied Vilna. On the 20th September, the Germans announced that the battle of the Vistula was "one of the greatest battles of extermination of all times". On the 29th, the Russo-German Treaty, partitioning Poland, was announced.

> Macmillan, who are beginning to take the Ministry of Information seriously . . . the Nazi-Soviet Pact for a common frontier and an obliterated Poland.

As in the first World War Geoffrey continued to advocate the reduction in the size of the Cabinet. The article in *The Times*, "War Cabinets", dealt with changes in the structure of the War Cabinet and claimed that the case for a smaller War Cabinet was certainly growing in strength. The following extract from this article shows that Geoffrey was no more backward in criticizing the Government than he had been in the first World War.

> Mr. Chamberlain dismissed it (the case for a smaller War Cabinet) very briefly on Wednesday afternoon by the statement that he would have formed such a Cabinet already if he had thought it the best plan. But there can be no doubt at all—his own answer implies it—that he did give the subject very serious consideration, and it is equally certain that he will some day be compelled to consider it again.

The diary for the day on which this article appeared reads: "to see the P.M. at his suggestion in Downing Street. He hadn't studied it (Hitler's much heralded speech) but gave me his general ideas—explaining also why he had come to form a larger cabinet (*vide* this morning's leader) than he had intended at first." This shows how ready Neville Chamberlain was to discuss matters of importance with Geoffrey.

On Mr. Churchill the leading article made this comment: "Mr. Churchill, for instance, without whom no War Cabinet would be complete, might well be allowed to range over the whole field of War, and not merely over the oceans, with his fertile imagination and his inimitable powers of expression"—Geoffrey could not anticipate that this was exactly what Mr. Churchill would be doing in seven months' time, at the moment of supreme crisis.

"The fog of War" did not disperse in the last months of the year. Whenever possible the Editor would go to the House of Commons to hear Neville Chamberlain make his survey. Early in October he heard the Prime Minister state the Government's general attitude towards any peace offer, which "was very well received in the House". There are frequent mentions of talks with Lord Halifax ranging over a wide field—one of the problems discussed was the necessity of finding the right man from the Labour Party to succeed Sir William Seeds, the retiring British Ambassador at Moscow.[1] Other subjects commented upon in the diary included the retreat of Hitler before Stalin in the

[1] Sir Stafford Cripps was ultimately appointed.

Baltic countries; news from the Admiralty of the sinking of three U-boats; the performances of the bureaucracy at Oxford in the matter of commandeering Colleges which were "incredible—Brasenose standing empty, Queen's asked to transfer bodily to Headington. There was a gathering of some 25 in Hall (All Souls) for dinner, 3-course and no dressing—Most people seemed to be working in Balliol on summarizing weeks-old foreign papers." There was the receipt of the tragic news of the sinking of the *Royal Oak* with "some 800 good men gone" and three days later there was a statement in the House of Commons "from Winston on the sinking of the *Royal Oak* in harbour (a deplorable affair)". In the same week came the news of a German air-raid on Rosyth when four of the *Luftwaffe* planes were shot down; and the War Office had to issue a statement on the German canard about British gas in Poland.

Early in November Geoffrey received the following letter from Arnold Wilson[1] which moved him deeply:

Pilot Officer A. T. Wilson,
No. 1 Air Armament School,
MANBY. Nr. Louth, Lincs. Nov. 3rd, 1939.

. . . A line to say that—*laetus sorte mea*—the above is as from tomorrow my style title and address. I go thither for a month's training as Air Gunner (a job I knew last war) before posting to a Fighter or Bomber Squadron, with I. Maccabees III 59[2] in my heart, and Psalm 144 verse 1[3] on my lips, and with my wife's full consent, and she lost her first husband in the R.A.F. last war—killed in action—so any credit is hers. I did not "wangle" the job, I passed with ease all the exacting medical and physical tests exacted of men of 25. . . .

I hope no one will suggest that my action was either impulsive or ill-judged. My military experience is 25 years out of date; the Admiralty said I was too old to sweep mines; the F.O. and C.O. could not, I agreed, use me in the Middle East; my old friends are out of office. I could only be useful at the top or near it. But the R.A.F. know me as a lecturer at Cranwell and in 1918 gazetted me an "Observer" and gave me my "Wing" after three air combats with Turks in one of which I was "shot down" with my pilot though we landed on the right side of the line.

[1] Sir Arnold Talbot Wilson (1884–1940), soldier, explorer, civil administrator and politician, characteristically, at the age of fifty-five years volunteered for service in the R.A.F. He was killed on May 31st, 1940, when the aeroplane in which he was serving was shot down and crashed behind the German lines.

[2] I. Maccabees III, 59.
For it is better for us to die in battle, than to behold the calamities of our people and our sanctuary.

[3] Psalm 144, v. 1.
Blessed be the Lord my strength, which teacheth my hands to war, and my fingers to fight.

Anyway a man with five orders of Chivalry from his sovereign has given a pledge which he must fulfil to the limit. If Orders have any meaning he is not a free agent like others. . . .

You know how grateful I am to you and your staff for the ever-recurring hospitality of and liberty of expression in your columns. . . .

On November 1st, on a brief visit to the House of Commons, Geoffrey "ran into Winston, just back from a visit to the Fleet". On November 2nd, the Editor noted that there was news of the final Neutrality division in Washington. Two days later President Roosevelt signed the revised Neutrality Act, which was very important from the standpoint of the Allies, for they were then enabled to obtain munitions and much-needed supplies from America, provided that these were not exported in American ships and that the title to their possession had passed out of American hands. On November 7th, a peace offer from "Leopold and Wilhelmina, who had been in nocturnal colloquy at the Hague" is mentioned, and a day later as the Editor was leaving Printing House Square came the news of a bomb attempt on Hitler at Munich. On November 9th, the diary states, "all the talk was of the Hitler bomb which was taken as a signal for violent warfare." On the 11th, the Queen broadcast a message to the women of the Empire. On November 16th, the Editor lunched with the Churchills in the flat they had made for themselves at the top of Admiralty House. . . . "Winston in very good form. I left him about to take his regular hour's sleep." On November 20th, "The news was all of the sinking of ships by 'Magnetic Mines'." (The Germans did much destruction especially among neutrals by laying these mines from aeroplanes.) There were several bad days at sea; the entries in the diary for December record that a wave of indignation swept the country when the news reached England of the Soviet's unprovoked attack on Finland. This referred to the splendid stand being made by the Finns for their freedom against 50 to 1 odds. The entry in Geoffrey's diary was: "No news whatever except of medieval fighting in the snows of Finland, reindeer and skis instead of tanks and lorries . . ."—wrote again on "Stalin and the unhappy Finns".

Of a rare day of relaxation, when staying with Major Astor, Geoffrey wrote:

Saturday, 9th December. A day's shooting at Hever. My second this season, and a lovely day out, sunshine and early mists and only the vestige of a drizzle in the afternoon. A wonderful shoot moreover. Home again soon after 4 for a peaceful time, reading and dozing, mostly in my bedroom, with the strains of John's organ for a lullaby; and a dose of Lord Haw Haw on the German wireless after dinner.

The month of December brought inspiring news from the South Atlantic to offset the series of unpleasant bulletins of Naval losses—apart, of course, from the number of German submarines sunk. The Senior Service had all along been on the watch for the German pocket-battleship used for commerce raiding. On December 14th (the morning had been spent by Geoffrey in enacting a final scene of *The Times* film) news reached London of what was so far the most important naval battle of the war. The pocket-battleship *Admiral Graf Spee* was tracked down by three British cruisers, much inferior in gun power, and driven, much damaged, into Montevideo harbour, where it was scuttled by order of Hitler to avoid internment. Extracts from the diary during these stirring days follow:

Friday, 15th December. . . . The eyes of the world were on Montevideo, where the *Admiral Graf Spee* was apparently refitting feverishly—with British reinforcements assembling outside. There was some doubt about the time limit:[1] but it seemed to be established in the end, that it expires on Sunday night.

Sunday, 17th December. . . . a walk with Michael round Regent's Park to see the animals on the edge of the Zoo, and an enthusiastic woman addressing a small gathering in favour of Tom Mosley (Sir Oswald Mosley) and peace with Germany. She had little sympathy from her audience. . . .

Monday, 18th December. . . . The news of the day should have been the last scenes of what Winston called "the Glorious Battle of the River Plate" but on this were super-imposed the sinking of another German cruiser in the Elbe; a great air combat over the North Sea; and late at night the safe arrival of the 1st Canadian contingent (in the United Kingdom), let out by Winston in his broadcast—though it was to be secret till tomorrow, which involved great changes in the paper. . . .

Wednesday, 20th December. . . . in the afternoon came the news that the Captain of the *Admiral Graf Spee* had committed suicide, poor man—a "Sacrifice (as we called it) to the Swastika."

[1] i.e. the period which damaged vessels of war may remain in a neutral port for repair.

XXXIV

THE END OF PEACEFUL WAR

THIS strange war was four months old on New Year's Day, 1940. For three months more the struggle, as far as the Allies were concerned, continued to be "peaceful", "counterfeit", or "phoney". The real war between Nazi Germany and the British Empire and France may be said to have begun when the Nazis embarked upon their well-prepared attack on Norway and Denmark in April. In Eastern Europe, as we have seen, Poland had been divided between the two strange bedfellows Hitler and Stalin.

During the first months of the war the attention of the British public was largely concentrated on the heroic struggle put up by Finland against the overwhelming might of Soviet Russia: the tactical successes secured by the Finns aroused great enthusiasm in Great Britain and many British volunteers wanted to go to Finland to fight for her. The would-be crusaders on behalf of a gallant nation fighting for her existence were confronted by the strict neutrality of the Scandinavian peoples and there was, accordingly, no means by which they and urgently needed supplies could reach Finland.

Early in the New Year Geoffrey had a "good invigorating talk" with Lord Trenchard and wrote: "(I have a doubt about his strategy), but he knows his men and I agree with him both about the weaknesses in the Government and about the risk of frittering away pilots and machines, R.A.F." On January 9th, the Editor lunched at the Mansion House "to hear the Prime Minister discourse on the war effort to a crowded and distinguished gathering. The most interesting point was his almost literal reproduction of this morning's leader (which dealt with the resignation of Mr. Hore-Belisha)." On the 11th there was good news from Finland, ". . . a vivid dispatch came in about the Finns' fourth and biggest victory, which apparently wiped out a Russian division".

On January 15th *The Times* returned to the Editor's conviction, based on experience of the first World War, that a small Cabinet was essential for the efficient direction of the war. The paper said, "there is a growing school of thought which would drastically reduce the numbers of the present War Cabinet (already brought far below its peace-time strength); would leave the three Service Ministers, who are greatly overworked in their several departments, to be represented in it by a single Coordinator of Defence." On the "domestic front" in January, the rationing of bacon, ham, butter and sugar was in operation.

Geoffrey received the following letter from General Smuts in South Africa:

26. 1. 40.

. . . You will be glad to hear that the moves made in fear and trembling in September of last year have worked out better than was expected, and the position of my Government is today stronger than it was then. As for me personally there was no other way. I am a firm believer in the Commonwealth, not only for its own sake and that of South Africa, but as the first tentative beginnings of great things for the future of the world. I was not going to desert or betray that great cause. *Gladstone once said that the Constitution of the U.S.A. was the greatest attempt in human government ever made. In the British Commonwealth we see the beginnings of something incomparably greater.*[1] The League experiment based on it has for the moment failed. But who knows whether that will not yet, in one form or another, be the only way out. I do not believe in "Union Now" or similar Utopian aspirations, and I shudder to think of the peace settlement which will have to follow this terrible conflict. My mind continues to move on the lines of our solid British experience and precedents.

I am glad you like my young Ambassadors; they are the real stuff and you need not speak in anxious whispers to them.

It is pleasant to think of Philip Kerr at Washington. That is the key position in our diplomatic world, and he will please the Americans . . . but the end may, now again, once more depend on them. This is going to be a terrible war; Germany has her hands free in the East and can mass all her resources at the vital points. In air and on land she is very strong, and the ordeal for us will be fearful. The Americans are subject to violent gusts of public opinion, and if things go too badly with us the Middle West mentality may suddenly disappear as it did in 1917. Let us woo and cultivate the U.S.A. They may yet be there before the end.

I am just afraid we may be induced by German frightfulness to be too hard on the small neutrals who are driven by abject terror. Let us keep public opinion with us in that neutral world also. Those imponderables will be formidable reserves in the long run.

[1] My italics.—E.W.

It was pleasant to read about our other friends—God bless them. And with all good wishes for you and blessings on you.

Yours very sincerely,

J. C. Smuts.

Some brief entries from the diary follow:

Feb. 8. . . . Nevile Henderson . . . had a good deal to say to me about his forthcoming book (for "the common people", and therefore to be serialized in the *Daily Herald*!) and its vast proceeds to be directed to the cause of the British refugees from Germany, etc. I undertook to help him. . . .

Feb. 9. Cecilia . . . picked me up to lunch with Evelyn Wrench and his wife at the Ivy Restaurant to meet the Seeds's lately home from the Moscow Embassy.[1] Thence for a long, friendly, discursive talk in Downing Street with the Prime Minister who was in very good form, looking fit and well on the top of his job. We discussed the battle front and the home front, the Finns and the Nazis, the new American peace feelers, the policy of bombing, the construction of the Cabinet and every other conceivable topic. . . .

Feb. 10. . . . Edward H. came to lunch and half an hour's walk across Regent's Park. . . . E., like the Prime Minister, obviously a little nervous of a bad Peace Offensive, for which there might be an excuse in the dispatch of Sumner Welles, the European observer for Roosevelt, who, however, delivered a strong anti-Soviet speech. . . .

Feb. 12. . . . The news of the day was of the arrival of the Australian and New Zealand contingents in Egypt. Anthony Eden had flown out to meet them. . . . The Russians were evidently making a tremendous effort to break the Finn defences.

Feb. 13. . . . Finns fighting hard . . . a German submarine sunk in the Clyde.

Feb. 15. . . . There was a statement on the Government's new evacuation plans. Finnish news not too good—Russians going all out before the March snows.

Feb. 18. . . . The world was all agog since yesterday with a good old-fashioned scrap in a Norwegian fjord in which the *Cossack* grappled and boarded the *Altmark*, prison ship of the *Graf Spee* slinking home, and rescued 300 British seamen—great indignation on the part of the Germans, protests from Norway, and general rejoicing elsewhere—especially in America!

Feb. 19. A long day in the office—not such a cheerful one, as yesterday destroyer *Daring* torpedoed (up North?) with nearly all hands and Finnish situation not too good. . . . A spate of letters about the neglect of religion in education. . . .

[1] Sir William and Lady Seeds. The former was British Ambassador in Moscow in the months before the outbreak of war and during the first weeks of the struggle.

Feb. 20. . . . the Prime Minister made a much applauded statement on the *Altmark* exploit, replying to a very lame note from Norway.

Feb. 23. London welcome to men of *Exeter* and *Ajax* (who had fought in the River Plate battle)—a wonderful demonstration and such crowds in the streets from Westminster to Guildhall as have not been seen since the Jubilee.

Feb. 29. Belinda's Deb. Ball. Office morning, afternoon and evening, only emerging to go as Mason's guest to a lobby journalists' lunch with Winston as the guest of honour and all the Cabinet and other notables there. I had Oliver Stanley for my neighbour and the Prime Minister two away. . . . An excellent speech from the Chair (Trevor Smith) and a stirring reply from Winston pledging support to Neville Chamberlain for the duration. I encountered him again, when at 11 p.m., after producing the paper, I went to join our party at the Grosvenor House Deb. Ball, a tremendous affair which they all thoroughly enjoyed. . . . Michael . . . 3 or 4 other boys in the Guards. There was something a little tragic about it all, but for the night it was a *great* success.

Geoffrey's diary for March tells, among other things, the tragic story of the last days of the Russo-Finnish War:

March 4. . . . There is a growing sense, which I share, that we are not yet doing enough for the Gallant Finns.

March 7. . . . Things were not looking good in Scandinavia, where the Swedes were obviously the pivot of some very dubious "Peace Talks". Edward hinted that the Finn Minister was coming to see him, probably about this. Harold Macmillan sent in a remarkable diary of his visit to Finland, which I read in bed till a late hour, absorbed in it.

March 8. . . . The Finn situation was becoming more and more confused and depressing. . . .

March 13. A black day. It was clear at once that the Russo-Finnish "peace" was definite—on most onerous terms.[1] . . . The Prime Minister's statement was very brief and rather surprisingly well received. . . .

March 14. . . . Riette brought "X", an interesting Finn. . . . He confirmed that his people had no grievance against us and the French, but a good deal against Sweden and some against America.

March 18. We showed *The Times* film at 12.00 to the Ministry of Information. . . . The Dictators were meeting on the Brenner—no news of their villainous conversations.

[1] Peace was signed in the gallant town of Viipuri on March 12th. The Finns negotiated an armistice, early in the month, when it became obvious that no direct help would be coming from the United Kingdom and France, ostensibly because of the refusal of Sweden, under German pressure, to allow the passage of troops through her territory.

March 19. Alastair Fraser[1] turned up for breakfast—very late—full of the raid on Scapa. I saw little of him, having an early assignation with the Prime Minister who was both to open and close an important debate on the war. He had a pretty good case on Finland, made light of the Scapa Raid, and was quite prepared to discuss the strengthening of the Government, the inclusion of Labour and the Service Chiefs. As a matter of fact he had a great success in the House in the afternoon.

During the next ten days there was little important war news. A week passed without loss to British shipping. Meanwhile, as usual, Geoffrey moved daily among those who were at the centre of national affairs. He exchanged views with Churchill, Halifax and Trenchard on many subjects, including strategy, the pursuit of "more active warfare", and Reynaud's succession to Daladier in the French Premiership; the reconstruction of the British War Cabinet, and the appointments of new Ambassadors to Moscow and Madrid.

On March 28th the Supreme War Council met in London and produced a "Solemn Declaration" to the effect that it would not negotiate or conclude an armistice or treaty except by mutual agreement. Admirable intentions but, alas, destined, owing to the subsequent collapse of France, to last only a few weeks.

In Geoffrey's diary for April 1st there is this entry, "There was a hitch today in the 'more active warfare' which the Supreme War Council was supposed to be starting. . . ." If the Supreme War Council appeared dilatory, Hitler certainly was not. He was preparing "more active warfare" which the Allies would have to meet and which within three months was to make him master of Western Europe from Norway to the Pyrenees.

On April 4th, *The Times* greeted the last of Ministerial changes unenthusiastically in the main—on the appointment of the Food Minister, however, the Editor commented in the leading article "Reshuffle", "a new man (and on his record a very good one) has been found in the person of Lord Woolton". Geoffrey ended thus: "And it gives ground for still more confident hope that the co-ordination of defence in all its branches will now pass in effect into the hands of Mr. Churchill. His official recognition as the Senior Service Minister should pave the way before long to the release of the other Service Ministers from the daily sittings of the War Cabinet, in which they might well have been represented from the beginning by a single spokesman."

The British nation can surely never, not even in Napoleonic times, have been through such black months as during the spring of 1940.

[1] Brother of Lord Lovat and an old Magdalen friend of Geoffrey's.

The very foundations of our western civilization were at stake and a seemingly unending series of disasters confronted the Allies—till in June the British Empire alone stood between Hitler and his bid for domination of Western Europe.

The Dawsons and their two daughters spent a few happy days at Tenby in South Wales in a little "seaside hotel with grand views over the bay of Caldey and a lovely little walled city", before the full fury of Hitler's attack on the West began in Scandinavia. A day in Caldey Island is thus described in the diary:

> *April 9*. Caldey Island. After various preparations we all went over to Caldey in the Monks' motorboat, landing by the Norwegian wreck *Belpareil* of Oslo where the salvage men were full of discordant rumours of events in Scandinavia. On their advice we went to the cottage, where the Captain was living and there heard on the wireless of the German invasion of Denmark and Norway. The Captain was optimistic—"the more in it the better"—but his mate was almost in tears. Neither had seen their homes for three years—having been in the Far East, Cuba, Antwerp with sugar, South Wales for coal before coming to grief in a lighthouse black-out. I made up my mind to get back at once: telephoned to the office, which had been trying to telephone to me: and got a sleeper on the 7 train. . . .

There was no doubt that this was the end of "peaceful war". The Norwegian expedition had been carefully planned by the German High Command and the failure of the British campaign was in truth "a tragedy of unreadiness". On Sunday, April 7th, a force of Nazi battle-cruisers put to sea. It was located by British air patrols and every effort was made by the Royal Navy to engage it but without success, except for "a brush at long range on the morning of April 9th between H.M.S. *Renown* and the *Scharnhorst*"; thanks to superior speed the Germans escaped and carried out simultaneous attacks on a number of key points in Denmark and Norway as far north as Narvik, the port through which the iron ore from the great Northern Swedish mines at Kiruna was shipped along the coast of Norway to Germany.

The entries in the diary for these fateful days follow:

> *April 10*. . . . Naval battles were raging all along the coast of Norway and an early statement of destroyers beaten off Narvik (2 of them lost) looked black. The Prime Minister put a better complexion on this by announcing in the House of Commons the extent of the damage done to German transports. Meanwhile the big ships were in action further south in the Oslo fjord etc. and there was constant news of the sinking of German cruisers. Oslo itself, Bergen, even Narvik, were

apparently occupied by German troops—but no first-hand intelligence was available and we awaited in vain a constantly promised Admiralty communiqué. Late at night it appeared that we too had troops on the coast and had retaken some of the places. . . .

April 11. . . . The world was all agog for news from the North Sea—last night's stories from Stockholm being repeated and growing in the evening papers. Everything was saved up for Winston's speech at 3.45 and the result, as it turned out, was rather an anti-climax. As I listened to his long and rather laboured narrative I kept hoping for some dramatic revelation but there was none. However the Navy was there and all seemed to be going well, and Ironside (C.I.G.S.), next to whom I sat at dinner, was very confident and enthusiastic about the sailors. . . .

An article by Geoffrey entitled "Relief for Ministers" appeared in *The Times* (April 16th). It is almost as though he were thinking aloud with no very definite scheme in mind, beyond the urgent need to lighten the burden on the shoulders of certain key men in the Government, among them Mr. Churchill. The article began thus:

A well-known member of the House of Commons, writing on this page at the week-end, gave it as his opinion that the Mr. Churchill to whom he had just been listening was "a very tired man". That, as he said, was not surprising in view of the burden which war inevitably imposes on the First Lord of the Admiralty. He might perhaps have added that the particular moment at which Mr. Churchill spoke came at the very height of those first critical operations on the Norwegian coast which must have involved him during the preceding hours in peculiarly intensive work and vigilance. . . . The difficulty—as was pointed out in these columns at the time of the last Cabinet reshuffle—is that certain Ministers (including Mr. Churchill himself in a notable Triumvirate[1]) are at this moment as nearly indispensable as any Minister can ever be, and that "their efficiency would unquestionably be diminished if they were no longer to be in close contact with their respected spheres of work. . . ."

The Editor, after pointing out that Mr. Chamberlain, in addition to restoring former Ministers (like Mr. Eden), had brought in new Ministers from outside, such as Lord Chatfield, Sir John Reith and Lord Woolton, continued:

. . . In the House of Commons alone, without going outside the ranks of those elected as Government supporters, there are at least half a dozen competent potential recruits for any Government, kept in the background, as Mr. Bartlett[2] and others believe, by the dislike of the Prime

[1] The other two were the Prime Minister (Mr. Chamberlain) and Lord Halifax.
[2] Mr. Vernon Bartlett.

Minister's advisers for anything like an independent spirit. Apart altogether from the case for giving a rest to some of the Ministers who are in obvious need of it, the infusion of new blood into the Administration might itself be made the means of concentrating, and affording relief to, those key men of the War Cabinet whose services at the present moment are rightly held to be essential. . . .

Some further extracts from the diary concerning the increasingly critical situation follow:

April 19. . . . There was no news to speak of from Norway, where things were apparently going according to plan; but the Italians looked like being stoked up more and more to intervention.

April 21. . . . News still indeterminate but not unsatisfactory. An admirable account of the German seizure of Copenhagen . . . a leader . . . on "Imperialism" based on the French Canadian Guard at Buckingham Palace: and some first-rate photos of the Narvik sinkings. . . .

April 22. . . . the landings, tho' sticky, were apparently going all right and it is believed that we have not yet lost a man in the process.

April 23. . . . The Budget—Simon speaking for 2½ hours till 6 and a leader to be written by 7! However there was nothing to be done but to grin and bear his enormous taxation—stamps, telephones, beer, whisky purchases. . . .

After a brief visit to Langcliffe, Geoffrey returned to London on April 29th to find that Barrington-Ward had spent a difficult week-end at Printing House Square and was worried about the news from Norway. Small wonder, for in fact the failure of the British effort to save Norway was to be announced in the House of Commons on May 2nd. Despite the fight put up by the Norwegians under their gallant King and the presence of the British expedition which landed on April 15th at Harstadt near Narvik, the Allies faced overwhelming odds and lacked a suitable aerodrome for fighter aircraft to protect the land forces. The Nazis dropped soldiers from parachutes, a method which had already been successfully exploited by the Russians in Finland; and they established a fifth column—described in *The Times* as "the suborning of traitors in the ranks of the Norwegians themselves", the chief of whom, Major Quisling, added a new word to our vocabulary.

Geoffrey's article in *The Times*, "A Warning and an Opportunity" (May 6th, 1940), dealt with the critical debate in the House of Commons on the strategic aspect of the campaign in Norway. He wrote:

But the purely strategic aspect of the campaign is by no means all that has troubled the public during this last anxious fortnight. . . . There has been in fact what it is the fashion to call a stock-taking both of the structure and of the personnel of the Government; and the conclusion everywhere has been that there is abundant room for improvement. The machinery, it is felt, is too cumbrous for rapid and vigorous initiative. The War Cabinet is still too large, and its meetings are attended by too many experts and advisers . . .; and indeed Mr. Chamberlain's weakness has always been his devotion to colleagues who are either failures or need a rest.

. . . That Labour will be found in the ranks of the Government before the war is over is as certain as anything can possibly be. The great twin problems of man-power and supply will never be solved satisfactorily without their willing and responsible help. They may say, as some of them are saying already, that the time has not yet come for so radical a change; but time waits for no man in such a struggle as that to which we have set our hand. The setback in Norway is happily not a national disaster, but it is a warning and an opportunity.

Some further extracts from the diary follow:

May 6. The general agitation in the Press showed that I was right to get my reflections on the direction of the war into the paper this morning and the article had many repercussions during the day. . . .

May 7. First day's debate in the Commons on Norway and the general conduct of the war . . . to a crowded House to hear the Prime Minister —rather a lame performance. . . . There was a good deal of criticism later—notably from Roger Keyes who made a fighting speech in full uniform. . . .

May 8. Second day's debate and division. . . . It was one of those desperate nights when the paper had to go to press 9.30 with a division at 11 after the most important speeches. I went down to the House at 10, heard Winston wind up and came back to Printing House Square to alter a few headlines. Government majority was only 81 in a crowded and excited assembly and there was a general conviction that it meant a reconstruction at once. (In spite of a loyal speech by Mr. Churchill in support of his chief, the motion of confidence had been carried by a majority of only 81, as stated above, instead of the usual majority of 200. It was in this debate that Mr. Amery, using Cromwell's words to the Long Parliament, addressed the cry to the Prime Minister: "You have sat here too long for any good you have been doing. Depart, I say, and let us have done with you. In the name of God go!")

. . . . .

On May 9th Neville Chamberlain consulted the Labour leaders: Mr. Attlee and Mr. Greenwood said the only conditions on which they would join a reconstructed Government would be under another Prime Minister; the Liberal leaders made a similar statement. Neville

Chamberlain, on May 10th, resigned and the King asked Mr. Churchill to form a Government. It is not an exaggeration to say that Great Britain faced probably the greatest danger which had confronted it since 1066.

On May 11th it was announced that the new Government's War Cabinet would consist of five members: Mr. Churchill, Prime Minister and Minister of Defence; Mr. Chamberlain, Lord President of the Council; Mr. Attlee, Lord Privy Seal; Lord Halifax, Secretary of State for Foreign Affairs; and Mr. Arthur Greenwood, Minister without portfolio.

On the day of Mr. Chamberlain's resignation, the diary commented:

May 10. Blitzkrieg: New Government. I was awakened by the news that Hitler had invaded the Low Countries—. . . things moved quickly both in the war and in our own politics. Labour passed a Resolution at Bournemouth offering full co-operation under a new Prime Minister: whereupon Neville Chamberlain went to the Palace and resigned in favour of Winston (Edward having presumably ruled himself out) and then proceeded to broadcast at 9. . . .

Geoffrey received the following letter from Lady Oxford:

44, Bedford Square,
London, W.C.1,
5 a.m. Sat. 11th May, 1940.

Dearest Geoffrey,

I had a wonderful talk with the P.M. last night. I did not hear his broadcast as I seldom listen in, but my taxi-man said it was very fine. I shall probably read it later on this morning before I go to the country (till Tuesday).

Feeling rather lonely, I thought I would chance seeing the P.M. and Mrs. Chamberlain, and went in a taxi at 10 last night. Their man-servant —whom I know—came down to the corridor—(which I know so well!) and said they would be "delighted to see me". It was not without emotion that I kissed her, and shook hands with him. They were both rather moved. He said that no one could have been nicer than Winston and that our orator (Archie)[1] had said to him "I've often said harsh things about you on platforms and in the House—I hope that you will forgive me for them." He then added—what I thought so sweet of him— "I know that you have not approved of the line your party have taken about me, and about my visit to Munich, so I thought you would like to know this." He told me (what I did not know) that he was going to remain in the new Government and serve in whatever capacity they thought he might be of use; that nothing just now mattered in *any* way

[1] Sir Archibald Sinclair.

about *him*, or about *any* individual; all that mattered was that they should be *United*. The only person of whom he spoke with biting words was Ll.G. "There are people in the world—as your husband found out—who are frauds; and but for Ll.G., Europe would have been easier to deal with. The day may come when my much cursed visit to Munich will be *understood*. Neither we nor the French were prepared for war. *I* am not responsible for this lack of preparation, I blame *no* one. None of us is always wise; I did what I thought right. I am the last person who would claim immunity from criticism."

I looked at his spare figure and keen eye and could not help comparing it with Winston's self-indulgent rotundity. I shall always maintain that tho' Neville has made many mistakes and not chosen the right men in his futile reshuffles, that he has a magnificent character, and less self-love, or self-pity than any man I know.

Yours,
MARGOT.

P.S. I am not vain; but there are two compliments which have been paid me in my long life. The first was when my husband said "You have more political insight than any woman and most men": the other when the Chamberlains saw me last night.

XXXV

ALONE THE BRITISH COMMONWEALTH DEFENDS WORLD FREEDOM

AFTER the "Black Month" of April, 1940, there were two even blacker months to follow. Surely never in the history of our island have its inhabitants had to face such a series of calamities involving their future, as in the late spring and early summer of 1940. The final withdrawal from Norway; the losses at sea; the collapse of the Netherlands and Belgium before Hitler's mechanized onslaught when the defences of the Low Countries collapsed like nine-pins. The downfall of France—foreseen by some wise men. The uselessness of the Maginot Line, once its flank had been turned, to hold up the onrush of the German Army, and the consequent downfall of France. The entry of Italy into the war at our darkest hour in June—the only rays of comfort during those terrible days were the "Miracle of Dunkirk" and Franklin Roosevelt's memorable broadcast in which he referred to Mussolini's act as "a stab in the back".

To steer *The Times* safely through such turbulent waters required the highest qualities and exceptional physical stamina in the case of a man in his sixty-sixth year. As we have seen twelve months previously, in April, 1939, the Editor had informed Major Astor quite definitely that he felt the year 1939 must be his last one at Printing House Square. If peace had been preserved Geoffrey would therefore have retired at the end of the year 1939. Once war came, however, everything changed: there were urgent staff problems, young men had to be released, economies had to be effected and Geoffrey's one concern was to make his utmost contribution to the Nation's war effort. What more natural then that he felt his duty was to carry on with his job? Surely this was not the time for swapping horses and however admirable a journalist his approved successor, Robin Barrington-Ward, might be, he had not Geoffrey's experience of having already edited *The Times* through the whole period of the first World War.

The eight months covered by this chapter witnessed the completion of Hitler's conquests up to the Spanish frontier; the evacuation of most of the original B.E.F. from Dunkirk, which, although not a victory, sent a thrill around the Empire and the United States; the necessity of keeping the Mediterranean open to British vessels with urgently needed supplies for Malta—after Italy had joined the ranks of our enemies—became doubly important with a French Government, under Pétain and Laval, in power. The question, "what would the French Fleet do?" was of supreme importance. Inevitably and reluctantly, the Prime Minister, a life-long friend of France, had to take the decision—after the British Government's generous offer of enabling it to withdraw in safety—to put it out of action at Oran; then came the recognition by the Axis of Japan's special place in the Far East as the dominant Power in a "new order" for Asia and Italy's dastardly attack on Greece; and finally the whole problem of heartening the splendid "home front" where the casualties among the civilian population had grown from 336 deaths in air-raids in June, to a total of over six thousand deaths from air-raids in both September and October.

The change-over from Neville Chamberlain to Churchill on May 10th was a matter of but a few hours and the new Prime Minister had no more loyal colleague than his predecessor, whose only desire was to defeat the menace of Hitlerism. Geoffrey's first leading article under the new Administration, called "Mr. Churchill's Administration" (May 13, 1940), began thus:

> It is a high tribute to British institutions and to the British temper that in the space of a single week they have been able, without rancour and without interruption of national effort, to transform the supreme direction of the war at the hour of its greatest crisis. . . .
>
> The basis of Mr. Churchill's reconstruction has been the retention from the old Government of the triumvirate (Mr. Churchill, Mr. Chamberlain and Lord Halifax) which at the moment was as nearly indispensable as any Ministers can ever be held to be. . . . The War Cabinet emerges as a body of five in place of nine who originally composed it. It contains a majority of Ministers—Mr. Chamberlain, Mr. Attlee, and Mr. Greenwood—without departmental duties.

Six months earlier in the leading article "War Cabinets" (Oct. 6, 1939), Geoffrey had suggested that Mr. Churchill—"without whom no War Cabinet would be complete—might well be allowed to range over the whole field of war, and not merely over the oceans with his fertile imagination and inimitable powers of expression". In his leading article, "Reshuffle" (April 4th, 1940), Geoffrey had returned to this subject and had expressed the hope that co-ordination of defence in all its branches should then pass into the hands of Mr. Churchill. Once more in his leading article dealing with the new Prime Minister, "Reconstruction" (May 13th, 1940), the Editor commented on Mr. Churchill's assumption of the Ministry of Defence with warm approval.

On May 13th the diary gives Geoffrey's second thoughts. He wrote: "quite a good little warlike speech from Winston and a solid vote of confidence. His new Government was daily enlarged by new appointments, *not* too well chosen: . . . too many friends! . . . X wrote on the campaign which was in full blast. We were not too happy about it—the Dutch Government and Royal Family came across to England."

But the battle was going badly. Then came the news of the replacement of General Gamelin by the veteran General Weygand, of first World War fame. The British public took heart and hoped that he would be able to stem the headlong rush of the German mechanized columns. Alas, an idle hope, as the events of the next few days were to prove. Heaven knows only a great captain of war like Napoleon could have improvised resistance. The Nazis gave Weygand no time to consolidate his position; they swept forward on a broad front, driving before them hosts of terrified French civilian refugees, whom the *Luftwaffe* machine-gunned with the deliberate intention of hampering the movement of the retreating French Army.

In its early days the Churchill Government announced the formation of Local Defence Volunteers against parachutists. Meanwhile the Dutch forces surrendered, and *The Times* printed an article on the last scenes in Rotterdam. A German mechanized column broke through the French line on the Meuse, and Geoffrey's diary records "Winston flew over to France (though this was not known to the public), presumably to say that this was their moment; and our R.A.F. was doing great things by night and day".

Geoffrey's diary records:

May 21. A *black* day . . . presided over a small meeting of Rhodes Trustees and returned to Printing House Square to find the place buzzing with the afternoon German communiqué. They had Amiens, Arras, Abbeville: the 9th Army was in dissolution: Giraud a prisoner. All this was confirmed later in a very frank and courageous speech by Reynaud. . . .

May 22. . . . Winston flew to Paris and back, as was announced in the evening. It was not announced that the C.I.G.S. had spent yesterday in and out of the contending armies in an open car and had returned well satisfied with French and British morale, though not apparently with all the French leadership. . . . House of Commons put through a new 1-clause Emergency Bill, taking powers over persons and property and also a Treachery Bill of some importance. . . .

May 23. Germans now in Boulogne. The Prime Minister made a short unadorned statement to that effect in the House. Curiously enough both Falls and McDonald seemed rather more cheerful when they came in with their news—perhaps a reaction from the last two days . . . and so back afoot to rather more than the usual scrimmage and a Board at 5 of "inspissated gloom". . . .

May 24. Rex Benson came in after breakfast. He'd been at G.H.Q. the day before in a Blenheim, which landed with 14 holes in it, and took a pretty gloomy view of the situation, though he reported all the troops in good heart. . . . Then I got writing—an admirable leader on the grave military position and the need for stout hearts—and spatchcocked into it a few sentences about the King's Broadcast (Empire Day)—also well composed and delivered. . . .

May 26. Oxford. Day of National Prayer. To church at St. Mary's . . . so to the office after tea to take over from B-W. News from the battle was being rightly damped down. Dill had become C.I.G.S. *vice* Ironside, who went to Home Defence. The French had sacked 15 Generals—Reynaud was in London.

May 27. . . . There was little positive news, but the situation was clearly becoming critical, and the 9 o'clock B.B.C. bulletin contained an anonymous and rather mysterious statement to this effect. . . .

May 28. Blackest day yet. We heard on the wireless at 8 that Leopold (of the Belgians) had surrendered the army in the night, and Reynaud confirmed the news in a bitter broadcast half an hour later. . . . I heard Winston make a short, simple and courageous statement in the House of Commons, and then settled down again in the office with a team of leader writers . . . and a spate of fatuous and irrelevant letters to the Editor. It was a grim situation for the B.E.F. and the Government didn't try to conceal the fact.

When the two French divisions, posted in the line near Sedan, broke, German tanks passed through the gap. The Germans then swung right to the Channel ports. The Belgian Army, as a result of the French failure, was in a hopeless position, and, as stated in the diary, King Leopold as Commander-in-Chief surrendered. His action meant that the British Army, under Gort, was cut off from its allies and isolated between the Germans and the sea. The operation of the re-embarkation of an army in the face of a vastly superior enemy is always one of extreme difficulty. Staff officers had at the time held that if one tenth of the British Army could manage to escape, Lord Gort would be lucky. Hence the national rejoicing and the entries of intense relief in the diary, when, through the improvised methods on the Dunkirk beaches, those 335,000 were rescued (with total losses of 30,000 killed, wounded and missing).

. . . . .

May 29. Another grim day—with little real news of the B.E.F. except that it was fighting desperately on the Coast. . . .

May 30. . . . Edward now cheerful over an amazing exploit of the new Defiant fighters, who, going out for the first time a party of 12, shot down 37 *German* machines without loss to themselves. Also over the extrication of more of the B.E.F. than he dared to hope—said to be 80,000 up to date. . . . Philby and the other correspondents went down to Dover late to get stories from the returning troops. . . .

May 31. Evacuation from Dunkirk apparently going well, and no fresh débâcle so far . . . at B-W's earnest solicitation, took train to Winchester and went out to spend a couple of nights with Fred Pelly[1] at Preshaw (in Hampshire).

June 1. Preshaw, Hants. Early awake and a walk to see my puppy before breakfast. He has grown into a very good looking dog and very friendly. Then a morning's farming with Freddy, circumambulating the whole estate in a small open car—shorthorns, sheep of 2 varieties, pigs, Jerseys, crops and woodlands. A little sleep in the garden after lunch. . . . Diana Ryder heard of her elder brother's arrival from the Dunkirk beach.

June 2. Preshaw. Another gorgeous morning, which (as usual in these days) I saw far too early. Some more talk with Freddy after breakfast and then Diana Ryder drove me into Winchester to service at the Cathedral before catching my midday train to London. Bishop of Southampton preached an excellent sermon and read a singularly appropriate lesson about Sisera, cut off from his army, and his 900 chariots of iron. . . . The B.E.F. was coming away fast, in a wonderful flotilla. Anthony Eden in a broadcast said 4/5 but the tale of casualties was growing. . . .

June 3. . . . Evacuation from Dunkirk still going on, but now more of a trickle than a spate. . . . Another sad casualty list. . . .

June 4. . . . to hear Winston make a most stirring speech in the House of Commons. . . . This was the end of the "Miracle of Deliverance" and the fall of Dunkirk was recorded late at night. . . .

. . . . .

During the first few days of June the Nation gave itself up to rejoicing over "the miracle of deliverance" of Dunkirk. Tens of thousands of homes in the land heard at first hand the amazing story of the escape from Dunkirk from members of their families who had been rescued, due in part to local air superiority gained by the R.A.F. and also to the smooth seas in the Channel for the vital days. On June 5th, Geoffrey noted in his diary a talk with Neville Chamberlain

[1] Fred Pelly and his wife were very old friends of Geoffrey's and there were many visits to Preshaw in pre-war days. The keeper there broke in many Labradors for Geoffrey.

who was "rather worried about a growing campaign, based on soldiers' stories, over the lack of tanks and aeroplanes". On June 8th *The Times* published a leading article called "The Secret Session", which explained that the demand for a secret session came at bottom from the very natural complaint of men returning from the great battles in Flanders, that they were pitted against weapons more powerful and far more numerous than their own. The paper stated, "the fact remains that the Allied Armies in the North were confronted with a devastating superiority of war material".

Before long, however, stern realities compelled the nation to recall that wonderful though the escape of 300,000 British soldiers from the grasp of the oncoming Nazis was, Germany under Hitler now controlled all the ports of Western Europe from Narvik southwards to the Belgian coast, and, with the collapse of France, right up to the Spanish frontier. Breathlessly the British people watched the rush forward of the mechanized Nazi columns and hoped that somehow or other the French would hold up the invader. The "battle for France", as Weygand called it, was getting very critical. The Germans continued to attack all along the line. After June 10th the diary became pessimistic:

June 10. As black a day as any yet (except May 28) and physically black, with a thick pall of hot mist over London, as dark as night. The French were fighting desperately all along the line from Switzerland to the sea. Narvik was evacuated and King Haakon and his Government arrived in England. Mussolini declared war in the late afternoon and about the same time came the news that we had had serious naval losses, including the *Glorious* off the Norwegian coast. It was a grim catalogue. . . .

June 11. . . . There was world-wide contempt for the Italians (after Italy's declaration of war), and the war was already spreading to the Mediterranean—bombs on Malta and in Libya and movements on the Abyssinian border. But the Battle of France was still what mattered and it was becoming more and more urgent and critical. . . .

June 12. Another grim day—with the Germans drawing closer and closer round Paris. I had a long talk in the morning with Trenchard, just back from a tour of R.A.F. stations and far more moderate and judicial than he was. . . . Winston had been in Paris but was back again—having, I hope, heartened the French, a task to which we were all devoting ourselves.

June 13. Germans ever nearer to Paris. Winston (and I think Edward) was over there again (or still over there) and there were grim messages as the day went on from Reynaud and the British Government, and moving appeals to Roosevelt. But it was getting pretty tense. . . .

June 14. Grimmest day yet. Germans *in* Paris—and though the bulletins kept recording orderly French withdrawals on either side, it became increasingly doubtful as the hours went on whether they would hold on and hold together.

June 15. . . . France still on the edge—more exchanges with Roosevelt. . . .

June 16. Things get grimmer and grimmer. The three-cornered conference about "help in time", and ability of France to hold out, went on all day. By midnight the Reynaud Government had been replaced (at Bordeaux) by a Pétain-Weygand administration. . . .

June 17. . . . soon after midday a slip brought in to me at the office, announced that the French Army had been ordered to cease fighting. This is rather numbing and it took a bit of effort to get going again. . . . Edward H., who opined that, having touched bottom,[1] we should now begin to rise.

June 18. Hitler and Mussolini met at Munich in the afternoon to discuss their plans and terms—meanwhile bits of the French Army were apparently still fighting and very late in the evening came a broadcast from General de Gaulle (now in England) urging them to do so. The situation in France, in short, was complete chaos. . . .

On June 16th the French Government asked to be relieved of its obligations under the Anglo-French Agreement. In the hope of saving something from the wreckage, the British Government telegraphed offering to conclude an Act of Union with France—but the days for such an arrangement were gone. On June 22nd, while at Langcliffe, Geoffrey heard that France had signed an armistice with Germany. Two days later he was back at Printing House Square and *The Times* published a leading article on the French surrender. The news was also received that French delegates were now at Rome and an armistice with Italy was signed. *The Times* correspondents "lately in France" returned to the office to produce "excellent retrospective articles" on the French tragedy; they had been "made as mystified as others by the conduct of the French Government and the Higher Command". It was indeed a melancholy story. On June 25th the Editor went to the House of Commons for half an hour "to hear Winston—quite good, very restrained, but not very informative about the fate of the French fleet". Problems of Home Defence received urgent attention. Now that the Germans occupied all the Channel ports, the danger of invasion seemed more imminent—but only if they were able to achieve complete air mastery over the Channel and South-Eastern England. There was a great expansion in the Home Guard, composed of part-

[1] On the day of the collapse of France I entered a chemist's shop in St. James's Street and said to the man behind the counter, "Well, we've had a bit of a knock today." Quickly and almost indignantly he replied: "I don't agree with you, sir, what I say is, thank God we have no more Allies. Now we know where we are."

time soldiers, to assist in the defence of factories, bridges and other key-points. All the French Colonies were collapsing and the Russians were in Bessarabia. The month of June ended with the occupation of the Channel Islands by German troops.

July opened with air-raids on both sides. The diary tells us that "some thought this was Hitler's date (July 1) for invading England and there were various rumours but there was nothing more extensive than an evening daylight raid on the North-East Coast". During these days the R.A.F. was doing "wonderful work on military objectives in Germany and the conquered coast". On July 3rd, owing to the threatening situation in the Mediterranean, a British Fleet appeared off the Algerian harbour of Oran and of Mers-El-Kebir, "having first offered the French Admiral several honourable alternatives, designed to give security against the use of his ships by the enemy, all of which were refused. The British Commander ordered his squadron to fire on the French Fleet at anchor and put the principal ships out of action.

Extracts from Geoffrey's diary covering these days follow:

July 3. . . . a big story of the sinking of the *Arandora Star* (with German and Italian internees fighting one another aboard) . . . and a more important statement about the rounding up of the French Fleet released at 3.30 a.m., an impossible and quite unnecessary hour. . . .

July 4. . . . The Germans were exploding over the Oran affair, but the world outside regarded it as inevitable.

July 5. . . . Not much news except of air activity on both sides. The Germans were bombing our coasts every night now, with considerable losses, and the R.A.F. were hard at it. X wrote another leader on the "tragic necessity" of the action at Oran—to which I got him to append an "uplift" peroration on our proud position and responsibility single-handed for the defence of freedom in the world.

On July 18th came the welcome news that Franklin Roosevelt had received the nomination by the Democrats and next day a most admirable broadcast to the Chicago Convention by the President. Not so pleasant was a speech from Hitler—"a paean over the war and an honours list for Goering, Ribbentrop and the Generals, a vague desire for peace, a sneer at Winston and the 'warmongers' ". On July 24th, the diary gave the general opinion on the Budget, which was that it was "interim and inadequate and didn't touch the real problem of the newly rich workers".

The middle of the month of August witnessed the beginning of the Battle of Britain and for several weeks large-scale air operations were of almost daily occurrence. The nation can never forget what it owed to the R.A.F. in those first anxious weeks. Then by degrees came the joyful realization that although greatly outnumbered the R.A.F. fighters were asserting their individual superiority over their opponents.

Some extracts from the diary follow; they include many references to the fighting in the air:

August 7. . . . More fulminations about invasion (now apparently fixed for August 12).

August 8. . . . A great air battle over the Channel which destroyed 53 German planes to our own 16.

August 11. . . . The only news was of air battles on the coast—60 German planes down to 26 of ours.

August 12. . . . The air battle raged again—principally at Portsmouth and all along the south coast. The latest relative score at night was 39 to 9.

August 13. . . . Lunch with Edward and Dorothy, Lady Northampton and General Wavell (home very secretly from Egypt) whom I was deeply interested to meet. . . . The *blitzkrieg* in the air was raging successfully and becoming more intense. . . .

August 14. . . . Air battles still raging round the coast—a very good day yesterday—and rumours late at night of the dropping of empty parachutes inland.

August 22. . . . The news was of a general bombardment of a convoy in the Straits, then of Dover itself, and there were isolated bombers over England. . . .

August 23. . . . The Germans had evidently begun a new phase of air attack—isolated bombers all over the country, but surprisingly little damage anywhere. . . . Afternoon busy sorting out leaders against emergency Air Raid warnings which are apt to send the whole establishment into the cellar. . . .

August 26. Air Raid. To the office in the morning . . . and thence to 10, Downing Street to lunch. The Cabinet was all emerging. . . . The luncheon party was a curious quartet—Winston, the Archbishop (Dr Lang), Henry Strakosch[1] and I. Some talk with Winston about the Independent Companies or Commandos (storm troops). . . . This partly in his Air Raid room, to which he and I adjourned on an early afternoon warning. He was in excellent form, fit and confident, and full of Beaverbrook's achievements in production. I was in the office by about 4; got home to dine with Cecilia and her mother: and then went back to an intolerable night of continuous air-raid. We were just going to press when the red warning went at 9.30—missed 1st edition trains—then 2nd, and were in the underground workrooms (with nothing to work at and the men forbidden to work) till 3.40 when we got going again. I satisfied myself that *The Times was* coming out and went home at 4.

[1] Sir H. Strakosch, closely connected with the South African gold-mining industry.

August 27. . . . And so the office—to get ahead with the paper in preparation for the nightly raids. A meeting of N.P.A. and Unions during the afternoon reached an agreement[1] to let work continue under conditions and though the warning came again at an awkward hour (9.30) the thing went smoother and the withdrawal was shorter. . . .

August 30. . . . There was a warning and raid in mid-morning. . . . Our serious trouble in London began about 9 and went on till about 4.00 a.m. . . . I decided to take Webb (one of the Editor's office secretaries) to his 11.19 train and went on home to bed. But not to sleep! It was a horrible night—geese cackling, planes overhead, guns, bombs, house shaking, no doubt remote explosions. . . .

The Management at Printing House Square had created an A.R.P.[2] organization as early as 1938. Over 300 members of the staff, all volunteers, had been trained in A.R.P. duties. Fire, gas and first-aid squads were organized in day, evening and night shifts covering the whole twenty-four hours. In anticipation of more severe raids of longer duration, the Management had gradually transferred staff and plant downstairs. That the staff was so well prepared for the terrible air-raids in September was in part due to the Chairman's (Major Astor's) wise decision that the second stage of the rebuilding of Printing House Square should be started in June, 1938; it was fortunately (despite the war) completed early in 1940. Below street level accommodation for the Editorial Department, the Composing Room, the Reading Room, the Moulding Room and the Publishing Department was ready before the bad raids began. The Machine Room and Casting Foundry were already at basement level. Later, bunks were fitted in the Air-Raid Shelter and in a tiny cubby-hole were two bunks where Geoffrey, Major Astor or B-W. used to snatch a few hours' rest.

Geoffrey received the following letter (August 20, 1940) from Smuts in Pretoria:

> . . . What you say about public opinion in Britain is also most encouraging. Adversity seems only to have steeled the temper of that gallant people.
>
> England will stand, in spite of the German attempts at invasion.

[1] At the discussion between N.P.A. (Newspaper Proprietors' Association) and the Trade Union it was agreed that in future production should be continued in spite of the air-raid warning, subject to three main conditions: (1) that only those who volunteered to work should do so; (2) that a "roof-spotter" system should be set up in which "spotters" appointed by the Management and Chapels (association of workmen in a printing office) should signal "immediate danger" to the workers below, upon which the workers could take shelter; (3) that the N.P.A. would create a fund to provide compensation in cases where employees were killed or injured in the course of their work or in travelling to it.

[2] Air Raid Precautions.

What we have also to watch and guard against is attacks on the British Empire. When the invasion of England fails, the vast hordes of Germany will be turned against Africa and Asia, and I hope we shall be sufficiently strong in the Middle East and in North Africa to counter the blows there too. That may come next winter, when fighting in Britain will be necessarily limited.

I am glad to hear of the activities of our old friends of the Kindergarten who are still making history—and in one case religion! Philip is doing grand work in the U.S.A. and when the elections there are over we shall reap the harvest. . . .

. . . I look upon this country as a key position in the Commonwealth and shall do my best to keep it safe and steady.

The diary tells the story of these never-to-be-forgotten nights, though by way of contrast the entry for September 1st portrays a very different scene, when the Dawsons were paying one of their periodical visits to their intimate friend Tom Hutchinson[1] at Sarsden.

Sept. 1. . . . so home to change for dinner, before which Cecilia and I had a wonderful experience of creeping round the edge of a copse in the park and waiting on shooting sticks while a whole family of badgers emerged from the earth and rollicked in the gloaming almost at our feet. It was my first sight of a badger family at large.

Sept. 3. Anniversary of the War. A morning warning which rather postponed the day's work by immobilizing the telephone. . . . Thence I took Cecilia to hear Henson's inaugural at Westminster Abbey where the congregation was almost eliminated by an Air Raid warning at about 2.50 when we were all asked to clear out and Their Majesties told not to come—a great pity. Still most of the Cabinet were there. . . . And so back to the office to deal with the difficult but most satisfactory arrangement with America over the 50 destroyers and the West Indian bases.

The above entry refers to the joyful news of the arrangement with the United States Government whereby a number of strategic sites in the West Indies, Bermuda and Newfoundland were leased for ninety-nine years to the American Navy in return for over-age destroyers transferred to the British flag in order to help to fill the gap caused by the withdrawal of the French Naval Forces.

Geoffrey was spending the week-end of Saturday, September 7th, in the country when London had its first very heavy night raid, the bombing lasting several hours, the most savage attacks being in the dock area.

[1] Captain G. Thomas Hutchinson, Treasurer of Christ Church. He contributed articles to *The Times* on agricultural subjects.

Sept. 9. . . . Cecilia met me at Paddington after a horrible week-end in London and we drove home past the wreck of the Tussaud cinema—every window gone in York Terrace and the neighbouring streets, and even one of our own. . . . I tried to sleep a bit in the small hours on a camp bed (at Printing House Square) down below. . . . The All Clear went just as I reached home in daylight—with a great fire illuminating the City.

Sept. 10. . . . in Printing House Square from early afternoon till 5 a.m. . . . It turned into the worst night yet—bombs all over London—many up our way (Bryanston Square, Marylebone etc.) Children's Hospital, 3 fires at least blazing, but particularly heavy round the office. . . .

Sept. 11. Another day much like its predecessors. . . . Walked out in the late morning to see the devastation in Bryanston Square and to ask after some of its denizens. . . . early start of the all night attack just as we were about to get the Country Edition out. It never ceased till getting on for 6 a.m. differing from the others in being met by a tremendous and very noisy barrage of gunfire. There were many bombs near the office (one going near to making us an "evacuated area"—a time bomb near St. Paul's). . . .

Sept. 13. An air raid warning all morning and again in the afternoon, in the course of which a good deal of damage was done and 5 bombs dropped on Buckingham Palace,—this time quite deliberately by a dive from the clouds. . . .

Sept. 15. Oxford—London. . . . Oxford was seething with people—evacuees from Kent and Londoners (like us) wanting a night's rest . . . we left early to enter London during a warning and, as it turned out, a terrific air battle, in which the Germans ultimately lost 185 machines.

Sept. 17. . . . *tête-à-tête* with Beaverbrook who was very forthcoming and interesting. He was more appreciative than before both of his colleagues and of the Service Chiefs: and insisted that the 2 great problems of the moment were to keep work continuous and counter night bombing. . . .

By the middle of September it became evident that despite the enormous losses in the *Luftwaffe* the Germans were no nearer to their objective of obtaining sufficient mastery of the air to launch their long-heralded invasion of Southern England. They therefore made a complete change in their tactics and abandoning the massed assault by daylight, adopted the policy of night raiding. They especially directed their attacks on London and the large towns. As *The Times* said: "The British civil population, facing an ordeal unique in their history, showed a fortitude that became the wonder of the world. The King and Queen set a royal example by refusing to leave their own bombed home, except to pay visits of sympathy to whatever town seemed for the moment to be suffering most acutely. . . ." After spending a week-end at Langcliffe, where the sad news of the sinking of a ship with child refugees going to North America was received and listening to the King's broadcast from Buckingham Palace, Geoffrey returned to London on September 24th. The raid which took place the following night just before 2 a.m. wrecked every room in the front of Printing House Square; the diary's account of this sad day follows (owing to the censorship the story of the disaster at Printing House Square was only published some days later):

Sept. 24–25. . . . To London by early train. . . . So to the office to take over from B-W. and cope with an appalling mass of letters (no use forwarding any in these days). The paper was well ahead of the new and very early time-table . . . dinner at the Connaught where I was temporarily lodged, and returned to the usual sort of evening—a very noisy one—retiring to my camp bed below about midnight. Two hours later there was a terrific and very near bang and a general buzz of excitement. I came up to find that 2 bombs had struck the front of the office—sub-editors' and messengers' rooms were wrecked. So were those immediately above. My own was deep in glass and debris but otherwise intact—windows of course gone everywhere. It was impossible to do much in the dark and Kent arrived to see to the salvage[1] and John (who'd been in the Board Room) and I went home to sleep. When I returned about 11 the clearing up was going well—whole Editorial Dept. transferring itself to other parts of the building. Many messages of congratulation and sympathy—Trenchard, Camrose, Kemsley, R. Jones (Sir Roderick Jones), etc. We went ahead throughout the day with a good deal of running to and fro to find essential people and eventually produced an orderly paper on a quieter night.

Sept. 26. Another rather difficult day's work. But the various displaced departments were gradually settling down—most of them in groups filling the whole length of the Old Composing Room. And the debris was being cleared away. I worked in my own room till dinner time—windows boarded, electric light and a fire, for it was bitterly cold. At 7 all lights were turned off on our side of the office—for reasons of black-out and the yawning gaps in the outer walls.

On the day of the bombing of Printing House Square (25th September), Geoffrey received the following letter from Neville Chamberlain:

Privy Council Office,
Whitehall, S.W.

Just a line to send you my sympathy upon your misfortune in being bombed and to congratulate you upon getting to press all the same. It is a great achievement, but only what one expects from *The Times*.

[1] In the report of Mr. C. S. Kent, published later, which deals with the damage done to Printing House Square, we learn that within an hour the interrupted printing and publishing of the day's paper was resumed.

The following day the diary records: "to the office where people seemed harder to find than ever amid incessant daylight raids. This battle over London, which resulted eventually in the loss of 130 German planes to our 30 (with 14 pilots saved) was one of the great pieces of news. The other was of the signing of a pact between the Axis Powers and Japan."

Early in October the reconstruction of the Government and the retirement of Neville Chamberlain were announced. On 9th October Geoffrey wrote to him:

My dear Neville,

The Conservative meeting this afternoon seems to set the seal on your decision to retire from active public life, and I, for one, am profoundly saddened by it. As I told you the other day, I am an impenitent supporter of "Munich"—whatever that may mean to the people who use it as a term of reproach. No one could have sat in this place, as I did during the autumn of '38, without realizing that a war at that time and on that issue would have bewildered and antagonized all the British Dominions and found even this country deeply divided. I have never admired anything more than your courage in averting it then—unless it be your courage in recognizing that, in spite of all your efforts, it was inevitable when it eventually came. I have no doubt at all that history will take this view.

For the moment I cannot think what the Prime Minister will do without you at his side. I only know that I shall feel the Government to be definitely weaker for the loss of all that you gave it to the end.

In October the diary entries are very similar to those in the previous month. Continuous air-raids, the wail of the siren, of a couple of hours rest snatched in the bowels of the earth at Printing House Square, of returning to the Connaught Hotel before dawn, as likely as not to the accompaniment of further warnings.

On October 12th the diary relates that "Another whopping bomb dropped just outside the office about 11.00 p.m. (the previous evening), bursting gas and water mains. It looked like the inferno . . . flames ascending from one end of a huge crater and a waterfall at the other!" As the Prime Minister saw no further need for secrecy about the bombing of Printing House Square, the paper published a brief account of the damage done seventeen days before and described how the part of one building facing Queen Victoria Street was badly damaged, while the actual Printing House Square, "where stands what was the home of the Walter family in earlier centuries, and the first home also of the newspaper they produced, escaped most of the surrounding destruction". Mr. Churchill sent a line of congratulations to Major Astor on the remarkable way the paper had carried on. Tributes to "The Thunderer" appeared in the Press throughout the world. Especially generous was the reference in the *New York Times* to Londoners, *The Times* and the British Press:

> The London newspapers of these terrible days are in themselves documents that deserve to be treasured. They explain how millions in London have been able to endure a month of terror from the skies. . . . To look at the unchanging front page of *The Times* one would hardly know that London was being bombed, apart from a pathetic death notice now and then, telling friends that some man, woman or child had died "owing to enemy action". . . . With such a spirit the free Press of England is now writing a chapter of courage and devotion which will take its place among the finest records of the newspaper profession.

Other events recorded in the diary were the formation of the American Eagle Squadron; Princess Elizabeth's first broadcast; "Another devastating night. Much damage, e.g. in Leicester Square—great dislocation of traffic; bidding farewell to Joe Kennedy, the American Ambassador off for good". On October 21st Geoffrey wrote, "I also found time to scribble a little leader about Joe Kennedy so as to leave a good taste in his mouth." In it the Editor wrote, "He (the retiring Ambassador) has never allowed his private friendships to turn him into an Englishman, and thus to weaken his influence with his own people." Mr. Bate, of the National Broadcasting Corporation of America, telephoned from New York to Printing House Square to say that Mr. Kennedy told him that nothing that anyone had said had made him as happy as what *The Times* editorial had stated this morning, and their judgment that he had remained an American. It was just another indication to him of British fair-mindedness.

During the last days in October news came of the meeting of General Franco and Suñer[1] with Hitler on the Spanish frontier—"Hitler in France intriguing on a wide scale from Spain to the Balkans". During a week-end at Langcliffe the Editor listened to news of the outrageous Italian attack on Greece;[2] on October 30th interest was concentrating on the "Middle East and the Balkans, the attitude of Spain, and the wriggles of the Vichy Government. 'Off the record'—

[1] Ramon Serrano Suñer, Spanish statesman and brother-in-law of General Franco.

[2] Italy had launched a treacherous attack, without declaration of war, across the Albanian frontier into Greece. Mussolini had apparently expected to meet with little resistance, but the Greek Army defended its territory with great courage and the Italian attack was soon brought to a standstill.

Smuts was on his way to meet Anthony Eden in Kenya and Cunningham (Admiral) was at sea covering a landing in Crete?"

The entry in the diary for October 31st was:

Oct. 31. . . . It looked as though Musso's aggression on Greece had gone off prematurely and that Hitler and he were not quite so much in accord as they professed. Both Greece and Turkey were apparently standing firm, and Spain and Russia at least not supporting the Axis. . . .

On November 3rd there was an announcement that British help was reaching Greece: on the eve of the Presidential Election in the United States "the betting . . . was going strong for Roosevelt", who was in fact safely elected for his third term; on November 5th the Editor was in the House of Commons "just in time to hear the Prime Minister's usual statement on the state of the war. It was short, confident and restrained: but the House was obviously nervous that the landing in Greece and Crete might go the way of Narvik and Dakar."

Further excerpts from the diary follow:

Nov. 6. . . . one of the long night raids, though not in great force. There was an amazing and horrible fire close to us, throwing up the dome and cross of St. Paul's with extraordinary brilliancy. John, Bishop (Assistant Manager) and I who had dined together, went on to the roof to see it at midnight. The paper of course was full of the triumph of Roosevelt. Greeks still apparently doing well. . . . Neville Chamberlain's private secretary gave me a very bad account of him and I got on with that. I slept well on my camp bed.

Nov. 8. . . . Edward told me of his sad little visit yesterday to Neville Chamberlain, who is dying. . . . News came late of a wonderful fight of a Hurricane squadron downing a whole German attack.

On November 8th Geoffrey wrote (in his own handwriting) the following, which must have reached Mr. Chamberlain on the day of his death:

My dear Neville,

I was grieved indeed to hear from Edward, with whom I have been lunching, that he had found you so stricken when he went to see you yesterday. I had hoped that before long you would be back in your place in Parliament and seeing this appalling conflict through to its only possible conclusion.

You did your best to avert it—far more than any other man would have dared to do. As I told you when I last saw you—how short a time ago it seems—I shall always be an impenitent supporter of what is called the "Munich policy". No one who sat in this place, as I did during the autumn of '38, with almost daily visitations from eminent Canadians and Australians, could fail to realize that war with Germany at that time would have been misunderstood and resented from end to end of the Empire. Even in this country there would have been no unity behind it. We know now that it was inevitable sooner or later; but we owe it all to you that it was later rather than sooner and that we are assuredly going to win it.

I don't know where you are—I didn't ask Edward any questions—but your faithful Hendriks tells me that he sends you letters, and I feel moved to send you a line of cheer and sympathy tonight.

Bless you for all that you have done for this country.

Among the events referred to in the diary in November were air battles over Britain "which yielded 26 victims, half of them Italians"; a great Armistice Day speech on democracy by President Roosevelt; talks at Berlin between Hitler and Molotov; on 13th the joyful news was received of the crippling blow delivered by the Fleet Air Arm "on the main Italian Battle Fleet lying in Taranto Harbour" which restored to the United Kingdom the balance of naval power in the Eastern Mediterranean, which had been in the enemy's favour since June; the final details were received in England the same day of the "suicidal gallantry" of the British ship *Jervis Bay*, whereby 30 vessels out of a convoy of 38 escaped to safety; on the 14th Geoffrey was present at the funeral of Neville Chamberlain in Westminster Abbey and he wrote, "It was arctic (I hadn't realized the broken windows and went without a coat)"; on 20th November, Hungary, not unexpectedly, was swept into the Axis; on 21st a new session of Parliament was opened by Their Majesties.

The month of December opened with a "rising-tide of indignation all over the world at the murderous bombing of provincial cities". This entry refers to Hitler's new policy of bombing English towns which was then a main topic of conversation and notably in the United States. From the domestic standpoint the most important event was the taking of a flat at 24–26 Lowndes Street, called by the irreverent "The Gasometer", which was the Dawsons' London home[1] for the rest of Geoffrey's life. The building was given this name owing to the smooth rotundity of its achitecture; by others it was known as "The Gasworks". On December 5th there is this reference to the move: "A morning between the house and the flat where we arrived with the little car bulging with boxes and books. It is beginning to look more

[1] Their own house, 23 Sussex Place, having by now been rendered uninhabitable.

habitable." On December 11th Geoffrey spent his first night—"a very noisy one"—in the new flat.

The Headmaster (Mr. Claude Elliott) rang up about the direct hit, mercifully without casualties, on the Leys House at Eton. On the following day (December 5th) Geoffrey was able to help him with the Ministry in connection with an unexploded bomb. On December 7th he visited Eton and wrote:

> *Dec. 7.* Cliveden. Cecilia and I took Waldorf (Astor) in to Eton . . . and then inspected the damage done by the School-yard bomb which had gone off on Thursday night, just after my feverish telephoning, at 10.30. It was a sad sight—the Headmaster's room and chambers gone, Upper School yawning at that end, chapel windows blown in—and the Leys House in Westons Yard had disappeared. However there were miraculously no casualties at all.

There are references to the bombing of London in the following entries:

> *Dec. 8.* . . . the earliest, longest and heaviest raid on London yet—bombs thudding round the office and indeed everywhere else. John and I took to our camp beds at midnight. At 3 I woke him on a false dream of the "All Clear" and we retired again. Near 6 we both jumped up on a tremendous bang (in New Bridge Street) and went on the roof and then home.
>
> *Dec. 9.* . . . there were sad sights as the result of last night's attack. Middle Temple Library, Temple Gardens (my old lodging with Leo Amery) and much else that I didn't see. . . .

In December there was cheering news from Libya. On the 10th 4,000 Italian prisoners had been taken by General Wavell's force in the Western Desert. Before the end of the year by a great turning movement he had cut off two entire divisions and driven the remainder of the Italian Army out of Egypt and into Libya. On December 12th came "the stunning news" of the death of Lothian early that morning at Washington. Apparently the British Ambassador had been feeling ill for some days but the Editor was quite unprepared for the sad event. He wrote a short leader about him. In it he referred to Lothian's death as "nothing less than a disaster both for his friends and for his country".

On December 19th the Halifaxes came to Geoffrey's flat to talk over the Prime Minister's suggestions that Lord Halifax should succeed Lothian at Washington, which Geoffrey considered would be "flattering to the Americans but a terrible loss to the Government at home". On December 23rd the paper printed a leading article on "The New Ambassador" which began thus: "No higher tribute could be paid to Lord Lothian's work in Washington than the consent of the Foreign Secretary to take the vacant place himself. It is a signal recognition of the fact that Anglo-American relations are more important than anything else in our foreign policy."

XXXVI

FAREWELL TO "THE TIMES"

NEW Year's Day, 1941 was spent by the Dawsons at Langcliffe, and the first words in the diary for 1941 are "The New Year—may it be better than the old!" Geoffrey's first leading article was on Baden-Powell, a very congenial subject. It was entitled "B.P." (January 9th), and Geoffrey wrote:

> If any of us were asked to name the man, or the woman, who in our lifetime rendered the greatest service to the rising generation, we should find it difficult to find an alternative to Lord Baden-Powell. The creation of the Boy Scouts—with their counterpart the Girl Guides—was his work and his alone. . . . What is perfectly certain is that no one but "B.P." could have conceived it in all its details and carried it into effect with such amazing success that, from small beginnings in this country, the Boy Scout movement has long since captured the whole Empire and indeed the whole world.

In January the diary as usual covers meticulously the story of the Editor's varied life. At Cliveden he met a Canadian General "who was obsessed with imminent invasion and generally rather alarming"; the North African campaign appeared, early in the month, to be going "better and better", Tobruk cut off and "Electric Whiskers"[1] apparently in flight; a vast Pilgrim lunch to Lord Halifax at which the Prime Minister announced the former's continued membership of the War Cabinet.[2] On the 29th the Editor lunched with Kindersley at the Savoy to meet Wendell Willkie, the unsuccessful Republican Presidential candidate in 1940. "Willkie made a little speech, urging us to keep the flag of free enterprise flying, and paying this country many compliments. . . . An attractive creature, with his big boyish head, and expansive

[1] Annibali Bergonzoli, nicknamed by Mussolini *Barba Ellettrica,* on account of his glossy beard.

[2] In addition to the post of H.B.M.'s Ambassador in Washington.

smile"; 30th, "Hitler made a speech on the 8th anniversary of his accession to power. The usual denunciation of the British Empire and protestations of his love of peace—not a very convincing or inspiring effort", and the following day Geoffrey writes, "Hitler's speech universally derided, especially in America, where Knox predicted imminent invasion."

Early in February there were leaders on civilian duties in the event of an invasion; on the 6th, the appointment of John Gilbert Winant as United States Ambassador was announced; on the 7th there was the joyful news of the occupation of Benghazi—"an amazing feat of rapidity"; on the 13th "The news of the war was more indeterminate than ever. Franco had seen Musso and Petain. Bulgaria was in a twitter—the Japs looking nasty"; on the 19th a strong Australian Army had landed in Malaya. The entry on the last day of the month was, "The news seemed a bit better—especially from Turkey, where Eden and Dill concluded their visit. Poor King Alfonso died (at last)." On March 6th we read, "Eden and Dill were on their way to meet Wavell and Smuts in Cairo, but the situation in the Balkans was described by Winston as 'murky'."

Early in March the newsprint situation was becoming serious, and during the month the Editor had talks with Brendan Bracken and Beaverbrook about the paper's urgent needs, and he reported that the latter "was very sympathetic about paper for *The Times*". A Board meeting of *The Times* on March 6th had decided "for quality as against circulation, a standard ten-page paper and a rise in price at one definite point in the reduction of buyers".

On March 16th everyone was heartened by a magnificent speech by Roosevelt. On March 20th Geoffrey notes "Wavell was still sitting on the official news of the landing of British troops in Greece"; and on the 21st, "Yugoslavia still hung in the balance and there were many signs of popular and army resentment at the project of a pact with the Axis." The National Day of Prayer (March 23rd) was spent by the Dawsons at Hever with Colonel and Lady Violet Astor. "We kept it, the four of us, at the Hever Church, walking back through the woods for primroses and branches." On the 25th the Yugoslavs duly signed their humiliating pact in Vienna.

The entries in the diary for the last days of the month were more cheerful than they had been for some time:

March 27th. . . .—best day for a long time. I arrived at the office about noon to find that the Yugos had risen in the night, had turned out their Government and Prince Paul, and were now rallying under the new King and a decent set of Ministers. This news cheered the whole world as the day went on, and was followed in the evening by that of the fall of Keren and Harar (in Abyssinia).

March 28th. Another good day, though we did not know it—Matapan. . . . Ogilvie[1] wants me to broadcast to North America—but what about?

March 30th. Glowing news since yesterday of a considerable Naval victory in the Mediterranean, 3 Italian cruisers sunk and at least 2 big destroyers, and a battleship crippled. No naval casualties on our side.

March 31st. . . . News of the Naval battle getting better and better. 3 or 4 cruisers sunk, 3 if not 4 destroyers, probably a battleship and not a scratch on the British Fleet.

The month of April witnessed the capture of Addis Ababa (the capital of Abyssinia) but, alas, there was much bad news from the Eastern Mediterranean. Early in the month came the report of a set-back in North Africa and the abandonment of Benghazi. A spate of bad news was to follow:

April 6. . . . the 8 a.m. wireless recorded the launching of the German attack on Yugoslavia and Greece.

April 9. . . . Winston had made a great survey of the war in the House of Commons, a restrained but effective effort. The news from the Balkans was not good and he made no attempt to pretend that it was.

April 11. Good Friday. Cliveden. . . . I drove myself up to London after breakfast. . . . The war was not going well at the moment—vigorous German threats in Yugoslavia and a rapid advance in North Africa involving the capture of 3 good generals by sheer bad luck in a sand-storm (this was followed by the loss of Carton de Wiart[2] in a plane which mistook its landing-ground).

April 14. Rather a gloomy Bank Holiday spent almost entirely in the Office. The news was bad in every quarter. Germans in Sollum, Yugos hard pressed, sinkings claimed in various seas. However, the situation had improved before we went to press, notably by the repulse of the enemy tanks at Tobruk.

A leading article on "Colleagues from the Dominions" by Geoffrey appeared in *The Times* on April 16th, in which he referred to the good news that Mr. Menzies had been persuaded to prolong his stay in England at this critical stage in the direction of the war. The paper continued: "General Smuts, to take the most notable instance of all, would be an outstanding figure in any company of statesmen. Lawyer, philosopher, administrator and soldier—he has already played his part in the common direction of the war in Africa, which he naturally regards as his special sphere."

[1] Director-General of the B.B.C.
[2] He was taken prisoner.

London experienced what Geoffrey calls its "Heaviest Raid" on April 16th, thus described in the diary:

April 16th. . . . all hope of getting later editions away had disappeared with a terrific and most indiscriminate attack on London, beginning at 9 and never relaxing till 5. I had dined in the office with Kent, Anderson and young Oliver Woods who looked in, and John came down soon after. The scene from the roof, when I put out my nose for a few minutes, was horrible at midnight. Great fires in all directions and bombs thudding down, and so it still was, in the grey dawn, as we made our way home with difficulty, going as far as Regent's Park to avoid blocked streets.[1]

April 18th. Langcliffe. . . . Anxious news from Greece these days in every B.B.C. bulletin.

April 19th. Langcliffe. . . . Desperate fighting round Mt. Olympus.

April 22nd. Langcliffe to London . . . office by 4 p.m. The news there was not good. Greeks at the end of their tether and short of ammunition. Germans losing heavily but pressing on; strong German diplomatic offensive against Spain and Turkey. Only Tobruk holding out well. The House met, but got little out of the Prime Minister. Winant however made a strong speech at lunch and Menzies a broadcast to Australia. . . .

April 23. No relief in the news except that Franco was a little stiffer against the German "diplomatic offensive". . . . Half an hour's walk in Kensington Gardens and again through the devastation in St. James's. . . .

April 24. . . . It was rather uphill work producing a paper under the present strain—impossible to say much about Greece during the withdrawal. Australia slightly restive—Turkey and Spain still wobbling, though rather firmer today. However, we tried to impress the urgency of the situation on the workers in the country and commemorated Anzac Day. . . .

April 30. . . . At the office I found that Winston had just given the figures of the evacuation of Greece—a wonderful record— . . . To lunch later with Beaverbrook at Claridges'—a gathering of Air Correspondents addressed by him. . . . He gave me an impression of impending withdrawal.[2]

. . . . .

We can now return to Geoffrey's account of his "Second Resignation—1938–41".[3] The first section covering the events in 1939 has

[1] In order to reach Lowndes Street from Printing House Square.

[2] Lord Beaverbrook resigned from the Ministry of Aircraft Production the following day.

[3] *Vide supra*, pp. 384-385.

already been dealt with. What follows refers to the definite retirement which took place in 1941.

Second Retirement from *The Times*
(written September 23rd, 1941)

And so things stood[1] for the next year and a half—with complete goodwill on the part of B-W., from whom I had had no secrets throughout.

But late on the night of May 5 I found the Chairman in his room and was just parting with him when he suddenly suggested that the office seemed now to be running very smoothly, that it had been strengthened e.g. by the acquisition of Carr and the development of Iverach McDonald, and that it might be unfair to keep my duly appointed successor waiting indefinitely to step into my shoes.

This rather took me aback, but I agreed at once that I ought to have thought of it sooner myself. I said I was sure that B-W. was quite capable of taking over the Editorship at any time, though the Carr-McDonald argument did not really meet the problem of his assistants and deputies at the centre. Anyhow I would have a talk with him at once and see how he felt about it.

This accordingly I did when I reached the Office next morning. . . . Nothing, of course, could have been more considerate than his (B-W's.) attitude. He begged me to take my own time, said it would be a sad day for him when I left Printing House Square, suggested reconsideration in the Autumn, etc. But he left no doubt that he was prepared to take over, and I told him that in the circumstances I should not dream of lingering on the stage. I suggested the end of July as a natural breaking-point. He talked about the end of the year. In the end we agreed upon September 30, so that he might have a month's holiday with his family before settling down.

The general programme which I had in mind at this stage was that a brief announcement of the change should be published some time in August—to take place "next month". With this in mind, and thinking that there was plenty of time to spare, I began, as occasion offered, to tell a few friends about it both inside and outside the office. . . . The process was incomplete and would gradually have been continued. But on the evening of July 17 the *Star*, in its last edition only, came out with an accurate statement of the facts and let loose a spate of inquiries from newspapers all over the country: (then followed the notice which had appeared in the *Star*). This was not perhaps surprising in the circumstances, seeing how many people knew by this time: but it required attention, and after a word with B-W., Kent and the Chairman, I decided that it was best to make a clean breast of it at once. Accordingly I

[1] Since the spring of 1939 it was definitely understood that Barrington-Ward was to succeed Geoffrey as Editor.

suggested the following announcement (which they all approved) and published it in all editions of the paper on the following morning:

EDITOR OF *THE TIMES*

Mr. Geoffrey Dawson is retiring from the Editorship of *The Times* in September on reaching the agreed age limit. His resignation would in fact have taken place last year if it had not been for the war, and his successor had already been nominated at that time. He has been Editor from 1912 to 1919 and again since the beginning of 1923.

Mr. R. M. Barrington-Ward, D.S.O., M.C., who will succeed him, has been Assistant Editor for nearly 14 years. He first joined the staff of *The Times* as Secretary to the Editor in February, 1914: left it later in the same year on the outbreak of the last War; went to the *Observer* as Assistant Editor on the conclusion of peace; and rejoined *The Times* in a similar capacity in October, 1927.

. . . . .

B-W. had meanwhile composed the following draft:

Mr. Geoffrey Dawson is giving up the editorship of *The Times*.

Mr. Dawson originally offered his resignation in June, 1939, and Mr. R. M. Barrington-Ward was then designated as his successor. Subsequently the change was postponed in view of the extensive reorganization imposed upon *The Times* by the onset of the war.

Mr. Barrington-Ward will take over the editorship at the end of September.

But it seemed to me (1) to leave unexplained the reason for my retirement—the age-limit which I had set for myself, and (2) to ascribe to me an extensive reorganization for which I could claim no particular credit. I was anxious to make it clear, beyond the possibility of speculation, that there had been no quarrel and no breakdown in health.

As it turned out, the *Star* leakage was by no means inconvenient. There was a flood of personal letters—I found that within the next week or two I had answered some 200, partly with my own hand and partly by dictation; and B-W. must have had twice as many, for he had to suffer all the people who wanted to stake out claims for the future. Of these he was able to dispose before starting on a month's holiday with his family in Wales, and I got rid of most of mine in time to devote my last few weeks in the Office to sorting and getting rid of old correspondence and generally tidying up.

. . . . .

A two-days' debate on the war ended on May 7th with a "fighting" speech by Mr. Churchill and a practically unanimous vote. There was also a "good message" from Abyssinia about the Negus's return to his capital. The R.A.F. was keeping its end up and there had been (May 8) "a good night against the night bombers—24 in the bag—and another dozen picked up during the day. . . . They were very active again tonight—planes streaming over and keeping us awake."

The diary for the next few days records one of the most extraordinary episodes in the war:

May 12. . . . Just after dinner came (by Reuter and B.U.P.) the extraordinary news that Hess had baled out in Scotland, and this was reinforced later by official communiqués, both British and German, and was the feature of all papers in the morning.

May 14. . . . In the afternoon came an admirable speech by Winant, to whom I switched the first leader, and a series of fresh revelations from and about Hess including the "release" of his desire to see the Boxing Marquess (Marquess of Douglas & Clydesdale). . . . The Ministry of Information more incompetent and variable than ever.

May 16. Traffic conditions get worse and worse with the progress of demolition and the discovery of unexploded bombs. It took me nearly an hour to get to the office after dropping Cecilia at Selfridges, and nearly as long to get home by bus and on foot. . . . The Hess excitement was dying down in favour of the new German menace in Syria, where aeroplanes were fuelling by leave of the Vichy Government. . . .

On May 17th the Dawsons lunched at Cliveden, where they found Lady Astor having a brief respite from the horrors of Plymouth. Geoffrey wrote, "Nancy vehement about the importance of getting L.G. (Lloyd George) into the Government, and wanting me to see him, which I am always quite ready to do, but not on a formal mission." On May 20th the invasion of Crete was the news of the day—1,500 Germans, airborne and in New Zealand battle-dress. The last days in May were dominated by news—or lack of it—from Crete and alarming rumours began to circulate, as they had at the time of invasion of Norway in 1940. On May 22nd there was this ominous entry in the diary: "No real news of Crete till 5.00 p.m., when the Prime Minister made a statement—not too optimistic, though there were rumours of worse to follow. It is clear enough anyhow that a pretty grim struggle is in progress and may continue." A long week-end was spent at Langcliffe during which the wireless brought the tragic news of the sinking of H.M.S. *Hood*; the official statement that the King and Government of Greece had left Crete; news that pursuit of the German

Navy was taking place off Greenland. On the last evening at Langcliffe news was coming in of tremendous hand-to-hand fighting in Crete.

Wonderful war news greeted the Dawsons when they arrived back in London:

> *May 27*. . . . Horner (*The Times* chauffeur) met us with the news of the sinking of the *Bismarck*, the pride of the German Navy, who'd sunk the *Hood* on Saturday and I went straight off to the office. The news had come just as the Prime Minister was making a statement in the House, which added a dramatic touch to an epic story. We got everything going for news and comment, and then had to wait interminably for the full Admiralty communiqué.

The month of June opened with the official news of the evacuation of Crete, a meeting between Hitler and Mussolini on the Brenner and "a set of incredible terms" which had been issued to the Vichy Government. On June 4th the Kaiser died at Doorn in the Netherlands.

One of the most important events of the World War was about to take place—certainly the greatest surprise of this war of surprises. Geoffrey's brief comments on Hitler's attack on Russia follow:

> *June 11*. . . .—great German concentration on the Soviet frontier. . . .
>
> *June 19*. . . . Attlee, Willink, H. Strauss came to lunch there (at Printing House Square). Attlee convinced (by Cripps) of the imminence of a Russo-German war. . . .
>
> *June 20*. . . . The symptoms of a German-Russian war slightly stronger. Fraser[1] of New Zealand arrived by air. . . .
>
> *June 22*. Oxford. *Hitler invades Russia*. The Warden, who'd been up at dawn, told us as we came out of Chapel that Hitler was invading Russia before issuing an incredible manifesto. Molotov had replied, and fighting was in progress all along the frontier. I got on to Printing House Square and to B-W. by telephone and made up my mind to return to London. . . . Everything was in train. Preparing a Hitler-Stalin Diary (for tomorrow), Military Naval and Air Correspondents at work. It was a tight fit to get even the documents—Hitler, Molotov, Ribbentrop into an 8 page paper: and Winston came on the air at 9 with another column.
>
> *June 23*. . . . Very little positive news of the Russo-German war. . . . We also printed an anthology of Hitler's speeches on Bolshevism.
>
> *June 24*. . . . went down to the House of Commons (sitting in the House of Lords, where Gallagher was addressing them from the red benches). The old Chamber, which I saw for the first time since its destruction, is a tragic sight. . . .

[1] The Premier of New Zealand.

Geoffrey was suffering from acute and prolonged attacks of sciatica and spent a week-end at Langcliffe, during which he attended a meeting of the Board of Governors of Giggleswick. During the five days June 26th to June 30th inclusive the diary is as closely written as usual but it is entirely devoted to the journey to Langcliffe and local events, with the exception of two lines about the war on June 27th, "Leo Kennedy broadcast on Hitler's New Order in the 9.00 bulletin." This complete absorption in his immediate surroundings to the exclusion of all else in the diary was commented on at the time of Northcliffe's death.[1] On this occasion, in view of the immense importance of the U.S.S.R.'s entry into the war one would have expected some reference to the turn of events in the diary. Nothing shows more definitely that Geoffrey was not writing his diary for posterity, and therein lies its value—its purpose was to record his immediate surroundings and the things which engaged his attention most directly.

After his return to Printing House Square on July 1st there are several brief entries about Russia. On July 9th "the Russians, according to their Mission (just arrived) were full of fight"; on July 13th "the Anglo-Russian Agreement was signed"; on July 14th "The Russians appeared to be holding, though their bulletins and the German differed widely". On July 15th "the Prime Minister announced in the House . . . that Russia was definitely an 'ally'. So *The Times* was justified . . ."; on July 16th "The news from Russia seemed pretty good".

In a letter from Pretoria (10th July, 1941) Smuts wrote to Geoffrey:

> . . . I think there might be more decentralization in authority instead of responsibility being retained in London. Some of the matters are perhaps just as important as the character of the War Cabinet. Cairo now and Singapore tomorrow may be the important centres to work effectively from London. Our Empire is a decentralized affair and we are therefore well situated to run a world-wide concern like this war.
>
> I hope Churchill is keeping fit and not overdoing it. Without his leadership we should indeed be poor.

Among the events referred to in the diary in the summer was "the Atlantic Circus"—the meeting between President Roosevelt and Mr. Churchill. When Geoffrey was at Langcliffe, he heard on the wireless on August 14th, the joint Churchill-Roosevelt declaration of War Aims after their meeting in the Atlantic.

September was Geoffrey's last month at Printing House Square, and the coming retirement—however long he had been prepared for it—naturally weighed on his mind. There are many references in the

[1] *Vide supra* p. 204.

diary to long days spent in looking through his vast correspondence and documents accumulated during the years of his two Editorships. By September 3rd he was demolishing "G and H" files. September 5th was an uninterrupted day of clearance "bringing me down to the M's, but revealing to my horror a whole pile of papers untouched since I brought them back to *The Times* in '22".

On September 8th the last leading article written by Geoffrey ("Looking Ahead") appeared in *The Times*. In it he wrote that the House of Commons would have much to discuss when it resumed its sittings: the whole episode in Iran "with its fresh credit both to the Prime Minister for his firm handling of the political situation and to General Wavell for the rapid disposition of his troops. Above all, the attitude of the United States has steadily developed under Mr. Roosevelt's judicious guidance, and has reached a new landmark in the famous Atlantic Charter, the outcome of his dramatic meeting with Mr. Churchill at sea." . . .

"On the other hand some of the reflections suggested are rather more anxious. They are bound to include the problem—constantly debated in private, but never, it may be hoped, to call for an answer while the war lasts—of a successor to the Prime Minister if a successor were suddenly required. . . . Like no one else in sight he has the courage, the imagination, the power of leadership which are the attributes of a great War Minister. England is fortunate indeed as she has so often been fortunate in the past, in having produced the man to fit the emergency."

On September 14th the diary recorded that there was fierce fighting round Leningrad and indeed all along the Russian front. A wing of the R.A.F. was operating alongside. On the 16th: "through a surging crowd round St. Paul's, where young King Peter (of Yugoslavia) was celebrating his 18th birthday. All the Kings and Queens including our own there."

Among the entries in the diary during Geoffrey's last days at Printing House Square are the following:

Sept. 19. . . . The war was *not* going well—nothing much at Leningrad: but by nightfall the Germans were claiming the capture of Kiev and were clearly making great headway in the Ukraine. . . .

Sept. 22. . . . The news from the Russian front was not good. Kiev apparently gone. On the other hand, there had been a successful attack on an Italian convoy in the Mediterranean. We dined with Edward and Dorothy, who are on the eve of departure (i.e. return to the British Embassy at Washington).

Sept. 23. . . . And then some heavy work on the files brought me at last to Z (for Zetland and Zulueta!). . . . The news *felt* to me a trifle better, though it was still pretty grim round Kiev. Maisky made a speech appealing for more help from Britain and America. Winston was made Lord Warden of the Cinque Ports.

Sept. 29. Getting very near the end. Several farewell notes from friends in the office, who didn't quite know when the change-over would come. I'd settled in my own mind that I would do some day work tomorrow and turn over the actual production of *The Times* October 1, to B-W. Cecilia and I paid a visit to James Gunn, whom the office want to paint my portrait, and liked him and discussed it with him. . . .

Sept. 30. My last day as Editor of *The Times*. I paid a brief visit to the office before going down to the House of Commons to hear the Prime Minister review the war. A very satisfactory performance with good figures of the Atlantic battle and the air. Down in the lobby afterwards I had a talk with Oliver Lyttelton, who'd reappeared on the Treasury Bench, back from Cairo, and others. I joined Cecilia for lunch with old Goodenough[1] at his Club . . . then went back to rather an emotional afternoon in Printing House Square. They insisted on my attending the Conference (which I hadn't meant to do) in order that Brodribb might conclude it by delivering an unexpected funeral oration, to which I had to reply. After that Casey came and literally wept on my shoulder, and there was an equally tearful parting with Miss Dickie. I got home in the end rather exhausted.

Oct. 1. A full day—even without any responsibility for *The Times*. . . . then a most excellent lunch with Stanley Morison at Scott's (oysters, partridge and savoury) followed by a visit to the new film of the original Reuter (introducing Delane) which we thought we must see. And so together to the office about 5—rather a melancholy visit, but I wiped up some bills for teas, postage, etc. and some farewell letters.

Oct. 2. . . . I paid a final, rather melancholy, little visit to the office to pay (still remaining) small bills for teas, postage etc. and to say some farewells. After that I dined with the "Round Table."

[1] Admiral Sir William Goodenough.

XXXVII

YEARS OF RETIREMENT—1941–1944

ALL active men, who have filled positions of responsibility and importance, find the first months of retirement difficult, however wide their interests or absorbing their home pursuits. Geoffrey throughout his life had looked forward to the day when he could retire to Langcliffe and live peacefully among his fellow dalesmen. His interest in the farms and moors had never diminished, and his holidays snatched in the critical pre-war years had usually been spent on the Yorkshire hills, sometimes shooting on the wild slopes of Penyghent, sometimes riding with his family and friends on a tour of the dales. He delighted in the slow humour and stolid common sense of the Craven countryman. Had his retirement come at a less anxious time he would have settled happily to minding his estate and joining in local affairs as a J.P. and governor of the ancient Grammar School at Giggleswick. As it was, he left *The Times* when a grim phase of the war had been reached and when his personal anxieties were great. His son was in the Grenadier Guards and his elder daughter—having returned after a hazardous journey to Australia escorting a party of emigrant children to the Fairbridge Farm Schools—was now a W.R.E.N. in Dover under frequent bombardment. Geoffrey's thoughts turned at once to finding an opportunity to help in the war effort. His strength had been tried by the strain of two years at war, the nights of bombing spent in the shelter at Printing House Square and he realized himself the need for some respite.

But his energy was undaunted and, had his health permitted, he would have thrown himself into new work in the national interest.

The following letter to Richard Feetham, an old friend of Kindergarten days in South Africa, was written at this time:

Langcliffe Hall,
Settle,
Yorkshire.
October 11, '41.

My dear Dick,

How pleasant to get a handshake with you today in the shape of a superb gift of butter and tea! It was addressed to me at Printing House Square, which in fact I vacated at the beginning of the month, but is all the more welcome for that. I am for the moment taking a brief holiday in the country, where butter is undeniably difficult to come by and tea is likely to follow the same course. I want to get thoroughly fit after some years without a break, before committing myself to some other niche in the war effort.

For many reasons I am sorry to leave *The Times* before the war is won. It is the penalty for having an orderly mind which likes to see the succession arranged in good time; and having settled an approximate date for retirement, and got my successor appointed, I began to realize that it must seem unfair to keep him waiting indefinitely. But I don't want to spend my remaining years in repose (even if repose were possible at such a time), or to divide my time evenly between the odds and ends of voluntary work that we all accumulate in course of time—in my case the Governorship of three schools (Eton, Giggleswick and Cheltenham); the *Round Table*, which badly needs an occasional helping hand; and a variety of local jobs up here. I must try to find something rather nearer to the centre of things when I am back in London, and let these others be side-shows for the present. . . .

Well my dear Dick, I end as I began, with much gratitude to you and Leila for your kind thought of us. It's no good speculating on our next meeting. I suppose you will come home when you can, and we had long planned a re-visit to S.A. whenever we were free. But we must brace ourselves to the possibility that we may grow too old (or too poor) for any of these dreams before we have finally done with Hitler and his gang. Anyhow, it was comforting to be in touch with you again.

Yours ever,
GEOFFREY DAWSON.

Shortly after his retirement *The Times* arranged to give Geoffrey a farewell luncheon when he knew he would be called upon to speak. All through his life, public speaking had come hard to him but even the most accomplished orator might have quaked in his shoes on such an occasion. This was no ordinary function but the outward farewell to his own past life and to a remarkable group of men with some of whom he had worked by day and by night for a quarter of a century—the "Company" of *The Times*—who, with Geoffrey, had shared the privilege of making the paper worthy of the greatest traditions during two world wars. Sir Bruce Richmond put into words, in the following letter, what many of his colleagues at Printing House Square were feeling when he retired:

> Just a line, not of condolence (for that is only of the moment), but of congratulation, both looking back and forward. None of your predecessors can have had so hard a time—two wars and a scarcely less harassing time between them. How you have stood it I can't think—how *The Times* has stood it, with steadily increasing authority, we of your staff are proud to think.

The diary for October 31st is given in full.

October 31. Farewell to *The Times* luncheon. I devoted some time in the morning to dictating a speech in advance, lest I should be overcome by emotion, and got early to the Waldorf, where there was an enormous gathering of Editorial Department past and present—some 150 in all, including very old hands like Bruce Richmond and Jenkins. The two Johns—Astor and Walter—were there and Kent and Bishop (Manager and Assistant Manager). Non-editorial people otherwise rigorously excluded. Speeches by Barrington-Ward (in the Chair), John Astor, self, Casey and Barrington-Ward again. I think they all went well, though I was glad of a little preparation! After that, with a load off my mind, I spent the day in a variety of interviews—Indian Comforts, Waldorf (the *Observer*)[1] . . . etc., at the Club and elsewhere.

On the menu card was printed "Times Portrait" by G. F. R. Anderson, the chief sub-editor:

TIMES PORTRAIT

G.D. departs; the last page goes to press;
His footfall echoes through the darkling Square,
His wisdom still irradiates the Chair,
The shadow of his greatness grows not less,
See in the magic glass of P.H.S.
The glancing smile, the devastating glare,
The Jovian nod, the rapt Olympian air,
The eagle puissance, ample graciousness,

[1] Geoffrey was a member of the small *Observer* tribunal which was seeking to advise "on the interminable question of Waldorf Astor, Garvin and the *Observer*". Despite its efforts a severance between J. L. Garvin and the paper took place at the end of February, 1942.

The sunset hour in flaming arabesque
Traces his name. The scribes of night assign
The columns of his praise: cut not a line—
No word too strong, no phrase too picturesque—
This truth marked "MUST" on Time the Printer's desk:—
The sun may set but does not cease to shine.

G. F. R. A.

October, 1941.

Geoffrey's retirement received a great amount of attention in the Press throughout the English-speaking world. I was in Australia when I heard the news, and was astounded; I had assumed that Geoffrey would remain in the editorial chair till the end of the war. In a way my sensations were somewhat similar to those I experienced at the time of the death of Queen Victoria—an era had passed. *The Times*, under Geoffrey, had so conspicuously stood for Imperial Unity and a frank understanding with the Dominions. I wondered whether the paper would ever again be controlled by one so essentially an Imperialist. No previous editor, as far as I was aware, had so felt the Empire in his blood from personal experience. I wondered what important niche he would fill as I was convinced that there would be many people who would want to make use of his exceptional gifts and experience. I assumed that he was perfectly fit, although I had always wondered how he stood up to the strain of his most exacting job. From his papers it appears that there were various attempts to get him to take on special work. One of Geoffrey's oldest friends wrote, "To all who know G.D. there seems something fantastic in reading that he is retiring from the Editorship of *The Times* on reaching the age limit." It was true that he was in his sixty-seventh year but those who knew him best and were acquainted with his physical powers regarded him as young in body and spirit with many years of active work ahead.

A forewarning, however, was given within five days of *The Times'* farewell luncheon when Geoffrey met Lord Dawson of Penn with whom he had a friendly talk about his health; he was troubled by sciatica and failing eyesight—in Lord Dawson's view both were common signs of overwork. But Geoffrey did not take these signs too seriously. He was occupied with the affairs of the *Round Table*, which he had now begun to edit. Oxford, since he was less tied, drew him, still more frequently, to All Souls and to Rhodes House, where he was for many years a trustee. One evening, in the Warden's Lodgings, he had a long talk with Keith Feiling about the *Life of Neville Chamberlain*.

Most of November, 1941, was spent at Langcliffe where Mr. James Gunn completed his "conversation piece" of Geoffrey and Cecilia which was being given to him by the members of *The Times* staff.

In the last three years of his life Geoffrey kept full diaries with nearly as many entries as in the busy years of his Editorship. These show the great variety of his concerns and his never-failing interest in the affairs of his children, of his friends, and Yorkshire neighbours. At Langcliffe he discussed the business of Giggleswick School with the headmaster; sat on the Bench; worked in the garden, lopping and sawing up branches or visited the hill farms. In those days of petrol rationing, he walked many miles or drove in a pony-cart. The house was then occupied by several small evacuees from Bradford as well as by his own children and their great-aunt; any friends, in need of a few weeks' rest, or soldiers on leave were sure of a warm welcome. In London Geoffrey's chief occupation was to attend meetings of the *Round Table*. He also had much work to do in clearing up papers in Printing House Square accumulated over nearly thirty years. The Archbishop of Canterbury wanted Geoffrey to take the chairmanship of a committee to deal with a fund from overseas for rebuilding the devastated churches in Great Britain. Montagu Norman, the Governor of the Bank of England, wanted him to undertake a mission; both proposals, however, Geoffrey refused to entertain. He was also invited to become an Alderman of the County Council in Yorkshire.

In February 1942, Lord Dawson's words of warning were fulfilled when Geoffrey was taken suddenly and seriously ill with a bad heart attack while attending a Governors' Meeting at Giggleswick School. The effects of overwork brought their inevitable consequences and Geoffrey was never to regain his physical robustness and vitality which had been such marked characteristics. For many weeks after this he remained quietly at Langcliffe and he was sadly forced to give up any idea of returning to the centre of affairs.

He could no longer walk with his alert and springing step or see well enough ever to shoot again. But he had the compensation which a scholar can always find in his books, returning again to the Aeneid and the Georgics and the novels of Dickens and Trollope.

As far as the war was concerned, although there were many anxious months to live through the tide may be said to have turned after the battle of El Alamein and the landing of American troops in French North Africa from Algiers to Casablanca, with the help of the Royal Navy. In May 1943, there was great rejoicing over the glorious news that the North African Campaign had been brought to a successful conclusion. In the last year of Geoffrey's life, his diary records the thrilling story of the invasion of Europe on June 6th, 1944, and on August 15th of the invasion of Southern France. Geoffrey lived therefore to realize that sooner or later the Allied Forces must triumph over Hitler and Nazism.

In mid-August 1942 there was one very happy entry in the diary at Langcliffe—"our family all together at home again for the first time for ages". In March 1943, Geoffrey wrote once again from Langcliffe to Richard Feetham in South Africa:

> We were so grateful to both of you for the box of delicatessen which awaited us here the other day, and for the kindly remembrance that inspired them. You struck just the comestibles that are rarest in the country nowadays—a superb variation of our Government cheese (no other may be made in England now) and raisins, which we haven't seen for months. I was thinking yesterday, when I got an unusual lift in a car up to the remoter farms at the top of Wharfedale, of the day you once spent with us there when you were staying with Hudson at Hellifield, and of the spot where we lunched by the river—Do you remember it? Those poor farmers are struggling now to turn their hillside pastures into arable, and doing it with very good will, though they realize that much of it is waste of effort—But they have little to complain about in general—thanks to an unnecessarily large Government subsidy on hill sheep.
>
> Cecilia and I came up here last week, I'd been in bed for a solid month in London with the universal 'flu and an intractable temperature and it was thought that country air would restore me. Happily this has coincided with Belinda's leave from the Wrens at Dover, where she is in the forefront of the battle, and also with Betsy's first vacation from Oxford where St. Hugh's (to her amazement) offered her a scholarship in History. Michael, as I can't help being glad, is still in England with a very highly trained Guards Armoured Division. He had a night in London before we left, after three weeks of tremendous exercises during which he never entered a house or even a barn and was in a grimy condition but extremely fit. So the whole Dawson family was reunited. For the rest, I am fairly busy with a variety of jobs—editing the *Round Table*, rather active for the moment with the Governing Bodies Association, serving on some of those same Governing Bodies, on the Rhodes Trust etc., etc., etc.
>
> I long to be doing something more directly connected with the "War effort", but it isn't very easy to find at this stage of the war, or indeed at this stage of our own lives. . . .
>
> I mustn't write about the War. This is one of these moments when it is going pretty well (after the capture of the Mareth position)—but I see signs of caution in my admirable old Military Correspondent's message in *The Times* this morning and I feel that we haven't quite done with Rommel yet. It is anxious work waiting—with all the children's friends, the boys who were in Michael's house at Eton, who have stayed here for Cricket or shooting, in the 1st or the 8th Army; and I know that there are heavy casualty lists to come—
>
> Goodbye my dear Dick—love and gratitude to you both from all of us.

In February, 1944, Geoffrey wrote to Colonel Deneys Reitz, High Commissioner for the Union of South Africa in London:

> Leo Amery, to whom I was singing the praises of your latest book yesterday afternoon, urged me to write and tell you how much it had interested me. This seemed to me to be rather an impertinence on a very slight acquaintance; but he assured me that authors like such letters, and he has had a good deal of experience. At any rate this one expects no answer.
>
> I associate "No Outspan" particularly with Leo because he and I, with Cecil Rodwell, who afterwards governed Rhodesia, made a memorable trip on the veld as soon as the South African war came to an end. My cherished possessions include a snapshot of the Secretary of State flanked by two of Lobengula's queens and another of him half immersed in the Bembezi river. We did not travel your distances, but we had a grand time.
>
> More seriously I was enthralled by your vivid account of the state of South African politics at the crisis of 1914. I had never seen so detailed a narrative before, and it increased, if possible, my admiration for your Prime Minister and his faithful supporters.

The last occasion on which Geoffrey visited All Souls was when he and Cecilia spent from August 9th to 13th, 1944, in Oxford. Much of the time was occupied with the task of seeing the issue of the *Round Table* to press. On August 21st they went to Langcliffe where they remained a month—it was to be Geoffrey's last visit to his beloved Yorkshire home. Shortly after their return to London there was "a capital letter from Michael about his entry into Brussels. His company was the first in". On October 10th Geoffrey arrived back in London for the last time. A week later he and Cecilia lunched with the Barrington-Wards and the following day he was picked up by Barrington-Ward to dine at Grillions, "a small and rather controversial party"—it was the last occasion on which Geoffrey ever dined out.

The last two entries in the diary were on October 24th when he attended an informal meeting of Eton Fellows to discuss the Provostship. "We duly assembled—7 of us, in Coutts's board room, and got through a surprising lot of business." The last entry was made on October 25th, his 70th birthday, and ended with the words "cheery letter from Michael in Holland".

Thirteen days later, on November 7th, Geoffrey died at 24, Lowndes Street.

XXXVIII

RETROSPECT

Geoffrey Dawson had a deeper sense of duty than anyone else I have known. I remember a talk I once had with him, which has always remained impressed upon my mind. It did not matter, he said, what your reputation was—it did not matter whether what you did was known or unknown, it did not matter whether you obtained any recognition for what you had done: what mattered was that you should be conscious yourself of having tried to do what was right. I think that we shall all feel that this was the right attitude for a journalist, who is expected to preserve anonymity, and that whether in South Africa or in the still more important position that he held in England, this was the motive that guided him.

(From the sermon at All Souls Commemoration Service, 3rd November, 1946, delivered by Bishop Headlam, Fellow of the College.)

ESSENTIALLY a modest man, Geoffrey would have appreciated few things more than the thought that he would be remembered by the brethren of "Chichele's House" and by his friends in all walks of life, as a man who tried to do what seemed right, without any thought of public recognition. The day will assuredly come when he will be recognized, however, not only as a great editor, but as a public figure who left his impress on events during the reign of King George V and the first years of that of King George VI. Below an attempt has been made to compare Geoffrey's tenure of office at Printing House Square with that of his three greatest predecessors. In one respect he certainly differed from them: while he was as capable a craftsman as any of them he was more than a journalist. His life shows that it is possible to have outside interests and still be an excellent editor. Geoffrey was a patriot throughout his life and gave much of his time to causes associated with the Commonwealth, and to those centres of learning with which he was so closely associated at Oxford, Eton and in Yorkshire.

In the 170 years since *The Times* was founded as *The Daily Universal Register* (the name of the paper was changed on January 1st, 1788, to

The Times or *Daily Universal Register*), four men between them have occupied the editorial chair for 113 years. They were:

Thomas Barnes	1817–41	24 years.
John Thadeus Delane[1]	1841–77	36 years.
George Earle Buckle	1884–1912	28 years.

George Geoffrey Dawson (he changed his name from Robinson to Dawson in 1917)

1912–1919	6½ years	Total period of over 25 years
1923–1941	18 years 9 months	
		113 years

The conditions under which each of these four men worked were so different that it does not seem possible or desirable to make a list of their respective merits, as one would place competing candidates in an examination. What we can say is that these men in their different ways were great editors and devoted their lives to the great newspaper they served.

Thomas Barnes must always occupy a unique position in the history of Journalism for he conceived, or anyhow put into operation, a new and original idea—an idea which is accepted today throughout the civilized world—namely, that a newspaper is "not an organ through which the Government could influence the people, but an organ through which the people could influence the Government". It was because *The Times* under Barnes became just such an organ by his thundering from Printing House Square that Barnes can be regarded as one of the chief founders of the modern daily press. Mr. Derek Hudson in his monograph is surely correct when he suggests that if any individual is entitled to the nickname of "The Thunderer" Barnes no doubt has the right to it. Barnes, like Delane, Buckle and Geoffrey, was a firm believer in the practice of anonymity. He probably agreed with William Cobbett, who saw the great weight which attaches to anonymous writing and said: "The mysterious WE that they make use of, gives men an idea that what they are reading proceeds from a little council of wise men, who have been sitting and deliberating upon what they wish to put forth. Each paragraph appears to be a sort of

[1] From the death of Barnes until the death of Walter II in 1847, Delane exercised only a delegated authority, thenceforward he was endowed with complete editorial authority.

little order-in-council; a solemn decision of a species of literary conclave." We can only fully understand Geoffrey's feelings at the time of his decision to resign the Editorship in 1919 rather than continue to work for Northcliffe, if we realize how imbued he was, as were his three great predecessors, with this concept of a newspaper, so loyally served by a group of men—the "Company" of Kinglake—whose individual personalities are lost in the "personality" of the paper. To Geoffrey, for the proprietor of *The Times* to scatter his name about the pages of the paper and to use his position to advance his personal aims was beyond endurance. Barnes or Delane would have agreed with him, as did Buckle.

On May 7th, 1941, *The Times* published a leading article entitled "Thomas Barnes", as was fitting a century after the death of the great journalist who had accustomed the country to ask "What does *The Times* say?" There seems today to be general agreement that Barnes may be regarded as "the greatest of all editors in the first half of the 19th century". It is, however, only in comparatively recent times that the magnitude of his contributions to journalism has been realized—a realization due in part to Northcliffe, to the Editor of *The History of "The Times"*, to Mr. Derek Hudson's biography and to Mr. Harold Child's Selection of Thomas Barnes's critical essays edited by him.

The leading article published in *The Times* on the Centenary of Barnes's death began:

> When the compilers of *The History of "The Times"* asked the keeper of the archives for information about Thomas Barnes they received no more than a half-sheet of notepaper, containing notes of the memories of a member of the editorial staff who had recently died at the age of ninety-five. It imparted just two facts—that Barnes was accustomed to have his hair cut in the office by one of the compositors, and that he habitually dined on tripe in the Editor's room. . .
>
> That being the limit of the tradition handed down by the servants of the journal that Barnes had edited with unprecedented power and distinction for twenty-four crucial years, it is plain that the remainder of his career had been expunged from the records at the instance of Barnes himself. In a sense the blank page is his characteristic memorial; for the kernel of the professional faith to which he clung was his belief in the anonymity of journalism. He held that honest writing needed not to carry, and could not carry, any weight but the weight of the argument, to the validity of which the name of the arguer could add nothing. By rigid adherence to this doctrine he raised *The Times* to an authority in public affairs that no newspaper had attained before, while totally suppressing his own robust personality. But on the hundredth anniversary of his death piety insists that his reluctant shade be summoned to take his call in front of the curtain.

Such indeed was the accepted practice of anonymity at Printing House Square in the days of Barnes that when he died there was no mention of the event in the news columns of the paper. Only a year later, owing to his connection with some litigation, did *The Times* refer to Barnes as "a gentleman connected with us who died last year and whose valuable services we must ever most highly appreciate".[1]

It is a curious coincidence that Barnes was born in 1785, the year in which the paper which he served so devotedly first appeared.

The status of an editor was vastly different during Barnes's lifetime from what it was during Geoffrey's two terms. Editors did not move in the highest social circles in the years 1817–41, for when Lord Lyndhurst gave a dinner to Barnes on December 2nd, 1834, the uncommon act of a Cabinet Minister in entertaining a journalist caused an uproar. There is a pleasant picture of Barnes, a Cambridge man, going a year before his death to record his vote for Lord Lyndhurst, as High Steward of the University of Cambridge, given by Disraeli who was present in the Senate and said, "Fat old Barnes of *The Times* waddled up to give his vote; he was recognized and the undergraduates mightily cheered 'The Thunderer' to his infinite satisfaction."

Of John Thadeus Delane much more is known and two biographies tell of his remarkable editorship, which lasted from the death of Barnes in 1841 to 1877. (Delane died at the age of sixty-two in 1879.)[2] If Barnes was born in the same year that the "Thunderer" first saw the light of day, Delane was born in 1817, the year in which Barnes became editor. Before being appointed to the editorial chair Delane, like Geoffrey, had spent a short period of initiation at Printing House Square: Delane for a year performed parliamentary and other work. He was only twenty-three when he became Editor, and was in his thirtieth year when he was vested with complete editorial responsibility. (Geoffrey was appointed Editor of the *Johannesburg Star* when he was thirty.) Both Geoffrey and Delane were born in October—both died in November. Of Delane it was said "No man was so little spoiled by society"—the same could have been said of Geoffrey. Both men were possessed of an imperturbable calm however momentous the news that arrived at Printing House Square. Both men made a practice of attending important debates in the House of Commons. Dasent refers to Delane as the "best informed man in Europe"—this could hardly have been said of Geoffrey—in his case it might have been said that "no editor was better informed concerning conditions within the Commonwealth and Empire". Both men went out in society, but Geoffrey could not compete with Delane in this respect; during a

[1] *The History of "The Times"*, Vol. I, p. 201.
[2] Geoffrey was five years of age when Delane died.

London season the latter dined out a hundred nights in succession. Geoffrey led the life of an efficient editor, but he would never, after his marriage, have consented to become a mere slave to the social round, as did Delane, the bachelor. No one can understand Geoffrey who fails to realize what an important part his family played in his life, and few men more truly deserved the happy home life which was his.

Both Delane and Geoffrey, however, would probably have agreed with Lord Houghton that "the intimate conversation of important men is the cream of life". It is thought that Disraeli had Delane in mind when he once, in a speech, referred to "the once stern guardian of popular rights simpering in the enervated atmosphere of gilded saloons"—a description which by no stretch of imagination could have applied to Geoffrey. In his case many of his most useful talks were made with members of the groups he was associated with, such, for instance, as the Governing body of Eton, the Rhodes Trust, the *Round Table*, Grillions, or the Royal Literary Society. Delane, however, like Buckle, had practically no interests outside *The Times*, although the latter shared with Geoffrey the bond of All Souls.

Geoffrey and Delane certainly held in common a place in the confidence of Prime Ministers and political leaders of the day. As a young man Delane had a deep respect for Lord Aberdeen who was Prime Minister in the years before the Crimean War, though in 1854 he thought that Aberdeen was not a fit war leader. His attitude to Aberdeen was somewhat similar to that of Geoffrey's towards Asquith in 1916. During Palmerston's premiership, Delane was frequently consulted about important appointments just as was Geoffrey during the Baldwin regime. "How do you get the secrets?" Diana Warwick asked Mr. Jonans in Meredith's novel. "By sticking to the centre of them," was the reply. This is what all four editors did. Both Delane and Geoffrey certainly overtaxed their constitutions, though ten years before he died Charles Dickens wrote: "I dined at Greenwich with Delane. . . . He looks as if he had never seen a printing office, and had never been out of bed after midnight." (In Delane's days the hours the editor worked were different as the paper went much later to press. Delane seldom left Printing House Square before 4 or 5 a.m. He claimed to have seen more sunrises than any man alive.) Delane was essentially a journalist, while Geoffrey, in addition to his role as a family man, had other interests, besides editing *The Times* during two world wars.

Delane, unlike Geoffrey, was "an editor who did not write".[1] No

[1] E. T. Cook's *Delane of "The Times"*, Constable, 1915, p. 191. Though the author qualified this statement, he says: "It seems that he wrote a few (leading articles)".

editor who frequently wrote leading articles himself could have found time and energy to lead the full life in society which Delane did. George Brodrick, Warden of Merton, wrote thus of Delane's methods, "He possessed in a rare degree the art of inspiring articles by short pithy notes, suggesting but not dictating the line to be taken." Like Geoffrey, Delane was an expert at sub-editing. In a letter to a member of the staff he wrote, "I believe not a column has been published in *The Times* which had not some of my handwriting in the margin." The writer of the obituary notice of Delane in the *Standard* said that none of Delane's writers "ever disputed the value of his criticism, or failed to agree cordially in his revisions, alterations and suppressions. Thousands of times when, in the heat and haste of writing, expressions had been employed which the writer had some little doubt about, and felt to be weak points in his composition, he found the editor's pen falling with sure discernment on the faulty passage, and justifying the writer's own suppressed misgivings."[1]

Every now and then Geoffrey writes in his diary of the tedious and difficult task of revising leaders, "the revision of an appalling leader by 'X'—one of those failures that take years off your life", and again "another bad night transforming a hopeless leader by 'Y', who went clean off the rails". In his ability to revise leaders speedily and effectively, Geoffrey has never been surpassed at Printing House Square. His colleagues, including one or two who did not always agree with his policy, state that he was an expert at swift revision. He would make a few excisions, add a word here or a sentence there, or perhaps alter a heading; and in an amazingly short time he would have transformed the article from the commonplace into the arresting. Many of his colleagues told me that it was a rare privilege to watch Geoffrey, the craftsman, at work on revision; with the addition or deletion of a word, the whole emphasis and balance of a leader would be altered and brought into line with the policy of the paper.

Geoffrey, always on the lookout for advance news, records in his diary on January 12th, 1916, how he put two and two together when attending the funeral of Lord Burnham, the chief proprietor of the *Daily Telegraph*, and afterwards going to Hall Barn. ". . . Decided after much reflection to predict Chelmsford as Viceroy. I had come to this conclusion (and written it to Valentine Chirol) earlier in the week and something said at Hall Barn made me fear it would get out." Two days later Geoffrey was glad to find that his venture of "intelligent anticipation" had been justified by events. There is another example of Geoffrey's foresight. In the memorandum of June 14, 1916, when he was studying ways and means for ensuring a better direction of the

[1] *John Thadeus Delane*. Arthur Irwin Dasent. Murray 1908, p. 344.

nation's war effort he suggested that it was essential "to get Lloyd George (he served as Minister of Munitions, and Secretary for War under Mr. Asquith) bracketed with someone" who thought as he did about the war. Geoffrey had in mind Carson. As an alternative to a Lloyd George-Carson combination, he suggested a Lloyd George-Milner union: Milner to be associated with Lloyd George, inside the Government. The Editor wrote, "The two of them would either control affairs in the Cabinet, or bring it down with a run if they were both to resign together."

If ever there was a case of "intelligent anticipation" it is in the last paragraph of this memorandum, written by Geoffrey to clear his mind. Lloyd George was appointed to the War Office to succeed Kitchener and within six months Geoffrey's scheme for getting Milner—the "someone who thinks as he does about the war"—within a small War Cabinet was realized.

Instances of "intelligent anticipation" can, of course, be found in the case of Delane, once described as "as quick on news as a toad's tongue on a fly". On one occasion an eminent physician told him casually that Lord Northbrook, a mutual friend, had asked him how a hot climate would suit his delicate daughter. *The Times* next morning announced that Lord Northbrook had been appointed Viceroy and Governor-General of India.

Delane, as we have seen, was first and last a journalist, with no other ties such as Geoffrey had. His interest in the passing cavalcade has been said only to have existed in so far as it needed recording in the columns of *The Times*. In this sense, he seems to me more to have resembled Northcliffe than Geoffrey. They (Delane and Northcliffe) both were news-gatherers *par excellence*, whose thoughts every hour of the day were concentrated on the passing scene in so far as it affected their papers. The Editor of *The History of "The Times"* rightly devotes much space to Delane, the news-gatherer, and quotes a typical remark of the great editor in a letter to his deputy Dasent—"That was a good murder you had last week"—an absolute parallel to the kind of remark often made by Northcliffe to members of his staff. As *The History of "The Times"*[1] rightly points out, Delane, "lacking political conviction, was hardly interested in affairs until public attention gave them journalistic importance". Such a remark could never have been made about Geoffrey. His most successful policies were those about which he had a deep conviction, and therein lay his strength.

There is, as far as I am aware, no biography of Buckle, Geoffrey's immediate predecessor in the editorial chair, and it is not possible therefore to compare their methods and outlook as in the case of

[1] Vol. II, p. 332.

Delane and Geoffrey. There are, however, certain bonds which united them, above all else the tie of All Souls which lasted during most of Geoffrey's second Editorship (for Buckle only died in 1935). In their devotion to Oxford and All Souls there was a strong link. Buckle was a man large in body and heart. There was nothing petty about him and he rose to heights of greatness in character, when he was deposed by Northcliffe—at the age of fifty-eight—to make way for Geoffrey; a smaller man would have found it difficult to enter wholeheartedly into the fortune of his successor. Two most moving and characteristic tributes to Geoffrey on his appointment as Editor of *The Times* in 1912, and on his retirement in 1919, came from Buckle. Geoffrey naturally throughout his life had a real respect for his predecessor. The fact that Buckle had been recommended as a likely young graduate for *The Times* by Sir William Anson, the Warden of All Souls, whom Geoffrey so deeply admired, probably always remained at the back of his mind (John Walter III had consulted R. W. Raper, the famous Trinity tutor who was also a close friend of Anson's). Both Buckle and Geoffrey were imbued with a deep devotion to *The Times*, and shared the anxiety lest Northcliffe might come to regard Printing House Square just as one more undertaking in his vast organization and not *The Times*—which was unique and must not be too closely linked with Carmelite House or his other interests. Buckle was offered, and refused, a baronetcy by Arthur Balfour, just as Geoffrey was sounded by Arthur Lee, on behalf of Lloyd George, about whether he would accept a title—presumably a similar honour. Unlike Geoffrey, Buckle disliked innovations such as the typewriter and telephone. I have among my possessions a typical letter from Buckle in his own handwriting about some trivial matter, which his successors would have dictated to their secretaries. Above all Buckle was as wedded to the practice of anonymity as either his predecessors or successors in the editorial chair. Unlike Geoffrey, he refused to sit on boards and gave his whole allegiance to *The Times*.

Geoffrey became a journalist by chance or rather through his association with Milner. The child was not the father of the man, as with Northcliffe, who at the age of thirteen founded for his schoolfellows at Henley House, Hampstead, the *Henley House Magazine*. The only indication we get of any interest in journalism during Geoffrey's boyhood is the youthful diary he kept, at the age of fifteen, during a Scottish holiday with his parents in 1890. On the flyleaf he wrote: "Inscribed with the author's compliments to His Parents and published by Knowboddy Bros. in the township of Sumware, and the County of Blankshare—13th Thousand. Entered as a newspaper at the Stationers' Hall." How surprised he would have been had he been told that in fifteen years he would be Editor of the *Johannesburg Star* and even more surprised, Editor of *The Times* within twenty-two years. None of those who knew him at Eton or Oxford have given me any anecdotes testifying to an interest in journalism. When he was at Wren's, the crammers, in 1897, he wanted to enter the Indian Civil Service. The only reference to Geoffrey's doing any writing in the early years occurs in his diary while in camp with the Volunteers at Sheerness in 1900, at the time of the South African War, when he reviewed "a wildly sensational book called *Caged*" at the request of his friend Richard Austen-Leigh, for a periodical then owned by Messrs. Spottiswoode. Milner had been a journalist and had served under John Morley and W. T. Stead on the *Pall Mall Gazette* and he made Geoffrey an Editor, so that the *Star*, under his guidance, would support the Milner policy after he himself had returned to England.

Within three months of joining the *Star* Geoffrey became correspondent for the *Daily Telegraph*. On April 29th, 1906, in a letter to his father, he writes, "I am beginning to think my connection with the *Daily Telegraph* may be a useful ladder back to England, but it's no use looking too far ahead." It was certainly lucky for Geoffrey that seven months after becoming Editor of the *Star*, Moberly Bell asked him to become correspondent of *The Times*—a position he had held for two years before coming on leave to England in the summer of 1908. This meant that Northcliffe, who had read *The Times* most carefully long before he acquired it, was familiar with Geoffrey's cables from South Africa. It was also very lucky that he should have taken his first leave from the *Star* three months after Northcliffe had acquired *The Times*. Although he hoped for a "ladder back to England" also through his cables to *The Times*, it was his political work on the *Star* which was to be of such value to him when he came to Printing House Square. Johannesburg, in the immediate years after Milner's departure, provided a wonderful training ground for a young journalist. His work as Editor of the *Star* was talked about. Both in 1908 and especially in 1909, when the first Imperial Press Conference was held, Geoffrey made many lasting friendships with journalists. I recall at various functions in 1909 how Geoffrey enjoyed meeting newspaper proprietors and editors from all parts of the Empire. After these two visits to Europe he certainly returned to South Africa with wider horizons and above all, with a greater belief in the Commonwealth despite the setbacks to the Milner policy in South Africa.

The experience which Geoffrey gained in his last years in South Africa, not only as a publicist for a cause—the great cause of uniting South Africa—in which the Kindergarten played so noble a part—was of the utmost value in his career. His work as a member of that remarkable group of men—the full story of the Kindergarten has never been adequately told—gave him first-hand experience of how great ideals can be achieved. The lessons he learned in South Africa in the campaign for closer union had a lasting effect on him and made him appreciate the possibilities of the judicious use of the Press. How well he did his job in South Africa is shown by the views of two such different writers as J. L. Garvin and John Buchan. When Geoffrey was appointed Editor of *The Times* by Northcliffe in 1912, Garvin wrote to him, "For two years I have said you would be and ought to be Editor of *The Times*." Buchan wrote: "I congratulate *The Times* on getting the best Editor now in existence. . . . I am delighted to think that your long and difficult years in the *Star* have borne their proper fruit."

From among the many tributes to Geoffrey's Editorship of *The Times* made either on his retirement in 1941 or on his death, we may select the following:

Arthur Mann, Editor of the *Yorkshire Post*, and very critical of some of the views expressed by *The Times* during Geoffrey's second Editorship, wrote: "Mr. Dawson has had to cope with dismaying and nerve-testing events both inside the office and out of it. He has borne himself with the moral self-possession of the best kind of Yorkshireman . . . (after referring to the divergence of views between Northcliffe and Geoffrey). . . ." The writer continues: "On the death of that dynamic and too impulsive personality and the return to a steadier proprietorship, there was never any doubt that Geoffrey Dawson was the man to control the paper again on its lines of sober news, policy and weight of statesmanship. He stood for the power of moral ideas, the self-respect of intelligent readers, and the value of honest discussion."

A writer in the *Yorkshire Evening Post* said: "There was never a man who wielded such power and influence in journalism, who was so completely unknown to the community at large, and who is, moreover, as much a stranger to the people of his own county as to those in the great throbbing Metropolis.

"Geoffrey Dawson owes his status in his profession and in the world at large to three predominating, overwhelming influences. The first, his own native ability, which embodies shrewd caution and an always active mind; the second, that wholesome influence of early days in Yorkshire; and the third his fortuitous association at an impressionable age with one of the greatest minds of the 19th century, the late Viscount Milner."

The letters from his colleagues on the paper on his retirement for the most part convey a sense not only that a great era was ending, but record a deep personal loss. Many of his young men speak with gratitude of the encouragement he gave them early in their careers. One successful member of the staff wrote: "You have taught me many things; not least, the virtue of being able to maintain an Olympian calm in a naughty and vexatious world. I have always been impressed, too, by your tolerance of the views of your spirited young scribes who have sometimes dared to disagree with you about this or that; and by your achievement in serenely presiding over and successfully managing as a team in the difficult days before the war, the often discordant politicians among us."

This is how Geoffrey appeared to a young Canadian, G. V. Ferguson, who wrote in *The Winnipeg Free Press*:

> In the early summer of 1924 a somewhat diffident and nervous young man crossed the famous portals of P.H.S. near Blackfriars Bridge in London and timidly asked an impressive commissionaire if he could see the Editor of *The Times*.
>
> Had the nervous young man an appointment with the Editor?
>
> The nervous young man had.
>
> Shortly thereafter he was ushered into the editorial sanctum where, behind his desk, sat Geoffrey Dawson, but lately returned to the chair he had occupied from 1912–1919, having left it, so the story goes, because he and the owner of *The Times*, Lord Northcliffe, had fallen hopelessly out.
>
> Dawson, ruddy-faced, square jawed, square-set, was kindness itself. Would the young man care to come into *The Times* office and begin to learn the rudiments of journalism? The young man nearly fell off his chair. The young man would. He started work next day.
>
> After that his contacts with the Editor were as strictly limited as the average cub's are to the average editor. But, when he left *The Times* office, he had a further interview with Geoffrey Dawson and once more the abiding impression he left on him was of the keen, kindly interest he took in the younger members of the staff. Why, asked Dawson, was he leaving? Because he wanted to go home to Canada. Did he propose to pursue newspaper work? He did. Could he help with a letter or two? He knew some of the Canadian editors. He would be glad to write to them.
>
> It was all done very simply and in a most friendly way. It may be that vein of kindness was born in him. It may be that he had himself learned from Lord Milner, one of whose kindergarten he had been in South Africa many years before, that it was worth while to encourage young fellows at their beginnings. . . .

Among Geoffrey's friends were some who disapproved of his support of the appeasement policy, others who thought that he should have appointed a foreign editor to have succeeded Harold Williams. As readers will be aware, Geoffrey felt his loss of Williams very deeply and was for several years seeking a successor to him, whom he never found. Among those who urged on Geoffrey the need for finding an adviser on foreign affairs in the category of Donald MacKenzie Wallace or Valentine Chirol, was R. H. Brand, not only one of Geoffrey's oldest friends, but also a director of *The Times*, who was therefore in a very special position to advise him. In the spring of 1939 Brand wrote a letter to Geoffrey on the need for a good foreign editor. Unfortunately he did not keep a copy of his letter and asked Geoffrey to destroy it when read, which he did—but Geoffrey's reply is given here:

> I am really *most* conscious of our weaknesses. Taking a long view, I have always thought them more dangerous on our Managerial than on the Editorial side, where I have got together some very good young men who are now ready for promotion.
>
> I see no one on the other except Bishop, of whom I have a high opinion. A really good Foreign Editor would be a great support. . . . For various reasons, I doubt whether we have anyone on the staff, at home or abroad, who could *take charge* of the Foreign Department as a whole.
>
> One of the weaknesses of which I have been most conscious is in the sphere of attractive "make-up", where the "D.T." competes most obviously. But I think I have a remedy for that at once, and hope to get it going this week. The fundamental difficulty with a staff of journalists is that the strain on them is very great, and that their work suffers if they are disgruntled. You can't deal with them as you could with a regiment or a house of business. In that respect, the Manager's task is a much simpler proposition. I would like to have a talk with you about all this. I am thankful that you and Harold Hartley are on the Board.

With the passing of years, many who were inclined to criticize the policy of appeasement, realize, as stated in an earlier chapter, that two arguments were fundamental in Geoffrey's case: (1) the Dominions were strongly in favour of it; (2) it brought the whole nation together in 1939, in a manner which would not otherwise have been possible. On the subject of not appointing a foreign editor there is, so it seems to me, a fundamental reason why this appointment would not have made the difference which some of its advocates think. In modern journalism a successful editor is all-powerful. No forceful editor would agree to divided control, for the ultimate responsibility is his and his alone. If his assistant disagrees with his policy, beyond making a protest, he can do no more. If a clash of opinion came the foreign editor would have, ultimately, to fall in with the views of the Editor or resign, for the Editor alone is responsible for the contents of the paper.

Few editors of *The Times* can have been more widely mourned than Geoffrey, for surely none of them had a larger circle of friends, not even

Delane. His widow received tributes from friends and admirers from most parts of the Commonwealth and Empire and from the United States. One came from Edward Impey (his tutor at Eton) who survived him; from friends who were at Aysgarth, Eton or Oxford with him; from members of the staff of the *Johannesburg Star*; from his intimates of the Kindergarten, from colleagues on the Rhodes Trust, from humble fellow dalesmen; and other Yorkshiremen to whom he had rendered some service; and above all, from his associates at Printing House Square. These letters pay a tribute not only to a great editor but to a true and kind friend, endowed with a rare gift of sympathy, ever ready to enter into the problems and sorrows of his friends; and to a man whose profound faith in the British Commonwealth never wavered even in the darkest days.

Geoffrey, who had a high regard for Charles Brodribb, would assuredly have liked to think that his colleague's lines, written after the funeral service (at which the ex-Archbishop of Canterbury, Dr. Lang, paid a tribute to him) in St. Paul's, Knightsbridge, would appear in the last chapter of the story of his life. Geoffrey's ashes were interred in the North Ribblesdale Churchyard of Langcliffe, a Celtic Cross marks the grave, and from it can be seen Penyghent.

IN MEMORIAM G.D.

The church; the moving bier; the Psalmist's span
Used to the full! This was King Henry's man,
Waynflete's and Chichele's pledge, once far from hence
Blessed by the Southern Cross's influence.
Bone of his Yorkshire's bone, none truer bred,
The sportsman's temper and the statesman's head;
Who bore like knight magnanimously spent
His own and other's honour to his tent.

C. W. Brodribb.[1]

November, 1944.

[1] Taken from *Poems*. C. W. Brodribb. Macmillan, 1946, p. 50.

INDEX

Abbreviations—G.—Geoffrey Dawson
N.—Northcliffe
P.H.S.—Printing House Square
T.T.—*The Times*